The Natural Musician

Д.К.КИРНАРСКАЯ

Музыкальные способности

«Таланты - XXI век»
2004

The Natural Musician
on Abilities, Giftedness and Talent

Dina Kirnarskaya
Professor of Psychology and Musicology
Russian Gnesins' Academy of Music, Moscow

Translated from Russian by Mark H. Teeter

OXFORD
UNIVERSITY PRESS

OXFORD

UNIVERSITY PRESS

Great Clarendon Street, Oxford OX2 6DP

Oxford University Press is a department of the University of Oxford.
It furthers the University's objective of excellence in research, scholarship,
and education by publishing worldwide in

Oxford New York

Auckland Cape Town Dar es Salaam Hong Kong Karachi
Kuala Lumpur Madrid Melbourne Mexico City Nairobi
New Delhi Shanghai Taipei Toronto

With offices in

Argentina Austria Brazil Chile Czech Republic France Greece
Guatemala Hungary Italy Japan Poland Portugal Singapore
South Korea Switzerland Thailand Turkey Ukraine Vietnam

Oxford is a registered trade mark of Oxford University Press
in the UK and in certain other countries

Published in the United States
by Oxford University Press Inc., New York

First published in Russian as 'Musical Abilities' by Creativity-XXI Publishers in 2004

This edition first published 2009

British Library Cataloguing in Publication Data

Data available

Library of Congress Cataloging in Publication Data

Data available

ISBN 978-0-19-9560134

10 9 8 7 6 5 4 3 2 1

Typeset in Minion
by Cepha Imaging Pvt Ltd, Bangalore, India
Printed in Great Britain
on acid-free paper by
CPI Antony Rowe, Chippenham, Wiltshire

Foreword

by Gennady Rozhdestvensky

One of the world's leading performers of orchestral music, Gennady Rozhdestvensky has served as artistic director and principal conductor for a broad range of Russian and foreign musical organizations including the Soviet Radio and Television Symphony Orchestra, the Bolshoi Theater, the Moscow Chamber Opera, the Stockholm Philharmonic and Royal Philharmonic Orchestra, the BBC Symphony Orchestra, the Vienna Symphony Orchestra, Berliner Philharmoniker, and Concertgebouw.

The volume before you, *The Natural Musician*, is the fruit of many years labor by the author, a psychologist and musicologist. In this book the author-psychologist and author-musicologist complement each other wonderfully, together rendering their 'joint' study of musical ability the more authentic and reliable for this unique collaboration. I do not know of a book analogous to this one in the literature on musical talent, as no book so actively and extensively draws upon the whole spectrum of contemporary scientific and scholarly knowledge in the field. Every judgment expressed here is based on and fed by a wealth of scholarly and scientific material. Every musician judges musical talent 'from his own bell tower', basing his opinions on his own experience—yet this book is nonetheless as objective as it is possible to be. Musicians of all kinds who read it will be surprised at the remarkable breadth of a field of knowledge, musical psychology, which is located 'next door' to them—and is busily studying their abilities, their perceptions, and their memories.

The Natural Musician will dispel a number of popular myths. Many people believe, for example, that the study of music demands a very fine ear, and that this study must begin practically in the cradle. These people think that *wunderkinder* are simply those musicians whom Fate treated as it did the young Mozart, and that such a destiny, albeit on a smaller scale, is repeated in the lives of most musically gifted children. Yet this is demonstrably untrue, and the author of this book dismisses this and other illusions in cheerfully methodical fashion. It turns out, among other things, that: one may study music with both pleasure and success without a remarkable ear for it (as such is usually understood); one may start music studies at any age and be successful; and that musical talent, like every talent, consists of many discrete components—each of which may be mastered to but a certain extent for someone to deem herself, quite rightly, a 'musical person'. Music is open to all, it is ready to interact with anyone who will meet it halfway; readers will become convinced of this by *The Natural Musician*, noting the practical experience of contemporary psychology the world over.

The relationship of talent and ability is a theme of interest to all of us, perhaps even an intimate theme. No one is indifferent to his own abilities or lacks interest in his talents. And even if the reader is endowed with wholly different gifts, far from the realm of things musical, this book will reveal a great deal. In the final analysis we are all created by nature from a single design; all talents are to a certain extent related in their construction, and the reader will find it easy to place himself, his talents, and abilities, within the array of human knowledge proffered in this book. A better understanding of the musical gift will lead any of us, as the author shows, to a deeper understanding of the essence of *any* gift in our possession.

Not only does the content of this book attract me, but its form appeals as well. It is written clearly, with a light touch and without the burden of heavy-duty terminology which one so often finds in Russian scholarship. Perhaps this derives from the fact that the author is not only a professional psychologist and musicologist, but a journalist as well. Or perhaps it owes to the author's interest in her hero. The music student, the composer, the musical performer—all these summon the author's affection, and all draw her empathy as they go through their creative torments and strive for perfection. This affection is particularly evident in the last chapter of the book, 'Homo Musicus', where the author, armed with abundant data, recounts how music enriches humanity, how it refines our thought, how much more observant and sensitive it renders people who love it and willingly give their time to it, equipping them with communication skills so critical for all of us today.

Those who pursue music are rewarded. I agree wholeheartedly with the author's call to everyone to get to know music better. This closer relationship will not only be better for Music, which will acquire new devotees, but, more important, for the individuals themselves. If anyone remains uncertain of his need for music, let him begin reading this book with the last chapter—after which he will undoubtedly want to learn everything about musical abilities that rest of the book has to offer. All who take this book in hand will find interesting encounters with music and musicians—and with their own musical abilities as well.

Preface

My first degree was in musicology, my second in psychology. I have spent my whole life among musicians. And having dealt with them for 40 years, 20 years studying musical giftedness, I can say with certainty that there is no more contentious and troubling question for musicians than that of how to evaluate musical talent—first their own, in childhood and youth, then later the talent of their students. The questions are indeed hard ones: 'Am I capable of reaching the real heights in a musical career? Will my efforts be rewarded? Do I have what it takes to become a soloist, a composer, or a conductor admired by thousands—or will my career be more modest? Would it be better, perhaps, to love music from a distance and commit myself to something more practical and less risky?'

The authors of the classic monographs on the psychology of musical abilities, Carl Seashore (1919; 1938), Boris Teplov (1947), and Rosamund Shuter-Dyson (1968; 1981), confirmed, specified, and decoded the fundamental musical abilities in all their details: the musical ear, the sense of rhythm, and musical memory. These were exactly the abilities that music teachers looked for in the little girls in bows and little boys in short pants who stormed the gates of Russian special musical elementary schools during the previous century. From the ages of 5 or 6 to 18, pupils in these schools were raised as future professional musicians. Yet despite the Herculean efforts of the teachers and their students, and despite the tears and agonies of many parents, some of these budding musicians still played tediously and mechanically, like little robots, while others amazed and enchanted listeners with their spark and inspiration. Where caused this? And why? Perhaps the great musical psychologists had not, in fact, uncovered all the components of this magical alloy called talent. Perhaps an outstanding ear multiplied by hellish labor cannot turn a child into a Sviatoslav Richter or David Oistrakh. Richter, by the way, was self-taught and showed up in Heinrich Neuhaus's master class straight from the foyers of Odessa's movie theaters, where he worked part-time as a dance pianist, occasionally playing whole operas by heart and improvising a little here and there.

It was noted long ago that composition is the nerve and center of musical talent and creativity. A good performer is congenial, a kindred spirit to a composer: he or she is like Anna Holtz, heroine of the popular film '*Copying Beethoven*', who practically breathes in rhythm with the composer as she senses and confirms every movement of his quill pen and every turn of his authorial mind. This congeniality, called the architectonic ear, is something I studied for many years. And indeed, it turned out that talented musicians feel and understand an author's style as if they themselves were its creators—not a single note or pause seems random or incidental—and as testing indicates, they can recreate the composer's motif if it has somehow been violated. The architectonic ear governs the correlation of all the musical elements to one another and to the piece as a whole, and this is one more attribute essential to the talented musician—and an attribute which does not proceed automatically from the development of the known musical abilities.

The sense of the beauty of a musical thought, the feeling of a musical form as a necessity born of some primeval impulse—all this demands a certain experience and acquaintance with musical styles. But there is something else important which also goes into the undefinable yet capacious concept of 'musicality'. This is what music teachers, following Boris Teplov's lead, call the 'ability to react to music emotionally'. From my study of the earliest forms of folklore, I have called this attribute the 'expressive ear'. It is older and more deeply embedded than the architectonic ear, appearing almost in the pre-musical era of human development. And indeed, as studies have shown, it is not the combination of various pitches and rhythms, but the sound itself, its timbre, amplitude, and articulation, that define the meaning and message of a musical phrase. Is it not these qualities of sound which distinguish one performance from another when all the notes and their relationships to each other have already been defined by Bach and Mozart?

Those who are greatly gifted with the expressive ear—people highly sensitive to the non-notational qualities of sound, perceiving it as a living 'voice' addressing them—such people react authentically and genuinely to music and love it very much. Can there really be a talent without the unbelievable attraction and love for music that the expressive ear oversees? As psychology experiments tell us, a wondrous expressive ear is the great gift of music soloists and those people dearest to musicians: the truly passionate music lovers.

So a more scrutinizing look at the musical talent reveals that along with the architectonic ear, the focal point of the musical intellect, comes the expressive ear, the indicator of sensitivity to the emotional and articulative ideas borne in sound. Both the architectonic and the expressive ear have been broadly tested in recent years to determine which Russian children should be invited to enroll in musical elementary schools and which students should continue musical studies as a profession.

Like all manifestations of culture and civilization, music and musical talent appeared in stages rather than all of a sudden. Human musical talent created music as it was establishing and developing itself—creative processes that in turn were influenced by the music being created. The research of ethnomusicologists indicates that in the beginning came sound invested with a certain expressive meaning; then came rhythm, which organized time and movement. After these came the musicalized word, and sound took on a certain pitch. Then oral-musical forms for the organization of sounds appeared—keys and tonalities. Only after all these did musical styles, manners, and directions appear. In my analysis, I constantly refer to the 'phylogenetic principle', whereby the course of the historical development of human talent, its historical evolution, determines its structure.

Thus the general principle of life—the idea of evolution, that the origins of higher and later forms of life emerge from simpler and older ones—also predetermines the construction of one of the most perfect creations of nature: musical talent. At its base lies the expressive ear, which let our distant ancestors differentiate crash and rustle, roar and chirp, all of which clearly had different meanings. With the help of the sense of rhythm, second in seniority among the components of musical talent, early humans distinguished different movements and the rhythms they produced—fast and slow, smooth and broken, jumping and flying. The third element to arise was the analytical ear—what people tend to call simply the musical ear. The sung syllable gave birth to melodies, which consisted of sounds of different pitches. And finally, at a later stage of history, humans learned to make complex musical constructions. For this we needed the architectonic ear, the 'quality controller' of musical compositions, and our musical-production capability, which creates new musical elements. These last two abilities are a sign of a composer's talent—the highest stage of musical evolution.

Why do we need to know which elements of talent arose earlier and which later? For two reasons, the first pedagogical. Talent, as a whole and in separate components, wants development. It is easier and more natural to direct and nurture this development if the developmental system proceeds in the same way as history itself, pushing off from the more basic and primitive abilities and attributes and moving toward the later and newer. That way talent becomes more firmly implanted, and it is easier to compensate for and correct the deficiencies everyone has. Talent is organic, it grows like a tree—outward, from the roots to the branches and leaves, not the reverse.

The second reason that underlines the significance of the phyilogenetic principle is scientific. More is known about musical talent than about other kinds of talent; it has been studied in more detail and more widely tested. Thus it is not surprising that all the constituent elements of musical talent are easier to represent and systematize.

So why not use this experience to assemble a schema of the other human talents? Each of them contains some sort of foundation like the expressive ear; this foundation of talent goes back to the earliest roots of the human activity that gave it birth. Like the sense of musical rhythm, all human talents organize space or time or both. Each activity uses its own 'language'; the analogue of the musical analytical ear in the make-up of other talents can manage the mastery and use of this 'language', no matter what it may be. Finally, in any activity there is a 'composer's gift': the architectonic ear, which evaluates the beauty and suitability of what has been produced, and its own productive ability, offering up for the judgment of the architectonic ear a great variety of elements and combinations for them.

All of the above is from the realm of hypothesis, of course. Nature, in any case, has wonderful news for each of us: we are all talented. Sometimes we simply don't know exactly where our talent lies.

The familiar adage for encouraging striving—'A person can do anything, all it takes is desire and drive'—is in fact illusory, a psychological mirage or urban legend. The study of musical talent offers us yet another proof of this. It's hardly a very good idea for psychologists to encourage everyone to inhuman efforts by giving false hope of success. Shouldn't we instead heed Socrates' injunction to 'know thyself'? Don't we need wider research on all special abilities and all forms of intellect? In this struggle for everyone's self-fulfilment psychologists and specialists in all kinds of activity will enrich and support each other. Perhaps then the Philosopher's Stone of psychology will appear: we will be able to discern all our talents in a timely manner and, most important of all, identify the talents of our children and direct them along appropriate paths. If the study of musical talent which I offer in this book is able to move us closer towards this great and admirable goal—even in the smallest degree, by a single iota—then probably what I've done was worth doing.

Acknowledgements

The publisher is grateful to Creativity-XXI Publishers for allowing them to reuse the foreword by Gennady Rozhdestvensky and illustrations by Nikolai Yudin that were published in the first Russian edition (2004) of this book under the Russian title 'Muzikalnie sposobnosti/Musical abilities'.

Contents

Music is something innate and internal,
which needs little nourishment from without,
and no experience drawn from life.

J. W. Goethe

Part 1

On special abilities

Individual differences and the idea of equality

'Man can do anything', 'The talented are talented in all they do'—such claims inspire optimism in humanity and assure each of us as individuals that nothing is beyond our reach. If we but show the requisite desire we can become Olympic champions, articulate jurists, or inspired poets. In reality, however, even very gifted people seldom shine with talent in every area; indeed, talent is very selective, and the true titans of human endowment—people on the scale of Da Vinci—are extremely rare. The ancient Greeks, demonstrating the selectivity of talent, assigned only one gift apiece to each of their gods: Hermes' talent lay in commerce, Apollo's in art, Demeter's in agriculture, and that of Zeus in governance. As a rule humans are likewise blessed to shine brightly, to amaze their contemporaries, in but a single area. Finding this area, a person's natural calling, is no simple task, but it is one in which the science of psychology can and should help.

Looking at people favored by Fortune, those who have proven themselves to be enormously successful at something, it is well nigh impossible not to pose the question: Why them? Why not others? Did nature grant certain special qualities to the successful, allowing them to overtake everyone else? Or perhaps these people simply showed such powers of exertion that they overcame all barriers and left the weaker and less determined behind? Or perhaps they were simply lucky: others set them upon their journey to success in earliest childhood, giving each an enormous head start over those who were left on their own until much later, forced to lose precious time before finally finding themselves under starter's orders. Or did the great masters simply have the greatest teachers, people who imparted priceless secrets of their professions to a select few while the great majority, lacking these crucial mentors, languished in ignorance? Or finally, and from the standpoint of common sense, most likely, perhaps all these factors were present, in greater and lesser degrees. In which case, of course, the question becomes how to account for each influence individually, how to determine the actual role of each factor in each specific case—itself an enormously complex undertaking.

All these questions, their sometimes contradictory character notwithstanding, are addressed by what has been called 'the psychology of special abilities', a subdivision of the psychological sciences which itself fits into a larger field called 'the psychology of individual differences'. The general field of psychology looks upon this division as something of an Achilles' heel because, primarily, it concerns itself with an extremely sensitive aspect of society's self-definition. It is here that the science of psychology bumps up against an enduringly popular conception of equality. All social development is directed toward compensating for the inequalities of birth and upbringing through equality of educational opportunity, and toward blunting the inequalities borne of social origin with the instruments of democracy—giving everyone a chance to move up and ahead to a position of prominence in society. Every one of us is led to understand that he or she is in no way worse than anyone else, and if something in one's life is somehow lacking or amiss, one can blame such shortcomings on a perseverance deficit, on teachers' insufficient skill or dedication, or simply on unfortunate turns of events, but never on an undemocratic Mother Nature, who might simply have deprived the unsuccessful of a fair share of this or that talent.

A tendency toward political correctness has thus come to loom large over that part of psychology which concerns itself with distinctions between and among individuals, not least in the area of ability, giftedness, and talent. At the same time, however, an impetus to discover the unvarnished truth can also be strongly sensed: it is no accident that Harvard University's coat of arms bears the lone word *Veritas*. Terms such as liberty, equality, and fraternity, for all the noble social and political intentions they suggest, convey nothing scholarly or scientific. And research psychologists, despite society's unrelenting pressure upon them to do otherwise, continue to search for and discover the reasons for individual differences—differences whose very existence simply does not suit everyone all the time.

IQ as the universal cure-all

IQ, the Intelligence Quotient, has become not merely a scientific and scholarly concept, but an influential factor in social development as well. IQ is measured everywhere: in elementary school, in the college admissions process, as part of job applications, and so on. The IQ measurement did not appear *ex nihilo*, of course; it rose to prominence as the practical instrument by which the theories of psychologist Charles Spearman were brought to life. In research conducted at the beginning of the twentieth century, Spearman attempted to measure 'general' intelligence, calling the indicator of such the 'g-factor'. The level of one's g-factor could, it was held, account for all human success in all fields of endeavor; a hypothesis reminiscent of the famous folk saying, 'The talented are talented in all they do.'

This g-factor, which is exactly what IQ testing came to measure, harks back to the intellectual faculties which allowed mankind to survive its early history—the ability to note in objects and natural phenomena the repetition of certain characteristics and relationships, on the basis of which, in turn, the beholder can form certain specific expectations.

In other words, people and animals for whom the past serves as a lesson for the future—that today's banana may be knocked off the tree with the same stick which served that purpose yesterday—have a higher g-factor than those out searching for another stick. Or to use a more complex example: on a certain day of prehistory, a high-g-factor person concluded that thunder and lightning were inseparably linked and produced certain observable phenomena; on the next occasion when thunder boomed forth, this person could (and did) deduce that it was not advisable to stand beneath a tree for shelter; lightning, he had concluded, was more apt to strike there than other places, reducing certain of his lower-g-factor friends and competitors to a state of toast.

When a toddler who is acquiring the power of speech suddenly understands on a given day that the word 'my' stands for 'things that belong to me', he immediately extends this principle indiscriminately to everything that he considers his: suddenly one hears 'my mommy', 'my brother', 'my toys', even 'my dreams'. It is the g-factor which allows us to reason with a degree of abstraction, by analogy, finding in objects and occurrences various parallels and similarities—thus saving us from the endless reinvention of the wheel, since that which has once been decoded and understood serves again for all analogous instances.

The most appropriate name for the psychological property associated with the g-factor is educability: the person possessed of a high g-factor quickly and effectively masters the algorithms to which various processes and procedures are subject, and is capable of putting these algorithms to use. American psychologists, led by Lewis Terman at Stanford, refined the methodologies for assessing the g-factor and named the resulting measurement, in an article published in 1916, the Intelligence Quotient. Terman simplified Spearman's measurements of the intellect to some extent, rendering them more practical and understandable; now they could be used, for example, in the assessment of soldiers being readied to fight in World War I.

Some years later Terman's testing was further refined so that it might help in determining which of the British soldiers who volunteered for service in Africa in World War II were in fact well-suited for the assignment—after a raft of such volunteers, unable to adjust to the new conditions, had requested return posting home following a mere month on African assignments. It was important to understand who could recognize and adjust to new and different realities of life and acclimatize to them, and who could not. This problem was resolved brilliantly with a set of 'pencil and paper' exercises: using only these basic instruments the soldiers were required to indicate similarities and differences between spatial figures and among series of lettered symbols, numerals, or words; the soldiers had to deduce, for example, the patterned regularities by which series are turned into distinct systems, from the simplest numerical line (3-5-7) upward to much more complexly related elements.

It turned out that those who mastered the algorithms used in IQ-testing exercises, and could work with the artificially created systems therein, not only knew better how to adapt to new circumstances but were markedly better learners in general: they learned better in school, in college, in professional training, and so on. The people with high IQs, one could say, had won a free pass to success in life, and psychology, in identifying this, had finally become a science whose conclusions were of interest and import to someone besides other psychologists. The creation of IQ testing rendered psychology a serious experimental science in the eyes of the public, as it appeared to offer concrete aid in solving tasks of critical importance.

Interest in IQ became fashionable in many countries, but particularly in the United States. Where more than in America, the land of immigrants, was there a need for practical people, people with minds 'quick on the uptake' who could orient themselves easily in different environments as they rapidly acquired new capabilities? How tempting must it have been to announce that from this time forth, society would no longer allow unrecognized genius to languish in obscurity, as we would discover as early as the elementary school level those with the potential to become, in Lomonosov's phrase, 'our own Platos and nimble-minded Newtons'? The developer of the IQ methodology, Lewis Terman, decided to mark psychology's ascendance over society's skepticism by committing the rest of his scholarly life to research on IQ and proof of its omnipotence.

Ironically, Terman's great experiment succeeded in proving almost exactly the opposite of what he had initially set out to demonstrate (Terman and Oden 1947). Terman collected data on over a thousand school children with IQs measured as 'high' (over 140 points) and 'exceptionally high' (over 180), following their progress for over the quarter century it took them all to reach age 45. In an effort to assure his triumph, Terman had measured the IQs of certain already-acknowledged major talents, in the hope that these people would emerge at a very high level of accomplishment. But instead, alas, what emerged were the first signs of 'system failure': two future Nobel science laureates, William Shockley and Luis Alvarez, did not even qualify for inclusion in Terman's experiment: their IQs had not been high enough.

A second disappointment followed: IQ scores did not yield direct correlations and did not subscribe to the rule 'The higher the score, the greater the success in life.' When Terman compared 26 people with 'exceptionally high' IQs against 26 with merely 'high' IQs, he found that both the former and the latter came out on similar rungs of the social ladder: all of them were successful businessmen, respected political figures, well-known physicians, and so on—but not one of them had become an outstanding poet, an actor beloved of the public, a famous scholar, or inventor. Beyond this, among the values most esteemed in life by the high-IQ subjects were things wholly unanticipated by Terman. Disdaining the joy of creativity and ignoring professional accomplishments, the high- and highest IQ people held that the principal things of value in their lives were their families, friends, social responsibilities, and relationships with other people—precisely those things which true talents are ready to sacrifice for the sake of their discoveries and creative successes.

Indeed, Lewis Terman himself might have foreseen the result of his grand experiment. In 1922, in an address to the American Psychological Association, he had observed that 'Gifted children are defined not only as academically superior but also superior to unse-lected children in physique, health and social adjustment; [and] marked by superior moral attitudes as measured by character tests of trait ratings'.[1] Much practical wisdom of unique value to humanity—such as the inclination to pose questions after answers have already been accepted, and the ability to find solutions in places which no one would expect to look for them—was left out of Terman's description. And indeed, after a quarter-century the data confirmed these lacunae: no outstanding creative potential was discovered among the children. It was not their lot to become the great showcase of human genius, nor did their labors serve as the source of study and imitation for generations to come.

The participants in Terman's experiment were affectionately referred to as 'the Termites'. As it turned out, the lives of the Termites were but one more scientific demonstration of the traditional maxim that 'All that glitters is not gold.' Human consciousness had once again proven itself to be an extremely complex 'mechanism', the essence of which could not be determined with the aid of one simple test. Upon closer examination, moreover, it also turned out that on matters of political correctness, IQ measurements also proved lacking as an instrument: as a rule, those with very high IQs are the children of very successful parents. These parents are people who set themselves apart from their friends and neighbors not only by their social status, but also by the high fences they build: successful representatives of the middle class do not live where the impoverished do; they have their own neighborhoods and suburbs, where they tend to interact only with people like themselves. In this regard American psychologist Howard Gardner has facetiously posed the question: 'Why should we measure IQ when it's enough to know someone's zip code?'

With a sigh of disenchantment the scientific world was forced to admit that, as Stephen Ceci and Jeffrey Liker put it, 'In many circumstances general intelligence does not limit final levels of skilled performance, and a number of researchers have questioned the view that the existence of a general intelligence factor ('g') has direct bearing on questions about the causes of individual differences in abilities'.[2] Nevertheless people are not in a hurry to part with the notion of IQ forever: the idea of leaving someone alone for an hour with a pencil and paper and then being able to predict what can be expected of him in the future is simply too enticing. Despite the doubts of the scientific community as to the efficacy of IQ testing, the use of this instrument continues to this day—not to discover tomorrow's Einsteins, but to identify promising candidates for clerical and middle-management positions, a task for which IQ assessment is, if not a panacea, at least a reasonably reliable instrument. As Howard Gardner once observed, 'I have sometimes suggested, half seriously, that the IQ test was perfected in France and Great Britain a century ago as a means of selecting individuals who could function as adequate mid-level bureaucrats dispatched to a remote colonial post.'[3]

---

[1] Cited from Winner, E. (1996) *Gifted Children*. New York: Basic Books, p. 9.
[2] Ceci, S. J. and Liker, J. (1986) A day at the races: a study of IQ, expertise and cognitive complexity. *Journal of Experimental Psychology: General*, 115, p. 259.
[3] Gardner, H. (1997) *Extraordinary Minds*. New York: Basic Books, p. 41.

The failure of IQ and its universal g-factor to predict giftedness in all its manifestations forced scholars to continue their search. It was necessary to recognize the fact that even in IQ tests not all tasks were handled with the same competence by the tested: some people coped better with spatial relationships, pictures, and drawings, while others preferred letters and words. Did this mean that the so-called 'general intelligence', if it acted so selectively, was not, in fact, so general? And that the concept of so-called 'general abilities' was simply a convenient abstraction behind which hid unequally developed elements of mind and soul, sometimes working wonderfully and other times weakly? The American psychologist Ellen Winner, a specialist in giftedness among children, hastens to disenchant remaining admirers of the g-factor and IQ:

> Those with mathematical talent most readily retain numerical, spatial and visual information; those with verbal talent most readily retain words. Thus, contrary to what many assume, there is no general enhancement of memory capacity in the gifted. Rather, enhanced memory is a function of a match between the kind of information to be recalled and the kind of talent possessed. . . . Experts have superior memories not for any kind of information, but specifically and only for information within their field of expertise. Ten-year-old chess experts, for instance, have superior memory for chess positions but not for numbers. High ability in one area does not mean high ability in general.[4]

The ideas of g-factor, IQ, and general abilities work only in a limited context, one in which the subject's task is confined to the mastery of existing algorithms. In those regions where the highest abilities begin—in the rarefied air of great achievement and original discovery, where man is given to leave his tracks, great and small, in human history—IQ retreats. To such basic questions as to why one person has panther-like agility while another is as strong as an ox, or why the chemist August Kekule could literally dream up the benzene ring while the composer Hector Berlioz dreamed up an entire symphony—IQ and the g-factor have no response.

IQ plus creativity equals . . .?

Exceptional people, it has long been observed, master things exceptionally quickly. What would have been the measure of the great ballerina Anna Pavlova if it had taken her years to learn an elementary *plie*? Hardly anything, as it would have taken her untold ages to master *The dying swan*. Or what if Newton had had terrible trouble fathoming the multiplication table? He would not have come up with his classic binomial theorem if he had had three lifetimes to do it. No matter how lazy exceptional people are (given that the lazy occur even among their ranks), when they get down to business, the business takes off. As scholars of the gifted like to observe, the exceptionally talented 'immediately see words while others are still connecting syllables'. Exceptional people are likewise possessed of exceptional memories in their fields, and of analogous growth rates in their professional competence. But history records such people not for their remarkable speed, adaptability,

---

4 Winner, E. (1996) *Gifted Children*. New York: Basic Books, p. 52–3.

and skillfulness, but rather for their great discoveries and revolutionary new ideas, the unique creations of their minds, hands, and fantasies.

Psychologists are unable to determine with any degree of certainty exactly which qualities are necessary to master material in some area to the level of known achievement, and which qualities propel us beyond, to the broadening, lengthening, and extension of the previously attained. But there is a general agreement that these two sets of qualities are fundamentally different. Experiments on the human brain were essential in making this demarcation: these revealed that it is possible to identify various brain functions visibly and with the help of certain instruments produce 'pictures' of various brain activities which clearly differ one from another. As Isabelle Peretz, one of the renowned contemporary neuroscientists, states, 'Recent evidence suggests that music might well be distinct from other cognitive functions, in being subserved by specialized neural networks, under the guidance of innate mechanisms.'[5]

Neuropsychologist Hellmuth Petsche (1996) conducted an experiment, in which 76 subjects at first completed purely computational-functional tasks—such as remembering various kinds of data, comparing them and entering the same onto charts, after which the same subjects were required to re-cast themselves in the role of creators: this time they drew pictures, composed melodies, and wrote poetry. It turned out that the brain acts differently in performing the two types of assignments, leaving correspondingly different 'pictures' of each: in the creative assignments the lines of the electroencephalogram depicted greater harmony and interaction among various regions of the brain, as if the process of creation required them to exchange information more often and 'listen' to each other more intently. This experiment, along with a host of other similar ones, convinced the scientific community by stages of the unique sources of and psychological dissimilarity among acquired, taught, and learned knowledge, on the one hand, and that which is composed, created, and imagined on the other. Those mental processes which were gauged by IQ testing resemble a psychological foundation, a base instrument with which humans master the use of already attained knowledge, but which does not enable us to proceed beyond it.

The mysterious ability of the mind and soul to rise above reproduction of the old to the introduction of something heretofore unknown was given the name 'creativity'. To better understand the creative phenomenon, American psychologist Ellis Torrance created tests in which the main emphasis fell on the number and originality of the mental 'products'. Creative personalities were virtual fountains of ideas, proposing scores of potential applications for bricks, needles, newspapers, balls, and various other innocuous items, in usual and unusual ways: the more and the stranger the methods proposed by the subjects for use of the items, the more creativity points were awarded. If the newspaper became something beyond a simple item for reading, serving by turns as a hat, a bird, a boat, and a fish wrapper, then the subject had reason for optimism as a Creator. But if a brick remained only a brick in a wall, never emerging as a tray, a hammer for nailing things, or

---

5 Peretz, I. (2005) The nature of music. *International Journal of Music Education*, 23(2), p. 103.

a bus stop indicator lying lengthwise on the pavement, the subject had every reason to be discouraged as to his creative potential.

Testing of this kind could identify a certain creative initiative; but what to do if neither a brick nor a newspaper could inspire a subject who wanted to do experiments with ancient alphabets, soil samples, or live frogs? Creativity tests had no answers to questions of this kind. The principal similarity of these tests to IQ testing lay in their extreme non-specificity: Ellis Torrance, just like Lewis Terman before him, could be stumped by the subject's simple question 'What should I be?' What exactly will my high intellect and creative possibilities do for me that others cannot match? Should I be a poet, an attorney, an artist, or an athlete? To which psychologists could only nod approvingly as they shrugged their shoulders. Yet society wanted answers to such questions, and the earlier in a subject's life the better, in childhood if possible, or at least by the early teenage years.

By the 1970s, it had become clear that practical psychology and psychodiagnostics were quite limited in scope: they could not predict where a bright future lay for every individual; their recommendations were vague and inexact; and their test results often correlated with a subject's origins, upbringing, and experience. Also mitigating against IQ and creativity testing was the fact that the tests had begun to turn into a sort of school subject unto themselves: those who wanted to get higher scores could, with sufficient training and determination, do exactly that. To clear up the situation, the scientific community decided to get back to theory: the time had finally come for the science of psychology to set its terminology straight and codify its concepts in the realm of individual differentiation in mental activity.

The term most widely used, *abilities*, is commonly associated with the speed and quality of information assimilation. There is also the term *giftedness*, a useful if ungainly derivative of *gifted*—a term also widely used, and one approvingly applied to exceptional children who demand greater attention and particular educational approaches. *Gifted* also bespeaks great promise and definite aspirations for the future. Beyond these there is *talent*, a collective term signaling something in people who demonstrate marked superiority, in both potential and actual accomplishments, over mere mortals. This is a term almost identical in all Indo-European languages (the Russian is *talant*), and it conveys a sense of something at once elevated, grandiose, and monolithic.

Then there remain the terms *intelligence* and *creativity*, each with its own nuances. The former, with or without its *quotient*, denotes an inclination toward mental calculation and manipulation; toward comparison and contrast, assembly and disassembly; and toward the ability to discover the critical link in a chain, the essential factor, the nerve center or kernel of truth—the heart of a matter, if you will. (In line with this universal term one also finds the Russian word *um*, which the psychologist Sergei Rubinshtein succinctly defined as 'the ability to perceive the essence'). *Creativity*, finally, represents the newest and most mysterious term in this lexicon, suggesting as it does the potential to make (up) something original, a productive ability (or admixture) involving innovation, invention, and intent.

Such are the five principal concepts: abilities, giftedness, and talent, plus intelligence and creativity. The sum of these attributes determines success in life. The more we have of these qualities, individually and *en masse*, the greater the cause for optimism in each of us as we look ahead.

Acquisition, diligence, and creative work

Of the five terms under consideration, talent is the most significant; all the others constitute preconditions of one sort or another, critical prerequisites which precede the appearance of exceptional success. Talent, on the other hand, is something closer to a result than a stage of development: in speaking of 'talented poets', for example, one can safely assume that the group we are referring to includes at least Marlowe if not Shakespeare, at least Tvardovsky if not Pushkin. Or of a 'talented physician'—the subject may not be the author of a new philosophy of healing, a Hippocrates or Paracellus, but is surely someone on the order of Sviatoslav Fedorov, the creator of optical microsurgery. This explains the efforts of psychologists to discover the essence of talent, and their disappointment at the imperceptibility and vagueness of the elements which comprise it. As distinct from the concept of abilities, which are most often defined as 'rapidity in learning and the acquisition of competence in a given field', Polish psychologist Maria Manturzewska has observed:

> Talent is known as a specific quality of personality which signifies, first of all, unrelenting effort toward the achievement of the best possible result, that far exceeding average indicators. The great minds of Europe have been pondering the problem of talent—its nature and structure, its origin and development—for some two thousand years now, from Plato and Aristotle to such modern-day psychologists as Sternberg, Csziksentmihalyi, Gardner, Heller and others. But despite their efforts, the problem of talent is far from resolved. An avalanche of publications and conferences notwithstanding, the very concept of talent has become no clearer. It has already become a habit to substitute for it such concepts as 'giftedness' or 'exceptional abilities', but scholars and contemporary psychologists are virtually incapable of explaining how these three terms stand in relation to one another—which is why they tend to be used as synonyms even though this simply does not correspond to the reality of the situation.[6]

This can be taken as both good news and bad news. The bad news is clear enough: two thousand years of thought and effort have yielded nothing close to an unambiguous result; the essence of talent, its basic conception, remains undiscovered. One of the most authoritative researchers in the field Francoys Gagné states that terms and definitions within the emerging theory of giftedness and talent are as many as there are scholars in the field—17 chapters of the renowned book on the topic (*Conceptions of giftedness* [1986] [ed. R. Sternberg and J. Davidson]. New York: Cambridge University Press) offer 17 different approaches to terms and definitions: 'Within that book, no one ever adopts another scholar's definition; each of them prefers to create his/her own. All these

---

[6] Manturzewska, M. (1994) Les facteurs psychologiques dans le développement musical et l'évolution des musiciens professionnels. In *Psychologie de la musique*, (ed. A. Zenatti), Presses Universitaire de France, p. 260.

conceptions develop in parallel, without ever confronting their respective contradictions and divergences'.[7]

The good news, on the other hand, is that the search process has shed light on the important difference between abilities (as a psychological attribute which 'feeds' the character of the acquirer) and talent (a psychological attribute of the creative, constructive character). Thus the psychological make-up of abilities and that of talent are no longer indistinguishable from one another, surely a victory of sorts. Was it not toward this that both the developers of IQ and of creativity theory were working? Through their joint efforts they demonstrated to mankind that certain basic human functions, understanding, mastery, recognition and learning, are all skills which demand the acquisition of certain algorithms; and enabling these skills, easing their realization is, in the end, what is done by what we call intelligence.

Intelligence is not a simple characteristic; it exists in various forms or aspects. Some people easily grasp mathematical information, for example, while others more easily assimilate information conveyed in an artistic and visual format. In the first instance it is said that the person possesses mathematical abilities, meaning that he has a particular inclination toward the mastery of numerical, spatial, and similar formalized operations. In the second case, by contrast, it is said that the person has artistic abilities, meaning a particular inclination toward the mastery of visual-figurative operations. If intelligence is the instrument of thought, then abilities are the instrument of thought trained on—and revealing itself exclusively in—a defined field of activity. Intelligence and abilities are, at base, synonyms: both are specific entities, never appearing in a 'general' form; and both intelligence and abilities allow man to carry out analytical and synthesizing operations on this or that object with particular success and the sense of naturalness characteristic of a fish in water.

Without possessing abilities and intelligence it would be impossible to make a genuine breakthrough in one's field: man without abilities is incapable of assimilating that which has been achieved by his predecessors: he cannot speak the language, as it were, of the realm in which he wants to distinguish himself. But the fortunate possessor of abilities still cannot progress beyond imitation and successful assimilation of the known. Countless epigones in the world of art, people whose abilities are undeniable, find that these abilities alone are insufficient for independent artistic creation. To produce something significant and lasting, there remains a further necessity: talent, the most mysterious concept in the psychology of giftedness, whose nature scholars and scientists have been attempting to fathom for untold generations.

Talent is connected with the creative imagination, fantasy, and the necessity of expression that psychologists call *creativity*, which acts as a sort of motor of talent, its psychological center (wouldn't it be reasonable to call creative part of any specific talent *giftedness*?). Abilities and giftedness as specific creativity form the base of talent: they are the principal components of its structure. Put otherwise, talent presupposes that man is at once possessed of both abilities and giftedness as specific creativity. Talent may be called that

[7] Gagné, F. (2004) An imperative, but, alas, improbable consensus! *Roeper Review*, 27, p. 12.

particular integrative property to which all great actions may be ascribed. Abilities or specific intelligence compose one side or component part of talent, and specific creativity, or giftedness, the other.

People often liken giftedness with talent—the highest creative potential for the fulfillment of a certain activity. In this case giftedness and talent are synonyms. Nevertheless some researchers suggest that it is better to call giftedness 'potential talent' waiting to be developed and threatening not to become talent if trained insufficiently—this is the platform supported by Francoys Gagné (Gagné 2004b). But the border line within talent theory looks more visible between 'abilities' as opposed to 'talent' and 'giftedness' as different types of human psychological potential: 'abilities' as the instrument for quick learning and 'giftedness' and 'talent' as instruments for creative input into the domain. Without consensus among researchers on this sensitive matter it is possible to accept 'abilities' versus 'talent' opposition as more widespread and clear than others.

The difference between psychological attributes of talent, leading to outstanding achievement, on one hand, and 'school abilities', helping to master the domain, on the other, was specially considered by Vadim Krutetsky, Russian expert in mathematical abilities:

> Whether to speak about distinguishing two different aspects of mathematical abilities—school and creative abilities, we find total consensus on the latter: creative abilities of a scientist-mathematician are the inborn entity—favorable environment is needed only for their revelation and development. That's the point of view of mathematicians A. Poincaret and J. Hadamard—both of them were interested in mathematical creativity research. W. Betz also referred to the inborn nature of mathematical talent, insisting that he has in mind the ability to independently unveil new mathematical truths while everyone, of course, is able to grasp already existing ideas.[8]

This kind of dual-component structure of talent, with its base of abilities and an 'upper-level' creativity (suggested here to be called 'giftedness'), suits many scholars. Robert Siegler and Dale Kotovsky (1986), for example, hold that the first part of the proposed *schema* can be termed as the 'educative-familial' part, since the family exercises great influence in the process of education and the mastery of ability functions; the second part, on the other hand, they term as the 'creative-productive' division, relating not to learners but to adults ready to introduce a unique contribution in any area of activity. Siegler and Kotovsky's conclusion would seem promising indeed for the general two-part *schema*: 'The results of a great number of empirical experiments describe a weak correlation between these two types of giftedness'.[9]

That is, once more we see an assertion that giftedness or talent, on the one side, and abilities, on the other, form something like psychological 'parallel lines'. The question of the specific attributes of abilities and talent—what kind of talent, where does it lead to and in what does it appear?—remains an open one: the *schema* and structure are suitable

----

[8] Krutetsky, V. (1998) *Psikhologia matematicheskikh sposobnostei shkolnikov/The psychology of schoolchildren's mathematical abilities*, Moscow: Institut prakticheskoi psikhologii, p. 27–8.

[9] Siegler, R. S. and Kotovsky, K. (1986) Two levels of giftedness: shall ever the twain meet? In *Conceptions of Giftedness* (ed. R. J. Sternberg and J. E. Davidson). Cambridge University Press.

for the very reason that they work for all cases and explain everything, from the talent of a master detective to that of an eminent performing artist. Maria Manturzewska, like many of her colleagues, emphasizes in her considerations of these questions an element of voluntary effort. The same is true for Joseph Renzulli's concept of giftedness (1978) including 'academic giftedness', 'creative-productive giftedness', and 'task commitment'. To take the moon from the sky—and such are the strivings of the talented, often extending beyond the bounds of the possible—is something that may be pursued if and only if one is consumed by an insane idea of this type and approaches its realization with maniacal dedication. Without this kind of unusually high motivation or striving toward a goal nothing is ever accomplished in any difficult enterprise. So it would seem that the two components comprising the structure of talent in the *schema*—*abilities* plus *giftedness*—so far are not in themselves enough. The first of them would be the nearest to intelligence as mental adaptation mechanism and the second would be the nearest to creativity as productive and innovative potential. To complete the picture a third, motivational component is required. This third element plays the role of the emotional fuel by which man propels himself toward a goal. It is hardly surprising that psychologists have taken to calling this creative motivation *drive*.

Among the first to note the leading role played by motivation was a group of Russian scholars of creative psychology led by Yakov Ponomarev (1983). They discovered that in experiments using challenging tasks which all members of a subject group could eventually perform, the winners were not the most intelligent, but rather those who could become obsessed with the task, consider its completion a matter of honor, and suffer genuine despair if a solution could not be found. The subject who knows only too well that the task she is performing and her personal well-being are actually far removed from one another usually abandons the search for a solution halfway through, and suffers not a twinge of regret if the solution does not emerge. It turns out that success and motivation are intimately connected: without a will, there is no way.

A summary of the thoughts on talent among late twentieth-century psychologists was undertaken by Dean Simonton, an American expert in the area of giftedness and genius. Simonton hastened to disabuse all those who hoped to find the answer in a single place, somewhere near IQ or perhaps close to creativity. He announced that talent was a property at once complex and of multiple components, presupposing particular attributes of thinking (a bow toward IQ); a particular kind of activity (meaning the connection with creativity, i.e the continuous production of new ideas); and, finally, an entire bouquet of personal qualities having nothing to do with the intellect: motives and needs, peculiarities and tendencies of the heart and soul, and interests and values as well. For the sake of convenience this exotic mixture of psychological attributes and qualities can be divided into three groups: an intellectual component, close to abilities and IQ; a productive component, close to creativity; and an emotional component, to which motivation is the key. Lest the scientific community demand too much of him, Simonton soberly cautioned:

> What really matters is whether there exists some innate endowment that enhances exceptional performance, not the exact nature of that endowment or how it especially operates. That is, talent

may be a much more complicated process than assumed in most investigations. By working with overly simplistic conceptions of talent, investigators might have looked for evidence by methods that necessarily underestimated its significance. Hence, my purpose here is to present what might constitute a more realistic, but thus more complicated, model of talent and its development.[10]

A multiplicative model of talent

The word *model* is simply a convenience of scientific terminology; it can be applied to any object or phenomenon which has a structure of some kind. A model of talent had in fact existed before Simonton's, and its apogee may be considered the announcement by Boris Teplov, a Russian psychologist who worked in the area of ability and giftedness, that a talent may have its weaker and stronger sides: pianist A may be talented in one way—his play is lyrical, refined, and sensitive, yet he cannot play three octaves in a row without missing a note—while pianist B shows talent of a quite different sort, with play that is thunderous, agile, and technically masterful yet never moves the listener, never touches the heart (Teplov 1947). The pianists are both talented, but differently. While the example is arguably imperfect, it is in any case certain that pianists A and B themselves get to decide whether they can live with their deficiencies—or go looking for work in some other profession. If pianist A thinks that the public will sigh and get along without the technical mastery, and pianist B concludes that deep musicality is not really necessary for a master of fleet, high-decibel playing, then both may be termed adherents of the so-called 'additive model' of talent. This means that not only switching the position of the elements but losing some of them altogether does not, in essence, change the sum total: the presence of certain of the elements in some way or another excuses, replaces, and softens the absence of others. 'Distorted' talents are, nevertheless, still talents.

Dean Simonton proposed another model, one which was less forgiving toward pretenders to the ranks of the talented. If, for example, a talented pilot reads instruments wonderfully, enjoys excellent health, has good balance, a fine sense of spatial orientation in general and mid-air orientation in particular, and yet has a slow reaction time, then this sole failing may negate all his wondrous virtues: in an emergency in the air, the absence of one of the components of talent, in this case quick reactions, may prove fatal. This talent model is called 'multiplicative', meaning that if even one necessary component of talent in fact amounts to zero, then all other attendant qualities, when multiplied by it, inevitably lose all their value—the entire talent structure zeroes out, leaving neither trace nor hope behind it.

The multiplicative model is particularly discouraging when the components of the talent in question are independent of one another and do not correlate, which is in fact the way things most often work out. A would-be ballerina may have wonderful physical characteristics but weak musical abilities and a poor sense of rhythm. This is a ballerina who simply cannot dance, as her outstanding athletic qualities can neither replace, lessen,

---

[10] Simonton, D. K. (1999) Talent and its development: an emergenic and epigenetic model. *Psychological Review*, 106(3), p. 437–8.

or otherwise compensate for her absence of musicality. As if that were not enough, ballerinas also need good artistic abilities and a certain stage presence. It stretches credulity to presume that all these outstanding qualities can ever occur together in one and the same girl: a gymnast's agility and endurance, a good pianist's musicality and a performing artist's communicativeness. And if one recalls that each of these qualities is itself a complex function with its own complement of elements—the ballerina's physical characteristics, for example, must include endurance, dexterity, agility, flexibility of joints, and autonomy of leg and arm movement, plus a strong sense of balance for the many multiple rotations, along with litheness and grace of figure—then it quickly becomes clear that any single ballerina who is in fact a *good* ballerina has emerged from among thousands upon thousands of candidates.

Using probability statistics based on two necessary components of talent (though there are actually many more), Simonton came to some rather harsh-sounding conclusions about any single talent:

> Almost exactly half of the children would fall in the lowest group, and 12% would have no talent whatsoever. In contrast, less than 0.5% would boast the highest possible talent potential. Obviously, unlike the bell-shaped curve of the two participating factors, their multiplicative combination is very much skewed right. The highest levels of talent will be as extreme as they are rare.[11]

More scrupulous inspection, however, reveals that Simonton's conclusions are not actually fatal. It may be that the majority of people do not possess actual talent; yet even in whose creative professions which are closest to natural giftedness, one hears the opinion that any creative field needs not only geniuses, but simply able people as well. Talent is a combination of abilities, creative potential plus motivation, and yet it is not a critical component of success in a given profession.

Despite the fact that talent is a multi-component phenomenon—that each component may be taken as the combined total of various sub-components; and that none of the components can equal zero—it is still true that the components are not all of equal importance. Psychologists have noted the presence of a certain 'core ability'. Ellen Winner and Gianvito Martino (1993) maintain that from the whole assortment of qualities necessary for an artist, the most essential is video-motor coordination—that which allows him to translate the three-dimensional items he observes in nature into two-dimensional ones on a stretched canvas or paper. The sense of color, composition, and all other attributes of artistic giftedness are less important than this core ability.

Winner and Martino (1993) identify the analogous ability for music as a 'feeling for musical structures: tonality, harmony and rhythm'. This 'feeling' is in fact the leading ability, the starting point without which there simply is no musician. All the other qualities—musical imagination, musical memory, and so on and so forth—all these are, in a certain sense, derivatives. In other words, the absence of a connection among the components of talent, a complete and utter lack of correlation among them, is purely

[11] Simonton, D. K. (1999) Talent and its development: an emergenic and epigenetic model. *Psychological Review*, 106(3), p. 442.

theoretical (just as physics has the concept of a vacuum, yet a perfect vacuum is something that exists only in the minds of physicists). In reality there are, in the structure of talent, very substantial components by which other components seemingly align and orient themselves; and there are less substantial components as well. In this light the talent model becomes more natural, more in keeping with living beings, taking on flexibility and variety: some components have to be present in utter completeness, in their 100 percent essence—while for others it is entirely satisfactory if their presence is marked but a modest degree above zero.

Alongside with Dean Simonton and Ellen Winner one of the Russian leading researchers of abilities and talent Evgeny Ilyin suggested the 'non-compensatory model' of talent, also marking the importance of 'core ability':

> Possibly, if one meets the highest demands of a certain activity, it's hardly possible to speak about full compensation of underdeveloped abilities (if it wasn't like that everyone could be gifted in all kinds of activities; but it's not the case—giftedness is basically the conglomerate of non-compensated human abilities). If core abilities are not shining brightly, compensatory mechanisms may only provide a very average level of this activity's success.[12]

Least autonomous in the structure of talent is the emotional part, the motivational component. It has been noted that the desire to give oneself over completely to one's chosen undertaking—understood as an absolutely selfless feeling, unconnected with a striving for glory or personal enrichment—is proportionate to the creative component of one's talent. Exceptional geniuses cannot be dragged away from their essential business even when thunder booms and lightening flashes around them. Marginally less imposing talents can sometimes be bothered by the trivia of life. The composer Balakirev, possessed of exceptional pedagogical gifts but only a fair endowment as a composer, confessed that he needed absolute freedom and a total absence of worries in order to write anything worthwhile. In all probability Apollo summoned Balakirev to the 'holy sacrifice' of composition in a voice none too loud, a voice too often drowned amid a sea of other calls, claims, and appeals. Such was not the case with Balakirev's more talented contemporary Nikolai Rimsky-Korsakov. Rimsky's friends were justifiably amazed by the totality of the creative attention he summoned in order to perform—along with all his teaching, directing, administrative, and other responsibilities—the principal task of his life: composing.

So, the Simonton talent model presupposes a multi-component nature of talent, a characteristic which expands when each component has the ability for further subdivision—just as any body consists of crystal and molecules which are invisible to the naked eye but under the microscope reveal a rich internal life. The multiplicative model of talent does not allow for complete failure in any one of its critical attributes—a malfunction by the smallest stay or bolt can derail the most complex machine. The talent model in statistical analysis is a source of what might be judged a politically incorrect set of truths: exceptional talents are extraordinarily rare; they are invariably people whom nature has

---

[12] Ilyin, E. (2004) *Psikhologia individualnikh razlichii/The psychology of individual differences*, St.Petersburg: Piter, p. 272.

simply blessed (with, e.g. the goodness of Mother Teresa or the strength of Hercules); and the majority of human beings in connection with any particular talent belong to neither group, figuring in a kind of 'golden mean'.

Simonton's most debatable assertion seems to be that of the complete absence of inter-dependence among the components, which in a mathematical model is an unavoidable given. In reality the interdependence of the components and their unequal weight in the structure of talent softens the strict mathematical model, allowing us to treat it simply as an initial attempt to bring order to chaos—to put, one might say, some preliminary analytical ground beneath our feet.

Nature versus nurture: god-given or pedagogue-driven?

Among the problematic issues related to the psychology of abilities and talent, one of the most prominent and socially controversial is that of the origins of these qualities. In Anglo-American scholarly parlance the issue has been framed as 'nature vs. nurture', and in its baldest elaboration it emerges as a fairly provocative question: 'Can someone become a Mozart if he is willing to try hard enough?' In other words, is it possible to create, to 'make' all these attributes—intelligence, creativity, giftedness, talent, and so on—through training, education, and upbringing? Or is it a matter of fate, meaning the gifts of intelligence are simply passed along to certain members of society by a benevolent Fortune while others are ignored? Consensus has yet to be reached on this question. The struggle of prejudices and passions, a desire to flatter society's collective ego and at the same time tell the truth has made for a most extraordinary tangle of contradictory opinions.

The nature–nurture argument dates back to the most ancient pre-historic times when it became clear that the quality of music making is like a demarcation line between indi-viduals. Pierre Boulez in his 'Le temps musical' lecture given in February 1978 at Centre Pompidou tells a naive story of ananga and basonga tribes living side by side in space and time. The former were deeply convinced that practice and desire to succeed is all you need to excel in music; the latter were not less deeply convinced in quite the opposite: in order to conquer hearts and souls by music there must be a certain inborn 'spark'. 'So, the basongas definitely support the idea of the gifted person whose talent was passed along through hereditary chain (the notion very much like our own in the Western world)'.[13] There is no need to say that both tribes' convictions didn't seek any support in science, evidence, objectivity, and so on. And their argument proceeded through centuries untouched without a resolution until now. As Joanne Haroutounian very fairly puts it: 'If you are seeking a heated discussion between colleagues in music, simply bring up the subject of musical talent—then sit back and listen'.[14]

[13] Boulez, P. (1995) Le temps musical. In *Homo Musicus: Readings in Psychology of Music* (ed. M. Starcheus). Moscow Conservatory, p. 66.
[14] Haroutounian, J. (2002) *Kindling the Spark. Recognizing and Developing Musical Talent.* Oxford University Press, p. xiv.

It seems logical to suppose that given extreme sensitivity and social alertness of the 'nature–nurture debate', the views on the problem are largely the servants of cultural preferences. Well into the nineteenth century the great heritage of medieval craftsmanship and respect for the guilds largely guaranteed that humanity's accomplishments would be ascribed to His Majesty Labor. Admirers of Bach heard the master voice as an opinion widespread at the time: 'I had to apply myself with great diligence. Whoever shows the same assiduousness will achieve the same result.' For some reason musicians of similar diligence have not appeared to this day, and the assiduous Bach continues to tower like Everest above all his contemporaries and successors.

At the end of the romantic nineteenth century, with all its reverences before the mystery of genius, the views of Francis Galton came to the fore. An expert in physical anthropology and the genealogy of the famous, Galton maintained that it was in fact heredity which dictated the inequality of ability and the resultant level of achievement. In Galton's works he managed to reconcile the irreconcilable—the finest subtleties of the human psyche and the blunt instruments of mathematical statistics—in order to find, with the help of the latter, the average level of giftedness and genius among various races, ethnicities, and social groups. Statistics, wrote Galton, are 'the only tools by which an opening may be cut through the formidable thicket of difficulties that bars the path of those who pursue the Science of Man'.[15]

Galton attempted to predict the probability of the appearance of great talents. With no intention of offending anyone in particular, he announced that among certain human communities and even certain races the appearance of genius was less likely than among others, and that neither poor teaching nor poor social conditions could be blamed for this: it was simply that Mother Nature had, over eons of hereditary baton-passing, put clusters of favorable characteristics together to create a stock of 'bluebloods'. In our age of democratic idealism it is difficult to read such a conclusion without shuddering; in any event, Galton's views were never refuted and were discussed by the scientific community of the time in complete seriousness. In full accordance with post-romantic heritage next generation of scientists were easily captivated by 'g-factor' and 'IQ' ideas. Carl Seashore's views of inborn aptitude for music and its pitch, rhythm, and memory measurements were totally up to date in 1919 when the first edition of his first famous book appeared.

In the twentieth century, with the dramatic increase in population and the growth of mass media, the ranks of the famous of the world swelled significantly. The biographies of outstanding people of the past and present became widely known, as did the processes by which they became such. In this connection no small part was played by the phenomenon of 'folk psychology', which began to influence public opinion, as much as, perhaps even more than, psychology in the scholarly sense. A good example of folk psychology at work would be a judgment rendered by Irina Viner, the internationally known trainer of

15 Pearson, K. (1914) *The Life, Letters and Labours of Francis Galton*. Cambridge, UK: Cambridge University Press.

artistic gymnasts.[16] A curious journalist posed a question to her in which one could hear a sort of timid rebuke: 'Ms. Viner,' began the journalist, 'I am a great admirer of gymnastics and gymnasts, but I simply can't understand one thing: how is it possible in principle to form such unbelievably intricate figures with your arms and legs?' Viner, not in the least put out, answered: 'The question is not how but who. The person who can do this is someone who has received the natural gifts of agility and extension. One day this person met a coach who, in turn, also enjoyed a natural gift—the ability to recognize and identify these qualities, and put them to use to their best advantage.' In place of Bach's diligence and assiduousness as an explanation for the achievements of the outstanding, we now find the endowments of kind Fortune—the gift of a pupil matched by that of a teacher.

Public opinion, in the main, has tended to support this view. Education has long since ceased to be the province of the wealthy, and thanks to the relative equality of various conditions, the inequality of people's results (which remains marked, of course) now calls forth a perfectly reasonable question: 'How is it, given that access to the means of individual development in certain countries is all but universal, that the number of talented people in these countries remains at the same small-percentage level as before?' The social conscience of a democratic society could not let this and related questions simply hang fire. The zeal and striving of the people, their struggle toward the victor's laurels, had to be encouraged and developed.

Toward the end of the twentieth century research psychologists responded to this public need with the theory of 'deliberate practice', set out by a group of highly acclaimed psychologists: K. A. Ericsson (of Florida State University), J. A. Sloboda (University of Keele), Jane Davidson (University of Sheffield), and M. J. A. Howe (Essex University). In the beginning of the 1990s they started a new circle of 'nature–nurture' debate saying that the concepts of 'abilities, giftedness and talent' were but a 'cultural myth'. Stating that it's just the amount of hard work or 'deliberate practice' that brings achievement, they concluded:

> People assumed to possess talent are seen as capable of very high levels of performance when given sufficient opportunities for training. As evidence the authors note that the same amount of practice time creates equivalent amounts of progress in most and least successful musicians (in other words, very capable musicians do not profit more from practice time than do unsuccessful musicians, thus suggesting that the two groups do not differ in innate talent).[17]

To those who wanted success in grasping the brass ring of life, they recommended several conditions (Ericsson and Charness 1995b; Howe 1995; 1996; Lehmann 1995; Sloboda et al. 1994a; 1994b). First, study and train more, more often, and more diligently than others. Second, start measuring your efforts as early as practicable, from the diaper stage if possible and get the support and encouragement of your parents in these efforts.

---

[16] Sozdavaia championov/Creating champions. *Sovetsky Sport*, May 11, 1998.

[17] Howe, M., Davidson, J., and Sloboda, J. (1999) Innate talents: reality or myth? In *The Nature–Nurture Debate: The Essential Readings* (ed. S. Ceci and W. Williams). Malden, MA: Blackwell Publishing, p. 257.

And third, find an instructor of the highest qualifications, and go full bore under his guidance for no fewer than ten years in your chosen field of science, art, or athletics. The observance of all three conditions would lead anyone to international recognition. No doubt, 'deliberate practice' theory is a well-elaborated scientific concept, and thus having many examples and nuances within it. But basically these three are the preconditions of success if to put them in the shortest possible way.

One of the most convincing of the experiments published under the 'umbrella' of deliberate practice theory is the one with conservatory violin students: from this experiment the claim for the necessary 10 000 hours of practice first emerged:

> Ericsson and his coworkers (Ericsson, Krampe, and Heizmann, 1993; Ericsson, Tesch-Romer, and Krampe, 1990) have found strong correlations between the level of performance of student violinists in their twenties and the number of hours of formal practice they had engaged in. By the age of 21 the best students in the performance class of a conservatoire had accumulated around 10 000 hours practice, compared with less than half that amount for students in the same institution who were training to be violin teachers.[18]

There are several questions arising from this famous experiment. (1) Isn't it possible that the most talented are at the same time the most interested and motivated, so they practice more? (2) Isn't it possible that 'the solo group students' pursue their practice goals because they are successful in their training efforts, and it's a matter of talent to benefit from practice? Doesn't it seem logical for those who don't gain by practice, simply not to overburden themselves with useless practice hours? This second possibility was invested into the discussion by Joanne Haroutounian in her latest book (Haroutounian 2002). (3) And finally, isn't it possible that the 'talent' of everyone under observation in this experiment is practically average, so quite fairly those who practice more succeed more? The fact that some students were included into 'the solo group' is not confirmed by any further biographical evidence. So, couldn't that be a typical case of 'school success' that not too often leads to creative success, and we don't know what 'the appointed solo group' could boast in their mature years? Chopin practiced not more than conservatory students, three hours a day, and he was Chopin. (Milshtein 1967).

The idea of family support suggested as one of the preconditions of any child's success is also far from being faultless. Thus, for example, the well-known musical psychologist Jane Davidson and her colleagues state that all the parents of children who later become successful musicians were, in fact, their charges' great friends and allies from earliest childhood (Davidson *et al.* 1996). If the great jazz musician Sidney Bechet were to hear of such a conclusion he would be surprised indeed. His altogether respectable parents, who dreamed of something rather more substantial and reliable than a career in music for their son, actually hid his clarinet from him—whereupon young Sidney, having recovered the instrument from a local trash heap, was obliged to hide it all over again! (Chilton 1987).

---

[18] Howe, M., Davidson, J., and Sloboda, J. (1999) Innate talents: reality or myth? In *The Nature–Nurture Debate: The Essential Readings* (ed. S. Ceci and W. Williams). Malden, MA: Blackwell Publishing, p. 262.

Robert Schumann's mother, the widow of a publisher and literary translator, reconciled herself only with difficulty to her son's choice of music as a profession; while Christoph W. Gluck, the great reformer of opera, was forced to roam about Italy and Bohemia after being expelled from home by his forester-father. Even some of the great musical geniuses, it is clear, were given switches and coal by an unkind Fate instead of the presents other youngsters received. The 'universal support' given by parents to beginning musicians turns out, upon closer examination, to be yet another myth.

And couldn't it be that, perhaps, one more alleged precondition for success, the observation and support of a mentor-instructor, stands up better under closer examination? In a word: no. Far too many musicians had to scale the heights of Parnassus entirely on their own: the classical composers Hector Berlioz, Michael Glinka, Alexander Borodin, and Modest Mussorgsky; such leading lights of popular genres as Vassily Solov'ev-Sedoi in Russia and Irving Berlin in the United States; and legions of performing artists, including Konstantin Igumnoff and the twentieth-century idol Sviatoslav Richter—all these went through an early period of establishing themselves in music entirely without the assistance of any instructors; some, in fact, got on quite well without them even later. And even this considerable evidence elides another crucial fact: that far from all musicians of talent, even when they had teachers, were satisfied with them. Far too many secrets of the profession, as in the cases of Yehudi Menuhin and Arthur Rubinstein, for example, had to be discovered by the artists themselves (Menuhin 1979; Rubinstein 1960). So the assertion that the great composers were cradled from childhood in the loving arms of their teachers is worse than an exaggeration. The direction of an instructor is, like the support of a musician's parents, in no way a necessary precondition for musical success.

Musicians who achieve exceptional success are workaholics, it is true. But why? Does a musician show exceptional results because he or she is a dedicated striver, or are they in fact such strivers because they are talented? Ellen Winner, an eminent American psychologist and specialist in the psychology of giftedness, often speaks of supreme motivation as one of the greatest riddles of talent. It is talent that drives the musician to try dozens of chord variations, the mathematician to go through reams of paper in search of the best proof, and the artist to refine the composition and color scheme of a picture already painted. A striving for the ideal leads the talented person forward, and from here is born the enormous love of labor. This is all the more so in a democratic society, where it is unacceptable to force children to study and there is no possibility of instilling in the average child the kind of drive and commitment to purpose which talent commands with no goading whatsoever. Motivation and talent are bound by a tie of such intimacy that it is hardly possible to disentangle it: time spent on lessons is directly proportional to the strength and stubbornness of motivation, which is, in turn, a recognized component of talent.

In attacking her opponents, Ellen Winner takes pleasure in pointing out their clearly loaded choice of examples: somehow they are enormously inclined toward classical music and athletics. But what about the realm of science, in which we see a future Niels Bohr and a future high-school physics teacher sitting in the same college classrooms listening to the same professors? Or what of rock and pop music, where some of the kids playing in garages on broom handles and air guitars go on to become The Beatles or Led Zeppelin, while others never escape their own neighborhoods? If one looks at the experience of Russia's specialized music schools, a convincing case emerges: under conditions of equal strictness on the part of parents and instructors, who hover Cerberus-like over every student, the success attained by the students is nevertheless very uneven: alongside such outstanding soloists as Gidon Kremer and Evgeny Kissin studied great numbers of average orchestral musicians and run-of-the-mill music teachers, although almost all the students gave their best, as the schools simply would not tolerate less.

Summing up the 'nature–nurture' argument Ellen Winner writes:

> Research on the nurture hypothesis has failed to demonstrate that giftedness is a product of hard work and intensive training. Research has failed to demonstrate that any particular kind of family environment causes giftedness. . . . To be sure, no research has demonstrated that hard work, perseverance, and practice is sufficient.[19]

The attempt at a 'democratic breakthrough' in psychology at the end of the twentieth century could be one more indication of the growing dependence of science on the demands of society, especially when the issue at hand was (and is) as sensitive as that of the psychology of the gifted: the psychological well-being of every member of society depends too much on this area of science, apparently, for science to be left entirely to its own devices. In turning itself over to public opinion, however, the scientific study of the psychology of giftedness is capable both of causing wounds and healing them, of comforting our collective ego and disturbing it. Raymond Cattell, a specialist in heredity, sent us a following warning:

> There is perhaps . . . deeper opposition in many people to the notion that their freedom is to some extent constrained by hereditary potentials . . . . At times we would all wish that the law of gravity, the laws of thermodynamics and the law of compound interest could be suspended. As A. Housman wrote: 'To think that two and two are four And neither five nor three The heart of man has long been sore And long 'tis like to be'. The more appropriate attitude is that the laws of heredity, like scientific laws generally, may be understood and managed toward human good: they can be denied and ignored only at our cost.[20]

Genealogy and talent

Traditional psychology holds that abilities and talent are to a great extent 'granted from above', although, no doubt, they need to be nurtured and developed. A word for it is once again pronounced by Isabelle Peretz:

> In fact, the functional and the morphological differences were related to musical aptitude, implying influence of innate determinants. These findings re-open the debate about whether the observed brain differences between musicians and nonmusicians arise from genetic or other predispositions (e.g. talent) as well as from practice and experience.[21]

---

[19] Winner, E. (2000) The origins and ends of giftedness. *American Psychologist*, 55(1), p. 167.

[20] Cattell, R. (1982) *The Inheritance of Personality and Ability. Research Methods and Findings.* New York, London: Academic Press, p. 16.

[21] Peretz, I. (2006) The nature of music from a biological perspective. *Cognition*, 100, p. 22.

No scientific evidence has yet cancelled the inborn nature of talent, and alongside this cornerstone the concept of a 'hygiene of labour' ascribed to talent—meaning that much work and untiring refinement are necessary to show one's talent in its full glory—appears the merest of trivialities. However, another question arises in this connection: does the inborn nature of talent signify a hereditary nature? Can one assume that talented parents should necessarily produce talented children, and that the forbearers of the talented were themselves talented as well?

A statistical analysis performed by Dean Simonton indicates otherwise: the concept of 'inborness' is not synonymous, it appears, with that of 'inherited from one's parents'. Talent is a structure of many components and multiple elements; the more inputs it has, the more difficult it is to receive all of them along with the genes of the parents. As Simonton puts it, 'The familial heritability of the talent declines, as accomplishment in the domain becomes increasingly emergenic and the odds of inheriting the entire configuration ever more small'.[22]

In other words, if the talent of a lawyer demands an analytical mind, an orator's gift, and (if possible) a winning personality, then each of the progeny of the lawyer will most likely inherit but one of these qualities: like the division of property in a will, the son may receive only the lawyer's analytical mind, and the daughter only the verbal dexterity. Relying on this genetic 'inheritance' the children may in fact become lawyers, of course, but most likely, lawyers of a lower order than their father. Hence the complete appropriateness of the folk wisdom concerning the children of geniuses: 'On the next generation Nature takes a break.' Such is indeed the case, since inheriting the entire brilliant constellation which made up the endowment of their great progenitor is statistically almost impossible.

Then again, if a family accumulates a certain number of able people in one or another field of endeavor, the likelihood of the appearance of an exceptional talent in a subsequent generation increases. This newborn reaps the 'harvest' from the great 'field' sown by his ancestors. As two experts on musical abilities, Rosamund Shuter-Dyson and Clive Gabriel, have noted, 'The chance that a child will be very musical is 86 per cent where both parents are talented, about 60 per cent when one parent is musical, and about 25 per cent when both parents are unmusical.' In the latter instance, the authors conclude, 'the ability may have been inherited from remoter ancestors'.[23]

The multiple-component nature of talent and its essential heterogeneity allow for an explanation of this: for example, a child may inherit auditory characteristics from his father who, having no other particular gifts to speak of, is a musical person, as we say, but not the possessor of talent. The mother may stand out for her musical feeling, a great musical intuition, but that is the extent of it; the mother's musical intuition turns into a passion for music in the child, feeding his motivation to pursue musical studies.

[22] Simonton, D. K. (1999). Talent and its development: An emergenic and epigenetic model. *Psychological Review*, 106(3), p. 446.

[23] Shuter-Dyson, R. and Gabriel, C. (1981) *The Psychology of Musical Ability*. London: Methuen, p. 177.

And from one of his maternal cousins the child received outstanding performing abilities; the cousin might have been an amateur singer with average musical characteristics but a born sense of stage presence. In the end, the child is potentially prepared for musical-performance endeavors, having collected 'a little here and a little there' from several of his forbearers. Naturally, the likelihood of receiving from nature the gift of the entire bouquet available from the musical 'garden' will be less if the child has fewer musical relatives.

Nevertheless, no phenomenon in the natural world can be entirely dismissed. Inherited characteristics can both appear in later generations and by an indirect line. Thus two parents may behold their son, an outstanding composer, and have no idea where his talent came from: the mother is a history teacher with a tin ear and the father an engineer without the slightest interest in music. The parents do not recall, of course, the obscure great uncle whose balalaika virtuosity won the heart of their great aunt. This was precisely the state of affairs in the family of the pianist Arthur Rubinstein, where not a single relative evinced an interest in music. The boy was sent away to study music at his own insistence, and the musical heritage of the family was left hopelessly lost in the depths of the ages.

A contrary and thus entirely traditional example can be drawn from the Dargomyzhsky family, where the father of the great composer Sergey Dargomyzhsky was a 'natural' son of the Ladyzhensky family, among which figured N. N. Ladyzhensky, a dilettante composer of great promise and a member of the Balakirev circle. Sergey liked music well enough, but did not demonstrate any outstanding abilities, choosing a career in administration. Here his considerable managerial talent came to the fore: he was a great success at the imperial Bank of Commerce, spent several years as the guiding light of the Romanov royal theaters, and in his youth served in the postal administration, where he won the recognition of departmental leadership. The composer's mother was a very musical person, but in rather limited doses: she regarded music with respect but without the passion of the fanatic.

It was nature's wish that the family's musical gene, having tried out different compositions and variations of giftedness, settled in full measure on the children: Dargomyzhsky's brother Erast, who died at the age of 21, was an outstanding violinist; his sisters Ludmila and Erminia both played the harp, and the latter, in the spirit of the age, also composed romances. Only one of the genetic 'probes' proved to be remarkably fruitful: Aleksandr Dargomyzhsky brought together various components of musical talent in the most advantageous of combinations—and became a great composer, the pride of Russian music. His sister Sof'ia, alone among the siblings in lacking any musical inclinations whatsoever, nevertheless inherited the administrative abilities of her father and handled all the managerial, publishing, and real estate concerns of the family. Her example serves as but one more illustration of the fact that not only artistic abilities are inherited, which is traditionally recognized by popular psychology, but more pragmatic talents are as well, in this case managerial talent.

The Dargomyzhsky family's example points out that it is not merely ill-defined general abilities or vague inclinations toward creativity which are inherited, but rather entirely concrete and special abilities, abilities which had been previously noted in other family members. Children, brothers, and sisters show strength precisely in those areas in which their ancestors and parents showed it; and a great concentration of musical abilities in a family suggests that it is unlikely that such a family will produce a painter of genius—just as a family with a great concentration of acting talent will be unlikely to see a great explorer emerge from its younger ranks. All this speaks once again of the fact that all abilities are special abilities. So it goes: the Bachs are a family of musicians, the Sadovskys are actors, the Belottos, whose most illustrious member, Canaletto, was the idol of eighteenth century Venice, are artists.

Alongside inherited origin there is a legend in psychology that can neither be entirely refuted nor confirmed: this is the assertion of a relationship between genius and madness. The idea of Cesare Lombroso, who named his study exactly that, continues to this day to occupy the minds of great numbers of people considerably less romantically inclined than the author of the hypothesis. Intrinsically agreeing with the still unarticulated idea of the component structure of talent, Russian psychologists of the 1920s set forth the following idea in the *Clinical Archive of Genius and Giftedness*:

> A person of genius or outstanding qualities is the result of the crossing of two biological family lines, of which one line of forbears, let us say the paternal line, is the carrier of potential giftedness, while the other line, the maternal one, is the carrier of inherited psychosis or psychic abnormality.[24]

In fact, both psychosis and giftedness may come to a genius from one and the same line of family. For example, in the Tchaikovsky family both the grandfather and maternal uncle suffered from epilepsy; the poet Simon Nadson died in a psychiatric hospital; Niccolo Paganini's father was a passionate lover of music and an extremely psychopathic personality; and the parents of the astronomer Johannes Kepler suffered from such acute psychological disturbances that the boy in effect became orphaned with his parents still alive.

One can elaborate and ponder the statistical significance of such observations at length. Suffice it to say here, in any case, that both an elevated nervous sensitivity and an inclination to succumb to various stresses, which the greats can indeed inherit, flow organically into the inherited 'cocktail' that is talent.

Happy message for everyone

It might seem that there is not much of the encouragement for all of us in the hereditary nature of talent, in its 'multiplicative model', not allowing the slightest 'spot' or weakness to crawl into it. But there are two optimistic points to make. The first is that psychological research with much evidence shows that musicians and non-musicians don't differ greatly in their aural capacities, and the former show superiority only in tasks connected with

[24] Klinicheski archiv genialnosti i odarennosti/Clinical Archive of Genius and Giftedness (1925) (ed. G. Segalin). Sverdlovsk: Uralskiy institut psikhiatrii, p. 29.

their professional training (Bispham 2006; Besson and Faieta 1995; Crummer *et al.* 1994; Duke 1989; Evans *et al.* 2000; Koelsch *et al.* 2000; Nilsonne and Sundberg 1985; Radvansky *et al.* 1995; Schweiger and Irving 1985). The message here is that a cat may look at a king: non-musicians given the opportunities to study music seriously could well replace the majority of existing musicians. Not only highly talented survive in music and are accepted into the ranks of experts—music industry is flourishing due to the endless labors of thousands and thousands music teachers, sound producers, orchestra and choir members, jazz, pop- and rock-musicians, both instrumentalists and vocalists, and other professionals, including those in the realm of world music, not speaking about music editors and publishers, music managers and many others who are neither renowned soloists nor great composers. All those people, devoted and faithful adepts of Her Majesty Music in fact make the musical world running: it could never survive by the efforts of the few giants such as Sebastian Bach in the past or Glenn Gould in the twentieth century. Who will turn pages for them and tune their instruments after all? So, practically everybody but about 4 percent of totally tone-deaf, as Andreas Lehmann and his colleagues remark (Lehmann *et al.* 2007), are invited to join 'the Musicians' Guild'. All of us are very welcome!

Only those musicians who wish to conquer the world and look onto the rest of the humanity from TV screens and newspaper photos will do a good job for themselves if they think twice whether they really have enough natural gifts and perseverance to make their dreams true. As Joanne Haroutounian puts it, 'When we hear a performance, do we only hear what has been developed through training, a gestural bag of tricks, or environmental influence? Or is there a unique talent that allows a student to personally interpret through sound in a creative way? There is always that one student you *cannot* not notice.'[25] In other words, there are musicians and Musicians, experts and Experts, and it's our choice whom of those we would like to join.

The second good news is that musicality as any other gift is specific: much evidence, especially in neurosciences, speaks in favor of special brain mechanisms responsible for music processing which doesn't exclude certain overlap with other functions (Gruhn 2006; Peretz 2005). It prompts that all our functions might be specific too. Born writers must not at the same time be born architects and those who are known as masters of *haute couture* could hardly become movie stars. Is it only music where all of us could gain self-respect and professional fulfillment? Do we really have a good reason for disappointment if composing hits like John Lennon or playing the violin like Gidon Kremer is simply not our cup of tea? Before coming to analyze musical talent in more detail it's very encouraging to know that musical talent is only one out of many other talents people are endowed with, and even if you can't sing in tune 'Mary had a little lamb' you very well have a chance to become the chief of Intelligence Service or the stock-exchange guru.

---

[25] Haroutounian, J. (2002) *Kindling the Spark. Recognizing and Developing Musical Talent.* Oxford University Press, p. 56.

What career to follow to be able to join the narrow group of elite experts? What talents are put to our service by Mother Nature and which of them are those that make our 'road' to excellence more straight and easy? One of the most acclaimed psychologists of our time Howard Gardner has shown 'the repertoire of talents' we could be looking for when we think of our future or the future of those we love. Any book on any of the human talents is to include his findings: guided by Gardner's ideas it would be easier to follow the wisest of all advices ever given to a human being—and that was the one given by Socrates: 'Cognize yourself'.

Howard Gardner and the theory of multiple intelligences

People are accustomed to marveling at the diversity of our natural surroundings: many and varied are the plants, birds, and animals around us, and rocks and minerals no less so; indeed, the harmony achieved by the wild jungle growth and the arid desert plain, the massive mountain ranges and the great yawning valleys, is nothing short of awe-inspiring. Curiously, however, man seems less surprised at himself, at the remarkable nature of human diversity. This diversity includes the obvious—giants and midgets, heads bald and curly, skins colored black, yellow, and white. Yet the real diversity of man lies in human talents, which at first glance seem almost to defy simple enumeration: a qualification listing of human professions runs to several volumes, each single entry representing a set of particular skills and abilities necessary to perform a given function.

At first the science of psychology, finding itself at something of a loss before this apparently immeasurable expanse of the human mind, attempted to render the enormity more manageable by forcing it all into the Procrustean bed of IQ. If someone has a good dollop of intelligence, the thinking ran, we can teach him the rest. The introduction of creative ability into psychology's range of study did not serve any better to lead all our talents to a common denominator, since creativity is just as pale, colorless, and lacking in individuality as its predecessor, intelligence. The science of psychology was forced to admit that human talents have their own characteristics, particular earmarkings which do not extend to other spheres of activity. Certain physicians, for example, for whom the complex human organism is an open book, cannot hit a tennis ball when equipped with the best Titanium racket on the market; there are likewise theoretical physicists who cannot draw, given ample paper and their choice of crayons, a house with a chimney. History confirms the high specificity of our gifts: Alexandr Pushkin's lycee contemporaries recalled that in their mathematics classes, x always came out equaling zero for the great poet, regardless; and the outstanding artist Vladimir Lebedev could not for the life of him tote up exactly how many objects figured in Samuel Marshak's famous Russian children's ditty ('a sofa, a suitcase, a satchel, a picture, a basket, a carton and a little doggy').

In studying the human brain, psychologists have noted that traumas caused by accidents can lead to the loss of certain abilities. An injury to one part of the brain can deprive someone of the power of speech, while an injury elsewhere may produce spatial disorientation. If a man loses the ability to think logically, he may still retain many other gifts: he may well continue to sing and dance wonderfully, garden with enthusiasm, and lovingly look after his pets. The base-level, fundamental abilities of any person enjoy distinct localization in the brain, so that if one area is damaged, other activities, which are controlled by other brain sectors, are not as a rule affected: the separate location of each ability provides it with relative autonomy. This arrangement of mind and ability has not been long known, as the instruments which allow for the observation of actual brain processes have been perfected only in the last few decades.

Together with the advances of neuropsychology, research in the pedagogical sciences has also been providing food for thought apropos of the variety of fundamental properties possessed by the human brain. The scourge of schoolchildren and their parents, slow learning, has been positively affected, it turns out, by allowing chronic D students in the early grades to learn through pictures: texts which use visual illustrations provide associations and parallels which significantly lessen the 'torture of learning' for some pupils. Other problem learners are hampered by the stationary nature of classroom study: given the opportunity to move about the room occasionally, and even skip a bit, these children can grasp things that had completely eluded them when they were permanently parked behind a desk. Still others flourish when lessons are accompanied by music, others learn best when regularly chatting with their friends, and still others perceive the information being proffered only if they can play with a favorite kitten during the process. Given today's approach to children—with a new respect for both the freedom of the individual pupil and the diversity of humankind—the discordances between the inner lives and minds of children could hardly go unnoticed.

Howard Gardner was, as fate would have it, both a neuropsychologist and a teacher. Studying activity of the brain, Gardner became convinced that each of its parts has a special 'zone of responsibility' which facilitated one of the human abilities. This enormous diversity of brain functions could not be tied to IQ, nor to any other single 'factor'. The world of the mind, it transpired, was just as multifaceted as the world itself. Observing children in the course of his psychology experiments, Gardner perceived the extent of their differences one from another: even in childhood, when life experience is still minimal, children displayed extremely dissimilar natural inclinations and turns of mind. Systematically categorizing these differences, turning the data into a *schema* of basic characteristics of human consciousness, creating a 'psychological spectrum' from which, as the colors from the rainbow, spring all human abilities—such were the tasks Gardner set for himself. The result was the theory of 'multiple intelligences', first published in 1983 in a volume titled *Frames of Mind*. This study turned out to be enormously influential in (and outside) the field of psychology, and Gardner has been expanding and adjusting the theory of multiple intelligences ever since. A thumbnail rendition of the principal points of Gardner's still-evolving *schema* will serve our ends well at this point.

In the beginning was the Word, and Gardner did not dispute the Biblical wisdom, awarding *verbal intelligence* first place in his system. The verbally gifted individual easily expresses all that he sees and feels, all that he has been able to note, understand, and evaluate, in words. For her, the word is the principal form of contact between her consciousness and the world around her. The distance between thought and word is reduced almost to nil: she does not search for words, they come to her, easily and naturally integrating into her thoughts and sensations. She understands patterns and connections best when they are expressed in words rather than conventional signs, visual symbols, or gestures. The verbally gifted person is attuned to texts: she is ever seeking and finding them, she likes to read them, discuss them, write them and bury herself in those written by others; in this way she refines her ability to collect words and give them form. Yet not every verbally gifted person can become a writer or a poet: verbal intelligence is not a professional gift and certainly not a talent, but rather a predisposition toward life in the world of words and texts. Such a predisposition is critical for success in many professions, and expresses itself in different ways, depending on the other talents and inclinations present in a given individual.

The second constituent part of Gardner's 'psychological spectrum' resembles IQ, although it is not actually related to intelligence. This is *logical-mathematical intelligence*, in which the word intelligence most nearly approaches its original meaning. The accent in 'logical-mathematical' falls on the first part: the person gifted in this area is endowed with logic, he is a rational thinker. He accepts nothing on faith, waiting until an established chain of logical deduction proves the truth of the postulate in question. He clearly sees cause and effect relationships when such are present; what follows from what, and what will come after what are obvious to him from his own judgments, as if past, present, and future all stood visible before him.

The logician is the master of relations between and among numbers, figures, and all other such abstract entities. The relationships of the very relationships which lie at the base of the mathematical process are entirely clear to him: the multiplication of components and participants in the relationships do not unduly complicate his thought processes, because he can always recast the problem, perceiving as he does what is extraneous and simplifiable. The person endowed with a logical-mathematical mind is always prepared to see analogies, symmetries, similarities, proportions, and all the cardinal numerical combinations of relationships, the manipulation of which presents no particular difficulty. He is ever ready to turn the particular into the general, the concrete into the abstract, and the incidental into the predictable.

Despite the fact that almost any educational procedure, and especially those of the elementary-school type, is to a large extent based on logical-mathematical abilities, the type of person in question here is far from a magician and is not even a genius at mathematics. The ability to think logically can be effectively used in many activities: in all the technical and accounting specialties (including finance but not bookkeeping), in construction and inventing, in the computer disciplines, in all the sciences and the humanities, in the work of detectives and prosecutors. But despite this seeming universalism, logical-mathematical endowment is not merely single talent. It is, rather, a necessary component of many talents, just like the various other 'intelligences' elaborated by Gardner.

Spatial intelligence may be called a relative of logical-mathematical giftedness, as spatial abilities are critical for any good mathematician. Spatial intelligence is no less individualized and specific than all the others. It arose from the critical necessity of locating oneself in place: without it the hunter could hardly find his way home after following an animal

into the woods, the mountains, or the jungles. An intuition for the direction of movement and a mental capability to take in big spaces lie at the base of the seafarer's being—
without them he could not find his way across the ocean or orient himself by the stars. For
this he has a psychological internal compass.

The spatially gifted person can mentally manipulate spatial objects: he 'sees through
walls', perceiving the internal arrangement of things otherwise visible only on the
exterior. This gift of mental sight allows him to sense all the categories of space as physical
reality—length, width, height, area, and volume, along with all the categories of measurement, are utterly clear to him. Spatial abilities are one of the most widespread components necessary in many professions: in geology, seafaring and travel, in aviation, in
architecture and construction, in all that concerns machines and mechanisms, including
practical engineering (as opposed to theoretical engineering, where logical-mathematical
abilities may sometimes suffice). Beyond these, artistic labors, design, and many sports,
golf and tennis immediately come to mind, require significant spatial abilities.

The oldest of the intelligences is that termed *bodily-kinesthetic*, the essence of which lies
in the effectiveness of connections between mind and body. The person whose body
obeys commands, taking orders effectively and fulfilling them with optimal economy and
maximum grace, a 'movement-gifted' person—this is the individual blessed with bodily-
kinesthetic intelligence. People of this order do not need to be taught techniques of running, for example; the outstanding African distance runners 'learned' their methodology
from nature, in the same way an antelope 'learns' to run optimally to stay out of reach of
a tiger. The movement-gifted are strong and enduring; physical activity is as necessary to
them as the air they breathe, for without movement they wither, losing critical body tone.
They understand the different intentions and modes of organization behind various
kinds of movement: the trajectory and character of running, jumping, turning, and
throwing are granted to them to perceive in the same way artists are given to grasp
the character of circles, squares, zig-zags, and undulations as well as all manner of color
and form.

Bodily-kinesthetic giftedness is a bodily 'mind' which will not allow resources to
be wasted, wisely moderating exertion and relaxation. The ordinary person expends
attention and imagination on this regulatory process, whereas it comes naturally to the
movement-gifted: the target is always hit, the hurdle remains untouched as the hurdler
flies over it. The bodily-kinetic person resembles Caesar in that she can organize many
movements at once, as her arms, legs, and neck enjoy sufficient autonomy. The applications of this kind of endowment are broad indeed: appropriate professions include athletes, dancers, and all those requiring exactitude in movement and hand-eye coordination,
such as surgeons, artisans of various sorts, and those occupied with the preparation and
restoration of any kind of equipment.

Musical intelligence, for its part, is the natural understanding of the organization of
sound, including the principles of the connection between individual sounds and the
patterns of their confluence into larger sound structures. The musical person easily
understands all aspects of the hierarchy of sound coordination: tonality, mode, chords,
themes and melodies, harmonic complexes, and consonance are his natural province.

She has the ability to distinguish sounds and consonances, joining them with one another, if necessary, according to defined rules. The mastery of different means of sound organization is given to the musical person, as is the recognition of various principles of the mutual attraction and repulsion of sound structures. She knows how to assemble a musically sensible whole from different links, and what elements, in turn, may lead to the disintegration of this whole.

A person blessed with abundant musical intelligence 'sees through' music as though beholding it in an X-ray. She is the ideal listener of whom philosopher Teodor Adorno dreamed, a listener who can take pleasure in the displacement and transformation of sound constructions, which for her possess a particularly satisfying self-sufficiency. For this person music represents order, regulation, and harmony, the secrets of which are not secret to him. For the musician musical intelligence is one of the components of talent; and like any component, it further breaks down into sub-components. Acting in concert with other constituent elements, finally, it serves as one of the bases of musical talent.

The sixth and seventh varieties among Gardner's multiple intelligences—*intrapersonal* and *interpersonal*—can be said to resemble two brothers who are unalike except for being raised in the same family. The inter- prefix signals a direction outside, into the larger world; those with the interpersonal gift have a knack for bringing people together. They are extremely sociable, their greatest pleasure comes from being among a crowd of like souls; all people are interesting to them, everyone diverts them, entertains them and arouses their curiosity. They are at home among friends and strangers alike; it does not occur to them to wonder whether others are interested in their company, in need of it or glad to spend time with them. The answer to such questions, if they were somehow to be posed to these people, would be a self-evident Yes.

Everyone who finds himself in the company of the interpersonally intelligent feels extremely relaxed and comfortable; the sense is that one does not meet such nice people, so well disposed to you, very often! An absence of embarrassment and self-consciousness among the interpersonally gifted is somehow passed along to their interlocutors: prejudices melt away, social boundaries disappear, and the interpersonal types get all they seek from persons in positions of authority: permissions, resolutions, licenses, privileges, and everything that can be shared with them. This gift, no rarer than any of the other intelligences, is part of the structure of all the talents connected with communication. It is a gift needed by lawyers, journalists, politicians, public relations people, diplomats, spies, managers—in short, all who regularly communicate with people with the goal of convincing them of something, drawing them to their side, obtaining from them some kind of information or some manner of boon.

The ability of the intrapersonal soul is exactly the opposite, although it is also connected with relationships with others. The person possessed of this attribute is not a communicator, but rather a psychologist. He has a penetrating mind, perceiving the essence of people—their secret strivings, hidden intentions, and the things that disturb them. He is capable of all this because, unlike his 'brother' of interpersonal endowment, the natural psychologist functions less on an exterior level, favoring the profound: his feelings, as a rule, are sincere and strong; the world of the inner human 'I' is for him more real than the outside, alien world around him. His 'real' life takes place in the interior space of his soul. The intrapersonal man is often timid, the external rituals of life threaten him; he has little sense of how to start a social conversation or how to end it once he has— yet you will not find a more patient listener, a more attentive confidante. This is someone who knows the internal causations of human behavior, and is therefore capable of giving good advice.

A proposed eighth type of intelligence harks back to man's earliest period and his earliest communication with the natural world—earth, water, plants, and animals. This is the gift of *natural intelligence*, the possessor of which brings to mind Kipling's Mowgli, the boy raised by wolves, panthers, and tigers: he is on intimate terms with living nature, knowing which berries are edible and which are not; what the weather will be like tomorrow and some weeks from now; what the gulls are thinking and when the next storm will roil the sea; and when an earthquake is on the way, as he senses its approach like a snake. The naturally intelligent have no fear of the animal kingdom, relating to it without words and as an ancestral commonweal, the point of origin of mankind.

The basic senses most people have lost or relegated to the role of secondary qualities are in the naturally intelligent extraordinarily developed: smell, touch, and taste are the most vital of these.

Everything that is organic, flowers, trees, living organisms, forms the province of the naturally intelligent; and even the elements—minerals, metals, ores, and other naturally occurring substances—are understandable and somehow close. Natural phenomena never intimidate, not even storms at sea, tropical monsoons and sandstorms, as these are but part of a comprehensible Nature. In general, everything that is natural, up to and including the failures in natural organisms, is understandable to the naturally intelligent. Nothing natural is tragic, including death itself—which is perceived as a part of life, distinguishing it from 'the opposite'.

The naturally talented are often people of few words and deliberate pace and manner; but when they speak and act, they do so clearly, distinctly, and with gravity. A good example of a person possessed of this type of talent is Robinson Crusoe, whom Defoe took from an actual historical prototype. The 'natural' gift is extraordinarily important and necessary in many professions: good doctors have it, as do hunters, farmers, chefs, and research chemists. All who deal with matter and substance, the concrete rather than the abstract, the intuitive doers among us rather than the theoretical ponderers, are blessed with this remarkable gift.

Finally, a ninth member of Gardner's group: *spiritual intelligence*. This is a gift quite as old, most likely, as its 'natural' counterpart—yet it is the form of intelligence most difficult to discuss, since it is the least perceptible and tangible. It is possessed by seers, shamans, and religious figures, the leaders of nations, prophets, and gifted teachers as well. These people enjoy a particular sense sometimes called the 'third eye', which seems to connect them to another and greater world—the cosmos, the universe, the world of the mind—which goes by different names among different people. The gift of insight and the ability to discern the underlying truth of things; to be able to see the higher meaning of human affairs, in our quotidian lives and in human history—these allow the spiritually gifted to predict the future, which for them is only the next open page(s) of the world's Book of Fate.

Those possessed of spiritual intelligence draw others to them without visible effort; their instruction on the truth of things is sufficient in itself to inspire the belief of people in that truth. The ranks of the spiritually gifted include Mahatma Gandhi, Jesus, Buddha, and others, all figuring among humanity's great teachers. Even teachers of the more mundane variety can claim some measure of this gift: when they inspire, by the power of suggestion alone, a student's belief in himself, they are really performing a small miracle. Such people project a kind of beneficial energy, elevating all around them and multiplying their powers. In the lives of these people an act which is regarded by the public at large as heroic is transformed into something at once inevitable and unavoidable—as it was unavoidable for the Polish teacher Janosz Korchak to go to the gas chamber along with his pupils, or for Jesus to redeem the sins of the world on the cross. For all its mysteriousness, the spiritual gift is present in the world, sustaining various forms of human activity, particularly instruction of all varieties, including the religious and political.

Such, then, are nine different types of intelligence as elaborated, at various stages of his work, by Howard Gardner: verbal, logical-mathematical, musical, spatial, bodily-kinesthetic, intra-personal, inter-personal, natural, and spiritual. Gardner's theory stands as a distinct alternative to the notion of general abilities as psychological universals independent of fields of activity. Each of us, Gardner maintains, is possessed in some measure of all these different intelligences—otherwise we would not have survived as a species—but our individual endowments tend to be in very limited quantities. Only one or two of these abilities are highly developed in any given person.

But is this not a cause, after all, for some well-founded optimism? Each of us, it turns out, is given the chance to win the endowment lottery and discover himself? The nine abilities represent such a broad spectrum of possibilities, offering mankind such diverse perspectives: each of us is given the joy of finding in him/herself at least one or two of the intelligences developed in some significant measure. This in turn means that Gardner's theory is in fact incomparably more democratic than that behind IQ. While Gardner surely was not aiming for political correctness as he developed his *intelligences* framework, it so happened that in this case the muses of scholarly-scientific discovery and concern for mankind's social and humanitarian dimensions not only did not conflict, but indeed came fortuitously together.

It also follows from Gardner's theory that the various intelligences serve as keys to our personality type. Behind each variety we find not only individual peculiarities of perception and a particular cast of mind, but a defined human type, with attendant interests and values. So it is that engineers, geologists, and explorers, all of whom possess significant spatial intelligence, tend to be positive, practical, and thorough, and at the same time not averse to the romantic, to which they are drawn by the winds of distant journeys. These are people unperturbed by difficulties and unpretentious in daily life; they are capable of much and like to take much upon themselves. Their descent from mankind's early hunters and seafarers has left them such.

By comparison, poets, prose writers, journalists, and others who live by the printed word tend to be more delicate, distracted, and capricious; they live in an imagined world of the Word, which means they cannot always be relied on in matters temporal. Everything takes its meaning through words, and since these are the people who bring words into existence, they can see themselves, at times, as rather more significant beings than they are in reality—which is another way of saying that they are inclined to a certain narcissism. All these attributes and qualities, having on the face of it no direct relationship to abilities, are in reality their direct continuation, which is why the psychology of personality, which brings together all the disparate branches of the science, must necessarily also be the psychology of abilities, the abilities which give birth to human types.

Gardner's work has turned the limitlessness of our abilities—which would seem to be as many and varied as human activity itself—into an orderly system. Of the most fundamental human abilities, those which make up intelligence as we know it, there are some nine varieties. Mixing them as the artist mixes colors on his palette we get the entire spectrum of human endowment. This is not yet talent as such; talent requires a creative component (on which Gardner is silent) as well as a motivational component. But it is clearly no longer mere IQ, and not a vaguely defined 'creativity' either, but something involving altogether palpable natural gifts. If one or more of Gardner's intelligences is (are) present in an individual in large measure, this constitutes a solid indication of talent. With the presence of a creativity component and strong motivation, this talented individual may leave a mark on history.

The innate nature of giftedness and talent may perhaps disappoint some people; yet this very innateness is also itself a cause for optimism. It was Socrates, after all, who framed the oldest injunction of psychology: know thyself. This is also what the theory of multiple intelligences indirectly summons us to do, as by its lights people need not seek the abolition of talent (as a disruptive 'myth'), but on the contrary should increase their efforts at self-discovery, each of us searching to identify our own primordial abilities. Whether this search should lead to digging in one's genealogy, to the careful and scientifically monitored development of children's early childhood or, perhaps, to the reorganization of education to fit the needs of different children—these are all questions for which answers are being sought by the psychology of the gifted.

Psychological testing is one of the active instruments of this search. This testing shows indirectly, via analysis of human behavior in games, in solving problems and in answering simple questions, that psychology can take on the role of prophet, predicting the subjects' future. The innateness of ability gives mankind a great head start in life, as predictions via testing can be made at a very early age—and there is no part of the human psychological repertoire, including abilities, that cannot be identified with the aid of the appropriate psychological instruments. Tests for special abilities should also be special: future musicians should deal with sounds, future philologists with words; spatial abilities should be tested in work with cubes, cylinders, balls, or in spatially-related games such as chess or *nards*. Pretenders to the mantle of Pirogov, the great anatomist, should be allowed to play with cats and fish, and future diplomats should be required to relate to their peers and educators by special protocols. As the history of twentieth-century psychology demonstrates, neither IQ scores nor creativity testing can reveal a future champion sailor like Fedor Koniukhov or a future screen legend like Marilyn Monroe. The testing of the twenty-first century should be conducted with the same materials which the talented use in their work—in the demonstration of the talent itself.

Testing children's abilities presupposes one condition which is particularly difficult to fulfill: the influence of experience must be lowered to a minimum. The test must be solvable for the gifted child, and must make a gifted professional ponder a bit before resolving it (brilliantly); but at the same time the test must not be something that an ungifted professional, however experienced, can ever solve. It is a test with a certain secret—one based not on knowledge or the skills wrought of training but on intuition, on the instantaneous recognition of a Truth. This is something only the genuinely talented possess. In age-indifferent testing for special abilities, experience does not lead to success, and the absence of experience does not hinder the outstanding resolution of the problem.

Armed with such a multiplicity of tests, ability psychology will genuinely be able to enrich mankind. However distant such a goal may seem today, the way lies open toward it—if we choose, as the Russian proverb has it, to 'master the road as we travel it'. If each of Gardner's intelligences can be equipped with tests appropriate for children, society will doubtless recognize, at length, that all the labors of the scholars of giftedness have not been in vain: mankind will receive a key to the realization of creative talent, and thereby to a measure of happiness for every member of society.

In summary, by the end of the twentieth century the theory of abilities, giftedness and talent had reached the following six conclusions:

1 There is no such thing as general ability. There are specific abilities which define a person's predisposition toward a certain kind or kinds of activity. There are up to nine fundamental abilities; these correspond to the kinds of intellectual attributes described by Howard Gardner in his theory of *multiple intelligences*.

2 Abilities are psychological attributes which facilitate assimilation and training rather than discovery and invention. Abilities are not equal to or the same as talent, which is something through which mankind's greatest achievements are born. Talent does not arise from abilities and is not their highest stage, but represents something different: an integrated and multi-component psychological attribute which includes an operational part (abilities), a creative part (which can be called giftedness), and an emotional part (motivation).

3 The structure of talent is multiplicative. This means that the absence (or zeroing out) of even a single one of the necessary components cannot be compensated for by anything else—the entirety of the potential talent, multiplied by the absent factor, still comes to nil. Every talent must command the entire selection of essential psychological attributes and qualities—operational, creative, and emotional. Thus the tremendous rarity of talent, its extraordinary nature is something exceptional.

4 Talent is the result of inborn factors of a hereditary nature and cannot be derived from more time spent working on the discipline in question although hard work is necessary to bring talent to its full blossom. Talent is likewise not the result of qualified training by teacher or mentor, and does not depend to a decisive degree on the support of a family (or the lack of it) during the early stages of its development. The theory of 'deliberate practice' is one of the steps on the everlasting path of 'nature–nurture' debate.

5 The inborn nature of talent does not of itself mean that it results from direct and immediate inheritance. Talent may be inherited from various members of a family, including distant ancestors and indirect relatives. The entire structure of a talent is almost never passed along *in toto* to the children of the gifted; but the likelihood of talent-passing increases with the number of children in the family (as in the case of the Sebastian Bach family, where three sons from more than twenty children by two wives emerged as outstanding musical talents).

6 Abilities, giftedness, and talent become evident and can be assessed only under conditions and using materials which are maximally matched to the specific activities which make up their functional profiles. Special abilities demand special testing procedures: success in such testing cannot be dependent on the age or experience of those being assessed.

The phylogenetic model of talent

The various aspects of natural human ability, named and catalogued by Howard Gardner as man's nine *intelligences*, define the whole of human intellectual and spiritual development. No great discovery, no achievement of the mind, and no practical advance could have been made without them. These nine forms of intelligence resemble the nine muses of Greek antiquity, each of whom was the mistress of a particular realm. To a certain extent each of us, as a descendant of the human evolutionary process, can boast a certain mastery of all nine talents. In each of us, after all, there is a bit of the poet, at least insofar as we understand and value poetry; each of us has a certain logical-mathematical facility, at least insofar as mastering the multiplication table and understanding the concept of square meters; and each of us has a certain interpersonal gift as well, as we all have friends and learn to reach compromises with those in authority.

But the mastery of Gardner's nine intelligences was the result of a long evolutionary process: these various human gifts did not all appear at once but gradually, sometimes with intervals of many thousands of years between them, because they arose only in conjunction with the development of the human activities for which they were necessary. Civilization was formed in stages, step by step; the human talents which marked its development naturally proceeded the same way.

The first to appear was the most basic and essential gift—the ability to move, to govern, and control the movement of one's body (*bodily-kinesthetic intelligence*). This ability stands first on the evolutionary ladder and unites humanity with the other living organisms, for the mastery of one's bodily movements is a primary condition for survival. Along with this form of intelligence arose another, *spatial* intelligence, which allowed early man to find his way in the woods and waterways, to build shelter and master the most ancient of crafts—working with stone, iron, and clay. Spatial intelligence helped early humans to act upon their environment, because without a practical understanding of spatial figures and the rules of their intersection man could not create the tools of labor and put them to use: bodily-kinesthetic and spatial intelligence were the psychological focus of primitive culture.

The Stone Age, during which man fed himself by hunting and fishing, established the primeval unity of humanity and the natural world. The mastery of physical movement and travel across territory signaled the full maturity of the human organism, its oneness with the surrounding environment. But the complete realization of this unity required the establishment of a dialogue with the natural forces and an understanding of the laws that governed their lives: knowing the signs of the cycle of seasons; recognizing the characteristics of plants and learning to grow them; knowing the habits of animals and how to tame and domesticate them. For this man needed *natural* intelligence, which allows him to fathom the secrets of the natural world and promotes relationship with it. Without natural intelligence we could have remained forever in the Stone Age, for this was the intelligence which ushered in the era of agriculture: the earliest humans tended livestock, and from there moved on to the working of the land and thus to the era of tribal and clan communities.

The first three abilities of Gardner's nine established the basis of the human psyche, its particular root structure and its point of departure. These abilities are the most ancient, they stand first on the phylogenetic axis of evolution—and are thus the most deeply embedded genetically. The masters of these three abilities are literally innumerable: the overwhelming majority of humans possess strength and agility; if we do not degrade our bodies through a sedentary lifestyle or overeating, neither of which was known to early man, then bodily-kinesthetic intelligence will unfailingly make itself felt. Modern men and women quite willingly devote their time and energy to various forms of sport; almost everyone understands what sports are and takes an interest in them. This is our bodily-kinesthetic intelligence rediscovering its ancient origins.

The vast majority of humans likewise possess a sense of *spatial intelligence*. In every culture there are great numbers of skilled craftsmen capable of, if not putting horseshoes on a flee a la Leskov, at least something useful with their hands; millions can handle an axe, a saw and other simple instruments, and millions more can sew, knit, and embroider. Spatial intelligence leads people to the conquest of rivers, seas, and mountain passes. By various means, some involving considerable risk, modern man like his distant ancestors overcomes enormous distances. At least as many people comprehend and revere the natural world: of amateur gardeners there are untold millions, people who enjoy and know how to dig the earth despite leading altogether urban lifestyles. And the ranks of animal lovers, people who cannot imagine life without such companions, are equally large. These manifestations of the ancient forms of intelligence by their near-total dissemination speak to the phylogenetic nature of the 'family tree of talent': its roots run wide and deep, encompassing almost every single human being. Many people possess the three oldest human abilities, the first three forms of intelligence: bodily-kinesthetic, spatial, and natural.

The next stage in the development of our place in the world was the appearance of human society. Having mastered their own physical being and found a common language with the natural world around them, people next had to understand themselves and others. Without mastering communication skills man and woman would be unable to advance along the path of civilization. Here they needed a 'duet' of talents: *interpersonal* and *intrapersonal* intelligence, the one for interaction with others and the other introspective, for understanding oneself. With the help of these two we became able to identify ourselves and our goals in life; to cooperate with other people, seeking compromise and consensus; to give and to take, creating conflicts and resolving them.

Humans became shrewd, they learned to attune themselves to the 'frequencies' of others, to sense the moods and thoughts of other people as though they were their own. Social communication put before humanity a plethora of new tasks: men and women now needed to support their friends and oppose enemies, to be sincere and hypocritical; to use deceit to gain their own ends; and to take into account numerous conflicting interests to determine where among them lay support for the realization of their own goals. We became politicians and psychologists: we made possible the formation of communities of common interests—tribes, clans, ethnic groups, and nations. All this came about through the good offices of intrapersonal and interpersonal intelligence.

Social communication and the demand for it presupposed ever more refined and developed means by which one could relay feelings and intentions. Wishing to be understood, man put himself at the service of sound—that of his own voice, which proved to be an ideal natural instrument of social intercourse. At the dawn of history, when human speech was still in its formative stages, the voice and its various intonations could already pass along a great deal. Thus was formed proto-language, the ancestor of music and the spoken word. It encompassed the critical parameters of social communication: in the form of the simplest voiced signals humans passed along information about themselves to one another and inspired their interlocutors to respond in kind. It was at this point that in the human psychological mechanism the element of intuition took root: without words, using half-gestures and hesitant sighs, humans learned to divine the relationship of a speaker to his conversation partner, to open his hidden intentions. The language of sounds played an important role in this. As a consequence of the need for social communication, early man availed himself of musical intelligence—the ability to pass along and receive oral information, sent consciously and with significance, in the form of aural data which could be decoded from a consecutive series of different sounds— different in timbre, loudness, pitch, and length. In this capacity music acted as the forerunner of all forms of art, as the sign of their belonging to the most important civilized sphere, the sphere of social communication.

Interpersonal, intrapersonal, and musical intelligence—the three forms which followed the three most ancient intelligences into being—were a signal of humanity's unification into variegated societies and the establishment of relations within and among them. This stage occurred later relative to the most ancient times, when the single goal of humanity was survival; the ability to communicate and the talents attendant to it are a later result of evolution than are the three oldest forms of intelligence. According to the phylogenetic 'pyramid' of human gifts, the older the intelligence, the more people possess it; and conversely, the higher we climb on this pyramid, the newer this or that form of intelligence is, the fewer people share it, as it has not yet succeeded in genetically embedding itself in humanity, its imprint is less 'durable'. Thus it is that people endowed with the talent of social communication, who penetrate into the sequestered *id* of others, people capable of leading, of convincing and inspiring their peers, are far fewer in number than natural-born explorers or gardeners. People who are predisposed toward communication with others in any form, including the realm of the arts, are far fewer than potential athletes or people capable of successfully making their way in the world via physical labor.

Finally, the smallest group of gifted individuals—the thinkers. The three last talents in the Gardner hierarchy—*verbal, logical-mathematical,* and *spiritual intelligence*—belong to this group, the most recent in origin. Language and speech, logical thought and the creation of philosophical systems belong entirely to the noosphere, the realm of spiritual life. These talents appeared last, signaling the final maturity of human reason and its multifaceted development. It is on these talents that science, the latest-developing form of thought, with its search for global generalizations and eternal truths, must depend. And although language and verbal talent grow from social communication and serve as a sort of bridge between our second and third groups of giftedness, the only thing that is impossible to express without language is thought. Everything else can be passed along by exclusively communicative means which arise, like all forms of art, from non-verbal forms of communication, from gesture and intonation.

People endowed with verbal, logical-mathematical, and spiritual intelligence are born 'systematizers', creators of structures and algorithms which open new avenues. A new poetic text, a new formula, or a new religious-philosophical doctrine is by nature a combination of elements, constructed according to certain rules; all are structured and systematized. The progress of civilization relies in the main on these newest forms of intelligence—thus it is that those endowed with these latest gifts to *Homo sapiens* enjoy such authority in human society.

These nine natural gifts, the nine forms of intelligence, are divided by their origins into three groups: gifts born of Nature, of Society, and of Thought. And although every human enjoys many gifts to a greater or lesser extent, each of us gravitates toward one in particular of these groupings. Humanity's need for representatives of each is proportionate to their natural occurrence: the need for physical laborers is greatest, while the need for scientists the smallest. The same phylogenetic regulatory pattern occurs in the structure of each different human gift: the properties and qualities which make its structure appear gradually: the older various skills are, the more people are blessed with them, while the later the 'upper stories' of a gift's structure were added, the fewer people will be endowed with their use.

The 'phylogenetic model' is simply a probable-theoretical *schema* of the structure of talent which transforms it into a structure of the hierarchical type. The layers of the

ON SPECIAL ABILITIES | 39

structure possess a defined interdependence, they are joined by a commonality of origin; when the upper-lying layers flow out, they 'grow up' from those lying below. People possessed of the lower, fundamental components of one or another gift, are often conveniently labeled 'able', and only those whose giftedness covers the entire 'phylogenetic model' (including its higher, latest 'floors') are called 'highly gifted' or 'talented'. At the same time it should be noted that talent, like any phenomenon of living nature, does not submit itself to artificial schemas depicting but the most general order of its functioning. Abilities and components of later origin do not always appear in people who are greatly endowed with abilities of earlier provenance; there is no direct correlation.

The phylogenetic model of talent proceeds from a historical description of certain activity. Its analysis yields information on the phylogenetic order of the appearance of talent's components; thus it becomes clear which of them appear more frequently and are more widespread, and which are later and thus occur more infrequently. In order to build such a model for all human talents, we must return to the farthest reaches of antiquity and examine the history of each form of activity. In musical activity we have the happy opportunity to do just that, since in music there is an entire subdivision, ethnomusicology, studying traditional forms of music, and ancient folklore. From ethnomusicological research one can determine what music was like even as far back as the period when the subject would be difficult to call music. A second source of information on the phylogenesis of any kind is ontogenesis—the process of child development—it seemingly follows the same path which all humanity has taken. Musical ontogenesis is remarkably illustrative; it gives us the possibility of being convinced that the components of musical talent of presumably earlier origin really did originate earlier, and the later ones really later. Musical ability gives the best possibilities for the creation of a phylogenetic model of musical talent, which, it is possible, will serve as an example for the creation of an analogous model of other kinds of giftedness.

The universal nature of musical talent

By the dawn of the third millennium ability psychology has painted a 'portrait of talent', which is really less a portrait than a sketch, with the overall composition, basic contours, and the proportions of its constituent parts all visible. Here and there certain blank spots and omissions remain, and some critical details are missing; consequently, the finished portrait is still far from realization. This is the case because to date the issue has been one of 'talent in general', which, strictly speaking, does not exist. 'Talent in general', as an abstraction, applies to all talented people equally, past, present, and future—and yet to no individual in particular. Thus the portrait of some nonexistent Talented Persona has necessarily emerged as somewhat vague and indistinct, since a concrete model for this 'portrait' has been lacking.

A synthesized model of human talent presupposes a trinity: an operational part (ability), a creative part (giftedness), and an emotional part (motivation). The nature of the connection between and among these components is not known; at present it is accepted practice to consider them relatively independent. But there are more questions: does each part further break down into its own components? And if so, what exactly are they?

How do these sub-components interact, and what is the function of each in the structure of talent? What, in the end, is the necessary and sufficient level of development of the parts and components which permits the whole structure to work effectively?

To refine the proposed model one has to fill it in with specific content, to draw the portrait of the talent in full measure, with all its characteristics and particularities, and illustrate it using a concrete example. The model must be such that other talents, as they behold it, can 'see themselves'. Musical talent is ready to become just such a universal model, demonstrating through its own example how all our gifts and talents are arranged. A universal model must be broadly understandable, so that people investigating, say, the giftedness of a chef or that of an actor can both glean something useful from it. Musical talent satisfies this condition: no one has to explain what musical activity consists of—musicians compose and perform music. In this process they develop the material of music, its sounds and tonal combinations; they create new compositions; and they attempt to interest the public in the fruits of their labor and fantasy, all of which together is produced amid agitation and creative torment. For all the mysteriousness characteristic of the creative professions, the musical profession is still far more universal than, for example, that of the phlebotomist, who can extract blood from a vein with virtuoso skill, or the ornithologist, who knows all there is to know about birds. In short, many people can understand exactly what is under discussion when the model is based on the example of a musician's talent, which would not be the case if the talent were that of an air traffic controller.

It is not enough, however, to understand what a model consists of and how it works: one also needs to form an opinion of it and join in the discussion of it as well. And here also the talent of the musician shows itself to be more universal than many others. For music is all-encompassing: it has been known and loved always and universally. In terms of geographical universality, the model of musical talent breaks all records: there is no such profession as 'system programmer' among the inhabitants of the jungles of Brazil, for example, yet almost every member of an aboriginal community knows music as a composer, performer, and listener. The historical universality of music is also beyond doubt, as Adam and Eve surely sang, perhaps even played the flute, without knowing so much as the multiplication table.

Musical talent can also aspire to the role of universal model as its exceptional nature was recognized long ago, and because over the course of the ages no one has ever attempted to encroach on this exceptionality. In ancient Greece nobody thought to challenge an individual's ability to harvest grapes or olives—all Greeks were presumed to know how to do such things, and no one would have deigned to test a compatriot for such a talent (which is a mistaken assumption, since 'natural' talent is just as much a full-fledged talent as many others). Yet the ability to sing and play instruments was always subject to question, and the heavenly origin of these functions was disputed by no one: the voice of the deity resounded in the voice of the singer, and this heavenly voice dictated wondrous songs to the performer. Not everyone is capable of hearing and capturing the songs, and not everyone can convey their beauty to an audience—so it was supposed in the era of the

Greek heroes. The symbol of music, the lyre, was handed down from above not to all the Greeks together, but to the legendary Orpheus alone.

The very idea of talent, its status as a rare gift, has long been connected with music: it is thus unsurprising that the presence of musicality, whatever one means by that term, has always been subject to verification. In the West boy choristers were tested to the point of torment over their sense of pitch; in the East people tried to predict whether the musical taste and fantasy of potential practitioners of *raga* (in India) and *makom* (in the Middle East) would be sufficiently developed for the task. The musical attributes of the maidens whose play soothed the ears of the Chinese emperors were also verified. Musical assessments were rendered, and continue to be, for children who are candidate pianists and orchestra musicians in modern-day specialized music schools.

Over the course of these centuries of verification a great deal of expertise in identifying musical gifts has been accumulated. Indeed, no other human talent can boast of such a large and historically verified data base—which, moreover, has served as the basis for the prediction of future success. This accumulated knowledge represents material of enormous value, material which may serve as the basis for a model of talent. For if the representations of parts, components and subcomponents of 'talent in general' leave questions and lacunae, our knowledge of musical talent has had everything verified and supported by the experience of generations.

It is easier to formulate a model of talent in music than in other realms since different levels of musical giftedness may be delineated by examples. If, for instance, it is relatively difficult to distinguish a capable archeologist from a talented one, and a talented one from an archeological genius, then in music the word 'capable' will suffice to denote certain individuals, 'talented' will identify others, and 'genius' will be set aside for a third group. A hierarchy of talent levels will form itself within the model, and it will become clear what these levels have in common and what distinguishes them. A hierarchical arrangement is an essential element of any proper working model, and an analysis of musical talent can in this respect lead to a more complete *schema* than analyses of other kinds of endowment.

The experimental psychology of music has amassed extensive data which may serve as a solid base for the formation of a model of musical talent. The past 50 years has seen the birth of an entire field called *cognitive psychology of music* which studies the mental processes of perception, cognition, and thought as they apply to music. In this field the musician's entire operational apparatus, all the analytical procedures that she employs, come under greater or lesser degrees of scrutiny. The field examines the process by which people distinguish musical elements; how they form patterns, kinds of base structures; how musical clichés are formed; how people remember music; and how they forget it. For the time being experimental psychology has concentrated less on music than on its bits and pieces—artificial aural residues and constructed phrases—but nonetheless the soundness and conclusiveness of its results and their grounding in science compensate to an extent for the relative paucity of the materials. Put otherwise, a methodology for the scientific study of the 'micro-world' of musical talent has emerged, its underpinnings are in place; and the operational mechanisms of musical cognition—what has been called the 'musical mind'—have become clearer.

Beyond this, finally, there is the strenuous growth of the neuropsychology of music, which now stands proudly in line with the rest of the neurosciences. The various accomplishments of musical neuropsychology cannot be counted on the fingers of both hands, but we can in any case note a few of them here. For one thing, the functions of the hemispheres of the brain during musical activity are known by this field. In general, without reference to the musical arts, the left hemisphere is held responsible for the 'three R's' and the right for the 'three I's' (reading, writing, and arithmetic versus intuition, inspiration, and imagination). Neuropsychologists know that the left (logical) side of the brain primarily answers for the musician's sense of rhythm and her interpretation of signs and elements (what has been called *sintagmatics*); this side is also the province, as a sort of special gift from the muse of music, of absolute pitch. All this makes considerable sense, as the left hemisphere is easily handling the organization and chronological arrangement of signs, signals, words, and more.

In the province of the right hemisphere, the home of spontaneity, are located frequency distinction and the processes of musical synthesis, the awareness of the unity of music and its individual character—however its living 'I' may be expressed. Thus integrated melodies, integrated works as well as everything in music which needs to be memorized as a unified expression comes under the competence of the right hemisphere—as opposed to the disintegration, fragmentation, and analysis functions assigned by nature to the left side. The right hemisphere is on intimate terms not with time—it cannot count, add, or multiply seconds, hours, or minutes—but rather with space. It can grasp in a moment the contours of something which in real time takes much longer to complete. Thus without the right side it would be impossible to experience the unalloyed unity of all the parts, synthesized and subsumed into the wholeness of a musical composition.

Neuropsychologists have been able to isolate exactly where, in which areas of the brain, this or that musical function has its roots—and this location can now be identified with considerable greater exactitude than merely one of two hemispheres. Thus the perception of familiar melodies and that of unknown ones are, to neuropsychologists, somewhat different things. Rhythm, on the one hand, and meter (beat) on the other, have their own separate localities in the brain, as do sounds which enter into the melody and sounds which do not, and a good deal else. In other words, the neuropsychology of music has graphically discerned just how narrow the specialized sections of the brain are, and exactly what these sections actually do. On the other hand, functions of the musical brain are mostly based on mutual input and cross-sectional interplay between different parts of the brain, and the idea of 'localization' in many cases is not the best to explain such a complex task as music production and perception.

Everything that neuroscience of music brings is priceless information, which may be used to reveal the localization of analogous functions in other spheres of human activity. It is no accident that the discoveries of musical neuropsychology often appear on the pages of prestigious scholarly and scientific publications such as *Nature* and *Science*. Using the scientific apparatus of the neurosciences, the psychology of music can discuss a great deal both very exactly and very convincingly, which for the formation of a model of musical talent will, undoubtedly, prove to be of great significance: the judgments and conclusions at the base of the model will be authentically scientific and rigorously proven. Possibly, that's why the neuroscience of music is most rapidly developing and most popular among scientists in the last two decades and until now.

In sum, the model of musical talent is today the most complete, the most reliable and scientifically based talent model which the science of psychology can proffer for society's judgment. The virtues of this model can be formulated in a few propositions:

1   Musical talent is, from the standpoint of history and geography, the universal talent: music has existed always and everywhere, so referring to music means referring to something everyone understands.

2   Musical talent is a talent which can be ranked. Its gradations and levels are 'calculated' by history, and confirmed and polished over the passage of time as well. Ability, talent, and genius are for music not so much metaphors and subjective distinctions as historically and publicly probated understandings, the very formation of which renders the model of musical talent more hierarchical, bringing it closer to the demands of the scientific *schema*.

3   Musical talent is a talent which has been verified over the course of centuries. In music it has been possible to contrast predictions and actuality, desires and their realization. Distinct views have emerged on what musical talent consists of; what constituent elements are necessary for its effective work; and how, by which procedures and observations, it is possible to discern—long before they flower into extraordinary success—the buds of undiscovered talent.

4   Musical talent is one which has for decades undergone scientific observation under laboratory conditions. It is studied by two well-developed fields of knowledge: cognitive psychology of music and musical neuropsychology, each of which has its own scientific apparatus, its own experimental base, and its own approved methods. The data of these sciences on the processes of musical perception and thinking, and on the work of the musical memory and the musical imagination, will become the basis for our model of musical talent.

Part 2

Musical abilities

The expressive ear for music

The expressive ear and musical communication

Exactly when it was that music first appeared in the world cannot be determined with any more certainty than where it came from. In any case we can say one thing: the process was complete at some point before man had come to understand that man was what he was, that is, a thinking, reacting being. Music predates speech, as organized sound signals were and are used by birds and other animals. The sounds these beasts use for communication remind us of music: dolphins sing, wolves howl, birds chirp away merrily. Science at this point does not doubt that music and spoken language are two sprouts which grew from a single stem. There is a growing conviction that at the beginning of time—meaning the dawn of human civilization—music and language were one, an undifferentiated whole (Fitch 2006; Masataka 2007; Mithen 2006). People communicated by means of uttered units, half-words and half-sounds, whose meanings were conditional, developing in the context of the very process of communicating them: mutually enamored cave dwellers cooed and moaned; enemies threatened each other with shouts, roars, and wails in various combinations; and approval was expressed by a short, calming sound, while disapproval was registered in tones strong and sharp.

Sound was and is an invariable sign of the presence of someone or something. If no one is at hand, blissful silence reigns, or perhaps a frightening silence ('It was quiet, . . . *too* quiet'). But once a friend, neighbor, or some other being appears, silence retreats and communication begins. By communicating man discovers the world; and in this process he continually relies on the help and support of other people—as an infant, on the care of his parents; as a child, on the admonitions of his teachers. And in subsequent years, communication continues ubiquitous—with friends and colleagues, with his own children—and its modes and contexts define life for him (joyful and sad, interesting and tedious, for business, and for the good of his soul) to the end of his days. Almost all of this array of communication normally takes place with the help of sound, which has been a communicative means since time immemorial, absorbing into itself the essence of the process of communication.

Music, the quintessence of sound, is ordered in such a way that man perceives it almost as a living being, as a voice addressing him. As music communicates with its listener, it creates the effect of a second presence, an interlocutor who relieves us from solitude. Regardless of whether we consciously enjoy communicating or consciously avoid it, at the subconscious level the state of being alone is perceived negatively. And in the end, the difference between extroverts (who love company) and introverts (who shun it) really only consists of the method of communication chosen by each: the former want to hear and see the immediate reactions of others to their words and gestures, while the latter prefer to 'listen', that is, read, look, and perceive. In the psychological sense, of course, both groups communicate constantly.

Communication is the bread, water, and air of the soul, and music provides us with an ever-present opportunity to sense community, that we are not alone. But perhaps humans have artificially invested music with this property, mistakenly inflating its meaning and anthropomorphizing it? Recent psychological experiments have confirmed those of the earlier periods in demonstrating that humans have, in fact, assigned music the status of a second presence: people really do communicate with music—not simply with each other *through* music, but with music *itself*, by which we mean that to listen to music is to perceive the 'speech' of another and to form, internally, a reaction to it. Put otherwise, the phrase 'music as a means of communication' is neither an image nor a metaphor but an authentic psychological reality for human beings. As musicologist Boris Asafiev phrased it, 'the source, the culture of the musical ear, composition and reproduction—all this is created and directed as communication by sound and the articulation of music as thought'.[1]

American psychologist Carol Krumhansl measured the pulse, blood pressure, respiration, and skin temperature of a group of test subjects as they listened to music (Krumhansl 1997). Their reactions were telling: to music that the subjects described as 'frightening' the physiological response was one of genuine fright—the subjects' pulses raced at a pace approaching that of someone encountering a bear in the woods. By the same token, 'joyful' music elicited reactions of real elation (with quickened breath) and 'sad' music brought down the heartbeat, blood pressure, and skin temperature as though the subjects really were experiencing the pain of separation. The lesson of Krumhansl's experiment (and others like it) is that music is not merely a means of communication—it is a means of *emotional* communication as well, and a means at once powerful, active, and responsive.

School children put on music while doing their homework, as we know, to make a more pleasant setting for the chore; the presence of such a 'companion' gives a sense of being in 'good company', and this 'friend' carries the advantage of never bothering one with questions or interfering with the actual homework—to a certain point, at least. Recent research in the field of psycho-acoustic of aural and musical perception has established that when the music played in such homework settings is very light and does not exceed the role of background accompaniment, students listen to it with only 'half an ear' and proceed with their work apace (Furnham and Allass 1999). But when music more complex and interesting is put on, the extrovert students are more inspired and introvert students more distracted from their studies taking music for a 'friend's voice': for extroverts it turns to be helpful and for introverts harmful. It turns out, unsurprisingly, that there is music and there is *music*. Some music seems to act like a capricious little girl,

---

[1] Asafiev, B. V. (1971) *Muzikalnaia forma kak protsess/Musical Form as a Process*. Leningrad: Muzyka, p. 117.

refusing to be modest and undemanding, but rather drawing all attention to herself and jealously excluding all other people and things. Only a genuine companion/interlocutor, a real living being, can behave that way.

As a valued and influential companion, music has the ability to persuade—and even to alter reality with its persuasion. Valerie Stratton and Annette Zalanowski (1989) at Pennsylvania State University decided to determine whether human decision-making was influenced more by sight or sound. A group of independent experts arranged two sets of pictures of faces, one set reflecting happiness and brotherly love and the other showing expressions of tension and aggression. A second group of experts compiled a series of musical fragments reflecting the same two sets of positive and negative emotions. Then the pictures and musical fragments were joined randomly and presented to a group of subjects who were asked, 'What kind of expression do you see in this person's face?' The subjects responded as if the music they were hearing was whispering the answer in their ears: if negative music was being played, they identified a face expressing nothing but sweetness and light as 'frightening'; if positive music was playing, they saw in the face of someone apparently auditioning for the role of serial killer nothing but friendliness and good will. The experimenters thus confirmed the fact and extent of the 'personification' that takes place, the direct transfer of emotional values that listening to music, as a 'person' one trusts, can engender. It is hard to accept the wisdom of 'Seeing is believing' in the wake of such results, as hearing is evidently so much more powerful an agency, capable as it apparently is of persuading people not to believe their own eyes if their ears tell them otherwise. Naomi Ziv and Maya Gochen (2006) also concluded that music was the most influential commentator for 5–6 year olds, deciding whether the story they were listening to together with music fragments, was 'happy' or 'sad'.

The ability of music to influence emotions and participate in the communicative process derives from the properties of sound. Unlike light, which can be ignored by closing one's eyes, and unlike an unpleasant vision, which one may turn one's back on, sound provides no easy escape from its powers: it is obtrusive and active, demanding a response. Sound insistently signals something, and usually something of critical importance: if one hears thunder there will soon be a storm; if there is rumbling in the mountains, a landslide is on the way. The signal from nature in such instances is clear: run, hide, save yourself! On the other side of the ledger, the gurgling of a stream, the rustle of tree branches and the gentle lapping of the tide all signal to the creatures in their sound range that it is appropriate to relax, go off guard and enjoy a necessary interlude of peace and quiet. Every sound possesses a certain authority which urges living beings, man among them, to actions of one kind or another. The ability of sound to convey important information, attuning humans to a specific mode, became an internal capability of the art of music; and no matter how complex this ability becomes or how multifaceted are the forms it assumes, thought-bearing sound remains the very soul and essence of all music perception.

In order to pass along the necessary information, sound exploits a wide selection of essential properties. First it distinguishes for us who and what is calling, whose 'voice' we are hearing. Large and imposing objects have a 'voice' that is low on the register, rough and crude, such as the roar of a wild animal or the crack of the splitting earth during an earthquake. Small and light objects, whose potential as sources of danger is not as great, have a correspondingly less imposing sound: birds sing softly and in a high register, children's voices sound a jingle, grasshoppers dryly and piercingly chirp in the grass. The timbre or general coloring of the sound as well as its register (meaning the location of sounds in a high or low diapason) differentiate the voices of all humans; indeed, it is the timbre of voice by which we distinguish those we know from those we do not. Musical instruments proclaim their difference from one another by timbre and register: the bass viol is low and 'thick'; the trumpet is high and penetrating; the bassoon grumbles with a nasal twang; the French horn sings freely and fluently. Even as we hear a sound, its timbre and register are conveying to us a great deal, suggesting what to expect from the sound's source and how to react to it.

It is no less important to know, of course, how far away the source is and whether it is capable of cutting through great distances. Loud sounds tell us that the 'object', or rather the 'subject', since it is possible that we will have to get better acquainted, is quite near. A quiet sound, on the other hand, tells us that we can wait, sharpen our arrows and squint, as the rumble of enemy horses is still far beyond the bend. The degree of volume along with the character of the articulation convey the most important information: what the 'subject' wants or expects of us and what his intentions are. A mad dog is going to bark in *staccato* fashion, roughly and often, as if fit to burst, while a gentle kitten will purr, its melody merging into the most tender of 'songs'. It is unimportant whether one can distinguish the pitch of separate sounds in these 'messages', or whether their continuity (or the lack of it) forms a rhythmic pattern; the various attendant properties of the sound are entirely sufficient for the listener to orient himself effectively vis-a-vis the 'subject'. The timbre, register, loudness, articulation, and accentuation of its 'speech', along with the tempo of its delivery, fast or slow, hurried or casual, reveal everything about the 'subject's' communicative intentions.

While these aspects of sound do not appear in the written form of notes, it is in fact they which define the character of music, its real sound and our reaction to it. If one digresses from the exact pitches of the sounds and their rhythmic pattern—and these are the things which are affixed by the notes in a musical score—the idea, the musical intention inherent in a passage will nevertheless come through. Light and airy, dynamic and seemingly rustling, Prokofiev's Juliet will trip along in our mind's eye, just as the elves in Mendelsohn's *Midsummer Night's Dream* will seem to slip away, flying off airily. The non-notational aspects of sound are analogous to the intonations of a person's speech, which can convey the idea of what is being said even if words are omitted. This is the origin of Boris Astafiev's notable phrase to the effect that 'music is the art of the intoned thought', the intoned thought which is manifest in even the crudest, most primitive qualities of sound, in the direction of the melodic movement, the volume and power of the sound, the greater or lesser degree of its activity, the level of accentuation and the particularities of vocal or instrumental pronunciation. The music scholar Viacheslav Medushevsky termed the ideational and emotional side of musicality the 'intonational form' to distinguish it from the pitch-rhythmic side of sound, the form he called 'analytical' (Medushevsky 1993).

The intonational form is based on the intonational–integral principle of the construction of a musical fabric which is

> . . . based on the all-encompassing use of all the properties of the musical material. Not only pitch and rhythm but also of timbre, tessitura, register, volume, articulation, and on through to such subtleties as methods of vibrato and agogic nuances. Historically, it was on this soil that the flourishing gardens of expressive-fabular organization arose: here we find the incalculable variations of types of intonation—of oration, song poetry, ballads, of the intonational types of melody, the multiplicity of methods of organization of the artistic world of music in the framework of texture and composition.[2]

The property of the human ear specially geared for the perception of the emotional–ideational aspects of music is called the *intonational* (or *expressive*) *ear for music*. The ear's capability of distinguishing the pitch of sounds and fixing the length of their duration is called the *analytical ear for music*.

The expressive ear cannot tell the sounds of *do*, *re*, and *mi* apart. On the other hand it can (and does) distinguish the ideational fulfillment of Debussy's stealing and gliding *Sails* from that of the insistent, elastic gait of Ravel's *Bolero*. The expressive ear differentiates the tortured moaning of Tchaikovsky's *Sixth Symphony* from the comfortably sleepy-headed modulations of his *First*. And yet with the help of the expressive ear it would be impossible to perceive or remember a single melody: the expressive ear is interested in the gesture, tone, direction of movement, and general character, but it cannot fix the details of a melodic sketch or the nuances of harmony—this is the function of the analytical ear, which assesses the relationships of sounds to each other.

The expressive ear is universal: everyone possesses it, at least to some extent. Without it the human race would not have survived its infancy, as it would have failed at interpreting the signals nature sent to the still-adapting early *homo sapiens*. The roots of the expressive ear lie in the deepest recesses of our life-matter, with roots extending back to parts of the unconscious which must rank among those formed earliest. The expressive ear, like the most of the unconscious mind, is the provenance of the brain's right hemisphere; it connects information about the emotional tone of communication with musical sound. In this sense the expressive ear serves as the nerve of musical perception and creativity, the focal point of the vivacity and ideation of the art of music. The expressive ear, in short, is the starting point of the development of *homo musicus*.

The expressive ear in scientific experiments

The business of science is to pose questions and subject the unproven to the rigors of examination. No matter what theoreticians may claim, brass tacks practitioners will harbor reservations about the musings of such colleagues until proof is offered. The concept

---

[2] Medushevsky, V. V. (1993) *Intonatsionnaia forma muziki/The Intonational Form of Music.* Moscow: Kompozitor, p. 57.

of the expressive ear was the subject of such skepticism, of course; it was necessary to prove that it really *was* ancient, part of our nature, indeed, a part so innate and natural that its functions can be observed even among infants. The youngest of our species can distinguish musical timbres and the general coloring of sound, the most characteristic sign of which is consonance/dissonance. The sound of musical consonance resembles the tender voice of a friend and produces a sense of peace and concord; the sound of dissonance, rough and sharp, can be compared to the voice of an enemy.

Analyzing the reactions of infants aged four to six months to consonance/dissonance, researchers have successfully demonstrated that the expressive ear is entirely ready for work in humans at these early stages of development, effectively doing its natural duty by distinguishing 'friends and foes'. Psychologists were convinced that infants do not like dissonance: exposed to dissonant sounds, they behave nervously, turning over constantly and attempting to keep away from the source of the sound. Consonant sounds, on the other hand, brought welcoming reactions from the same infants, as if they had been given their favorite rattle: they would go still, looking fixedly at the speakers from which the sound came, and begin to smile (Trainor and Heinmiller 1998). In another experiment, the infant subjects joyfully welcomed the euphonious accompaniment of a Mozart min-uet, dancing in their cribs; when the speakers put forth scratchy dissonance to accompany the same minuet, the same infants began to groan and sniffle—clear expressions of dissatisfaction (Johnson 1998). Thus scientists confirmed that the expressive ear does not need great experience to be able to tell potentially friendly sounds (consonance) from those of potential enemies (dissonance). The expressive ear works on a genetic basis, and thus infants lacking any musical experience at all nevertheless are already in possession of the so-called sense of consonance, which is what the human ear for timbre relies on.

The ear for timbre and the sense of consonance are already present in apes, as demon-strated by Scottish researcher Colwyn Trevarthen (2002): the physiological reactions of human brains and those of macaques when exposed to consonant and dissonant chords are identical—the same sections of the two species' brains react, and do so in the same fashion. Trevarthen thus concluded that those sections of the human brain which respond to consonance and dissonance were in fact formed relatively early in the evolutionary process, before primates had begun significant differentiation.

Not only is the perception of timbre fully functional among young children; so is their perception of the emotional character of music. Two Dutch psychologists asked 3-year-old children to select pictures showing sad and happy faces to fit corresponding music (Terwogt and Van Grinsven 1988). Similarly Joseph Cunnningham and Robert Sterling (1988) also asked 4 year olds to explain the emotions and moods of classical pieces by Grieg, Wagner, Lyadov, and Debussy, indicating which pieces they associated with anger, fear, laughter, and sadness. In both experiments the children showed themselves to good advantage, making few mistakes—indeed, adult subjects, it turned out, could complete the same tasks no better. The expressive ear as an indicator of musical emotion develops very early, beginning to work almost immediately and claiming as its provenance not only the simplest contrasts but more complex functions of the recognition of moods in music as well.

While it was well and good to note the success of the children tested for musical responses in cases like these, some researchers expressed doubts as to how they actually recognized musical emotions: it is entirely possible to suppose, after all, that it was not the 'rough' properties of sound controlled by the expressive ear— timbre, volume, tempo, and articulation— which helped the children solve the tasks, but completely different ones, such as the rhythmic pattern or interval construction of the melody, which unarguably in Grieg's *The Death of Oze* are one thing (sadness) and in the overture to Wagner's *Flying Dutchman* something else altogether (anger). Moreover, some of the pieces used with the children were in a major key, traditionally more positive and peaceful, while others were in minor keys, traditionally associated with negative, saddened emotional states. How is one to tell which qualities of sound actually assisted the young subjects in identifying the emotional tenor of the given works?

Swedish psychologist Patrick Juslin (2000) of Uppsala University entered the fray on the side of the expressive ear and its limited but very simple and stable properties. Juslin employed the mood labels already in use in musical psychology (happiness, sadness, anger, fear) but decided to have them demonstrated for his experiment's subjects using the same pieces all played on the same instrument, the guitar. While the listeners sat in another building and heard the guitar music through earphones, Juslin's guitarist would play a piece unknown to the adult subjects while internally frowning, grimacing, and otherwise projecting things negative—then the same piece with a light heart, peacefully smiling and trying to inject all the good and joy of life into the music. The effect was astonishing. All the listeners could distinguish the musician's projected emotions, although the notations (the pitch of the sound) and rhythmic pattern were exactly the same in each performance. The listeners' responses, in short, were based exclusively on the expressive ear. In addition it was proved that we unveil the emotional meaning of the music as quickly as less than one second from its start—too little time to be aware of anything but its tempo, volume, manner of pronunciation, and other very general qualities (Bigand *et al.* 2005).

To prove once and for all that it is not the pitch–rhythmic parameters of sound, but rather its 'rough' properties which are the basic carriers of emotional expressiveness in music, another experiment was conducted in the psycho-acoustic laboratory at Oxford University (Rosner 1999) in which the subjects were tasked with understanding and sensing the thought and character of 'foreign' music: for white English subjects, Indian *raga* music was played. The subjects had no knowledge of how *raga* is constructed or of its cultural significance; and they likewise knew nothing of the pitch arrangement of *raga*, having no idea of its modal organization or of how the sounds were connected with each other. The subjects also knew nothing of the rhythmic patterns in which *raga* exists, and would surely have been lost in its flowing, ineffable rhythmic phrasings which lack the time measures and accents the European ear is accustomed to. As the experimenter Bob Rosner put it: 'Can people identify the intended emotion in music from an unfamiliar tonal system? . . . If they can, is their sensitivity to intended emotions associated with perceived changes in psychophysical dimensions of music?'[3]

[3] Rosner, B. S. (1999) A cross-cultural investigation of the perception of emotion in music: psychophysical and cultural cues. *Music Perception*, 17, p. 101.

Tempo, the general direction of melody and rhythm and register were the parameters on which the subjects posed their judgments of happiness, sadness, or anger expressed in ragas. Judgments of emotion were significantly related to judgments of psychophysical dimensions, and, in some cases, to instrument timbre. In other words, once again the resources of the expressive ear proved essential for the subjects' success; in correctly solving the 'emotional riddles' of the music as they were assigned to do, the subjects had no other tools available: they were hearing music of an alien culture, coded in unfamiliar pitch–rhythmic systems.

An experiment in the same spirit was conducted by Kate Hevner, who investigated the significance of different parameters of sound in the perception of a musical thought (Hevner 1936; 1937). She found that tempo and register led the listeners when they attempted to interpret what the emotional conditions inherent in the music were. Second in importance were articulation and direction of movement. Kate Hevner was most surprised, in any case, when she played a melody backwards for her subjects, not one of whom reported any difference whatsoever in the mood of the piece. Rosamund Shuter-Dyson and Clive Gabriel report about that: 'Interestingly the direction of the melodic line, varied by inverting the melody, was found by Hevner's method to convey nothing very much at all'.[4] These represent only a modest selection of the experiments on record which demonstrate that the idea and essence of a musical message are entirely perceived by means of the expressive ear, which is what it exists to do.

As in many scientific disputes involving brain functions, the debate over the nature of the expressive ear was ultimately resolved by neuropsychology. In an experiment conducted by two Canadian neuropsychologists (Boucher and Bryden 1997), subjects were first required to identify a melody which they had heard before from among a number of unfamiliar ones; in a second task, the subjects were to identify the timbre of the tuba among that of other bass instruments (bassoon, bass viol, cello, bass clarinet, etc.). It turned out that for the performance of these two tasks different sections of the human brain were put to use, leading the authors to conclude: 'No relation was observed between lambda measures for the two tasks, suggesting that laterality for melody processing is independent of laterality for timbre processing'.[5] The recognition of timbre, as is well known, is one of the principal functions of the expressive ear.

In another notable experiment, conducted by Isabelle Peretz and Louise Gagnon (1999), a woman with severe brain damage—musical agnosia, meaning she had no musical memory—could not distinguish familiar and unfamiliar melodies; and yet, without being able to recognize pieces, she could detect and characterize their emotional tone and character. This suggests that the perception of the emotional character of music and the musical memory travel along different paths and have their own separate 'residences' in the brain; thus the expressive ear, the manager of emotional expressiveness in music,

---

[4] Shuter-Dyson, R. and Gabriel. C. (1981) *The Psychology of Musical Ability*. London: Methuen, p. 253–4.

[5] Boucher, R. and Bryden, M. P. (1997) Laterality effects in the processing of melody and timbre. *Neuropsychologia*, 35, p. 1467.

is a separate and autonomous psychological formation. This experiment surely convinced many previous skeptics of the real existence of the expressive ear. Another patient with a brain damage restricted only to one area, amygdala, was unable to experience fear and sadness coming from music, and yet could enjoy happy music in the way we all do. This is to say that our perception of musical expressivity is highly specialized and there exists a special brain 'instrument' for responding to each emotional stimulus. So, the researchers concluded that 'the amygdala appears to be necessary for emotional processing of music rather than the perceptual processing itself'.[6]

The expressive ear, working with the non-notational aspects of sound, justified all expectations: it appeared extremely early among primates (apes and infants possess it); and it coped successfully with the recognition of the emotional side of music in any circumstances—where musical and cultural experience could not do so and direct perception had to be used exclusively. The expressive ear proved itself autonomous and independent, confirming that in music, analyzing and memorizing are one thing, while experiencing, empathizing and being moved are something else altogether—nature envisioned different psychological mechanisms for each.

How the expressive ear works

Man's nature is an integrated one: it is quite difficult for us to break down into parts the components and elements which compose our life impressions. A person may or may not like a specific set of circumstances, which either pique his curiosity or turn it off; the relationship of an individual to a situation encompasses everything present in an integrated whole. The greatest quantum leap a child makes in perceiving the order of things in the Big World comes when she realizes that the chair she sits on when she drinks tea, the cup the tea is in and the chocolate which makes the tea so tasty are, in fact, furniture, crockery, and food, that is, things which are essentially different. When a person learns formal classifications of objects and understands the essence of the mental activity of analysis—that person ceases to be a child, as he has begun to practice abstract thinking. In childhood humans think concretely, situationally and in images; this type of thinking, in the terminology of Lev Vygotsky (1993), may be called 'complex'.

In encountering art man returns to his childhood: he becomes a direct, feeling, perceiving creature, and his childhood inclination to the sorting and linking of objects on the basis of emotional and situational proximity returns—everything goes into one psychological 'complex'. Everything becomes one, everything melds into everything else: color, light and sound, sound and smell, weight and sound—all merge into each other with ease, united as they are by the power of one human being's perception. Sound may become heavy or light, oily or wooden, smooth or rough, any of a number of things: it answers no longer to the laws of physics but to those of synthesis, presupposing strong psychological

6 Gosselin, N., Peretz, I., Johnsen, E., and Adolphs, R. (2007) Amygdala damage impairs emotion recognition from music. *Neuropsychologia*, 45, p. 236.

associations between the perception of different modalities, visual, aural, tactile, or olfactory. As musicologist Henrikh Orlov puts it,

> The last thing that we can define with a word in our non-verbal impressions of music are syntheses—the innumerable 'inadequate perceptions' of sounds, as if they were not aural sensations but visual, tactile, gustatory, mental and so on. . . . Should we not see in these syntheses remnants of our primitive experience with sound—sound as Presence—and thus relics of the primitive mystical participation in the organic undivided unity of the world? Are these syntheses not intimate symbols of a magical self-identification with reality?[7]

Syntheses in music are the provenance of the expressive ear. The timbres of voices and instruments are easy to associate with weight and color: the sound of the bass is velvet, dark and heavy, while the sound of the soprano is light, bright, and crystalline. Penetrating and powerful sounds, like dumbbells dropping on a floor, can seem like a giant-magician, with his broad gestures and leaden gait, while the quiet rustle of harps and violins can remind us of the rustling of the tree branches in a wood, the gurgling of a stream and the summer grass as it ripples under a breeze. The note E and the note A, taken without timbre, as mere abstractions, do not summon such images and associations; nor does a rhythmic figure, deprived of timbre, tempo, and character of movement. It is in fact the expressive ear, through motor, visual, tactile, and other associations, which connects music with the greater world of life and culture.

One of the principal channels of communication between music and the rest of existence is movement, the conscious gesture. Music moves and gesticulates, it is filled with abrupt movements and smooth ones, hasty and relaxed ones; it flies like an arrow, crawls turtle-like and strides along smartly like a soldier on parade. Our reaction to music is inseparable from motion (Eitan and Granot 2006; Medushevsky 1993). Swedish psychologist Bjorn Salomonsson (1989) confirmed the connection of music and body-motor movement in a series of experiments which demonstrated the deep psychological interdependence between sound and the obligatory bodily reaction to it, which should hardly surprise us, in the end, as sound is itself movement: a sounding string or the column of air from a woodwind vibrate, that is, move. The infants in Salomonsson's studies 'vibrated' like a string when hearing sounds: their perception was an active response by the body to the vibration of sound; if you changed the nature of the sound, Salomonsson found, the nature of the infants' movement likewise changed immediately; different timbres and different registers called forth different movements as well. As Salomonsson concluded,

> To the infant, in whom hearing is already active, primitive affects consist mostly of bodily changes and the infant's perception of them with the ideational content in the background. Sound, later tone sequences and music will therefore be suited for symbolizing these affective bodily expressions. The infant and the adult listener associate similarities between the affect-expression and the world of sound which is accomplished according to archaic meaning schemata.[8]

---

[7] Orlov, H. (1992) *Drevo muzyki/The Tree of Music*. Washington-St.-Petersburg: Kompozitor, p. 174.
[8] Salomonsson, B. (1989) Music and affects: psychoanalytic viewpoints. *Scandinavian Psychoanalytic Review*, 12, p. 126.

Older children trying out the role of composer for themselves draw various movements. As Rosamund Shuter-Dyson and Clive Gabriel put it: 'Children's first compositions reflect their motor energy with uncontrolled gestures. When listening to recordings of their compositions they often repeat the actions involved'.[9]

Market research studies also confirm the connection of music and movement in a curious way, and a way that should serve as a warning to us of the potential danger of music: listening to music, we run a real risk every day of buying things we do not need. Anyone who thinks that the quiet hum of background music in a store has nothing to do with her, or no effect on her, is seriously mistaken. Human muscles react to music entirely involuntarily; indeed, they start 'dancing' to it. When the store plays slow, lullaby-like music which allays our natural vigilance and slows our movements, the customers move deliberately along the aisles, slowly and languidly piling up everything that falls to hand in their carts and baskets. Supermarket profits rise considerably under such circumstances, some 39.2 percent according to the research of Ronald Milliman (1982). Store managers who risked playing lively, upbeat music in hopes of charging up the purchasing masses and putting them in a good mood involuntarily activated their customers' musculature—and the natural motor reaction was 'Move out of the store!', a development that had the managers quickly rethinking their strategy.

Sound and its various properties call to life not only motor associations and body-movement reactions but visual impressions as well, sight images which one might not initially assume to be directly connected to aural stimuli. The existence of such associations was demonstrated in the work of four American scientists (Feierabend et al. 1998), although the possibility itself had been discussed 15 years earlier by Claude Levi-Strauss in his classic book *Structural Anthropology*: 'Practically all children and some adolescents automatically associate sounds, phonemes or the timbres of musical instruments with colors and forms'.[10]

A group of Japanese researchers (Oyama et al. 1998) identified two universal trans-modal factors, lightness and sharpness, which subjects had to discern in colors, forms, sounds, groups of words, facial expressions and film fragments; and the subjects succeeded. Sharpness occurs in visual impressions as an obvious form: everything that can penetrate and cut, in the world of visual impressions, is sharp—sharp corners, sharp noses, sharp twigs—which in the end go back to the same tactile and motor sensations, for they extend to objects with the help of which the actions are accomplished: a soft and stroking movement cannot be sharp. In aural impressions sharpness is inevitably connected with the capacity to pierce, the 'keenness' of sound which would certainly elicit in infants something like a lunge, a jab, a blow—the sound slices the ear just like sharp objects potentially slice and puncture: the sharp sound of a horn, sharp like the series of aural 'punctures' in Khachaturian's 'Saber Dance'.

[9] Shuter-Dyson, R. and Gabriel, C. (1981) *The Psychology of Musical Ability*. London: Methuen, p. 107.
[10] Levi-Strauss, K. (1983) *Strukturnaia antropologia/Structural Anthropology*. Moscow: Nauka, p. 86.

Equally revealing was the work of Robert Cutietta and Kelly Haggerty (1987) who assembled 1256 subjects, aged 3 to 78, to test sound-color associations. The researchers concluded 'that the association of color with music may not be the result of experiential conditioning or early chromesthetic experiences as has been theorized. Instead, color associations may be a kind of sensory processing of music that appears to be widespread and consistent across a broad age spectrum'.[11] In other words, musical impressions take on color directly, through the emotion perceived in the music. For example, the martial blaring of horns easily becomes red, never blue; a blindingly extravagant major is too vivid and bright, too colorful and challengingly open to become brown or purple. The emotional–ideational meaning of music perceived by the expressive ear and the analogous meanings of color pile upon one another in such proximity that they merge; it is not clear whether in the human experience 'red' music preceded the 'red sun', red banners, the red cape of the toreador or, as researchers affirm, everything bright, strong and triumphantly threatening of itself becomes red, and for the eye and ear in equal measure.

The expressive ear is capable of seeing spatial images in music, almost pictures. Bringing to life definite gestures and movements, music can—under the law of complex and synesthetic thought, which wants to see a whole situation in its entirety—'screw on' to them a spatial frame; the listener, turned by the strength of his own imagination into a viewer, must 'see' where the events described in the music take place. If she hears a heavy, trampling tread with great leaps interspersed, which Prokofiev describes in 'Montekki i Kapuletti', it is impossible to imagine that this movement could take place in some tiny space: the knights are dressed in heavy armor, their broad gestures and heavy treading about demand a surface of some breadth and depth: the actors in the play need such space to move about, to overcome the resistance of their own weight and strength.

Musical perception is closely connected with spatial imagination, a theme which musicologist Mark Aranovsky (1974) treated in an article called 'On psychological prerequisites of object-spatial aural imaging'. Some specialists consider spatial representations the basis of musical perception. Musicologist Valentina Holopova, for example, holds that

> It goes without saying that music exists only in man's perception of it, and the reality of a work can be examined and evaluated only in terms of someone's psychological reactions to it. Here one discovers the principal paradox of music as a 'temporal art form': from the point of view of psychological perception, a work of music enters the human consciousness first and foremost through spatial representations.[12]

The psychologists Dean Delis *et al.* (1978) have established the ability of listeners to draw integrated spatial pictures. To an undistinguished symphonic piece— something so nondescript it could easily have served as muzak in a retail outlet—the psychologists affixed various labels: in the first case the fragment was named 'Winter Forest'; in a second 'The Rebirth of Justice'. The first title evoked visual associations, while the second

---

[11] Cutietta, R. and Kelly, A. J. (1987) A comparative study of color association with music at various age levels. *Journal of Research in Music Education*, 35, p. 78.

[12] Holopova, V. (2000) *Muzyka kak vid iskusstva/Music as an Art Form*. St.-Petersburg: Lan', p. 161.

one forcibly repressed them—although the inherent significance of the pale, bland musical fragments, the experimenters held, was far from anything that might be considered image-representational. The experiment, at all events, demonstrated clearly that the listener's soul thirsts for visual associations: having found them, it takes in and remembers everything associated with them. But those who heard 'The Rebirth of Justice' and could not visualize anything could not pick out the fragment later from among other works. The researchers thus concluded that visual associations stimulate aural impressions and facilitate their recall, while aural impressions which lack visual equivalents easily fade from memory.

The non-notational aspects of sound and the expressive ear which perceives them mitigate toward psychological theatricalization, something which performers recognize before anyone else. Pianist Gerald Moore, the legendary concertmaster for many outstanding singers, recalled that he had reached the end of Brahms' 'Futile Serenade', through the bows and lamentations of the hero, and there occurred a sharp and terse chord—the composer called for its performance exactly that way, *sforzando*, meaning sudden, short, and powerful (in the nineteenth century composers began to suggest to performers how their works should be played because music no longer fit into one great tradition, in which composition and performance were the province of one and the same people).

'Without a doubt', wrote Moore, 'Brahms shows us that the girl closes the window with a bang'. Continuing, Moore likewise describes his impressions from 'The Grave of Anacreon' just as concretely and strikingly, unconcerned with accusations of vulgarization: 'the piano postlude gently takes us by the hand and leads us out. We leave unwillingly, turning back time and again to look once more at the poet's resting place'.[13] The pianist's thought is fairly bursting with motor associations of smooth and unhurried movements which are written into the spatial image of the road from the cemetery. Associations of this kind constitute a classic pattern of the work of the expressive ear.

The expressive ear saturates sound with muscular-motor and visual-spatial associations which, being psychologically tied to the aural sound, become very personal and intimate impressions. Sound demands response, engagement, participation, and invariably gets them. The mechanism of this kind of participation, as many music scholars have noted, is the unconscious singing or humming of a melody. Thanks to the expressive ear, for whom moaning and whining as well as shouting and whispering are exactly the same as singing, every listener makes music internally whether he knows it or not. It is in precisely this invariable participation in a performance that many musicians identify the great strength peculiar to music. As the conductor Ernest Ansermet observed:

> The art of representative portrayal does not, in the end, afford the listener the same experience of sensation as the art of direct expression: before an image the listener becomes in some measure a spectator, as he also sees the image externally, from without—whereas listening to music of

---

[13] Moore, G. (1987) Pevets i akkompaniator. Vospominaniya. Razmyshleniya o muzyke/ Singer and Accompanist. Remembrances. Thoughts on Music. Moscow: Muzyka, p. 256.

subjective expression, the listener experiences it for himself, and the author's act of expression becomes his own.[14]

The psychological mechanism of this appropriation of the sound process, under which the listener himself seemingly 'utters' the music being played, is connected with the mechanism of speech intoning which is localized in the right hemisphere of the brain: as distinct from the lexical-grammatical resources of language, intonational (expressive) properties are situated namely in the right (spatial) hemisphere. This makes sense, of course, as the melody of speech, like any other melody, can easily turn into a line, into a contour—it becomes a rising zigzag if the speaker uses an exclamatory tone; or it turns into a wavy line lightly interrupted by bumps if he coos like a pigeon. Without such an individual 'melody line' there can be no integrated speech intonation.

Experiments in neuropsychology show that injuries involving the loss of the 'singing' function in speech also render the mechanism for the personal appropriation of music inoperative. Music in such cases is no longer experienced as a living expression, although its idea and essence remain entirely clear to the handicapped listener. The music may be sad but the listener does not grieve; it may be majestic, but the listener's head does not rise nor does his carriage straighten: he takes in the music at a remove, not engaging it and not experiencing it as an event which is part of his emotional life. The journal *Brain and Language* recorded a case in which four neuropsychologists (Patel *et al.* 1998) studied a patient whose right-hemisphere functions, including speech intonation, had been lost. The man could not combine individual sounds into a melodic line and because of that, as he explained, he 'listened to music without any pleasure at all', although he could correctly answer questions about the emotional content and significance of the music in question. He simply could not appropriate the meaning in a personal sense; in a word, he could not experience the music.

Experiment and observation have confirmed the integrated and all-encompassing nature of the expressive ear, whose action mechanism includes both the human muscular apparatus (through the association of sound with movement and gesture) and the speech apparatus (through the internal 'singing' and 'voicing' connected with the intonation of speech, a kind of 'co-intonation' which invariably accompanies musical perception). The expressive ear also facilitates the appearance of the visual-spatial and color associations which are incorporated in the process of listening to music and enriching aural impressions. The expressive ear is the least specific kind of aural perception, the least connected with pitch and rhythm, the purely musical features; it opens up the aural field of music, revealing for *homo musicus* the world of sight and sensation.

The psychological vocabulary of the expressive ear

The science of psychology traditionally connects the art of music and the world of human emotions, assigning as traditional labels for joy, sorrow, fear, and anger. Experimenters readily use these definitions. There is considerable good in them, above all in their limitation.

[14] Ansermet, E. (1976) *Besedy o muzyke/Talks on Music.* Leningrad: Muzyka, p. 48.

Musicians may note with an air of injury that psychologists commit sacrilege trying to force the whole rich variety of musical experience into the Procrustean bed of these four labels; yet the truth is that the world of emotions is an ancient world, and the situations in life which bear genuine significance are actually quite few in number. These include acquisition—of sustenance, a wife or property, results which made early man happy; and the loss of such, which made him sad. When something threatened him, the emotion of fear arose to defend him without fail. And finally anger, which spoke to one thing alone— 'Do not fear! Forward, attack the enemy!'—which early man would do, hurling himself at the offending party. Thus the four emotions—happiness, sadness, fear, and anger—are sufficient to describe in principal the human emotional mechanism; further complication of this mechanism would be superfluous: the emotional oppositions of 'positive-negative' (happiness and sadness) and 'defence-attack' (fear and anger) are the necessary and sufficient conditions for the survival of man in the surrounding world, which means the fundamental functions of emotions in the human psyche are basically fulfilled. So it is that despite its seeming narrowness this primitive selection of emotional qualities is entirely representative and altogether adequate for modern scientific and scholarly analysis.

Emotions, as one sees from the above-mentioned examples, are the result of some sort of interaction, its dry residue, the result of an occurrence which by itself has no form of companionship. Yet music is not a result, but rather a process, a process of communication. It is emotionally colored, yet it demands in addition to purely emotional description a complementary set of concepts to take into account the particularities of music as the 'voice of the other', as a message coded in sound. How does man experience the process of communication, and what does this process mean for him? Where do the emotions which the process arouses come from? Thus for the classification of musical perception the so-called communicative archetypes—no less ancient than happiness, anger, or sorrow—will become fundamental; these archetypes are stereotypes, 'eternal models' of human communication in which the content and external attributes reveal its permanent bases. The concept of 'archetype', the focus of the ancient remnants of the human psyche which lurk to this day in the depths of the unconscious, was introduced into scientific discourse in the 1920s by Carl Jung (1981).

There are four basic kinds of communication among people, four communicative archetypes (Alexeev 1986; Kirnarskaya 1997; Kirnarskaya and Winner 1999). The first is the interaction of a leader to a crowd, a boss to a subordinate, a higher-up to a lower-down. The second is the reverse, communication from a hierarchically lower person to someone higher, in which the former appeals/requests/hopes and his interlocutor listens and decides. The third type of social communication is that among equals, the most natural and simple. The fourth type is communication with oneself, with one's own heart and soul. Communicative archetypes dictate a certain emotional tone, motive equivalent and spatial coordinates of the process of communication, creating its general image, which has an intermodal character—visual, motor-motive, and aural, in which all these modalities abide in indissoluble unity. Some researchers suppose that music had been born as a form of adaptation, as a survival tool, first of all giving way to signal-like expressive forms of communication (McDermott and Hauser 2005; Mithen 2006).

> Music and dance may have evolved as a coalition signaling system that could, among other things, credibly communicate coalition quality, thus permitting meaningful cooperative relationships between groups.[15]

If one imagines how, over the course of human history, communication between leaders and crowds, rulers and ruled, commanders and troops has ever been, one invariably comes to a significant similarity among all the examples which is dictated by the situation. The leader seeks to command the crowd so that it will recognize in him the strongest among them. The ruler must summon the people to battle, to the achievement of victory, and they follow him unconditionally. Not only is this the conduct of the leader of great multitudes, but also that of the construction foreman at a work site; and even, come to that, of the rooster in the hen house: he proudly strides to and fro, chest pumped up, and crows loudly, piercingly and with exceptional assurance letting others know of his superiority. In short, the nature of power is the same always and everywhere, no matter who does the ordering.

The spatial-motive archetype, the energized analogue of the communicative archetype of *invitation* in aural form, presupposes a certain cover; the intonations of the invitation archetype are unquestionably loud, ascendant and rise in such a sharp and decisive way, moreover, without the slightest hesitation. The 'voice' embraces a wide range, it is sweeping and strong, the character of its movement is large-scaled, sharp and powerful, taking in great spaces. The motor equivalent of the invitation archetype often includes a summoning gesture which is interpreted as a gestural 'exclamation':'Forward! Follow Me!' The monuments to rulers are cast in such poses. The most ancient models of the invitation archetype—those relating to the incantations of pagan priests (the shaman *kamlan'* of the north Asian Evenk and Chukchi) and to the earliest military and hunting rituals were all in this vein.

Communicative archetypes absorb into themselves generalized constructs, patterns which reflect in sound the idea of the communication, its spatial, muscle-motor, and intonational characteristics. The expressive ear, aimed at identifying the primary, the most 'coarse' properties of sound, first of all recognizes the communication archetype through its intonational profile, general character of movement, through its spatial and energy qualities. If the communicative archetype of the invitation is the one in question, then that fact predetermines the type of melodic movement, its tempo and general character, the dynamic characteristics of the sound, the articulation and accentuation profile of the music, independent of its stylistic and aspectual qualities. The invitation archetype in African hunting dance rituals, in the war cries of Wagnerian knights, and in the young heroes' arias in Verdi are in principle one and the same from the standpoint of their realization in sound, since the content of the communication and its emotional and ideational equivalents are also in principle the same.

---

[15] Hagen, E. H. and Bryant, G. A. (2003) Music and dance as a coalition signaling system. *Human Nature*, 14, p. 21.

The invitation archetype, extraordinarily rich in its musical applications, has another popular variant, in which the leader communicates with the crowd not as a commander to his army, but rather like the toastmaster at a wedding reception addressing the guests, or in the way a soloist in a popular musical revue communicates with the audience by gestures. The content of such communication is encouragement, an attempt to kindle spirits, to get people to follow one's lead in matters less critical than the common victory over an adversary or defense against a common foe. Natural for this variant are leaps, sharp but not very powerful blows and tosses; the space for the 'action' is no longer so wide and unlimited as in the military version of the invitation archetype, and may even be constricted into a circle (as Tchaikovsky's Odille moves with aggressive coquettishness in a circle during her 32 pirouettes [fuete]). The intonational profile of this variant of the invitation communicative archetype will be recurrent, resembling the hitting of a ball, when the voice stubbornly leaps to one and the same interval as though jumping away from a support. To this variant of the archetype belong the genres of the drinking song (including the famous example from Verdi's *La Traviata*), the Russian canticle (Glinka's '*Slav'sia*' is the classic example), and all manner of sporting and campaign songs (such as Isaac Dunaevsky's '*Marsh entuziastov*'). Among the non-classical hits of the genre one finds the British World War II song 'It's a Long Way to Tipperary', the heroine's aria 'I Could Have Danced All Night' from the musical *My Fair Lady*, Carambolina's aria from *Violets of Monmartre*. Even from such a brief list it is clear how beloved the invitation archetype has become in all the light musical genres, as its entertainment variant (which is second to the basic, or 'heroic' variant) serves for everything from songs of daily life to the operetta and the musical.

The second communicative archetype, also a very old means of communication, draws on the *request*, the act of petitioning for something. Traditional rituals have many such situations; here one finds the request by a suitor for the hand of a bride, a prayer to the heavens for rain and the mourning of the dead, which is in essence also a request (for the healing of the wounded souls on earth and the peace of the deceased in heaven). This request is directed at the god-figure in pagan religions, when the god-figure is also human, only stronger and more powerful. The social idea of the request archetype is communication of the lowly with those higher-up: here it is no longer a case of a strong leader talking to an obedient crowd, but rather of a subordinate who senses his dependence directing his voice at the one in whom he envisions the fulfillment of his desires. All the lyrical genres of communication, all the confessions of and pleas for love, belong to the communicative archetype of the request.

In 'request' form of communication the intonational contour is more often wavy: the petitioner is unsure of himself and this lack of assuredness is reflected in an inevitable wavering of the voice; and because his feeling is both great and sincere, the waves are rather large, 'hump-backed', with vivid rises and descents. The muscle-motor element of the request archetype relies on the bow, an inclination of the head and the entire body, an intonational profile corresponding to the basic form of forgiveness which such a bow produces. Such melodies sometimes issue from the so-called 'summit-source', such as, for example, the famous question the character Lensky poses in Pushkin's *Evgeny Onegin* ('What does the dawning day prepare for me?') or the analogous question from Tatiana in the same work ('Who are you, my guardian angel?'). The spatial element of the request archetype is somewhat more modest and compact than in the invitation archetype, but in the former there is a certain modicum of convenience of the spatial distribution: in relative terms, this is not the space of the greater world, where gods and heroes test their strength, and certainly not the unlimited field of battle, but more likely a room, a garden, a tree-lined path. In short, a space which is readily visible and scaled to the size of a human being, one who can turn to another such being in this intimate space with heartfelt openness and trust.

The request archetype is the one upon which all lyrical music relies. The limitless storehouse of the lyrical provides for all aspects of musical culture, from opera-symphonic and chamber music to jazz and pop. The love song, the lyric aria and all manner of moaning, sobbing, plaint, and their delicate reflections in music (to which belongs the blues tradition within jazz) figure here; so do various lyrical outpourings, including those rendered up-tempo, in symphonic music—the main theme in Mendelsohn's *Violin Concerto* for example, and both themes from Schubert's *Unfinished Symphony*—and, without question, all the pop music hits of the sensitive, touchy-feely type (Ennio Morricone's theme from the movie *The Professional*, with its mournfully falling melodic sighs, comes to mind)— these are merely some examples, and any number of others could be adduced to demonstrate the ubiquitousness of the lyrical; but we will limit ourselves to citing two other vivid entries from the world of cinema, the leitmotif from the music for the movies *The Umbrellas of Cherbourg* and *The Godfather* (with its quasi-Italian emotionalism so reminiscent of the Russian-Gypsy song '*Ochi chernye*'). A more guarded and gallant variant of the request archetype is based not on low bows but on soft curtsies, not on the intonations of plaints of love and loss, but on coquettish breathiness. Space here is intentionally chamber-oriented, like a snuffbox, even sort of dollish; such is the general minuetish character of the finale of Haydn's *Farewell Symphony*, Barbarina's song from Mozart's *The Marriage of Figaro* and all music whose context is unvarying deference, timidity, and delicacy, up to and including Debussy's 'Sails' and 'The Girl with the Flaxen Hair'.

A third kind of social interaction is based on the equality of the participants in the communication, with no weaker or stronger among them and no leaders or petitioners. This kind of communication is a remnant of childhood innocence, a focusing of simple joy, or, in any case, evidence of absolute freedom of thought and action, with no pressure or tension from within or without. This communicative archetype is that of *play*. Its intonational signature is somewhat agitated but by no means obtrusive; it may remind one of the chatter, chirping, and cawing of birds. There are no strong accents or broad lines; the whole of the sound assembly fits into a modest and compact space. The muscle-motor equivalent of the play archetype is often circular and closed off, as in Rimsky-Korsakov's 'Flight of the Bumblebee'. The motor nature of the play archetype is one of inertia, the movement is reminiscent of a spinning top, the flight of a moth, the passing of wind over grassy fields or the movements of the dancers in the traditional Slavic maidens' dances (*khorovody*), with their repeated separations and reunions.

The musical embodiment of the play archetype is virtuoso music, extremely light and lively. Also pertinent here is a 'danceable' quality of the 'Sylphide' mode; one of the hits of this genre is Bach's 'Gavotte for Flute in G Minor'. This is music which flows away, babbles like a brook, whistles, bounces along (jumping just a bit the while), flying and turning in the air. Likewise in this archetype one finds the galliard dance of times long past along and its progeny, the kurant and the gigue; here also is much of the virtuoso music of the Baroque and classical periods, including all the symphonic finales of Haydn and Mozart, many of the rondos of both, many fragments from the *opera bouffe* and much of the virtuoso etude music of the romantic period. All amusing, comic, and scherzo music, such as Prokofiev's famous 'Mercuzio' figures in the play archetype.

Finally we come to the last communication archetype, one whose origins hark back to the traditional culture of antiquity: the *meditation* archetype. This is associated with a state of isolation and internal involvement, with one's innermost thoughts: this is the archetype of communication with the self, calm and unhurried, devoid of life's irritants and the unwanted interruption of 'the other'. The meditative archetype can be traced to the ancient genre of the cradle song in which the singing mother seems to communicate with herself, with her best 'I', which is embodied in the cradled infant. In this archetype the intonational profile is calm; it is distinguished by the recurrence of themes, an attraction to supports already attained. Like a metronome, the meditative intonation is seemingly tied to itself, rotating the while alongside unvarying and proven intonations, as if afraid of being torn away from them.

The tempo of meditation is calm and measured, its body-motor equivalent is wandering, indecision, a reluctance and difficulty in taking over new space and a preference for an already-established diapason. This is a closed space of thought in which every step may lead to the Universal but is connected only with the step adjacent to it, and the entire journey can be seen with difficulty through the series of steps to come. This is characteristic of the majority of Christian musical cultures, such as the Gregorian chant of western Europe and its Russian counterpart, the *znamennoe penie*. Their principal ploy is the repetition of the already established, the return to the already articulated which, somewhat unexpectedly, produces the impression of one more turn of a spiral which is losing itself in the infinite. To this archetype belong musical works which draw on reflection and empathy; this includes many slow parts of European symphonic music and the music of mystical revelations of the twentieth century (such as Olivier Messiaen, Sofia Gubaidulina, Arvo Pyart and many others).

All of written music, of course, cannot be fit in indivisibly and in its entirety into one of these archetypes. Real, living music is to be found more often than not at their intersections, where the archetypes are mixed about, yielding mutual enrichment and mutual fulfillment. In great, large-scale works it is rare for a single archetype to predominate; different fragments tend toward different ones. It is likewise important that archetypes are the most ancient reference points of the expressive ear, and this means, inevitably, that at issue are the very performance parameters of sound. The communication archetypes resound and are realized through performance, and thus one and the same work—taking the example of Chopin's 'Prelude in F Sharp Minor'—can draw toward either an angry call to arms (in the performance of Maurizio Pollini) or a lyrical petition (with Ivo Pogorelich).

The communicative archetypes represent the fundamental psychological lexicon of aural images, the peculiar aural thought-formations on which all musical culture relies and from which, in reality, it developed. But in the same way that an alphabet is not a language and a dictionary is not speech, so these archetypes are but the frontal supports which bear the construction of an incalculable number of variations of musical experience and expression. The expressive ear masters the communicative archetypes as the bases for rich musical perception. Relying on them, the expressive ear interprets the musical idea as a living word addressed to it, the primary meaning of which is as clear as *ra* and *pta* were to an Egyptian or alpha and omega to a Greek.

Testing the expressive ear

Recognition of the communicative archetypes lies at the base of decoding a musical thought, and thus understanding the essence of a musical message. In a certain sense the communicative archetypes are the basics of musical language; no matter what culture a musical language belongs to, in the distant past it was a language of primitive sound signals which retained their original meaning in the framework of communicative archetypes. They are the source of music [and an essential guardian], not permitting the disappearance of man's primitive memory of what sound is or what its critical life-functions are. Penetrating into the contents of the communicative archetypes, the listener becomes a participant in the imagined situation of communication; thus it is easier for him to take in and experience the musical content, which he perceives as a message directed at him. Given the ancient origins of the communicative archetypes and their connection with the most basic properties of sound (loudness, articulation, timbre, and tempo), distinguishing the energy and pressure of the invitation archetype from the calm and self-exploration of the meditative archetype is a simple matter.

The art of music, even in its highest manifestations, remains a peculiar proto-language, a basis of communication in which the essence of the expression, its idea, cannot be interpreted incorrectly: there is no one who cannot understand the powerful summoning call of the 'Ride of the Valkyries', even without a love for classical music or a knowledge of Wagner and his passion for the medieval epos. Nor is there anyone who could not recognize the meditative archetype in the mystical meanderings of Ligeti's 'Atmospheres', fading and dissolving away into infinite space; even without liking the music of the twentieth-century avant-garde (and preferring melodious pop music), the listener is not hindered in decoding the primary idea of the musical directive with the help of the communicative archetypes.

At first glance the recognition of communicative archetypes has no direct bearing on musical talent, since this is a facility which virtually everyone enjoys. The level of development of one's expressive ear necessary for archetype recognition does not have to be very high. At the same time the necessity of a highly developed expressive ear, especially among performing musicians, is indisputable. As the outstanding Russian specialist on musical talent, Boris Teplov, noted over fifty years ago:

> It seems to me that the enormous significance for performance of the sense of timbre and the dynamic ear has been far from fully acknowledged. Timbre and dynamics— this is exactly the

material with which the performer works most of all; pitch, after all, has been decided for him in advance (or for the pianist in any case). Thus the performer's ear should be a highly developed ear for timbre and dynamics.[16]

Teplov broadly interprets the notions of timbre and dynamics here, since accentuation and articulation (additional parameters of the expressive ear) are also timbre and dynamics of a sort: an accentuated sound is louder than an unaccentuated one; and a continuous *legato* sound is softer than a disjointed *staccato*, meaning articulation becomes part of the timbre, enriching and detailing it. In other words, the expressive ear for music (the ear for timbre and dynamics, to Teplov) is an invariable component of musical talent.

All music teachers work on the expressive ear of their charges, calling it forth to do its duty: 'Don't pound the keys, draw out the sound, bring the line together', says the pedagogue, explaining how to play Bach. 'Sharper, more active, don't nod off', the teacher tells the student taking on the music of Prokofiev. Suggestions of this type can be successfully implemented only in the presence of a keen expressive ear which can differentiate the subtlest nuances—those of sharpness and dampening of a sound, its thickness or transparency—or countless other qualities, some inexpressible in words, that attend to timbre and dynamics. Is it possible to identify a good expressive ear in someone who is not a performer, who cannot demonstrate such an ear directly through achievement in performance? Can one predict the extent to which someone is predisposed toward the perception of a musical message? A person who has never heard or understood music will never be able to create the necessary palette of sound nuances in her own play.

In testing for the expressive ear, that is, in the prediction of its level of development in a given person, it is entirely possible to rely exclusively on the communicative archetypes: it is precisely they that have a direct bearing on the work of the expressive ear, on the entirety of all the non-notational aspects of sound which it encounters. The seeming primitivism and prehistoric nature of the communicative archetypes are in no way a hindrance since any task, including the recognition of these archetypes, can be conducted in both simple and complex forms, with an alternate context of activity rendering it easier or more difficult. It is well known, for example, that mathematical problems involving distance, time, and speed can be very simple, accessible even to a first grader. But an analogous problem, one with different ends in mind (philosophical rather than didactic) can turn into Xenon's paradox of Achilles and the tortoise, the former never catching up with the latter. To resolve such a paradox one must have a real logical-mathematical intellect rather than the primitive faculties of a schoolboy, even though the basic ideas involved in the problem—distance, time, and speed—are the same.

Identifying communicative archetypes in music is not difficult if their idea is explained beforehand to a test subject tasked with finding them. Or, in the case of 3-year-old subjects, if the archetypes are defined in the context of simple key words (happy, sad, afraid), whereupon the said 3 year olds will demonstrate, as has been shown, that they listen to music as discriminatingly as adults. Much depends on the musical examples: if a tester denotes three musical fragments with the words 'request', 'invitation', and 'play' and

16 Teplov, B. M. (1947) *The Psychology of Musical Abilities*. Moscow: Pedagogika, p. 94.

chooses extremely contrastive and characteristic fragments for each category, then there will be no mistakes in identification: children and adults, with and without musical education and practical experience, successfully distinguish the three archetypes from each other—which means that the task does not test anything. But if one adds other musical parameters to the task (genre and form of music) and increases the number of examples while withholding key-word explanations, the test becomes considerably more challenging.

In an experiment conducted at Harvard University (Kirnarskaya and Winner 1999), a group of adult and child subjects was asked to break down six musical fragments into three pairs according to the message which they perceived in them. 'Musical fragments should be like musical brothers and sisters who resemble each other in their habits, character, manner of speech and movement', the subject children were told. Among the six fragments were two possible ways of finding pairs: grouping them by communicative archetypes and by genre and style. Each method was possible, but the first presupposed the engagement of the subjects' expressive ear, while the second relied on a knowledge of musical styles and genres appropriate to the first grade level.

For the pair created to represent the invitation communication archetype the experimenters chose the wedding march from Wagner's Lohengrin and Edith Piaf's rendition of *Non, je ne regrette rien (No, I regret nothing)*. In both cases the non-notational aspects of the sound were identical: a low, strong sound, a rising melodic movement, a broad sweep, and a victorious call—the 'voice of a strong person'. In other respects, beyond the invitation communicative archetype, these fragments were completely dissimilar: they were music selected from different centuries and national cultures, vocal and orchestral music, classical and popular; to pair them together one would have to pay attention to their psychoemotional, 'coarse' sound parameters, which the expressive ear relies on, and ignore the knowledge acquired via musical experience.

The pair representing the play archetype consisted of a Russian folk song *Vdol' po rechke shla* and the *Sonata in F minor* by Domenico Scarlatti (as performed by Wanda Landowska). Here the attention of the subjects should have been attracted by the similarity of the abrupt jerky articulation, the circular movement within a small diapason and the general liveliness and passion characteristic of the play archetype. The trickiness and difficulty in identifying this pair arose from the genre/stylistic opposition: classical vs. folkloric, performance on an antique harpsichord vs. the singing of a folk chorus, and likewise the opposition of major and minor—the song in the former and the sonata in the latter (this is a critical detail which proves that those subjects who paired these two fragments did not do so because both were in major or minor keys).

Finally the third pair, the request archetype. Here one fragment was chosen from a romantic sonata by Caesar Franck for violin and piano, while the other was a well-known melancholy jazz piece performed by Sidney Bechet. Both fragments were slow, with wavy, flowing melodic lines and a lyrical manner of expression which imitated deep sighing. The principal distinction between the two was the dissimilarity of classical music and jazz—different eras, different cultures, and different worldviews.

The music chosen for the fragments was relatively familiar and not difficult, in order to render the memorization factor of minimal importance. For example, the Piaf song was met by all the subjects, children and adults alike, with smiles and applause; from the Sidney Bechet saxophone the subjects were on the verge of dancing. The subjects marked their answers at the bottom of a sheet, placing the numbers of the selected fragments in the appropriate boxes. During their time listening to the music selections the subjects could draw, record, and make themselves as comfortable as possible.

The task was assigned to several different categories of listeners: children with no musical experience and from different racial and educational/social backgrounds (black and white, private and public schools). Along with the children there were three groups of adult subjects in the experiment: gifted performing musicians with careers as soloists; modest music teachers—professionals in most of the cases lacking outstanding musical talent per se (their talent lying in pedagogy); ordinary adults without special musical education or particular musical passions; and adult music lovers, passionate amateurs.

A certain number of the subjects succeeded at the task, not succumbing to the clever traps and identifying the correct pairs according to their communicative archetypes. But most of the subjects chose as their basis for pair formation only timbre in its purest form, first pairing Piaf and the Russian chorus (female, non-academic song) and making a second pair on the basis of a relatively lively tempo and common membership in the genre of music classics (Wagner-Scarlatti). These subjects did not heed the 'suggestion' of their expressive ear because, most likely, it was too quiet, meaning not very active. The method of musical perception used by the subjects who found the communicative archetypes was termed by the experimenters 'expressive', while the other methods were termed 'formal'—underlining by this the expressive role of the intonational ear (and thus the alternate appellation) in the formation of the mental image of music, its ideational direction.

The statistical results of the experiment completely confirmed the correspondence between the level of development of the expressive ear and musical talent: despite considerable knowledge and musical experience, the overwhelming majority of concert performers (78 percent) made their pair choices on the basis of expressive parameters and found the communicative archetypes. Only 20 percent of the music teachers were able to reject what they had been told and give themselves over to the direct perception of music in accordance with its internal composition. Present in this is one of the principal signals which allows us to deem the task a real test of professional giftedness: successful professionals completed the task wonderfully, while people doing the same thing for living without such success performed the task significantly worse. If between these groups there is also equality of experience (which there was, since the median age of all subjects was around forty and all had specialized higher musical education), then the task has even more claim to consideration as a test for professional giftedness.

Among the adult nonmusicians a slightly higher group (30 percent) used their expressive ear; the remainder followed the music teachers in orienting themselves on the other parameters, those having no connection with musical thought or the content of a musical message—that is, they acted 'formally'. The greatest success in demonstrating the possibilities of the expressive ear was recorded by the separate group of adult music lovers: almost all of those, the people who adored music but had not made it their profession, used the expressive strategy of musical perception. Among them some 93 percent of the subjects oriented themselves by the communication archetypes in making up the musical pairs.

The subject children performed approximately the same as the adults tested: 125 of the children (to age 14) found the communicative archetypes, which suggests all the more that the experiment may be used as a test for musical giftedness—some of the children with no musical training complete the assigned task just as well as trained, educated adults. Thus one may suppose that it is these children who are 'infected' with the 'musicality virus'; some 88 percent of their peers cannot complete the same function, as their expressive ear is less sensitive and subtle. Moreover, it turned out that among the children who correctly performed the assigned task there was a remarkable balance: black and white, privileged and underprivileged, boys and girls were all represented in equal measure. These results indirectly suggest once again the genetic origins of the expressive ear, which is awarded in the same way to representatives of 'all sorts and conditions of men'.

In conclusion the experimenters summarized their findings as follows:

> Our results demonstrate that the predominant, most likely response of most people is to listen formally rather than expressively to music. Only those subjects who chose music as a career or who chose listening to music as a serious hobby, showed a strong tendency to listen to music expressively. It is our contention that this tendency is an indicator and a predictor of talent. The next step would be to conduct a longitudinal study to test this hypothesis. Of children given training in music, those who show a tendency to listen expressively should be those most likely to stay with music, continuing to play throughout adolescence and into adulthood. [17]

Phase II of the experiment turned to be the longitudinal study, conducted in Russia in 2001. The original experiment had already laid claim to the status of a serviceable test for musical giftedness, as it had been used to distinguish talented musicians from mediocre ones; now the field could be expanded—and 10 000 Moscow first graders became the subjects. The function of the test was to identify the most musically inclined children. The test could be used on such a large scale because of its practicality: the assignment of matching the musical pairs can be completed in 20 minutes by all the children in a school classroom simultaneously; there is no need to devote time to each individual student, as has been the case with traditional methods of testing for the musical ear.

The Moscow experiment yielded some 1 124 successful results, that is, children who completed the assigned tasks using the communicative archetypes, thus demonstrating a good expressive ear for music. These children were enrolled in special elementary schools with musical emphasis, where the great majority of them are continuing their studies today with no thought of doing otherwise. The 'expressive ear test' during five recent

---

[17] Kirnarskaya, D. and Winner, E. (1999) Musical ability in a new key: exploring the expressive ear for music. *Psychomusicology*, 16, p. 15.

years has become the instrument of involving musically gifted children into music education from Yakutia to South Siberia and from Kaliningrad to Krasnodarsky region.

In any case, one may already speak of the intimate connection which exists between the expressive ear for music and musical talent. This comes as no surprise: the liveliness and directness of perception and its responsiveness, which cannot be suppressed by educational stereotypes or years of lessons, serve as a sort of bridge between the experiment described above and the experience of observing the talented in a wide range of areas; paradoxically, the talented unite in themselves a depth of thought (and its technical equipment) with a spontaneity and openness of perception.

A telling observation was made by one of the experimenter's assistants after talking with the parents of the children who had been recommended for enrolment in special music schools: seventy-five percent of parents mentioned that a musical gene was clearly present in the family tree, that in each case at least one or more of the relatives of the child whose expressive ear for music was extraordinarily developed—parents, grandparents, aunts, and uncles—sang and played various instruments. Many of them were self-taught, some had learned several instruments, certain among them even had professional music training, although economic concerns prompted them to pursue their livelihoods elsewhere.

In any case, the notion of the heredity of musical talent received one more indirect confirmation. The 'environment idea' as the explanation of the child's musicality is dismissed by the rest of musical children with good expressive ear: according to the interviews 25 percent of them couldn't boast any hereditary links with the music—their parents and other relatives didn't carry any signs of musicianship. Isn't it a prompt that musical abilities may really carry a heavy footprint of inborn origin, in some cases clearly hereditary while in other cases not? Rosamund Shuter-Dyson and Clive Gabriel report of almost the same data on the family roots of musical and unmusical children: their findings appear later in this book in more detail (Shuter-Dyson and Gabriel 1981).

The expressive ear and musical motivation

The experiment described above demonstrates, on the one hand, that the expressive ear belongs to the structure of musical talent: gifted professional musicians and music-loving amateurs are possessed of the expressive ear to a very high degree, as are children who are drawn to music and wish to take it up seriously. On the other hand, the exact place of the expressive ear in the structure of musical talent, its role in the work of the many components that make up that talent, remains unclear. This experiment leads us to the assumption that the essence of the expressive ear within musical talent should be sought at the point of intersection of the professional performer's talent and that of the music-loving gifted amateur: these two groups demonstrated identical success in the work of the expressive ear, which functioned for each as the decoder of musical meanings that revealed the essence and idea of a musical expression.

Three American psychologists (Juniu *et al.* 1996) conducted an experiment which confirmed that among working musicians of middling talent, in comparison to music lovers per se, there was a singular absence of musical enthusiasm. The psychologists studied the attitude of professional musicians and amateur music lovers to the act of performing, determining that for the former this was work, motivated by compensation (i.e. externally), while for the amateurs it was relaxation and joy, motivated purely from internal sources. At first glance one would think from this that all was as it should be: some render unto God and others unto Caesar. But no. Unlike their less-talented colleagues, highly gifted musicians, paradoxically, never perceive music as a way of making one's living. As Leonard Bernstein wrote, defining what, exactly, everyone involved with music should do, 'Fun is the X of the equation that tries to solve the riddle of why art exists at all. . . . we, musicians and dancers, have this to say to ourselves: Relax. Invent. Perform. Have fun'.[18]

From observing the musical life it is known that the similarity between highly gifted professionals and passionate amateurs consists precisely in the attachment of both to the art of music; neither can envision themselves outside of music, which can never be for either a heavy burden or routine occupation; and no matter how much time is devoted to it, music will never begin to bore nor will the need for communion with it ever weaken. The 'blame' for this great and passionate love may fall squarely on the expressive ear: the fact that concert performers and music-loving amateurs function identically under test conditions confirms the relational affinity of the expressive ear in both, as it is always ready to put the internal content of a musical expression ahead of such formal qualities as style, form, and genre.

One may draw a confirmation of this supposition from a 'negative proof' as well: people possessed of an outstanding analytical ear, even perfect pitch, do not in all instances love music. And the reverse: some people blessed with a highly sensitive expressive ear, which opens to them the richest world of musical communication and all manner of associations—visual, picturesque, poetic, muscle-motor, and so on—are not always capable of carrying a tune and 'lighting up' musical texture. Stendhal defined the difference between 'music analysts' and 'music expressivists' in the nineteenth century in his book *The Life of Rossini*, and his account so edified two major scholars of musical ability, Boris Teplov and Rosamund Shuter-Dyson, that both cited Stendhal, the music lover, in their work.

When in Italy Stendhal knew an old shipping clerk at a military procurement office who was endowed with perfect pitch, and did not like music at all: 'He always preferred the theater where they did not sing', notes Stendhal. 'I think music affords him no pleasure at all except in that it gives him a chance to exercise his talent at naming notes; the art of it says absolutely nothing to his soul'. Yet another example rather inspired Stendhal: a certain young nobleman, Count C., could not sing even a few notes without hitting a very false one—yet he was a fervent music lover. 'It was particularly striking', observed Stendhal, 'that the off-key singing not withstanding, he loved music with a passion rare even for Italy. It was clear that among his most varied successes, music was for him an essential and significant part of his happiness'.[19]

[18] Bernstein, L. (1982) *Findings*. New York: Simon and Schuster, p. 105.
[19] Cit. from Shuter-Dyson, R. and Gabriel, C. (1981) *The Psychology of Musical Ability*. London: Methuen, p. xiii.

As if to add to Stendhal's observations, a group of contemporary researchers reported something very similar to 'Count C. effect' when part of tone-deaf people called themselves unmusical while the other part exactly as Count C. found themselves very musical (Sloboda *et al.* 2005).

When Boris Teplov (1947) and Rosamund Shuter-Dyson and Clive Gabriel (1981) both cited Stendhal's example they emphasized how important the direct and emotional perception of music is. According to Teplov, 'the capacity for emotional response to music' comprises the 'nucleus of musicality', that is, the qualities which are, as he put it 'essential for musical activity as distinct from any other'. One may justifiably consider the expressive ear this nucleus of the 'emotional response to music'; the expressive ear, in fact, is the essence of musicality. At least among musicians, music teachers, performers, composers, and music students, musicality is the term for the elusive inclination of the soul toward music, the ability to find it to be of true and immutable interest, to admire its beauty, react and respond to the musical message and the content of a musical expression. This is exactly what the expressive ear does: these are precisely its functions in musical perception and creation. And if musicality, which is not a psychological term and can be used fairly broadly, may contain some other qualities and properties beyond the expressive ear for music, there can hardly be, in any event, such a thing as musicality *without* the expressive ear.

Rosamund Shuter-Dyson and Clive Gabriel (1981, pp. 253–5) expressed similar thoughts in commenting on the experiments by their psychologist colleagues Kate Hevner, Ralph Gundlach, and K. B. Watson (Gundlach, 1935; Hevner 1936; 1937; Watson 1942). They asked their nonmusician subjects to identify the significance of a number of musical fragments. Twenty professional musicians had already performed the task in advance, and in the main study the only fragments used were those whose meaning had been agreed upon by consensus of the experts. The psychologists established that the ability of their subjects to judge the musical significance of the fragments and to distinguish among them was associated neither with IQ nor with the analytical ear based on pitch and rhythm discrimination (both of which had been assessed in advance). The sole factor with which the participants' ability to make penetrating musical judgments was connected was, in fact, their love of music. The greater this love, the more exact and nuanced were the subjects' judgments: love and understanding went hand in hand. As Rosamund Shuter-Dyson and Clive Gabriel concluded,

> The work of Hevner, Gundlach and Watson (as well as that of other early workers in this field) can leave us in little doubt about the existence of a language of music which may be primitive and incomplete but which is basic to our comprehension of music. The function of melody in this language remains a problem. Indeed, as has been suggested earlier, the perception of melody may sometimes be the conscious experience relating to a cognitive coding of other more basic attributes of music rather than being one of the attributes itself.[20]

---

20 Shuter-Dyson, R. and Gabriel, C. (1981) *The Psychology of Musical Ability*. London-New York: Methuen, p. 256.

Shuter-Dyson's and Gabriel's desire to assign a fundamental role in the formation of musical meaning to more primitive properties of music than, for example, melody, coincides completely with Russian musicologists' conceptions (Alexeev 1986; Asafiev 1971; Kirnarskaya 1997; Medushevsky 1993) of intonational form, the expressive ear and its functions. The main point here, in any case, is that the intimate connection of one's level of understanding of music and one's musical motivation is once again confirmed.

The Moscow first graders who were recommended for enrollment in music special schools after the experiment in 2001 also demonstrated total musical motivation (Kirnarskaya 2006). Unlike many children who are unable to avoid music lessons because that is what their mothers want, these children, selected on the basis of a demonstrated expressive ear for music, on occasion dissolved in tears when directors of music schools did not want to admit them as pupils: among some of the children the analytical ear was not highly developed, and they could not impress the directors sufficiently with their rhythmic drumming and precise repetition of a well-memorized standard tune. The conservative directors were dismissive of the children's desires—a serious misconception indeed! A musical person, child or adult, is ready and willing to love music unrequitedly, even if he or she enjoys no other components of musical talent beyond the expressive ear. Children such as these will hardly abandon music studies, as happens with certain 'sharp-eared' types who resemble Stendhal's shipping clerk and are ready to run away from music as far and as fast as they can, even if they have gotten straight A's in all their graded exercises.

Society's conceptions of musical abilities are rather conservative, putting too much weight on the accuracy of pitch perception and musical memory, and no matter how much music teachers insist on the primacy of musicality as a criterion, alternatives to the traditional methods of determining musical talent among the young are introduced and find acceptance only with great difficulty. What is needed are long-term studies and active propaganda to raise the expressive ear from the status of a sort of incidental curiosity, a 'recently discovered' component of musical talent, to the position of significance such a component deserves in the daily world of musical pedagogy.

The expressive ear, as the nucleus of musicality, organically enters into the motivational component of talent: it explains how and why people who have the expressive ear begin to feel a heightened interest in music, why music moves and occupies them, why they feel a deep inner relationship with it. The reason is not hard to fathom: music is something they understand. Its language says much to them; they easily penetrate into the hidden ideas of music, they have been privileged with the art of musical 'co-experience' since a musical expression, through the mechanisms of the expressive ear, turns into their *own* expression, one adopted by them. People with the expressive ear find their imagination easily stimulated: their path from the aural to the visual, sound to motor sensation, to color, to spatial, and other associations is a short one, as music for them easily broadens its boundaries. For these people understanding musical speech requires no effort: decoding musical meanings is something done automatically. All this leads us to the possibility of significant conclusion: that people with a good expressive ear for music may be more motivated; they are inclined to love music.

Biographical evidence from the lives of outstanding performers also confirms the connection between love of music and the expressive ear. One sees this when for the performers the desire to study music was closely tied to one of the components of the expressive ear—timbre. These people could not love music 'in general': they wanted to (and in fact could only) love it exclusively in a definite, timbre-related guise. The great cellist Pablo Casals related his own experience this way:

> Once I caught sight of the violoncello, I could not take my eyes off it. From the very moment I first heard its sound I was completely stunned. I could not breathe. There was something so tender in the sound, so beautiful and so human—yes, yes, very human. I had never heard such beauty before.[21]

Although the young Casals had certainly heard music before, without the timbre of the cello, 'his timbre', it had not produced such an impression on him. Some outstanding performers cannot even imagine themselves playing another instrument: 'If everything on the piano came easily to me', recalled the pianist Walter Gieseking, 'this ease disappeared almost completely when I played the violin'.[22] Perhaps it was not so much the particular structure of Gieseking's hand that was at fault as it was the timbre of the second instrument, its irreplaceable voice through which, by means of the expressive ear, love for the instrument and for music itself enters a person.

The expressive ear, being the motivational component of musical talent and the launch mechanism for the love of music so necessary to musicians, cannot for all that be equated with musical talent as such. For musical talent is a multi-component, complex organism no single element of which can make the whole function in the absence of the others. This is no less true for the expressive ear than for any other component of the musical talent whole. The expressive ear is extraordinarily basic and primary. Because of its ancient origins, its closeness to the deepest sources of life, there are probably more people with at least moderately developed expressive ear than people who can boast of other musical abilities. Everything begins with the expressive ear and the motivation that derives from it: the love for, interest in and desire to study music, as well as all musical growth and development. Hardly any musical talent is imaginable without an extraordinary love for music, which is to say without its launch mechanism, the expressive ear. Possibly, the great majority of talented musicians, no matter their ultimate numbers, are drawn mostly from the ranks of people whose expressive ear is commendably developed. Presumably, the possession of every subsequent musical ability should limit the number of potential pretenders to musical talent: the count will begin with the approximately 12 percent of children who demonstrate a high degree of development of the expressive ear. Is it much or not? If compared to zero percent of music majors that are able (or better to say 'unable') to discriminate between the interpretations by very different conductors of the same

---

[21] Kazal's, P. (1977) Radosti i pechali. Razmyshleniya Pablo Kazal'sa, povedannie Albertu Kanu/ Joys and sorrows. Reflections by Pablo Casals as told to Albert E. Kahn. *Ispolnitel'skoe iskusstvo zarubezhnyh stran/Performing Art Abroad*, 8, p. 241.

[22] Gieseking, W. (1975) Tak ya stal pianistom/So I've become a pianist. *Ispolnitel'skoe iskusstvo zarubezhnyh stran/Performing Art Abroad*, 7, p. 196.

well-known piece (Madsen *et al.* 2007), these very musical children bring extremely good news about humankind's overall musical sensitivity. There is a possibility that all above-the-average musicians—very capable, highly gifted, outstanding and genius-level—proceed from this original 12 percent group.

One may suppose by analogy that the structure of other talents is built in similar fashion. They all rely on a certain primitive base, a kind of meta-ability which is of ancient origin and is deeply connected with the given field of activity. In searching for the motivational basis of the activity, at all events, one should explain its root sources, its function in the survival of man as a species: how the activity was born, what facilitated its appearance in the primitive human world—that is the question which can shed light on the origin and essence of the key ability, which sets off the motivational mechanism of talent. In music this was the necessity of exchanging signals which allowed people to recognize immediately the communicative intentions of a subject (sender) and react to these intentions appropriately.

From the function of this basic ability will flow the ability's structure. This will become clear through analysis of the specific material with which the given form of activity is connected. While in music this material—sound and its properties, as well as the organization of these properties into primary conscious constructs— consists of communicative archetypes, in every form of activity there will emerge some primary form of the material's organization, in a way related to communicative archetypes in music. It will become clear how and thanks to what the material of the given activity becomes a fact of the psychic life of man and how the first becomes the second. The basic ability, which serves as the ground for the given form of activity, will draw in its wake a motivation toward the activity and a love for it. One can hardly imagine a talented person of any kind for whom motivation did not represent the most important quality. Perhaps in other forms of activity the connection analogous to music professionalism and amateurism will reveal a deep psychological kinship which traces back to the same ancient ability, the great grandmother of the given activity.

Talent begins with love; where does love begin? In music it begins with the expressive ear.

To summarize our discussion of the expressive ear for music:

1　The expressive ear is a psychological mechanism of perception and decoding of the content parameters of music, based on music's psycho-physiological properties—timbre and tempo, dynamics, articulation and accentuation—and also on the general direction and contour of melodic-rhythmic movement. The roots of the expressive ear go back to the origins of aural communication, which from the earliest times facilitated man's orientation in the surrounding world and his reaction to it. In close connection with the expressive ear were formed the two principal communication systems—music and speech, the former predating the latter.

2　The expressive ear arouses in the listener natural synesthetic and muscle-motor associations which are inter-modal in nature: thus aural perception turns out to be connected with visual, color, spatial, and tactile sensations. By means of the expressive ear musical perception broadens its boundaries and opens to music an entire world of human representations.

3   In the recognition of musical content the expressive ear orients itself first of all on communicative archetypes—inter-modal stable constructs which carry a generalized idea of the basic means of social interaction. There are various distinct communicative archetypes, including that of the invitation, request, play, and meditation, each of which is predetermined by the social relationships of the participants in the communication. The communicative archetypes rely on a synthesis of spatial, motor-movement, and intonational parameters.

4   The expressive ear is the motivational component of musical talent whose function consists in supplying internal emotional connections between a person and the art of music; this function has traditionally been called musicality. On it is founded the interest in and love for music which accompany a person all through life. The distribution of the expressive ear among children is approximately 12 percent: talented musicians, from the very capable to the outstanding, may come from within this group, since the expressive ear is the fundamental and primary property of the musically gifted individual.

5   The expressive ear is analogous to the ancient base components of other talents. The search for this type of component leads back to the earliest origins of every form of activity, to the earliest function of this form of activity in the survival and refinement of the human species. The basic role of this component in the structure of talent is connected with the idea that from it comes the motivation for the given form of activity as well as the love and devotion to it. The discovery of the motivational component of all talents involves the analysis of the common psychological properties of highly qualified professionals and also devoted amateurs in the given form of activity.

The sense of rhythm

In the beginning was the beat?

Rhythm really was there in the beginning, and Heinrich Neuhaus was right when he insisted on exactly that in his book *Ob iskusstve fortepianinnoi igry/The Art of Piano Playing* (1994). Let us not mince words: without rhythm and outside of rhythm nature itself does not exist: all functions visible and audible, and all that are mysterious and hidden as well, are completed in rhythm. The stars twinkle, their light grows dimmer and then more vivid—they 'wink'. And no matter how this actually takes place—in rare flashes with long periods of darkness, or the other way round, in long and vivid bright periods marked by sudden 'power failures'—the fact is that a certain rhythm is obtained in the process, be it an even one or an irregular 'limp', smooth or abrupt. Rhythm invariably represents the alternation of events of even or uneven length in combination with pauses spaced between them. Waves lapping at the shore, a woodpecker pecking in the forest, birds chirping in the skyway—all is rhythmic.

Strictly speaking, rhythm has no need of sound. Sound merely signifies and underlines the rhythmic nature of the events taking place, and even inspires this 'rhythmicness'. If work is to be undertaken together with another party, then rhythm is essential; in order to act in coordination with one another audio signals are a necessity, as they provide rhythm for the joint action, indicating the optimum variant of joint movement in any situation. All work which demands spurts or bursts of energy takes place in the rhythm 'light–heavy, weak–strong'—a pattern immortalized in the Russian 'Song of the Volga Boatmen' ('Ei, ukhnem'). First there is the 'ei', that is the upswing, and then comes the 'ukhnem', that is the act itself—to throw, heave, or pull with all one's might. If it is necessary to work on some object evenly and persistently—such as sawing down a dead tree or breaking up a boulder with a sledgehammer—then the accompanying rhythm will be different, becoming exactly as persistent and periodic as the work itself.

The role of rhythm was just as great in man's communications with higher powers: the shaman's dance is constructed on a steady increase in the activity level of a movement—a slow, swinging rhythm gradually turns into a rhythm of rapid gyration. This rhythm seemingly 'corkscrews' itself up into the space of the world, creating an energy pole between the heavens and the earth. In many traditional cultures the performance of mystical ceremonies does not require song, limiting itself to the rhythm of a drum: the dry, sharp sound of small drums and the deep, resonant sound of great kettledrum percussion establishes contact between the people and their heavenly protectors. Rhythmic dances to a drumbeat accompany all the most important events in the life of the tribe; rhythm seemingly joins a man to his relations and peers, making his life part of the common life of the group. The birth of a child, the ritual initiation into adulthood, weddings, and funerals—all are impossible to imagine without a rhythmic accompaniment.

The association of rhythm with the collective labors and ritual ceremonies of the earliest humans invested rhythm with its main idea: it became a sign of the attachment of a single individual to the common affairs of all, both the common weal and the common grief. Acting rhythmically meant acting together, adding something to the collective and becoming a part of it. It is exactly for this reason that the most rhythmic forms of the art of music, jazz and rock, presuppose an unconditional collectiveness of perception and reaction to the art as performed. And for the same reasons the most individualistic and elite form, classical music, does not resort to rhythm in its primary function as a collective organizer; rhythm and rhythmicness are organically written into different parameters of sound in the classics and rarely become dominant in them.

Musical rhythm is movement in the form of sound, since rhythm is born in movement and appears to describe it, and preserves its residue even if the movement has since ceased. The inseparability of rhythm and movement in daily reality turns the former into the aural echo of movement, its perceived 'record'. Rhythm's relationship to movement parallels that of written language to speech: reading a written text one can 'hear' the speech, with its various sounds, intonations, and accents. In the same way, when one hears a rhythm one can see a live movement, feel it, and recall it. Dance music uses this property of rhythm, inserting moving events into a rhythmic shell: the movements of the hands and feet, the turns of head and body. At first the gestures and movements form the dance, then the dance gives birth to an accompanying rhythm—steps, jumps, and slides are added with the help of rhythm. Then the melody and harmony wrap the rhythm, decorating and adding color to it, revealing the accents of the discovered rhythm and highlighting its beauty. And when all these events take place in the necessary order, a new dance has appeared in the world; in its rhythm, recorded with the help of music, there is everything necessary to recall the movement which gave it life. In essence movement gives birth to rhythm, and rhythm gives birth to music.

Movement is always emotionally colored and ideational; man cannot move and remain indifferent: in order to strike his enemy, he must hide himself, focus his strength on a single point and turn into a coiled spring. In order to stroke a kitten, a person must be calm, relax all his muscles and, purring internally, give himself over to communication with his four-legged friend. Movement always signifies emotionally colored activity, directed arousal; and even if a man is not moving but merely watching or even simply imagining movement, then he perforce joins into it, feeling it as the movement of his own body guided by his own intentions.

In order to understand what rhythm consists of, one must begin by breaking down a movement into its parts, its origins and the idea behind it; the most obvious characteristic of a movement is its tempo. Movements can be regal and calm, in which case the tempo would be slow; sometimes it is even called slow rhythm (rhythm understood broadly) to match with the tempo that goes with it—the clouds float slowly across the sky on a clear day, slowly the waves break on the ocean under a quiet breeze. But it also happens that a slow movement arises from the fact that something is hindering it, meaning the movement has to overcome resistance; so moves a ship through an ice floe, and so a mountain flower emerges into the sunlight after growing through a rock.

Fast movements also have their own character. A top spins fast, an arrow flies fast; fast movements are particularly inclined toward inertia, toward the spontaneous and the end-lessly continuing: man imagines the *perpetuum mobile*, the eternal engine of fantasy, in just this way. In this case only the original impulse will be energetic, then the subsequent movement will resemble that of a ball which has been pushed off the top of a hill. Fast movements are not only inertial, but often very energetic, when every explosion requires an additional push or pump. So moves a herd of antelope frightened by a tiger, and so move the opponents in a fistfight. And every time, depending on the goal of a movement and its character, the tempo of the movement will be slightly different. Tempo is born of the emotional tone and the idea behind the movement; thus in music finding the proper tempo is half the battle. It is not accidental that tempos have so many different designations, including the following nine:

Grave—awesome, extremely slow movement making its way along with great difficulty, as if frozen, carrying its own impediments with it;

Adagio—powerful, strong movement, slow largely because it is weighed down by its own mass and significance;

Largo—broad and sweeping movement, slowed by its limitless breadth and extension, from striving to occupy a large space.

The character of fast movements is also quite varied:

Allegro—signifies moving gaily, actively, with spark, with pressure;

Vivace—lively, is the closest thing to allegro, but it is a tempo associated with somewhat more inertia of *movement*, with a greater sense of lightness and flight than the more frequently used *Allegro*;

Presto—the tempo of a stream, flowing or flying, made up of hardly distinguishable fine particles; *everything* flows together and becomes one line where the speed is so great that there seems to be no movement.

There are also three common moderate tempos:

Andante—a march, the tempo of one's pace on a walk where the movement will not impede daydreaming, reminiscing, and pondering;

Moderato—the most measured and most undistinguished, a characterless and indifferent tempo;

Allegretto—almost Allegro, in which calm and excitement are at odds and produce a tempo-compromise.

Naturally, the sense of rhythm begins with a sense of the tempo of movement, with expe-riencing its speed, as this determines the muscular tone of the movement and its basic parameters.

When the tempo to move at has been decided it is essential to understand how, by means of what tiny units this movement will be formed. In the real world movement is seldom continuous and completely of a piece; on the contrary, it is generally divided into several stages and phases. Movement independent of speed can approach a run or jump, it can trip along in mincing steps, or it can fly as if in the air. A body in movement may swim, smoothly crossing a surface, or walk standing on it. These parameters of movement are communicated in music through shades of articulation or captured bits of sound: the signal of flowing together, *legato*, is closest of all to swimming or crawling; flying and running are also conveniently rendered by *legato*, otherwise the separation of every sound will hold up the movement. *Portamento*, a separated movement, is close to a step; and *staccato*, a short, jerky movement, recalls jumps.

Beyond tempo and means of motion, the perception and experience of rhythm are formed by accents. It is these accents which turn the undifferentiated flowing mass of sounds into a conscious rhythm: for any structure, after all, including a sound structure, inequality is essential—multi-functionality is necessary, so that different elements in the structure can perform different roles. Accent, beat, and sharpness create this difference and inequality of sounds, even if they are equivalent in terms of length of time sounded. The even striking of a woodpecker on a tree is actually nowhere near as even as it sounds at first: some of the sounds will undoubtedly be more noticeable than others since the blow creating these sounds is somewhat stronger. And for the sensation of a beat or the accentuation of a sound it is in no way necessary for it to be longer. But the reverse pattern, nevertheless, does exist: a longer sound does indeed seem more accentuated; this accent does not even need to be underlined, it emerges by itself.

By means of accents and uneven length of sounds music forms its version of patterns—figures which are called a rhythmic pattern: sounds accumulate into groups, each of which is united by a common accent. This accent creates something like 'rhythmic gravity', analogous to modal gravity—the sounds are drawn to the accent, but the time after it seemingly relaxes, simply hanging there. Thanks to accents music resembles the phases of muscular exertion: there is an aural up-swing, a pre-accent period which is often called 'the predykt'; then comes the accent, like the blow itself; and then follows a relaxation, the resting of the muscles after the blow has been struck. So even here, in the area of accentuation, rhythm copies movement, filling in its general picture, which already includes speed of movement (tempo), means of movement (articulation), and phases of movement (rhythmic groups held together by an accent).

Rhythm identifies the aural image of a movement, recording all its main features. Yet many attributes of movement may be recognized with the help of the expressive ear: this establishes the general tempo of movement, its articulation profile and character of accentuation, differentiating movements such as the tread of a bear in a dense forest and the flight of a butterfly in a field. But the expressive ear does not establish the length of sounds and does not compare them with each other—a unit of musical movement for the expressive ear is not a practical reality, though at the same time there can be no sense of musical rhythm without the perception of the temporal relations of sounds. Both the 'bear' and the 'butterfly' can be identified relying on the resources of the expressive ear. But repetition of the movement can be done only with the help of the sense of rhythm. If the expressive ear reads the general idea of a musical communication, then the sense of rhythm recognizes its temporal organization and manages the time relationships of the sound elements.

The expressive ear can identify the overall flight-like character of movement or its generally jumpy nature. It can also note that the movement in general is continuous or in general jerky. But at what moment which accent arises and what follows after it, when and how the next accent comes, to which patterns its appearance will be subject? These questions cannot be answered by the expressive ear, since it cannot separate the flow into units of any kind, which in turn means it cannot recognize the relations between such units. The sense of rhythm, on the other hand, knows when and how one or another accent arises in music and what its appearance depends on; the sense of rhythm has command of the hierarchical principle, meaning that it perceives the sound flow as the relationship of greater and lesser temporal units, which are divided in turn into units even finer in their dimensions.

And it also perceives the reverse, such as the relationship of smaller units joined into ever greater ones: movement along the hierarchical path in both directions is equally possible for the sense of rhythm. Movement as a whole will be divided into segments, segments into phases, phases into groups, and groups into units; and on each level will arise chains of elements in which there are main, leading elements (such as accents) and subordinate, accompanying elements. Where the expressive ear senses an integrated picture, the sense of rhythm sees the details of temporal relationships; where for the expressive ear there is an aural blank space, the sense of rhythm is presented with a complex life of sounds, intricately united into a rhythmic pattern.

The expressive ear is older; any sound-making body is relevant for it. Even a single sound possesses, for the expressive ear, a significance of its own. Everything that sounds, the roar of the ocean in a storm, the cry of an infant, the song of the wind in the reeds, is experienced and identified by the expressive ear. For the sense of rhythm this is not enough: it needs disassembled movement, divided into phases, having its own hierarchy, where every moment has its own function and plays its role in the general picture of movement. The sense of rhythm presupposes not spontaneous movement but willful movement, directed and goal-oriented, which gains from this not only a general character but a defined means of organization of temporal units. Yet in its origins the sense of rhythm proceeds from the depths of the expressive ear and grows out of it: the sense of rhythm begins from coarse qualities of movement such as tempo and articulation—not yet co-subordination of the moving units, but the speed and general character of movement is already present. The sense of rhythm is born from the expressive ear, grows out from it but outgrows it, reaching greater refinement and fixing in much more detail that process of movement which the expressive ear could only sense as a whole.

The body-motor nature of the sense of rhythm

When we say 'In the beginning was the rhythm', what we really mean, of course, is 'In the beginning was the body', since a moving body precedes rhythm. And the sense of rhythm, that is the experience and interpretation of temporal relationships in music, cannot fail to take that into account. Over the course of the millennia man has perceived rhythm as a collective-organizing beginning point and, having sensed a rhythm, he involuntarily subordinates himself, orienting his movements to it. If he hears a military march, he begins to stride like a soldier; if he hears the bumptious grinding of a twist, he begins to wriggle and writhe with his whole body. The deep and inevitable connections of rhythm with bodily movement are followed in contemporary research (Bispham 2006; Dogantan-Dack 2006).

Music penetrates into man through rhythm just as it does through intonation: a person unconsciously sings along with the music she hears, and by this act takes it in, absorbing it via the vibrations of vocal chords; in exactly the same way a person moves along with the music she hears and absorbs it through the motor functions of her whole body. As the great expert on the sense of rhythm, E. Jaques-Dalcroze wrote 'Rhythm, like sound dynamics, depends entirely on movement, and its nearest prototype is our muscular system. All the nuances of time—allegro, andante, accelerando, ritenuto—and all the nuances of energy—forte, crescendo, diminuendo—can be perceived by our body, and the acuteness of our musical sense depends on the acuteness of our body's sensations'.[1]

Rhythm is so all-powerful that not only do the arms, legs, trunk, and head move in conformity with it, so do the muscles of the throat and breathing apparatus as well as the deeply embedded muscles of the ribcage and the abdominal cavity. Psychologists have identified these 'micro-movements', establishing that man, in the embrace of rhythmic movement, 'gives himself up' to rhythm both with his entire musculature and each individual part of it. In this rhythm can be likened to musical sound: the vibration of an entire string gives a basic tone; but each part of the string, vibrating at the same time, also gives a certain 'in-sound'. These 'in-sounds' add their nuances to the common bouquet of sound, which is how overtones are formed, elements without which musical sound would be quite pale and flat. The same thing happens with rhythm: without the 'micro-movement' of internal muscles which accompanies rhythm, the experience of it would not be as deep and all-encompassing.

In traditional cultures movement and rhythm are indivisible: music cannot be separated from dance, from walk-arounds, or from the motions of labor which are accompanied by song. The uniting of rhythm and movement in rock 'n' roll and jazz represents one of the great strengths of these genres of music: the listener frees himself from the constraints of modernity and behaves just as man behaved when listening to music at the dawn of history, when it joined with the movement summoned by it. The musical classics, which force one to suppress motion reactions, translating them to the internal level and rendering them hardly noticeable, lose a great deal in terms of direct perception. Yet they gain just as much on the level of cultural self-definition—the imagined hero of classical music is not a savage but an educated being who knows how to restrain his physical manifestations; in this respect the restraint of body-motor reactions becomes a sort of calling card of the intellectual, the admirer of the art of classical music. In any event,

---

[1] Jaques-Dalcroze, E. (1965) *Le rythme, la musique et l'education*. Lausanne: Foetisch, p. 105.

no matter what the external (bodily) manifestations of the listener, the psychological nature of the sense of rhythm is based on audio-motor coordination, when sound provokes movement. As Boris Teplov noted:

> The perception of rhythm is never exclusively aural. The majority of people do not recognize their motor reactions unless they pay special attention to them. Attempts to suppress these motor reactions lead either to the appearance of the same reactions in other organs of the body or bring about the cessation of the rhythmic experience. The experiencing of rhythm is in its very essence active. One cannot simply 'hear rhythm'. The listener only experiences rhythm when he 'co-produces' or 'co-creates' it.[2]

The experiments of Lazar Stankov and Georgina Spilsbury (1978) provided indirect evidence of the unbreakable connection between sense of rhythm and movement. They were comparing the perception of rhythm among people blind from birth and sighted people. The blind people lacked a sense of the spatial coordinates of movement. Despite the fact that they could experience rhythm bodily and attune themselves to it, as though trying to 'dance', they were nevertheless limited in their knowledge of how different types of movement are expressed in space. They did not know how a top spins or how a horse jumps. Experiencing movement is impossible without movement's spatial profile, without being able, mentally, to sketch the movement, assigning it spatial coordinates. In addition, the blind subjects were limited in their movements: they were afraid to move, afraid to bump against something, they had to 'feel their way' before advancing in some direction, meaning their freedom of movement was practically nil. The experiment confirmed the original hypothesis about the limited nature of the sense of rhythm among the blind, who completed the assigned tasks far less accurately than the sighted subjects: the limitation in movement and the very concept of it led to limitations in experiencing rhythm.

Beyond this one should add another point: deaf subjects who hear no music at all are nevertheless capable of sensing it indirectly through sound vibrations and the muscular sensations they cause (if these vibrations occur close enough to the body). The deaf experience rhythm directly through their bodies, not hearing music but, paradoxically, reacting to it (Thackray 1969; Tarasova 1988). Their experience of rhythm, according to measurements of muscle tone, follows the music even more closely than do those of the blind. Thus once again the body-motor nature of the sense of rhythm is confirmed: it can function even without music, but cannot function without body-motor sensations.

Not only the blind imperfectly perceive rhythm, but so do all people who are limited in their movements. It is sad to note that invalids with disrupted motor abilities are mostly unmusical because their sense of rhythm is underdeveloped. The great expert in child musicality, Henry Moog, conducted a series of experiments on the identification of sound figures among child invalids aged 11 and 12 years (Moog 1979). The subjects were to distinguish simple rhythmic patterns both within and outside the confines of

[2] Teplov, B. M. (1985) Psihologiya muzykal'nyh sposobnostei/The psychology of musical abilities. In *Izbrannie trudy, t. I/Selected Works*, vol. I, (ed. M. G. Yaroshevsky). Moscow: Pedagogika, p. 196.

a melodic movement. Despite their normal mental capacities the subjects could not fulfill the task, which was easily done by their non-handicapped peers of similar mental capabilities. Put otherwise, not only the body-motor nature of experiencing rhythm, but the body-motor nature of the very *recognition* of rhythm was demonstrated in the experiment: without directly 'plugging into' the rhythmic sensation, it is impossible either to recognize or to remember rhythm by purely speculative means.

A 'reverse experiment' conducted by Daniel Levitin and Ursula Bellugi (1998) produced the same results. The subjects tested were suffering from Williams Syndrome, which causes pronounced mental fatigue. The task, assigned to both healthy subjects and Williams sufferers, was to reproduce rhythmic figures by clapping hands. As Levitin and Bellugi summarized:

> The Williams syndrome individuals performed as well as the controls, including meter change and beat maintenance. Moreover, their production errors were more likely to make rhythmic sense than the errors of the controls. The findings are taken as evidence that at least one aspect of musical intelligence is normal in otherwise retarded individuals, supporting Gardner's view of multiple intelligences, one of which is specific to music.[3]

Thus the connection of rhythm and man's body-motor functions was once again confirmed.

The sense of rhythm is deeply subconscious and reflexive. Among all the musical capabilities, sense of pitch, modal sense, and musical memory, the sense of rhythm is closest to the pre-civilized phase of human development. At the very least, the subconscious element in the sense of rhythm plays a great role. Michele Biasutti (1990) performed one of the experiments which confirmed this. The experimenter had a group of subjects who had previously been tested for various musical abilities, hypnotized and tested again. Their results after the hypnosis sessions were the same, except that the scores for sense of rhythm improved. By acting upon the sense of rhythm through the subconscious, the psychologist was able to get in contact with it, refresh and strengthen the mechanisms of its work; yet the same hypnotic efforts had no influence at all on the ear, the musical memory, or any other musical functions.

Experiments with infants also confirm the pre-historic roots of the sense of rhythm and its very general character:

> Temporal grouping processes and categorization on the basis of rhythm are evident in non-human listeners and in human infants and adults. Although synchronization to sound patterns is thought to be uniquely human, tapping to music, synchronous firefly flashing, and other cyclic behaviors can be described by similar mathematical principles. We conclude that infants' music perception skills are a product of general perceptual mechanisms that are neither music- nor species-specific.[4]

---

[3] Levitin, D. J. and Bellugi, U. (1998) Musical abilities in individuals with Williams syndrome. *Music Perception*, 15, p. 357.

[4] Trehub, S. E. and Hannon, E. E. (2006) Infant music perception: domain-general or domain- specific mechanisms? *Cognition*, 100, p. 73.

The rhythmic image of music is easily remembered, coming second only after the image associations created with the help of the expressive ear. That is, aspects of sound are retained by the memory 'by seniority': the oldest image-memories connected with the general tone and character of a musical expression settle into the memory first, immediately followed by the body-motor tracks of music identified by the sense of rhythm.

Speaking of the primacy of image associations and content parallels in musical perception, John Sloboda (1985) noted that clearly the listener was totally unable to reproduce or recall a single theme from the music just heard, but nevertheless he was eager to speculate on it metaphorically. For example, as a heroic struggle triumphantly finished. In the same way, continues Sloboda, children remember music using metaphors: 'like in a church', 'snowflakes falling', 'horses racing', when they cannot recognize or recall a piece of music.

Next comes rhythm, when children try to remember a melody, they first recall its rhythm. John Mainwaring (1933) noted that while listening to music children involuntarily moved as if creating a dance that corresponded to the music. Subsequently, when asked to remember the melody, the children could not immediately recreate it, but began to jump, quiver and turn about exactly as they had when they were listening to the music. And Eureka! One of them managed to start singing the melody, although the children had heard it fairly long ago. Without the 'hook' of movement, in any case, they would never have been able to remember it. Rhythm is identified first and brings after it all the other musical parameters, a conclusion reached by psychologists who have studied the work of the musical memory in children (Moog 1976; Spiegler 1967; Tarasova 1988; Thackray 1972).

Rhythm serves as the legal representative of the entire musical whole in the memory of many people: remembering rhythm, people use it to identify musical fragments, even in cases when the differences between them are much more complex and varied than the differences of purely rhythmic dimensions. Being such a fundamental instrument of musical perception, the sense of rhythm is perfected quite actively—going hand in hand with the physical maturity of children, the sense of rhythm overtakes other aspects of musicality. Steven Demorest and Ronald Serlin (1997) asked school children aged 7, 12, and 14 to 'measure' how far certain musical variations had departed from a theme played for them. Relying on rhythm the children divided the variations into the necessary groups; but when they were asked to do so using other, non-rhythmic properties, the results were rather less pleasing—the melodic differences had completely escaped the childrens' attention. Moreover, the older the children, the easier it was for them to orient themselves in various rhythms, which could not be said of the other, non-rhythmic aspects. As the authors concluded: 'Results using a new, contrasting test melody confirmed the findings of the first study regarding the increased importance of rhythmic information'.[5]

Experimental research on the sense of rhythm once more confirmed its extremely close connection with the body's motor mechanics. Rhythm is experienced only in and through movement; in movement it is sensed and remembered, and its role as representative of

---

[5] Demorest, S. and Serlin, R. (1997) The integration of pitch and rhythm in musical judgement: testing age-related trends in novice listeners. *Journal of Research in Music Education*, 45, p. 67.

the musical whole continually grows. Such is the perception of the majority of people, and one may immediately suppose that like the expressive ear—the oldest musical ability—the sense of rhythm, which is almost as old, is also fairly widespread. Those of us who experience music as movement, in bodily-motor terms and kinesthetically, are many indeed. It's not by chance that both the sense of rhythm and Howard Gardner's 'bodily-kinesthetic intellect' are connected with the cerebellum, the phylogenetically oldest part of the brain (Levitin 2006).

Beat and rhythm: order and freedom

Nature prefers a periodic rhythm expressed in regular units of time. Rain drums steadily on the roof, waves break steadily on the shore, the heart beats steadily in the breast, and if not, doctors note a 'cardiac arrhythmia' and proceed to treat it. The pulse rate, even breathing, a measured stride—such are the fundamental rhythms of the human experience. And it is precisely from this that the art of music sets off, proposing the basic unit of musical time as the beat. The musical tempo is oriented on the human pulse: *andante* is somewhat slower than this measure, at 60 beats per minute—a natural pace for a pleasurable stroll. A very lively tempo, somewhat more energetic than *allegro*, would be approximately twice as fast, 120 beats per minute (a typical *allegro* is 100).

An infant receives her first experience of steady rhythm even before birth, sensing her mother's pulse rate: thus from the very beginning a steady movement at a tempo of 72 beats per minute is perceived by humans as the norm, as a symbol of the accustomed order of things, and the normal flow of life. Science has, in fact, verified that newborns do indeed take the sound of a heartbeat as a calming influence. D.M. Spiegler (1967) demonstrated that 40 English infants, two days after birth, would react differently listening to an ordinary heartbeat and an arrhythmic one: the former put the infants to sleep while the latter left them disturbed, as they clearly perceived that something was not right, and expressed this sense by crying.

A year before Spiegler another experiment had been conducted by Yvonne Brackbill and her colleagues (1966) in which infants were comforted not only by heartbeat but also by the sound of a metronome striking at 72 beats per minute and by a lullaby in a foreign language. The two-day-old subjects were completely satisfied with the assembled material, demonstrating that they liked things in general with a steady beat and a monotonous sound—not only that of a heartbeat. True, by the time they have reached two years of age children already perceive music as a conscious message directed at them and the sound of a metronome as an irritant; and two year olds go to sleep much better to the sound of a heartbeat than to other external noises. Yet any sound is better than no sound at all: in silence children express more discomfort than they do under the steady ticking of a metronome. Such is the power of an even, repetitive sound—one–two, one–two, and so on *ad infinitum*—as was demonstrated in a series of three experiments in the beginning of 1960s (Salk 1960; 1961; 1962).

The beat, the basic measure of time (called over the past four centuries the *metrical unit*) can be divided into smaller units. The simplest variation of this further subdivision can be understood if the left hand counts the beat at a tempo of the normal pulse rate (or slightly slower) while the right hand counts twice as fast. The result is that in the left the count of metrical units is maintained, while the right counts something very simple in the form of a rhythm. Rhythm can, in the time allotted to it, perform very complex tricks: inserting itself into the established metric scheme, it can play three or five sounds; it can insert into the meter sounds of unequal length, some shorter, some longer. But the left hand, despite all this slight of hand, must keep the tempo, continue the beat. If it fails to do that, then the rhythm falls apart immediately, as it has nothing to subscribe to; the net of metric shares disappears, which is the same for the tempo as the disappearance of the pulse rate for the human body.

The rhythmic relationships of sounds are the relationships of their time proportions, their mutual interdependence and cooperation. The entirety of the time relationships of the sounds in a piece constitutes the rhythm, and the speed of their movement is the tempo. If one plays a piece much slower or faster than normal, one can nevertheless recognize it. Yet if one changes the internal time proportions and relationships of the sounds, then recognizing the melody will be almost impossible. Thus it is that the art of music, because of the great role allotted in it to the notions of proportionality, symmetry, equality, and inequality, is often likened to architecture. Indeed, architecture is sometimes referred to by those in the arts as 'frozen music'. In such instances tempo may be likened to the size of an architectural ensemble and rhythm to the entirety of the internal relationships between the ceilings and the walls, the planes and the columns—all the constructs and artistic details. Reduced a million times in size, the pyramid of Cheops is the same pyramid, with the same relationships of planes and angles but at a 'very fast tempo'; if one could imagine the same pyramid at a 'very slow tempo', then it would take up all of Cairo.

The sense of tempo or beat is the basis of the sense of rhythm, its point of origin. One can at the outset count off the tempo, get a feel for how the metrical shares go, and then, in the given tempo, begin to play; this is how conductors give orchestras the tempo. But one can also go about it the other way: hear music with a complex rhythm and, nevertheless draw the beat from it by tapping on a table or clapping one's hands. This second exercise is often used to check the sense of rhythm. Normal children, according to the data of Baldwin and Stecher (1925), kept the beat with hand-clapping, as did retarded children suffering from Williams syndrome.

Problems in keeping the beat are encountered not only by children, but by adults, and by adult musicians, as well. Robert Duke and his colleagues (1991) asked subjects—under conditions of a steady beat, without dividing the units in half or more complex units—to identify the beat and tap to it. Duke had already made matters complicated enough by including in the nine different tempos presented to his subjects both very slow examples (less than 60 beats per minute) and extremely fast ones (over 120). The musicians among the subjects fared no better than the others as 'rhythm masters'; it was as difficult for them as for any other humans to sense that metrical units can have both very great numbers of sounds in them and very small numbers as well.

If there are many sounds at a very slow tempo, the movement seems quite lively while the tempo is turtle-like. At a quick tempo an entire metrical unit may be given over to a single sound, or even less; the measure may have only one whole note. In this case the movement will not be particularly agitated, but the tempo may nevertheless fly like an arrow. In this exercise the tempo had to be taken from the music, no matter how primitive it was; for in real music making (other than that of an orchestra) there is no 'helper' next to the musicians to keep the beat, which means that in real music making the tempo is an imagined beat, a mentally postulated movement of metrical units. And not everyone can feel this beat, although, as in this experiment (Duke 1989), everyone has a solid musical background. This means that a good sense of tempo is a rarity; even being a member of the musical profession is no guarantee that a person has it.

As if to confirm Robert Duke's results beforehand, in the nineteenth century life itself set an analogous experiment. A 5-year-old boy named Leopold Auer, a resident of a small Hungarian village through which passed various military brigades, decided to try himself in the role of drummer (Ginzburg 1966). He took a small drum and so crisply and steadily drummed away that the soldiers drew themselves up, turned their mustaches and followed after the boy at a determined gait. The regimental commander was delighted and asked the boy's father to let him come along with the soldiers. But the father was not inclined to agree, not wishing to expose the boy to the risks involved, great sense of rhythm or no. And thus it was that Leopold Auer, who was to become head of the famous Russian school of violinists, was preserved by history for a greater role than arch-drummer boy. In any case Auer's childhood experience underscores a known truth: that a sense of rhythm is a sign of musical talent. It rarely occurs in complete form (which is why the phrase 'perfect rhythm' sounds so unusual—unlike 'perfect pitch'), yet everyone is possessed of it in one degree or another.

Why is this quality so rare in its perfect form? At first glance it seems strange indeed that a human cannot do the same thing that is so easily accomplished by a human creation, the metronome; especially since the human heart and, by extension, the pulse indeed do what a metronome does, sensing the regular time intervals and tapping along with them, internally or aloud, without hurrying or slowing the pace. But for some reason all things mechanical call forth in humans a certain resistance. Thaut *et al.* (1997) conducted a rather simple experiment in which the subjects, 20 and 70 year olds, were asked to beat time on a table, first to the rhythm of a musical selection, then to the rhythm of a metronome. It would seem that with a metronome everything would be easier: the instrument gives the same 'ticks' with the same intervals every time, and one need only mechanically repeat this process. With music it is a different matter: one has to extract the tempo and feel it through the movement of rhythmic sketches and figures. Yet the musical task proved the easier of the two: both sets of subjects, college students and retirees, successfully aligned themselves to the musical tempo and kept time quite well. To the relentless 'play' of the metronome, however, both groups adjusted only with difficulty, repeatedly falling behind or overtaking it: the metronome's lifeless knocking suppressed the subjects' natural sense of musical rhythm.

Perhaps counting off identical time intervals is too tedious and humans simply tire of it quickly. Such was the supposition of Pavel Lamm, whose experiments are recounted by Boris Teplov (Teplov 1985). Lamm's subjects were to take some rhythmic figure, then play it somewhat more slowly, and then, a third time, still more slowly, but at exactly the same degree of diminution of tempo as between the first and second renditions. The musician-subjects who had an enviable sense of rhythm performed the exercise just as badly as did the weakest music pupils. The mechanical considerations in question (subtracting a percentage, and then the same percentage again, from a given tempo) turned out to be extremely harmful to the sense of rhythm—although one cannot deny that the request to slow down the tempo in regular stages does not in itself represent anything exceptional, happening regularly, as it does, in music. Commenting on Lamm's experiment, Teplov noted that

> Those subjects who in the course of a musical performance can reach rhythmic perfection better than others lose this advantage in those cases where there is no chance to rely on musical-rhythmic sense. What were they forced to rely on? Obviously, on counting, trying to do every figure slower than the previous one, with the diminution in tempo identical each time. The tests showed that the rhythmically stronger students were no stronger than the weak students when it came to 'counting'. Obviously, in musical performances they do not use this sort of 'counting'.[6]

It follows from this that masters of rhythm and people with a good sense of tempo do not measure or count anything, and the regularity of metrical units or, if necessary, their regular alteration to faster or slower, comes about not from the fact that the people 'counted' the time intervals and their relationships well. The sense of tempo is not of metronomic origin, and it most likely does not derive from beating as such—the very word 'beat' here disguises more than it reveals.

In order to understand the origin of the sense of rhythm musicians and psychologists assigned four organists and music teachers to play five hymns (Ivanchenko 2001). According to official musical logic, the different rhythmic units, half-notes, quarter-notes, and eighth-notes, should all be equal to one another at different points in a piece, that is, all the halfs-, eighths-, and quarters- should be of the same duration in a given piece played at a given tempo. Traditionally a quarter-note is equal to one metrical unit; a half-note should equal twice as much and an eighth-note half as much. However, when the notes were measured in the actual performance of the hymns, all the musicians playing all the hymns registered disparities in the arithmetic relationships among the notes they played, and notable disparities at that. If, for example, a note was accented, then it would seem long and the musician would 'cut it down' slightly; if, on the other hand, the musician felt that a note was too 'weak', he would underline it by 'holding' it somewhat.

All sounds transcribed into musical scores as identical are, in reality, not identical at all: they are in the event longer or shorter, sharper or weaker, lighter or deeper, and this difference in coloring and character, the difference in their role within a musical phrase,

---

[6] Teplov, B. M. (1985) Psihologiya muzykal'nyh sposobnostei/The psychology of musical abilities. In *Izbrannie trudy, t. I/Selected Works*, vol. I, (ed. M. G. Yaroshevsky). Moscow: Pedagogika, p. 199.

is necessarily expressed in the arithmetic duration of the sounds. The notes are like peas in a pod, like sections of an orange, like the seeds of a pomegranate—no two are ever exactly alike. These micro-deviations from the mathematical exactness of the duration of the sounds are the very breath of music, without which it would seem dead. Real musical tempo is maintained in exactly these 'uncomfortable' conditions, when these micro-deviations occur (as they must) and yet the tempo must be observed, nevertheless, in its original sense to the extent possible.

In other words, the sense of tempo is an indivisible part of the sense of musical rhythm, and the necessary regularity of the metrical units is maintained at the expense of living rhythmical breathing, the 'pacification' of which is exactly what the sense of tempo is for. Thus we arrive at a paradox: if there is nothing to pacify and nothing to struggle against, the sense of rhythm becomes dull, as an unused saw goes dull out of season. And it is impossible to sense the tempo and maintain the beat if live rhythm is not resisting. Regularity arises in the regularizing of a thousand irregularities; a regular tempo is born as the median size, as the measure of communality of the rhythmic movement of the living sounds. That is why the sense of tempo is such a great rarity possessed by so few musicians. It is the result of a highly developed sense of rhythm; and despite the external impression, tempo is born of rhythm, from its generalization: it regularizes the progression of musical time, which is filled by hundreds and thousands of irregular rhythmic events.

A-one, and -two . . .

When someone studies music, the performance of rhythm brings forth masses of difficulties, even if the subject only intends to play the simplest of ditties, such as the Russian 'Chizhik-pizhik'. In this little song there are three kinds of rhythmic duration: eighth-notes, quarter-notes, and half-notes, in a relationship of 1:2:4. All the units should be of equal length, and the music teacher will not allow deviations here or there, or nothing will remain of the musical rhythm. Only the great masters can render rhythmic breathing free while the listeners still perceive that everything is proceeding perfectly regularly. Some of the sounds of 'Chizhik', the accents, are stronger than others, but one cannot hit them too hard: sounds are accented in accordance with the style of the work, sometimes very distinctly and roughly, and sometimes almost unnoticeably. Every performer decides for himself how to deal with 'Chizhik', but listeners should be able to recognize the piece.

To aid matters music teachers have come up with a trick in which the metrical unit (the quarter-note) is broken into two 'oral counts'—'a-' preceding the actual 'ONE', recalling Lawrence Welk's famous 'And a-ONE, and a-TWO'—but despite such clever ploys it is still difficult to reproduce even relatively simple rhythmic figures accurately. One can successfully play a rhythmic figure only in those cases when all the temporal relationships within it are understood by the performer and she understands the figure as a kind of whole, a sort of ta-ta-ta-ta-Ta-a-a, ta-Ta-a. Repeating a rhythm one has heard is somewhat easier, as such an already-prepared rhythm does not have to be 'made'; but without sufficient practice not everyone is capable even of this, for that matter.

A good many quasi-mathematical formulations are included under the aegis of rhythm, including the apportionment of units of measurement, the concept of proportional division and division in general, the concept of symmetry, and that of equality/inequality. At the same time the actual practice of music as such mitigates against the intellectualization of the sense of rhythm: there is simply too much for the performer to take into account; if all the rhythm-related actions were not accomplished reflexively (or nearly so), the musician would need an artificial intellect on the scale of a computer to perform.

Refusing to recognize the significant role of an intellectual component in the sense of rhythm (and thus 'mathematizing' it), Boris Teplov (1985) cited the judgments of the musician and psychologist Leonid Meiman, who pointed to the abilities of the pianist, which lie on the verge of what is humanly possible. One hand plays one thing, the other something else, and something completely different; in the first case we have two sounds to a count, in the second—three. The speed of the movement involved is dizzying, and suddenly the player takes up a *new* tempo, one corresponding to 'a certain fractional part of the previous speed'. The equality of the temporal units (now somewhat different than before) is maintained at this breakneck speed, and everything may begin all over again: the division into two is split into a division into three, or five; on one hand tiny rhythmic units march along as though on parade, while on the other hand they leap and skip about as though possessed, yet observing as they do this a predetermined tempo. Under these circumstances, Teplov quotes Meiman,

> . . . we stand before an alternative: either performers and listeners have at their disposal an utterly exceptional auxiliary means of judging time, or the computational metric instructions in music have for the performer, in the best case, the significance of orders for undefined acceleration/ diminution and expansion/reduction of the tempo which are perceived in the same vein by the listeners as well.[7]

This last sentence may be taken as a voice crying in the wilderness, as the acceleration/ diminution and expansion/reduction in question are normally measured in temporal 'microns'—such 'microns', if they are a bit more noticeable, give rise to the so-called agogics—but on the whole music is entirely prescribed into the boundaries of a tempo, the micro-deviations from which speak to the liveliness of the rhythm, its anti-mechanical nature, and not in the least to some notion that rhythm is distorted, stumbling, and bumpy.

Great flexibility of rhythm inserted into steady tempo beat means that we are perforce left with Meiman's first assumption, that of the presence of some 'auxiliary means of judging time'. These means are, in fact, of muscle-motor origin, where as a unit of time measurement we have not a frozen temporal interval but a temporal interval which is equal to the movement—a broad step or a mincing one, a deep breath or a quickened one, an open wave of the hand or a rapid one like the gesture for 'no-no'. All our movements take up a certain amount of time and, merging with this time, provide for its measurement.

....

[7] Teplov, B. M. (1985) Psihologiya muzykal'nyh sposobnostei/The psychology of musical abilities. In *Izbrannie trudy, t. I/Selected Works*, vol. I, (ed. M. G. Yaroshevsky). Moscow: Pedagogika, p. 196.

Thus the sense of rhythm depends on units of time derived from movements written into them. Movement begets rhythm, and the sense of rhythm again turns to movement, each time giving birth to and imagining that movement which stands at the origins of a rhythmic figure.

The musician experiences rhythm in his imagination; micro-movements of the body are fueled from the imagination and passed along to the music. The sense of rhythm turns this sensation into an idea, and an unconscious one at that. The sense of rhythm appeals to the body-motor intellect and feeds off it, and thus rhythm cannot be calculated or miscalculated—it can only be experienced by the whole body reacting to it with motor impulses, identifying with its own movements, real or imagined, all the contours of the rhythm—otherwise it would not be rhythm but a mechanical rendition of something in Morse Code (and Morse Code, for that matter, works on the basis of rhythm, as its signals are subconsciously associated with the corresponding movements indicating long and short signals).

All rhythmic units are born of movement and experienced as movement—the examples are legion. Here one sees evenly running drops, in a group of 16 notes. Or there jumps up a so-called dotted rhythm which can 'blow the doors off' and 'wake the neighbors' if it really gets going. Or over there we have sprays of water, flowing and gurgling along—they provide the rhythm for several of Chopin's etudes. People who suffer from Williams syndrome should have no particular deficiency in their sense of rhythm since their body-motor intellect is practically untouched by the ailment. Some other mentally retarded people called 'oligophrens', do not understand rhythm because they do not know how the coursing of a herd of wild animals differs from the rustling of tall grass in the wind: they cannot identify the differences in the character of the movements, they have nothing with which to fill in the rhythmic figures, which suggest nothing to them.

The weakness of the oligofrens' kinesthetic intellect is connected with a weak conceptualization of movement, with a lack of understanding of its various functions, ideas and its varying energy and speed. Normal children understand all of this and have a sense of rhythm. And if they have this sense, then counting a-one and a-two is not a requirement: the intuitive-motor sensation of tempo and rhythmic proportion of sounds will appear from the movement itself, and from its conceptual representation—one need only sense what kind of movement lies at the origins of this or that rhythm.

It is, of course, rather easier to say that one need only sense this or that rhythm than it is to do so in reality. In musical-pedagogy circles there is a widespread opinion that while the musical ear may be subject to influence and training, things are rather less promising with the sense of rhythm. At first blush such pessimism would seem unfounded: after all, the ear, taken as the ability to identify, remember, and reproduce the pitch of sounds—is a very refined property which, not surprisingly, far from everyone possesses. But the sense of rhythm, at least in its most elementary form, should be present in all humans: everyone walks, breathes, jumps, runs, and performs a mass of rhythmic movements while engaging in sports and all manner of other physical activities—chopping wood, carrying water from a well, even washing a floor. And nevertheless the evidence points to the fact that a creditable sense of rhythm, one good enough for the professional performance of music, occurs far less frequently than we would hope and expect (Ivanchenko 2001; Tarasova 1988).

Part of the reason for the rarity of the good sense of rhythm lies in the fact that in classical European musical culture, the people who make music are by no means only those who are naturally predisposed to, and these people are able to be musicians because European culture invented the musical score. The score serves as a sort of prop, a crib sheet for those who without it would possibly remain among ardent listeners. If in folklore, jazz, and rock their music is born in oral experimentation, the European tradition of musical notation proceeds from 'the other way around': first comes the written score and then the music which reflects it. In oral musical cultures an excellent sense of rhythm is essential, for without it there would be no way to accumulate that musical material on whose basis the work of the next composer is going to develop. Without remembering by ear the rhythms and rhythmic figures, the student will not be able to create music. Someone with a less-than-stellar sense of rhythm will never become the lead singer of a rural choir or a musician in a jazz band. In the European classical tradition the music teacher takes it upon herself to instruct practically any and all comers, as long as they will attentively look at the printed notes and do what is written there.

What exactly is the pitch of the note inscribed on the sheet of music before her is something the student will understand as soon as she learns where such a note is written; this is the same thing as learning what one or another letter looks like on paper and learning to pronounce it aloud. A thoughtful child can learn to read notes in two weeks, and just as the beginning reader soon begins to put together printed letters into syllables and words, so the beginning piano player rather quickly learns to do the same thing with simple pieces. But there is one catch. The rhythm inscribed in the text, which is plainly visible there, is completely understandable—the second note is twice as long as the first, say, and the third and fourth are four times as short as the first—but playing it is, nevertheless, not so simple.

The arithmetic approach, pronouncing a-one and-two, and-three aloud, helps to an extent; but as Teplov suggests, this practice may do as much harm as good. Explaining why it is so difficult to teach people to play in rhythm, Teplov notes:

> If the student is going to follow the instructions of the score exactly, then *as a result of that alone* the pitch movement necessary will be obtained. This is not the case with rhythm. If the student follows the score exactly, as a result of that alone the desired rhythm will not be obtained; what will be obtained is only a nearly exact reproduction of certain relationships of duration. The pupil who does not have prior conceptions of pitch will, as a result of his performance, at least hear the necessary pitch movement. But the student who has no prior conception of rhythm cannot hear any rhythm at all as a result of his performance. The method of 'arithmetic counting' represents the substitution of one rhythmic criterion for another. This method acts as a means of getting, without the help of the sense of rhythm, some sort of arithmetically acceptable movement—a harmful surrogate for musical rhythm. This arithmetic scheme is derived from the printed score; the student who uses it is going to hear something completely alien to rhythm and, it is entirely possible, is going to mistake this alien entity for actual musical rhythm. This one factor alone would be enough by which to understand why the task of developing the musical-rhythmic sense

entails such great pedagogical difficulties and why the legend of the unteachability of the sense of rhythm arose in the first place.[8]

The arithmetic method helps to stuff the necessary number of sounds into the necessary interval of time: saying 'one' and playing two sounds during the time produces relatively even eighth-notes; saying 'and-one', but playing only one note over both counts gives the quarter-note indicated in the score. But if one removes the counting 'training wheels' and asks the student to play the already-learned ta-ta-Ta-a segment, nothing will come of it: everything will emerge distorted, lopsided, and irregular. The student has not experienced physically, by motion, the sounds she has articulated; the rhythm she played emerged not as a portrait in sound of completed movements, but rather as empty durations, lacking any experience of movement. If one says along with 'One-and-two-and' something like 'Do one big jump, and then two little ones' then the rhythm Ta-a, ta-ta with the jerky articulation of *staccato* will appear of itself and will neither be forgotten nor distorted. Musical-rhythmic relationships are born of movements of differing intensity, duration and energy investment, thus the sounds which reflect them are longer or shorter, harsher or milder. The auxiliary stimulus for the sense of rhythm is not counting numbers aloud but motor-movement experience and its activization.

The intensity and richness of motor experience serve as the basis for the appearance of the sense of rhythm, which is why black musicians and Africans in general have such an acute sense of rhythm: their motor experience has been broad and various as well as continuous and intensive; over the course of thousands of years white people spent much more time than Africans in enclosed spaces, where they sat and lay more than their black counterparts, untold generations of whom lived in the open air and in constant movement. The regular physical labor performed by Africans also facilitated the collection of motor impressions. It is thus unsurprising that Africans and African-Americans have such an acutely developed sense of rhythm, and why so many outstanding athletes have emerged from their ranks. Both have the rich and 'high-quality' motor experience, which successfully entered the genetic fund of the people and became a natural characteristic.

A sense of rhythm is further not inherent in many people because in it there is the moment of transition of a first signal system to a second—the transition from real experience to mental representation of it. It is not enough to experience movement and feel it throughout one's entire body; one must also complete its sound portrait, express in sounds the tempo, character, intensity and structure of this movement. Here the motor experience turns into the image of experience, its spiritual reflection. But even that is not enough: one must also be able to retain in the memory an entire rhythmic structure together with all its sound relationships and accents. That is, on the path from actual movement to the expression of the rhythm which reflects it, there are two intermediate stages: translating the movement into sound and remembering the result. Here the

---

[8] Teplov, B. M. (1985) Psihologiya muzykal'nyh sposobnostei/The psychology of musical abilities. In *Izbrannie trudy, t. I/Selected Works,* vol.I, (ed. M. G. Yaroshevsky). Moscow: Pedagogika, p. 204

distance is the same as between the contemplation of a running bison, the creation of a drawing on a rock wall with the bison's likeness, and the subsequent retention in the memory of the drawing with all its lines and streaks. An analogous journey is made by Moving man, *homo mobilis*, on the road to becoming Musical man, *homo musicus*.

Experiencing movement, expressing it in sounds and remembering the accumulated impressions—this is the path of development of the sense of rhythm, or rather, toward its exposure and awakening in the mind of the student. The life of man as a historical living being is so long and so intimately connected with movement that proper encouragement should be able to arouse this sense. The arithmetic approach yields little here, but even given appropriate methodology, different people's sense of rhythm will be different. One person, without a single regular lesson, by mere exposure to music and unsupervised practice, may become a legend of jazz, a Charlie Parker or a Sidney Bechet, which was, in fact, true in both cases. And someone else will only be able to play, and this after a month of 'one-and two-and', a modest version of 'Yankee Doodle' for his father's birthday.

The sense of rhythm in experiments and in musical practice

The art of music is the art of organization of time to the same extent that the plastic arts, painting, sculpture, and architecture, are the art of organization of space. From this flows the leading role of the sense of rhythm in the structure of musical talent: it is the principal 'manager' of musical time without which the art of music cannot exist. There are certain temporal universals—'segmentation, predisposition and active search for regularity, temporal zone of optimal processing and predisposition towards simple duration ratios'—that give birth to our sense of rhythm regardless of acculturation or experience (Drake and Bertrand 2003). In all cultures except the academic culture of Europe, the rhythmic component has been worked out immeasurably better than that of pitch. From the earliest times the musician was, first of all, the 'king of rhythm', and only after that the possessor of a remarkable musical ear. It is easiest to see and appreciate the properties of the sense of rhythm as a part of musical giftedness through a process of comparison, looking at how it manifests itself among outstanding musicians and how rhythmic qualities are possessed (or sometimes not possessed) by ordinary people.

All outstanding musicians, and particularly rock musicians, are endowed with an acute sense of rhythm. The sense of rhythm appears among these people in an elevated motor reaction to music, which speaks to the very close audio-motor connection—sound and movement beget one another just as invariably as the movement of waves gives rise to the roar of the surf. The beat of this music, its tempo and character, makes rock singers dance about, rock back and forth, and jump up and down as if they cannot stand in one place. This was exactly the case with Elvis Presley, the king of rock 'n' roll and the idol of American youth in the 1950s. He freed the sense of rhythm, letting it go outside, by allowing himself what performers had never allowed themselves before: the sense of rhythmic pulsation, the beat, was in Elvis' presentation no longer merely audible; it was visible. In Elvis rhythm merged with movement.

Elvis's heightened sense of rhythm was a particularity of his personality, practically his calling card. His level of motor activity, which music simply stirred up all the more, was already considerably higher than that of ordinary people. 'I can't seem to relax ever and I have a terrible time falling to sleep at night', Elvis explained. 'At the most I usually get two or three hours of broken sleep' . . . As to movement as such: 'I guess the first thing people want to know is why I can't stand still when I'm singing. Some people tap their feet, some people just sway back and forth. I just started doing them all together, I guess'.[9]

Elvis sensed in the rhythm of his songs the rolling gait of the cowboy and, at the same time, the drumming tap-beat of the jazz dancer. This combination symbolized freedom and strength of character, light bravado and stubbornness—all passed along through the musical rhythm. This was the way that truck drivers, with whom Elvis liked to be compared, not least because he had been one himself, carried themselves in public. Elvis's success, in the end, came about because his sense of rhythm built a bridge between a socially recognizable type of music and movement. The gait of the average American, the suppleness of his movements, is imprinted forever in the songs of Elvis, which is why Presley remains even now the idol of many; the love of the American public for him has hardly ebbed in the three decades since his death.

The directness of the audio-motor connections as one of the components of the sense of rhythm is also characteristic of classical performers, although in the classical tradition extraneous movement on stage is not welcome. Nevertheless, psychologists have successfully analyzed how one of the most restrained of the world's great violinists, David Oistrakh, actually moves with the music he plays. Vezio Ruggieri and Alexander Katsnelson (1996) studied videotape footage of Oistrakh performing Bach's Brandenburg Concerto No. 4 and Mozart's Violin Concerto in D-major. They discovered that each work was connected with a particular Oistrakhian 'dance': the violinist continually performed characteristic movements, and different ones in each case. The Bach music brought forth a regular stepping movement, the continual shifting of the body from the left foot to the right—and an analogous swaying is clearly sensed in the music that emerges.

Ruggieri and Katsnelson concluded that Oistrakh's movements made up part of the context of his performance. Thanks to the exactness of his audio-motor connections, the performer extracted rhythmic movements from the music and they continued to accompany it. These movements at the stage of creation of the composition could be a part of the creative process, its launch mechanism; such a proposition is entirely natural since rhythmic rhetoric, the popular in Baroque era rhythmic figures-cliche were those into which Bach eagerly prescribed his thoughts. Every work that David Oistrakh performed had its own 'dance'; this speaks only to the fact that it is the music alone which gives rise to the onstage movements of the violinist—these are not simply habitual gestures and mannerisms which are the same in all instances. The liveliness of the rhythmic experience, its directness, the mutual attachment of music and movement—all these are properties of the wonderful sense of rhythm characteristic of the great artists.

---

[9] Presley, E. (1977) *Elvis in his own Words*. London-New York: Omnibus Press, p. 17.

We should note here that the 'onstage dance', in classical music or rock 'n' roll, constantly emphasizes the beat, pointedly inserting itself into the given tempo. The presence of metrical units and the role of the peculiar grid, which they describe for rhythmic figures and sketches, makes one devote special attention to the sense of tempo. Yet some people can hardly distinguish metrical units from ordinary rhythmic units; in the popular consciousness the two merge all the time, and almost every step seems to be a metrical unit. Sometimes subjects tend not to hear the various functions of sounds, their accentuation or the lack of it; they may miss their joining into rhythmic groupings. Thus we see the weak hierarchical nature of rhythmic perception, the inability to separate rhythm into two structural 'floors'—tempo (the passage of metrical units), on the one hand, and the rhythmic groups inscribed into these units on the other.

The constant attempts by psychologists to discover the essence of the sense of rhythm are connected with its seeming simplicity. A group of children aged 10–12 years are played two musical fragments and asked whether the second was faster, slower, or at the same tempo as the first (Kuhn and Booth 1988). If in the second fragment there were more sounds, the music's movement seems more active to the children and they will say that it was faster; if there were fewer sounds, they will say it was slower. Virtually none of the subject children in an experiment on this principle were able to sense the key difference between metrical units and the sounds that go into them. The psychologists who conducted the experiment, Terry Lee Kuhn and Gregory Booth, warned the childrens' teachers against heightened expectations of the sense of rhythm in untrained adolescents. Only music students succeed in analogous experiments separating rhythm and tempo, ascribing to the metrical allotment as many sounds as there are in reality. And in this operation they succeed only when dealing with the simplest, best-known rhythmic figures and in the most popular, relatively moderate tempos. All attempts to get results with more refined differentiation by the subjects have ended in failure.

Musicians know how hard it is to sense the relative independence of rhythmic figures and the tempo of their movement. The great violinist Fritz Kreisler offered some useful advice in this regard: 'In those places where there are few notes and they are significant, do not slow the tempo down; and where there are many notes and they are not critical, do not hurry it'.[10] It is true: there is always a risk of confusing the intensity and the frequency of the 'sound' and the musical tempo, if the metrical unit allotment has many sounds, the tendency is to speed up, if few, to slow down. The composer Arthur Honneger created his most popular work as a balance between ever more 'wordy' rhythmic figures and a constant, even lessening tempo. This juxtaposition gave the piece, 'Pacific 231', an air of extreme tension. As Arthur Honegger recalled:

> In the process of composing Pacific I admit that I was guided by the rather abstract notion of creating the impression of such a quickening movement, which would seem to be done with mathematical precision, despite the fact that during this time the tempo of the piece would in fact be becoming slower. From a purely musical point of view what worked out was something like

10 Yampolsky, I. (1975) *Fritz Kreisler*. Moscow: Muzyka, p. 33.

a broad choral variation shot through with contrapuntal lines in the spirit of Bach. I originally called the piece 'Symphonic Movement.' But having thought it over a bit, I decided that title was too pale. Suddenly I was struck by a romantic idea and, having finished the score, I titled it 'Pacific-231'—such was the name of a type of boat which was supposed to pull heavyweight cargoes at extremely high speed.[11]

In other words, she who does not fall into the trap of confusing winding rhythmic figures and the severe tempo of their movement, she who easily surmises both tempo and rhythm, maintaining the former and elaborating the latter—this person has a marvelous and highly developed sense of rhythm.

For a musician blessed with a good sense of rhythm time is not chaotic; indeed, it gravitates toward order. Whether or not man can sense this order and support it was the subject of an experiment by a team of Czech psychologists led by Marek Franek (Franek *et al.* 1994). The group took a simple rhythmic figure of six sounds of equal length and repeated it, each time raising it a tone higher so that the subjects could identify each new appearance of a rhythmic group. At first the original figure was repeated rather infrequently—waiting for a repetition of it took some while—but each successive waiting period was shorter than the previous one, and to such an extent that as a result what emerged was a very even, although slow, acceleration. The subjects were supposed to adjust to this acceleration, registering each appearance of the original six-sound fragment by clapping their hands. If they were expecting this appearance, they successfully clapped when they should have; if they were not expecting it, they clapped at the wrong time.

It turned out that subjects who were musicians easily formulated the temporal inertia—a regularly accelerating tempo was to them completely understandable and they easily adjusted themselves to it. Non-musician subjects, on the other hand, were unable to grasp the inertia of evenly diminishing time intervals and clapped at the wrong places. The psychologists concluded that the musicians more easily formed the temporal conditional reflex, the inertia of time, since the sense of tempo is nothing more or less than the same inertia which must be kept up under conditions of a changing rhythm.

The Czech results confirmed those of Russian psychologist L. Belenkaia from two years earlier, which had included another assertion: 'The results testify to the existence among musicians of skills of particularly subtle differentiation of time'.[12] That is, musicians can easily evaluate how much longer or shorter a time interval is in comparison with that which precedes and that which follows it. Despite the scientific value of such experiments, the degree to which they can assist testing for the sense of rhythm is unclear. If the skills demonstrated by musician-subjects are those which they have learned, then the fulfillment of tasks like this is connected less with ability than with experience. Or vice versa: the inborn factors play greater role in 'rhythmic qualification' than the learned ones. As Isabelle Peretz puts it: 'the available data are compatible with the idea that there are two

[11] Honegger, A. (1963) *Ya – kompozitor!/I am a Composer!* Leningrad: Muzyka, p. 132.
[12] Belenkaya, L. (1992) Ob uslovnyh refleksah na vremya u muzykantov/On conditioned reflexes for time among musicians. In *Muzykal'naya psihologiya/Psychology of Music* (ed. M. Starcheus). Moscow Conservatory, p. 96.

innate factors guiding the acquisition of the musical capacity, with one related to temporal sequencing and the other, pitch sequencing'.[13]

In order to clear this up, the same task must be assigned to children with no musical background, successful musicians, and less successful musicians; having evaluated the differences among the groups, one can deduce what exactly the researchers are dealing with—acquired skills of rhythmic labor or natural qualities which yield to external influences only with difficulty. Since researchers to date have not set themselves such goals, the question remains an open one. But one thing is clear in any case: the formation of reflexive time expectations, an ordered inertia of foresight before events of one kind or another is something that comes easier to musicians than to other people.

An outstanding sense of rhythm is connected with the skill of coordinating and supporting actions which are being completed simultaneously in several different time frames. This kind of skill is often needed by performers of contemporary music, where different orchestra groups, different instruments of an ensemble and even different hands of one performer are playing different music at a different tempo in a different rhythm. The great conductor Herbert von Karajan was a subject of study at the Institute for the Study of Music Perception where he stunned psychologists with his ability to walk at a speed of 120 paces per minute while singing at a speed of 105 beats per minute (Osborne 1991): this kind of dual tempo is something that can be maintained only by uniquely rhythmical individuals. Von Karajan's sense of tempo was not only multi-planned but extraordinarily precise as well—he accelerated and diminished the tempo no more than 2–3 percent, a record which was, according to the researchers, the lowest level of error they had ever witnessed. In von Karajan's case, if a soloist in his orchestra began his performance the slightest bit faster or slower than necessary, the conductor was physically distressed.

The unity and conflict of opposites—the strict periodization of tempo and free rhythmic breath—creates the basic content of musical rhythm. Thus the ability to keep a sure tempo, on the one hand, and while doing so also maintain a sense of rhythmic freedom, on the other, creates the basic content of rhythm as a component part of musical talent: if a musician cannot handle a strong tempo and a free rhythm, then a musical career is not a realistic option. Free rhythmic breathing is in a literal sense connected with musical air, that is, with pauses. The difficulty of working with them is that for the most part these are micro-pauses, those same microns of time torn from musical durations, the agents which shorten a sound unnoticeably yet give the musical whole a light breath. The conductor Kirill Kondrashin was exceptionally distinguished in this art form; when he was praised for the rhythmic freedom of his performances, he would respond 'One must give the quarter-notes air. I do not do anything unusual, I simply let the quarter-notes breathe'.[14]

---

[13] Peretz, I. (2006) The nature of music from a biological perspective. *Cognition*, 100, p. 16.
[14] Kondrashin, K. (1976) *Mir dirizhera/Conductor's World*. Leningrad: Muzyka, p. 38.

The quarter note, by which the metrical unit is traditionally measured, can be narrowed by this micron relatively painlessly, giving the rest of the music 'air'. In order to sense rhythm on the level of microns of time, one must experience in detail every rhythmic figure, entering into every micro-movement, sensing it almost bodily. Here one needs a certain motor impressionability which distinguishes outstanding musicians. The rhythmically gifted person will always sense micro-differences in the articulation of a musical phrase: are there in it the tiniest diminutions or aspirations? Studies show that some people do not have this kind of sensitivity; hearing musical phrases articulated differently by a performer, they can hardly identify the differences—the expressive nuances connected with them escape the attention of these subjects, even when most of them are themselves student musicians.

American psychologists William Frederickson and Christopher Johnson (1996) had a group of 120 music students listen to a fragment from the First Part of Mozart's Concerto No. 2 for French horn and orchestra. The selected fragment was played by two different performers, both of whom drew out the notes, as if holding them longer, for maximum expressiveness, but since they understood the music differently, they did this in different places. This kind of rhythmic difference can occur within the framework of the so-called *rubato* or free tempo: the rhythmic picture nonetheless remains entirely recognizable. The subjects were asked to note where they felt particularly accented or emphasized moments in the fragments—slowing-down always indicates such an emphasis. All the subjects answered independent of the rhythmic nuances of the performances, which were simply not noted—indeed, they were completely ignored.

Yet another study (Repp 1998c) examining the rhythmic abilities of student musicians has shed light on the reason for this conservatism. It turned out that the future musicians had certain rhythmic sets or frameworks which they had worked out during their prior experience, and their perception of music was too strongly connected with the expectations born thereof. If the musician-subjects were played a metronomically exact performance, they would ignore it, assigning the music a nonexistent *rubato*, which they were used to hearing in the given Chopin etude. Then Bruno Repp from Yale University offered the subjects a fundamentally different performance, in which the pianist very originally and highly musically interpreted the same etude, using interesting rhythmic effects. Yet the subjects still continued to hear not what was played, but what they were accustomed to, the stereotypical rhythmic decisions already familiar to them. In their perception the real sound was replaced by that of the memory.

Unlike such students, outstanding musicians avoid hard and fast decisions; for them rhythm each time is suborned to the individual musical thought and freely expresses it through rhythmic nuances of performance. Pianist Gerald Moore, the well-known accompanist of many famous singers, writes about one of the outstanding baritones of the twentieth-century Dietrich Fischer-Diskau:

> If I had to identify what differentiated Fischer-Diskau from other singers, I would express it in one word—rhythm. He is masterfully possessed of this true source of the living strength of music. I cannot remember a single song in which he observed a metronomically precise count. In the

piano introduction to the first of Wolf's *Songs of the Harpist*, the metronome and I would part company in the first measure, since the third and fourth quarter-notes there are longer than the first two, the second measure in shading is close to the first, but the third measure explodes into the fourth and, generally, is performed faster. The fifth one is very slow. Such is the schema created by Fischer-Diskau, a schema disguised behind fiery emotions. It seems that way to me, at least: the colored spots and nuances naturally reveal the durable and flexible construction'.[15]

The demand of free rhythm, the ability to divert oneself from the metronomically precise durations of sounds, was given to musicians by the composer Claudio Monteverdi (1567–1743), as if proving that over 400 years the understanding of the role of the sense of rhythm remained the same: 'He who does not know how to conceal, to subtract from the duration of a note at the expense of another in singing, he certainly will not know how either to compose or to accompany himself. He will turn out to be devoid of refined taste'.[16]

Observation confirms that the sense of rhythm is different in gifted musicians and mere mortals. The former are distinguished by audio-motor sensitivity, which makes them react to rhythm physically, engaging in rhythmic movement as if becoming part of it. The latter can remain calm under the thundering of drums and the pulsing beat of rock music; in the latter case the motor activity of the hall can be the result of the most sensitive listeners being 'infected' directly by music, while the remaining part of the audience reacts not so much to the music as to the behavior of the rhythm enthusiasts next to them. For rhythmically gifted people the beat is very infectious; they react, like David Oistrakh, to every rhythm with different movements, which is not true of the audiences at rock concerts, who 'go nuts' over everything, with the possible exception of ballads in the rhythm of a lullaby.

Outstanding musicians easily distinguish rhythmic movement and the movement of metrical units, which produce tempo. They hear rhythm simultaneously on two planes, as both the rhythmic figures which latch onto each other and as the beat which governs them. In their perception both rhythmic planes remain autonomous, while the majority of us is inclined to mix them up, confusing intensive rhythmic movement with quick tempo and restrained rhythmic movement with slow tempo, although in reality these are very different things. An understanding of the relative autonomy of tempo and rhythmic scheme is a sign of good rhythmic abilities, and exercises which check this aspect of musical perception can be used as rhythmic tests. It is understood that the large-scale use of any tests demands appropriate procedural checking, but the ideology of rhythmic testing should without fail take into account this two-planed rhythmical perception.

It is impossible to imagine a good musician who lacks a sense of living, anti-mechanical rhythm, in which there is a necessary and natural unmetronomic articulation of phrases. People without highly developed rhythmic skills cannot distinguish phrases played differently, as they cannot identify the subtle rhythmical nuances. For the gifted rhythmatist,

[15] Moore, G. (1987) *Pevets i akkompaniator. Vospominaniya. Razmyshleniya o muzyke/Singer and Accompanist. Memoires. Thoughts on Music.* Moscow: Raduga, p. 74.

[16] Konen, V. (1971) *Claudio Monteverdi.* Moscow: Sovetsky kompozitor, p. 121.

the slightest diversion from mechanical rhythm will be noticeable; most important of all, she will recognize in which direction the diversion was made and what brought it forth from the point of view of musical logic.

The sense of rhythm in the structure of musical talent

The place of the sense of rhythm in the structure of musical abilities comes directly after that of the expressive ear. This order signifies, first of all, a historical succession: the sense of rhythm separated itself from the expressive ear millions of years ago and developed from it, forming its own independent structure. The sense of rhythm closes ranks with the expressive ear towards certain ends, fulfilling along with it various emotional-expressive, content-oriented, and communicative functions of the art of music. The general tone of a musical expression, reflected in its articulation, in the character if its musical movement as well as in its tempo and degree of energy in fulfillment—all this comes under the joint aegis of the expressive ear and the sense of rhythm. There is but one difference involved: the sense of rhythm, relying on the parameters of sound, strives toward the building of a musical structure, organizing sounds in a successively larger continuum—rhythmic sketches, phrases, sentences, and parts of a whole work.

The expressive ear and the sense of rhythm are the lowest and deepest 'floors' of musical talent. Without an understanding of the idea of a musical expression, its general content and direction (the expressive ear) as well as the principles and structure of its time organization (the sense of rhythm), no musical activity of any sort can take place. Given the antiquity of these properties, the majority of people possess them in one degree or another; more people are endowed with an expressive ear and sense of rhythm than with a musical ear in the traditional sense—comparing sounds by length and accentuation is easier than reacting to the precise pitch of a sound and comparing sounds by pitch.

The expressive ear and the sense of rhythm are widespread among humans because in many cultures they are sufficient for musical activity. Musical cultures of the pre-historic world got along without exact identification of the pitch of sounds; pitch simply appeared, sometimes resembling weakly differentiated 'thinner and thicker' sounds. The art of playing drums, on the other hand, was of more moment: the drumbeat accompanied the life of early man for thousands of years. Such is the case today with the traditional cultures of a number of peoples who continue to live by the patterns of their ancestors—Australian aborigines, islanders of Polynesia, Indians of the Amazon jungle, and certain African peoples. In their music a general hue of sound, its communicative direction, formed by the expressive ear, and an incredibly finely honed sense of rhythm together create miracles: the music lives, it infects people with its mood, it accompanies all the important events in the life of the tribe, practically performing the role of principal mass media outlet. Timbre, tempo, direction of movement of quasi-musical sounds, the calling up of spirits, the shouting and shrieking of the singers, their half-speech/half-song, accompanied by drumbeats—all this ancient cacophony, tied into acute rhythmic patterns, is the great grandmother of music. By themselves such phenomena would serve only as reminders of the sense of rhythm's deep past, if they did not play such a great role of the genetic baggage of musical talent—which has remained in large part a rhythmic-expressive talent, taking under the term 'expressive' the resources primarily of the expressive ear.

In a paradoxical way the avant-garde music of the twentieth century with its timbrous and sonorous effects, which the sense of rhythm turns into structures and musical forms, represented a return to the roots of musicality. Some of the compositions of the avant-garde and post-avant-garde do not need a developed analytical ear, brimming as they are with shouting, growling, shrieking, wailing, and various other quasi-musical types of sound, formed into miraculous rhythmic continuums. Here there is no room for refined differentiation of the musical fabric: sound clusters, the opposition of timbres and groups, the sharp accents and fading vibrations for its perception and interpretation do not summon the highly developed analytical ear. Such works are perceived more generally and directly than the music of the 'basic classics' from the Renaissance era to the first third of the twentieth century. Ancient folklore and contemporary music often get by without the analytical ear, which simply demonstrates once more that this is not the critical, the main musical ability.

The imagined 'law' of the hierarchy of talent holds that the older the psychological property at the base of the given area of activity, the higher for this activity the significance of the required property. The second article of this 'law' goes as follows: the older and more essential for the given talent is this or that psychological property, the more widespread the property is among humans and, correspondingly, the more people who possess this property in a high degree—in comparison with the number of people who share the abilities of later origin.

The most fundamental property for musical talent is the expressive ear for music, which answers for the perception of the communicative and emotional content of a sound message. More people possess the expressive ear than musical abilities of later origin. Some 12 percent of children are endowed with wonderfully sensitive expressive ear. The concept of the hierarchy of talent holds that the sense of rhythm may be ranked in second place; thus very good rhythmatists are significantly fewer in the general population than those with a good expressive ear, a fact which pedagogical practice confirms.

Dean Simonton's concept of the multiplicative structure of talent (1999) maintains that the successful performance of any activity, including musical activity, requires the application of all the psychological properties that go into the structure of talent. This means that pretenders to the title of highly musical individual can only come from the ranks of people possessing both the expressive ear and the sense of rhythm; the absence of either signifies that musical talent itself is incomplete. Because of the internal kinship of the expressive ear and the sense of rhythm, outstanding rhythmatists are drawn from among those people endowed with the former. While it is impossible without special studies to pinpoint the number of people who may boast of a very good expressive ear and an equally good sense of rhythm, the laws of dual competence suggest that the fall-off from the greater (the 'expressivists'') to the lesser (the 'rhythmatists'') is not a matter of several percent, but several folds more.

In light of a certain expendability of the highly developed analytical ear and possibly, the second place that the sense of rhythm occupies in the hierarchy of musical talent, one might perhaps alter the interpretation of musical abilities for practical purposes of musical pedagogy (i.e. determining who might best study music). Testing of the expressive ear and sense of rhythm should be done before (or instead of) the usual testing for the analytical ear. If the first two of these are present in a subject in good measure, then a highly musical individual is almost ready. To be convinced of this one need only look at the stars of non-classical musical genres: their ear for pitch manifests itself only in singing relatively simple, at times primitive, melodies, whereas their expressive ear is so infectious and their sense of rhythm so perfect that they turn into stars of pop and rock music for many decades. This means that an ear for pitch is not the only ticket up the musical Olympus. In any case, the current testing practice in Russian musical pedagogy for future professionals—half-hearted, pro forma testing of the sense of rhythm in the special music schools, and universal, country-wide testing for the ear for pitch—may be reversed. The first testing could be for the expressive ear, then for the sense of rhythm, and only third for the analytical ear. The musical art as practiced in Russia will only gain from such a rearrangement of priorities; there are, after all, pianists of the author's acquaintance who are of all-European caliber—but whose analytical ear is far from perfect.

In order to test someone's sense of rhythm one must first know how it is set up. The expressive ear is a homogeneous property, an integral unit which is not divisible into internal structural 'cells'. The sense of rhythm, as a sense of later origin and a more refined one, has an entire complex of properties and qualities that go into it, each of which, by the law of multiplicity, is absolutely essential to musical talent. A part of these properties hone to the expressive ear, that is, they are included in the visual-content interpretive component of musical talent, in its motivational bloc. Another part relates to the operational component of talent. Here the functions of the sense of rhythm and the analytical ear are very close, as together these two abilities form the internal organization of music, its pitch, and temporal structure.

* * *

All the components of the sense of rhythm fit into the three properties mentioned earlier: motor sensitivity, or the ability to react emotionally to movement, remembering its outline and temporal characteristics; the ability to translate motor impressions into aural ones, as well as the ability to retain and identify received impressions with an acute discriminating ability, which may be called the rhythmic memory. Our experience in teaching the sense of rhythm and evaluations of the process allow us to arrange the components of the sense of rhythm according to experimental data already available.

The primary property of the sense of rhythm is its kinship with movement. The replicate of movement is the rhythmic figure, and the most important rhythmic ability consists in the ability to create such aural replicas of movement, establish the internal kinship between the bodily-kinetic form of movement, its direction, energetics, and the corresponding properties of rhythm. Thanks to its aural-motor component the sense of rhythm does not lose its connection with reality, but is reinforced by it. This component is functionally close to the expressive ear. The audio-motor component of the sense of rhythm determines the most general qualities reflected in the rhythmic figure, in its articulation, tempo and direction of movement, smooth or abrupt, circular or zigzag, determined or inhibited.

Insofar as it is possible the test subject can himself move to the music, trying to depict it, to play out his own pantomime. Music should inspire a rhythmically gifted person to appropriate movements; while they may not be smooth and attractive in all instances and people, the important thing in any case lies elsewhere, in the internal content of the movement: it should show to what extent the subject has captured the essence of the given rhythm, how much he senses the movement as a possible arousal motive of the heard rhythmic figure. Some of the exercises of this kind are most easily done individually, but group testing is also possible if the testing teacher can conveniently follow all the participants.

The second component of rhythmic giftedness is the ability to form a rhythmic image. This ability appears when movement has already crossed over into rhythm, has *become* rhythm, in fact. This ability signifies that a person can distinguish one rhythmic 'portrait of movement', one rhythmic drawing from another. Such task is widely used in existing testing, and the question is traditionally posed in the accepted form for such tests: same or different. It is possible to include another, more subtle variant of the same question: if the original figure includes several rhythmic groups, and one of them is altered by the tester before the second round, the question may be posed as: Which element of the rhythmic figure has been changed? Tests of this kind of the formation of a rhythmic image check the level of durability, the lastingness of the rhythmic images. Exercise of this nature is very convenient for those who allow wide variance in the complexity of the tasks. If the subject compares, for example, the rhythm of a running triplet in the first instance and a march-like dotted line in the second, finding no difference between them, then her sense of rhythm is rather weak. If, on the other hand, she can distinguish between two marches, one with 16th notes and the other with 32nds, then her sense of rhythm is close to ideal.

In the translation from the audio-motor component to the ability to form rhythmic images lies the sense of accent. No movement can be entirely without accent, and neither can its audio image. The most popular exercises for testing the sense of accentuation in music are comparing the accent in a real movement with the accentuation in a musical fragment; identifying which of the various sounds played is the accented one; identifying where an accent falls at the beginning of a phrase and where at the end; and indicating how many rhythmic groups there are in a phrase.

The third component in the sense of rhythm is the sense of tempo, the beat. The tester can play several musical fragments for the subjects, then bang out the tempo of each of them and ask the subjects to match each fragment with its hallmark tempo. This kind of 'forced abstractioning' will demonstrate how securely the music and its tempo are merged in the mind of the subject. One can also ask questions about which music is faster and which slower. These can be very simple tasks, if rhythmic figures do not confuse or distract the subject; there can also be extraordinarily complex questions, for which one must have very solid ideas on the differences between tempo and the rhythmic pattern inserted into it.

Various accelerations and decelerations can be included in testing for the sense of tempo so that the tester can see how the subject hears them. It is best to use exercises which do not require personal contact between the examiner and the subjects or exercises which can be performed by an entire class at the same time.

And finally, in evaluating the sense of rhythm one must check the inclination of the subject toward rhythmic freedom, the absence of the mechanical in his understanding of rhythm as such. Here exercises with vividly expressed fragments with *rubato* are appropriate. One may ask the subjects to indicate in which place in a short piece they found moments which departed somewhat from the established rhythmic pattern, or to differentiate among several performances of *rubato* (demonstrate this). Even better are active exercises: have the subject sing a phrase insistently, then pleadingly, then tenderly. From this the tester will hear the extent to which the expressive ear of the subject will grow into the sense of rhythm, arousing a freer, more artistic approach to the articulation of a rhythmic figure.

The role of the sense of rhythm in music became more noticeable during the twentieth century, as non-classical genres came to the forefront of world musical culture. It is essential to add some new accents into music teaching: creating special workbooks for developing the sense of rhythm, the variety of which could be compared to the breadth of the 'listener's library', the library which mankind has been assembling and studying for several hundred years now. Contests aimed at the sense of rhythm should be organized in the music institutions, including the conservatories. One has to wonder whether the performance of classical musicians today is sometimes so colorless and uninvolving because of an inactive, underdeveloped sense of rhythm. If they love rhythm and develop a keen sensitivity to it the public will flock to musicians. The sense of rhythm paired with the expressive ear has worked miracles even when the sound of a certain pitch only loomed in the distant future.

Rhythm as a sense of organized movement, breath, and gesture is not only a part of poetic and prose speech, where its role is almost the same as it is in music—rhythm in its original, bodily-motor form is part of all forms of activity in which there is organized physical effort—in sports, in dance, in hunting and farming, in construction and industry. Rhythm as a system of proportional-symmetrical relationships among elements has a wider meaning, ranging far beyond the bounds of the art of music and bodily-motor manifestations. Neuropsychological data, probably the most reliable of all, underline that in the brain there are certain areas processing structural relations, and rhythmic relations are only ones among many others: 'The processing of structure (and perhaps meaning) in music, may thus involve many of the same neural correlates as the processing of structure and meaning in other domains'.[17]

It is impossible to name a sphere of activity in which there is no rhythmic influence: there is rhythm in spatial figures, which means in the fine arts, design, and mathematics.

[17] Levitin, D. J. and Menon, V. (2005) The neural locus of temporal structure and expectancies in music: evidence from functional neuroimaging at 3 Tesla. *Music Perception, 22*, p. 572.

Spatial-rhythmic relations are a key part of construction and inventing, mechanics and geology. Here the sense of rhythm aligns with the spatial intellect and becomes genuinely all-pervasive. The function of organizer of time, which rhythm fulfills in music, is comparable to the function of organizer of space, which it can fulfill in other forms of activity. Most likely the sense of rhythm will also be the second in seniority in other kinds of giftedness, following the original fundamental ability which gave rise to the activity and lies at its origins. The analogue of the sense of rhythm in the structure of other talents will also be that of 'manager' of the organization of elements into structures.

To sum up our discussion of the sense of musical rhythm:

1 The sense of rhythm is born of movement. The most important properties of movement, strength, speed, direction, and general character, are embodied in musical rhythm. The sense of rhythm identifies these fundamental properties of movement together with the expressive ear. The sense of rhythm grows out of the expressive ear, occupying itself with the detailing and structuring of a generalized 'portrait of movement' which it receives from the expressive ear.

2 The sense of rhythm organizes musical time, dividing it into allotments (metrical units) defining the speed of its movement. It groups sounds into rhythmic figures and drawings by singling certain sounds out and accenting several of them. The internal part of the sense of rhythm manifests itself through the resistance and reconciliation of opposites: on the one hand there is the regular passage of metrical units, musical tempo; on the other there is free breathing of sounds, the relative length of which is defined not by mathematical but musical logic—the expressive intentions of the performer.

3 The components of the sense of rhythm which are suitable for testing are: audio-motor coordination—the ability to translate muscle-motor impressions into aural ones; the aptitude for rhythmic 'gestalt-ness'—the ability to sense the proportional relationships of the duration of sounds and to group them, separating out and accenting some elements and subordinating them to others; tempo-rhythmic ability—the ability to distinguish the passage of metrical units from the rhythmic designs inserted into them and reconcile the equal-length of units of the musical tempo, its certitude, with the freedom of mutual combination of sounds within rhythmic groups (that is *rubato*, musical agogics).

4 The place and role of the given component in the structure of talent are also defined by the rule of hierarchy in talent: the role of the given component in the structure of talent is proportionately bigger and more important in relation to the seniority of its origin. This rule in relation to musical talent is confirmed by the very history of music: there are styles and directions of the musical art, which make relatively low demands on the analytical ear, but there are no styles or directions in music which do not require a highly developed sense of rhythm.

The analytical ear

Many millions of years ago man could distinguish only the crudest differences in pitch—the deep *basso* of a bearded hunter, say, was easy to tell from the gurgling of an infant—and such obvious contrasts could be recognized by the expressive ear alone. But if two sounds differed in pitch only marginally, bamboo pipes of different lengths, perhaps, or the ring of two similar vessels holding different amounts of water when one struck them with a stick, many thousands of years had to pass for humans to learn the distinctions; our early forbears had to develop a new proficiency, this time with the *analytical ear*. This is the capability of human hearing which identifies the finest shades of sound frequency and assigns them each a separate name. The best known of them is the sound designated by the note A of the first octave which has a frequency of 440 hertz (cycles per second). How important are these finely calibrated distinctions? If people could not distinguish that even the slightest movement up or down by the voice produces a sound which is in fact different from the previous one, there would be no such thing as melody, songs, or musical instruments.

Melody, defined as musical thought, a musical expression consisting of sounds of different pitch and length, was born with the development of the analytical ear. Primitive man took in melody's ancestors with his expressive ear, perceiving the various vocal ascents, glides, risings, fallings, and zigzags of his own invention, and in nature as part of a continuous and unbroken line of sound. This line as yet had no fine points for the separate sounds which appeared later, with the advent of the analytical ear. This event (or completed process) gave man the capability of perceiving and creating music not only as a means of summarizing and emotionally coloring the image of movement, but of carefully and in detail identifying the process in which every micro-turn, micro-vibration, and micro-step is experienced and invested with thought, validated, in fact, by the human voice or an instrument in its place. Where the expressive ear and the sense of rhythm created the general contour of musical design and composition, the analytical ear added to this the finest shades of colors, highlights, and half-tones in order to complete the sound portrait so worthily begun. Thanks to the analytical ear we can distinguish one sequence of sounds from another. The slightest change in aural configuration now becomes noticeable; even a single sound whose pitch does not match that of a neighboring note already constitutes a melodic step. If the sequence of sounds is preserved exactly, then an exact repetition, a confirmation, will take place; if the melody changes insignificantly, then a variant repetition, a development, will occur; and if the melody is entirely different, utterly unlike the original version, then it will become a new musical idea.

As music specialists put it, everything there is in music, the whole of the phenomenon, amounts to a single process: the evolution of different kinds of repetition (Holopova 2000). And the capacity for distinguishing between the levels of similarity and difference within the various 'degrees of repetitiveness' is the province of the analytical ear. It perceives whether a sound (or series of sounds) is in fact a repetition of a previous thought, a variant of it, or something novel; thus the analytical ear lays the foundation of musical forms. The relationships of variant repetition between A, A1, A2, and A3, and the relationship of utter dissimilarity between A and B is, when all is said and done, all that is necessary for the organization of the most complex musical forms. Musicologist Boris Asafiev (1971) termed these relationships 'identity and contrast'. They alone are capable of creating the form of a symphony, opera, or any other large-scale, multi-part composition. All these relationships are controlled by the analytical ear.

The role and functions of the analytical ear in music are distributed as though on two separate levels. On the micro-level the analytical ear creates and distinguishes nuances of pitch, offering up sounds differentiated qualitatively even if their physical frequency differs entirely insignificantly; the analytical ear identifies the subtlest movements of sound, each of which reflects a barely noticeable movement of thought and feeling. On the macro-level the analytical ear occupies itself with insuring the intelligibility of the musical whole by identifying the similarities and differences of themes and melodies: from the musical threads it insures, as it were, that musical tapestries are woven. The analytical ear penetrates into musical development, identifying the unbroken chain of changes of musical units, following the course of musical events, resembling musical poetry, a musical story, or a musical novel.

The speech origins of the analytical ear

The analytical ear is a logical and highly differentiated instrument which appeared at a relatively late stage of man's development—when he began to speak. In this respect the difference between the analytical ear and its predecessors, the expressive ear and the sense of rhythm, is great indeed. The expressive ear can exist passively, reflecting reality and signaling its 'intentions' in relation to man. In the sense of rhythm the degree of joint participation by man is much higher: it is impossible to merge with rhythm, to feel it, without executing movements, however small and unnoticed. But rhythm itself is an expression of the collective origin, of general and concerted movement, group actions which an individual joins and experiences together with the collective. One may move along with everyone else in a group entirely subconsciously, almost reflexively. The general movement will of itself direct the participant in a ceremony, take charge of him and orient him; the bodily-kinesthetic intellect, strengthened by sound, will work in an unconscious mode.

The analytical ear is a new step on the path of musical evolution, since recognizing the precise pitch of a sound is something only Singing Man, a being who expresses himself individually and as a thinker, can do. Even singing together, in chorus, demands from each individual singer a conscious effort to form the sounds of various pitches: the human voice can only form them intentionally. As distinct from the reflexive nature of the sense of rhythm, the nature of the analytical ear is entirely conscious and under the control of the intellect. The analytical ear is like language and speech: it is impossible to talk without understanding what one is saying. The very act of speech presupposes an intellect, just as does every musical act—the singing of sounds of different pitches. Each of the sounds must be just as consciously formed as phonemes and words are, just as well understood as the goal of an act of speech, its content and its structure are. Otherwise what will emerge will not be singing, not the creation of a musical expression, but rather a spontaneous and emotional outburst formed by the vocal elements, a mere shout, wail, or cry.

The appearance of the analytical ear is similar to the appearance of the human intellect; the sign of the completion of this process was the birth of articulated oral speech which arose from the merger of spontaneous vocal signals. But speech did not arise directly from them. Researchers speculate that somewhere on the road from the first vocal signals to language and articulated speech stood song (Alexeev 1986; Mithen 2006; Wallin *et al.* 2000). As anthropologist Bruce Richman has noted, 'Singing and speech seem very different; singing is more expressive of emotions than speech. And singing also served as an evolutionary transitional state between primate-like vocalizations and speech'.[1]

Singing is beyond wailing, roaring, and even rhythmic shouts. The melodious extension of a vowel sound is, in and of itself, a version of conscious pronunciation. To move on with one's voice to the next sound is again to take on a certain 'pitch', to locate and identify it. Melodic activity presupposes two inseparable conscious steps: the division into parts, into micro-stages of the diffusion-integration process of 'pre-singing'—laughter, crying, sighing, and the unification of the micro-steps, the vocal micro-actions in the integration process. But in distinction from a rhythmic pattern the sung thought will be experienced not only bodily and reflexively; its line of pitch will become a constructed whole created by the efforts of the awakened intellect. 'I think, therefore I am', as Descartes had it; one might justifiably paraphrase the great *philosophe*: 'I sing, therefore I think'. I divide and unite, I articulate and summarize, I see at once both the individual sound movement and the entire integrated line into which figure all the vocal steps I have taken. Singing is movement from the reflexive to the conscious, from the indivisible to the articulated, it is the step from primitive sound syncresis to aural analysis and synthesis—and the agent which took this step, forged as it was in pre-melodic practice, was the analytical ear.

The ancient predecessor of speech, which we may term proto-language, began to turn into language as such not with the advent of words but rather via communicative units in the form of melodic signals. The vestiges of this language can be seen in a number of animal species, including our fellow primates. The gibbon, for example, alone among the ape family, can sing; its song serves an honorable and naturally critical role—the continuation of the species (Mitani and Marler 1989). While rams butt each other and bucks charge with antlers atilt, the male gibbon, and it is only the males who have the capacity

[1] Richman, B. (1993) On the evolution of speech: singing as the middle term. *Current Anthropology*, 34, p. 721.

to sing, communicates his interest in a closer relationship with a female as well as his worthiness as a sire by demonstrating his ability at the fine and demanding art of song. Nature taught the male gibbon to arrange and perform only the simplest of melodic signals, but they are sung so loudly and female gibbons are so attuned to them that those males who lacked the singing facility were, in essence, doomed by the evolutionary process—females could fail to hear them and, in consequence, ignore them as potential mates.

The singing of birds is considered a predecessor of speech; indeed, some scholars consider it the single best model for the study of how speech was acquired (Konishi 1994; Saito and Maekawa 1993). Just as a child must hear the spoken word in order to learn to talk, birds must listen to the singing of their progenitors to learn to sing themselves, and just as in humans, this must be accomplished early in life. Bird species have their own languages: the singing of robins is incomprehensible to goldfinches and vice versa. And in the same way that the human brain has particular areas which are responsible for speech, so the avian brain contains special areas which answer for singing.

The singing of animals, including the roaring of mammals and the whistling and trilling of birds, most resembles a rhythmic growling in which the melodic phrases are in fact integrated rhythmic-intonational signals. This kind of sound derivation is syncretic to the highest degree: all the characteristics of sound are merged in it—timbre, tempo, dynamics, register-tessitura, and rhythm. The voice of 'singing' mammals and birds slides and makes glissandos; in this singing, as a rule, there is no breakdown of the source into separate sounds with their own pitch characteristics. Birds and gibbons know only a few quasi-melodic signals; and in distinction from human speech, there is nothing in the animals' 'language' of the consciously intentional: the melodic 'words and phrases' play the same role as other animals' barking, wailing, and so on—oral manifestations which neither change nor develop. The existence of such 'language' merely testifies that the connection of singing and speech was created by nature itself and semi-singing/semi-speech phase on the path of human development becomes more and more visible (Masataka 2007; Mithen 2006). The brain structures capable of directing the singing and speech function emerged over millions of years of evolution.

From the earliest stages of the process the function of differentiating sounds by pitch, on which the analytical ear relies, and the function of speech production went hand in evolutionary hand, their properties formed as one.

The ancient origin and kinship of the speech and music compartments of the human brain were demonstrated by the group of neuropsychologists in an article in the magazine *Science* (Gannon *et al.* 1998). The left hemisphere (*planum temporale*), which answers for both the perception of pitch and the speech function, appears exactly the same in humans as it does in one group of chimpanzees, the Pan troglodytes. Both groups show this brain compartment slightly enlarged, since the evolutionary process invested such an important role in it—the comprehension of speech and music. This means that the speech–musical kinship at the brain level emerged some eight million years ago, and we are correct when we refer to 'musical speech'—a precise term, it transpires, rather than a metaphor.

The enlargement of this brain region, the *planum temporale*, is particularly noticeable among professional musicians. And not only professionals, but all those musicians blessed with perfect pitch, for whom distinctions of pitch, obviously, represent child's play. American scholar Albert Galaburda explains this coincidence by the fact that those with perfect pitch can identify the pitch of separate sounds by name: 'that's C of the first octave, and that's E-flat of the second' (McNamara *et al.* 1994). The extraordinary development of the left-hemisphere *planum temporale* explains why it is so easy to identify by name the pitch impressions: beyond the names of the sounds one does not have to 'go far'—at the same time as one hears the sound, its name immediately rises to the surface in the same compartment of the brain.

Other scientists opine that not only are the common 'place of residence' in the brain of the sound-distinguishing and word functions involved here, but that there are other factors at work, including the deep internal kinship of music and speech, both of which are occupied with the categorization of sounds (Brown *et al.* 2006; Delogu *et al.* 2006; Hoskins 1988; Merkur 2000; Moen 1991; Patel 2005; Richman 1993; Tervaniemi *et al.* 2006; Zatorre *et al.* 2002). Music differentiates sounds by pitch and length, speech distinguishes phonemes (vowels and consonants) and recognizes the sound properties of different languages. Scholars speculate that the first languages to arise were the tonals, many of which are of Oriental provenance. In these languages the pitch of the speech sounds fulfills the function of naming and signification; in most European languages this role is played by the combination of linguistic phonemes. Tonal languages demand a good ear for pitch; children who are beginning to speak have no fear of the most complex demands of pitch—their ear is attuned to the assimilation of different languages, including the tone-based. The analytical ear in infants is always in excellent form, especially when compared to the minimal 'musical experience' that they have, but researchers regretfully acknowledge that this facility is clearly not permanent: quite soon in the child's life, during the first stage of the mastery of language, the wonderful inborn sense of pitch will disappear.

Sandra Trehub and her colleagues (1986) decided to determine whether infants between the ages of 9 and 18 months could recognize the smallest interval between sounds—the half-tone in a five-note melody. The initial variant of the task was easier from the point of view of adults, since the melody resembled a phrase of a song, and in the phrase, not particularly disguised, came the half-tone. In this situation, preschoolers in the 4–6 year age range fared fairly well, as did, in fact, the infants: all identified the half-tone successfully. But when both groups of subjects were asked to find the same half-tone within a five-note melody of a twentieth-century avant-garde type, many of the preschoolers lost the half-tone and could not locate it. The infants, on the other hand, were not a bit put out by the new task; indeed, whether they were played pop music or Schoenberg, all the infants reacted with assurance to the sound of the target half-tone. Two conclusions may be drawn from this: that the analytical ear in infants is excellent—would that we all could retain it over a lifetime—and secondly, that this marvelous operating condition of the infants' ear for pitch may be connected with the high aptitude of humans at that age for learning languages, including those which are tone-based, if the sound-distinguishing ability and the language ability itself is located in the same area of the brain.

Rosamund Shuter-Dyson has noted in this context that 'Accurately reproducing the pitch of sounds can be a matter of routine for infants, but the majority of them lose this ability when they begin to master language and the surrounding environment no longer facilitates its retention'.[2] The author refers to European languages, the mastery of which really does not require a good sense of pitch, and among the developing speakers of those languages the corresponding ability naturally falls away. Infants developing into native speakers of tonal languages, which require subtle differentiation of pitch, can retain the musical pitch-reproduction facility longer; but over time they also lose it, since in the use of mature speech the subtle differentiation critical in the formative stage of language is no longer necessary.

Michael Lynch and his colleagues (1995) established that in the first months of life the ability to identify musical pitch is not connected with musical experience but with experience that is purely aural. Normal infants aged 6 to 12 months distinguish the pitch of sounds considerably better than do infants born prematurely, whose aural experience in the womb was naturally less. 'These findings suggest parallel developmental tendencies in the perception of music and speech that may reflect general acquisition of perceptual abilities for processing of complex auditory patterns'.[3]

The psychological mechanisms of music and speech demonstrate such close kinship that musical pitch may be counted as a part of a single music–speech mechanism (Don et al. 1999; Kirnarskaya 1995; Patel 2003). This unity is so intimate that a person attuned over the span of a lifetime to the frequencies of his native language perceives all frequencies, musical and speech, accordingly. As Diana Deutsch has noted (1978), it is for this very reason that acoustic speakers of English and Japanese manufacture sound different: they are attuned to different language frequencies, those typical of the speech zones of their origin. At a later stage of the mastery of a language the ear for pitch defines how well a person reads and understands what she has read. It is considered that variations of vocal frequency or speech intonation is a leading factor in the transmittal of the idea of a text: voice intonation plays the same role in relation to speech as the non-notational properties of sound do in relation to music—the idea of the transmitted 'word-information' is clear without actual words, relayed exclusively by their intonational profile, the vocal risings and fallings, into which is inserted a text.

A group of psychologists (Barwick et al. 1989) came to analogous conclusions when they posed the question of whether there existed a connection between musical abilities (the analytical ear, in the instance) and the mastery of reading skills among early elementary school students. The experimenters assembled 50 such pupils and tested their musical

[2] Shuter-Dyson, R. (1994) Le probléme des interactions entre hérédité et milieu dans formation des aptitudes musicales. In La psychologie de la musique, (ed. A. Zenatti), Presses Universitaire de France, p. 216.

[3] Lynch, M. P., Short, L. B., and Chua, R. (1995) Contributions of experience to the development of musical processing in infancy. Developmental Psychobiology, 28, p. 377.

abilities (i.e. distinguishing pitch) and their reading age. It turned out that reading ability and the musical ear have a clearly demonstrable positive correlation: the better the musical ear, the better the reading ability. That is, speech intonation is better remembered and more thoughtfully transmitted by children with a good analytical ear, since speech and music are closely related. This means that the entrance exams for Russia's theater institutes are acting wisely when they test an applicant's ear for music—not because contemporary theatrical performers are necessarily going to sing and dance in productions, but rather because someone wholly lacking this gift is less likely to give a good reading of anything in prose or poetry.

The characteristics of childhood music making tell much about the origin and stages of the evolution of musical abilities. The ontogenesis (the course of a child's development) in its main points is copied from phylogenesis, the evolutionary path of man: the child passes through, at an accelerated pace, the same stages which all of humanity before him traversed. If infants have a good analytical ear, this speaks to the fact that fine differentiation of musical pitch was, at some point of historical evolution, critically important for the survival of the species. It is entirely possible that a good ear for pitch stands at the origins of human speech, closely related to singing. The oldest languages may well be tonal; it is not incidental that the most ancient bearers of civilization on earth, the Chinese, spoke (and speak) tonal languages and dialects.

In their spontaneous musical games children divide melodic music (resembling musicalized speech) and the rhythmical music they associate with movement. The first they term 'chant' and the second 'song', a distinction noted by the psychologists Moorhead and Pond in 1941. Commenting on these findings, Rosamund Shuter-Dyson and Clive Gabriel have noted that

> Chant appears to evolve from speech. In fact, the first type of chant is merely heightened speech; its rhythm is that of speech, but it differs from speech in that the most important syllable is strongly accented melodically. The second type of chant has a definite rhythmic pattern to which the words may be forced to conform. The distinguishing characteristics of the second type (song) are that it seems indifferent to melody; it is rigidly rhythmic and closely associated with physical movement; it is repeated through rises in intensity and pitch till a climax is reached, then stops. A chant may be started by an individual but is most often sung in groups. [4]

This description highlights the different relationship of children to rhythmic movement (song) and musicalized speech (chant). Does the phylogenetic contrast between music which relies on the sense of rhythm and music connected with speech not signify a similar difference? The sense of rhythm, which leads song behind it, and the analytical ear, which leads chant, have different origins—and thus children sense song and chant as 'different musics'.

The analytical ear is a subtle sound-distinguishing instrument which expresses a musical thought: it differentiates the stream of sound, dividing it into micro-bytes and collecting them into a consciously integrated whole. The analytical ear arose with speech, or even

---

[4] Shuter-Dyson, R. and Gabriel, C. (1981) *The Psychology of Musical Ability*. London: Methuen, p. 109.

preceded it, and it shares with speech the same means of sound organization; for speech and the analytical ear have, in many respects, a common goal, that is, to create a consciously integrated unity of sound and insure that it is correctly understood. Michael Lynch, who has studied the establishment of speech and music among humans, put it this way:

> Music and language are parallel in their hierarchical, temporally organized structure, and the evolution of hierarchical representation in hominids may have provided the basis for musical representation. Because music could have been produced manually or vocally before the production of spoken language, it remains possible that language emerged from music and that music thus served as a communicative precursor to language [5] (see also Aranovsky 1991).

His assumptions are largely confirmed by neuropsychological data: scholars find distinct overlap between 'music zones' and 'speech zones' of the brain, serving phonological and syntactical needs of both 'languages' (Brown *et al.* 2006; Koelsch 2005).

The setting-apart into distinct musical expressions, that is, the breaking-up of a stream of sound into units of greater and lesser size, is a significant step on the path to hierarchization. The sense of rhythm splits up the flow of time in accordance with the logic of movement, while the analytical ear disassembles it according to the logic of the train of thought; these two forms of logic may, in many cases, simply fail to correspond. If the logic of rhythm gains the upper hand then the pitch origin in the music will be required to submit and 'write itself into' the phases of movement proposed by the rhythm. This often happens in the oldest genres of traditional music and in certain branches of contemporary rock and pop music, such as disco and heavy metal. When the logic of thought predominates, on the other hand, then rhythm, as with the children's chant, has to play a secondary role and create a rhythmic core for the vocal intonation decoded by the analytical ear. This logic is most often followed in classical genres, jazz blues, and rock ballads. In all aspects of music thought-directed movement is the rhythmic origin and moving thought is the melodic origin; they naturally supplement one another, but one of the elements of musical speech, pitch or rhythm, always takes the lead role.

The sense of completing a thought is very important for the analytical ear, which forms a musical expression. In pedagogical practice, the sense of the completeness of a musical phrase is used as the roughest criterion when checking the analytical ear. Edwin Hantz with his colleagues (1995) performed an experiment to test whether the sense of completeness of a melody was identical with the sense of completeness of a speech phrase in a psychological sense. Their subjects were played musical themes with different endings—completed, uncompleted, and loud. The neuropsychoplogical data showed that the subjects identified the completion of a melody almost with a nod of the head: the measurements of brain impulses corresponded with affirmative 'peaks' on the screen. If a completion did not take place in the music, then the sense of anticipation hung in the air—and the peak measurement was truncated, registering lower on the screen. When similar operations were done with vocal sentences, the peaks were like the musical ones both in the

---

[5] Lynch, M. (1996) And what of human musicality? *Behavioral and Brain Sciences*, 19, p. 796.

case of a completed phrase and an uncompleted one; and these peaks were identified as residing in the same area of the brain. The experimenters drew the conclusion that the speech–musical mechanism which marked the divisions of the sound stream was in fact a unified one: the syntax of music, recognized by the analytical ear, and the syntax of human speech are controlled by the same brain structures. It has long since been noted that with the loss of speech (aphasia) the analogous musical functions of the brain often die out, while the loss of musical ability (amusia) often leads to dysfunction in speech skills (Benton 1977; Patel 2005; 2003). Despite the considerable specificity of speech and music skills they have many joint mechanisms which regulate both spheres of activity. At the dawn of civilization music *was* speech; while their paths later diverged, the internal communality of these two agencies continues to make itself known.

The structure of the analytical ear

A musical texture is often metaphorically called a musical fabric. This is an attempt to underline its variety, the multifaceted nature of its layers. Like a woven fabric, music has a 'face' and an 'inside', meaning there are obvious, highlighted strata and hidden or less obvious ones. Some melodies, musical lines, and themes are brought out on the first plane, where they cannot be missed, while others play a subservient, accompanying role, one in which they can easily go unnoticed. Like a fabric music embraces a defined area. If one can represent a musical work as completed, played through and set as if in the past tense, then it may be taken in at one glance, as the sequence of sound events which have already taken place—melodies sounded through, the development of experienced musical themes, chords and consonances replacing one another. Then music, like a fabric, takes on two dimensions, the horizontal and the vertical: every consonance, chord, and singly-taken complex of sounds become the verticals, while a melody or any other musical events, melodic lines, and developments completed one after another become the horizontals. Like a fabric music may initially seem sheer and indivisible, and only through more attentive listening will it become clear that it consists of 'musical knots' and 'musical threads', that in it there are in fact a wealth of sound elements, lines, and extraneous features, both more independent and more subservient. Music has an internal structure which may be revealed, heard, and understood to the last sound, to the slightest pause. The psychological instrument which allows us to do this is the analytical ear.

The structure of the analytical ear is defined by the structure of the musical fabric, the possible perspectives from which may be aurally examined. And the first perspective, unarguably, will be melodic, both because of melody's seniority status and by the role which the melodic voice plays in the majority of musical genres and styles, from traditional music to the newest, nonacademic compositions. One hesitates to term melody the unquestioned soul of music only because of its competition from rhythm; in some musical genres melody rules, in others rhythm does. But in our perception melody always dominates; in the search for the ideational center of music man is always ready to give preference to melody because singing-along always takes first place as the moving force in transmitting musical experience. Even if there is nothing to sing along with, which happens all the time, people will artificially 'melodize' music they have heard to find the basic line, the leading voice, and the main idea in it (Aranovsky 1991; Asafiev 1971; Nazaikinsky 1967).

The melodic idea is the closest relative of an expression of speech. In traditional music and in folklore it is impossible to tear it away from the word, from the poetry with which melody became related many thousands of years ago. The analytical ear, speech-oriented by origin, acquired in melody its leading stronghold: it developed as a speech-melodic ear, acquiring melody in the chanted pronunciation of verse. This recitation could be extraordinarily expressive, like the ancient incantations which were used to call forth heavenly powers, or done in a monotone and intensely focused, like the recitation of ancient prayers—but the pronunciation of the text always remained melodic. Word and music sensed their indivisibility precisely by and through melody, and through it the analytical ear nourished this very indivisibility. In our time, when music has come such a long way and emerged in such endless diversity, for the majority of people the concepts of music and melody are practically identical. The concept of an 'ear for music' is interpreted by most as an ear for melody, whose absence or presence is established in the simplest fashion—by whether or not someone can sing a given melody in tune.

Musicians speak of a melodic ear in the same sense, only for them melody signifies more than the main musical idea and not only the lead voice, but all the horizontal threads of a musical fabric. All the extended musical lines drawing across the horizontal are recognized by the melodic ear: whether it is a *basso* voice that the musical fabric relies on, or a less noticeable *mezzo* voice, it in any case draws the line which cuts the musical fabric along a horizontal axis. In multi-part vocal music the melodic ear brings along several melodies at once, hearing them all at the same time and each one individually. But no matter where the melody is situated, no matter in what voice of the musical fabric one hears it, the melodic ear will differentiate the entire melody overall, all its motifs and phrases, all its intervals, the 'steps' or 'stages' on which they are situated—the analytical ear under any and all conditions will disassemble the musical whole into its parts.

Certain musical cultures, including many traditional and some oriental cultures, are monodic, not knowing polyphony. European music, however, has inclined since the thirteenth century toward music with a multitude of sounds, planes, and components. In Asia the tendency is to delve deeply into a subject and grasp all its details and nuances, whereas in Europe the opposite tends to obtain: the desire is to broaden the borders of a subject, put it in a larger scale context, and examine it from different sides. Thus it is that in European music alongside the horizontal arises the vertical measurement, where sounds taken simultaneously make up consonances and chords, and those in turn enter into certain relationships among themselves. The aspect of the analytical ear that deals with the relationships of the vertically organized units is called the harmonic ear.

The harmonic ear is a two-faced Janus, at once illuminating the vertical and uniting the consonances it receives into a new horizontal sequence. It knows how and why exactly these sounds ended up together in the same chord and what the sound will be if one sound disappears or is replaced by another. The harmonic ear also knows how these consonances create a certain sequential chain to form a logical musical 'story'. Penetrating the vertical with the ear, making each chord transparent, clarifying its sound composition, and joining these consonances into phrases and structures according to certain rules—such is the function of the harmonic ear, which is also analytical by nature because it turns that which is merged into something divided, the hidden into the visible. Without the work of the harmonic ear music would seem a random collection of sound holes and multi-sounding blots, the logic of whose appearance together would be unclear. Thus the harmonic ear is not only harmonic, meaning it recognizes multiple sounds and harmony; it is also harmonizing, which means putting things into order, explaining the logic of the sounds which lie at the base of a stream of music.

One particular aspect of the analytical ear is the internal ear. It forms the basis of audition, holding and preserving the musical idea when this has already become clear and revealed its components and layers. Now, everything that has been brought out and understood must be identified and remembered in order to reproduce it, to bring to life once more music heard at some previous time. The musical memory uses material which is supplied to it by the internal analytical ear since that which has not been understood and not disassembled cannot be recalled—chaos does not yield to rational identification. And man does not recall any and all material suddenly or immediately, but more often than not by a gradual process, out of necessity, arranging the material into elements and layers, stages and subdivisions which one after another are placed in the memory. The preliminary stage of recalling music will always be the internal ear, the completing component of the analytical ear which plays the role of a photographic negative or of the pre-printing examination in a computer printout: the whole of the music, with all its internal proportions and relationships, is already present in the image of the internal ear; the end result is almost ready to sound out, and it remains only for the internal ear to forward the finished musical image to the musical memory which will then reproduce the work heard before.

The work of the analytical ear proceeds from the general to the specific, from synthesis to analysis. At first it takes in the entire work, with its sections and fragments merged into a whole, at a point when the sound composition of the musical fragments and consonances is still undifferentiated. The analysis of the musical fabric begins with the assignment of a work to a musical system the listener is familiar with, a codex of rules to which the sound constituents, the rules of formation of consonances, and the rules of their coordination are all subservient. When the system which governs the musical fabric as a whole has been defined, the analytical ear, like an x-ray, illuminates the entire 'musical insides' of the composition, perceives its entire structure, its entire sound composition, all the connections, and elements. Analysis to this level of detail is not always necessary and does not always take place in practice, but nevertheless it is this kind of photographically exact and detailed sound scheme that the analytical ear strives for.

When the internal ear understands the entire picture—all the musical elements at hand and the various possibilities for their combination, successfully taking all this in at the ideational level—then the analytical ear has done the maximum of which it is capable of: it has created the basis for a new synthesis. At this point new elements and new combinations can arise from the 'old' elements and combinations at hand. This is why it is impossible to be a composer without a highly developed analytical ear: without disassembly into parts there can be no new assembly of elements and parts, or put most simply, without analysis there can be no synthesis.

A preliminary overview of the possibilities and functions of the analytical ear, a preliminary listing of its components, leads one to think that such a multi-elemental and complex activity could hardly be within the province of mere mortals, the great majority of us. But we are not speaking at this point of a very good analytical ear, the kind on which someone must depend to become a professional musician. Even a middling degree of mastery of the operational mechanisms of the analytical ear is not something granted to a great many people. Sometimes one hears the opinion voiced, apropos of the musical ear, that in the past, when people sang and played more and there was no option of giving oneself over entirely to a passive enjoyment of music through recordings, there were considerably more people with good voices and good ears. The celebrated singer Sergei Lemeshev, himself of peasant origin, would answer such pronouncements this way:

> Why did people sing so well in the old days? Was it really true that everyone was talented, everyone had a great voice? It is more likely that the real singers in the past were simply limited to those who had a voice and an ear for music. If, for example, forty people were coming home from work, no more than 20–25 of them would sing while the rest would blissfully listen to them in silence, as they lacked the ear. And if one of these non-musical types would occasionally begin to sing along, then someone next to him would say 'Stepa (or Grisha or Vanya), hold on there, you're spoiling the song'. And Stepa, embarrassed, would go silent.[6]

From Lemeshev's story one can draw two items of good news and one of bad. It is good that the musical ear of the general public is, in all probability, not getting worse; according to Lemeshev, the public's ear in the past was not all that great. It is also good that people with a passive analytical ear and the capability of distinguishing false notes from true are somewhat greater in number than those who sing beautifully and purely: there is always someone to keep the Grishas and Vanyas from ruining the song. The bad news is rather subjective: the number of people with a good ear is somewhat smaller than one would like. The spontaneous total that Lemeshev offered gives a fairly accurate starting proposition: people with a natural ear make up a little more than 50 percent of the population—which is not a small group, of course, but quite a sizeable contingent.

But an analytical ear at the professional level, as opposed to the ordinary 'good ear' that Lemeshev was referring to, is something which only an extremely small number of people can boast of. Singing a simple song in tune is one thing; recognizing the entire aggregate of complex pitch structures in all the interconnections of the elements which make them up is quite another. A very good analytical ear, as a later-appearing component of musical

---

6 Lemeshev, C. (1987) *Iz biograficheskih zapisok. Stat'i, besedy, pis'ma, vospominaniya/From Biographical Notes. Articles, Talks, Letters, Memoirs.* Moscow: Sovetsky kompozitor, p. 13.

talent (compared to the expressive ear and the sense of rhythm), is something one comes across rather more infrequently than the other musical abilities. This is hardly surprising, as reasoning in music, which is governed by the analytical ear, is a higher stage of development of the musical intellect in comparison with the spontaneous appearances of the ancient components of musicality.

The sense of musical pitch

Musical pitch is the sensory reflection of the frequency of sound. Large, deep, and weighty objects sound low and heavy. The sound itself and the image of the object which makes it both go into the definition of the sound. A long and heavy string vibrates slowly, with a frequency of around 30 hertz; large kettledrums sound low and booming. Huge, heavy objects naturally lean downward, toward the earth; as they have great weight, their 'voice', by association, calls forth a sensation of something foundation-like and supportive, a deep and large-scale sense of 'the depths', a low sound. Objects of lesser volume and mass, short strings, longitudinal pipes, sound light and fine, meaning high. The small weight, airiness, and fragile appearance by association seem to attract the object upward; and the 'voice' of such flying objects also seems light, drawn toward the heavens, in a word, high. Here we encounter a certain type of synesthesia, wherein different modalities are sensorily united: the visual and tactile impressions connected with volume and weight grow into aural impressions by association.

There is another significant basis for this tendency—to call low-frequency sounds simply 'low' and connect them with the earth, as we call high-frequency sounds 'high' and connect them with the sky—which is the acoustic, frequency-based composition of sound. If a long, low string vibrates, in its entirety and with all its parts, each of which also gives off its own sound, then all these sounds also fall into our aural range and can be recognized by the listener. This listener perceives the low sound together with many side tones and overtones, and thus the timbre of the low sound will be crude, rough, thick, even a little dirty. These quasi-tangible associations only strengthen the impression of weight and depth. If a short string vibrates, in its entirety and in all its parts, then the overtones which it issues are too high for our ear to hear—the majority of these frequencies go unregistered by humans and are cut off from the basic sound, which as a result sounds light, smooth, clean, and fine. Here the quasi-tangible associations strengthen the impression of the height, weightlessness, and fragility of the sound. So in the main musical quality of the sound, in its pitch definition, come together tactile and visual-spatial associations.

Children easily perceive the connection of musical pitch with the spatial concepts of height and depth. Kevin Durkin and Julie Townsend (1997) set out to demonstrate the presence of this perception in 6 year olds. In one subject group, the children simply sang and listened to music; in another, a teacher reminded the 6 year olds that a melody can 'walk' up and down and constantly pointed out where and how a melody was taking such 'steps', thus helping the children make aural-spatial associations. When both groups were tested later for musical pitch, it turned out that the groups in which aural-spatial associations were constantly emphasized managed to improve its test scores significantly since their previous testing before the experiment. In the group in which the children merely sang and listened without aural-spatial reinforcement, the re-test scores for musical pitch showed no improvement.

Aural-spatial associations also arise outside the analytical ear. The existence of aural-spatial connections is determined by the function of the ear in nature: hearing can function in the dark, informing man of what is going on around him during the most dangerous time of day for the species. It was critical for early man to know where a threatening sound was coming from, where a stream whose sound he had detected was located. Then as now, the connection of sound and spatial perceptions in the perception of musical pitch reflects more general qualities of aural perception. Riccardo Barbarotto and his colleagues (2001) put sound speakers from which issued loud bursts into the center and along the periphery of a dark room. The subjects, made up of musicians, conductors, and nonmusicians, were to identify where the sounds were coming from. Everyone except the conductors distinguished a single central source of the sound; only the conductors perceived that the sound emanated not only from the central speakers but from those on the periphery as well, and they correctly identified where these speakers were. The psychologists concluded that the facility for aural-spatial orientation was so well developed in conductors because of their professional experience. However the reverse is no less probable an explanation: the only musicians who can become conductors are those who were granted a voluminous sense of sound by nature, a sense which lets them correctly define what kind of sound is coming from where.

Neuropsychologists who study musical talent constantly draw attention to its connection with the spatial intellect (Hassler 1992; 1991; Hassler and Birbaumer 1986; Hassler et al. 1987). The connection has been noted in many experiments in which gifted composers and others who know how to improvise and compose demonstrate much higher results on tests for spatial perception than nonmusical people, or even people whose musical ear is not bad but who do not demonstrate creativity. Marianne Hassler and her colleagues (1985) who studied the connection of the spatial intellect and musical abilities over the course of many years confirm that a high level of musical ability, including a developed analytical ear, is inevitably connected with an understanding of spatial relations. A particularly profound connection of this type has been observed among gifted male musicians as compared to gifted females.

The connection between musical activity and spatial abilities is also in evidence in children who play keyboard instruments; as they advance in their studies, their scores in spatial tests progress likewise (Aranovsky 1974; Hodges 2005; Stough et al. 1994). Children who do not play piano, synthesizers, xylophone, or accordion have less of a chance to realize their spatial intellect to the full. Researchers claim that in the psychological sense the aural-spatial connections which stimulate play on the keyboard sharpen the understanding of spatial relationships: keyboard-experienced children perform better than their peers at tasks involving the representation of objects in cross-section, at the drawing of figures in which a folded sheet of paper is turned over, and in general at any and all spatial activities, including spatial tasks in the context of IQ testing.

Japanese psychologist Takeo Nakada (1998) demonstrated that the reading of musical notes is a specific spatial operation. A special area was discovered in the right hemisphere of the brain which is responsible for the reading of musical scores to the exclusion of all other functions. Much of the data demonstrate that our accepted understandings of 'high' and 'low', rising and falling, taking off and receding and other definitions of musical pitch are by no means metaphors. The sense of musical pitch is closely tied with spatial sensations—through the sensing of musical pitch the intellect becomes sighted. So the analytical ear, the instrument of pitch perception, makes music a spatial variety of art.

The sense of musical pitch which the analytical ear relies on is perfect in very few people. And difficulties in the recognition of the pitch of a sound have objective, indeed unavoidable, reasons as well, since musical sound is heard in the entirety of all its characteristics and qualities. The note A of the first octave with a frequency wavelength of 440 hertz can be played loudly or quietly, insistently or imploringly, sharply or softly; and the main thing to note here is that it can be played on the cello, the horn, or the violin. The sound will be perceived differently, since it is heard not only by the strict analytical ear, but also by the expressive ear, which reacts to the emotional tone of the sound's articulation. The expressive ear brings a certain confusion into our aural impressions, and thanks to its interference any differences of timbre and dynamics hinder the understanding that this is all the same A no matter who or what tries to reproduce it.

A live or complex sound is always the unity of various sound qualities, but in laboratory conditions researchers artificially remove side tones and overtones, making the so-called clear sounds, the frequencies of a certain pitch. Simple sounds are rather colorless and inexpressive, but subjects in experiments with enviable stubbornness continue to call low simple sounds 'dark' and 'thick' and high sounds 'light' and 'thin' (Ivanchenko 2001; Pitt 1994), although in reality these sounds have lost their connection with timbre and character—assigning them anything beyond a number of hertz is mere fancy. The sensation of a change in the pitch of a sound necessarily draws with it a change in the sensation of its timbre. Commenting on this reaction among subjects, Boris Teplov noted that 'in experiments with simple sounds there is a second factor involved—the carry-over into these unusual conditions of those categories of perception which were worked out during the perception of complex sounds'.[7]

Separating pitch from timbre and recognizing it as a separate and autonomous quality—this is to acquire the analytical ear. And if the expressive ear perceives sound in the integrated whole of all its qualities, as if 'percolating' the pitch of a sound in its timbre, loudness and articulation, then the analytical ear, on the contrary, separates out the pitch of a sound as its main quality and works only with it.

The inevitable kinship and connection between the expressive ear for music and the analytical ear consists in the fact that the latter is separated from the former both phylogenetically and ontogenetically: children begin to recognize the pitch of a sound as a separate quality not immediately, and not all children ever recognize it. In the scientific

[7] Teplov, B. M. (1985) Psihologiya muzykal'nyh sposobnostei/The psychology of musical abilities. In *Izbrannie trudy, t. I/Selected Works*, vol. I, (ed. M. G. Yaroshevsky). Moscow: Pedagogika, p. 124.

usage of the first half of the twentieth century the term 'musical ear' was understood to mean the dual unity of the expressive and the analytical ear, or, at other times, exclusively as the analytical ear. Boris Teplov noted that

> If we look at the definitions of the musical ear given by various authors, we find that from the point of view which interests us now they may be divided into two groups. The first group (Kries, Hacker and Ziehen) accepts those definitions which include considerations of timbre and dynamics, or both, alongside those of pitch. The other group consists of those who do not include the timbre and dynamic sides, understanding, in consequence, the musical ear exclusively as the ear for pitch (Rimsky-Korsakov, Varro and others).[8]

(B. Teplov refers to: Kries J. Ueber das absolute Gehor. Zeits. f. Psychol., 3, 1892; Kries J. Wer ist musikalisch? Berlin, 1926; Hacker V. u. Ziehen T. Ueber d. Erblichkeit der mtisika-lischen Begabung Zeits. f. Psychol., 88, 89, 90, 1922; Rimsky-Korsakov, N. A. Muzikalnie statii i zametki, St.-Petersburg, 1911; Varro M. Der lebendige Klavierunterricht, seine Methodik und Psychologle, Leipzig, 1929).

It is more convenient, of course, to separate the concepts of the expressive ear and the analytical ear so as not to confuse in the future those aspects and sides of sound which each controls.

If melodies could consist of one single repeating sound, then the analytical ear in principle could not have arisen, since it is born in the comparison of sounds by their pitch. In just this way the expressive ear is born of the comparison of sounds by timbre, loudness, and the character of sound. Light and darkness, warmth and cold, as well as all the other properties of matter (including sound) are recognized only in comparison, when we sense how a scale of measurement of this quality is formed. The pitch of a sound is revealed to the ear only in the movement of sound, when sounds or musical tones go in a defined direction, either higher or lower, after a given first sound.

The process of comparing sounds with each other is continuous up through the time when the melody ends, and the pitch of the sounds is determined only in relation to each other: a person with a good ear, even someone unable to read music, will always say that the last sound of the first phrase of the popular song 'Podmoskovnye vechera' ('Moscow Nights', or 'Midnight in Moscow' in the Benny Goodman rendition) is exactly the same as the first; that the second and fourth sounds of this phrase are identical; and that the fifth one is somewhat higher. If a soprano sings the song instead of a bass, all the sounds will move upward, but everyone who knows the song will nevertheless identify it immediately. Put otherwise, the pitch of sounds in the context of real music making is defined not so much by a scale of hertz-vibration as by the relationships of pitch within the song or piece. In vocal practice songs and romances are often specially transferred up or down in conformity with the capabilities of various voices; but for all that no one ever mistakes one song for another, whether sung by a tenor or a bass.

Two processes are at work in the establishment of the analytical ear: the separation of pitch from timbre and the recognition of musical pitch in the process of sound movement,

---

[8] Teplov, B. M. (1985) Psihologiya muzykal'nyh sposobnostei/The psychology of musical abilities. In *Izbrannie trudy, t. I/Selected Works*, vol. I, (ed. M. G. Yaroshevsky). Moscow: Pedagogika, p. 171.

in the process of comparison of sounds by pitch. In childhood musical development (ontogenesis) these two processes take place in parallel, although in certain exercises one or another side may be emphasized. In real music making the most essential thing is the continuous comparison of various sounds by pitch, the evaluation of pitch relationships of musical units from which is constructed the image of music in our understanding. The analytical ear in its most often encountered form (and almost always) acts as the so-called relative ear. The relative ear is the term used to describe any analytical ear which depends on the comparison of sounds by pitch. Only in the rarest instances is the evaluation of the pitch of a sound done without comparing it with other sounds, but by means of identifying and assigning a name to every frequency vibration, to each sound separately—an analytical ear of this kind is called perfect (or absolute) pitch.

The analytical ear manifests itself in the ability to distinguish the timbre of a sound from its pitch—and not to confuse them, even when circumstances conspire toward that end. Emmanuel Garcia (2000) assigned a group of young amateur musicians, all wind instrument players, to demonstrate their ear for pitch by two means. The first employed one of the methodologies most beloved of psychologists: 'same or different?' The subjects listened to a pair of sounds; in some instances the sounds differed in pitch, while in others the sounds were the same, but the same note was played by a French horn and a trumpet. The second means of demonstrating the analytical ear was a test of the ability to attune one's instrument to a given sound—to reproduce that sound, in short. The subjects were always inclined to 'raise' light and vivid timbres and to 'lower' dark and thick ones: if they heard the trumpet play A, in repeating it they always wanted to play higher notes, B or C. If they heard the same A from a bass clarinet, in repeating they would play it as A-flat or G, as their ear told them this thick sound was lower than it was in reality. The same held true in the exercise in comparison: the trumpet sounds seemed higher than those of the French horn simply because they were lighter and clearer. Similar experiments have only affirmed the leading role in our perception of music of the expressive ear, which controls our reaction to timbre. Can professional musicians, however, avoid mistakes in such experimental exercises? The results obtained by Mark Pitt (1994) show that they can: the professionals in Pitt's experiment distinguished timbre and pitch with assurance and without error.

Cornelia Yarbrough and her colleagues (1995) did a study of the sense of musical pitch among elementary school students who were learning to play wind instruments. In one group, the students' instruments were tuned too high; in the other, too low. The subjects were to correct the situation, of which they were told at the beginning of the experiment, and put their instruments in tune. Almost no one in either group could successfully complete the task: the 'high' group lowered their tuning, but not as much as they should have; the 'low' group, similarly, adjusted their instruments upward, but no matter how close they came to the right level, they never reached it. Of some 197 participants in the experiment, only 6 demonstrated a good analytical ear—a really highly differentiated sense of musical pitch. Such a result is hardly surprising, since in trying to tune their instruments the subjects were only allowed to use their internal sense of the right pitch—they had no model to refer to and no one to compare their results with. When the students were asked to complete an easier task, such as repeating a given note on their own instruments, twice as many succeeded (12 of the 197). Is that many or few? Probably many, because hitting the necessary note exactly and correctly tuning one's instrument are functions of which only people blessed with a good analytical ear plus considerable experience are capable. Even from this experiment it is clear that the selection of music professionals must be carried out from among an extremely limited field of candidates: one of the most important components of musical talent, the subtle and sensitive analytical ear, is very rare indeed.

Absolute pitch

Those who possess perfect (or absolute) pitch make many people green with envy. Ordinary people with a relatively good ear for music recognize the pitch of sounds by comparing them: if they have no marker, no control point for comparison, they cannot name a given sound, which someone with perfect pitch (an *absoliutnik* in Russian) can do without turning a hair. The essence of this ability has not been entirely explained; the most widely held version, in any case, is that for the absoliutnik every sound has an 'appearance' just as defined as timbre. In the same way that ordinary people easily identify their family and friends by recognizing the timbre of their voices, so those blessed with perfect pitch recognize the 'face' of every sound. As Boris Teplov put it:

> Timbre acts as a property of a separate sound as such, while pitch, as a property which characterizes sound in relation to other sounds. These definitions however, apply only to those people who do not have perfect pitch. The perfectness of perfect pitch lies in the fact that for people who have it pitch is exactly like timbre, a quality which characterizes every sound as such. [9]

It is quite probable that perfect pitch is a kind of supertimbre: when the distinctions of timbre are so fine that they touch every individual sound, which is invariably just a shade subtler and 'lighter' than its neighbor (if it is higher) or a barely noticeable shade 'darker' than the sound next door if it is lower. Gary Crummer and his colleagues (1994) assembled a subject group comprising musicians with perfect pitch, musicians without it and nonmusical people. The subjects were asked to identify the timbre of various instruments. All kinds of people recognize timbre very well, of course, so it was unsurprising that all the subjects handled the assignment quite well. But the people with perfect pitch responded much faster and with more assurance than their peers. This tells us that perfect pitch includes a timbre element, or may be taken in its entirety as a super-sensitive branch of the ear for timbre.

A number of observations by musicians themselves support the 'timbre version' of the origin of perfect pitch. The composer Sergei Taneev, for example, recalled:

> For me the sound of the note C had a very special character. I recognized it quickly and easily by this particular character of its sound, just as one immediately recognizes the face of someone one knows. The note D, on the other hand, had a completely different, but equally distinct, appearance,

---

[9] Teplov, B. M. (1985) Psihologiya muzykal'nyh sposobnostei/The psychology of musical abilities. In *Izbrannie trudy, t. I/Selected Works*, vol. I, (ed. M. G. Yaroshevsky). Moscow: Pedagogika, p. 192.

one which I could recognize and name in a moment. And indeed, so it was with all the other notes as well. [10]

The second popular version of the nature of perfect pitch puts the accent not on the timbre-sensation factor but instead on that of a super-memory for musical pitch (Levitin 1999). An ordinary mortal can remember the pitch of a given sound for a minute and a half, meaning she can repeat (recreate) it or identify it among other notes. Among musicians the memory for a note is rather better: they can reproduce a sound over the course of some 8 minutes after they have heard it. People with perfect pitch retain the pitch of a sound indefinitely. Daniel Levitin assumes that perfect pitch is, in fact, merely perfect memory, or a long-term memory which simply does not expire before its owner does.

The super-memory version is supported by data of teachers of Baroque instruments, which have a lower register than contemporary ones (Wilson 1994). On a modern violin the note A registers at 440–444 hertz, whereas on a violin from the Baroque period one hears A at 415. Students with perfect pitch initially feel a certain discomfort when they encounter the discrepancy between what is written in the score and what they hear when they play the lower tuned Baroque instruments. But then they adapt, and their perfect sense of pitch begins to 'divide', to work in two different regimes: they instantaneously recognize and name two types of sound: the first, the old one, with its computation of A as 440 hertz, and a second, a new one, in which A has 415. In this new tuning, all the sounds change their names; the sound which is now E was formerly called D. The *absoliutnik*, moreover, never confuses the two systems: he remembers the pitch of every sound in each system exactly, remaining perfect in the Baroque and contemporary registers. Beyond this, the indivisibility of pitch and timbre in any given sound does not allow one to settle on either of the two competing versions. It is entirely possible to remember the face and character of every sound both from its unique timbre and through the fixed position of its pitch and its name in the memory.

Perfect pitch comes in both active and passive forms. In the passive version the *absoliutnik* can recognize and name the pitch of a sound but if asked to sing a particular note at random she is not likely to be able to produce it at will or without trial and error. The possessor of the active version, on the other hand, can not only produce a note at will and without error, she can recognize any sound as well. In discussing the nature of active and passive perfect pitch, researchers find evidence for both timbre and pitch versions of its origins. Some suppose that passive recognition of sounds depends on timbre-perfect pitch, while the ability to reproduce sounds depends on perfect pitch as such. The question of the nature of perfect pitch remains an open one but no matter what it is that the *absoliutnik* remembers, timbre, pitch, or something else altogether, she is in any case a very rare bird: some sources say 1 percent of the general population in Europe and the United States (Ivanchenko 2001) are absolute pitch possessors, others (Takeuchi and Hulse 1993; Sacks 1995) name one in ten thousand estimation or one in 1500 among amateur musicians (Gregersen *et al.* 1999). The question of the nature of extraordinary

---

[10]   Cit. from Maikapar, C. (1938) *Gody ucheniya/Years of Studies.* Moscow-Leningrad, p. 103.

memory for sounds is specific to this very small community, but nevertheless researchers devote sufficient attention to it.

Career music professionals spend much of their time on masses of aural exercises, from their days in elementary music schools, music high schools, and then conservatories: they write musical dictations, sing by note, identify chord progressions by ear, and so on. In the work of a conductor, chorus master, singer, and in many and varied kinds of musical activity, perfect pitch helps a great deal. The colleagues of those fortunates who have perfect pitch often assign themselves the task of acquiring the gift, to work it out and earn it somehow, even when it is not in their nature. People have reported about the success of such attempts with a certain amount of optimism, especially with children, since the so-called passive version of perfect pitch, particularly when it manifests itself within familiar timbres, can be developed artificially (Miyazaki and Ogawa 2006; Russo *et al.* 2003). In Russian tradition those who wish to succeed as *absoliutniks* make themselves concentrate on the barely noticeable differences among sounds of varying pitch (Starcheus 2003; Tarasova 1988). Here is C of the first octave, weighty, a bit thick, sustained; here is C-sharp—this note is a mite sharper, seemingly more determined and compact. Then D—self-assured, somewhat brighter, flatter than C. Or E-flat—dull, off-white, mother-of-pearl-like. And so in the course of many hours of training the fanatics eventually do acquire an otherwise-heavenly-endowed perfect pitch and for a certain period can use it, if only in this passive form. But once the intensive training ceases, the 'learned' perfect pitch disappears without a trace; the skills acquired at such a cost turn out to be elusive and ephemeral.

Infants, who are in any event inclined towards manifestations of perfect pitch, can learn it even in its active form. William Kessen and his colleagues (1979) asked the mothers of a group of 3-month-old children to instill in them a particular love for the note F of the first octave. This note is convenient for a child's voice, and when the infants would start gurgling at their own pitch, the mothers were supposed to remind them of the note F, as if suggesting exactly this pitch of sound. After 40 days of such lessons the 23 infants in the experiment happily gurgled exclusively in F: they succeeded in remembering exactly this pitch and did not waiver in reproducing it. After a certain amount of time, when the idea of this particular love for F no longer obtained and the mothers had ceased their endless repetitions of the note, the infants returned to their normal gurgling, and thus the short life of this hardly emerging perfect pitch came to an end. Of many analogous trials and errors with infants, children and adults, researchers came to the preliminary conclusion that real, lasting, active perfect pitch, which does not require additional practice for maintenance, simply cannot be taught. On the other hand, the absolute pitch in its original condition may well be the result of intensive exposure to music and special music training in 'critical period' before 7 years old—one more version of its emergence supported by some researchers (Chin 2003; Levitin and Rogers 2005; Russo *et al.* 2003).

The reason behind various fiascoes in attempts to acquire perfect pitch may lie in its genetic origins, which have been demonstrated on many occasions. A report given at the American Society for Human Genetics in 1997 cited statistics from a study conducted with 600 people who possessed absolute pitch—along with their siblings, of whom an additional 25 percent also turned out to have it. When similar measurements were taken of the siblings of professional musicians who lacked perfect pitch, only 1 percent were revealed to be *absoliutniki*. Thus the geneticists confirmed the possibility of inherited origins of perfect pitch: among the relatives of those possessing it there were 25 times more with perfect pitch then among the relatives of musicians without it.

Some neuropsychologists also assume that perfect pitch may be inborn and genetically conditioned. A group led by Gottfried Schlaug (Schlaug *et al.* 1995b) conducated studies of a section of the left hemisphere of the brain, the *planum temporale*, which is slightly larger in humans than the equivalent right hemisphere. This section answers for sound differentiation, including the distinctions among phonemes, and as noted above a certain enlargement of this brain function in 'speaking man' began some eight million years ago, at the chimpanzee stage. Closer examination of modern humans reveals that the *planum temporale* among musicians with perfect pitch is even larger than it is among mere mortal *Homo sapiens*, and even larger than that of musicians who lack this gift. As the Schlaug group concluded, in an article in the *Science*, 'Research indicates that outstanding musical ability is associated with increased leftward asymmetry of cortex-subserving music-related functions'.[11]

Helmuth Steinmetz (1996), one of the neuropsychologists who conducted this experiment, added his own results to the data gathered. He measured the *planum temporale* in people who had difficulty distinguishing speech phonemes. Steinmetz found that those with a limited ability to differentiate sounds had a *planum temporale* even smaller than other people: the comparative asymmetria with the right brain hemisphere which is normal was almost altogether absent. Musicians with absolute pitch had a *planum temporale* significantly larger than people in any other group. Steinmetz theorized that all the work of differentiating the speech-music stream can be given to the *planum temporale*, and perfect pitch then can be not only a heightened ability to remember musical pitch, but a broader ability for extremely fine sound distinctions, including speech phonemes, timbres of voice and all other qualities of sound. Williams syndrome patients are also inclined to possess absolute pitch to a very high degree, that also speaks in favor of its 'nature' not 'nurture' origin (Brown *et al.* 2002).

Judging by the data of neuropsychologists and geneticists, perfect pitch, as a super-enhanced ability in sound distinction and aural memory, is not something that can be taught and developed, but something innate. 'Abandon hope all ye who enter here' should be written not only on the gates of hell but above the door of the *solfeggio* classroom of certain zealous music teachers who attract gullible students with promises of teaching them absolute pitch. The more important question lies elsewhere: does the musician really need this gift of nature? Is perfect pitch such a valuable commodity that a real musician cannot do without it? Since public attention has been focused on the

---

[11] Schlaug, G., Jaencke, L., Huang, Y., and Steinmetz, H. (1995b) In vivo evidence of structural brain asymmetry in musicians. *Science*, 267, p. 699.

phenomenon of perfect pitch many tales have been bandied about as to the almost unbelievable aural capabilities of man. But these quasi-anecdotes do not bring perfect pitch closer to music; on the contrary, they cast doubt on its usefulness as a purely musical quality, making it appear all the more a mere curiosity of nature with only the most oblique relationship to the music as an art form. There is even an assumption that the origin of absolute pitch 'may be relatively independent of musical experience' altogether (Ross *et al.* 2005).

Perfect pitch works automatically, examining everything that comes its way. Miss Sauer, a famous American *absoliutnik* and the principal keyboardist of the Chicago Symphony Orchestra, recalled how her dentist distracted her from the unpleasant business at hand by asking questions about which note the whistle of his drill was playing (Weinberger 1995b). Like the young Mozart, who could tell what notes a glass filled with water, a ticking clock and a squeaky door played, Miss Sauer could distinguish the pitch of every audible sound. At one point while she was learning of a piece of music Miss Sauer heard an unwelcome accompaniment in the form of the sound of a neighbor's lawn-mower, which whirred at the pitch of G. From that day forward, every time Miss Sauer played that unfortunate piece, in her consciousness resounded a lawnmower at that very note, and the concert piece was irretrievably lost. A colleague of Miss Sauer's, the Rev. Sir Frederick Ousley, Professor of Music at Oxford University, was likewise possessed of legendary perfect pitch (Weinberger 1995b). At age 5 he told his mother, 'Imagine, papa blows his nose in F'. He could also determine that thunder roared in G and wind howled in D. At the age of 8, listening on a hot summer day to Mozart's Symphony in G Minor, the young Sir Frederick confirmed that in reality he heard not G minor, but A flat-minor, a half-tone higher. It turned out that the boy was right: the instruments had been so heated by the weather that their tuning had risen slightly.

The conscious, logical nature of the analytical ear, including its connection with ideational speech, and the extreme, almost reflexive automatism of perfect pitch make one wonder about the different natures of the two. Much speaks to the early origin of absolute pitch, which is even more ancient than human speech. People play and sing the same melodies at different pitches, the same music can be heard anywhere you like at higher and lower pitches. The relative ear, for which is important not the absolute pitch of the performed music, but the relationships between the constituent sounds, reigns in musical creation. The same is not true for birds, who sing their 'music' at one and the same pitch: they remember not the bird-melodies but the absolute pitch of the sounds that go into them (Konishi 1994; Saito and Maekawa 1993). This aggregate of sounds is for them a sign, a signal, but not an artistic message. Dolphins likewise send out sounds at a certain pitch in which each frequency plays the role of a certain sign-signal. Animals who must communicate at great distances use the frequency of sound as the most reliable of its characteristics, that least subject to distortion. From the earliest times the frequency of sound vibrations was used to convey information in rain, snow, and storm, cutting through forests and oceans and overcoming all sound impediments. For this reason in certain kinds of animals perfect pitch evolved, making them capable of distinguishing several usable frequencies and putting them to work.

Akihiro Izumi (2000) played sounds of differing pitch, not connected by any musical idea, to adults and 8-month-old infants. The infants attempted to remember them by their absolute pitch; the adults, on the other hand, tried to interpret the sounds and turn them into something like a melody, thus remembering them as some sort of musical expression, albeit not the most successful or beautiful. Izumi concluded that 'Unlike the infants, adult listeners relied primarily on relative pitch cues. These results suggest a shift from an initial focus on absolute pitch to the eventual dominance of relative pitch, which is more useful for both music and speech processing.' [12]

English psychologists Sergeant and Roche (1973) asked children aged 3–6 years to remember melodies, judging the quality of their recall by several different parameters: the absolute pitch of the sounds, the melodic contour, the exactness of the internal-melodic intervals and the correctness of the supporting sounds in the middle and at the end of the melody. The 3-year-old subjects proved best at the exactness of reproduction of the absolute pitch; in everything else they trailed the older children by a considerable margin. The conscious perception of a melody with an understanding of the idea of the melodic contour, which reflects the general design of the intonation as well as the intervals which define this design, is an ability formed in children by exactly this time, age 6. This conclusion has been confirmed by such experts in the filed of child musical psychology as David Hargreaves and Howard Gardner, the latter having conducted a number of experiments in the field of children's artistic (including musical) perception (Gardner 1971; Hargreaves 1986).

Sergeant's work has shed light on many phenomena connected with perfect pitch. One of his claims is that almost anyone can acquire perfect pitch, if she starts the study of music in early childhood. A survey of 1500 members of the English Musical Society by D. Sergeant showed that there is a clear connection between the age at which one begins music lessons and the possession of absolute pitch. It falls away because the same music played in different tonalities is taken as practically the same; if the phenomenon which musicians call transposition did not exist, perfect pitch could be retained. Proposing this, however, would amount to utter fantasy—singing as the basis of music making could not exist without the performance of the same melodies by soprano, bass, or tenor. All the available data, including that on absolute pitch in animals (musicians sometimes refer to perfect pitch as 'dog's ear') and the ease with which infants perceive the absolute pitch of sounds, makes one wonder whether perfect pitch may not be, in fact, the highest achievement of the human ear (as is sometimes held) but rather just the opposite: an aural rudiment, a disappearing shadow of the evolutionary process, a mere trace of the aural survival strategy of our distant ancestors. In ontogenesis, in child development, which reflects phylogenesis, the historical development, one can easily see how perfect pitch, almost unnoticeably, dies out for lack of practice and support: it is necessary neither for music nor for speech, and without demand for it the vestigial remnant quietly goes the way of the human tail.

----

[12] Izumi, A. (2000) Absolute pitch in infant auditory learning: evidence for developmental reorganization. *Journal of Acoustical Society of America*, 108, p. 3073.

The musical perception of people with absolute pitch is in many respects incomplete, which to some extent blunts the envy of them on the part of their musician colleagues. Ken'ichi Miyazaki (1995) conducted an experiment to determine whether those with perfect pitch could function appropriately under conditions of out-of-tune and flawed sounds. Miyazaki's subjects were asked to compare certain sounds played for them with false-noted standards. Hearing these false standards, the out-of-tune C, E, and F sharp, the subject *absoliutniki* were so upset that they could not make any comparative comments. Musicians with relatively good natural ears went about the assigned tasks normally; the falsely set standard notes were not perceived so forcefully by them, and did not hinder them in defining distances between the false standards and the other sounds. Musicians know that those with perfect pitch often shrink away from assignments in which relative ear is necessary, since they can only rely on their perfect ones—which while a great and useful gift is clearly not all-powerful.

Yet the *absoliutniki* have their revenge, so to speak, when time comes to tune an instrument, to fix its frequency range exactly. People without perfect pitch hear musical intervals, the distances between sounds, with a certain margin of inaccuracy; within this inaccuracy the interval remains constant, even if one of the sounds is slightly raised or lowered. The aural 'measurer' of the distance in the framework of the non-perfect ear can approach a centimeter, for which the distance from one to seven will consist of six units, and if in place of one you place 1.3 or in place of seven you put 6.8 then nevertheless for the relative ear the distance will be around six. The absolute ear, on the other hand, cannot make peace with any kind of approximation of this kind, sensing any and all violations no matter how minor. Jane and William Siegel (1977) asked non-perfect-pitch musicians to identify false musical intervals in which certain sounds were slightly higher or lower than necessary; the subjects in this situation reacted very uncertainly. In actual fact, 77 percent of the intervals presented to the subjects were off-key, but the non-perfect-pitch group could identify only 37 percent. Their perfect-pitch colleagues, naturally, fared considerably better: any *absoliutnik* can distinguish the slightest false note; her internal standard of the pitch of a sound never fails her.

Knowing the ability of people with perfect pitch to recall the pitch of individual sounds, a group of four psychologists led by Edwin Hantz (1995) hoped to confirm once more their superiority, creating a task of identifying a single sound among a melange of others. The subjects were supposed to signal by saying 'There it is!' when they heard the correct sound, as various other sounds resounded around them. Confounding the researchers' expectations, those with perfect pitch and those without it performed the task equally well. That is as it should be: if there is a standard for comparison, a musician lacking perfect pitch can lag behind only in the speed of reaction, since he needs some minimal time for comparison. But when that time is not measured in milliseconds and the experiment is carried out in a normal pace, the difference in reaction time practically disappears, and those with a good relative pitch do not underperform those with absolute pitch at all.

Among the advantages ascribed to musicians with perfect pitch one often hears of so-called 'colored sound', in which musical tonalities are perceived by the listener as seemingly decorated, colored, insistently calling forth in the memory certain color associations. Nikolai Rimsky-Korsakov thought of E major as 'dark blue, sapphire, shining, night-time, dark azure' thanks to the prompting of his composer colleagues. Glinka wrote the chorus 'Lozhitsia v pole mrak nochnoi' in this key and Mendelsohn used it for the overture to *A Midsummer Night's Dream* and his famous *Nocturne*. How could one avoid 'night-time and dark azure' associations *there*? Beethoven used F major as the basis for his *Symphonie Pastorale*, which was connected to the lives of shepherds and peasants in a setting of nature, and from then on this key began to draw naturally, in the composing fraternity, toward things green. E flat major was associated with water by both Rimsky-Korsakov ('*Okean-more sinee*') and Wagner ('*The Golden Rhine*'), although Rimsky was blessed with perfect pitch and Wagner was not. This further encourages the thought that 'colored sound' is a historical and cultural phenomenon unconnected with perfect pitch. Scriabin, further, was drawn toward color-key associations, but like Wagner he did not possess perfect pitch.

Comparisons between musicians who do and do not have perfect pitch reinforce their basic equality in the principal thing: both hear and identify sound relationships and remember the pitch of sounds, but they do so using different strategies. The *absoliutnik* neither ponders nor compares, acting instantaneously, while his non-perfect pitch colleague gets the same result with a certain (minimal) amount of exertion, except in those cases in which the exactness of the tuning of an instrument must fall within a few hertz or the identification of a false note is in question. Thus one wonders whether those with absolute pitch are really to be so envied; and how, in the end, are we to interpret this gift of nature, thinking of the possibility of its rudimentary origins and the fact that a number of great composers, including Tchaikovsky, Wagner, and Scriabin, obviously got along wonderfully well without it.

The very phrases used to describe the phenomenon, 'perfect pitch' and 'absolute pitch,' clearly lead to notions of something ultimate, supremely high and unattainable. These terms reflect society's piety before perfection, at the very least because of its extreme infrequency in the population as a whole. The very possession of it suggests a superior musicality in the possessor. Yet even a cursory glance at the facts of the matter and the expert opinion available tells us that this public piety is misplaced. 'Perfect pitch is not a panacea', says Miss Sauer, who can identify the notes played by dentist's drills and lawn-mowers. 'It is only as important as what you can do with it and how you can use it' (Weinberger 1995b).

Some statistics reflect the tone of these calming tirades. If the world's population at large can be said to consist of 0.01 percent or even 0.0001 percent with perfect pitch, and among the conservatory students of Europe and America one finds a level of 10–15 percent, there is a clear quantitative break among Asians: about 65 percent of Chinese music students possess perfect pitch (Gregersen *et al.* 2000). Discussing the input of genetics and early exposure to music to the formation of absolute pitch the authors couldn't give the palm to neither of these: any of the two—early and intensive or no exposure to music under the age of 7 could neither exclude nor guarantee the appearance of absolute pitch.

Couldn't that bond between the absolute pitch and the Asians emerge most likely because of the genetic affinities of oriental languages with tonal languages? Was it not for this reason, the aural resources of Asians so exceeding those of Europeans, that the complex classical music of Europe so quickly won popularity in the Far East? It is easy for Asians to perceive the global sound constructions of sonatas and symphonies since the Asian ear is so well developed. Yet the percentage of outstanding musicians among Asians is no higher than among Europeans. One can find entirely ordinary musicians all around the world who have the gift of perfect pitch, along with various piano tuners and numbers of people who do not like music at all and take no interest in it, like Stendhal's military supply bureaucrat. As Dr. Atovsky, a professor with perfect pitch who taught a *solfeggio* class at DePaul University, put it: 'Having perfect pitch by no means makes you a good musician. It doesn't mean that you understand relationships, it doesn't mean you're good rhythmically, it simply means that you do actually have perfect pitch. Many people think that it means a lot more'(Weinberger 1995b).

That said, it is also true that among outstanding musicians, the number of *absoliutniki* is very great. At the very heights of the musical Olympus, on the level of Mozart, Bach, and Debussy and their like, the absence of perfect pitch is a rare exception. The same can be said of outstanding performers on the level of Svyatoslav Richter, Isaac Stern, and Mstislav Rostropovich. Seventy percent of outstanding violinists are reported to have the gift (Ginzburg 1966). There is clearly a certain non-correspondence here: on the one hand, perfect pitch and musical talent are obviously connected, and among musical geniuses the non-possessor is a rarity on the order of a white musician among the black titans of jazz. At the same time perfect pitch does not guarantee even passable musical abilities: indeed, beyond simple pleasures of the parlor-trick variety—being able to distinguish your front door from all others by the unique musical properties of its squeak—this gift of nature offers no promises whatsoever.

Even a superficial analysis of the aural capabilities of the great brings a certain clarity to the mythology of absolute pitch. As Camille Saint-Saens observed:

> When I was two and a half years old I found myself in front of a little piano which had not been played for several years. Instead of banging away in any old fashion, as children usually do, I played one key after another, not striking a new one until the sound of the last key had completely died out. My grandmother explained the names of the notes to me and sent for a piano tuner to bring the instrument back into playable form. As he was doing this I was in the next room, from where I amazed everyone by naming the notes as each was played by the tuner. I know these details not from the recounting of others: I remember them wonderfully myself. [13]

The surprising thing in Saint-Saens' story is by no means the early appearance of perfect pitch (which normally manifests itself quite early); nor is it not the fact that the child could identify all the notes after having heard them only once (which is the essence of absolute pitch). What surprises is the early awakening in the child of the love of music— the attentive listening to the sounds, the enormous interest in them, the treatment of the

---

[13] Cit. from Teplov, B. (1947) *Psihologiya muzykal'nyh sposobnostei/The Psychology of Musical Abilities.* Moscow: Pedagogika, p. 136.

piano as a conversation partner who needed to be heard out rather than a toy which one whacked at to produce a jingle-jangle response. The composer Darius Milhaud also recounts something similar when he, as a toddler who could barely reach the piano keys, discovered perfect third intervals with his fingers and cried for joy at their beauty (Milhaud 1995). In the St.- Saens' story the depth of the impression produced on the boy by the as yet unorganized sounds also strikes one; the impressions were so great that they remained with the composer into his adult years. For many typical perfect pitch possessors it is more important and entertaining to describe how they heard the sound of their soccer ball as A natural and how they can distinguish (as could one of Boris Teplov's subjects) that their house keys used to jingle a half tone lower than they do now.

The boyhood story of composer Charles Gounod who heard the complaining cries of a woman selling street wares in the minor third interval 'C-E flat' is quite characteristic (Teplov 1947). 'That woman who is crying—she is shouting in C!' the boy remarked. First to react to the woman's shouting was the boy's expressive ear for music, which gave him to understand that the cry was one of complaint, that the music was crying. The thought behind what was said, expressed in musical intonation, solidly merged in the young Gounod's mind with the notes which expressed the thought. This is a model of genuine, high-level perfect pitch which is brought forth as the strengthening of all the musical resources of the mind—the expressive ear, the sense of rhythm, and the analytical ear which relies on them both. Perfect pitch may be rudimentary in origin, an atavism, but it is retained in gifted musicians, on the one hand, and ordinary 'tuners', on the other, for different reasons. Outstanding musicians are gifted in things aural not specifically with perfect pitch: their common elevated musicality, their sensitivity to the ideation of sound strengthens all their sound differentiating capabilities, including perfect pitch. The latter does not fade away in the mind of outstanding musicians because it includes itself into the context of other aural data, among which necessarily figures an excellent relative ear: an outstanding musician equally freely uses his perfect pitch and relative ear, if such is needed. Highly gifted musicians are recruited, as a rule, from among people with perfect pitch of the 'first sort'—who make up the expected majority among the residents of the musical Olympus.

Those who have perfect pitch of the 'second sort'—those who might be called the 'tuners'—are hardly musical: their perfect pitch might be only a rudiment, a vestigial curiosity of nature. Sometimes in a family of musicians this rudiment is retained because a child is overwhelmed with aural impressions, his hearing apparatus has to work overtime. Beyond this, the children of musicians have an inherited tendency toward the retention of perfect pitch. However in all such cases the tendency toward retention does not come from inside the mind, from inside the awakening musicality, and as a result what sometimes develops is 'dead' perfect pitch, which can spur one toward the choice of music as a profession. In this the recognized fetishism of the phrase 'absolute pitch' will play its treacherous role: the apparent mastery of the principal assets of the profession hide a bitter truth from this pseudo talent: nature presented him, in perfect pitch, not with a real creative gift but only a surrogate.

Even if perfect pitch and its retention are summoned by internal reasons, and a child is really favored with a wonderful expressive ear, a good sense of rhythm, and even a fine relative ear, all these qualities together do not mean that musical talent is necessarily present. These aural qualities are operational ones which allow one to disassemble the musical fabric, understanding why it is constructed in this way rather than some other. But these aural qualities do no signify that the *absoliutnik* has even a dollop of musical fantasy, imagination, and artistry. He is still far from meeting the demands which society puts before gifted performers and composers. In addition, in the musical profession it is altogether possible to get by with a good relative ear—a fact which once again saves society from indulging in too extravagant transports of delight before the 'magical' qualities of perfect pitch, whose yet unknown, but possibly rudimentary origins and basically unconscious, reflexive nature once more underline that the concept of 'perfect pitch' is but another myth. Whether to believe in it or not is something we all decide for ourselves.

The sense of the musical interval

Musical speech, just as the speech of words, is divided into expressions, each of which is a relatively complete thought. In music the thoughts expressed are colored by a certain communicative intention, a certain relationship to what has been said and a relationship to the listener. In the cultures of antiquity there were no purely informational or philosophical modes of communication, where the emotional-affective side would be relegated to the background; the communication of the ancients was quite direct and pragmatic. From this point of view musical expression in its earliest forms resembled dramatic dialogue which was always directed at the listener and engendered a certain interaction with him: it delivered the intention of the speaker to the interlocutor and inspired the latter to a certain responsive reaction. It is no accident that the art of the theater is the oldest form of art, growing as it did naturally from the ritual dance-songs of antiquity. As the theater historian Vladimir Volkenshtein pointed out,

> Live dramatic dialogue always involves finding out, ferreting, investigating and interrogating; or coaxing and admonition; or request and extortion; or seduction, temptation and revenge; or reproach and accusation; or indignation, affront, challenge and attack; or warning and advice; or defense, justification of someone and the like. Or it is a diversion away from attack, seduction and so on, diversion by means of hiding something, silence, removal to one side. In a word, dramatic dialogue presupposes willed force—it is action in the form of words. [14]

In music the communicative intention of the speaker is discerned by the listener's expressive ear, which identifies one of its external manifestations—the direction of the melodic movement, its curve formed by the rising and falling voices. If it is a case of 'challenge, affront and attack', then this will be a strong speech 'gesture' with a vividly expressed culmination, as if driven from the bottom up, exclaiming and affirming—the communicative archetype of invitation corresponds to such an expression. If it is a case of 'coaxing, admonition or request', then the likely approach is that of a descending melody where the voice is insistent and at the same time complaining about something, moaning to

---

14 Volkenshtein, V. (1931) *Dramaturgiya/The Drama*. Moscow-Leningrad: Academia, p. 113.

someone; the voice creates amphibrachic phrases with relieved beginning, a deep sigh and a soft conclusion.

In order to distinguish the type of melodic contour which surrounds diverse musical rejoinders, the resources of the expressive ear are sufficient: it easily identifies the direction of the melodic movement, its ascents and descents, its loops and zigzags. However, on this territory the expressive ear encounters the developing analytical ear: the focused and integrated perception, attendant to the expressive ear, already contains in itself the seeds of a more detailed penetration into the audited expression, a more detailed audio perception of each combination, each sound streak and each sound point. And in the same way that the sense of musical pitch was derived from the syncresis of the timbre and pitch of a sound, so from the syncresis of the musical contour and the direction of movement is derived the sense of interval, the feeling of distance between two sounds, two points on the integrated melodic line. The appearance of the sense of interval, which differentiates separate steps on the wide melodic curve, signifies a new step in the formation of the analytical ear.

In the early stages of its establishment the sense of interval exists in the context of the expressive ear, only promising to appear—such is the process of development of the analytical ear, both in phylogenesis, over the course of the development of the human race, and in ontogenesis, over the course of the formation of a separate human being. In this period the whole expression is thought of as some sort of synthesized 'meta-interval', with its beginning, culminating point, and end. Musical styles, taking their beginnings from the most ancient forms of music making (such as the Gregorian chant in the west and the *znamennoe penie* in Russia) imagined any musical expression in exactly this way: it had a point of departure, a central supporting tone, and a completing foundation.

The sense of interval, which fixes the distance between two separate sounds—melodic points—was formed as a psychological instrument-marker between the beginning of the movement and its center, and between the center of the movement and its completion. Each of these points was invariably lower or higher than the other: in order to overcome the small distance an almost-insignificant voice tension was necessary, while to overcome a large distance, tension of the vocal cords became more obvious. The overcoming of the distance between sound points was sensed as the given interval, experienced by the audio-motor voice tension. In its formation the sense of interval also relied on the sense of musical pitch and the sense of audio-spatial relationship between the noted points of a melodic curve. The interval could be felt as wide or close: it could cover a wide distance, demanding great 'vocal expenditures', or a small one, which did not. So it was that in the sense of the interval its two components merged: on the one hand was the audio-motor, which fixed the degree of tension of a vocal step; on the other there was the audio-spatial, which relied on the synthetic, audio-visual representation of the melodic distance which was crossed.

At the beginning stages of the establishment of musical abilities and musical perception, the contour of the expression and the melodic curve embracing it form the main distinguishing feature which indicates that namely this melody, and not some other one, is in force here. In exercises making this kind of identification the analytical ear is the leader, despite the fact that the internal-melodic relationships of the sounds thus escape the subject's attention, remaining unidentified: the entire melody is perceived as one integral expression, as a particular 'meta-interval' with a beginning, a middle, and an end. Henry Chang and Sandra Trehub (1977) demonstrated in an experiment that infants have the ability to distinguish melodies from each other by melodic contour, without reference to the absolute pitch of the sounds.

Five-month-old subjects were played six-tone melodic phrases. Over the course of the experiment the phrases were played higher and lower, alternatively, that is, at differing levels of absolute pitch (the process of transposition, as musicians call it), but each time the phrases were themselves the same, with the same melodic contour. In some cases, however, the sounds which formed the first phrase were regrouped in such a way that the general melodic contour was changed: an adult listener would say that the melody was no longer the same. The infants were, as it turned out, of the same opinion—their sense of interval had already begun to be formed.

The technology used for this experiment was quite clever and, in a certain sense, unique. The infant listeners' heartbeats were monitored: when such subjects hear something new, their heart rate slows down: they freeze in uncertainty, struggling to recognize the new phenomenon and take in the new information. If the infants do not perceive anything new in their environment, then their heartbeat registers as normal. Hearing the transposed melodies during this experiment, where the initial melodic contour was maintained (the rise and fall of the sounds remaining the same), the infants continued to enjoy the sound peacefully: their heartbeat did not react to anything. But if the melodic contour was changed, independent of whether the music was played in the initial absolute pitch or as a 'spoiled' melody which moved higher and lower, the infants' heart rate immediately slowed down regardless, as if to say 'Attention, we are encountering a new object!'. Such was the idea behind the signal which the audio perception sent to the young listeners' brains. As the experimenters concluded, 'The infants reacted to the new melody by means of slowing their heart rate, but did not so react to the transposed old one—thus indicating their sensitivity to the change of musical contour'.[15]

American psychologists William Dowling and D. S. Fujitani (1971), relying on similar experimental technology but using adult nonmusicians as subjects, tested for a more highly developed sense of interval. In this case the subjects did not simply have to understand whether they were dealing with a familiar melody in transposed form or with a new melody using similar intervals: they were played three variations of the melodies—some which retained the general contour of the melodic movement, but contained within them certain micro-deviations (an initial step of D-E-G might be replaced by one of D-F-G, say); some with a similar, but not identical, motif inscribed into the same contour; and some which were simply not the same melodies, disrupting the initial contour altogether.

---

[15] Chang H. and Trehub S. (1977) Auditory processing of relational information by young infants. *Journal of Experimental Child Psychology*, 4, p. 324.

The experimenters did not impose their criteria of old and new on their subjects and did not tell them which differences they should evaluate as 'the same melody' and 'another melody'. The overwhelming majority of the subjects preferred to orient themselves using the melodic contour as the leading indicator, the basis on which a melody would be judged 'the same, not a different one'. In other words, for adult subjects the sense of interval is 'a leader' more often than not in the same condition as it is for infants: listeners are concerned only about the beginning, middle, and end in their principal pitch relationships; lesser variations of pitch within the melody are of lesser concern. In similar cases professional musicians are not inclined to qualify melodies with a similar contour but with different internal-melodic relationships as identical: their analytical ear and sense of interval are much more highly developed and they perceive each internal-melodic step as significant. Such differences between professional and amateur listeners have been noted by psychologists studying the audio resources of nonmusicians (Cutietta and Booth 1996; Siegel and Siegel 1977).

Lyle Davidson asked a group of adult nonmusicians to sing the well-known tune 'Happy Birthday' and in the course of his experiment he came to understand that the sense of interval predominates like the sense of melodic contour, without internal differentiation: the subjects sang, merely approximately observing the correct direction of the melodic movement. The author thus concluded that 'Melody's understanding by non-musicians is static, it's mechanical recall without reflection, like rendering without understanding. Song is a formalized musical sign taken as a whole but not as the interconnection of independent parts, involved into some relations'. [16]

One's own singing as an active function imposes on the development of the ear higher demands than mere identification. Nicholas Long (1972) asked a group of school children to perform a relatively easy task—differentiating an original melody from distorted versions of it. In the first test case the melody retained the general melodic contour but the internal-melodic relationships were changed; in the second the opposite was in effect: the entire melody, completely retained and without distortions, was simply transposed higher and lower. The majority of the subjects could distinguish the true melodies from the distorted ones—that is, their sense of interval extended further than the identification of the melodic contour in its most synthesized form. But they could not indicate, the author observed, where exactly, in what particular place, the melody had been 'injured'; they could not identify which melodic fragment it was that had been distorted, much less what exactly constituted the distortion.

The retention of the melodic contour as the representative of the melody and as the leading sign of its identification and recognition was a great evolutionary step in the developmental path of the analytical ear and the establishment of the sense of interval. In nature an integrated expression is firmly tied with its purely audio characteristics, with its absolute pitch: neither the spatial design of the melody nor the tensing–relaxing of vocal

[16] Davidson, L. (1994) Songsinging by young and old: a developmental approach to music. In *Musical Perceptions*, (R. Aiello and J. Sloboda). New York: Oxford University Press, p. 127.

cords during its enunciation serves for further formation of the sense of interval in birds or in other singing animals. The inability to transpose the expressed musical thoughts, to carry them over to another pitch is the chief sign of the absence of the sense of interval. Stewart Hulse and Suzanne Page (1988) made a special study of this question based on the singing of the starling, and came to the conclusion that birds memorize pitch patterns on the basis of the absolute pitch of the tones that go into them—they do not know transposition and have no sense of interval.

The sense of interval in humans is a sign of the merging of the affective-ideational direction of an expression and its audio integrity, its intonational profile. The sense of interval is born, embracing entire melodies as individual expressions and not knowing yet how to distinguish within them finer ideational units. However in the course of the evolution of the analytical ear the sense of interval becomes increasingly differentiated and detailed, and it can 'pick out' as if with a magnifying glass the most subtle melodic steps and turns, identifying each as a micro-expression. Thus each tiny stage of a musical thought acquires comprehensibility and independence: now it is both a constituent part of a larger thought and also a relatively independent internal movement, a micro-phrase which the analytical ear, refining and sharpening, already notes and identifies. Evidence of this may be found in the well-known technique of memorizing musical intervals as starting points of familiar melodies, in which each interval is a micro-thought, a micro-step, a micro-exertion.

The piano keyboard features only 12 sounds; the possible distances between them, before all are used up, number 11. Musicians know their names well; each name is a defined distance between sounds, a kind of micro-melody of two tones which has a character of its own. This character is connected with the overtone relationships between the sounds; if the neighboring sounds have very few corresponding overtones, then the interval will consist of sound-competitors which try to overcome each other in a kind of enmity. If, however, there are many common overtones, then the two sounds will strive to merge into one another, providing each other with a kind of echo, reverberation, and reflection. When the quantity of overtones is neither great nor small, the effect of joint singing of sounds arises, a consonantal duet: the sounds neither merge entirely nor do they strive to crowd each other out. Thus music creates a sort of ideal for the relationships between all elements of matter, the best version being a golden mean: both similarities and differences, if they are too great, will prove equally fatal to harmony and concord.

The octave is the biggest interval and resembles a melodic echo of the basic sound, its repetition in another register. The fifth is a sense of spaciousness, of the lightness of overcoming a melodic step, but also conveys a sense of a certain emptiness and transparency; it is a sign of doubt and instability. A fourth is aggressive and tenacious; thirds and sixths, minor and major, sing, merging agreeably; seconds and sevenths, also minor and major, slither onto one another and resound sharply, pointedly. These intervals took on their significance inside the melodies, particularly when they stood in the most noticeable place—first. The potential of the meanings of intervals, their spatial and vocal image became settled, migrating from one melody to another; then the best method of recognizing melodic intervals and, correspondingly, the best means of forming the sense of interval, became singing them aloud for further comparison with popular melodic examples. The beginning of the revolutionary '*Internationale*' and of the Soviet (and now once more Russian) national anthem consist of martial fourths. The beginning of Glinka's romantic '*Ne iskushai*' is a melancholic minor sixth. If one hears any interval and repeats it vocally, a well-known song will easily suggest exactly what interval the person is singing.

James Smith and his colleagues (1997) confirmed once more the melodically ideational nature of the sense of interval which is formed at the point when the distance between sounds is conceived and realized in accordance with known melodic examples. One group of early elementary school subjects could recognize intervals when prompted: the experimenters explained to the children that the intervals to be played for them could be found in the well-known tunes '*Greensleeves*', '*Cumbahyah*', and '*Here Comes the Bride*'. At first the subjects repeated vocally the intervals they heard played on the piano, and then they tried to name them, comparing them with the sung examples. A second group of children of the same age worked without prompting: they were simply given abstract examples of intervals, told their names, and tasked with remembering how each interval sounded. When asked to identify intervals subsequently played for them, the childrens' only basis for comparison was the abstract sounds they had heard, which they may or may not have been able to commit to memory.

The experimenters recorded that the successes of the first group, which was helped by familiar song melodies, and the second group, which was not, were not at all comparable: very few of the children in the 'abstract' group could recognize the same intervals that the 'song' group members could identify easily. The researchers concluded that only conscious pronunciation, the inclusion of an ideational context, could noticeably stimulate the formation of a sense of interval—a sense which is stored up in the course of conscious musical-vocal intoning and, if divorced from conscious musicalized speech, which is what singing is, the sense of interval cannot be established and will not function. During the stages of its establishment the sense of interval should rely on expression-intoning, and only later can it give the analytical ear particular 'constructs' of sound distances (interval patterns). These observations once more confirm the wisdom of viewing the musical art as the art of intoned thought—without melody, through the sense of interval as 'micro-thought', one of the primary components of the analytical ear cannot be formed.

The ideo-aural path is the way of the formation of musical ability, the sense of interval in the given instance. But the very existence and growth of the sence of interval presupposes an already defined degree of abstraction, assuming a distinct independence of the concept of the interval. By analogy, geometric abstractions such as the circle, rectangle, and triangle need, in the beginning stages of their formation, both substantive and visual support; only later can they function separately, as abstract-spatial categories of consciousness. The components of our intellectual and sensory abilities are formed in a pragmatic and logical manner, in life experience and practice; in music they are formed in the realization of elements and means of conscious sound communication.

At the same time in professional activity that sort of pragmatic approach is not enough: here one needs abstract representations of sound categories, formalized and generalized, relatively independent of their original affective content. The ability to form such categories serves as the basis for a good analytical ear; in relation to the sense of interval this ability signifies the skill of recognizing intervals without any melodic support, relying solely on the knowledge of the corresponding construct pattern.

A team of three psychologists led by David Howard (Howard *et al.* 1992) divided a group of adult subjects according to their musical ability. In addition to their musical accomplishments (or lack thereof), criteria for the division of the group included various standard tests which were administered to determine the subjects' musical data: ear for music, sense of rhythm, memory for pitch, and so on. All subjects were required to perform two tasks: in the first they were to distinguish between major and minor thirds; both intervals are harmonious and singable, the distance between the two sounds is in both cases rather small, but if you play and sing them one after another, one can get by without a highly developed sense of interval. In short, the task is one that will rarely seem difficult to a subject. In the second task the subjects were no longer to distinguish these same major and minor thirds one from another, but instead use them as abstract patterns. The subjects were played major and minor thirds in random order and required to name them. There were many examples, and without a formed sense of interval, including on the abstract level, the labeling of major and minor thirds proved very difficult.

There was a marked correlation between the musical abilities of the subjects and success rates at the second task. Those for whom the sense of interval became the center for particular musical understandings, who knew how, on the basis of these formed understandings, to act in a situation requiring labeling, were the most musical. Thus the experimenters conformed the link between the formed sense of interval and musical abilities. At the source of these abilities lies the sense of interval as an integrated melodic contour. In the most musical among us the sense turns into a highly differentiated and detailed categorical awareness of the 'musical molecules', the melodic micro-movements, each one of which occupies a definite and distinguishable place among others like it, being the 'cornerstone' of musical expression.

Modal sense/the sense of tonality

In deepest antiquity, at the origins of music and speech, all peoples expressed themselves in similar fashion. Threat and supplication; ingratiating flattery and harsh insistence; a mother's lullaby, and the cry of the victorious soldier—all these differed very little from one person to another. Thus ethnomusiclogist Edward Alekseev (1986) speak only of types of musical expression, their social and communicative role, and say nothing of differences in their purely musical formation. At the dawn of civilization the human ear reacted only to the primordial thought of an expression; if there had been a musical chronicle in those primitive times, something which recorded the first musical manifestations of ancient man, it would have had little specific to set down: the ancestors of the Greeks, Egyptians, Chinese, and Hindus simply formed the idea of a sound and a sound relationship on the simplest, most rudimentary ideational bases. This was the kingdom of the expressive ear for music, a time before even the first signs of national identity—in terms of language, society, or culture—had appeared.

The emergence of the analytical ear began with the sense of musical pitch and the sense of interval; the expressive ear, perceiving the sound fabric ever more subtly and with ever greater differentiation, gave birth to ever more perfect audio instruments—now it could separate sound into timbre and pitch, and could perceive the simplest two-tone intonation as a sort of micro-expression—an independent interval. The sense of pitch and sense of interval came to distinguish themselves more and more clearly from the expressive ear, turning into a starting point for the next, higher stage of musical consciousness—the analytical ear which details and distinguishes the musical whole.

In the joint process of the birth of music and speech, an increasing 'manners of speech' of different peoples manifested themselves; in the course of time people began to live in different conditions, each formed its own daily routine and social system which, as the distance from the primitive world grew, became greatly individualized. Reflecting the difference among human types with a particular type of thought pattern and feelings, some hundreds of thousands of years ago national languages began to form. Each was marked by its own scale of sounds and intonations, giving birth to the melody of speech of each national group. The bird-like chatter and water-falling melodiousness of Chinese speech could not be confused with the measured descending cadences, moving like a cavalry column, in the melody of the language of the Romans.

The music of a people, having given birth to a language and expressing a frame of mind, had its own characteristic melodic movements and its favorite motifs. This music was constantly drawn toward the same intervals, while at the same time seemingly repelled others; the melodies of peoples and races, their songs and ditties insistently cultivated the same refrains, phrases, and sequences. Along with the speech and language of a people its musical speech was formed: these two types of speech, born together, strongly resembled each other. The people of the Orient preferred flowery melodies which fluttered like a kite—these melodies were themselves like the languages of the east, which remind one of the rug fabrics and designed links of Asian ornaments. The people of the west preferred direct and clear lines, where the sound bases did not slide and did not vibrate as in the Orient but related to one another instead on the ground of multi-functionality and mutual deference. A different logic of thought gave rise to different logic of language and speech— and a different logic of sound connections, which shone through, and continues to do so today, in the music of different peoples and races. Even now, in the times of 'global village', as Aniruddh Patel and Joseph Daniele found, French-composed tunes show a great rhythmic and phrase-pattern relativity to French language and English-composed tunes to English language. 'Thus',—conclude the researchers, —'there is an empirical basis for the claim that spoken prosody leaves an imprint on the music of a culture'.[17]

---

[17] Patel, A. and Daniele, J. (2003) An empirical comparison of rhythm in language and music. *Cognition*, 87, p. B35.

After many thousands of years, along with a typical selection of speech phonemes and rules for their combination into words and phrases, the typical selections or 'registers' of musical sounds and possibilities for combining them were also formed: characteristic and typical melodic phrases in the context of a one particular musical culture might be extraordinarily rare in another. The beloved musical sequences and melodies, like every living organism, gave birth to the main characteristic of any system: multifunctionality. And just as movement in the natural world is stimulated by differences in pressure, which direct matter from the area of highest pressure to the area of lowest, and just as electric current is channeled by the difference of positive and negative charges, the stream of sounds is directed by the notions of a musical base and non-base, and musical support and non-support. The concepts of base and support in music are analogous to the speech tone which makes itself felt at the ends of phrases through a natural falling of the voice. Thus it is with speech itself: an expression begins as a search for a thought, as a process of rummaging around—and eventually arrives at its destination, completed and articulated, relaying the thought behind it by forming it into the appropriate words and phrases.

Every nation formed a selection of necessary and usable sounds to express its musical thoughts, organizing and creating both 'active' sounds, which in turn attracted others, and 'passive' sounds, which themselves needed support and strove toward it. Yet the concrete organization of such intonational systems, born of the particularities of the musical speech of a people, was directed by these very particularities. In some sound systems non-base was drawn to base very emphatically and definitively, in others very softly and to an extent voluntarily, in various fashions; in some sound systems there were certain bases which competed against each other in the course of the development of the melody, while in others there was but a single base. Sometimes the base sound was manifest in the very beginning, as often happens in European music of the seventeenth to nineteenth centuries, and sometimes the melody itself, as in certain Oriental and Middle Eastern cultures, takes on the search for that base by means of self-development and self-movement and confirms it only at the end of the path. The composition of possible sounds included in the melody might be given at the beginning or, on the contrary, might be developed in the course of the musical movement. It is impossible to describe the whole cornucopia of sound organisms, with their differentiated sound composition and the relationships of their base/non-base rules of formation, which gave birth to the music of various peoples. The historically formed systems of sound, which regulate the integrated whole of the sound relationships in the context of musical cultures, came to be called the modal systems or modes. There are also more individualized modal systems which regulate the life of separate aspects and genres of music.

The role in the musical arts of modal systems resembles the roles which language groups and even racial 'root languages' play in speech. The storehouse of musical languages-modal systems of the nomadic steppe peoples (Kazakhs, Mongols, Kirgiz, and Buryats) are related, although even here national-modal particularities can be found. Also related are the modal systems of the Far East peoples and those of European musical cultures in which they manifest the peculiarity of restrained and underemphasized musical speech, as for example the Estonians and Finns, in contrast to the broadly sung and seemingly limitless 'flowing' speech of the Russians. The psychological instrument with the help of which modal systems are attached to the consciousness and with the help of which the analytical ear recognizes the algorithms lying at their base is called the *modal sense.*

The word for mode in Russian (*lad*—pronounced *laht*) brings to mind agreement, peace, and a harmonic system of relationships; it also suggests a storehouse (*uklad*) where it is understood that at base there is a certain order, arrangement and law, and the rule of peaceful co-existence among variegated things and elements is in force. In English the corresponding word for the Russian understanding of *lad* is *mode*—which suggests arrangement, manner of action, and form. The Russian concept of tonality or the pitch position of *lad* is expressed in English by *key*—bringing to mind the essential bases and relationships which form a system. The historically formed sense of *lad* presupposes the understanding of the laws to which the system is subject. In comparison to the sense of interval, at whose base lies the relationship between two sounds, and also in comparison with the sense of musical pitch, for which the sensation of sound movement (to another pitch, even a neighboring one) is sufficient, the sense of *lad* lies much higher on the evolutionary axis. It presupposes the ability to act within the formed system and understand its algorithms.

The sense of interval is born of separate expressions; the sense of *lad*/mode is born of language relationships which regulate the unlimited entirety of such expressions. That is the modal sense, in comparison to the sense of interval, is the next step in the structure of the analytical ear; this step signifies the mastery of musical language, positioning itself amid the field of other languages. In other 'musical languages' the system of sound relationships is arranged differently and governed differently. In the sense of mode the analytical ear moves from the single to the general, from a selection of various element-intervals to the rules of their life inside the system; with the help of the modal sense the analytical ear masters musical speech. If with the help of the sense of musical pitch and the sense of interval a person can master phonemes, words and sentences of musical language, then with the help of the modal sense *Homo musicus* began to speak: all his expressions became part of a unified stream of speech, directed by the logic of a musical thought.

The modal sense relies on the knowledge of stereotypes of sound relationships, accepted in a given mode. When someone acquires great familiarity with melodies which belong to a certain mode, he begins to treat this particular mode as something like a 'musical native language'. The sound order of the mode becomes known to him, the entirety of its component sounds; he begins to sense the basic sounds of the mode as the centers of gravity to which the other parts are drawn and sense the non-base sounds as incomplete sounds which strove toward resolution. In the oldest and simplest modes the system was constructed on a minimal representation from the roles of the mode, which then consisted of several sounds among which the base sound would be only one; the other sounds would gravitate toward the central sound with approximately the same strength—thus between them, the non-base sounds, there was no particular differentiation. Such a mode can suit an 'authoritarian musical regime' where there is no complex system of checks and balances, where there are no 'alternative centers of power' in the figure of several bases and where there is no division of functions between non-bases—they all sound like 'non-leader' before the 'sole leader'. The sense of mode was historically formed in the context of just such very simple modes.

More complex modes, to which the European major and minor belong, consist of a much larger number of sounds. In major and minor there are formally only seven stages, in reality all the non-base stages—II, IV, VI, or VII—can be raised and lowered, producing several more sounds of the mode. The base sounds—I, III, and V—are divided by the degree of stability, retaining, however, their supportive functions, and there are only three of them; non-base sounds in different ways gravitate toward the main, central foundation and toward neighboring bases. All this creates a very rich system of possibilities, in which each sound, each stage of the mode, possesses an enormous potential of degrees of gravity and degrees of support: the functional relationships in such a mode are extraordinarily rich, and the modal sense raised by such a mode, is distinguished by the finest differentiation of sound relationships: each stage has its own aural tint defined by the modal function of that sound and its role in the multivarious system of modal sound relationships. This kind of complex mode in certain respects reminds one of a 'democratic system of musical government' as it has several centers of power, with internal differentiation, both in the framework of the power structures themselves and in the framework of the structures of the governed. Coincidentally or not, modes of the 'authoritarian' type are most often found in the east, while those of the 'democratic' profile are preferred in the west.

In knowing a certain modal system, the listener receives a unique opportunity to enter into a dialogue with sound matter: a musical tone can hardly sound out before the listener responds to it internally, as though continuing its movement; she hears the subsequent step of the musical thought, anticipates it and, hearing the real next sound, either conforms her expectation or is disabused of it. In this way the modal sense magnifies by several orders the degree of the listener's involvement in the musical experience, making her a participant in the music making even if she is not really singing or playing. Any musical perception is built on the mechanism of anticipatory hearing since 99 percent of the music performed in the world is written in one mode or another. Even avant-garde music, which denies the modal sense, is nevertheless perceived willy-nilly in the context of a modal orientation, the only possible one for the majority of listeners.

Is a dialogue of listeners with music reality or illusion? In other words, does the sense of mode really direct the musical perception into dialogue, where certain musical events are expected in the highest degree and others are unexpected? Many musical-psychological experiments have tried to establish the phenomenon of anticipatory hearing, including those performed by Marion Pineau and Emmanuel Bigand (1997). The first of the sequences played for a group of adult nonmusicians ended on the central base of the mode, called the tonic. The second sequence was constructed in such a way that its ending sounded unexpectedly off-base—the listeners would sooner expect to hear in this place a tonic, but instead heard a non-base chord of a subdominant. In the measurements of the brain's reactions to both sequences it emerged that the reaction of the brain to the expected ending of the first sequence happens faster than the reaction to the unexpected ending of the second: in the first instance the brain of the subjects seemingly 'hurries on' the expected event, as if trying to hasten it. The sense of mode really does make us hear music as a system of events which come about with different degrees of expectation. This experiment and others like it confirm that mode and modal sense belong not to the theory of music as such but in fact make up the reality of music perception.

The activity of the modal sense explains why simpler melodies are more easily remembered: all the sound relationships in them are more predictable and more expected—a person can easily become a participant in the music making when he understands entirely how and why every musical sound came to be in its place. Mark Schmuckler (1997) confirmed these suppositions when he asked college students to identify melodies recently played for them, some of which consisted of predictable and expected sound sequences and some of unexpected sound combinations. The melodies of the first type were remembered much more easily. These small melody segments were then put inside other, broader melodies; in these more complicated conditions the melodies with the expected and predictable melodic turns were found easily by the subjects, while the unexpected melodies, the internal logic of which was not understood, completely dissolved in the new context—none of the subjects recognized them as familiar.

The modal sense is the systems operator of musical abilities, harmonizing the entirety of the interdependencies between sounds, the whole system of their functional relationships; it defines how the lower lying layers of the analytical ear, the sense of pitch and the sense of interval are going to work. The modal sense is capable of swallowing the sense of interval, replacing it and forcing it out. The great pianist and composer Ferucco Buzoni conducted a clever experiment using his musician-guests as subjects (Barinova 1964). He played them a chromatic scale in which the sounds stood apart from one another not by half tones, as usually happens, but by one-third tones—and the guests did not realize that the scale was completely off-key and consisted entirely of incorrect intervals. If in any mode any of the half-tones were to be replaced by a one-third tone, the wrong note would be detected instantly. In this case the changed degree of the mode would have been completely unlike itself, it would have lost the uniquely inherent level of gravity which every musician senses as the irreplaceable face of this and only this degree. In the chromatic scale all the sounds are equally great and equally significant; in this artificial mode there are (were) no modal functions. And Buzoni's guests were right in a way in not recognizing anything wrong since the chromatic modal system as a system of relationships of equally significant sounds in essence is the same, independent of the distance interval which separates these sounds. So Buzoni showed his friends and the world the all-powerful nature of the sense of mode, overcoming as it did the sense of interval and the sense of musical pitch.

The sense of mode creates in man a certain inertia in the perception of musical pitch which he cannot imagine outside the mode. Marc Perlman and Carol Krumhansl (1996) asked six Javanese and six European musicians to judge how on-key or off-key were some 36 intervals. The Europeans made mistakes in judging the pitch of the sounds, coming from typical European-tempered modes, where the tuning is carried out in half-tones; the Javanese made completely different mistakes, 'drawing out' the sounds they heard toward the two systems of tuning accepted in Javanese music, *slendro* and *pelog*. And while the Europeans all made the same mistakes, trying to imagine the sounds by elements of a tempered system, the Javanese made different kinds of mistakes among themselves: some thought that the sounds gravitated toward the *slendro* system but others thought the *pelog*. No objective evaluation of the pitch of the sounds as such took place: the majority of the subjects stubbornly tried to hear their 'native modes' in places where there were no modes at all. That is why the avant-garde music of Europe is so radical for any listener: it is extraordinarily difficult for anyone to part with the inertia of the modal sense. According to the observations of musicologist Boris Asafiev (1971), the musical community is more conservative because aural inertia is deepened by the corresponding system of education which is built on a modal upbringing.

The sense of mode, if it is already in place, is capable of facilitating a dialogue between the listener with unknown modes: the presence of a certain sound-order and the presence of relationships of base/non-base are phenomena known to virtually everyone. Glenn Schellenberg (1996) played certain melodies for groups of adult nonmusicians—some of them had grown up in China and some in the United States—and asked their opinions as to how well certain new sounds he then played for them (after the initial melodies) fit into the context of and advanced the original music. Independent of musical background, the Caucasian Americans chose appropriate sounds to continue Chinese melodies, and Americans of Chinese origin chose equally well for American folk tunes. Schellenberg thus demonstrated that mode possesses such a high degree of systematization that the human ear cannot accept crude violations of it: such would amount to attempting to continue an English phrase in Greek, or a Greek phrase in English. Even someone who does not know either language will not, upon initial acquaintance with their sounds, make a continuation error of this kind. Sounds and the rules for their combination, stipulated by the sense of mode, are unconsciously grasped by the perceiving ear so that jarring mistakes cannot take place. Simple and passive manifestations of the sense of mode are accessible to almost everyone. That may well be why traditional cultures, based on simple, usually 'authoritarian' modal principles, so easily attract all the members of a tribe into the music making—the sense of mode by its very nature is just as fundamental as the sense of language, and there is no one utterly incapable of sensing a mode as the basis of musical speech.

It is also true, however, that a highly developed sense of mode is neither something one encounters frequently nor something which develops very quickly. Arlette Zenatti (1980) conducted an experiment to determine how well children under age 13 remembered melodies in the accustomed European modes and melodies outside them (atonal melodies). The girl subjects did considerably better in modally organized melodies: they had already developed their sense of mode, which hindered them in perceiving atonal musical phrases. The boy subjects in general did worse at the assigned tasks, and for them the melodies in modes were no easier than the atonals: their sense of mode had not yet formed and thus had not created in them modal inertia.

Commenting on her results, Zenatti suggested that perhaps the boys heard contemporary atonal music more often, or in general are less interested by the art of music and did not succeed in forming sufficient modal inertia. Such a supposition is entirely believable: boys really do, especially in childhood, sing less and take less interest in music than girls. But why? Since ontogenesis is a brief repetition of phylogenesis, it is entirely possible that over the course of thousands of years women, as the basic performers of many rituals, sang more: marriage, birth and child rearing, funerals, daily work, and calendar holidays were always accompanied by music making, the basic actor of which was the woman. On the strength of this the sense of mode among girls was more deeply genetically rooted than among boys; thus in the process of ontogenesis, girls more easily 'remember' their musical past, and their sense of mode is formed sooner.

In some of her remarks Arlette Zenatti addresses the weakness of the sense of mode among children. They cannot extend the sense over sufficiently long melodic fragments. When singing, children badly maintain the pitch position of the mode (tonality). The sense of modal base (tonics) turns out to be in their consciousness a weak 'magnet', incapable of holding in order all the articulated sounds and governing their relationships. A good modal sense, in fact, is characterized by two main parameters: on the one hand, durability when the tonality is held for a long time—here an analogy arises with the sense of rhythm, which always disciplines the course of metrical units. On the other hand, a good sense of mode is highly differentiated: each modal function possesses its own degree of gravitation toward a base which recognizes itself as a characteristic of exactly this modal function and exactly this degree.

The harmonic ear

The harmonic ear was the last and the most complex manifestation of the sense of mode; it realizes entire consonances and chords in their modal role. There are musical cultures which get along without the harmonic ear: they are called monophonic. But European man naturally gravitates toward polyphony: if someone utters 'A', then someone next to him should pronounce 'B', or at least 'A1'—the European consciousness cannot imagine itself without polyphonies of opinion, as the European will always prefer dialogue to monologue. And it is exactly that—the simultaneous mutual-positioning of parallel musical expressions—which the harmonic ear controls. The harmonic ear unites the sounds, turning them into a certain sound *gestalt* which subsequently, using their most divergent criteria, evaluates whether something is euphonic or not by degree of consonance or dissonance.

Akira Izumi (2000) observed a certain species of simians, the *Macaca fuscata* monkeys, as he played them two types of chord sequences: the first was based on the transition from consonance to dissonance, that is from softer consonance to sharper; the second type of sequence, by contrast, proposed a transition from dissonance to consonance, that is from sharper sounds to more harmonious ones. The monkeys reacted differently to these two types of chord sequences, vividly demonstrating the opposition between them. Movement from consonance to dissonance made the monkeys fidget and react—since time immemorial dissonant sound, resembling rustling or scraping, has inspired an answering reaction. The reverse, movement from dissonance to consonance, often went ignored by the monkeys: why bother, indeed, if soft consonances, signaling peace and quiet, do not require a reaction? The researcher noted not simply the monkeys' ability to distinguish rough and sharp sounds from soft and smooth ones, but to make this kind of distinction under the conditions of complex musical sounds. Here the monkeys clearly demonstrated the seeds of the harmonic ear, once more confirming its origination from the ancient expressive ear for music.

Man's harmonic ear is distinguished by its ability to perceive musical sound groupings not only by timbre as consonances, but also as chords possessing a defined modal function. Here consonance plays practically the same role that in melody belongs to each modally ideated sound. If one unexpectedly inserts into a piece some completely alien chord—one which disrupts the modal logic of a sequence of chords which make up a coherent phrase in the European modal system, for example—then the listeners cannot fail to notice, at least subconsciously, this violation. In speech such a sequence of words can be likened to a correctly constructed sentence into which one suddenly inserts a grammatically incorrect turn of phrase.

Four psychologists led by Stefan Koelsch (Koelsch *et al.* 2000) performed an experiment to determine how sensitive listeners were to violations of musical grammar. The experimenters worked with nonmusician subjects whose brains were wired to measuring devices registering their reactions to violations of correct chord sequences. This sequence, like any modal construction, created in the listeners certain defined expectations which were disrupted by the insertion of a textually alien chord. The overwhelming majority of the subjects sensed the violation of context, and their brains sent out a corresponding electronic signal.

> This sophisticated brain 'knowledge', concluded the Koelsch group, 'might be hard-wired, so that it does not require experience. More likely, simple exposure to Western tonal music may be enough for the brain to extract rules of harmonic composition and automatically compute the types of chords that should be heard. Regardless of the cause, it is clear that we are inherently musical.[18]

The authors' optimism grows somewhat dimmer if the subjects are required to proceed on the level of conscious action, revealing the level of development of their harmonic ear. Then it is much harder for them to distinguish appropriate use of chords from inappropriate, correct harmonization, completely possible for the given melody and inappropriate, off-key harmonization. In the 1930s Boris Teplov (1947) tested to see to what extent the harmonic ear of subjects had matured in the modal sense and whether the subjects could distinguish how correctly a proposed accompaniment in fact goes with a melody and whether it suits it appropriately. Of the 47 teenage subjects, 27 successfully fulfilled the task, while 20 failed miserably at it, unable to determine that the chords which the

---

[18] Koelsch, S., Gunter, T., Friederici, A. D., and Schroeger, E. (2000). Brain indices of music processing: 'nonmusicians' are musical. *Journal of Cognitive Neuroscience*, 12, p. 520.

experimenter tried to use in support of the melody were completely inappropriate for the context. It is possible that if Teplov had had the use of apparatus which could register electrical impulses, such would have shown that the failing subjects had identified everything necessary on a subconscious level. But the answers which they gave in the usual conscious state disappointed the experimenter:

> The results of these experiments are often evaluated by musicians as extremely paradoxical and even incredible. And indeed, it is difficult not just for musicians but for anyone who likes music to force himself to listen to the end of those variations used in the experiments which feature off-key [fal'shivoi] harmony. Yet the facts of the matter are beyond dispute. Furthermore, they correspond exactly with the oft-noted observations in musical literature which refer to the fact that the harmonic ear in its development can strongly lag behind the melodic ear.[19]

The differences in the results of the American tests for sense of harmonic context and those of Teplov owe to several contrasting factors. In the American experiment the harmonic ear was demonstrated by adults, while Teplov's subjects were teenagers. Since the harmonic ear is the last component of the analytical ear to develop, in many teenagers it is simply not yet in place, not completely formed. Furthermore, eliciting the conscious judgment of a subject is, of course, more difficult than working with someone in an unconscious state, where the indications of the instruments rather than those of the subjects themselves are the source of data. The results of both experiments attest the fact that the reaction of the harmonic ear to the modal context is characteristic of many people, but by no means of all. And despite this, the sense of consonance/dissonance in tasks of this kind should help the subjects considerably, supporting their sense of mode.

The difficulties of establishing the harmonic ear lie in its very nature: the harmonic ear should enlighten the musical vertical, arranging a consonance which has been merged into a united timbre into its component parts and analyzing them. This feature should be highly differentiated and extremely analytical—for the identification of the modal functions of separate sounds in the context of a melody is not hindered by anything: every sound is revealed and does not disguise its modal affiliation. But a harmonic complex, chord or consonance, stands out for a certain diffuseness, and the sound composition of such a complex is much harder to hear. Even outstanding musician Yehudi Menuhin did not distinguish himself for an exceptional harmonic ear. As Menuhin recalled, 'My ear, very much advanced in the realm of sight-singing and other tricks with melody, was extraordinarily dull in harmony and its 'nomenklatura'.[20]

Menuhin's monophonic violin specialty does not serve here as an explanation or kind of justification; this example speaks only of how high the level of ability of a highly developed harmonic ear actually is—and how rare it is. In this connection the complaints of psychologists about the mistakes which a subject's harmonic ear makes can be explained by the very late origins of the latter—the ear of a European has to do with the harmony since sixteenth–seventeenth centuries, a period which is, of course, altogether insufficient

19 Teplov, B. (1947) *Psikhologiya muzykal'nyh sposobnostei/The Psychology of Musical Abilities*. Moscow: Pedagogika, p. 203.
20 Menuhin, Y. (1979) *Unfinished Journey*. London: MacDonald and Jane's, p. 33.

for development on a mass scale. Given this lateness, only a certain number of individuals should possess a good harmonic ear, which is exactly what one finds in reality.

Andrea Halpern and her colleagues (1998) designed and conducted an experiment in which they asked groups of musicians and nonmusicians to distinguish melodies which differed from one another only by rhythm, melodic contour, or only in modal relationships; among the latter, some of the melodies were in major and some in minor keys, but all other parameters among them coincided. Despite the fact that the subjects worked with melodies, major and minor are for the harmonic ear something like a take-off point. The basic chords of sequence and consonance have in major and minor keys a different sound composition. And if it were necessary in the context of modal sense to find the closest point at which the harmonic ear meets with it, this point would be the differentiation of major and minor. As the authors summed up: 'Discrimination of major from minor tunes was difficult for everyone, even for musicians. Mode is apparently a subtle dimension in music, despite its deliberate use in composition and despite people's ability to label minor as 'sad' and major as 'happy'.[21]

The authors' commentary does not take into account the huge influence of the expressive ear on our capabilities to judge the extent to which one piece of music or another is joyful or sad: here the most important factors are tempo and rhythm, the contour of the musical movement, its direction and, finally, the articulated parameters of performance, its dynamic characteristics. Major and minor in this regard are not as important as is often thought. On the contrary, distinguishing major and minor is one of the functions of the harmonic ear, and it is no surprise that like all functions in which the harmonic ear is involved it is far from perfection—and may happen to be an Achilles heel even among professional musicians.

Experimental data on the work of the harmonic ear confirm the phylogenetic bases of its structure: the most ancient parameters of the harmonic ear, connected with the expressive ear and the sense of timbre, are in most people well developed and fully functional—consonant and dissonant chords do not confuse even monkeys. But once one steps into the area of high differentiation of consonances, the necessity of performing an aural 'X-ray' and the understanding of modal functions, the harmonic ear tauntingly reminds us of its late origins; the majority of people, including musicians, experience significant difficulties. The example of Yehudi Menuhin confirms once again the multiplicative nature of talent: any essential element, once it rises above zero, can already occupy its place in the structure of giftedness. The later-added components of talent are the most vulnerable; and few people can boast of possessing them in a high degree.

Audiation ability and musical memory

The analytical ear in the most natural way possible manifests itself in singing: a person who can identify and fix the pitch relationships of sounds, sense the intervals between

---

[21] Halpern, A., Bartlett, J., and Jay, W. (1998) Perception of mode, rhythm and contour in unfamiliar melodies: effects of age and experience. *Music Perception*, 15, p. 335.

them and understand modal patterns should be able to sing accurately and well. At first glance, there would seem to be no intermediate link between accurate hearing and accurate singing. And yet there is such a link, and to understand this one need only recall the common origins of music and speech. Hearing and understanding speech is, of course, somewhat easier than speaking; passive functions, including those in the area of speech, are always simpler than active ones. The only people who can speak a language are those who perceive its structure and sense the rules of connection between its constituent elements. The mind of the speaker is in fact chock full of vast amounts of information about linguistic units, their significance, and the grammatical rules for their use.

Before pronouncing something, a speaker always imagines internally the phrase she has assembled and wants to articulate aloud. Without this internal representation, though fleeting and unnoticed by the speaker herself, there would be no human speech. The same thing happens in music: every articulation of music (or musical 'speech') is preceded by a musician's internal representation of it. When a melody sounds out, it means that a split second earlier, in the mind of the singer or player, it had already been 'heard'; without this internal aural image, no musical action is possible. Man's ability to conceive music in his mind, to hear it in his imagination, is called the internal ear.

Our modal sense helps us to experience and sense a musical thought in all its details, feel all the sound relationships in their interconnectedness, but the modal sense suffers from being mute, the entire depth of its understanding and experience are directed only at the perception of musical thoughts, not to their creation and production. The internal ear helps to assemble in the mind and preserve from disintegration those sound relationships which man has recognized with the help of the modal sense; the internal ear gives these relationships a final, fixed form. The differentiated musical perception progresses, with the help of the internal ear, to a conception—and now the completed image of a musical whole may ring forth.

After listening to a piece of music a person who possesses an internal ear clearly senses that the piece has left something in his consciousness. This remnant may be fairly vivid, practically a copy of the original just heard; but it may also be very weak and hazy. Yet the quality of the analytical ear is defined not so much by the degree of clarity of these aural 'tracks' as by the ability to engage them consciously, to call them up from one's memory. As Boris Teplov put it:

> We should thus define the internal ear not simply as 'the ability to imagine musical sounds', but as the ability to use and call forth at will musical sound representations. The differences among people in ability at aural representation are great indeed. But in the majority of cases the question is not whether a given person has aural representations or not, but whether he can call them forth at will and use them.[22]

Accurate singing proves beyond argument that a person possesses an internal ear. And off-key, out-of-tune singing, or the complete inability to sing, demonstrate just as clearly

---

[22] Teplov, B. M. (1985) Psihologiya muzykal'nyh sposobnostei/The psychology of musical abilities. In *Izbrannie trudy, t. I/Selected Works*, vol.I, (ed. M. G. Yaroshevsky). Moscow: Pedagogika, p. 205.

the lack of an internal ear in someone else. Optimists maintain that people who cannot sing can themselves hear that they are off-key, but their voices cannot adjust. Some research psychologists dismiss such comforting thoughts: if someone cannot sing, they hold, it means his internal ear is weak and unstable, and the signals his voice receives are so ephemeral and indistinct that he has no hope of relying on 'prompting' from them at all (Starcheus 2003; Tarasova 1988; Teplov 1985). Those who cannot sing but would like to be able to should undertake 'repairs' of their ear rather than voice lessons: coordination of ear and voice hardly exists as such—it's the internal ear, that arouses and supports such coordination. The internal ear reflects the 'battle readiness' of all the components of the analytical ear, since the internal ear is dissolved in the sense of pitch, the sense of interval and the modal sense. The internal ear is like cement in the construction of a building or the glue that holds a book's pages in place—without it the analytical ear could not work, as it would fall apart. To understand and entirely absorb the sense of any action of the analytical ear without the internal ear is hardly possible—any recognition, including the awareness of sound relationships, requires the active mastery and repetition of the already-understood: thus a pupil must repeat a lesson learned to demonstrate that she has really mastered the material. It is not incidental that Boris Teplov called the internal ear the reproductive component of the musical ear, accentuating the moment of repetition of what has been heard, its reproduction.

The internal ear is like the air of the analytical ear: each element of the analytical ear 'breathes' through the internal ear and turns toward the internal ear in its development; and just like air, the internal ear is not always evident—it's existence is taken for granted. When it becomes clear that a musical movement exists in which one sound is undoubtedly higher or lower than another, that means that the understanding of musical pitch is being separated out from the timbre—but until a person has repeated this movement with her voice, has actively assimilated it, one may say that the sense of pitch has not yet been awakened. When a person learns to distinguish intervals she begins to understand that broad intervals differ from narrow ones, and rough dissonances differ from soft consonances, but until her vocal chords have sensed the different degree of tension required for singing different intervals, the person has not yet experienced them, has not really mastered them—which means that the sense of interval which can lie at the base of a good analytical ear has not yet formed. The modal sense develops the same way: until the voice understands how much further there is to go to reach the most fixed sound and crosses this distance independently, the sense of mode will not be formed—the gravitation and resolution of sounds in their finest distinctions cannot be understood completely without the experience of active reproduction.

The ability to imagine a musical sound comes together in the process of real musical perception, in the process of musical participation, an active self-engagement (if only subconscious) in the process of performing the music. As one listens to music, the internal ear sings along, continuously attuning itself to the sound, trying to experience and sense it—and at some point it becomes capable of independently traversing the reverse path without any support—the sound and the internal experience of it through the voice have become inseparable. The catalyst of the internal ear, thus, is a sort of initiative of the ear: the person who loves music and wants to be closer to it will intuitively repeat it, stimulating his internal ear. But the passive, superficial listener will not stimulate the internal ear—and she risks never awakening it. The appearance of the internal ear testifies to a person's musical activity and initiative. That is why all musically gifted people possess an extraordinarily developed internal ear. They created it through the activity of their musical perception and their continual participation in musical performance.

The formation of the internal ear, as something spontaneous, involuntary and also conscious, always takes place in a dialogue between real sound and mental sound, sound imagined internally. Singing along, the mechanism which gives rise to the internal ear, also accompanies it into the future. 'I can summon forth a clear image of the sound of an instrument or voice', wrote one of Boris Teplov's subjects, 'only if I help my imagination with actual movement of the vocal chords'.[23]

Thus help in the formation of the internal ear can be rendered by the alternation of the work of the internal and the 'external' ear: singing melodies already begun through to the end, or attuning one's singing voice to the audible voice of an instrument. Esther Efrusi, a specialist in the development of the ear, emphasized the innate character of the internal ear, which can be assisted in its establishment but which can hardly be created *ex nihilo*: 'There is no exercise which can develop an ability that does not exist already to have living mental sound representations: it can only pass along the skill to better use inborn ability and put off the inevitable pressure and atrophying of this ability'.[24]

The internal ear of the musician is always working. No matter what a person plays or sings, the internal ear automatically reacts to the sound, repeating it like an echo, expecting some events but not other (Schon and Besson 2005), or being a regulator of performer's actions (Pfordresher and Palmer 2006). Steven Finney (1997) demonstrated that if one hinders the work of the internal ear, the entire process of music making will inevitably fall apart. Finney had a group musician-subjects play on a 'dead keyboard'—when pressing the keys the subjects did not hear anything, yet despite this continued to play, replacing the absent sound with their internal ear. Another group of musicians played on a 'delayed keyboard': playing a fragment, the musicians heard not what they were playing at that moment, but what they had played several seconds before. In the heads of these musicians chaos reigned: their internal ear played them one thing, while in real time they heard something completely different. All the musicians in the second group stopped playing, as this terrible discrepancy between the internal ear and real sound was simply fatal for the performance of anything. Finney thus confirmed the necessity of the internal ear in music making, as without its support the process cannot go on.

At the same time the internal ear is a rather dependent entity, as it needs help from other constituents of the performance process. Louise Banton (1995) did a study of various mistakes typical in the sight reading of music: under normal conditions the pianist looks

[23] Teplov, B. M. (1985) Psihologiya muzykal'nyh sposobnostei/The psychology of musical abilities. In *Izbrannie trudy, t. I/Selected Works*, vol.I, (ed. M. G. Yaroshevsky). Moscow: Pedagogika, p. 209.
[24] Efrusi, E. (ed.) (1939) *Muzykal'noe vospitanie nachinauschih pianistov v rukah pedagoga-pianista/ Music Education of Piano Beginners in Piano Teacher's Hands*. Moscow: Pedagogika.

at the notes and controls the result, monitoring the degree to which the sound sequence she hears corresponds to the one she sees on paper. At first Banton's pianist-subjects were deprived of aural control: what they played on the keyboard did not sound (the 'mute keyboard' again). And as in the experiment above, removing the sound element during sight reading did not hinder accurate play; in part the subjects supplemented the unheard music with that of the internal ear, in part controlled their playing visually, literally looking at the keyboard, and the end result was an altogether acceptable performance. A hindrance of the opposite kind, when the pianist-subjects were deprived not of sound but of sight, proved considerably more bothersome. With their view of the keyboard obscured, the pianists found that the faithfully rendered sound of what they were playing was not a great help: the number of mistakes rose dramatically, demonstrating that the internal ear works only in conjunction with visual monitoring of the keyboard, that is, with the help of audio-spatial images.

The dependence of the internal ear on real-time aural perceptions was confirmed by the experiments of a group of psychologists led by Gail Stwolinski (Stwolinski *et al.* 1988). A selection of 59 student musicians was divided into two groups, one of which sight read a piece of music using a keyboard while the other simply listened to a recording of the same piece. Both groups were then played the piece in a somewhat distorted form, with certain mistakes intentionally introduced into its performance; both groups of subjects were to identify the mistakes in the music. Those who had simply heard a recording of the music did better at the assigned task and did it with greater ease than those who became acquainted with the music independently, sight reading it. In sight reading, where the internal ear plays a great role, its imperfection leads to significant errors, and one's image of the music is distorted. How could subjects whose perception of the music was *already* faulty be expected to identify mistakes in it? The Stwolinski group's results confirmed once more the wisdom that in music it is better to hear something once than see it a hundred times, because only people with a wonderful internal ear can imagine for themselves the sound of a piece simply by looking at the music text: all the rest of us, whose internal ear is far from perfection, cannot rely on it entirely, as real ('external') sound is infinitely more helpful.

Experiments testing the role of the internal ear in performance show that it is a sort of secret component in music making, hidden as it is from the participants during performance. But for the majority of people the internal ear is extremely weak and dependent: it needs to be helped constantly, leaning on both visual images and the support of real (external sound). The nature of the internal ear is contextual in the highest degree: it is only a part, one side, of the 'lining' of any musical activity. Even a very bad internal ear—in distinction from a very bad sense of rhythm or a very bad modal sense—is in no way necessarily fatal: there are entirely capable musicians whose internal ear is a long way from perfect. The Russian saying 'A lone man on a battlefield is not a warrior' perfectly conveys the situation of the internal ear, as it reinforces the work of the analytical ear, activates it. The internal ear can replace the real, external one only in the rarest of instances, involving musical abilities of a very high caliber indeed.

Working with the internal ear is usually done in accordance with its nature: music teachers strive to include it in the context of musical activity, to refer to it but not to rely on it entirely. Anne Theiler and Louise Lippman (1995) had musicians study a piece simply by reading the notes, then alternating this reading with playing the piece, then endlessly repeating the piece on their instruments. The most effective methodology, it turned out, was the mixed version, in which the internal ear (the study of the sheet music) worked in alternation with 'external' (the playing of the piece). Pure playing and pure study were less effective, which means that turning to the internal ear is most effective when it is applied partially, in combination with other, simpler methods of getting to know a piece of music. The surprising thing here is not that the internal ear is not a panacea, which is obvious, considering its relative weakness and lack of development among most people; no, the surprising thing is that given this weakness and underdeveloped state, it is still necessary nevertheless. The internal ear provides real help; using it, in conjunction with other things, is much better than simply forgetting about it.

One can judge a good internal ear on the professional level by its manifestations. Singing on-key is a critical stage on the path of establishing the internal ear; the professional work of a musician demands a much higher level of its development. Heinrich Neuhaus (1999) extraordinarily highly valued sight reading, claiming that, with very few exceptions, the degree of possession of this skill allowed one to judge the musical gift of a musician. At first glance this claim is far from obvious: the ability to turn visual impressions from a text into correct finger movements does not tell us anything, and participation in this process of the musical ear is hidden from superficial inspection.

Revealing the connection between sight reading and aural data was the task undertaken by Andrew Waters, Ellen Townsend, and Geoffrey Underwood (1998). Thirty pianists were tested for the analytical ear, competing at the tasks of naming a note the fastest (indicating sense of pitch and modal sense), naming brief chords of succession (the harmonic ear), distinguishing musical fragments as types ('the same' or 'different'), testing the overall analytical ear, and comparing a written score with audited music (the internal ear). At the end of the testing the same subjects performed sight reading exercises again and their skills at this were again evaluated. It turned out that sight reading ability as a summary indicator of musical abilities correlated closest of all with the last task, that is, with the internal ear. The more active a musician's internal ear, the better he sight reads and the higher are his musical abilities.

The research of Vladimir Avratiner (1971) with students at the Russian Gnessin's Academy of Music in Moscow is interesting in this respect. Avratiner told pianists who knew the pieces they had prepared as part of their entrance exams wonderfully and by heart to write them down, leaving each student alone in a room with music paper and his internal ear. There was no help to be had either from muscle memory (the finger-motor movements) or from real sound. It turned out that the majority of students could not write anything down, that is their musical images were predominantly motor-spatial in character: the subjects remembered not so much music as the sequence of their finger movements on the keyboard, which was so well worked out that it did not even need aural reinforcement. It is well known that the majority of music students are people with rather middling musical abilities. The internal ear is a sign of high abilities and it is hardly surprising that its weakness corresponds completely with weakness of musical abilities overall.

Consistency in the fulfillment of various musical actions is a sign of a highly developed internal ear. In the Finney experiment described above the subjects could not play when the real sound of their playing trailed behind their expectations, putting off the work of the internal ear. John Gates and his colleagues (1974) obtained similar results, noting in addition that their subjects even tried to speed up their performance in an attempt to 'escape' the noise that so bothered them. Ward and Burns (1978) conducted a study using professional and non-professional singers, playing for both groups a distracting noise through earphones as they were singing scales. The noise bothered both groups, of course, but the professionals were able to stay within the bounds of on-key singing, while the amateurs repeatedly hit the wrong note and generally lost their way. The researchers paid particular attention to the extraordinarily individualized differences among the subjects in the development of the internal ear. Without the analysis of special experiments, these dissimilarities go unnoticed, since both professional and amateur singers are distinguished more by the beauty of the voice and vocal technique than by aural data, and both sing, on the whole, correctly and cleanly. Only particular procedures reveal the deep contrasts in their musical abilities—and most of all these concern the internal ear.

Great musical talents are marked with their outstanding internal ear—an ear so fine that the sound in the musician's mind is practically indistinguishable from genuine live sound. Thanks to the enormous resources of his internal ear Beethoven continued composing musical masterpieces after going deaf: he heard (or 'heard') these works in his mind as clearly as you and I hear them performed today. An English admirer of the great violinist Niccolo Paganini inadvertently revealed the secret of the latter's musical technology, which was the phenomenal activity of his internal ear (Shulyachuk 1912). This man would today be termed a fanatic (if not a stalker): he followed Paganini around for 6 months, staying in the same hotels as the violinist, and in adjoining rooms. The curious Englishman wanted to penetrate the mystery of the artist's holy of holies—to observe him practicing by himself. But no matter how hard he tried, he was never able to catch the master at this intimate musical occupation, from which the impression arose that the enchanting sounds which issued forth from his violin in concert were totally spontaneous and unprepared: Paganini apparently never practiced, and nothing but silence ever came from his room.

Then one day fortune finally smiled on the despairing admirer. Peeking through the keyhole into the maestro's room, he suddenly caught side of Paganini raising his incomparable Guarneri violin to his shoulder. Anticipating at this point the enjoyment of a concert to be performed for himself alone, the admirer froze in expectation. And then he saw the maestro barely touch the instrument's strings: he played soundlessly, controlling his performance solely with his internal ear. The music sounded in Paganini's head even when he did not play a single note—and this 'practice' was sufficient for him to remain in phenomenal artistic form. The curious admirer went away with nothing and fell into even greater confusion than at the beginning of his trip; he had the concept of the internal ear.

The internal ear of composers is particularly well developed; it is for them the final expresser and identifier of their musical idea. As Edison Denisov, a classic of twentieth-century Russian music, explained it:

> A composer has to have an internal ear. The richer and more developed it is, the better for him and his audience. If I did not have the internal ear, I would simply die. Just imagine the nine years I lived in conservatory dormitories, first in a 15-man room, then in a 7-man room on Dmitrovka, and only the last year or two in a double room with the composer Fliarkovsky. How could I write music in those circumstances?[25]

The compositions of Denisov, who had a wonderful internal ear, were born during those student years, but in the reading rooms of the Lenin Library, where the composer sat with his music paper. Incidentally, Denisov, like his colleagues Tchaikovsky, Wagner, and Scriabin, had an ideal and outstanding ear, but not perfect pitch, which is no guarantee of the internal ear and is unconnected with it in general.

The internal ear, the capability for aural representation in the mind, is an essential base for the development of one's musical memory. It is defined by the degree of durability of the aural tracks which the internal ear retains. The quality and exactitude of the sound representations, the level at which they correspond to the original—this is the area of responsibility of the internal ear. In some people the internal ear is distinguished by the liveliness and vividness of its aural images, yet the individual's memory for music is mediocre: the images are quickly erased, disappearing altogether. In other people, however, the internal ear can be quite imperfect, the sound images it retains being muddled and unclear, but muddled or not, they remain in the individual's memory essentially forever. There are, in short, two components to the musical memory, defined as the ability to retain musical images in one's consciousness and reproduce them at will: the ability to register a trail of sound in one's mind (the internal ear) and the ability to store this information (the memory proper).

As in many other cases having to do with the processes of musical perception and creativity, the launch mechanism of the musical memory is the expressive ear. People remember what they like; humans are inclined to retain in their memories things which interest and occupy them, and those who have a genuine interest in music give their musical memories an extra advantage: the expressive ear as the motivational nucleus of musical abilities stimulates the musical memory, acting as its catalyst. It is like the soil from which all man's musical abilities grow; various components of the analytical ear and sense of rhythm have a deep connection with the expressive ear, since to a certain degree they are its products—they focus and fine tune the overall image of music created by the expressive ear.

The love for music and musical motivation, which a good expressive ear supports, stimulates the appearance of the internal ear, strengthening the listener's participation in

---

25 Shulgin, D. I. (1998) *Priznanie Edisona Denisova/Edison Denisov's Confession*. Moscow: Kompozitor, p. 15.

music making; this love for music makes the person return to his musical impressions, awaken them again, which enables the development of the musical memory. Love for music through its representative in our psyche—the expressive ear—one way or another gives birth to many musical abilities, raising the chances and strengthening the probability of their appearance and development. The person who wants to remember will: this applies just as well to music as to any other activity.

It is well known that musicians normally have an outstanding musical memory. This memory arises as a result of continual music making in the mind and as a result of extraordinary activity of the internal ear. Mozart, whose musical memory has been legendary for centuries, dedicated every moment of his life to music. Because of this he was absent minded and socially awkward—he would spend his time at formal dinners scrawling something on napkins, heedless of his surroundings: his internal ear was taken up with the Herculean labor of creating and storing the music which his imagination was constantly churning out. His memory was so phenomenal that he could compose music, sometimes over periods of years, without writing it down: he always had a multitude of pressing responsibilities and could not commit to paper even those things which were already done (Abert 2007). His father Leopold, himself a very gifted musician, marveled at this, his son's ability, and, as if not entirely believing in it, constantly reminded his son of the necessity of writing down his compositions. Such a miraculous memory, in terms of quality (exactitude) of musical images and length of their retention, plainly put the fear of God into Leopold. The enormous tension involved in this kind of continuous labor by the musical memory was by itself enough to put someone into an early grave, even without serious illness that came to plague Mozart.

The well-known case of the 14-year-old Mozart, on a performing tour of Italy, memorizing Allegheri's mysterious *Miserere* at a single hearing, makes the point vividly: the piece was a polyphonic choral composition, which one of the monasteries of Bologna guarded like a special talisman: no one was allowed to transcribe the score of *Miserere* or take the written music outside the confines of the cathedral. The young Mozart, attending the service in the cathedral, committed the piece to memory and subsequently wrote it down note for note. Leopold Mozart, who was accompanying his son on the tour, wrote home about this miraculous feat of acquisition with a certain trepidation, and chose not to send the actual manuscript by post; only upon returning to Salzburg did the young Mozart's manuscript see the light of day, and the story of its origin become legend. What is stunning in the case is not only the young maestro's amazing memory for music, but also his ability to enter into a musical style entirely alien to his own: the light, refined and wholly secular manner of Mozart's writing was a long way indeed from heavy-handed solemnity and endless counterpoint of Allegheri. The irony of the story is that the fame, and indeed the very name of Allegheri might have been lost to history forever had not Mozart's phenomenal display of musical memory insured their survival for posterity.

In addition to the quality and exactness of musical memory, which depend on the internal ear, and beyond the length of retention of musical images, the level of development of the musical memory is also defined by its (geometric) volume. Recalling and exactly reproducing a few favorite melodies all one's life is one thing; remembering and playing whole musical scores note for note is quite another. A very good musical memory is characterized not only by recalling familiar music well and for a long time, but also for the sheer amount of music that can be remembered. There are musicians and music lovers who can play (or whistle) from memory entire operas; many of these people retain in their minds whole libraries of music and can reproduce at will whatever quartets or symphonies they happen to want to listen to.

Most mere mortals, on the other hand, do not suffer from an overloaded musical memory; indeed, we often enough find ourselves unable even to recall a tune we actually know. Here the passive resources of the human consciousness are much more significant than the active ones. The justice of this observation has been demonstrated by Z.F. Peynircioglu and colleagues (Peynircioglu *et al.* 1998), who asked a group of college students to look at a list of songs and recall their melodies. If they could not do this they were asked whether or not they had the sensation that they had heard the melody and remembered it, but simply could not reproduce it—such 'hidden' recollections were also recorded by the experimenters. Peynircioglu termed these recollections the 'feeling of knowing', meaning that in the consciousness of the subjects there arose the sensation that 'somewhere, sometime I heard this, it seems, and remember it', but the result of this memory could not emerge in the form of a sung melody. In the second half of the experiment the subjects listened to melodies, introduced into the 'feeling of knowing' list, and were asked to identify them. Peynircioglu concluded as follows:

> Although subjects could not recall certain melodies during the first part of the experiment, their feelings of knowing [FOK] predicted their ability to recognize the music when it was played; the greater the FOK, the better the recognition. This study demonstrates that FOK are a valid source of information about apparently forgotten music, emphasizing the fact that much of musical knowledge is not directly available to our conscious awareness.[26]

The musical memory awakens very early. British psychologist Peter Hepper (1991) put the fanatical devotion of a number of pregnant women to the soap opera *Neighbors* to work for the good of science. Having heard the theme music to the series dozens of times as unborn progeny, the womens' infants were then tested after birth to determine whether they recalled the same melody—that is, whether their musical memory was already at work before birth. The methodology for testing was monitoring the infants' heartbeat: recognizing a piece of music, the heart beats faster out of a sense of joy. If the infants were played other tunes, or the same ones played backward, their hearts registered nothing out of the ordinary. The remarkable musical memory of infants was once more demonstrated when they had to recognize very sophisticated pieces, *Prelude* and *Forlane* from *Le tombeau de Couperin* by Maurice Ravel, and they succeeded after a two-week delay (Ilari and Polka 2006). Such studies show that the musical memory is born very early, and quite literally,

---

[26] Peynircioglu *et al.* (1998) Name or hum that tune: feeling of knowing for music. *Memory and Cognition*, 26, p. 1131.

before its owner. And it is born in developed form—trying to turn a middling musical memory into an outstanding one through rigorous training seems to be a fool's errand. A phenomenal musical memory by its very existence demonstrates this. At its base, of course, lies an outstanding internal ear, since it is exactly the work of this feature which the musical memory supports and retains. Pianist Marina Barinova, a student of the legendary Joseph Hoffman, recalled that 'Hoffman possessed a phenomenal memory. He learned many piano pieces without benefit of the instrument, simply by looking at the sheet music and committing it to memory with speed and exactness that appeared unattainable'.[27] Recalling music exclusively from its written form, that is, using the internal ear only, demonstrates once more the deep connection between the internal ear and musical memory: if a wonderful internal ear can indeed in many instances be combined with a middling memory, the reverse is highly unlikely—an exceptional musical memory presupposes an exceptional internal ear.

Yehudi Menuhin recounted a remarkable case involving his teacher, the violinist and composer Georges Enescu (Menuhin 1979). In Paris in the 1930s Enescu was approached by Maurice Ravel and the music publisher Duran, in whose hands was the score of a sonata for violin and piano which Ravel had just written. The captious Duran kept insisting that Ravel play his compositions again and again, as though Ravel were a beginning composer the quality of whose work required further assessment—and here he was asking Ravel to perform this new sonata with Enescu. After they had done so Duran's enthusiasm knew no bounds—and he wanted to hear the masterpiece again, but this time, to derive even greater pleasure from the experience, he had decided to follow the performance by reading the sheet music, which existed, at this point, only as Ravel's own copy. Ravel and Enescu performed the piece wonderfully, the latter playing from memory— memory of a piece of music he had seen for the first time in his life a half-hour previously. The sonata had just been written, thus neither Duran nor Menuhin himself, who was also present, could suspect fraud: Enescu simply remembered the extraordinarily complex music from a single play-through. As Menuhin commented in his memoirs:

> Enescu knew by heart some 58 or 60 volumes of the collected works of Bach, given to him by Queen Mary in his conservatory years. I remember a day when he sat at an old piano and, counting the beat, growling and whistling several voice parts, performed *Tristan und Isolde* more dramatically than an operatic troupe—without a score, since he also kept all of Wagner in his memory.[28]

Such an outstanding memory demonstrates the extreme limits of the possible for the analytical ear: the perceiver hears all the sounds and chords which go into the performed piece: the logic of their combinations is entirely clear to him—hearing one motif or fragment, he seemingly hears in advance the next motif or fragment. The entire musical form is retained in his memory in an abbreviated, enclosed form and is later opened with the same ease and inevitability as that of a genetic code growing into a mature organism.

---

27 Barinova M. (1964) *Vospominaniya o Gofmane i Buzoni/Memoirs on J. Hoffman and F. Buzoni*. Moscow: Muzyka, p. 72.

28 Menuhin, Y. (1979) *Unfinished Journey*. London: MacDonald and Jane's, p. 37.

An extraordinarily developed musical memory points up the extraordinarily systematic and synthesized nature of musical perception.

A wonderful analytical ear is one of the essential elements of an outstanding memory, just as the internal ear is. However that extraordinary systematization and synthesis of perception which a phenomenal musical memory relies upon already exceeds the bounds of the ear itself and stands on the way to a musical thought. This systematization, as the apex of development of the analytical ear, is at the same time the beginning of musical-creative thought. He for whom the disassembly of a musical thought is logical and understandable can not only follow its development, to a certain extent anticipating it, but he can also identify the entire journey of musical elements, retaining them in his memory. An outstanding memory signifies an outstanding understanding of the laws under which a musical organism can be born.

The musical memory is an integrated quality of musicality, its summary indicator. Even the internal ear, which enters into its structure, is already integrated: it includes in itself a good analytical ear and musical motivation, without which the internal ear cannot arise. A middling musical memory relies on a middling internal ear—it is neither particularly fine nor particularly reliable and does not extend to great volumes of musical information. As soon as the memory becomes outstanding it already demands another level of analysis and understanding of the musical material that arises not by itself but uses other qualities of musical consciousness and thought, being a witness to their presence, their result and their continuation. Understanding here is primary and memory secondary—such, in essence, is the memory of the gifted musician.

The only exception to this would be the memory of those unfortunates termed idiot-savants. These people possess phenomenal musical memories, unconsciously recording enormous musical tapestries. There is not yet an unarguable explanation to savants' extraordinary abilities and so, field for hypotheses and speculation is free enough (Heaton *et al.* 1998; Miller 1999; Scheerer *et al.* 1945; Treffert 1989; Young and Nettelbeck 1995). It's possible to suppose that with savants another mechanism is at work, where in place of a highly structured perception which penetrates into musical algorithms we find simply an 'element-to-element' copying process. The memory of the idiot-savant uses its own, different from normal, memorizing strategy altogether; it is inaccessible to others, a dead end curiosity of nature, psychological syncresis without analysis or synthesis. Unlike that of the idiot-savant, the outstanding musical memory of the musician is an integrated characteristic of musical abilities, a sort of mountain peak: the path to the summit includes many stages and the shining musical memory crowns the rise as an indicator of what has been reached.

The analytical ear in the structure of musical talent

There is a tradition in musical culture: anyone who claims the title of professional musician must demonstrate a good analytical ear. This requirement is obligatory in folk music, jazz, and in certain divisions of rock and pop music. The musician-performer often takes up the role of composer—it is impossible to compose without knowing which elements are at the artist's command and how he can combine them. Among Russian musicians one hears the phrase *sniat'* sound from a record or a disc: this means that the musician should know how to write down in note form or simply repeat on an instrument the music he hears. Any composer needs a new synthesis of the accepted selection of possibilities or at least the ability to copy exactly and then in the future make variations of the copied models. The same is true in the culture of academic music, where every musician in the service of the feudal lord had to be able to compose, and if necessary take the place of an absent *kappelmeister*.

The tradition of checking the musical ear was strengthened by a multitude of vocal musical specialties—in all musical cultures, from folklore to classical European, singers were never, under any circumstances, to hit a false note. Choir and chorus directors are supposed to detect anything off-key and correct it. A sense of pitch is essential to musicians who are required to tune stringed instruments and woodwinds without help. But what level of development of the analytical ear is necessary for performing musicians? Is it really so great, and are there not significant differences among the needs of different musical specializations? It is clear that a conductor, who controls the pureness and correctness of the play of a hundred performers, must have an ear for music rather better than that of a mere orchestra musician.

Music teachers have always striven to evaluate the probability of success of their charges, hoping to identify in advance those who incontestably deserve their efforts and patience. Toward this end over the course of the centuries procedures have been worked out for testing the musical ear; procedures which only took into account the analytical aspect. The expressive ear, in whose province is located all the non-written characteristics of sound—that is to say, in essence, the entire arsenal of the means of performance—was given considerably less attention. Likewise, the sense of rhythm was given short shrift; it was the analytical ear alone which was assessed and measured, rigorously and in detail. In the twentieth century, the American psychologist Carl Seashore (1919; 1938) became the leader in musical testing who in various tests assessed the degree of differentiation of human musical perception. Seashore's subjects, answering on the principle 'the same or different' compared separate sounds, short motifs, and chord combinations. For example, children who could distinguish which note in a numbered group had been changed during a repeat playing of a three-note chord were considered more musical than those who could not. Seashore's tests, containing as many as 30–40 examples, were extremely tiring and far from live music; despite their psychological validity and reliability, the tests were a source of disenchantment for many musicians from the 1930s onward.

American psychologist E. M. Taylor (1941) compared the results of Seashore's tests and the musical success of the subjects during their student years and later, when they had emerged as professional musicians. The marks from the Seashore tests and the marks of the students in schools (in musical dictation and vocals) correlated rather poorly; the tests had not predicted neither the ability to analyze and set out the elements of the musical texture, which were necessary for taking musical dictation, nor the level of development of the internal ear, which comes to the fore in singing. The correlation with success at the professional level was likewise feeble, the reason for which was that Seashore had stopped at the level of sense of pitch and sense of interval—his subjects heard not music and not elements of music, but merely disparate sounds and elements. Even the level of modal sense was for his tests too high, so it is hardly surprising that real music making presented the analytical ear with demands incomparable to Seashore's finely tuned tests.

Many researchers followed Seashore, improving his methodology as they went along: the exercises were varied by differentiation and recall of sound elements, but the results of these efforts were nonetheless disappointing. In the year 1998, Joyce Gromko and Allison Poorman produced a summarizing article on the topic in the leading musical-pedagogical journal, putting the issue of testing for musical abilities into sharp relief: 'Why has musical aptitude assessment fallen flat? And what can we do about it? … Despite decades of research and at least modest evidence for the validity of such tests (particularly regarding their ability to assess a mechanical-acoustic factor), the objective assessment of musical aptitudes is not part of the standard career assessment battery'.[29] Gromko and Poorman concluded (as had many others) that testing procedures essentially threw the baby out with the bath water: dividing music into elements, the testers had lost sight of the actual music itself, its living, and vibrant context.

Studying Seashore's methods, Lazar Stankov and J. L. Horn (1980) arrive at the conclusion that at the base of the analytical ear lay one basic operation—distinguishing sound structures. Desmond Sergeant and Gillian Vhatcher (1974) departed somewhat from mechanical-acoustic procedures and dead sound structures. Working individually with 75 children aged 10 and 11, Sergeant and Vhatcher tested the ear for music of each by traditional methods: the children were given melodic phrases to study for a period, and then asked to identify them from among a selection including many others. Thus the subjects demonstrated their musical memory and their skill at comparing actual sounds with their own aural conceptions. The results of the procedure were quite revealing: the musical-analytical operations correlated solidly with the subjects' IQ scores, that is, the best ear for music was to be found among the children with the highest intellect. Moreover, the authors were able to shed further light on their results—a summary evaluation of the tests for musical abilities showed a direct correspondence with the verbal section of the IQ test. Thus the deep psychological connection between the analytical ear and verbal abilities was once more confirmed as the task which the verbal part of the IQ sequence tests is aimed at analyzing verbal structures. Yet no one has yet been able to use these tests to predict the level of future success in any particular professional field.

Many researchers and practitioners see the ineffectiveness of such tests stemming not from faulty construction but rather from the fact that the analytical ear itself is a long way from exhausting the concept of musical abilities. The outstanding violin instructor Boris Struve collected in one place the critical arrows fired at those who excessively admire 'measurement' of the ear:

> The whole complex psychological side, with its leading ideo-emotional conception, the central side of the performer's gift is, in the majority of cases, not subjected to even a pretense of being revealed

[29] Gromko, J. and Poorman, A. (1998) Why has musical aptitude assessment fallen flat? And what can we do about it? *Journal of Research in Music Education*, 46, p. 173.

by the experiment's subject. Thus the most important musical-performance data—such as, for example, the ability to perceive and understand a musical phrase, the activity of musical expression and the underpinnings of creative-performing initiative—are eliminated from the overall picture of the test score. Pedagogical experience leads to the conclusion that the absence of a distinct, good musical ear is in no way a sign of unmusicality, particularly among children. One meets also the combination of the person with so-called perfect pitch and a rather mediocre artistic-performance record, or no record at all.[30]

The essential presence of the analytical ear in the structure of musical talent is not open to question; people who have a 'cast-iron ear' should probably not try to become musicians. It is also true, however, that the analytical ear in the given instance is no guarantee of success—or talisman against failure. Given the multiplicative model of talent, it is entirely sufficient for the analytical ear to be, on the measurement scale, anywhere above zero in order for it to function at some acceptable level (though not brilliant or outstanding). The analytical ear comprises a middling, operational component of musical ability. Below it on the phylogenetic axis is the expressive ear, from which are derived certain components of the analytical ear. If one imagines a situation in which the analytical ear is rather good but the expressive ear rather bad, then this extra-emotional, dead analytical ear, cut off from the roots of musical motivation, is highly unlikely to be able to serve as the support base of a musical talent. As the evaluation experiments for the expressive ear have shown, the overwhelming majority of concert musicians have a very well-developed expressive ear (Kirnarskaya and Winner 1999); evaluating the analytical ear without allowing for the expressive ear in the process makes no particular sense—a 'dried up' analytical ear will not lead a musician to the heights of a musical career.

By origin the analytical ear is in part connected to the expressive ear; the active relationship to music and love for it positively bespeaks for itself in the development of the analytical ear, particularly the internal ear and the musical memory. The expressive and analytical ear are psychologically akin, and one may expect that people with a wonderful analytical ear come from precisely that 12 percent of all children who have been blessed with a high-quality expressive ear and 'suffer' from their love of music. In this case an analytical ear of a high level is formed in a very musical person, exactly the ear which musical soloists and music lovers possess: both of these almost always have, alongside the expressive ear, a wonderful analytical ear. The author's own experiments (2006) revealed that among conservatory students 67 percent have a good expressive ear: conservatory students' analytical ear is also quite good (they had to pass conservatory entrance exams, after all). All these data attest the fact that there is, among musicians, almost no divergence between a good expressive ear and a good analytical ear; they really are recruited by a natural phylogenetic method. Among those who have a good expressive ear, those who likewise possess a rather good analytical ear will prove the cadres who become musicians.

An analytical ear of a high level may arise on the base of a very ordinary expressive ear; but, as noted above, without motivation and the deep psychological roots of musicality

[30] Struve, B. (1952) *Puti nachal'nogo razvitiya yunyh skripachei i violonchelistov/The Ways of Early Development for Junior Violinists and Cellists.* Moscow: Muzgiz, p. 28.

which the expressive ear provides, such an analytical ear is almost useless. On the other hand, if the analytical ear is very weak, even though the expressive ear and sense of rhythm are good—the problem is not fatal. Not every musician is fated to compose and give solo concerts: there are also musical critics, music teachers, and music editors; there are musical specialties where enthusiasm, a subtle understanding of music and a real love for it are entirely enough to give a person all that is necessary for professional development, even if his/her analytical ear is at a minimally acceptable level. The more so as even a wonderful musical ear—expressive, analytical, and internal, along with a good musical memory—is still not sufficient for creative success in music.

The composer and the performer need a whole assortment of properties and qualities which are not part of the analytical ear. These are the components of talent which lie above the analytical ear and are later in origin: the whole complex of gifts which provides compositional creation—including musical fantasy, musical imagination and the ability to produce new musical thoughts—bears no direct relation to the analytical ear and does not depend on it. In 'The Musical Rules of Home and in Life' included in his *Album for the Young op. 68* Robert Schumann described his ideal: to hear for the first time an unknown composition (most likely of large scale) and immediately imagine it in the form of a score. Schumann was describing a high stage of work of the analytical ear: all the musical elements were identified, clear and correctly laid out. They were securely retained by the musical memory. If the composer Schumann entertains such dreams, then there really is nothing more to wish for—all the rest, including musical genius, Schumann has. But even a tremendous ear will not bring happiness to those with only modest gifts. He who has an analytical ear is possessed of a musical language. However, just as in oral speech a person who has command of the language is not necessarily a poet, so the possessor of a wonderful analytical ear is still not a composer. Such is the opinion of one of the most authoritative musical psychologists, Maria Manturzewska:

> A high level of specific musical abilities is a manifestation of one of the conditions for development of the professional musician, but is in no way a sufficient condition for musical activity of a high level. One should not see in a particularly high level of the manifestation of these abilities an indication of musical giftedness. [31]

In the structure of other nonmusical talents there is also an ability analogous to the analytical ear; in every area—agriculture, jurisprudence, diplomacy, computer science, and so on—there is always a particular and specific language. In everything there is a system of signals of the micro-level and an order of their connection; everywhere, as in oral speech and in music, there are certain sequences of these signals which 'encode' the 'messages' into this particular 'language'. If attention is focused on the language aspects of any activity, then one may approach the sum of the particular psychological properties and qualities which provide for the learning of the 'language' and the mastery of it in

[31] Manturzewska, M. (1994) Les facteurs psychologiques dans le développement musical et l'évolution des musiciens professionnels. In *Psychologie de la musique*, (ed. A. Zenatti). Presses Universitaires de France, p. 271.

specific activities. The disintegration into components of this multi-part 'language gift' will be dictated by the very make-up of the 'language' and, above all, the order of the origin of its characteristics.

It is entirely possible that just as with the analytical ear, the 'language ability' in different spheres of activity will by its origins be connected with a fundamental ability, with the motivational nucleus of this activity. And just as in musical activity, the analogue of the analytical ear in other spheres should represent an operational component of talent thanks to which the inclusion of the elements into quasi-linguistic structures takes place—by the same token the analytical ear in music must turn these connections into algorithms of the creation of 'phrases' on the micro-level and direct their perception and decoding. The analytical ear should read these 'messages' as ideational and predictable, it should expect certain 'events' and not others—thanks to the 'analytical ear' a 'dialogue' should be instituted between the sender of the 'linguistic messages' and the receiver.

To sum up our section on the analytical ear, some principal points:

1 The analytical ear derives from the expressive ear, detailing and refining the picture drawn by the latter of pitch movement. The analytical ear is born of the sense of timbre and direction of movement, from the sense of the musical 'up and down' connected with the sense of register; it recognizes the pitch of separate sounds and evaluates the pitch distance between them—thus is formed the sense of musical pitch and the sense of interval.

2 The analytical ear forms the modal systems, built on stable pitch relationships of joint subservience and hierarchy. The modal sense awakens the emotional experience of the function of each sound in the context of the mode and the effect of 'pre-hearing', turning musical perception into a process of dialogue.

3 Perfect pitch defines the pitch of a sound as such by memory, without comparing it to the pitch of other sounds. Perfect pitch outside of combination with a highly developed relative ear is not a sign of great musical abilities.

4 The analytical ear is the operational center of musical talent, responsible for the learning of a musical language; yet for the functioning of musical talent a modest development of the analytical ear is sufficient under the condition that the expressive ear and the sense of rhythm are highly developed; in this case the person in question will not be able to practice certain musical specialties which demand a high development of the analytical ear, such as those of the conductor, sound producer, or choir master.

5 The analytical ear does not define or control the musical-creative components of talent; the level of development of the analytical ear and the scale of musical talent are not directly proportional functions.

Part 3

Musical giftedness

The giftedness of the composer

The music of traditional cultures seems bestowed from on high, a gift that apparently appeared from nowhere, *sui generis*. It accompanies important events: agricultural harvests, the changing of seasons, weddings, funerals—yet no one knows who wrote this occasional music, all these dirges, festive marches, and holiday round-dances. The lead singers in the choruses say that they heard the songs from their grandmothers; the grandmothers, in turn, cite even older ancestors; still others recall that they heard the songs from neighbors or from wandering minstrel singers. The anonymity of the authors of traditional songs does not derive from an intent to conceal or from the inadvertent loss of an author's name; it is, rather, the result of the oldest technology of creativity, wherein music is born in the process of collective improvisation. In exactly this fashion various tribes who still live according to ancestral traditions compose their songs to this day. Observing the creativity of children leads one to the same conclusions. David Hargreaves (1999), a specialist in musical ontogenesis and the author of a monograph on musicality in children, modeled a case of ethnographic music-making using ten 8-year-old children; observing them for 5 months, Hargreaves formulated the main points of their musical practice as follows:

> (1) objectification, that is, joint creation of the notion of improvised pieces based on the development of a participation framework; (2) thoughtfulness, that is, the awareness of immersed involvement into self-determined musical thinking; and (3) shared intentionality, that is, a sense of being heard, and a sense of listening, a feeling that music making is essentially a form of joint action and communication of intentions.[1]

Early music arose from the process of collective improvisation, and the best examples of the art crafted by this collective creator were retained in the common memory and preserved for future generations. From the earliest times society has perceived music as its collective portrait, as an expression of common values; and the imagined hero of a society's music, the person from whose point of view it is recounted, becomes contemporary man. The connection between man and society received its loftiest embodiment in music—creator and listener came together in one person, each entering the soul of every music maker and everyone who appreciates music. The collective composer reaches the height of recognition when the listener feels himself a co-author and receives someone else's music as his own.

---

[1] Hargreaves, D. (1999) Children's conception and practice of musical improvisation. *Psychology of Music*, 27, p. 205.

The art of music, its inalienable essential quality, lies in this ability to convey a feeling of communality and the merging of all into one; the more openly this feeling is expressed, the more popular the kind of music embodying and supporting the feeling becomes. Such are all the non-classical forms of music, including jazz, rock and pop, as well as all the various youth movements, past, present, and future—techno, grunge, rap, rave, and interminable other 'musics' in which the collective subconscious and music reflect and extend each other in an effort to create a seamless unity. The popularity of rock and pop is connected to the fact that in the course of music's performance the audience comes to feel itself a part of the collective process of composition-improvisation: it is allowed into the holiest of holy places and becomes a participant in a ritual, just as all who observed the collective musical rituals of antiquity were. The most ancient of musical roots are awakened in today's rock concert audience, who sense the music being played as an expression of their own immediate, present-moment condition, as a manifestation of their souls—without which said souls would remain mute and unintelligible. The audience becomes part of the music-making collective and the collective in turn becomes part of them, voluntarily accepted by the audience as their own sacred 'I'.

Group leader Mick Jagger described collective authorship within the *Rolling Stones* this way:

> I just go in there [to the studio] with a germ of an idea, the smaller the germ the better, and give it to [the group], feed it to them and see what happens. Then it comes out as a *Rolling Stones* record instead of me telling everybody what I want them to play. That way no one's got any preconceived ideas. All they've got is a notion to go on. Which is exactly what Keith Richards is, a notion to go on. There are songs that start off as my particular riff, but they get taken up by others in the band and turned into something I didn't imagine … If I'm right along with them it helps even more. Which is exactly why the records sound like group efforts united by a common feel.[2]

In the process of the collective improvisation which gives birth to music, one person offers up a beginning idea-impulse, another takes this up and develops it, and a third decorates and completes it, giving the general thoughts a living form. Each participant has his own particular role in this complex process: together they must select, from a whole arsenal of possible choices, that one and only possibility which corresponds to and is right for the mood of the given moment. It is necessary to find an appropriate continuation for this thought, one which corresponds to its nature, in order that every subsequent move be an unavoidable continuation of the move before. It is sometimes necessary to return to the previously expressed, and to find the best time and place to make such returns: unending innovation cannot be retained in the human memory and renders the piece formless. Sometimes it is necessary to make pauses, bring a thought to a temporary conclusion and then begin again. It is also necessary to preserve the internal unity of the process of music making, not to let out of one's sight the original emotional impulse, its idea, and at the same time continually push forward. This function—that of 'keeper of the main key'—is, in the *Rolling Stones*, the province of guitarist Keith Richards, while the

2 *Rolling Stones in their own Words* (1985) London: Omnibus Press, p. 99.

role of generator of ideas belongs to Mick Jagger. If, however, all these roles are played by one person—then a figure is born which society has every reason to call a composer.

The composer appeared at a rather late stage of man's musical development, during the post-traditional period, when sufficient material for 'solo improvisation' had already been compiled, when many possibilities for the development of initial musical ideas had been noted, and when it had become clear that it was possible to give a spontaneous musical stream a controlling and logical base form. The composer is he who has gone through the musical school of the past and is ready to take upon himself the role of oracle and 'expresser' of the internal 'I' of an entire generation. He is master of the whole available arsenal of musical means; he knows how his contemporaries see the process of change, how they see development and its possible outcome, and how they see the universe as a whole. He who is prepared to write the spiritual message of his age in the language of music becomes a composer.

The architectonic ear

A composer's creation may seem like the embodiment of freedom: the author can call forth any theme he wants from out of nowhere, give it the form he desires, think up a continuation for it which suits him, and finally, when he thinks the time is right, complete the piece's development. Unlike, say, an architect, a composer is not constrained by the practicality of his conception—no one is going to live in his musical 'castle'; and unlike an artist, a composer is not bound by notions of verisimilitude, as his musical picture does not have to resemble anything or anyone. And unlike a poet, further, the composer is not restrained by the accepted meanings of words and the rules of grammar. And yet the composer is less free than any of these colleagues in creativity. A musical work derives all of its logic internally; it has no direct or visible correspondence with the real world; the degree of its internal coherence and the extent to which its form proves organic define its quality.

The listener, who takes music as his own creation, should be in a position to follow the thought of the composer and agree with it: he should appropriate this thought and at every stage follow along, now expecting, now not expecting to hear one or another of its turns. Finally, he should be in a position to recognize the work as something familiar when he hears it again. For music to become a means of communication, the composer must observe an organic-ness of development and completeness of form, so that everything naturally flows from what preceded it and so that everything together constitutes a connected and internally logical musical account. 'You can't take a word out of a song', as the Russian folk wisdom has it, seemingly underlining the principal quality of any artistic creation—its organic nature. Such a composition can be likened to a plant which has grown from a seed, or a living organism which has developed from an embryo: just as the 'plan' of the entire organism is set in a unique combination of genes, so a musical work invariably develops from the composer's conception and embodies his idea.

In analyzing musical compositions, Yehudi Menuhin found that the best method for him lay in noting when he could understand why certain motifs, and not others, turned up—and turned up namely *there*, and not elsewhere; and in understanding how, step by step, namely *this* work arose and not some other:

> How could I now be content with conclusions drawn from basic musical analysis, listing exposition, development, recapitulation and coda and noting a series of modulations in this or that major or minor key? Like a biochemist discovering that every human cell bears the imprint of the body it belongs to, I had to establish why these notes and no others belonged to this sonata. . . Such information remained in the end as unilluminating as the description that tells you a man has the normal furnishing of limbs and features, weighs so much, is dark haired and has brown eyes; the man himself slips through the categories. . . Laboriously the composer feels his way through the notes of his symphony to the last triumphant bar, only to discover that their choice and sequence were inevitable all along. The inevitability does not rob him of achievement, however, for only hindsight can preclude all other notes and only he could father these.[3]

The demand for internal coherence and organic-ness of continuation obliges the composer to look attentively after adjacent phrases and sound combinations; if he has used a certain A, and next to it placed a certain B, then for a subsequent C there are already a considerable number of limitations. This C cannot simply be dropped in out of the blue: it can be a variant of A, a variant of B, a synthesis of the two, or a contrast to them (and them alone, not other possible A's and B's) —but it cannot appear as though nothing had gone before it. All parts and stages of a musical phrase must together comprise a certain organic unity of possibilities and their realizations, each subsequent step of a musical thought must flow from those which preceded it and must lead to those which will follow.

Learning to 'put together music' by purely speculative means, as a child might assemble building blocks, is impossible. One can learn typical methods of connecting musical elements in one or another style; one can memorize an impressive collection of these elements themselves. But the entire diversity of their coupling and arrangement, built on the organic-ness of the connections between the past and future and on the unity of the conception which runs through all these combinations, is impossible to learn. On this level of musical structure, 'supergrammatical' in nature, the architectonic ear begins its work. It joins in the role of assistant in the development of a wondrous musical creation: it does not allow the appearance in the creation of internally illogical musical steps. It is the musical quality controller and creator of musical beauty fulfilling the function of overseer of the integrity of the text. The architectonic ear answers for the continuity of development and proportionality of the parts of the musical form; it creates musical harmony, insuring the correspondence of the parts to the whole and strengthening their internal unity.

The term itself suggests, of course, a certain affinity with mathematics. One of the first uses of the term can be traced to Rimsky-Korsakov (1911), who employed it in his musical-pedagogical works since the 1880s. Rimsky held that any composer worth mentioning was endowed with an 'architectonic ear'. The musical historian and critic Boris Astafiev later noted, in analyzing the talent of Glinka:

> The development of perfect pitch and the internal ear leads to the formation of an ability which can be termed the architectonic ear and the sense of musical logic. This is the ability to hear

---

3 Menuhin, Y. (1979) *Unfinished Journey*. London: MacDonald and Jane's, p. 136.

part-singing and sense the tonal and rhythmic relationship of chords between and among themselves; the ability as a result of which the musician instinctively senses the laws of unconditional beauty and the logical connection of the consequences, interpreted and illuminated by the course of the melody, i.e. of the musical phrasing.[4]

The Renaissance was the era of sovereignty for the architectonic ear in music; during that period, the process of composition saw the mind walk hand in hand with intuition, so to speak, and perhaps even a bit ahead of it. In the eighteenth and nineteenth centuries, with their outgrowing forms and quest for organic development, the role of the architectonic ear was also very great. And this role only increased in the twentieth century. This is particularly characteristic of representatives of the twelve-tone technique of the early part of the century. One of the leaders of this trend, the composer Anton Webern, remarked that 'From a single main thought one develops all those which follow—therein lies the surest connection!'[5]

In the work of the composers of the 'rationalist school' this striving to create an entire musical fabric from a single nucleus was a conscious endeavor. The 'rationalist' Sergei Taneev, a great admirer of the Renaissance masters, put the matter quite plainly: 'In composing I do not pay any attention to whether or not this or that combination of a musical idea will find a use for itself in my work; I concern myself only with exploiting fully, in all avenues, those musical conclusions which can arise from the given thoughts'.[6] Composers of a more intuitive cast of mind did the same thing completely unconsciously: Gustav Mahler, for example, recalled that 'Sometimes I begin in the middle, sometimes at the beginning, and sometimes even at the end—then everything else comes in and arranges itself around what is already there until a completed whole is achieved'.[7] Both composers were in fact speaking of the architectonic ear, which oversees the internal connection between the whole and the parts, directing development in such a way that this connection always appears faintly visible on the surface but is under no circumstances primitive or obtrusive.

The esthetic sense of the person endowed with an architectonic ear, who understands the correspondence of the parts and the whole in music, signals whether it is ready to accept the fruits of compositional fantasy for further development. The work of the architectonic ear—which man senses as the continuous discerning of Yes or No, Beautiful or Not Beautiful—constantly directs the process of compositional creativity. Without an active architectonic ear and esthetic sense the work of composition would become an empty 'musical eruption', lacking as it would anything to form it and turn it into a conscious whole. The architectonic ear is the creator of the musically sublime; because of it music turns from an information system, like that of speech, into art—and man from an

---

[4] Asafiev, B. V. (1952) Sluh Glinki/Glinka's ear. In *Izbrannie trudy/Selected Works*, vol.1. Moscow: Izdatelstvo Akademii nauk, p. 294.

[5] Webern, A. (1975) Lektsii o muzyke.Pis'ma/Lectures on Music. Letters. Moscow: Muzyka, p. 113.

[6] Protopopov, V. (ed.) (1947) *Pamyati Sergeya Ivanovicha Taneeva/In the memory of Sergey Ivanovich Taneev*. Moscow-Leningrad: Muzgiz.

[7] Mahler, G. (1964) *Pis'ma, dokumenty/Letters, Documents*. Moscow: Muzyka, p. 233.

ordinary mortal into a composer, whose beautiful creations are capable of surviving him for the ages.

How the architectonic ear works

A composer gets an idea, a vague image, really, which he wants to embody in sound. He searches, probes, sketches, and sometimes it seems to him that his concept is ready to be brought to life. If he were satisfied with the first thought that came to mind, if he seized on everything, joyfully and uncritically, that his tireless fantasy suggested to him, he would emerge as a nothing more than a musical hack, producing a stream of useless musical trash. To such a composer the pangs of creativity, sleepless nights, and the search for the Ideal are unknown: he has no sense of what one might strive for or where the unachievable musical perfection might 'live'.

The talented musician, on the other hand, has the architectonic ear standing guard Cerberus-like at the 'exit sign' of the probing and testing musical workshop of his mind. The architectonic ear knows the initial idea with which the author began; it senses the sound connections and relationships invested in this idea; and there at the exit it monitors what gets out of the planning stage for further development, allowing only those things which do not distract the work from its proper course and insuring that all the attendant musical phrases and fragments are strung appropriately together for the general line selected for further development. The architectonic ear is strict: the esthetic sense is often required to reject the fruits of the composer's labor, requiring the author to continue his search for usable musical 'parts', a process which can be, given the demanding nature of the esthetic sense, torturous. The nephew of the outstanding composer Nikolai Metner recalled:

> [Metner] occupied himself with composing from morning till night, with tremendous stubbornness and insistence. For hours at a time he would search painstakingly for just that expression of an idea of his which would satisfy him. He admitted to me that in composing he would have the feeling that he had to capture on paper something that already existed somewhere—all he needed to do was strip away all the unnecessary material around it and reveal the real essence of this music in the closest approximation possible to that ideal image which he sensed. It was a difficult and torturous process for him every time.[8]

The architectonic ear, lining up a flawless chain of mutually compatible musical fragments to form an integrated text, is continually occupied with the process of making difficult choices. If among the proffered material there is nothing useful or attractive, the architectonic ear repeats its 'demand' and the composer's imagination must return, again and again, to its storehouse, where the creative powers likewise must, repeatedly, invent, combine and construct some new fragment which can be sent along for review to the 'higher authority' (that same 'higher authority' which Pushkin said hung over poets: the esthetic sense which judged more truly and more strictly than the most captious critic).

8 Metner, N. (1981) Stat'i, materialy, vospominaniya/Articles, Materials, Memoirs. Moscow: Sovetsky kompozitor, p. 37.

Offering more and more new combinations of musical elements, continuously seeking to identify correspondences between the demands of a concept and its possibilities—which are present, as Boris Asafiev said (1971), in the 'intonational dictionary of the epoch'—the musical fantasy of the composer attempts to draw as close as possible to an ideal of beauty. And indeed, such is also true of the creative process outside the realm of music, and even outside that of art itself. Almost a century ago, in his book *Mathematical Creativity*, the outstanding mathematician Henri Poincaret noted:

> To create means not to put together useless combinations but useful ones, which are a tiny minority. To create is to know how to recognize and to know how to select the useful. The ability to select the best, indeed the only useful combinations, is always connected with the creative will and is one of the principal signs of giftedness.[9]

The work of the architectonic ear, acting through and revealing itself in the esthetic sense, unfailingly includes esthetic motivation, which holds before the mind's eye of the composer an ideal of beauty, never letting it fade or disappear. This ideal is sensed as the appropriate relationship of the elements, to each other and to the whole, which the creator envisions. The esthetic sense contemplates this ideal state of relations as peace and harmony—the complete and successful adjustment of the constituent parts to each other. If this harmony is for some reason not achieved, the esthetic sense cannot rest. Esthetic motivation is a fundamental component of the architectonic ear. It is esthetic sense that made Kai, the boy hero of Andersen's *Snow Queen*, endlessly rearrange the blocks of ice in his attempt to create a design of ideal beauty. But the heartless boy lacked, most likely, a fundamental component of the architectonic ear—the esthetic controller which takes a potential new piece for the picture, examines it and decides whether it fits or not. Kai spent hours with his blocks of ice but could not find the answers—what he lacked to complete his design.

The technology of the work of the architectonic ear is mathematical insofar as it relies on the practice known in logical thought as variant selection. The esthetic controller examines the outcome proposed by the musical fantasy and, depending on the evaluation of its esthetic quality, accepts or rejects it. This entire process takes place, as a rule, entirely unconsciously (Aranovsky 1991). Attempting to explain the technology of the work of the esthetic controller, Igor Stravinsky liked to draw on his mathematician friend Marston Morse, who very accurately defined on what basis and by what means, from a field of innumerable variants, the composer chooses the only usable one: 'Mathematics is the result of mysterious forces', he said, 'which no one understands and in which an important role is played by the unconscious comprehension of beauty. Of the numberless possible solutions the mathematician chooses one for its beauty, and then brings it down to earth'.[10]

Esthetic motivation as an eternally sensed striving toward the ideal makes up the emotional component of the architectonic ear. In this motivation there is something of

---

[9] Poincaret, H. (1910) Matematicheskoe tvorchestvo/Creativity in Mathematics. Yuriev, p. 16–17.
[10] Stravinsky, I. (1971) *Dialogi/Dialogues*. Leningrad: Muzyka, p. 233.

the much more primitive yet similar (in emotional 'side tone') feeling of modal attraction: not finding resolution, the sound remains poised in midair and the whole phrase cannot be completed. The esthetic controller is the operational-practical and logicalized component of the architectonic ear. It sets musical 'meanings' into a musical 'expression', where there should already be an unknown element, where a place has been prepared for it, and checks whether this is the necessary element or not; if not, alas, the search must continue. The joint action of both components—esthetic motivation and the esthetic controller—brings into action the architectonic ear and carries out its work. This gives a dual emotional–rational character to the activity of the architectonic ear.

If the architectonic ear is not an integrated part of the compositional activity and the esthetic sense is working in a passive mode, then the rational component comes to the fore: the esthetic idea, giving harmony to the sequence at hand, is already determined and understood, and the architectonic ear functions as a control to determine the extent to which the final 'product' corresponds to it. It analyzes the musical whole and defines to what degree this whole is appropriate to the harmony it bears within it.

Testing for esthetic assessment of music, Polish psychologist Andrzei Sekowski (1988) divided a group of schoolchildren into two sections according to their success in things musical. According to Sekowski's results, children who were successful in music were not distinguished by a high level of traditional musical abilities (i.e. musical ear, sense of rhythm, and so on) but rather by the exactitude of their esthetic evaluations of music, the nuanced feel for its beauty. The ability to make such evaluations correlated much more strongly with the general level of intellect and intellectual achievements of the members of the group than with their basic musical abilities. Continuing to question teachers and familiarize himself with the successes of children in various areas, Sekowski learned that the ability to form a true judgment of musical value corresponded to the general criteria of the participants in the experiment and to creative potential as a whole. As he eventually noted,

> Findings showed that ability for esthetic assessment of music was more strongly correlated with general intelligence level than was fundamental musical ability. This suggests that musical taste is determined not only by level of esthetic sensitivity, but also by intellectual level and factors connected with creative activity, requiring specific predispositions.[11]

Thus the author concluded that the musical-esthetic sense bears a multifaceted emotional-rational character, including as it does the work of the intellect as well as a creative component.

An experiment by Clifford Madsen (1997) confirmed the presence of a certain rationalism and logical orientation of the esthetic sense. Madsen sought to determine, with the help of computerized identification of the phases of a listener's attention, whether there exists a psycho-emotional relationship between the arousal-relaxation sensations summoned by music, on the one hand, and the esthetic perception of beauty-ugliness on the other.

---

[11] Sekowski, A. (1988) Personality predictors of music achievement. *Polish Psychological Bulletin*, 19, p. 131.

Adult non-musician subjects listened to a large (20 minute) segment of Puccini's *La Boheme* and noted the most arousing, 'spiritually uplifting' and touching moments in the music and the most esthetically satisfying moments. In many cases the subjects did not call the arousing moments beautiful or the beautiful ones arousing, meaning the emotional and esthetic approaches to the art of music did not correspond—proving that the perception of musical beauty is completely autonomous and does not depend on its emotional qualities. There is no strict correspondence between these two scales of measurement.

The expressive ear for music takes on the principal burden of recognition of the emotional expressiveness of a musical passage, whereas musical beauty is primarily the province of the architectonic ear. The lowest, least discriminating level of musical perception and the highest, most intellectual level work together in every act of perception. Each keeps up a man-music dialogue; the expressive ear maintains the simplest exchange of communicative signals, while the architectonic ear gives rise to a dialogue of esthetic dimensions in which the esthetic sense either accepts or rejects the musical 'product' the subject is hearing. Composers often complain of the inability of ordinary listeners to grasp both these levels in a musical work. Arnold Schoenberg (1949), for one, felt that relatively few people were capable of perceiving music from a truly musical standpoint—on the level at which the intellectual pleasure born of structural beauty can be of the same magnitude as that produced by the music's emotional qualities. The sense of participation in the process of communicating something, which the expressive ear creates, should ideally be reinforced by the sense of participation in the musical thought itself, which is what the architectonic ear creates. But this ideal is realized, like so many ideals, only very rarely.

A critical aspect of the work of the architectonic ear is its reliance on spatial perceptions. As the overseer of the integrity of the overall text, the architectonic ear takes in all the constituent elements at a single glance, contrasting them with each other in the process. It discerns the key idea which holds together the whole construct, seeing the musical form as a spatial object with its various proportions and structural patterns. These patterns do not apply to individual sounds and minor motifs, nor to the rules of musical language level; it is the analytical ear which regulates these simplest of musical connections on the level of cohesion of individual sounds and the sound groupings next to them. The architectonic ear, by contrast, works with larger blocks, each of which represents an individually formed unit of musical speech; it belongs exclusively to this phrase and fulfills its own role in the phrase's structure.

Far from all listeners are capable of grasping with their mind's eye large musical spaces and evaluating the beauty of the musical forms which arise only in such a wide-view spectrum. As some music scholars and psychologists have noted (Asafiev 1971; Clynes 1986; Davidson 1994; Kirnarskaya 1997), the majority of the audience listens fragmentarily, in excerpts, not attempting to imagine the entire work as a whole.

Ruth Brittin and Deborah Sheldon (1995) asked a hundred non-musician students to evaluate twelve fragments of European classical music in styles, Baroque, Romantic, and twentieth century. The same works were then evaluated by student musicians, with the evaluations (once again) performed in two stages—during and after the listening period. The non-musician students quite differently evaluated the material in both stages; in the post-listening period they immediately turned cooler toward the music which they had liked while hearing it. The student musicians, on the other hand, maintained the same evaluations before and after: for them the music retained the same attraction it had held previously and thus received the same high marks in the post-listening phase. In the context of these results one cannot but recall Asafiev's concepts of 'form-process' (1971), in which every moment is experienced only in contrast with the moments adjacent to it; and 'form-crystal', in which the entire form stands before the listener as a completed entity. The architectonic ear regulates the form-crystal, and musicians whose architectonic ear is more developed are capable of perceiving form-crystal and reacting to its beauty. Non-musicians are less prepared for such listening; their architectonic ear practically ceases to work after listening and the music they have heard dissipates into separate fragments which call forth no esthetic reaction.

The work of the architectonic ear demands a significant degree of hierarchical arrangement in musical perception: minor sound units come together into bigger ones, and these larger musical blocks and parts, entering into certain relationships with each other, remain in the consciousness of the perceiver as if transparent: the separate sounds and motifs of which they consist are realized and are fixed—the architectonic ear works together with the analytical ear and the two listening strategies combine with one another. Psychologists agree that the encompassing of an integrated musical thought takes place in the right (spatial) hemisphere of the brain, while the disintegration of this thought into smaller 'corpuscles' and individual sounds is handled by the left hemisphere, to whom the perception of musical pitch is assigned (Aranovsky 1974; Benton 1977; Levitin 2006; Levitin and Menon 2005; Medushevsky 1993; Patel *et al.* 1998; Peretz and Zatorre 2003). A good architectonic ear presupposes that the left and right hemispheres are working in tandem, that neither one is suppressing the other. In practice the ability to exist as if in 'two phases' is fairly rare and demands a good internal ear and musical memory.

Lucinda DeWitt and Arthur Samuel (1990) conducted an experiment to determine the extent to which subjects were capable of working on the level of an entire musical thought and at the same time on the level of the thought's smallest 'molecules'. Adult subjects were played familiar melodies which had been changed in various ways; in some cases entire phrases had been 'spoiled', while in others the changes had been limited to 'minor damage' on the level of individual sounds and chords. These second, minor disruptions were easily corrected by the subjects, relying on their musical-language perceptions: their sense of key and sense of rhythm told them how to act. In the deformations of the first type, in which comprehensible fragments of the whole had been affected, the subjects proved powerless to make repairs despite the fact that they knew, it seemed, the melodies—which would thus yield without great difficulty, one would think, to recreation from memory. The experimenters noted that without the support of the architectonic ear, which senses and evaluates the reciprocal distribution of the units in a passage as comprehensible and even inevitable, the musical memory refuses to work: the incorrect variant erases from the memory all traces of the correct one, and reconstructing it from a basis of musical-language and musical-grammatical patterns was impossible for the subjects.

An analogous experiment was conducted by a team led by Irene Deliége (1996). A group of 20 subjects, 10 musicians and 10 non-musicians, was asked to reconstruct the original version of a melody they had just heard in fragments. In a second task, the two groups were required to correct the mistakes in a melody made by violations of standard musical-grammatical rules. Here also the second assignment seemed to both groups much easier than the first, and many subjects could replace the incorrect sounds. However, the melody that both groups had heard in fragmentary form proved impossible to reconstruct anew for the majority of both groups. The subjects lost the logic of the musical thought; the interrelationship of the parts within the melody was incomprehensible to them. The subjects' architectonic ear proved too weak for the task, and their esthetic sense kept silent: they could not correctly evaluate the quality of the probes and supports attempts which they themselves undertook. An experiment conducted by Michael Karno and Vladimir Konecni (1992) at the University of California at San Diego with 42 music students became a scandal within the musical psychology community. The subjects listened to the famous first movement of Mozart's *Symphony in G-minor* in which the continuity of the alternation of the major fragments had been changed: certain of the experimental examples began in the middle, then moved on to the end, and for their conclusions returned to the actual beginning of the fragment. In eight of the nine cases the whole logic of Mozart's constructions had been brutally violated; only one original-author variant was hidden among the nine, quietly awaiting the subjects' highest evaluations. Yet such were not forthcoming: the students reacted equally positively to all nine variations, showing no preference whatsoever for Mozart's own version. Their architectonic ear did not grasp the structures presented to them in their entirety, as complete units; thus the students could not perceive the violations in musical logic. The authors of the experiment noted with a sense of disappointment that there are real limitations of aural resources in society:

> It would seem that many (armchair-based) claims made by musicologists about the role of structure in a work's impact can be called into question by empirical research; and structure may be less usefully viewed as a perceptible element in music appreciation and more as a conceptual tool of music composition.[12]

Many experiments have identified the weakness of the architectonic ear in the majority of people who do not sense the illogic of musical development and the lack of correspondence of parts to a musical whole. Musicians of average ability—a category which includes university and conservatory music students—are no exception to this general rule, which demonstrates once again the high level of musical giftedness the architectonic

---

[12] Karno, M. and Konecni, V. (1992) The effect of structural interventions in the first movement of Mozart's symphony in G minor of aesthetic preference. *Music Perception*, 10, p. 72.

ear and esthetic sense operate. They form the initial stage of the musical-creative gift since they define the artistic quality of the creative production of the composer: an inability to make esthetic judgments automatically speaks to an absence of a gift for composition. Even in evaluating a musical production created by others almost all people experience significant difficulty. It is not incidental that the great philosopher Immanuel Kant assigned such great significance to the esthetic sense, treating it as the sense bordering reason itself; he called his work on esthetics *The Critique of Judgement*. A spatial encompassing of the musical whole, the necessity of bearing in mind both the whole entity and the interrelationship of its constituent parts, which is provided by the joint operation of the right and left hemispheres of the brain—all this places very high demands on the architectonic ear. Meeting these demands is something that can be done only by a musician who possesses the signs of the composer's gift.

The architectonic ear and the esthetic sense of the composer

The architectonic ear grasps the patterns of construction of a musical form on all its levels. If the form is beautiful then the esthetic sense accepts it as a sort of law, whereby all things of this nature should be this way. The composer Anton Webern noted with enthusiasm in one of his letters that for the ancient Greeks the concepts of 'law' and 'melody' were rendered by the same word, *nomos*, underscoring a higher design that melody also represents. The architectonic ear received its name from architecture, where beauty and the mathematical calculability of proportions go hand in hand. Beautiful musical and architectural forms are always extraordinarily exact, and the slightest deviation from the author's conception may prove fatal. The architect Carlo Rossi, the author of St.-Petersburg's many treasures, maintained that in a good building one finds that the unity of all the parts follows the laws of the genre in such a way that nothing can be added, subtracted or changed—except for the worse (Nikolaev 1964). In an analogous way the esthetic sense of the composer seeks musical perfection. Sergei Rakhmaninov remarked of the music of Chopin that it was 'a pleasure to play one's through his perfect passages. Every note in his works seems to be in exactly the right place, the place where it must produce the most subtle effect. All is where it should be. It is impossible to add anything or take anything away'.[13]

If the logic of a musical form is violated, the architectonic ear of the composer reacts in exactly the same way as someone with perfect pitch reacts upon hearing a false note. There is a story told of J. S. Bach (Kushenov-Dmitrevsky 1831) in which he is invited to dine at a fashionable and important residence. One of the other invited guests played a bit on the clavier, but upon seeing Bach enter he abandoned his playing, ending the piece rather abruptly and awkwardly. Bach could not tolerate such cavalier disregard for musical beauty: without so much as greeting a soul, he hurried to the clavier, made up an ending for the piece which worthily completed its musical thought and, when he had played

---

[13] Rakhmaninov, S. (1964) Literaturnoe nasledie. Pis'ma, vospominaniya, interv'yu/Literary works. Letters, Memoirs, Interviews, vol. 1. Moscow: Muzyka, p. 92.

it through to its conclusion, offered the appropriate greetings to the host and the other guests. To Bach music was more important than the elementary social graces. A story from the modern era makes the same point. It is said that the young Leonard Bernstein, while still a student (Peyser 1987), once heard through an open window a toneless pianist making his torturous way through the labyrinth of someone's romantic opus. Bernstein immediately constructed in his mind what *should* sound forth in place of the musical nonsense that was grating on his ears. The future maestro climbed in through the pianist's open window: at the piano sat a young girl, whom Bernstein unceremoniously brushed aside as he began to play, starting in the place where the girl had gotten completely lost. 'This is the way it is supposed to sound', he is said to have told the dumbfounded girl, after which he disappeared whence he had come, back through the open window.

The composer's gift often makes itself known through an unusually keen esthetic sense. The future genius has yet to create all his future masterpieces, he has not yet been noticed for any reason, but the capability of his musical judgment is already distinguished by its extraordinary acuteness and subtlety. In every era the musical stage sees many and various authors, and it would be naive indeed to think that only masterworks are performed in popular music revues and the opera theater. Nonetheless, the young Tchaikovsky, while still a mere dilettante pianist and law student, immediately distinguished high-quality music from popular imitations.

> The music of *Don Juan* [he recalled] was the first music which produced a tremendous impression on me. It aroused in me a sacred rapture which later bore fruit. Through it I entered the world of artistic beauty inhabited by only the greatest of geniuses. For the fact that I committed my life to music I am indebted to Mozart. He gave the impulse to my musical powers, and made me love music more than anything on earth.[14]

The young officer Modest Mussorgsky similarly took to the musical masterpieces immediately, the same Don Juan and the works of Glinka and Dargomyzhsky, and tried to win over his comrades who were mired in admiration for the fashionable Italian operas of the day (Shlifstein 1975).

The great pianist and teacher Karl Meyer, who taught Glinka, saw his pedagogical role as sharpening his charges' esthetic sense and assisting in its further development (Glinka 1954). Recalling his years of study, Glinka particularly valued the development of his musical taste, a process which his teacher insistently and thoroughly pursued. Comments on his playing, demands that he demonstrate a good performing style, were more or less self-evidently useful and necessary, but explications concerning artistic quality were something for which Glinka gave primary credit to his first teacher.

> Meyer more than others abetted the development of my musical talent. He did not limit himself to taking a stand four-square against over-sophistication and refined expression in my playing, demanding from me a clear and natural performance; he also explained to me, naturally, without pedantry

---

[14] Tchaikovsky, M. I. (1903) *Zhizn' P.I.Tchaikovskogo/Life of Pyotr Iliych Tchaikovsky*. Moscow: Izdatelstvo Jurgensona.

and taking into account as much as possible my level of understanding at the time, the worthiness of pieces, differentiating the classic from the merely good, and the latter from the bad.[15]

The experience of hearing good music is a critical condition for the awakening of the composer's talent: a sleeping architectonic ear and esthetic sense will not allow a composer to compose; without experience at perceiving musical beauty, the composer's esthetic sense cannot become the regulator of the creative process. The architectonic ear must first learn to perceive music as a designed entity and, through the esthetic sense, perceive the higher integrity and perfection of the musical form. In his memoirs Rimsky-Korsakov complained about the extraordinary poverty of his childhood impressions:

> The Tikhvin ball orchestra long consisted of a violin, on which someone named Nikolai sawed away at polkas and cadrilles, and tambourines, which were artistically banged by one Kuz'ma, a house painter by profession and a great drunkard. As for vocal music I recall hearing only a single Tikhvin woman, named Baranova, who sang the romance 'Chto ty spish', muzhichok?' ('Why Do You Sleep, Little Man?') Then beyond my father's singing there was spiritual music, that is the singing done in the women's and men's monasteries. In the former they sang badly, while in the latter, as I recall, it went well enough. I could only seriously come to love music in Petersburg, where I first heard real music played in the real way.[16]

From this and similar reminiscences from other composers one may conclude that to a composer the masterpieces of his colleagues are important not simply as useful musical information but as an emotional stimulus as well, as a psychological catalyst for his own creative work. Maturity of the esthetic sense can only be achieved through the experience of hearing good music; only when sufficient maturity has been reached can the composer create independently. The great Russian composers of the nineteenth century—Mussorgsky, Glinka, Tchaikovsky, and Rimsky-Korsakov—were all children of the gentry estate and all belonged to the category of late bloomers: their gifts were discovered only after the age of 20, which is by European standards extremely late. While all four had the opportunity in childhood to hear not too many musical masterpieces, their esthetic sense did not find fertile ground for establishment and growth, and thus they began to compose late—and reached their full creative maturity late as well, as the delayed start inhibited the development of their genius.

The architectonic ear easily establishes the principles of connection among musical elements, and can predict what should follow what in this or that musical style, what their thematic roots are, and the typical methods of their development—just as the analytical ear masters modes [lady] and the simplest sound relationships, so the architectonic ear masters musical styles. They stand before the architectonic ear as complete systems, particular dialects of a musical language with its own lexicon and rules of syntax. The possessor of a good architectonic ear is not only capable of distinguishing different musical 'handwritings', he can in fact master them himself and write in them. The ability to understand someone else's musical language as you do your own—with complete

15 Glinka, M. (1954) O muzyke i muzykantah/On Music and Musicians. Moscow: Gosmuzgiz, p. 16–17.
16 Rimsky-Korsakov, N. A. (1982) Letopis' moei muzykal'noi zhizni/The Story of my Life in Music. Moscow: Muzyka, p. 14.

recognition of its internal algorithms and a sense of the connections of the sound elements in the context of a given style as patterned and predictable—is a quality enjoyed by all gifted musicians.

A highly developed architectonic ear may exist in the context of a musical system quite removed from said composer's own preferences or passions. The brother of the composer Karl Weber, the orchestra director for the Berlin opera, was quite surprised when Giacomo Meyerbeer, whose talents related exclusively to opera, presented him with a masterfully written eight-part fugue (Becker and Becker 1989). Meyerbeer easily mastered all the contrapuntal devices which were then the basis of a composer's education: he could imitate different musical styles, living and working within the framework which they described. This ability constitutes a particular 'specialty' of the architectonic ear, its highest expression. This imitation and variant copying is the beginning of all creative composition. The composer's architectonic ear draws him to 'write himself into' the framework of defined styles; he wants to feel at home in someone else's 'musical house' before he is capable of building his own.

A composer's architectonic ear is active. It does not simply puzzle out the algorithms of musical styles, it creates them as well. The esthetic sense of a gifted musician is equally busy. Teacher-composers are famous for immediately detecting violations in the assignments written by their students, and knowing how to indicate exactly the place where the violation occurred. A less acute esthetic sense in such a case could only perceive that something was 'amiss'—the necessary harmony was lacking—but could not carry out the immediate 'lifesaving' work necessary to right things. The beginning composer Emmanuel Muzzio took lessons from Giuseppe Verdi, 15 minutes at a session. As he noted at the time:

> The reason why the lessons are so short is that the Signor Maestro sees at a glance if there are mistakes in my exercise; if it's not right he indicates where I must correct it; I correct it and he gives another glance, and that suffices. Then a few words on tomorrow's lesson, five minutes playing— that's the lesson. Does that seem little to you? Nevertheless with these quarters of an hour I have reached a stage I could certainly not have reached with anybody else. Everything has turned out for the best. [17]

Such examples speak to a speed and exactness of the composer's esthetic judgments not characteristic of less gifted musicians.

The esthetic sense of the composer can also be prescient: amid the great musical current it can distinguish fragments which are, in essence, subordinate to different stylistic algorithms—and draw appropriate conclusions from these distinctions. The 17–year-old composer and critic Gustave Laroche was able, thanks to his highly developed esthetic sense, to discern in the music of the beginning Tchaikovsky the signs of a coming (if still far from realized) genius:

> I see in you the greatest—or better to say the only—hope for our musical future. You know perfectly well that I am not flattering you. I never hesitated to tell you that your *Romans in the Coliseum*

---

[17]   Walker, F. (1982) *The Man Verdi*. The University of Chicago Press.

was a pathetic mediocrity, or that your *Groza* was a museum of anti-musical mediocrities. Indeed, everything you have done, not excluding *Kharakternye tantsy* and scenes from *Boris Godunov*, I consider the work of a schoolboy, preparatory and experimental, if one may say so. Your creations will begin to appear, perhaps, in five years or so. But these, the mature, classic works, will exceed everything we have had since Glinka.[18]

The height of the composer's esthetic sense is his ability to judge his own creations and to evaluate their artistic work accurately. And indeed, this is the principal control function of the esthetic sense in the creative process. This control does not spare the author's vanity and never exaggerates the value of music it is called upon to judge. The composer Dargomyzhsky, influenced by the quartet groups which met to play Beethoven in his family's house, set about writing a quartet himself. 'I wrote three parts', he recalled, 'but two moths later they seemed to me so bad that I lost interest in writing the fourth'.[19]

At the same time, when a composer has written a masterpiece, he knows it: his esthetic sense never deceives him. Scott Joplin, the great composer of American ragtime, immediately and unabashedly announced to his friend Arthur Marshall the birth of a masterpiece after he had composed the '*Maple Leaf Rag*' (Gammond 1975), which was to be a worldwide hit. The accuracy of his esthetic judgment helped the author fight for the publication of his song with a total certainty that it would bring him wealth and fame. After being turned down by two publishers, Joplin went to see a third, John Stark; so confident was Joplin of the song's wonderful properties that he picked up a 7-year-old boy on the street on his way to the publisher's, then played the '*Maple Leaf Rag*' for Stark as the boy danced and made faces to the music. This 'argument' convinced Stark, whose esthetic sense had remained silent (he was not a gifted musician). The publisher believed the boy and believed the composer; and this belief earned both Stark and Joplin considerable wealth. But had the esthetic sense of the author been less insistent and sure of itself, who can say what might have become of the '*Maple Leaf Rag*'?

The young rock and pop composer Paul McCartney felt triumphant after producing his masterpiece 'Yesterday'. As he recalled some years later

> I like it not only because it was a big success but because it was one of the most instinctive songs I've ever written. I just rolled out of my bed one morning and there was a piano next to the bed in the place where I was living at a time, and I rolled out of bed and just got the tune. I was so proud of it, I felt it was an original tune, it didn't copy off anything and it was a big tune, it was all there and nothing repeated. I get made fun of because of it a bit. I remember George saying 'Blimey, he's always talking about "Yesterday", you'd think he was Beethoven or somebody'. But it is the one, I reckon, that is the most complete thing I've ever written. When you are trying to write a song there are certain times when you get the essence, it's all there. It's like an egg being laid, it's just so, there's not a crack nor a flaw in it.[20]

[18] Tchaikovsky, M. I. (1903) *Zhizn' P.I.Tchaikovskogo/Life of Pyotr Iliych Tchaikovsky*. Moscow: Izdatelstvo Jurgensona, p. 25.

[19] Cit. from Pekelis, M. (1966) *Dargomyzhsky*. Moscow: Muzyka, p. 141.

[20] *Paul McCartney in his own Words* (1983) New York: The Putnam Publishing Group, p. 19.

In McCartney's description one hears the euphoria of an esthetic sense which has found perfection: this unerring sense of the creator was the first sign to the author that he had produced a masterpiece for the ages.

Unlike the unsure and incomplete architectonic ear that most people have, the composer's ear is algorithmic: it can grasp 'stylistic formulas' and turn them into entire compositions. The esthetic sense of the composer is faultless, distinguishing itself by its activeness and quick response; and it is always capable of accurately evaluating its own compositions and the work of others. These qualities—of the faultless quality controller and overseer of the integrity of a text—are the heart of the composer's gift, a gift possessed only by the talented. The architectonic ear selects and filters musical material; it constructs with it, following certain defined rules; and it monitors the quality of its construction. Briefly stated, the architectonic ear and the esthetic sense stand at the origins of musical creativity and at the root of musical talent.

Testing the architectonic ear

The architectonic ear reacts sharply to violations of the integrity of a text: the crystal-form is already in place, with its critical underlying sound relationships, its structural regularities and its developmental logic. Any attempt to alter the crystal form or violation of the elements that go into it will unfailingly be registered by the esthetic sense, as it is impossible to change anything in the form without damaging the internal harmony of the musical idea, which is completely developed and has assumed its final form. Knowing this, the British musical psychologist Henry Wing began in the 1940s to put into practice broad-based testing for music appreciation. Wing (1968) proposed that the esthetic sense which the subjects would demonstrate in his tests would be the best indication of their musical giftedness. The introduction of new testing procedures was a kind of response to the methods of Carl Seashore: the replacement of Seashore's 'beep system' of recognition of sounds and intervals by tests based on music was significant indeed, as the new tests proved a very effective predictive tool.

Wing used real examples from the musical classics, altering them by various means. Indeed, the scandalous experiment involving the California music students listening to rearranged Mozart segments was a 'Wing-type' undertaking. The Wing subjects, in any case, were supposed to make their esthetic choices—accepting or rejecting the variants proposed by the controller—in response to the question Wing formulated as 'Which musical fragment do you like better?' If the subject selected the Wing-altered variants of the Bach chorale, he received a low score; if the subject's taste corresponded with that of the composer, a high score resulted.

Wing's psychology colleagues assumed that the Achilles heel of this methodology lay in the risk of previous familiarity with the music in question. It was entirely possible, they felt, that both professional musicians and amateur music lovers well acquainted with Bach's chorales would have an unarguable advantage in the testing. To the general surprise of all involved, however, it turned out that familiarity with the material had no effect whatsoever on test scores. In one of Wing's test samples, up to 45 percent of the subjects were familiar with the material—yet registered no appreciable difference in success rate at fulfilling Wing's tasks. These results were first obtained in 1948 (Wing 1968, first ed. 1948); they did not change for over two subsequent decades of testing. If the subject repeatedly heard a piece of music it did not follow that he would remember it well. Beyond this it transpired that altered variants possess a cunning all their own—an ability to erase from the memory all traces of the original works, substituting themselves in their place. The subject begins to think that it is precisely that variant—the altered one—which he had long known and remembered. Here, of course, the nature of the alternations made by Wing was of decisive significance: they did not violate musical grammar; all the musical-linguistic laws remained in force and the listeners' analytical ear was entirely satisfied. The experiment violated the musical logic and beauty of the *whole*, which is much less striking and can be detected only by subjects with an active, highly developed architectonic ear.

Compared with the exercises used to test for the analytical ear, Wing's test for the architectonic ear showed much greater predictive strength. They predicted very accurately who among the subjects would continue in music studies: only 2 percent of the 'Wing champions' left the field. No matter how researchers divided up the subject groups—into 'high' and 'low', 'high', 'low' and 'medium', or otherwise—the testing for 'music appreciation' invariably correlated with the musical success of the participants in the experiments. Wing assumed that musical talent was an innate ability (1963), and in this he was in complete agreement with Seashore (1919; 1938); but unlike the latter, Wing felt that sound-differentiating abilities were rather preceding qualities for those of a much higher order—the architectonic ear, musical taste, and the esthetic sense.

Other than musical success and love of music, the Wing test results did not correlate with anything—neither with the subjects' musical experience, with the intensity of their musical studies, nor with their families' social status. Certain individuals whose results showed that they possessed very refined musical taste were not involved with music at all; others with similarly high scores had for various reasons interrupted their music studies. But no such circumstances could influence the degree of success at Wing's tasks. The esthetic sense remained a stubborn indication of the quality of musical perception, regardless of any external circumstances. Such a 'harvest of experience' speaks to a very high quality test, one which measures only that which it is called upon to measure—the musical-esthetic sense, on which the musicality of the subject depends. Moreover, to the end of his scholarly career Wing devised tests which, in the majority of cases, remained remarkably 'democratic'. For example, students at the Rochester-Eastman School of Music, one of the best music schools in the United States, found Wing's tests too easy, claiming that they were more for amateurs than professional musicians (Newton 1959).

A series of experiments conducted by the present author in Moscow in the late 1980s used a methodology close in certain respects to that used by Wing (Kirnarskaya 1989a; 1995): at the heart of the test exercises lay altered versions of original melodies by classic composers. But at the same time significant correctives were introduced into the procedure: the participants were given 'violated' melodies, tunes disrupted according to the principles of the mathematical theory of errors. All possible violations of the whole were employed: elimination of connecting elements (in this case discrete sounds or short motifs; changes in the order of the elements; and substitution of the elements with others incorrect for the situation). The subjects were to correct these violations and reconstruct the author's original musical thought. Unlike the Wing tests, these tests were aimed at the evaluation of professional musical giftedness thus the methodology of the experiment relied on independent written work with a music score. This kind of work is closer to that of a composer and presented considerable difficulty for the subject—much more than expressing one's musical preferences among fragments played for you, as in the Wing exercises. To strengthen the creative direction of the test, the material chosen was the most elusive and least formalized— the melody. On the one hand, a melody already constitutes an integrated musical thought while on the other, however, a melody's internal laws do not subjugate themselves to any previously established rules; one can imagine an infinite number of melodies which satisfy the requirements of musical grammar. Some of these will be wonderful and others awful. As the composer Jean-Phillipe Rameau put it, 'The melody possesses no less power in the realm of the expressive than does the harmony; but it is almost impossible to lay out definite rules in this area, in which good taste has more significance than everything else'.[21]

In working with a melody the subjects are forced to rely on their intuition, that is, to demonstrate their talent and taste rather than their knowledge of the theory of music. All the test examples were of vocal music taken from the nineteenth-century romantics: Wagner, Verdi, Bellini, and Tchaikovsky. One example (of five) was from the Baroque— the first theme of the introduction to the aria for *basso* from Handel's *Messiah*. Working with vocal melodies in a familiar style should have represented a task which the student musicians taking part in the experiment could cope with easily enough: their entire education had been built on exactly this style, and none of the subjects enjoyed any advantage in this respect. The fundamental relationship of the tones which formed the melody was chosen as the basis of each melody's musical thought. The music scholar Mark Aranovsky (1991) calls the critical underlying sound constructions of the melodic whole the 'base layer', as distinct from the elements which decorate and supplement the musical thought, which he terms the 'layer of ornamentation'. Two or three supporting sound or minor motifs pertaining to the 'base layer' were removed from the melodies given to the subjects; but this was done in such a way that the tracks of this layer remained unchanged in other places; thus the 'base layer' could be reconstructed intuitively by replacing the 'disrupted' sections of the music. Two of the five tasks were of this nature.

In the third task the experimenter inserted wrong notes, sounds which violated the logic of the melody, in place of the excised tones. The task was phrased thus: 'Sing the given melody. Find the sounds in it which violate the melodic idea and correct them'. The fourth and fifth tasks focused on changes in the order of succession of the elements— parts of the theme. One task required that subjects correctly assemble scattered

---

[21] Rameau, J.-F. (1934) Traktat o garmonii/Treatise on harmony. In *Materialy i dokumenty po istorii muzyki/Materials and Documents on History of Music*, vol. 2. Moscow: Academia, p. 267.

fragments, while in the other they were to find where to restore time taken from the melody. Here the subjects had to demonstrate an understanding of the logic of musical development by finding the beginning, middle and end. The subjects in the experiment were drawn from three levels: undergraduates at a musical college (average age 22), students at a musical high school (18), and at a specialized musical elementary school (14).

The results of the experiment showed that the subjects' scores correlated to an extraordinarily high degree with the expert evaluations of the same students by teachers who had known them for at least three years. The subjects who scored below 50 were weak students whom their teachers had described as lacking in initiative, poor at academic tasks, and incapable of creative work. Scores of 50–75 went to middling students who had shown good musical qualities but consistently required the help of a teacher, to whom they looked for instruction. Only the group with scores of 75 and above was composed of bright, talented students capable of independently solving complex creative problems (Kirnarskaya 1989). This test was approved for use in the entrance examinations for higher music schools in Russia. And with the help of this test (administered before the competition), the identity of the leading group of contestants at a recent International Guitarists' Competition was predicted in advance: those who had the best test results proved the most successful in the contest, winning all the prizes awarded (Kirnarskaya 1992).

The performance of the subjects on tests for the architectonic ear once again confirms the necessity of a highly developed esthetic sense for successful musical activity: only he who possesses an architectonic ear, to whom a musical form is a designed entity and the principles of its construction clear—only this kind of person can undertake musical creativity. One more result of the experiment described above was the conclusion that the existing system of professional selection of musicians in Russia is ineffective. The percentage of gifted students in elementary, secondary, and college-level music schools is not rising; on all three levels 50 percent of the students are middling, 25 percent are weak, and 25 percent are strong. Even when competition for places in these schools was significant, students with little musical ability could be admitted. The selection system, whose methodology consisted primarily of the performance of learned material, did not command sufficient means to attract the strongest students and weed out the weakest.

An ideal system of professional career selection in the musical arts would be one based on a phylogenetic principle under which those students possessed of the highest and rarest kinds of musical gifts would be continuously recruited from the larger pool of students who have more basic and more common abilities. If the testing for the expressive ear for music were conducted on a mass basis, then the students of secondary music schools, the future music lovers and amateur musicians, would make up a large and solid base from which to make subsequent selections for professional training. Among them would naturally appear the people with the best sense of rhythm and analytical ear; these qualities would not pass unnoticed over the course of their music education. And the children motivated internally— those naturally inclined to love music and never give it up—would be reserved for the art of music regardless of their future choice of profession.

At the outset of a professional career it is desirable to have—in addition to the performance of a program learned long before and *solfeggio* exercises—testing for the architectonic ear. This would show the level of development of the architectonic ear in the future musician and the degree of activity and subtlety of his musical taste and esthetic sense. As the college-level entrance exams showed, the test scores of the majority of entering students correspond best to their results on the piano—the most gifted students proved to be those with the best architectonic ear (Kirnarskaya 1992). Given the extremely demanding competition one finds in the music world that the future professional will never be hindered by another opportunity to prove himself. No test, of course, even a very well-designed one, can pretend to the role of oracle or deliver verdicts on anyone; but each student could look at his test score at least as a kind of psychologist's analysis—and advice which might prove quite useful indeed for a musician who wants an objective evaluation of her prospects for a career in the field.

The composer in contemporary culture

From the earliest times through the eighteenth century the concept of 'musician' and that of 'composer' were, for educated Europeans, synonymous; the self-evident nature of the unity of composing music and performing it lasted for thousands of years. From antiquity to the era of Mozart and Beethoven it was impossible to imagine a skillful clavier player or violinist who could not write an accompaniment to an operatic aria, compose a choral arrangement for the mass or provide some musical couplets on the felicitous occasion of the birthday of some important personage.

In early pagan rituals music played a significant part, indeed, it served as the heart and soul of the event, becoming so integrated into the ritual procedure that at times it became unnoticed within or indistinguishable from it: the summoning of spring and the harvest festival would have lost much or all their charm had music not inspired and animated them, as would later be the case with the carols of Christmas. Yet traditional culture, while transferring the same values from one century to the next, preferred that the composer remain anonymous. The work was more important than the author, and the song disguised the face of its creator. Even in the image of the legendary Orpheus the artist-singer overshadows the artist-composer: music, in which a collective origin clearly takes precedence over the individual, necessarily put the composer in the background and gave the primary roles to the singer-performer. In traditional culture the roles of the composer and performer were thus united: people never tired of polishing and modifying the songs of their ancestors—the melodic kernel was 'tossed up' by one singer, taken over by another, continued by a third, and in the course of this collective improvisation a new oral masterpiece was born. In both folk music and academic music the composer and the artist-musician were taken as one and the same person. The musician was one or the other, depending on the situation and the social requirement in question.

The mass culture of the twentieth century, which was close to the music of ancient times and traced its ancestry to popular buffoonery and street carnivals, paid minimal attention to the figure of the composer. Hardly anyone knows who the author of Madonna's hit singles is, or who wrote the music for Edith Piaf or Yves Montand—pop music, which is part of the dance and mime show tradition, is indivisibly connected with context. It is part of the artist's legend which is created by video clips and media interviews; pop music blends with the texts of the songs, with the persona of the singer, with her movements and mimicry, and with her stage image—such music does not demand an individual role and its author remains anonymous. And the music itself modifies the existing selection of tunes with no pretense at originality; it expresses the 'spirit of the tribe' just as the traditional chanting of antiquity did. The music of the cinema and theater also frequently remains 'unheard': here the music belongs to the spectacle it accompanies and the composer sees a particular honor in not bothering the director, not getting involved in the plot and not distracting the viewer from the play of the actors. Like the music of the ancient rituals, the music of the movies blends with the screen, becoming an integrated element of the film, a part of it—this aspect of music appreciation rightfully prevails in the social consciousness since it duplicates genetically the deeply rooted habits of humanity. It is difficult for society collectively to register the very existence of the composer who creates all these musical riches: the anonymous author, dissolved in the musical-spectacular context, is the form perceived most naturally and with the most psychological comfort by and for modern man.

In academic genres of contemporary musical culture the position of the performing artist is also much more secure than that of the author of the music. The public goes to see performers, conductors, pianists, violinists, whose faces normally look out from the posters and whose images present themselves to the television viewer and newspaper reader. Only music professionals put the composer in a suitable place on the musical Olympus—without forgetting, however, to put the education of musical performers in the first place. In contrast to previous ages, musical education today is the education of music teacher, the music critic, and the orchestra player, none of whom is to even the smallest degree a composer or a master of the composer's craft. The language of contemporary academic music, directed at a narrow circle of experts, deepens the isolation of the composer in contemporary culture—the majority of listeners have no notion of the classics of contemporary music; while they can name their favorite actors, writers, and even artists with ease, only a very few could name their favorite contemporary composers; and the fewest among those would be the fans of the genres of popular music.

The flowering period of the composer's art and the attraction of society's attention to the figure of the creator of music is connected with four centuries in the history of Europe: from the seventeenth through the twentieth century the culture of European individualism created an oasis of classical music. The composer's art became the alpha and omega of musical culture; the leading role of the composer emerged into the front rank—and could not be forgotten thereafter, whatever historical vicissitudes awaited the musical arts. But even in those fortuitous times there were attempts to downgrade the essential status of the composer. Performers had no qualms about expressing their judgments as to the music being performed, and even tried, as circumstances allowed, to offer corrections to it. The story has been passed down of the composer Jean-Phillipe Rameau, whose opera *Hippolyte et Aricie* was deemed too difficult by the orchestra players and conductor.

In the heat of battle with the author of the music the conductor, enraged, threw his baton at the man's feet—this at a time when such batons were a good deal more substantial than they are now. Rameau flung it back at the orchestra and, before the rehearsal could degenerate into a fistfight, succeeded in proudly announcing 'In this temple of music I am the architect. You people—are merely the foreman and his bricklayers' (Bryantseva 1985).

The composer's position has always been unenviable. He was obliged to depend on the kindness of famous virtuoso artists willing to perform his works and make them popular. The honoraria of the virtuosos were always very high: prima donnas of the opera, famous conductors, pianists, and violinists can even today boast of the significant fees which their star status brings them. Composers, on the other hand, even using their well-deserved fame to the full, still depend (as they did in the past) on charity and sponsorship. A triumvirate of donors led by the Austrian Archduke Rudolf sustained the musical genius of Beethoven; during his greatest period of creativity Tchaikovsky lived on the support of Nadezhda von Meck; Wagner, of course, relied on the charity of King Ludwig of Bavaria. Débussy put his financial affairs in order through marriage to the wealthy Emma Bardac; and the father of musical romanticism, Franz Schubert, whom no one offered support, died in utter penury.

Disdain for the figure of the composer has led to a state of affairs in which research into the psychology of giftedness has never put the talent of the composer in the first rank; the experimental psychology of music has collected incomparably fewer data on composing than on the particularities of the musical ear of infants and even on singing among the great apes. Meanwhile, the 'architect' of whom Rameau so wisely reminded us cleared the way for and constructed all the music in the world. The inspirational ability of his musical imagination, his creative power—these are the principal assets of the whole of musical culture, the study of which is possible only through analysis of the accounts left by the creators of music themselves. Their observations and comments on their lives and work—which is what their memoirs and letters largely consist of—remain to this day the basic source of our knowledge of the Composer. Scientific research on the psychology behind the composer's creativity remains to be done, and the testimony of the Composer about himself will doubtless serve as the setting-off point for such studies.

Music, your own and others': the composer as listener

The composer is the ideal listener. He is attentive and responsive, he values musical impressions extraordinarily and actively pursues them; he needs them like air and for him there is nothing stronger and more memorable than music which enthralls him. 'Last week I heard *Ifigeniia v Avilide*', Glinka wrote home to Russia from Berlin. 'My God! Whatever was that on the stage! Madam Kestner (Ifigeniia) and Madam Wagner (Clytemnestra) were actresses and singers without peer. I simply wept from the depth of my rapture'. [22] He went on to describe many of the scenes from the opera as soul-wrenching,

---

[22]   Glinka, M. (1954) *O muzyke i muzykantah/On Music and Musicians*. Moscow: Gosmuzgiz, p. 62.

pointing to the enthrallment of the entire audience as proof to his addressee that it was not merely he who experienced these transports of delight. When he spoke of Beethoven's *Egmont*, he turned to the fragment 'The Death of Klerchen': 'It produced a deep impression on me. At the end of the play I grasped my hand—it seemed to me from the alternating movement of the French horns that my pulse had stopped'.[23]

A composer reacts to music with his entire body, which cannot be said of most listeners or even of most musicians. He breathes, trembles, and sobs in time with it. His musical sensitivity seemingly continues the sensitivity of his aural perception as a whole: Anton Webern loved reading aloud and took what was read with particular intensity (Webern 1975). All his life Igor Stravinsky remembered the sounds of St Petersburg that had excited him in childhood—the clopping of hooves, the cries of coachmen, the church bells and even the sounds of the first telephones, which he later imitated in the introductory measures of the second act of his opera *Solovei* (Stravinsky 1971). Gustav Mahler was possessed of a particular sensitivity to the sounds of nature, which he could never tune out—the sound of rushing water, the rustling of leaves, the voices of birds were never for him background noise but always in the plane of the conscious. As one of his friends recalled, 'in Steinbach-on-Brenner a tirelessly crowing rooster almost reduced him to despair, as the cock-a-doodle sound was distinctive for some peculiar modulation'.[24]

From his earliest years onward the composer communicates by means of music. He amuses his friends with it, uses it in place of speech, addresses his family with demands for reactions to his compositions and their opinions of them. This kind of musical and sound reaction and communicability, such a fine sensitivity to sounds in general and the ability to react so strongly to the performing means of music speak of one thing only: the basis of the giftedness of the composer is his expressive ear. In the composer this ear is distinguished for its unprecedented sensitivity; sound for the composer is always significant, and thus he cannot distract himself from it. The developed expressive ear always reacts to sound, which by its nature seeks a response. The first person who is ready to respond is the composer-listener.

The ear of the composer is motivated from the very roots of musicality, when sound was not yet music but rather only an aural signal. The connection of the composer's talent and the uncharted qualities of sound subservient to the expressive ear is demonstrated by the modern technique of composition, which willingly addresses timbre and sound-space associations. Even beyond considerations of pitch these have, for the composer, their own significance. The expressive ear of the composer is so active that he is ready with the help of synesthesia, with the help of connections with visual, spatial, and motor-tactile sensations, to turn music into a vital story. Is this not because the thirst of the Composer is so great to perform the music he has written? Here not only is the author's self-esteem important, but also the clear understanding that unsounded music is dead. Music for the Composer always sounds, it is not tied to any system of notation. Such a view of the musical

---

[23] Glinka, M. (1954) *O muzyke i muzykantah/On Music and Musicians*. Moscow: Gosmuzgiz, p. 70.

[24] Mahler, G. (1964) *Pis'ma, dokumenty/Letters, Documents*. Moscow: Muzyka, p. 474.

art is inspired in the author by his highly developed expressive ear. This ear plays a significant role in the quality of the motivational component of the composer's talent—from it begins the attraction of the Composer to communication by means of sound.

This 'listener immediacy' combines in the Composer with a highly developed architectonic ear. He easily grasps the musical logic of any style, discerning its attendant algorithm without difficulty. He understands the connection of the original compositional impulse and the entirety of its further development. In this sense every Composer is a hidden constructor, his perception is very efficiently organized. As Arnold Schoenberg observed, 'Whatever happens in the piece of music is nothing but the endless reshaping of a basic shape. Or, in other words, there is nothing in a piece of music but what comes from the theme, springs from it, and can be traced back to it'.[25]

The Composer can reduce all the seeming variety of the external forms of the music, the entire cornucopia of musical compositions, to the basic principles on which they were constructed. In non-classical styles, where familiar patterns dominate, the Composer particularly acutely senses the compositional monotonous quality of everything he hears: all his impressions represent to him variations on the same original idea, which is already boring to him. As Mick Jagger noted 20 years ago, 'I can't believe that rock 'n' roll still exists in the form that it does. Even with all its permutations it's very limited and its entertainment value is very limited. Everything going on I've seen at least twice before'.[26]

The combination of a sensitive expressive ear, which is the basis of music making, and the architectonic ear, which represents its apex, differentiates the perceptive ability of the Composer from that of the majority of people. This invariable combination once again prompts the thought that the higher stages of musicality depend on the lower ones, and the most gifted musicians are those few who have gone through the entire course from the foundation of musicality (the expressive ear), through the sense of rhythm and the analytical ear, and risen to the level of the architectonic ear—but in the case of the Composer, not merely to the architectonic ear, but to the level of musical-creative gift.

The desire to create music appears very early in the Composer's life, and often in rather unpromising circumstances: instead of showing himself a diligent pupil and delighting his parents with well-turned renditions of the pieces assigned to him as homework, the future Composer begins to experiment. At the age of 4 Andrew Lloyd Webber learned to play the violin and the piano; gradually and almost imperceptibly he turned the music he played while learning the instruments from that of others into music of his own (Mantle 1989). He would add something onto the endings, or change something in the middle; in the end, being tired of repeating somebody else's melody over and over he would substitute several of his own for it. His mother Jean, a piano teacher and admirer of the classics, was less than overjoyed that her offspring was taking liberties with everyone short of Mozart himself, but she made her peace with it. Her husband, the pianist and organist William Webber was, like the Webbers' young son, distinguished for

---

[25] Schoenberg, A. (1949) *Style and Idea*. New York: Philosophical Library, p. 102.
[26] *Rolling Stones in their own Words* (1985) London: Omnibus Press, p. 130.

his 'musical omnivorousness': he could be moved to tears by both the aria from Puccini's *Tosca* and a sentimental popular hit such as 'Some Enchanted Evening'. Young Andrew clearly preferred chansonettes to sonatas and by the age of 9 had written his first musical, *Games in the Theater*.

The Composer cannot repeat something without changing it. He is the ideal listener, empathetic and enraptured, but his architectonic ear so quickly captures musical thoughts that repeatedly returning to them becomes impossible. Most people hum away at the same popular tunes for decades; the Composer cannot satisfy himself with musical 'chewing gum'—a musical thought, once understood, begins to bore him and he moves on in search of new musical impressions. The music of others represents to him material for his own composition: it inspires his imagination, he begins to discern new possibilities in it, possibilities unnoticed by the original author.

> When people show me compositions for critical commentary', Igor Stravinsky recalled, 'I can only say one thing: I would have written this completely differently. No matter what arouses my interest, no matter how much I like something, I still want to redo it in my own fashion ... perhaps I am describing a rare form of kleptomania?[27]

The pro-active nature of the composer's ear, the 'co-author' position which he occupies as he listens to other people's compositions, derives from the fact that his own unwritten music is constantly alive within him; it searches for a way out, and the Composer has to try out the role of writer before he is really ready to do so. There is a story, long since of legendary status, of the 5-year-old Tchaikovsky: it was said that he heard music in his head all the time. His internal ear was at work constantly, he continually thought things up. As his brother Modest later recalled, 'There was a holiday celebration in our house once, which included music. Toward the end of the evening little Peter tired of it all and went upstairs to his room. A while later Fanny found him in tears, crying "O, the music! Save me from it, it's even up here, I can't get away from it!"'[28] Later Tchaikovsky himself said that he had begun to compose immediately upon hearing music for the first time—from a listener he turned instantly into a Composer and, by his own admission, sounds followed him continually all his life, no matter where he went or what he did.

The composition of music never arouses timidity in the Composer since mentally he has been searching, practically from infancy, for new and interesting sound combinations. The 4-year-old Mozart, crawling on the floor and covering a sheet of music paper with inkblots, announced that he was composing a concert for the clavier; the beginning author simply could not limit himself to something more modest, such as a minuet or an aria (Abert 2007). Recalling his own childhood, the twentieth-century classic Arthur Honegger wrote:

> In the beginning I was self-taught. Having mastered certain fundamentals, I immediately took to reading Beethoven's sonatas, which helped me get better acquainted with the principles of

27 Stravinsky, I. (1971) *Dialogi/Dialogues*. Leningrad: Muzyka, p. 220.
28 Tchaikovsky, M. I. (1903) *Zhizn' P.I.Tchaikovskogo/Life of Pyotr Iliych Tchaikovsky*. Moscow: Izdatelstvo Jurgensona, p. 19.

classical harmony. As a result of this, the idea that I should also write sonatas arose in me perfectly naturally. Whereupon I made my poor mother work out at the piano the feeble fruits of my ardor. Then it occurred to me that composing sonatas alone was too little—and I decided it was time to move on to operas. And soon, although it was still difficult for me to work things out in different keys, I already had two completed operas under my belt.[29]

The ability to independently master the principles of composition speaks of the highly developed architectonic ear of the Composer; his aural impressionability to his expressive ear; and the very fact of his composition and the persistence of sound 'in his head', in turn, to his internal ear. All these indispensable components of talent can be found in other people; in the Composer they secure the ability to express musical thoughts, they make up his operational apparatus. The sole psychological attribute unique to the Composer is an unusual creative need, one which makes him hear the music of others not so much for itself but as material for his own music; further, it does not recognize any tasks as too difficult or any problems as unsolvable. The Composer wants to express in music his thoughts and impressions; everything he sees and feels needs and tries to emerge as music—not as painting, not as a malleable form, and not in words. The musical-creative demand represents a launch mechanism for musical talent, its motivational nucleus; all the highly developed musical abilities help it come forth, but the need itself is an independent psychological attribute located at the source of the creative gift of the Composer. And this musical-creative need appears even when the Composer is only a listener, a student of the genre trying to look into its (and his) future.

The composer as the notional hero of a style

People sometimes voice a fear that all the books have been written, all the songs sung, and all the music composed. But despite the continual hand-wringing over the excess of creative production, more and more of it comes out, like clockwork. In traditional cultures this is always from the same circle of themes and the same rotation of means: the story of life and death, of man's departure from nature and his return to it, of the unchanging life of tillers of the soil, which is accompanied by seasonal, workday and wedding songs. In this kind of salt-of-the-earth milieu, social roles are few and well understood: mother, wife, pining fiancée, strapping young man, heroic soldier, or heroic laborer. In any situation and role there is always a person who fulfills, with majestic monotony, the duty of supporting and continuing the status quo of the given Way of Life.

But as man has moved ahead on the road of civilization, the number of these roles and of views of the world associated with them has grown astronomically. Nationalities, nation states, epochs, and generations each make their own cultures—and the worldview of people becomes so multifaceted that it seems they are moving in different orbits or spinning off in different directions. Culture halts the fleeting moments; as the Russian writer Andrei Bitov states, creativity helps people 'break the silence'. Every age and every people wants to establish itself in history, to be heard and understood, and assigns this

---

[29] Honegger, A. (1963) *Ya - kompozitor! /I am a Composer!* Leningrad: Muzyka, p. 27.

mission to the descendants of Orpheus and Apollo: with pen and paint, with word and sound, these inheritors of ancient mantles write the story of a given generation, each tracing a portrait in his own milieu. This portrait emerges in the music composed, the novels and poetry written, and in the plays and films of the era—all made to save the time and its people from the gaping maw of nothingness, of nonexistence.

In art one always hears the voice of the author, whose social role is understood and whose spiritual face is visible. In the poetry of Pushkin one hears the voice of a son of the Enlightenment, a troubadour of liberty and a fine hand at sizing up people—the Russian nobility's version of a European liberal; in the paintings of Francois Bouchet and Fragonard, on the other hand, one sees a sybaritic aristocrat, a cultivated lover of life and esthete of the pre-revolutionary era who cherished his ephemeral happiness even within sight of the guillotine and general anarchy. In any form of creativity, any genre of art or expression of the word, the historical type of the person who created it peeks through. In music the generalized type of the man who represents his people and his generation has been termed the *notional hero of the style* in the early 1980s by the scholar Vyacheslav Medushevsky (1993, second edition). It is through his eyes that the music regards the world, and in his voice that it speaks; the music conveys his thoughts, expresses his feelings, and each author chooses for himself his own notional hero from the gallery of contemporary social types. In Gregorian chants one hears the voice of the Catholic monk, mystic, and philosopher. In the music of Tchaikovsky, a Russian *intelligent* of the post-reform era pours out his soul, suffering for all and everyone, searching for answers to the eternal questions and vainly trying to avoid encounters with Fate, who is always but a step away from catching him. In the music of Sofia Gubaidulina the listener meets an esoteric sensibility and galactic thinker of the end of the twentieth century, a hero who hears the wind and the stones, knows the language of planets, and the idea of temporal movement. Gubaidulina's hero is reminiscent of the God Krishna, knowing all and savoring the harmonic peace of nirvana.

Music is a world of ideas and, as the musicologist Boris Asafiev noted (1923), the most valuable ideas in it are 'rays of thought'. To gather these rays, the beginning Composer tries to penetrate into the musical language of his notional hero and master the musical phrases which are (will be) typical of and for him. Many composers in the course of collecting notional material rely on their own experience and have no need of teachers: Music itself is their great teacher, and from the vast cornucopia of sound they select only that which is closest to the image of their hero. As a rule, the composer is himself from the same social class and milieu as his hero, the class from which he hopes to speak in his music. The creators of rock and pop music rarely belong by birth to the highly educated layers of society, and those who write symphonies just as rarely emerge from the ranks of craftsmen and farmers. In short, the Composer seeks a notional hero close to himself by birth and education; this salient feature made itself felt with particular acuteness in the twentieth century, when the Composer had an extremely wide choice: he could write academic music, he could become a pop hit-maker, he could turn to rock or to stage musicals.

Vasily Soloviev-Sedoi, the son of a Petersburg groundskeeper, from childhood onward played the mindlessly untaxing music of the middle classes and tradespeople; his talent did not strive toward a conservatory education. For the creation of gems of urban lyricism (such as 'Podmoskovnye vechera' and 'Vecher na reide', Russian classics in the genre), a serious education might have been an impediment; thus Soloviev-Sedoi limited himself to a musical *tekhnikum*. Aleksandra Pakhmutova, the daughter of a Donetsk miner, graduated from the Central Musical School and the Moscow Conservatory, but in what became her masterpieces of song her academic training was almost ignored altogether. The notional heroines of her style were deft young *Komsomol* women and good girls from the countryside who worked in the kitchens and at the factory looms, dreaming of a smiling and eligible machinist. Their lively patter suggested to Pakhmutova the melodies for her songs *'Po Angare'* and *'Devchata'*, which brought their author well-deserved fame.

So it was as well with Raymond Pauls, the great popular songwriter and revue composer: Pauls spent his entire youth as a restaurant pianist, despite the fact that his performances of Rakhmaninov and Beethoven invariably amazed and impressed the professors at the Riga conservatory where he studied. He could have been but did not want to be a classical musician —despite the constant urging of his father, the son of a Latvian peasant to whom the career of a classical pianist seemed considerably more desirable and respectable than that of a composer of pop music ditties. But to the younger Pauls the foxtrot, the charleston and the twist were far more interesting than Handel and Bach. In the future hitmaker's eyes, the philharmonic hall always lost out in the competition for his interest to the restaurant stages, and Raymond's career remained there, where his notional hero was—an unpretentious but hip young man with the bearing and manner of a provincial heartbreaker. Cases similar to Raymond Pauls' simply testify to the genetic depths from which the speech of the Composer resounds: how deeply implanted in his subconscious mind is the image of the notional hero, the choice of whom cannot involve anything artificial or incidental. The soul of the Composer is merged entirely with that of the person whose image stands at the source of his creative work, and no manner of education or outward influence can weaken this genetic connection. The Composer easily distinguishes the voice of his hero in the stream of contemporary music and hurries to his call, guided exclusively by his creative intuition.

Joseph Haydn, the Great Viennese, recalled that in his early years he never had 'proper teachers', learning instead by doing and listening:

> I always started right away with the practical side first, in singing and in playing instruments and later in composition. I listened more than I studied, but I heard the finest music in all forms that was to be heard in my time, and of this there was much in Vienna. Oh, so much! I listened attentively and tried to turn to good account what most impressed me. Thus little by little my knowledge and my ability were developed.[30]

---

[30] Geiringer, K. (1982) *Joseph Haydn*. Berkelee: University of California Press, p. 21.

In his youth Haydn learned the music of the Catholic mass which he sang in St Stephen's Cathedral; he heard opera during the visits to the court by distinguished guests; and he knew the early symphonic music which was played by the court *Kapelle*. But above all else he paid attention to the music of the city's streets, the music of popular (and secular) relaxation—the simple popular tunes and chivalrous minuets, the sensitive arias and holiday serenades to which the Viennese treated their ears during their time off—these were the real center of Haydn's interest. His architectonic ear had the ability to select the necessary musical elements and retain them in his memory: the notional hero of this style drew to himself, like a magnet, these indispensable means, preparing Haydn for his subsequent work.

In the years during which the composer's talent is being established, the architectonic ear is occupied with the selection of a musical environment. For this one must have a sense of the society around one and a capacity for directed selection: given a bewildering array of musical genres, voices, and styles to choose from, the Composer can stop only on those models and images which express the inner world of his notional hero. He is helped in this by a sort of 'musical compass' which is built into the apparatus of his architectonic ear and does not let him deviate from the selected course. Gifted non-composer listeners do not possess such selectivity; they are less critical in their selection of musical material, their musical taste is more universal. The ear of the Composer is not simply the highly developed architectonic ear, but a social and historical ear as well. It possesses a particular sensitivity to the origins of musical languages and dialects, and can distinguish within completed works their stylistic and generic origins.

As a young man at the end of the nineteenth century, the budding genius of ragtime, Scott Joplin, created a 'cocktail' from the popular music of black Americans—civil war songs, minstrel show tunes, and songs from the daily lives of plantation slaves. His musical nourishment in St Louis, where he earned extra money as an on-call piano player, were the popular tunes of the 1850s and 1860s: the very names of the songs tell a great deal about the way of life of Joplin's notional hero: 'The Arkansas Traveler', 'I Never Get Drunk at the Bar', 'Where are the Friends of My Youth?', 'O Them Golden Slippers!', 'A Flower from Mother's Grave', 'Carry Me Back to Ol' Virginia'. The hero was a deck hand on a Mississippi river boat carrying cotton, flour, and coal. He danced quadrilles and waltzes to the music of the violin and banjo during the evenings when the boat stood in port, and dreamed of building his own version of Uncle Tom's cabin one day. Joplin's talent heard in the musical sources he knew a sentimental nostalgia for the warm hearth, a stylish bravado and the bitter humor of his hero. Such creative observational eye differentiates the perception of the Composer from that of other people.

The selective ear of the Composer, following his notional hero everywhere, is extraordinarily reliable. It works quickly and effectively in any given condition. Unlike abilities which are aimed at gaining knowledge and mastering skills, the creative and productive nature of talent demands relatively little pedagogical support and assistance. A good instructor can do a great deal for someone who is able and is striving to learn things; here the teacher develops the potential inherent in the person to its maximum extent.

The talented, on the other hand, tend to go it alone, for better or worse; their principal instructor and chief creative stimulus is the music they hear, rendering additional teachers and outside stimuli largely superfluous.

The number of self-taught in the ranks of the composers is quite large. Commenting on this inclination of the talented toward independence, Mikhail Pekelis, an expert on the work of the composer Dargomyzhsky, observed that

> As was often the case with talented musicians, [for Dargomyzhsky] the study of theoretical rules took place when the basic patterns had already been discovered by practical experience, as a result of observations on literature, [his] own composing experience and intuitive aural 'nourishment.' In these cases this or that theoretical position represents something already long known, and lessons themselves are simply organization, an introduction into a system of familiar rules.[31]

Dargomyzhsky's 'school' was the music of Glinka, the culture of the Russian romance and, most important, his beloved theater and French opera, which brought to perfection the art of the recitative—musicalized speech. Dargomyzhsky's hero searched for sharp sensations and a pronounced 'attitude' and found them: hardly any teacher could have directed him to the sources which would later constitute the unique entirety of his style. The aural predilections of the notional hero of a particular style exclusively inhabit the consciousness of the composer himself, and he alone is capable of recognizing them.

The lifestyle of the musician class takes into account this particularity in the growth of the Composer, and there are always plenty of 'composers' schools': there are groups of like-minded composers, like the great *'Mighty Five'* of nineteenth century Russia, in which the composers make music together and exchange musical news; there is the friendly help of colleagues, who send each other sheet music and recordings; and there is direct demonstration, where a 'teacher for an hour' shows a pupil something in person. This method is particularly popular in jazz circles. As Duke Ellington recalled of his learning years in Washington,

> Back in those days if you were a constant listener and hanger-on like I was, any piano player in D. C. was wide open and approachable. If you were to ask any one of them something like: 'How did you do that, what you just played?' They would stop doing whatever they were doing and play it again, while I watched and listened to it and its explanation.[32]

This was all the instruction the great Ellington ever had.

The connection of the Composer with his notional hero gives the architectonic ear of the former two particular qualities—extreme selectivity and extreme independence. These signs of creative giftedness are not characteristic of the developed architectonic ear of music lovers and musicians of other fields; the Composer is the voluntary megaphone of the notional hero of a style, the voice of which speaks out only through the creative will of the Composer.

[31] Pekelis, M. (1966) *Dargomyzhsky.* Moscow: Muzyka, p. 182.
[32] Ellington, D. (1973) *Music is my Mistress.* New York: Da Capo Press, p. 28.

'Volk volku kompositor': there is no love lost between composers

The Composer is an empathetic and impressionable listener, but also an extraordinarily demanding one. He does not simply take in what he hears, limiting himself in the process to some sort of amorphous approval or disapproval; he is an active participant in the music played in his presence. He catches its stylistic algorithms, penetrates its secrets, and mentally takes apart its pieces like a child playing with an erector set. The Composer is always keen to know exactly how a piece of music was put together, and what it comprises.

As musicologist Boris Asafiev noted,

> Composers most often hear other people's music as though hearing their own, as they start from their own musical habits; and if these do not mesh with the 'counter-plan' of the work they are hearing, then it becomes almost an enemy object, something from which it only bears extracting whatever is interesting for one's own purposes. Exceptions to this are not rare, but 'egotism' in a composer's listening is nevertheless a preponderant nuance.[33]

The Composer's prejudiced attitude toward the music of others is connected with the creative type of hearing which he practices, that is, composing-while-listening. He penetrates into the author's conception, following the curves and contours of the musical thought and enjoying its beauty. But all these listening pleasures are there for the Composer only in those rare instances when he accepts the music wholly, when he is ready to take what he is hearing as his own: its construction and the tone of its speech are near to his heart; the author's chosen means of development seem logical to him; he agrees with the principles of construction used for the form of the piece; and if there were something that might be suggested or improved (always a temptation for a Composer), then it would be only a detail which would render the author's ideas that much more vivid.

Unlike the majority of listeners, the Composer divides his colleagues (living and dead) into musical friends and musical enemies. In this he is absolutely adamant, admitting no compromise of any kind. The music lover listens in order to surrender himself to the music, using it as transport to another spiritual realm—one which will by its very presence act upon and expand his own. The Composer, on the other hand, listens to music in order to make it surrender to him, to sense his power over it. The 'joining of souls' between a piece of music and the Composer can take place only in the case where the notional hero of the music in question is close to him, if they are joined by a common understanding of the goals and ideals of life. It is enough to glance at the 'map of musical prejudices' maintained by any Composer to convince oneself of this.

Shostakovich likes Beethoven because they each despise tyrants and believe that people, recognizing their own worth, are capable of overturning tyranny. Both Shostakovich and

---

[33] Asafiev, B. V. (1952) Sluh Glinki/Glinka's ear. In *Izbrannie trudy/Selected Works*, vol.1. Moscow: Izdatelstvo Akademii nauk, p. 266.

Beethoven analyze the course of history in their works: they study the reasons behind events, follow the logic implicit therein, and thus know that the Fate of nations is in one place alone—the hands of the people themselves. Both of them want to convince their listeners of this. The notional hero of both styles is a hero in the original sense of the word, a witness to and participant in the great events and catastrophes of the world. Shostakovich's musical form is drawn on the Beethoven model—dramatic and action-oriented, it has a plot which, like a historical drama, proceeds past the mental eye of the author. Shostakovich and Beethoven detest beauty for its own sake, allowing themselves to be abrupt and crude. Calling a spade a spade and all things by their proper names is the fondest desire of both. Beethoven often allows himself this, while Shostakovich uses an 'Aesopian language' of allegory and the grotesque. Yet the civil pathos and political temperament of both Composers lead them by the hand, as if into battle.

Shostakovich does not like the music of Debussy, which seems to him artificial and mannered. Debussy's hero, smacking of dawns and sunsets, breathing the 'sounds and aromas, wafting through the evening air' and not noticing the cannons pointed at Europe's forehead, does not seem to Shostakovich authentic and worthy of attention. Music of the age of gallantry, the music of Haydn and Mozart, is completely alien to Shostakovich: the motifs of the opera-bouffe—serenades and romantic intrigues, with attendant grimacing and running about—do not inspire him in the least. The perfect proportions, astute observations, and sharp wit of the old Viennese masters live as if in another reality altogether, a reality one hardly even dares to mention in the face of the *Gulag*. The composer Shostakovich uses neither the intonations nor the compositional discoveries of his least favorite authors, leaving all their achievements outside his field of vision—while generously availing himself of the language and compositional devices of his favorite authors; the common content and pathos he shares with them cannot but summon forth a certain commonality of both musical language and construction of form.

The composer's feelings about the music of his colleagues are in fact so strong that he is incapable of restraining them: no manner of social *politesse* will deter him from saying everything he deems it necessary to say about someone else's music. The expression *Volk volku kompozitor*, used as the title for this section, is in fact an ironic Russian paraphrase of a Latin proverb (*Homo homini lupus est*). The proverb speaks of man's intolerance of his fellow man—and was quoted to the present author by the Russian composer Viacheslav Artemov as a sort of shorthand summary of the relations between and among composers and their various schools: to Artemov, the appearance of enmity among these people and groups is approximately as remarkable as the appearance of snow in winter. Particularly intense dislike is often summoned by Composers who are at watershed periods in musical history and are not lacking at the same time, in a certain spirit of hooliganism; they end to 'bring it on themselves'—their notional heroes and their music itself are overt provocations. Such was the young Sergei Prokofiev, a coarse Scythian barbarian in the age of Russian Symbolism, Acmeism, Imaginism, and other such esthetic niceties. Prokofiev's conservative teacher was Anatoly Liadov, a musician of subtle tonalities who 'painted sound in watercolors'. He did not approve of Prokofiev's crudities and did not disguise this fact, although he was the kindest of men and the soul of politeness. Prokofiev wrote:

> I do not show my compositions to Liadov because he would probably throw me out of his class. . . if I did. He stands firmly for the old, peaceful music and above all else values good part-singing and the logic of sequence. But the new music, with its interesting harmonies—this he courses up, down and sideways. My latest works belong to this category, so I prefer not to show them to him at all.[34]

Nor did Alexandre Scriabin spare Prokofiev, for that matter, calling the latter's work: 'Such filth . . . And what a minimum of creativity as well. The saddest part is that this music really does reflect something very well—but that something is in fact something awful'.[35]

Scriabin spills the beans here: it is not the alien sound combinations that the Composer does not like, but the 'something awful' which lies beneath them and which emerges as the music's notional hero, with the understanding of reality that he brings with him. Behind the pseudo-technical arguments between composers about the relative beauty of sounds and compositional devices, there are actually reasons for mutual antipathy which are far more ideational than musical. At the beginning of the previous century there was a particular abundance of artistic directions and ideational platforms; the enmity between and among them sometimes became acute —and this extended, among composers, to biases and complaints against both contemporary colleagues and classics long since deceased. It reached the point where conversations among composers resembled, to outside observers, the wrangling of quarreling relatives. 'It was that beast Gluck who destroyed everything', announced Debussy. 'He was so boring, so pedantic, so hopelessly sententious. His success is simply incomprehensible to me'.[36] To the pianist Margaret Long, who came to play with him, Debussy confessed: 'I really dislike, of course, Mozart's concertos—but still not as much as I dislike the concertos of Beethoven'.[37] The clarity and definitiveness of classical thought and the civic *gravitas* in the phrasing of Beethoven and Gluck irritated the impressionist Debussy; they seemed to him tasteless and out of place, unworthy of a genuine artistic aristocrat who is more a contemplator of reality than its mere inhabitant.

The Composer's antipathy towards his colleagues and brothers in arms often leads him to make extremely subjective judgments. At the same time he can be an ingrate and forget entirely about favors done to him. The volatile, hot-tempered Robert Schumann, who was an influential musical journalist, welcomed the appearance on the musical scene of the young Frederick Chopin with great enthusiasm. With complete sincerity Schumann proclaimed 'Hats off, gentlemen, before you stands genius'. This weighty pronouncement from an authoritative critic was for the then-unknown Chopin a sign of acceptance by

34 Cit. from Nestiev, I. (1973) *Zhizn Sergeya Prokofieva/Life of Sergei Prokofiev*. Moscow: Muzyka, p. 45.
35 Cit. from Nestiev, I. (1973) *Zhizn' Sergeya Prokofieva/Life of Sergei Prokofiev*. Moscow: Muzyka, p. 45.
36 Cit. from Rytsarev, S. (1987) *Christophe-Willibald Gluck*. Moskow: Muzyka, p. 3.
37 Long, M. (1978) *Za royalem s Debyussi/At the Piano with Debussy*. Moscow: Sovetsky kompozitor, p. 31.

Europe; indeed, Schumann's welcoming article helped Chopin a great deal in his subsequent career. But the world of Schumann's music—sharp-angled, asymmetric, shot through with the fantastic, the world of Jean-Paul and E. T. A. Hoffman—was so alien to Chopin's Apollonian nature that Chopin could not disguise his hostility to it. As Chopin's students recalled, 'Owing to some sort of strange internal artistic antagonism Chopin did not like the works of Schumann. "Carnival—that isn't music at all", he would say'.[38]

In reality this antagonism represented enmity between different notional heroes of styles, and thus in the hostility there was actually nothing strange at all. To award recognition to music alien to his own hero seems to the Composer practically treasonous to his own ideals. Yet it would be the greatest of exaggerations to see in the Composer a malcontent and Dutch uncle critic who longs to fire poisoned arrows at his innocent colleagues. No one throws his arms open wider to welcome a new talent than does the Composer. Donizetti enthused over the young Verdi (wonderful! marvelous! splendid!) and made room for him in the musician's world most generously:

> My turn for sympathy is over; another must take my place. The world wants something fresh; people have given place to us; we must give place to others. I am all the happier to have given place to a man of talent like Verdi. In any case if his success does not answer the expectations of his friends, that will not prevent the good Verdi from occupying before very long one of the most honourable places in the ranks of composers.[39]

The two Italian masters of the bel canto easily found accord in the face of the German music which was equally alien to both of them. Donizetti's affection and respect for Verdi easily became mutual: composers who espouse the same ideals support each other just as heatedly as they vilify those whose views on life and art they oppose.

The Composer who is acerbic and unfairly critical of the notional hero in the works of others becomes as tender and enraptured as a lovesick schoolboy when expressing his love for the music of a colleague. He loves this music to distraction, he can see no flaws in it; his penetrating eye and strict esthetic sense go silent. Just as unstinting as the Composer's antipathy is to the music of some, so is his affection and ecstasy over the music of others boundless. 'Glinka was the musical hero of my childhood', Stravinsky admitted. 'He was and will for me forever remain faultless. In him lie the origins of all Russian music'.[40]

Stravinsky called Bach 'wonderful, wise and irreplaceable'. Tchaikovsky, who admired Mozart's music, often said that in Mozart he loved everything, as we love everything in any person we genuinely love. In his eternal idols Stravinsky admires the faultless beauty of form, and the construction and naturalness of development which he always strove for. Stravinsky's hero Glinka adored the Viennese classics Haydn and Mozart for the same clarity and finesse of style for which Stravinsky loved Glinka himself. 'Yet I did not cut off

38 Milshtein, Y. (1967) Sovety Shopena pianistam/Chopin's Advice to Pianists. Moscow: Muzyka.
39 Walker, F. (1982) *The Man Verdi*. The University of Chicago Press.
40 Stravinsky, I. (1971) *Dialogi/Dialogues*. Leningrad: Muzyka, p. 29.

my hand', Glinka remarked on the works of Haydn and Mozart, 'which after these great compositions still dared to write musical notes'.[41]

The most important thing in the love and hate of the Composer for the music of others was and is the supremely idealistic character of this emotion. The feelings of affection and antipathy were exclusively esthetic and philosophical; the Composer is least likely of all to turn things into the personal. Aleksandr Glazunov, director of the St Petersburg Conservatory, disliked the music of a certain beginning composer in the extreme; and yet between Glazunov and Maxim Gorky, who assigned special food provisions for starving artists during the Russian Civil War and the early Soviet period, there could be a dialogue such as the following:

> 'He is a composer, he brought me his works', Glazunov began his account of the boy-musician.
> 'And did you like them?' Gorky asked.
> 'Ghastly,' answered Glazunov. 'This is the first music I can't hear when I read the score'.
> 'Then why are you here?' Gorky asked.
> 'I don't like his music, but that isn't what's important: the future belongs to this boy, not to me. The fact that I don't like the music is simply too bad; but this will be real music, you've got to get him the special food ration for scholars.'
> 'All right, I'll take down the information. How old is he?'
> 'Fifteen,' answered Glazunov.
> 'And what's his name?'
> 'Shostakovich'.[42]

Cases like this attest the fact that the quibbles and biases of the Composer pale before his sincere love of music. The Composer always distinguishes wonderful music from the useless, the deep from the superficial, and no manner of subjective prejudice can make him call a Salieri a Mozart or a Mozart a Salieri. Music stands above all things, it alone possesses the soul of the Composer, and the apparent enmity of composer-colleagues simply reaffirms the wisdom of an old Russian saying—*Milye braniatsia, tol'ko teshatsia*—which holds that family quarrels are just that: voices may indeed be raised, but in the end everything is still 'all in the family'.

The creative abilities of the composer: variant copying

The Composer senses himself to be a future creator of music from his early youth, sometimes from his childhood. His unwritten creations already live within him, his musical-creative need searches for a way out, a way of expressing itself: it wants to communicate with the world by way of sounds. This musical-creative need is the active form of the expressive ear. It inspires people not only to communicate with the help of sound; the active expressive ear is enriched and rendered complex by the entire operational system of musical abilities. It has integrated into itself the sense of rhythm, the analytical ear, and the internal ear: having preserved its motivational potential and striving for

---

[41] Glinka, M. (1954) *O muzyke i muzykantah/On Music and Musicians.* Moscow: Gosmuzgiz, p. 64.

[42] Seroff, V. (1943) Dmitri Shostakovich: The Life and Background of a Soviet Composer. New York: Alfred A. Knopf, p. 60.

musical communication, the expressive ear passed through the crucible of all the musical abilities and, enriched by them, became the musical-creative need. The person who possesses it does not simply wish to but in fact can communicate with the help of music; he senses music as one senses a native language and feels the desire to speak it. The content of his musical speech is not something he chooses himself; it is the story of a generation, a living portrait of its thoughts and feelings: this is what is given to the Composer to create. The need to 'break the silence' creates the motivational nucleus of musical-creative activity and leads the Composer to his creative work. 'Great and sad is the fate of the artist', wrote Liszt. 'It is not he who chooses his calling, but the calling which chooses him—and unfailingly draws him forward. He feels himself the prey of some sort of unnamed ailment; an unknown power makes him express in words, sounds and colors an ideal which lives in him'.[43]

The musical-creative need plays the role of the 'ailment', forcing the Composer to convey this ideal living inside him in sounds. The inspiration for this ideal comes to him from the notional hero of the music's style, the Composer's 'brother in fate', his contemporary and his spiritual ego. Submitting to the needs and tastes of his hero, the Composer chooses the sound milieu for his future works, he masters the same genres and styles of music which his notional hero considers his own; of the many impressions which surround the Composer, he selects and reinforces only those which are capable of embodying and bringing to life in sounds the internal world of his hero and become musical brush strokes toward this hero's portrait. The architectonic ear of the Composer allows him to penetrate into the secret recesses of the musical form, to learn the secrets of its beauty and its seamless integrity. A highly developed esthetic sense stands on guard over and ready to work on everything that he can write.

But all these wonderful qualities are still not enough to allow a Composer to appear before the world. A sensitivity of the soul, a refined and subtle understanding of his contemporary man and an identification with him—the very gift of intra/interpersonal intelligence described by Howard Gardner, the perception of life and the world through the eyes of a hero-contemporary—is a quality necessarily possessed by all creative artists, and the Composer is no exception. A highly developed expressive ear, of course, is inherent in the Composer, and he shares it with the most sincere but least-gifted admirer of his talent. The Composer possesses a wonderful sense of rhythm and an equally fine analytical ear; without these a musical fabric would be for him an undifferentiated blank spot of sound and he would be incapable even of thinking of any kind of creative work: he would not even know what resources for creative work were at his command and what laws turn a chaos of sound into ordered musical language. This understanding is provided to the Composer by a wonderful analytical ear which combines with an excellent internal ear, often at the level of the outstanding and the phenomenal. The musical memory of the Composer stands out for its exactness and durability; it has no difficulty remembering what attracts his attention and gives the appearance of being useful. Yet even these high

---

[43] Lizst, F. (1959) *Izbrannie stat'i/Selected Articles*. Moscow: Muzyka, p. 72.

qualities are found in many musicians who are not composers; this is a level of ability which all professional musicians, to one degree or another, can be said to inhabit, even those with only modest natural gifts.

The musical-creative need, the motivational nucleus of the Composer's gift, inspires him to creativity; his architectonic ear and esthetic sense are ready to evaluate the fruits of his labor, but if the Composer does not produce musical expressions and texts, no manner of wonderful qualities will make him a creator of music. His esthetic sense can collect materials and evaluate them—but collect them from what? Who will serve as provider of the original material, what ability will create such a provider? This magic ability of musical invention can be called creative or productive; its essence consists in the Composer constantly producing music in his imagination. Wagner used to say that he composed music with the same inevitability that a cow produces milk. The fantasy of the classic French composer Camille St Saens, in the composer's own opinion, gave birth to musical ideas in the same way that an apple tree produces apples (Teplov 1985). The music itself comes to the Composer; he does not know the secret of its appearance, but his testimony can shed light on the most common skills and qualities from which musical-productive ability—an ability inherent in Composers but not in other talented musicians—certainly derives.

Musical-productive ability starts off from the capabilities of the architectonic ear: the future Composer, assimilating the stylistic algorithms of his colleagues, copies the manner of their writing—he improvises, in short, in known styles. At the same time his musical-productive ability invents musical elements and builds compositional blocks using a known model. The 9-year-old Sergei Rakhmaninov liked to play a particular joke on guests to the family household (Rakhmaninov 1964). He would announce that he was now going to play something by Beethoven or Chopin. With seriousness and dignity the young pianist would play something in that style but which he had in fact written himself—yet he did it so masterfully that no one suspected the trick; and when the boy finally revealed the truth, the guests were invariably awestruck. The ability to improvise in well-known styles is taken even by experienced instructors as the creative gift of a Composer. This gift so struck a friend of Scriabin's, the future mathematician Leonid Sabaneev, that he recorded the following:

> Once Taneev came to our place. He entertained warm feelings toward me and even recognized in me 'unusual' composer's gifts, in his expression. This conclusion of his was nourished by the fact that at that time I could play 'a la Mozart' in virtuoso style. I was sincerely taken with Mozart and in part due to the influence of Taneev himself, for whom Mozart was likewise a sacred name, I studied his manner and compositions so faithfully that it was almost physically painful to sense any and every departure from this clear and light style (the author was thirteen at the time).[44]

[44] Sabaneev, L. (1925) *Vospominaniya o Skryabine/Memoirs of Scriabin*. Moscow: Izdatelstvo Sabashnikovykh, p. 81.

Other authors, in distinction from the overt copyist Sabaneev, made independent creative attempts—but these also looked just as imitative. The Russian classic Rimsky-Korsakov recalled himself at age 14:

> In that year (1858–59) I was trying to compose something, partly in my head and partly at the piano, but nothing was coming of it; the thing was all fragments—unclear, dream-like meanderings. Taking the shards of pieces I had played by Glinka, Beethoven and Schumann, I cooked up with great difficulty something fluid and elementary.[45]

Witnesses to Scott Joplin's first attempts at composition likewise noted the extremely derivative nature of the works. As his biographer observes, 'Joplin's first sentimental songs, "*A Picture of Her Face*" and "*Please Say You Will*", could have been written by any sentimental lady composer of the Victorian era and show no intimation of genius'.[46]

Regardless of the area of the talent, its first steps are taken on 'musical crutches'; the beginning Composer looks like a plagiarist, more or less skillfully laying out other people's ideas.

From a phylogenetic point of view this order of development of the musical-productive ability is both natural and unavoidable. In genetic terms this ability was formed in the context of traditional musical culture, in the context of folklore, where independent creativity did not spread widely and was not supported. A composer was someone who knew how to copy already extant models, and do it well. Thanks to a highly developed architectonic ear and their musical-productive ability, traditional composers made high-quality variant copies of the music of those style-cultures in which they grew up. It was enough for them to have a large selection of examples of a given style in order to determine its algorithm. The early appearance in child composers of the ability to do variant copying and its ontogenetic primacy speak of deep phylogenetic roots: the development of a child composer's talent indicates the phases which the talent of the composer passes through on the path of phylogenesis.

Even earlier on the phylogenetic axis lies simple copying: all the members of the family who possessed musical abilities imitated the people who sang and copied the musical models handed down to them by their ancestors. The copying and imprinting in the memory of existing melodies is the earliest of all musical abilities, the first stage of musical-artistic practice.

The tendency toward direct and variant copying, the ability to imitate, is formed very early; thus in the psychological sense it is distinguished by the extreme depth of its installation. Having been born first, this ability likewise appears first. So it is that in a paradoxical way the ability to imitate and copy lies at the base of the giftedness of the Composer: without it his musical-productive ability, which ceaselessly creates combinations of musical elements, could not be formed. 'Plagiarism' arises in the Composer's work completely spontaneously and involuntarily. The outstanding guitarist and

[45] Rimsky-Korsakov, N. A. (1982) *Letopis' moei muzykal'noi zhizni/The Story of my Life in Music*. Moscow: Muzyka, p. 21.

[46] Gammond, P. (1975) *Scott Joplin and the Ragtine Era*. London: Abacus, p. 213.

contemporary composer Eric Clapton found himself in an unpleasant situation when he almost stole the compositions of a colleague, having published the other man's melodies with different titles under his own name. As Clapton's biographer put it, 'That original shortlist of two [songs] contained Scott Boyer's *"Please, Be with Me"* and *"Give Me Strength"* which [Clapton] inaccurately credited to himself, though by default rather than dishonesty'.[47]

The danger of involuntary copying has dogged Paul McCartney for years as well. Describing the creative process once to actor Dustin Hoffman, McCartney said,

> You don't know where it comes from, you just do it! How do you get all of your characterizations? It's just in you. The same with me. With a song, I just pull it out of the air. I knock a couple of chords off, and it suggests a melody to me. If I haven't heard the melody before, I'll keep it.[48]

In other words, Paul McCartney, a classic of pop music if the genre has ever had one, admits quite openly that the ideas of others come into his head just as easily as do his own; what he has to do is figure out what distinguishes the ideas from each other. His new melodies appear via the methodology of variant copying; but sometimes something absorbed and long forgotten simply surfaces from the depths of memory now apparently as one's own. The aural range of the Composer is so great that it extracts items from its musical storehouse without remembering how they got there in the first place; the ideas of others were understood and completely adopted by the architectonic ear, becoming digested as part of its musical nourishment—after which the artist's musical-productive ability offers them up for judgment and prospective use.

Copying lies at the base of the psychological mechanism of creativity, and thus various of its forms are a reflection of the utter naturalness and psychological inevitability of the creative process. The case of Beethoven has become a textbook example: he used as the first theme of his *Third Sonata for Piano* the beginning of Handel's oratorio *Samson*. Beethoven's notional hero recognized Handel's style as one of his favorite 'musical dialects': the declamatory nature and toughness of Handel's language, the precision and martial air of his rhythms completely suited Beethoven, whose mature style was formed under the direct influence of Handel's music. It is hardly surprising that the deeply secreted stage of study and assimilation of models—when Beethoven was learning, playing and rewriting the works of Handel—remained in his memory; and at some particular moment Beethoven's imaginative powers came up with this particular theme, which—although the conditions of its performance as well as its manner of execution, tempo, and tonality were somewhat different—was nevertheless clearly taken from someone else.

The borrowing of another style *in toto*, of another manner of writing, is sometimes encountered not as 'spontaneous plagiarism' but rather as a specific creative device: composers writing on special order for the theater and the film industry often resort to it. In such cases the tune is called, literally, by the one paying for it, meaning the director. The Composer has to have command of the technique of variant copying of styles well enough

47 Pidgeon, J. (1985) *Eric Clapton*. London: Vermilion, p. 89.
48 *Paul McCartney in his own Words* (1983) The Putnam Publishing Group, p. 63.

so that as the situation dictates he can avail himself of almost any of them. Edison Denisov liked to write special order music at the piano in order to compare what he wrote 'á la ...' with his memories of them: when he wrote 'for himself', he had no need of a piano to control his fantasy and there was no reason to check whether he had copied accurately or not.

> When I write what I myself consider important, everything arranges itself naturally, as if the result of submission to some sort of internally heard ideas—that is, here I am the only source, here is something mine alone, and I hear it all wonderfully well without any instruments at all. It's a completely different matter writing for the theater and the movies. There I must, as Alfred Shnitke says, put on an unfamiliar mask, something alien to me.[49]

In the early stages of the formation of the musical-creative gift the Composer relies on 'soft plagiarism' by creating variant copies of other people's music. Nevertheless he has (and senses) a need to take on a voice of his own, to discover his own unique musical self. On the one hand he wants to be contemporary, to reflect in his work the musical present—which means he is ready to assimilate other people's thoughts. On the other hand, the Composer wants to be himself, he wants to transform the material he begins with in such a way that everyone will say 'Yes, that's Composer X'. However, it is impossible to become oneself starting *tabula rasa*: to formulate new laws means overcoming the inertia of the past and re-examining the laws established earlier.

Edwin Gordon (1978) conducted an experiment using groups of musical and non-musical subjects. He played each group melodies which they were directed to learn, and then asked them to reproduce these melodies—first in the natural 'forward' mode (beginning to end), and then in the unnatural 'backward'. Gordon attached particular importance to the fact that the musical subjects experienced unusual discomfort when required to disrupt the settled order of inertia and play the melody 'back to front'. The non-musical subjects reacted to this direction with utter complacency: no pre-existing inertia had been established by them, hence they had nothing to 'get over'. However, the musical subjects as a result of the procedure learned to sing melodies 'backwards', and overcame their previously established stereotypes. Their non-musical peers, on the other hand, even when singing a melody 'forward'—which would seem simple enough—reproduced the melodies much worse than the musical people could sing them 'backward'. Non-musicality is connected with a lack of ability to perceive rules and patterns, and to form certain skills on the basis of this information. Such is also the case with composing, which is subject to the same psychological patterning: he who has not mastered an already existing style cannot create a new one. A new style can only appear from the nucleus of a previous one, transforming and superseding it. The copying stage is an unavoidable step in the development of one's own individual composing style. The Composer's colleagues in the common artistic workshop—masters of the fine arts, artists, and sculptors—never tire of copying. Through the creation of copies they move toward the achievement of a unified stylistic whole, toward the practical realization of that critical unity.

---

[49] Shulgin D. I. (1998) *Priznanie Edisona Denisova/Edison Denisov's Confession.* Moscow: Kompozitor, p. 15.

A particular feature of this stage of the formation of the musical-creative gift is eclecticism, the absence of esthetic integrity among the opuses which appear from the pen of the beginning Composer. He copies first one thing then another, his attention is drawn by an interesting harmonic phrase of one colleague, a beautiful transitional section of another; at one point his attention was riveted by the graceful melody in the spirit of Composer X, and at another he was entranced by the means of melodic development borrowed from Composer Y. As Rimsky-Korsakov rightly noted of his own ideas at this stage, 'all those were merely segments and ill-defined musings'. The beginning Tchaikovsky likewise got by with such music at the same point: banal ideas, trivial melodies, and slipshod melodic development peek out everywhere. Tchaikovsky was obsessed with the pseudo-pathetic patriotism of the national opera, where he was somehow taken prisoner by the teary romanticism and/or heart-rending gypsy emotionalism of the day. It was only with difficulty that the perspicacious Gustav Larosh managed to espy some glinting flecks of genius in the early Tchaikovky's 'uninspiring stream of compositional effluvia'.

But hurrah for plagiarism. In his youth the great Bach almost went blind studying and copying over the concertos of the young and fashionable composer of that day, Antonio Vivaldi. If Bach had not done this, he would possibly not have become Bach—and the world would never have heard the *Brandenburg Concertos*, which were written on the Vivaldi model.

The giftedness of the Composer first manifests itself as the ability to create variant copies of known styles. One of the component parts of this ability—the plethora of musical ideas which appear in the Composer's mind—is a sign of the maturity of the musical-productive ability. Both the people close to him and the Composer himself relate that the creative process really does bring to mind the condition of 'a cow continuously giving milk'. Ideas, motifs, themes, and musical turns of phrase simply 'flow' into the Composer's head, independently and in enormous numbers. Mozart's sister-in-law Sofia recalled how in the early morning, even before his daily ablutions, Mozart was already clumsily tripping over himself as he looked distractedly at the day ahead: musical ideas were already being born in his imagination. For despite his extremely outgoing nature and jocularity, Mozart always remained thoughtful, in the sense that his musical fantasy never knew rest. This kind of ceaseless labor goes on in the consciousness of every gifted Composer. It is a necessity: as great a volume of material as possible must be offered up for analysis and judgment to the composer's great arbitrator, his esthetic sense.

The musical-productive ability, which comes up with musical ideas on the model of existing ones by producing different variant copies, cannot *not* produce a certain number of successful, esthetically satisfying variants—such are the laws of statistics and probability. If the Composer does not work at his craft often enough, then it is possible that among what he does produce there will not be that one unique item that his esthetic sense has been subconsciously thirsting for. That is why Tchaikovsky liked to say that inspiration was a capricious guest who did not like to visit the lazy. The lazy mind cannot bring into the world that uncountable volume of musical probes which are necessary for further selection. When testing for creativity, psychologists quite rightly consider a large quantity of ideas appearing in the subject's mind a sign of creative giftedness. The same is true in music: without an avalanche of ideas coursing through the mind of the creator, it is naive indeed to hope that many successful ones will appear.

The creation of a plethora of variant copies within the framework of an exiting style model is a sign of a professional composer's fantasy at work, a sign of the presence of a musical-creative gift in the process of development. Jacques Offenbach, the founding father of operetta, demonstrated exactly this kind of stunning productivity as a teenager. Describing this wunderkind's ability, the magazine *La Danse* effused that 'Monsieur Offenbach regularly composes three waltzes after breakfast, a *mazurka* after dinner, and between lunch and dinner another four *gallopes*. This youthful wunderkind has asked us to report that he recently lost a handkerchief on which was etched the manuscript of one of his waltzes. A suitable reward will go to the finder'.[50]

When a surfeit of variant copies in the framework of accepted algorithms has accumulated in the Composer's mind—a collection which includes thematic kernels, variants of developing material and successful harmonic turns of phrase—a very important stage begins during which the initiative is taken over by the 'quality control officer' of the Composer's brain: his esthetic sense. The Composer's architectonic ear must cast its 'thoughtful eye' over the accumulation of sound figures and select from it the best which the Composer's fantasy has been able to create. 'When you are composing', Chopin confided, 'everything you write seems good—otherwise nothing would get written. Only some while later do you begin to ponder, and either throw things out or keep them'.[51]

In this Chopin underscores the well-known automatic nature of the compilation of material—a certain avalanche-like flow with its attendant 'unanalytical-ness'—which is typical of this stage of the creative process. A successful variant never appears immediately, in or from a single take. Mick Jagger has noted that a good melody for a song does not come into one's mind easily; and just like the classic Chopin, the master rock musician is inclined to overvalue the ideas that first occur to him. 'There's very few people who can actually sit down and write a single', Jagger testified. 'I've never done that. Nor has Keith [Richards]. I sat down and wrote one the other night, though, that I thought would be a single. I was quite excited about it, but then I just forgot about it'.[52] This is the typical cycle of composing work—attempt, hope, rejection—which is repeated an untold number of times.

When sufficient experience has been accumulated a moment comes when the quantity of successful ideas, productive notions of development, and interesting musical elements born of the Composer's fantasy reaches a kind of critical mass. Suddenly, as he is composing yet another opus—and by force of habit considering it but one more probe of the pen, one more copy composed of more or less successful drafts and outlines—the Composer notices that his composition is no longer imitative. It is *this* beginning (from all the successful impulses he has had) that is uniquely his, and *this* interesting phrase which belongs to him too. In the course of laboring away on the songs of X, the Composer came

50 Decaux, A. (1958) *Offenbach, Roi de Second Empire*. Paris: P. Amiot, p. 31.
51 Cit. from Milshtein, Y. (1967) *Sovety Shopena pianistam/Chopin's Advice to Pianists*. Moscow: Muzyka, p. 106.
52 *Rolling Stones in their own Words* (1985) London: Omnibus Press, p. 104.

to like the variant of the refrain which he himself thought up, and he immediately made a mental note of it. Continuing his thought, the Composer only slightly changed the order of the customary, already-established movements—but in this new form they played something completely new. His now-original culmination also pleases him, and once integrated it is very organic and good; it had come into his head when he had been, long ago, working on the fugue by Y, and now it falls into place as though *made* for it, and the coda of his new piece resembles the concerto endings of Z, which he has been using for a long time.

The Composer may not even recall where, in reality, these elements which now so please him came from; he may not consciously understand how his fantasy brought them to the light of day and how they, as if by the waving of a magic wand, merged with one another to form a complete musical idea. But at this point it is already *his* idea; he did not copy a known model from someone else to obtain it, and did not simply cook up some sort of awkward *pot pourri* from the leavings of others: his own experience is by now so considerable and the number of his successful formulations so great that in producing this original piece he in effect *copied himself*. All the elements which go into the opus now belong to him, the Composer himself: they arose here and there in the course of his work; the creative thought which lived in his soul and demanded embodiment finally found itself in the new creation of the young maestro. The Composer might think that it is all the same variant copy—yet another collection of well-known clichés slightly freshened up under his hand. But suddenly this ugly duckling, this batch of ungainly imitations of everything under the sun, has transformed itself into a beautiful swan of the Composer's own individual style. This means that the first stage of stylistic transformation is complete: from an untold number of borrowed elements, from their overlaps and patchings and from the different possibilities for their continuation and development, a new style model has emerged, one consisting of elements made by the Composer and offshoots from these elements. Put otherwise, what has emerged is a variant copy the Composer made from himself.

The first phase of the transformation is a joint enterprise of the Composer's musical-productive ability, which tirelessly produced a legion of different copies and sound combinations to choose from, and his strict and watchful esthetic sense, which toiled away at salvaging a number of 'diamonds in the rough' unique to the author's compositional fancy from the musical scrap heap. Sergei Prokofiev wrote of this process in his *Diaries*:

> The author splits into two halves—an inventor and a critic. The former serves up fragments of musical ideas quickly, one after another; among them are whole crowds of reflexive, derivative ideas and, lost among them, some original ones as well. It is as if the inventor were sifting through sand in which he occasionally finds gold nuggets. The author-critic instantly analyzes the material offered up—and continuously, endlessly rejects things as defective. But as soon as he comes upon a hint of something original, fresh, and beautiful, he grabs onto this hint like a hook and stays with it … Now it can be written down and set aside for a day or a month. The bullion has been located and secreted away, we can go look for more—and when we have several deposits saved up, we shall set about forging a link for a whole chain.[53]

---

53 Prokofiev, S. (2003) *Dnevniki/Diaries*. Moscow: Klassika-XXI, p. 308.

Put otherwise, the first phase of the transformation of incoming material is born of two 'parents', a creator (the author's musical-productive ability) and a controller (his esthetic sense). At a critical moment the architectonic ear uses the base built by this joint labor to form a new algorithm of style. Sometimes the entire process does not take very long—perhaps a year or two pass between the appearance of the first variant copies and the crystallization of the Composer's own style. But sometimes it takes as much as 10 years. This normally depends on the degree of affinity between the incoming material and the result which the Composer wants to hear.

A short and straight line leads from the first variant copy to the first example of the Composer's own style in pop music, for one, and in work done in the framework of existing mature styles, for another; the latter includes the example of the style of Mozart, which did not stray too far afield from the models of the music of the Age of Chivalry. The path is most difficult for innovative composers who are blazing new trails: there the period of trial and error continues for a long stretch, and the early models of the author's own style appear rather late, as in the case of Claudio Monteverdi. One of the most radical innovators of his time, Monteverdi only came to the complete realization of his own mature style at the age of 40 with his opera *Orpheus*. Before that he had been making variant copies in the madrigal genre, forging his writing style from various elements and discoveries of his composer-contemporaries.

One of the earmark features of the field of pop music, which is extraordinarily conservative in this respect, is the close proximity of authors' styles and the existing collection of stylistic algorithms. Niccolo Paganini, the virtuoso violinist sometimes cited as the first star of show business, composed in an improvisational manner natural for the pop music of his time—strumming away on the guitar he would sort through familiar motifs suggested to him by the sounds of the Italian streets. As his biographer noted:

> As a child of the people who had grown up among the voices of an animated quarter of the city [Paganini] transferred this atmosphere to his music. The themes he left germinating within him that overflowed from his soul... were spiritually akin to the simple flowing melodies of the Italian soul. Like these they were pure, natural, mellifluous, effervescent, capable of being engraved immediately and indelibly on the memories of all who heard them. We find no preliminary sketches, no revisions, no touchings and retouchings, no tentative drafts. Everything was apparently *ecrite du premier jet*, in the white-hot speed of execution. . . . His task, as he saw it, was simply to develop his own gifts—this prodigious technical skill with which the gods had endowed him.[54]

This was the gift of variant copying and rapid selection of the best variants for the creation of an original style. Copying the best of what naturally came into his head over his years of practice, and forming from that a new style—though one rather close to the original stylistic model—did not represent a difficult task for Paganini. In pop music the finding of one's musical self takes place quickly and painlessly. The creative method in question can be called 'variational': it psychologically gravitates toward traditional music

54 Courcy, G.de (1957) *Paganini, the Genoese*, vol.1. Norman: University of Oklahoma Press, p. 53.

and genetically it is the most limited form. Arthur Honegger was describing exactly this method when he wrote:

> The harmonies, melodic lines, modulations and rhythms used by a given Peter do not call forth the slightest reaction. But if Paul reproduces them almost note for note using a different manner of presentation, it turns out that these same elements are suddenly signs of the distinctiveness of his individuality, becoming manifestations, in fact, of his giftedness.[55]

Claude Debussy seconded this opinion: 'Where does this charm that unexpectedly sounds forth in familiar chords come from, coursing through all the music, if not from the [author's] introduction of places in the sound which cannot be learned because they are not written down anywhere?'[56] Such then is the first phase in the transformation of music: never too far afield from the originals, and yet ... Such was the early music of Mozart, when his contemporaries still liked it—before he became the Great Mozart who delighted the experts and frightened the ignorant.

Psychologically pop music strongly gravitates toward 'light plagiarism'. The whole of the genre can be thought of as one great meta-text which is sliced up and nibbled at by various composers, all of whom are essentially taking bites out of the same pie. Music scholar Mark Aranovsky has observed,

> There is no better example of the general striving of texts to merge into a single common Text, than the mass-entertainment genres. These texts not only draw towards one another, they often become as indistinguishable from each other as clones. In such situations one rarely has to talk about the phenomenon of a work, since an individual initiative normally does not enter into the esthetic programs of these genres. In essence they are only everyday forms of communication, that is, above all, statements, texts.[57]

Cases of variant copying, sometimes dangerously close to the source model, are in pop music entirely natural. The composer Mikael Tariverdiev, when composing the leitmotiv for the popular Soviet spy movie *Seventeen Moments of Spring*, unintentionally wandered into the zone of variant copying of another melody [shliager], that of composer Richard Clayderman's *Love Story*. Both themes are melancholy and sentimental, shot through with a light sadness; it is hardly surprising that they employ similar melodic turns of phrase. Yet Tariverdiev's melody hovers right over the border between variant copying and the first phase of transformation: using material common to all of pop music, Tarivardiev sharpened the nostalgic note which is part of such themes at the expense of reaccenting the supporting tones; in place of Clayderman's 'swinging back and forth' we get Tariverdiev's 'hanging in the air', a self-styled lightened *lamento*—a pop variant of the Russian *angst*. 'Soft plagiarism' as a means for working out a talent for composing in no way excludes creative individuality.

---

[55] Honegger, A. (1963) *Ya - kompozitor!/I am a Composer!* Moscow: Muzyka, p. 41.
[56] Debussy, K. (1964) *Stat'i, retsenzii, besedy/Articles, Reviews, Interviews.* Moscow: Muzyka, p. 164.
[57] Aranovsky, M. G. (1998) *Muzikalny tekst: struktura i svoistva/Musical text: structure and properties.* Moscow: Kompozitor, p. 31.

Many composers see their own styles as the product of the transformation of preceding styles: they know their model, they know exactly what they took from it for their own ends—and took in such a way that the model would, in their hands, reach its full potential, emerging as something new in the process. The group Led Zeppelin, which reached enormous popularity overnight in the early 1970s, was accused by unfriendly observers of 'dirty PR', using shady advertising and manipulating the public. The artists themselves explained their success saying they were using a different style model and successfully transforming it—a path to success well known in the musical arts in general, and in pop music considered the *basic* method. As Jimmy Page, the group's leader, put it 'The only people with a similar musical approach at the time were *Cream*, but I always felt their improvised passages used to go on and on. We tried to reflect more light and shade into the spontaneous pieces and also a sense of the dramatic. If there was a key to why we made it, it was in that'.[58]

Great talents and even geniuses long past the stage of establishing themselves once in a while return to 'light plagiarism'. As though unable to bear the creative pressure which arises from the ceaseless labor of the esthetic sense, the author's creative fantasy stops listening to him and the 'musical junk' of the early stages of creativity flows unhindered. It is in this way that geniuses produce unsuccessful compositions. Copying bad models, Beethoven created a variant of them in his melodic overture the *Battle of Vittoria*. Tasteless and trite ideas sometimes crept into Tchaikovsky's music, as they did into Verdi's as well. Most often, however, such breakdowns of the esthetic sense and attendant returns to variant copying happen to composers whose talent (and even genius) are not alien to the ideology of pop music, with its naive openness and pedestrian daily realities. Tchaikovsky and Verdi are just such composers. The strict esthete Debussy had no such 'misses' in his record, nor does one find them among the works of the reclusive Hugo Wolf or the philosophizing Bach. Only Haydn and Mozart were capable of remaining 'musical democrats' without ever lapsing into bad taste. One wonders whether perhaps this owed to the fact that the pop music to which they turned had already gone through the mill of the eighteenth-century academic traditions and thus came to them in a handily 'pre-cleaned' version.

After the first stage of the stylistic transformation, heralded by the appearance of an individualistic authorial manner, the same psychological schema continues to work. If the Composer moves further along the path of individual evolution, if the new content of his work demands a further replenishing of his means, then the author proceeds to the second stage of transformation, in which the psychological instruments of his talent act in the previously established fashion. He masters the style he has found, producing multiple copies of it; in the course of this process, the esthetic sense goes ahead with its selection of the most original ideas and most successful creative discoveries. Once again critical mass is reached, this time of new material bearing no resemblance to the old, and it threatens to blow up the earlier style model which had appeared as a result of the first

---

[58] *Led Zeppelin in their own Words* (1981) London: Omnibus Press, p. 40.

phase of transformation. Finally the Composer no longer copies himself in the previous mode, but his new self; now he relies only on new ideas, new thematic models, new means of development, giving birth to a new style model—which completes the second phase of transformation. The same components of his talent were involved as before: the musical-creative need stimulated the appearance of new ideas and goals; the musical-productive ability churned out copies of musical elements and combinations; and the architectonic ear took on the duty of selecting the most successful ideas and completing the construction of a new stylistic algorithm.

There are composers whose way leads through three or four phases of transformation. This happens with those whose notional hero is developing, whose view of the world is undergoing radical evolution—as did Beethoven's hero and Tchaikovsky's. There are also composers whose style is formed once and for all; such was the case with Bach, whose religious worldview and elevated mode of thought did not change over the course of his lifetime, as the Baroque period did not strive toward spiritual evolution. The more dynamic Handel came to a 'second style' in the latter half of his life: his notional hero changed and the author found new means for the expression of his spiritual being, having turned to new stylistic sources.

Yet none of this—not creative continuity, nor inclinations toward stylistic transformation, nor the genres and forms of music the Composer works in—can change the nature of his talent. The talent of a composer always depends on musical-creative need, musical-productive ability and the architectonic ear, including as it does the esthetic sense. Talent presupposes the ability of these elements to 'hear' each other and work together in concord. In this respect the talent of Beethoven is no greater than that of Rossini: the two men had different creative interests, different notional heroes and, one might say, different levels of spirituality. But spiritual power and strength of idea are characteristics of a personality rather than components of talent. From this point of view it can be claimed that the composer Paganini, in whose music one finds the portrait of a life-loving Italian untroubled by the eternal questions of being, and the composer Mozart, Paganini's senior contemporary who saw God in music, were equally gifted.

A talented person imprints upon his works a certain defined cultural reality, and the strength of the talent derives from the extent to which this reality is vividly and convincingly expressed and how esthetically satisfying the result is. In this respect the pop music classic Paul McCartney is in no sense less talented than his avant-garde contemporary Pierre Boulez: each of them accurately and profoundly expresses the internal world of his notional hero and creates an aura of thought and feeling around him; and each composer can justly claim as his own certain models of musical beauty in his chosen genre. Paradoxical as it may sound, it is not differences in the level of musical giftedness which give rise to such different kinds of music, but rather differences in the composers' philosophical *ustanovka*—point of departure and mindset—which they choose for themselves. Here the issues do not concern the psychology of talent, the definition of the structure of its components or the means of their interaction. These questions relate rather to the existence of different cultural milieus and mindsets, to the realm of philosophy, theology, hermeneutics, culture studies, sociology, and other areas in the humanities and social sciences well beyond the bounds of psychological issues.

Creative inspiration: the neuropsychology of composer's talent

A creative idea is born in the zone of the so-called 'Three I's': inspiration, intuition, and imagination. 'Who can penetrate the mystery of the writing of music?' asked Debussy.

> The noise of the sea, the curve of a line on the horizon, the wind in the tree branches, the cry of the birds—all these make various impressions on us. And suddenly, without asking anyone's permission, the memory of one of these sounds simply flows out of us, expressing itself in the language of music. It carries within it its own harmony; and no matter how hard one tries, it will never be possible to find a harmony either more exact or more sincere. Only in that way does the heart destined for music make its most beautiful discoveries.[59]

Anton Webern, whose creative impulses found expression far from the contemplation of nature, said much the same thing. In explaining to a colleague how he went about composing, Webern related that 'For me it goes this way: I carry around in myself an experience of some kind until it comes out as music—music connected with this experience, definitely and completely. Sometimes down to details. And the experience becomes music more than once'.[60]

The Composer wants to turn his life impressions into music, and one particularity of his perception is the peculiar 'closeness of the musical strain' to everything that touches and interests him. That which for others appears in the form of the seen, said, read, and understood is for the Composer always ready to emerge as the heard. Thus awakens the Composer's musical-creative need, which in turn arouses in him a musical concept.

The arrival of a creative idea is the most mysterious part of the creative process. At this stage the Composer already hears the entire piece as if in complete form, taking it in its entirety in a single moment. Mozart wrote:

> ... now I look over the piece spiritually in a single glance, as a beautiful picture or a beautiful person, and I hear it in my imagination not note by note, as it will come out later, but as if all together. What a sumptuous feast! Finding everything and doing it —all that goes by as if in a deep and beautiful dream. But the best thing of all is to hear everything together all at once.[61]

The composer Karl Weber likewise noted that 'The internal ear has the amazing ability to catch and envelop entire musical structures... This ear allows one simultaneously to hear entire period segments, even entire pieces'.[62] Both Mozart and Weber were talking

[59] Debussy, K. (1964) Stat'i, retsenzii, besedy/Articles, Reviews, Interviews. Moscow: Muzyka, p. 192.
[60] Webern, A. (1975) *Lekzii o muzike. Pis'ma/Lectures on Music. Letters.* Moscow: Muzyka, p. 39.
[61] Mikhailov, A. (1993) W.A. Mozart i K.F.Moritz, ili o videnii slukhom/ W. A. Mozart and K. F. Moritz, or on visualization via ears. In *Problemy tvorchestva Motsarta/Problems of Mozart's Creative Work*, (ed. T. Chigareva). Moscow Conservatory, p. 67.
[62] Cit. from Teplov, B. (1947) *Psikhologia muzikalnikh sposobnostei/The Psychology of Musical Abilities.* Moscow: Pedagogika, p. 244.

about the capabilities of the architectonic ear, which sets about its work at the beginning stage of an idea and establishes the so-called general outline of the work—that which musicologist Mark Aranovsky calls the *proektivnoe tseloe*, the project overview. On this are imprinted the spatial contours of the future composition and its proportions; also present are the intonational seeds and the principal sound relationships. All this appears before the Composer as if in rolled-up form, like a plan or a *schema* in which the details have yet to be written in.

The architectonic ear grasps the newborn conception and turns it into a definite plan for future composition, forming its aural-spatial image. In the initial stage of the concept it attracts the resources of the expressive ear, which senses the tensions and stresses of the musical statement and the general direction of its movement; then the architectonic ear draws a spatial portrait of the future work—as the pianist Laszlo Kovacs put it, he sees 'the piece as a whole, like a sort of dismembered architectonic, and [sees] its parts in audio-motor terms'.[63] In the initial generalized form one hears the contours of the principal sound relationships—as far as the melody is concerned, the first thing to fall into place is the 'base layer', where in coded form lie its fundamental tones (Aranovsky 1991); present in the initial form of the work, according to Aranovsky, is its style-genre model, which focuses and directs the creative attention of the Composer—he is concentrating on a certain collection of themes, of means of development and of form-delineating principles: from this collection his imagination will come up with his compositional ideas.

The architectonic ear provides the capability of 'musical overview', under which the entire future work is, in Mozart's expression, set before one in the form of a 'visible idea'. The architectonic ear acts as a 'musical excavator' which compresses the musical details, preserving in the form of a spatial image the basic sound relationships and proportions of the musical form. Speaking of the origins of a musical concept, Arthur Honegger recalled:

> At first I try to imagine the general scheme and the character of the entire symphonic work as a whole. This looks approximately like what one might see when, in the midst of an unusually thick fog, things gradually begin to delineate themselves, and the outline of something resembling a castle begins to appear. At times a ray of sunlight suddenly lights up one wing; though it is still surrounded by forest, this wing becomes my model. Then it is time to report all one's observations of this kind, and I concentrate on the search for the means with which to make this construction. Notes appear in my rough drafts.[64]

The comparison of the process of composing with that of constructing a building is quite apt: first a musical-creative need appears, which turns any kind of impression into a musical impulse, the spark for the musical fantasy. Then the architectonic ear creates a project plan for a future construction. Thus is formed a 'musical order': the Composer recognizes what he wants and what he expects to get as a result of the work. This 'order', thanks to its quasi-spatial and single-moment psychological nature, may be housed in the

---

63 Cit. from Teplov, B. (1947) *Psikhologia muzikalnikh sposobnostei/The Psychology of Musical Abilities.* Moscow: Pedagogika, p. 245.

64 Honegger, A. (1963) *Ya - kompozitor!/I am a Composer!* Moscow: Muzyka, p. 142.

right hemisphere of the brain. That is why artistic giftedness is traditionally assigned to that hemisphere: in it takes place both the gestation and birth of the creative idea, without which no creation is possible. And it is possibly to there, the right hemisphere, that the completed composition is eventually sent for comparison with the original concept. After the plan of the future work is ready, the center of creative activity moves to the left hemisphere, responsible for combination of elements and blocks which takes on the actual 'construction'.

Musical-productive ability, as a continuous production and combining of musical thoughts, presumably belongs to the left hemisphere—the one that thinks things up, invents things, compares them and lines up the chains created from musical elements. The linguistic left hemisphere specializes in linear consecutive signals, and without its work no musical statements could appear. The Composer's left hemisphere is in a state of continuous searching and endless combining activity; the esthetic sense monitors its results and selects the best of them, creating the resource base for musical creation. Arthur Honegger described the process in the following manner:

> In composing music one begins to resemble a person trying to set up a ladder—without leaning it against the wall. There is no construction lumber; the building under construction is kept from collapsing only by a miracle: a sense of the demands of internal logic and an inborn sense of proportion on the part of the builder. I have to be both the builder and an observer from the sidelines at the same time: I do the work and analyze how it is progressing as well. When any sort of sudden hindrance forces me to stop, I leave my work bench, sit down in the listener's chair and ask myself: 'What else would you like in order to sense, if not spiritual genius, then at least success? What, by the logic of things, should there be here to inspire in me a feeling of complete satisfaction?' And I set out in search of a continuation which satisfies me. I do not look for it in banal formulations which anyone can see coming; on the contrary, I look for it in elements of originality, in that which can intensify one's interest.[65]

The constant search for musical ideas exhausts the Composer: between the concept created by the plan and the building blocks found for its realization there passes a continuous exchange of information; and much of what is proposed by the musical-productive ability is subsequently rejected by the esthetic sense. The Composer naturally inclines toward any kind of repetition, since from a psychological point of view only the technique of copying does not demand particular exertion: all other material collected must be 'sent for approval', and in case it is rejected there the search must be started again. So Mikhail Glinka complained:

> Many have accused me of laziness. Let these ladies and gentlemen take my place for a time—then they will be convinced that with the continuous nervous stress and the strict view of art which has always guided me it is impossible to write a great deal. Those trifling romances flowed out by themselves in a moment of inspiration, but often they can cost me considerable effort—not repeating yourself is more difficult than you can imagine—and I have decided from this year to close the factory of Russian romances.[66]

---

[65] Honegger, A. (1963) *Ya - kompozitor! / I am a Composer!* Leningrad: Muzyka, p. 89.
[66] Glinka, M. (1954) *O muzyke i muzykantah/On music and musicians.* Moscow: Gosmuzgiz, p. 54.

An aversion to repetition and a fear of the banal constantly weigh on the Composer. The romantic Berlioz, who was not a pianist, rejoiced in this fact because he felt it lessened the risk of borrowing from others' common stock:

> I can only thank the stars which placed before me the necessity of creating freely and in silence, thus saving me from the tyranny of those accustomed movements of the fingers across a keyboard which are so dangerous for thinking—and from temptation by the sound of vulgar things, a temptation which is always capable of influencing the composer.[67]

Through strict selection, creative self-discipline and ceaseless labor the left hemisphere succeeds in compiling a resource base sufficiently extensive to include the 'building material' necessary for the future composition. And now here, in the left hemisphere, the material is worked into certain combinations. The process of combining is continually checked against the plan, which is kept in the right hemisphere; between the two hemispheres a constant 'exchange of opinions' goes on, leading to mutually agreed upon adjustments. Almost all composers admit that this combining process, which threads together and joins the musical elements according to a certain defined logic, is in essence mathematical. 'I have always maintained', noted Scriabin, 'that mathematics should play a major role in composition. Sometimes I have a complete computation in a composition, a computation of form'.[68]

Edison Denisov also held that the 'logic of the musician is in many respects reminiscent of the logic of mathematics'.[69] And Arthur Honegger, a composer far from enraptured with the musical avant-garde, agreed with his 'progressive' colleagues as to the relevance of a mathematical model: 'Architecture is often called frozen music', he noted, 'but I would put it differently: music itself is geometry moving in time'.[70]

A substantial part of these quasi-mathematical functions is performed by the sequentially combining musical-productive ability located in the left hemisphere; if an interruption occurs in its work, the whole composing process is derailed. The Composer's talent can only exist as an entity uniting all the components distributed throughout the brain's two hemispheres.

Neuropsychologists cite the illness of Maurice Ravel (Alajouanine 1948; Cytowic 1976; Otte *et al.* 2003; Warren 2003), who in the last years of his life suffered from both a severe speech impediment (aphasia) and disturbances of the motor apparatus (apraxia). Ravel claimed that he had never had so many ideas as when he suffered from these afflictions—but he could not commit them to paper: his ailing left hemisphere could not assemble combinations of musical elements, and thus the creative concept, the right hemisphere's image of the future music, perforce remained unarticulated. Beethoven likewise suffered from apraxia and agraphia: he had continuous problems with reading, writing, and

67 Berlioz, G. (1962) *Memuary/Memoirs*. Moscow: Muzyka, p. 39.
68 Cit. from Sabaneev, L. (1925) *Vospominaniya o Skryabine/Memoirs of Scriabin*. Moscow: Izdatelstvo Sabashnikovykh, p. 105.
69 Cit. from Shulgin D. I. (1998) *Priznanie Edisona Denisova/Edison Denisov's Confession*. Moscow: Kompozitor, p. 39.
70 Honegger, A. (1979) *O muzikalnom iskusstve/On the Art of Music*. Leningrad: Sovetsky Kompozitor, p. 139.

arithmetic, which speaks to a left-hemisphere functional deficit. His awkwardness became legendary. Food and drink dropped and dribbled from him, he broke dishes, glasses fell to the floor at his touch. Nonetheless some neuropsychologists suppose that left-brain functions were critical to Beethoven in his composing. Jan Ehrenwald (1984) has noted in this context that the composer's more narrowly gifted and specially focused left hemisphere had to play a role in the organization and development of his finished product; with experience an increasing 'migration' of musical elements from the right to the left hemisphere can come about—and that if creative giftedness is a combination of inspiration, invention, and communication, it is only logical to concede that the last two of these ingredients constitute the contribution of the artist's (and thus Beethoven's) left hemisphere.

Despite the deficit in left-hemisphere functions Beethoven brilliantly performed his compositional labors. This case and others like it may be interpreted as examples of one hemisphere substituting for the other—in the given instance, the healthy right taking over the functions of the ailing left. As some neuropsychologists suggest (Balonov and Deglin 1974; Bekhtereva *et al.* 1977; Ivanov 1983), in many gifted musicians, including Beethoven, these very functions themselves tend, in the 'musical brain', toward interpenetration; the functions of the brain hemispheres of talented musicians may be localized in a more mobile and variable setting than they are in the less musically inclined. According to a study led by S. E. Gaede (Gaede *et al.* 1978), an extraordinarily positive role in musical development is played by just this capability, that of alternating at will between the generalizing-spatial strategy of the right hemisphere and the analytical-combining strategy of the left. The absence of musical talent, concluded Gaede *et al.*, can be laid to a too-strict adherence by each hemisphere to its own strategy and an inability to regulate the strategies themselves. Referring to neuropsychological research Vyacheslav Medushevsky indicates:

> Anomalous dominance, defined as any pattern deviating from the standard one, is associated with more anatomically and functionally symmetrical brains, with language less lateralized to the left hemisphere, and visual-spatial functions less lateralized to the right side. And there is now some evidence that various forms of giftedness are associated with a more bilateral, symmetrical kind of brain organization, with the right hemisphere participating in tasks ordinarily reserved for the left hemisphere.[71]

One-third of such 'anomalies' are found among left-handed people: their brains are more balanced, with the functions of the two hemispheres seemingly 'lubricated' and less clearly delineated. Research by a group of neuropsychologists led by Marianne Hassler (Hassler *et al.* 1987) describes various experiments which confirm the connection between left-handedness and musical giftedness. A statistical study compiled by John Aggleton and colleagues (Aggleton *et al.* 1994) established that the percentage of left-handed people among conductors and composers was significantly higher than among the population at large.

---

[71] Medushevsky, V. (1993) *Intonatsionnaya forma muzyki/The Intonation form of Music*. Moscow: Sovetsky kompozitor, p. 46.

The Composer's giftedness constantly relies on a dialogue of the brain hemispheres: the right-brain architectonic ear and esthetic sense interact with the left-brain musical-productive ability, which creates new combinations of musical elements. The talent of the Composer presupposes the greatest degree possible of flexibility in alternations between left- and right-hemisphere functions. There have been cases in which, due to the exceptional development of these connections, musicians could continue their creative activity despite the loss of one of the hemispheres altogether. The composer Vissarion Shebalin, who suffered from aphasia and disruption of the left-hemisphere functions, continued to compose; and the talent of Alfred Schnitke did not suffer unduly as a result of a brain lesion. Musical activity in general and that of the composer in particular presumes exactly this kind of flexible and multifunctional work regime on the part of the brain.

The meetings of creative concepts worked out by the right hemisphere and the aggregate of musical-technical resources offered up by the left are not always of the happiest kind. Sometimes the two simply do not understand each other, and the concept remains unrealized. In just this way many ideas have died, among them Glinka's emotional *Cossack Symphony*. Recalling this episode the composer wrote:

> If I am demanding of others, then I am even more so toward myself. And here is an example of just that: in Paris I wrote the first part of the Allegro and the beginning of the second part of the *Cossack Symphony*—but I could not continue the Second, I was not satisfied with it. After reflecting on this, I found that I had begun the development of the Allegro in the German style, while the general character of the piece was Ukrainian. I threw out the score.[72]

The piece, in other words, fell victim to Glinka's desire to join the unjoinable: the popular-song material simply did not fit with the symphonic development which was forced to split it up and twist it, artificially creating bustle and commotion; the process was inappropriate to the material. In the given instance the mistake was made by the 'architect', his task was obviously not fulfilled and no matter how hard the left brain tried, it could not compile the necessary material for the job. If, on the other hand, the architectonic ear has correctly set out the basic contours of the composition and its main idea, and at the same time the 'building materials' which have come to hand, without requiring a long search all over everywhere, prove exactly the ones necessary —then the moment of creative inspiration can arrive.

The left and right hemispheres work in tandem like never before, almost overtaking each other: every request from the right-brain 'musical-architectural workshop' receives an immediate answer from the left-brain 'construction department'. An initial idea immediately appears, as does a way for its further advancement and the form of the entire composition. At that point it seems to the Composer that the work was dictated from above, that he has been waiting his whole life for this moment to arrive. In the creative biography of the Composer there may be more than a few such moments of happiness.

Tchaikovsky created his *Queen of Spades* in Florence in the course of 3 months, and the reasons for this are hardly mystical. The two constituent elements of the Composer's craft

---

72 Glinka, M. (1954) *O muzyke i muzykantah/On Music and Musicians*. Moscow: Gosmuzgiz, p. 77.

were ready to create this masterpiece. Tchaikovsky's architectonic ear had the experience of planning musical-dramatic tableaux, in the center of which lay the conflict between Man and Fate (the frequency to which the author's musical-creative impulse was always attuned). His musical-productive ability, providing themes, melodic lines, harmonic complexes and phrases, could have, in the given instance, gotten by without great effort: Tchaikovsky had been selecting the esthetically perfect images from the required genre mood all his life, and for *Queen of Spades* his imagination produced them with unbelievable ease—he did not have to search for anything, everything flowed into his head as if of its own accord. His entire experience as a Composer had anticipated the appearance of precisely this concept, polishing it up in various different examples; and exactly these stylistic means had come to maturity in his many other works. The right- and left-brain segments of his talent worked together effortlessly, drawing on labor performed long before—and thus the moment of inspiration, the moment of the merging of concept and realization, could not but arrive.

If, on the other hand, the Composer does not work, does not spend his time honing his concepts and checking the results against his true intentions; and if in doing this he does not amass an enormous collection of the musical elements he needs—then the architectonic ear can formulate an 'order' which is incorrect or inexact, and the musical-productive ability may not be able to find a sufficient quantity of ideas for the Composer to select from. This is why the moment of lucidity dawns only after long labor (something all researchers into creativity have noted). It is necessary to spend some time working on exactly that concept, to turn one's imagination in the direction the concept indicates, and to gather as great a quantity as possible of probes, mistakes, and new probes. The composer Arthur Honegger described his creative travails as follows:

> Usually I go over my notebooks in search of notations, hoping to find in them some kind of melodic or rhythmic sketch or some chord combinations ready for use. Then, having given a melody some time to mature, I mentally toss in everything that could be extracted from it. And how many disappointments there are! It takes no little courage to begin everything all over again—for the third, fourth and fifth time. Once when I was filling out a form I defined talent in the following way: 'The ability to begin everything over again'.[73]

There are composers who seemingly never search for inspiration—it is always right there beside them. Mozart belongs to this group: the masterpieces of his genius give off an almost magical impression of cornucopia and lightness. Yet there is not really anything mysterious in the creative productivity of Mozart or in that of Bach. The left-brain function in their creative process was greatly facilitated by the fact that they did not have to invent the necessary combinations of musical elements, appealing for help to heterogeneous sources. The stylistic aspect of their material had already been perfected and 'set in type': they arrived at a moment of the complete maturity of a style—Bach at the height of the Baroque period and Mozart at that of European classicism. They used the element base already present almost in its pre-packaged form, polishing it only slightly with the

---

[73] Honegger, A. (1963) *Ya – kompozitor!/I am a Composer!* Leningrad: Muzyka, p. 101.

touch of their genius. The means of realizing each concept flowed into their imaginations as if by themselves, creating the conditions for continuous inspiration.

Other colleagues had to create this element base themselves, writing with much more difficulty. Beethoven, standing at the musical headwaters of the new nineteenth century, had to bring a common denominator to the music of the French revolution and contemporary French opera, the music of Haydn and Mozart, the music of Handel and Gluck. He himself forged his own style, nothing coming to his mind in pre-arranged form; thus it is hardly surprising that Beethoven's inspiration was less generous and rarer than Mozart's. It is entirely possible that the number of masterpieces in the music of Mozart is greater: it was easier for him to create them.

The creative giftedness of the composer overlaps with other forms of giftedness in psychological content. It is particularly close to mathematical and verbal giftedness.

Critical in all three forms of activity is the combining of elements, with a result which must correspond to a defined esthetic concept. Analogues to the architectonic ear, which creates the plan for a future work—poetry, commentary, mathematical arguments, and so on—must be present in the structure of logical-mathematical and verbal giftedness. It is natural to suppose that in these structures there is also a psychological analogue to the musical-productive ability, which comes up with the elements necessary for creation (and combination) *en masse*. There should also be a 'control point' for the 'product' which issues forth—the esthetic sense. The multifaceted nature of talent should likewise be one and the same in all spheres of activity, and creative inspiration should everywhere be a sign of the coordinated work of both brain hemispheres—a sign, in sum, of the highest correspondence between an initial concept and the means selected for its realization.

To summarize, then, our section on the creative giftedness of the composer: the structure of this gift consists of three basic elements:

1 At its source stands the composer's musical-creative need. This need is located at the border between the spiritual-cultural content which the author wants to express and the musical form to which this content must be addressed. The musical-creative need stimulates the appearance of a simultaneous image of the future work—a multi-modal audio-motor and audio-spatial construct which is the embryo of the composition and the launch mechanism for work on it. The musical-creative need forms the musical-creative concept and is the motivational nucleus of the composer's talent.

2 The musical-productive ability is the left-brain component of the composer's giftedness. It supplies all the musical elements necessary for creativity and the means for their assembly. It combines musical structures of different hierarchical levels into bigger blocks, creating a broad element base. The musical-productive ability continually produces musical thoughts of various structural levels and combines them, supplying for the architectonic ear a sufficient selection base of creative possibilities necessary to and useful for every situation. The musical-productive ability is the 'builder' of the musical composition, as it holds all the material necessary for its creation.

3 The architectonic ear controls the internal logic of the development of a musical thought, intuitively sensing the relationship of parts to the whole and their concomitant interdependence. The esthetic sense is the psychological indicator of the architectonic ear, heralding the latter's presence in the structure of musical talent. The architectonic ear relies on aural-spatial associations and is the 'architect' of the future composition, controlling all phases of its construction.

The giftedness of the performer

The compositional talent of the performer

The profession of performing musician is a young one. A mere two centuries ago it would have been difficult to imagine a musician who would dedicate himself entirely to the performance of works written by other people. But over the course of these last two hundred years the musical art of Europe has become extremely complex and varied; it now includes many musical cultures, currents, and directions, among them early music, classical music of the eighteenth to the twentieth centuries, the avant-garde, the post-avant-garde, opera and chamber music, rock music, a plethora of youth-music movements, jazz, ethnic music, and a great deal else. Each of these cultures commands a great arsenal of ways and means used for performance, and they are continually becoming more sophisticated: today's youthful performers can boast, while still studying at primary music schools, of repertoires which in the past would have been commanded only by mature artists. In a jazz band of the 1920s or 1930s one could find a white-collar type enjoying himself after work; today, in order to play contemporary jazz, in the Winton Marsalis orchestra, say, a child must be trained practically from the first grade onward. If a Mozart symphony could be performed by an amateur ensemble, a Mahler symphony—a work much greater in size and many times more complex—can be played only by a professional orchestra. Music has ceased to be only a part of life—a part which pertained to religious rituals, city holidays, or rural festivals; instead it has become an independent realm of culture, with its own infrastructure of concert halls and venues, its own institutions for study and instruction, and its own multi-media press.

Up through the nineteenth century music continued to be regarded as a form of relaxation for amateurs; every capital of Europe could boast of hundreds of homes in which people made very nice music indeed, enriching their leisure time with the graceful tones of Brahms quartets or Schubert sonatas for four hands. Over the course of the twentieth century, however, people's perceptions of music changed fundamentally. Today's community of super-professionals, narrow but unsurpassed specialists in their fields, demands from musicians such a level of polish and perfection in performance, such flawless and beautiful sound, that even a very gifted amateur is, by comparison, simply out of his depth. Music has become big business, a commercial enterprise in which hundreds of soloists, orchestras, groups and ensembles compete for the public's attention. In this age of professionalism, the paths of the performer and the composer are simply bound to diverge.

The image of the composer in society's eyes is one of a person wholly given over to art—a servant of his muse, the soul of which resides in the world of sounds, and a person who commands this secret world with his ability to turn cacophony into a conscious message. Far removed from the petty concerns of the quotidian world, the Composer creates his musical manuscript, destined to capture Time itself. Society's image of the performer, on the other hand, is one of a person who has mastered not music as such but rather his particular musical instrument (or voice). She can realize, and to great effect, someone else's musical thoughts; she has a great stage presence; and she is unsurpassed in the delivery of sound *qua* sound and in the delivery of Music as well. It is really the performing artist who creates the image of music for society, as the music media focus their attention first and foremost on her, the Performer.

At first glance the talents of the Composer and the Performer would seem rather distant from one another: their roles in musical culture are different and their means of expressing themselves musically are different as well. But unlike social life, human nature, including the nature of talent, does not change dramatically. On the contrary, talent is, by way of structure, very conservative; it reflects the phylogenetic path of development of the human race over the course of many thousands of years. For almost all of this period the Composer and the Performer were a single being; each was the best of the improvisers, creating music before an audience and inspiring this audience with his art. The talent of the Composer and the Performer grew from one and the same seed; it was for ages a single whole, and as such naturally included the same principal elements in its make-up. Only the weight and the proportion of each in the structure of talent came to differentiate the talent of the Composer from that of the Performer.

The Composer is the king of music, the architect of the musical building. His talent is of such all-encompassing proportions as to include the performer's gift; in historical terms it was the rare composer indeed whose performing talents were not also notable. If a composer writes for the piano, such as Chopin or Lizst, then he is a piano virtuoso unique in his time. If his interests lie in composing for the orchestra—he is often an outstanding conductor, such as Mahler or Richard Strauss. The performing gifts of the great composer-violinists Corelli, Vivaldi, and Paganini are legendary. The entire musical world knew the work of the composer-organists Bach, Handel, César Franck, and Olivier Messian during their lifetimes, as it did that of Mozart and Beethoven, the virtuosi of the clavier and piano. Shostakovich and Prokofiev were outstanding piano performers, as was Gershwin on jazz piano. In pop music as well the composers are, as a rule, exceptional artist-performers: Elton John is an excellent pianist and singer, and the composers John Lennon and Paul McCartney were likewise unusually gifted as guitar performers and solo singers.

For the most part composers turn aside notions of a career as performing artists in order to concentrate on composing music—although in the ranks of composers you will hardly find a single one incapable of becoming a performing soloist if he so chose. Friends of the composer Arno Babadzhanian often told pianists they knew to be glad that Arno was content to compose and did not want to appear on stage; if he were suddenly to re-think and switch professions, the other pianists would have to give back all their performance medals. The sole exceptions to this rule are those composers who did not study an instrument in childhood; to this category belong Aram Khachaturian, who began his musical studies at the age of 19 and Edison Denisov, who began music school at 16. The Russian classics of the nineteenth century, none of whom went through a truly professional school of performance training, nevertheless played wonderfully: it is impossible to imagine better singers and accompanists than Glinka or the remarkable Mussorgsky, who toured Russia as a pianist with great success with the singer Daria Leonova. The talent of the Composer is the highest stage of musicality, and only a disinclination to commit his time to the necessary technical exercises keeps the Composer from occupying the first place among musical performers of his time and place. 'Can there be a composer with mediocre musical abilities?' asked Rimsky-Korsakov—and then hastened to answer:

> Definitely not. The musical abilities of even the least among the composers, meaning those who left the least behind them in the history of art, must still tower above the abilities of those on the middle level. The least significant composers in Western music were nevertheless great musical talents . . . Indeed, the very idea of a composer without great musical talent is absurd.[1]

Yet is the 'reverse theorem' true as well? Is it also the case that every great musical talent is necessarily a composer? Yes, it is—and this is true even if the basic occupation of the talent in question is musical performance. In such cases the performer is already outside the bounds of the middling. When among the technical equipment of the musician-performer one finds a composer's strength of musical imagination, a composer's flight of musical fantasy, a maximally developed esthetic sense and a wondrous architechtonic ear—all these qualities of the composer's gift lift the Performer above the level of his ordinary colleagues. The talent of this kind of Performer is phylogenetically based, nourished from the natural roots of human musicality; it originally appeared and established itself as the musicality of the Composer, then merged inextricably with his mastery of performance. The outstanding musician is in fact—as described by Rimsky-Korsakov, director of the St Petersburg Conservatory and an experienced instructor as well as an expert on talent in its various incarnations—he who has, necessarily, at least a modest composer's talent plus a great performing gift. There is hardly one that has since improved upon this formulation of the essence of a performer's endowment.

The conductor is distinguished by his highly developed expressive ear; every sound is significant to him, as his hearing is extraordinarily sensitive. The musician-performer is the same. A group of French psychologists led by Christophe Micheyl (Micheyl et al. 1995) did a study of the reactions of musicians and non-musicians to loud sounds and diminishing sounds. It turned out that musicians do not have the 'sound shield' that ordinary people do: if to non-musicians a very loud sound always seems somewhat quieter than it is in reality—the hearing of normal people modulates loud noises, subconsciously protecting itself from them—then musicians hear the sound exactly as it is.

----

[1] Rimsky-Korsakov, N. A. (1911) *Muzykal'nie stat'i i zametki/Papers and Notes on Music*. St.-Petersburg: Jurgenson, p. 77.

In the Composer's memory sound is retained for long periods. Stravinsky long remembered the sound of the Petersburg telephone which had so amazed him in his childhood. Musician-performers likewise easily distinguish sound from noise and store the latter in their memory. The musicians in Micheyl and colleagues' study, unlike their non-musical peers, could hear the sound of a certain pitch through noise interference and successfully recall it. The non-musical subjects, when the sound was 'covered' by hindrances and quickly faded out, forgot it much more easily. Thus the psychologists demonstrated that a musician's hearing, irrespective of whether the sound being perceived is musical, is more open and sensitive than others.

In the sense of responsiveness to sound's volume the musician's hearing does not differ from that of the Composer. The sensitivity of outstanding composers to various gradations of loudness is extremely high. In his memoirs the conductor and composer Richard Strauss noted, *inter alia*, that 'If it seems to you that the brass are not sounding loud enough, turn them down by two more degrees'; 'Do not let the French horns and the woodwinds out of your sight: if you can hear them, it means they are playing too loud'; and 'Always accompany the vocalist in such a way that he can sing without any exertion at all'.[2] Such observations from this maestro are nothing if not testimony to the performer's, and especially the conductor's, exceptionally sensitive ear.

The composer takes the sounds of nature and of the street as material for his creative work: the rush of water, the rustling of leaves in the trees, and the singing of birds all easily turn into music in his imagination. The performer is also possessed of a singular vividness of aural perception by which the sounds of the external world attract his attention and take on a particular beauty and significance. The great singer Sergei Lemeshev has noted, recalling the sound made by peasants' carts in the country:

> Invariably each wheel of this kind of wagon would sound off resoundingly, and sound off with its own individual creaking—its own 'melody' and its own 'tonality.' The trip to the field was about a *verst*, sometimes two. The road was uneven and full of potholes. And there were something like ten of these carts, which meant that some forty wheels were creaking away at once—that is, forty 'folk-music instruments.' You can imagine the kinds of 'symphonies' we played![3]

For Lemeshev as a future Performer the sounds of nature were potentially musical, and as a mature artist he remembered these aural impressions from his childhood: his perception was in essence entirely that of a composer, for whom sound was filled with beauty and meaning, and as a result served as a source of memories and vivid impressions.

The Performer, just like the Composer, hears vividly, in images: the timbre of sounds, their particular articulation—these are the character, the mood or even the very depiction of the hero. Herbert von Karajan recalled with delight how the young cellist Mstislav Rostropovich wanted to paint a musical 'portrait' of Don Quixote's long-suffering

---

2 Strauss, R. (1975) Razmyshleniya i vospominaniya/Thoughts and memoirs. *Ispolnitel'skoe iskusstvo zarubezhnyh stran/Performing Art Abroad*, 7, p. 35.

3 Lemeshev, C. (1987) *Iz biograficheskih zapisok. Stat'i, besedy, pis'ma, vospominaniya/From biographical notes. Articles, Talks, Letters, Memoirs.* Moscow: Sovetsky kompozitor, p. 15.

horse, Rosinante, with total authenticity—and his expressive ear selected for this task a particularly groaning, clanking, and exaggeratedly unpleasant sound.

> Rostropovich was wonderful. When we started rehearsing we arrived at the cello's first entry and he came in with a dreadful grumbling noise. I was so surprised, I stopped the orchestra and went over to him. I said: 'Slava, are you all right?' He looked at me and said: 'Yes, but you see it's a very old horse I am riding! Wonderful![4]

The Performer, just like the Composer, has need of a great many musical impressions. He puts these into his 'piggy bank' of sounds and minds that deposits into this bank are made continually. The need for musical input for the Performer is as active and lasting as that of the Composer—which is likely why the Performer psychologically feels himself a Composer, and perceives the language of music as his native tongue. As the conductor Bruno Walther recalled:

> From childhood I felt music as my element, the thing I was born for and the place I was really at home. And to the extent that music may be called a language, it is *my* language, I understand and speak it. Among all my self-doubts, amid all the sometimes torturous consequences of my search for self knowledge, I was comforted and assured by a 'tower of calm in the flood of events', my unbreakable connection with music— which proved to be the secret essence of my existence.[5]

Taking music as his spiritual 'daily bread', as the material of his life, the Performer submerges himself in music, eagerly and for the long haul—and never tires of it. It is impossible that his life, any more than that of the Composer, might have 'too much music'. As Elvis Presley, the king of rock and roll recalled:

> I take my time to do the right thing. I can't properly explain it but it all begins with listening and more listening. It all narrows down gradually. I listen for hours. For a week. When I'm down to the songs I think I'll want to sing, I call the session. I can cut 15 songs on a session. Me and the boys sometimes get together late at night and it's late morning when we call it a day.[6]

Just as the Composer needs to reach a critical mass of musical impressions in order to create, the Performer, as his psychological 'kinsman', also has need of an enormous quantity of music. The compositional nature of talent pushes the Performer toward the absorption of musical impressions in hypertrophic quantities.

Good performers possess a highly developed architectonic ear. Their sense of a musical whole leads them to feel, in the most acute way, the degree of appropriateness of every component step, every development in an unfolding musical thought. Bruno Repp (1996) asked 10 pianists to play from the sheet music a song previously unknown to them. Despite the lack of practice, the majority of the mistakes made by the subject pianists were entirely 'acceptable' in the context of the piece, meaning they did not tear its harmonic fabric. A different group of 8 pianists, who were already quite familiar with the music used in the experiment, had the task of identifying the mistakes their colleagues

4 Osborne, R. (1991) *Conversations with Karajan*. Oxford: Oxford University Press.
5 Walter, B. (1969) *Tema s variatsiami: avtobiografia/Theme with Variations: Autobiography*. Moscow: Muzyka, p. 22.
6 *Elvis in his own Words* (1977) London-New York: Omnibus Press, p. 83.

made—but in their collective best efforts could only note some 38 percent of them. Judging by these results, a concert audience will notice even a smaller percentage of an artist's mistakes: as Repp concluded, all these errors occur in the proper context, and thus do not affect the heart and soul of the musical thought—what the musicologist Mark Aranovsky (1991) has termed the 'base layer'. The mistakes performers make in the main involve only the 'layer' of ornamentation, sounds which can be changed or omitted altogether without significant loss to the musical whole.

The ordinary listener's perception is not focused on pitch and faultlessness of execution—nor is that of the musician, who judges both his own play and the play of his colleagues by their attendant degree of conviction and by the beauty of their dynamic profile, articulation and phrasing. Musicians listen to music with their expressive ear, and formulate their own performance likewise. Once the cellist Grigory Piatigorsky (1970) lamented to his colleague Pablo Casals that he, Piatigorsky, had played with a certain inaccuracy and lack of sharpness at a recent evening performance. Casals assured him that there was no reason to upset himself over these trivial shortcomings. Obviously, such tiny lapses in the play of an outstanding artist such as Piatigorsky would occur well 'in context' of the music and not be noticed by most listeners. 'Let us leave such things to the dull-witted and the uninitiated', said Casals with resignation',—those who judge performance by counting up mistakes. I can be grateful, and you can too, for even one fine note, for a single wonderful phrase'.[7]

Performers' architectonic ear and esthetic sense allow them to judge how beautiful or ungainly every musical fragment sounds, how harmonically positioned its constituent sounds are. The conductor Ernest Ansermet (1976), a specialist in the music of Stravinsky and the debut performer of many of his works, noted before the premiere of 'The Symphony of the Spirits' that there was in the score a not entirely appropriate note (a D) and sent the composer a telegram in which he insisted that by all musical logic what was needed here was in fact a D-sharp. Stravinsky turned stubborn: given his pedantic nature and meticulousness, he could not imagine that he had made a mistake or expressed a musical thought less than successfully. But on the day of the concert, before the work debuted, a telegram arrived: the author acknowledged the performer's rightness and ordered the correction in the necessary place to a D-sharp. Such cases speak to the fact that the Performer listens to and 'lives through' a work all the way down to the smallest sounds, adjusting to and trying to experience the musical logic proposed by the Composer to the greatest extent possible. Just like the author himself, the Performer senses what the logic of a piece is constructed upon and tolerates no violations of this construction.

The logic of all form, including musical form, is based on the variable significance of the elements of structure, on the assignment to them of different weights in the formation of the whole. John Sloboda carried out a study of the data from experiments on sight reading music. He noted that more qualified musicians, by simply casting their eyes over

---

7 Piatigorsky, G. (1970) Violonchelist/Cellist. *Ispolnitel'skoe iskusstvo zarubezhnyh stran/Performing Art Abroad*, 5, p. 148.

the musical score, already know before beginning to play the relative importance of one or another element or figure, and also know what in the music can be, if such a necessity arises, sacrificed without disturbing the whole (Sloboda 1984). In the ability to listen to music, paying attention to the varying significance of musical fragments and elements of the text, the musician's architectonic ear makes itself known. As conductor Kirill Kondrashin observed:

> Studying a score as a conductor—this means determining what, how and whom to conduct, and what exactly needs to be controlled at every moment. I think this can be defined as a conductor's stereoscope: you look at the score and before you arises a differentiated view of the relationship of the material according to its significance.[8]

The performance of a gifted musician, as distinct from that of a journeyman or an inexperienced pupil, never gives the impression of studied-ness or affectation. It is always fresh and convincing, as if the composition had only just appeared in the mind of the artist and now before the public. The psychological root of performing and composing is improvisation, and a performance will be vivid and impressive if this improvisational element remains in it, if it becomes the psychological vector which guides all the artist's actions. The great conductor Wilhelm Furtwaengler described it thus: 'The performer travels the composer's path in reverse, in that the composer, in creating his music, gave it a living idea before writing it down, or as he wrote it down. So the heart, the essence of the music is improvisation, which the composer tried his best to capture on the page'.[9]

Psychology experiments have demonstrated that improvisation and spontaneity distinguish the performance of more gifted musicians from that of their less-gifted peers. Caroline Palmer (1996) timed the performances of concert pianists and compared them to those of performances of the same music by student musicians. Among the mature artists she discovered the phenomenon of 'melody lead', in which the melody preceded all other aspects of the given musical facture by some 20–50 milliseconds. The students, on the other hand, played the same music note-by-note: the melody, in their consciousness, did not arise before the other voices; they did not mentally create it as they went along, enveloping it with the accompanying lines and supporting parts, as their elders had. And thus in the students' performances the melody easily fit into the framework of predictable mechanical computation—whereas the real artists' performances saw improvisational variance in rhythm, the so-called *agogika* which an improvisational perception of music calls forth.

Bruno Repp (1997) had student musicians and expert pianists play Schumann's *Traumerai* a technically undemanding but musically quite subtle and dense piece. All the details of articulation and musical nuances were tape recorded and subsequently analyzed in an acoustics laboratory at Yale University. A non-specialist would be inclined to think that the professional performers would be more stable and reliable conveyors of the music.

[8] Kondrashin, K. (1976) *Mir dirizhera/Conductor's World*. Leningrad: Muzyka, p. 23.
[9] Furtwaengler, W. (1953) *Entretiens sur la musique*. Paris: Albin-Michel, p. 102.

But the reality of the case did not confirm this seemingly natural expectation. The students were miraculously stable, playing evenly and without mistakes; their performances, moreover, were virtually indistinguishable from one another. Not one of the students 'recreated' the music as she performed it; on the contrary, all of them simply 'turned in' quality renditions of material they had mastered. The expert pianists, however, played unpredictably and spontaneously, giving performances that in no way resembled each other: all the increases and decreases in tempo, pedal movements, and other means of expression were applied by each in her own way. They adjusted their interpretations according to mood. In short, they improvised. The students demonstrated with robot-like reliability the acquisition of their skills, and the acoustic monitors registered the invariability of all the sound characteristics from one rendition to another.

In a later study Repp (1997) established that student musicians likewise preferred to hear, as passive listeners, performances that were predictable and mechanical rather than those of a more artistic and individualistic bent. He directed his listener subjects to choose the performance variant of Schumann's *Traumerei* which they liked best. The student group preferred those renditions which a computer identified as nearest to the arithmetical mean of the great number of standard performances. Commercial recordings by professional musicians were much less favored by the students; they were too individualized, less familiar and little reminded the students of that version of the piece which the students had learned and taken as their own. Through these and other similar experiments psychologists have demonstrated that giftedness is connected with an inclination toward co-authorship with the composer. Any form of studied-ness, mechanical-ness, or repetitiveness on the part of performer is a sign of mediocrity and of a lack of the spirit of improvisation—from which both composition as such and the very art of music itself arose.

The gifted performer retraces the path of the composer, as though he were himself creating the work he is performing; and he recreates it every time through. Outstanding performers have the knack of re-covering all the stages of the creative process, including the simultaneous envelopment of the work as a whole. 'And today, when you arrived', Pablo Casals relayed to his biographer, 'I was occupied with the study of one of Bach's recitatives. I have been working on it for several weeks now, first at the piano and now on the cello. A complete intuitive perception of this work has not come immediately; I sense that I will master it in the way I would like to, but for the time being I have not been able to grasp it in its entirety'.[10] The Performer traces the path of the Composer from the end to the beginning, from the piece as a whole, clear in all its details, to an unclear image of the whole, from which the work originally arose at some earlier point. If this path is not covered, then the work will not be reborn in each act of its performance—and the music will turn into a kind of lifeless entity of stone or metal, repeated only as a mechanical copy of itself.

[10] Korredor, H. (1960) *Besedy s Pablo Kazal'som/Converstions with Pablo Casals.* Leningrad: Gosmuzizdat, p. 258.

The Artist, following the Composer's path, arranges the form anew, gathers all the details and listens to the relationships between and among them as though he had collected them from scratch, as if it were *his* musical-productive capability giving birth to all these musical elements which his architectonic ear then organizes into a musical whole. Casals recalled apropos of the same Bach recitative: 'Someone in my family asked me concerning the recitative, 'How do you have the patience for it?' And I answered 'What is so remarkable about that?. . . It is so hard to find the desired form for all sounds, for their interaction with each other and with the whole! It takes a great deal of labor so that everything can fall into place!'[11]

It is exactly this imitation of the creative process which occupies the Performer as he works on a piece, and not the mindless technical exercises which the great artists have never considered worth the time involved. The mind and the ear, once they have understood a composition through all the internal connections of its elements and parts, will render a sense of the work which is so organic that technical labor will be unnecessary. During a performance the Artist is reincarnated as the Composer; at certain particular moments this subconscious reincarnation becomes conscious. So it was when Leonard Bernstein was playing his favorite compositions by his favorite composer, George Gershwin, on the day that Gershwin died,

> I went to the piano and played a chord to get the group's attention. I told them Gershwin had died and that I would play one of his pieces for them and wanted no applause afterwards. I played the Prelude No. 2 and there was absolute silence—a heavy silence. That was the first time I realized the power of music. As I walked off I felt I was Gershwin, not that I was there in Heaven but that I was Gershwin and had composed that piece.[12]

The composing faculty of the Performer is so strong that he does not merely improvise on stage, feeling himself the creator of the music, but willingly or unwillingly he allows himself to *replace* that creator. This happens unwillingly, as a rule, because sometimes the artist's memory betrays him and he forgets the written music. The performer of middling ability is inclined to go into a panic in such cases, but the great artists cope with such moments easily: their self-insertion into the work is so organic, they so completely understand its internal logic that they not only continue playing, but go on in such a way that the audience has no inkling that anything is amiss. Grigory Piatigorsky recalled:

> I was once playing Bach's *Suite in D-minor* in Hamburg and I forgot everything after the first note, which was a D. This was a very long prelude but, at length, I reached the final chord. Glancing into the auditorium, I saw professor Jacob Zakom and his cello students searching through their scores with looks of incomprehension. 'How entertaining!' said Zakom after the concert. 'I did not know this version of the prelude. Very interesting. I would like to have a look at it.[13]

The young Alexandre Scriabin somehow contrived to forget the music to Bach's *Gavotte* while on stage—and yet recreated it on the spot (Prianishnikova and Tompakova 1985).

---

[11] Korredor, H. (1960) p. 259.

[12] Peyser, J. (1987) *Bernstein*. New York: Beech Tree Books, p. 47.

[13] Piatigorsky, G. (1970) Violonchelist/Cellist. *Ispolnitel'skoe iskusstvo zarubezhnyh stran/Performing Art Abroad*, 5, p. 39.

The young Anton Rubinstein, having forgotten out of nervousness Mendelsson's *Duet*, likewise 'recomposed' it before the audience (Barenboim 1957). Professor Barth, Rubinstein's teacher at the time, exclaimed 'A hell of a lad! You're a scoundrel but a genius, too. I could never, not even in the next life, pull off a trick like that!'[14] The professor's ecstatic reaction merely speaks to the fact that such a self-insertion into the architectonics of the original is something only the greatest of talents can do. If there is no such merging and bonding with the Composer, at least to a certain extent, then the Performer is deprived of the true seed of giftedness, the composer's intuitive scent, without which his play will remain lifeless and schematic.

During their development outstanding performers pass through the same creative phases that their composer-colleagues do. Performers are capable of creating variant-copies of known styles, this 'soft plagiarism' done with sufficient subtlety and quality to elude detection even by professionals. A story of this kind of plagiarism was told by the great violinist Fritz Kreisler, who at the beginning of the twentieth century amazed Europe with the appearance of an entire line of most elegant musical *bagatelles*, allegedly composed by authors long since passed away. As Kreisler told a *New York Times* correspondent in 1909:

> I found these pieces in an old monastery in the south of France. I now have 53 such manuscripts. Five of them don't represent anything of value. Forty-eight are masterpieces. Among these are pieces which later became popular—Porpora's *Minuet*, Couperin's *Song of Louis XII* and *Pavanne*, and the *Andantino* of Father Martini. Naturally, they were not written for the violin. I rearranged some of them for my instrument and introduced some minor changes into the melodies; I modernized the accompaniment, changing the dimensions somewhat, but I tried to leave the soul of the original works untouched. Nineteen of the 48 pieces have become part of my concert program, and no one other than myself has played them.[15]

After this sensational announcement from the idol of touring performance musicians, reviews began to appear in the press in which critics noted that 'the miserable new-fangled things that Kreisler himself composes cannot bear the slightest comparison to those by the old masters, which he also plays in his concerts'; or 'Lanner's Waltz, which Kreisler plays incomparably, is, of course, far more elegant than the maestro's own compositions'. Kreisler's wife subsequently confessed that all the stories about mysterious discoveries in old monasteries were pure invention, and the enchanting pieces in the style of the old masters had in fact been written by Kreisler himself. Like many of the outstanding performers, he could stylize wonderfully, and although his own compositional 'signature' was not marked by the flights of fancy which accompany genius, Kreisler certainly enjoyed the composer's gift in its entirety.

While creating music the Composer hears it with his internal ear almost as though it were actually playing. He has his own idea of how the music should sound. The Performer may hear the music somewhat differently. The entire sound profile which the piece derives from the timbre, dynamics, articulation, and accents employed by the Performer

---

[14] Cit. from Barenboim, L. (1957) *Anton Rubinstein*. Leningrad: Muzgiz, p. 51.
[15] Yampolsky, I. (1975) *Fritz Kreisler*. M., Muzyka, p. 41.

can produce an impression quite different from that of the Composer's intention and from the impressions of other colleague-performers. The composer, as the author of the music, hears it with the ear of his era; it is known that in previous centuries music was played, on the whole, somewhat slower, with more reserve and more delicacy. In the eighteenth century the notion of music as pleasure for the ear and repose for the soul influenced the style of performance, which became, to a significant extent, just as *galant* as the music itself. In the twentieth century people saw something else in the music of the Age of Gallantry: wit, boundless energy and strict logic. To emphasize these qualities other means of performance were required: contemporary performance style and the style of each performing musician tend to emphasize one thing in the music and conceal another, changing its notional accents and the general character of its sound.

The possibilities of the expressive ear to influence the unwritten properties of sound are really limitless: the nuances in timbre, tempo, articulation and accentuation, and rhythmic *agogika* which the expressive ear moderates can transform the sound and transform the idea behind the musically elaborated text, and any given performance can differ from any other performance just as two different presentations of the same play can differ from each other. The plot and text of the play remain the same, but different stagings, different understandings of the theater space and different intonation and movement by the actors can together add up to a completely different interpretation of the play, a different thinking-through and presentation of it. So it is with the performing musician, who can change the actual sound image of the same compositions from performance to performance, sometimes rendering them unrecognizable.

The composer's authorial conception of his own music is not always ideal. Indeed, the ideal performance of a piece is hardly possible to imagine, as music is always very much wedded to the here and now: it cannot but be affected by the tastes and habits of the era and the host country it is performed in, by the mood of the given minute, and by the unique atmosphere created by the confluence of moment, venue, and audience. The improvisational nature of music always demands a certain variation in performances, and the performing musician can sense better and more finely than the Composer himself all the circumstances which can and should influence the presentation. At a rehearsal of Ravel's *Bolero*, the conductor Arturo Toscanini adopted a quicker tempo for the piece than was customary (Toscanini 1974). Ravel, who was present in the hall, remarked on this to the conductor. One would assume, of course, that to a conductor a composer's word would be Law. Nothing of the kind. Toscanini replied to Ravel, 'You don't understand a thing about your own music. This [tempo] is the only way to make people listen to it'. At the actual concert Ravel surrendered, but with the cautionary words 'You are the only one who is allowed to do this!'[16] Toscanini had convinced Ravel, using the latter's own music, that a certain forceful brusqueness which the conductor brought to the performance corresponded ideally to the tense, pre-war atmosphere of Europe in the

---

[16] Toscanini, A. (1974) *Vospominania. Biograficheskie materialy/Memoirs. Biographical Materials.* Leningrad: Muzyka, p. 69.

mid-1930s. The composer, having heard his opus in a new way, came to realize that at the present time such a performance would in fact be the freshest and most convincing.

Serving as co-author, mastering and adopting the Composer's music as his own, the Performer becomes very passionate about his performance. He is convinced that it is he, in truth, who gives the music its real life, its genuine sound. Here the Performer is as hypercritical and easily offended as the Composer is intolerant toward his musical detractors. Once Rakhmaninov got into an argument with a relative of his, the outstanding pianist Alexandre Ziloti, over Chopin's *Etude in A-Flat Major*. Ziloti, it seemed to Rakhmaninov, was unjustifiably holding certain notes of the melody too long, notes that should not have been held long at all. 'So I said to him', as Rakhmaninov recounted in a letter, 'Listen, that isn't there [in the text] at all. And he replied, 'That's the way I understand it.' And I said to him, 'Well, you understand it poorly!'[17]

The disagreement almost created a serious rupture between the two, and it is clear why: the Performer's understanding of the music is as dear to him as the opus itself is to the Composer. For both the Composer and the Performer the music which they hear in their imagination is their creation, which they are each ready to defend against the assaults of all comers. In this regard the issue is not really what exactly each of the 'authors' composed—certain pitches and rhythmic figures following in a certain order, or their formation as certain determined sounds. Both Composer and Performer feel that the work is his own creature and neither can remain casual or indifferent to its fate in performance, which is the fruit of his (own!) fantasy.

The expression 'there is no love lost between composers' applies just as well to the performing fraternity; the compositional nature of a musician-performer's talent is such that it makes him perceive his play in a very biased manner: it becomes his second self, just as the composer considers his work a second self. For the Performer, the music he has mastered and come to inhabit sounds the way—and only the way—he hears it. Other performances and interpretations of the same music seem to him flawed, poor conveyors of the idea within the music. The young Konstantin Igumnov, in his first time in Moscow during his conservatory days, plunged into the concert life of the nation's second capital (Teplov 1998); he discovered there that there were in fact *other* pianists, with *other* approaches to his favorite piano works. He reacted to other interpretations of these works with the same disapproval which the Composer reserves for music opposed to his artistic precepts.

> It seemed to me [Igumnov recalled] that I was playing brilliantly. What kind of artistic plans could I have had then? I liked my performance. I assumed that I was doing everything more or less as it needed to be done. When I heard the pieces in my repertoire performed by other pianists I felt they were completely different, alien, utterly unlike the way they sounded in my interpretation. Something unfamiliar had been introduced into them—as, for instance, when I first encountered Taneev—and that element, whatever it was, was something I did not much like.[18]

---

[17] Rakhmaninov, S. (1964) *Literaturnoe nasledie. Pis'ma, vospominaniya, interv'yu/Literary works. Letters, memoirs, interviews*, vol. 1. Moscow: Muzyka, p. 114.

[18] Cit. from Teplov, B. M. (1998) *Psihologiya i psikhofiziologiya individual'nyh razlichij/Psychology and psychophisiology of individual differences*. Moscow-Voronezh: Modek, p. 124.

The compositional nature of the Performer's talent makes itself known via a particular selectivity in the choosing of the performance repertoire. If the Performer, with the technical mastery he has acquired, merely played other people's music without taking part in it, without entering into the works, so to speak, then he would be able to play various styles equally well. But he does not simply reproduce music, he 'composes' it—and thus can only 'compose' anew such music as he believes in, music which is as close to him as it is to the actual Composer. Otherwise the Performer will play unconvincingly, without the strength of inspiration which comes to him as co-author of the music in question. Polyglot performers are extraordinarily rare. In the contemporary world of performance music, focused as it is on a particular perfectionism and with no room for any sort of sloppiness, incomplete understanding, or unfinished thought, the 'localization' of repertoires continues to grow apace. The great Glenn Gould is great only at Bach and the classics; Walther Gieseking and Alfred Cortot made their fame performing Debussy; Vladimir Sofronitsky loved the music of Scriabin. These performers, all outstanding artists, also performed other music on a very high level—but they became co-authors only for their favorite composers, and the audience could not help but notice this.

The genetics of the composer's art, its intimate connection with the world of feeling and with the thought processes of the composer's national heritage, bespeaks itself also of the fact that genuine co-authorship arises, as a rule, only between a Performer and the geniuses of his national tradition. This is music the Performer can master, it is understandable to him, and he is prepared with complete sincerity and genuineness to experience it and recreate it. No one conducts Italian opera better than Italian conductors, no one plays German symphonies better than Germans, Tchaikovsky and Scriabin better than Russians, or Debussy and Ravel better than the French. In the particularity of these connections the psychological co-authorship of the Performer gains another indirect confirmation.

Just as the Composer welcomes the appearance of other authors with ideologies close to his own, so the Performer extols the virtues of those among his colleagues whose style resembles his. The conductor Ernest Ansermet, an admirer of Stravinsky, very much favored the sharp, striking, and colorful manner of performance which so suits the work of that composer, especially in his early period. Ansermet praised these same traits in the performance style of the young jazz clarinetist Sidney Bechet, whom he heard in London in 1919:

> Extremely difficult, they [Stravinsky and Bechet] are equally admirable for their richness of invention, force of accent and daring novelty, and the unexpected. Already they gave the idea of a style, and their form was gripping, abrupt, harsh with a brusque pitiless ending like that of Bach's second *Brandenburg Concerto*. I wish to set down the name of this artist of genius; as for myself I shall never forget it: it is Sidney Bechet.[19]

The architectonic ear of the Performer extends not only over musical structures, but also gives him the ability to stylize other people's music, composing 'a la . . .' or 'in the style of . . .' And just as the Composer begins his career by copying known models, the

---

[19] Chilton, J. (1987) *Sidney Bechet, the Wizzard of Jazz*. London: Macmillan, p. 40.

Performer does the same in relation to those of his colleagues in performance whom he has chosen as his idols. The jazz saxophonist Charlie Parker oriented himself on the performance of the outstanding musician Lester Young. Gene Ramey, who was a witness to Parker's creative development, recalled: 'He knew every one of Lester Young's solos by heart. He sounded almost exactly like Lester Young, Lester playing alto but with something else of his own that was beginning to come through'.[20]

Just like the Composer, the Performer possesses the gift of musical synthesizing, he can discern the 'stylistic algorithms' of his colleagues and put them to use. These algorithms systematize for the performer not only the structures of pitch and rhythm, which make up the 'body' of music, but also the sound formation inherent in them: the Performer's expressive ear summarizes and systematizes the entire aggregate of sound accents, pauses, increases, and decreases in tempo, and nuances of phrasing which are peculiar to the masters of performance whom he has taken as his models. He possesses a particular receptivity to performing styles and knows how to copy them. John Pidgeon, a specialist on the work of guitarist Eric Clapton, has written that,

> There were other guitar players around, but he somehow had managed to latch onto the same kind of fire and attack and the same kind of flowing phrase that B. B. King and Freddie King were so good at doing.... That was where he scored: that he was able to reproduce it ... He could play all that stuff because he was into blues. But there were probably lots of other guitar players around at the time who were also into Freddie King and B. B. King, but who didn't have the technical ability to be able to translate it. And Eric had it.[21]

By technical abilities here one should understand not only a virtuoso performance capability but also the perceptive ability of the composer's type, in which the listener turns into the player—taking on his thought patterns, penetrating the world of his style and not attempting, as do others, to reproduce discrete moments characteristic to the style of play.

The nature of his compositional talent gives the Performer the capacity for self-instruction. The performer masters the musical logic of the pieces he performs, submerging himself in them completely; then they themselves lead the beginning musician after them, prompting him as to what to play and how to play it. Konstantin Igumnov grew up in the little town of Lebediani in the province of Tambov. He had no real teachers, and there was no one to whom he could listen: the local pianist, Varvara Ivanovna Pirozhkova, did not rise above the amateur level. 'I heard almost no one', Igumnov recalled of his childhood. 'My uncle, who died early [and] Varvara Ivanovna [who] ... played no better than I did, I think. So for the most part I only had myself to listen to'.[22]

By the age of 14 Igumnov had played all of Beethoven's sonatas; from the age of 11 he had begun to compose and improvise (Teplov 1998). This inclination toward composition was the nucleus and the strength of his musical talent. Upon arriving in Moscow, Igumnov

20 Cit. from Russell, R. (1973) *Bird Lives!* New York: Charterhouse, p. 93.
21 Pidgeon, J. (1985) *Eric Clapton.* London: Vermillion, p. 37.
22 Cit. from Teplov, B. (1998) *Psikhologia i psikhofiziologia individualnikh razlichii/The Psychology and Psychophisiology of Individual Differences.* Moscow-Voronezh: Modek, p. 118.

went to the well-known instructor Sergei Zverev, who was initially shocked by his technical awkwardness; but in half a year Zverev put the young pianist in sufficiently good working order so that he could enter Moscow Conservatory. Another 'self-taught wonder' was the 'pianist of the century', Sviatoslav Richter. Richter began his career path in Odessa; he worked there as a dance-hall pianist in theaters, transposing his own arrangements of the entire repertoire of opera music—but he was not a wunderkind and never had any sort of qualified guidance until in his later youth he landed in the Moscow Conservatory, where he joined the class of Heinrich Neuhaus.

Almost all the great names of jazz have been self-taught musicians who used only other performers as early models: trumpeter Louis Armstrong learned a little from King Oliver; Charlie Parker oriented himself on Lester Young, as did Sidney Bechet on Louis Nelson. But no one formally assisted their development as performers or composers; they all made personal observations, and took advice from time to time, but the main factor at work in their growth was simply life in a musical environment—indeed, total immersion in it. These future artists trusted Music: their minds were consumed by it, they absorbed the most revealing musical impressions and imitated the best examples; and thanks to their compositional gift, their self-education was always active, coming to include attempts at creation and improvisation which made their ear distinguish and follow a musical thought, grasping its logic and sensing its beauty. And these performers did not abandon, once they reached the heights of their musical careers, their attempts at composition; for the most part they wrote for themselves, simply responding to the demands of their innate musical-creative instincts. These attempts were sufficient to retain the musical 'muscle tone', the liveliness and immediacy necessary to them as performers. Like any Composer, even the most insignificant, the composing performer by the very fact of the creation of music confirms the breadth and scale of his musical talent.

We can see the notion of the compositional nature of musical giftedness reinforced in the observations and creative notes of performing musicians. In essence, the Performer possesses the same qualities as the Composer—but they are present to a lesser degree, less consistently, and on a smaller scale. Like the Composer, the Performer has an extremely refined sense of sound: his expressive ear is capable of finding sound analogies for impressions and models of reality, and can consciously interpret everything it hears. Again like the Composer, the Performer has a highly developed architectonic ear: he masters stylistic models and can sometimes write in adopted styles using the attendant algorithms. The Performer's perception, like that of the Composer, is blessed with a heightened selectivity; the Performer can successfully interpret only that which he can 'recompose', as the mechanical recapitulation of music is simply not an attribute of great artists.

In the creativity of the Performer there will always be present an element of the improvisational, which is psychologically most essential to a musician: good performance is always to some extent spontaneous and unpredictable, and composition and performance grow from one and the same seed—improvisation. During his period of learning apprenticeship, the Performer, like the Composer, is inclined to imitate models he considers successful; the Performer can independently orient himself in the world of music and reach significant success without the aid of the systematic instruction of a teacher. Finally, the outstanding Performers themselves compose, and do so throughout the whole of their musical lives. But having impeccable taste, they do not publish their compositions, as they find them insufficiently original. The compositional talent possessed by Performers is often insufficient to allow for creation in a composing style of their own, but entirely sufficient for the Performer to follow the Composer into and through a work, emerging as its co-author. As the great pianist Alfred Cortot remarked, 'To perform means to recreate in yourself the work which you are playing'.[23]

The virtuoso giftedness of the performer

Every listener finds different elements of attraction in music and thus loves music in his own way. Some people appreciate music as an invisible companion, chosen in accordance with one or another mood; for others music is valuable as a path to spiritual expression, as a means of grasping a higher truth; for still others music serves as a sort of 'audio narcotic' which calms and relaxes. Some listeners, further, see in music the height of esthetic perfection, sensing its hidden harmonies. And there are those who see music as an oasis of cordiality, sympathy, and goodness lacking in daily life, or as a pleasant background which can stimulate mental labor. The list, clearly, is a long one. But whatever it is that attracts listeners to music, everyone everywhere has always liked the 'sporting' side of the musical art—its stage character, its virtuosoness, the demonstration of the ability of the performing artist to play dynamically and precisely.

The speed of the pianist's hands as they race across the keyboard during the performance of a virtuoso etude can be compared to the speed of a racing car on a track, a speed measured in scores of miles per hour. The technical side of performance has always been that most accessible to audiences. Through virtuoso players music can attract thousands of admirers to concert halls, among them people who may be not too musical themselves. Fast and powerful play is the amusement-park attraction of music, with a power to draw audiences analogous to (and just as inextinguishable as) that of sports. Listening to the play of a virtuoso artist, everyone is ready to proclaim his mastery and give the art of music due credit for raising the possibilities of man to such otherwise-unattainable heights. It is hard to conceive of the perfection required of the apparatus which operates in the virtuoso performer's brain, allowing him simultaneously to control and co-ordinate a great number of fine movements. While the pianist's left hand produces thunderous octaves, the right can send forth wondrous trills or a rumble of elegant scales. While the left hand of the cellist accomplishes high-flying pirouettes on the instrument's neck, the right hand can at the same time pluck the strings with the strength of a heavyweight boxer. Virtuoso performing is a kind of public battle between man and instrument, with the performer always emerging victorious. Even professional musicians never cease to be amazed by the virtuoso mastery of their colleagues. The conductor Leoplold Stokowski (1943) considered that the hands and lips of virtuoso artists had something like a 'local

23 Cortot, A. (1965) *O fortepiannom iskusstve/On the Art of Piano Playing*. Moscow: Muzyka, p. 34.

brain' which directed their movements; the ordinary human brain, in Stokowski's view, could not cope with the fine delicacy required of this kind of work.

The secret of virtuoso play was revealed some three hundred years ago by the great J. S. Bach. Responding to the adulation of admirers of his organ play, Bach noted that 'the whole thing really only consists in hitting the right keys at the right time'. The wit of this observation lies, in fact, in its absolute truth, as Bach had reduced this most difficult task to its essence—precise action at a high rate of speed. Some people can play an instrument commendably, never missing a key or hitting a wrong one, but cannot do so at a fast tempo. Others can move their fingers and hands quickly enough, but the movement causes mistakes, and resulting missed notes ruin the piece. The combination of these two facilities composes the heart of virtuosity, and this heart is in essence the harmonious functioning of the right and left hemispheres of the brain. The left hemisphere mainly answers for the rhythm of movements, as in it together with cerebellum resides our sense of rhythm: this fixes deviations from the required tempo and any violation of the necessary evenness in the sequence of sounds being played. The right (spatial) hemisphere is responsible for the placement of the virtuoso performer's hands—where exactly on the fretboard, keyboard, or neck each finger should go. The body-motor side of musical play, comprised in rhythmic design and tempo, must be co-ordinated with the visual-spatial components. If the motor-spatial connections are made without hindrance, then the preconditions for virtuoso play are, literally, at hand.

Yet the main point here is that the entire process is directed by the musician's ear: however near perfection his movement capabilities have advanced; however lithe and flexible his hands have become; however good his ability to measure and however exact is his spatial sense of his instrument—all these notwithstanding, if his ear and his musical imagination are not directing his play, the other attributes will avail him little or nothing. Virtuosity is defined as that power which music has over man, the degree to which mood or attitude to the music is dictated by the contribution of an artist's entire musicality. If the expressive ear draws an inspiring image of sound and movement overall, if the sense of rhythm turns this image into a definite rhythmic pattern which arouses a certain motor-muscular reaction, and if this impulse to movement gives rise to an exact spatial equivalent on the neck of the instrument or keyboard, then the fact of virtuosity is accomplished. This fact will be the result of a joint action of the emotional, motor-muscular, and spatial forms of music in the consciousness of the player, the fruit of his mastery of all the sensory components of musical expression. The music will create a 'dance' of fingers and hands, which will be its motor-spatial analogue.

Virtuosity, as a rule, goes hand in hand with giftedness, confirming as it does each time that the 'command center' of fast and precise play is located in the consciousness of the musician—*pace* the great Leopold Stokowski, there really is no 'local brain' in the fingers. Gifted musicians master several different instruments without difficulty. They can do this because the aural image of music, the entire complex sound construction, can be turned into various spatial analogues. The musician 'hears with his hands': on the piano his movements may be broader and more sweeping, and on the violin more compressed and compact, but on any instrument the proportional relationships of these movements will be a sort of copy of the proportional relationships among the sounds—greater distances between sounds will likewise produce greater 'steps' of movement. This kind of audio-motor 'copying' of a piece on his instrument allows the musician to play the same music on other instruments, in different spatial conditions. No matter what instrument he takes up, he will sense that he is reproducing the same sound relationships.

The young Alexandre Scriabin, who was later to distinguish himself in particular through the power of his musical-spatial and geometric associations, played many instruments as a child.

> He was always very pleased [recalled the aunt who raised him] when people gave him children's musical instruments. He had a little barrel organ and many different fifes. Once when he was six years old we went to the train station to see off an uncle of his on his way to the Russo-Turkish War. The band at the station broke into the lively *V"iushki* quadrille. Upon his return home, little Sasha immediately raced to the piano and immediately played the last figure of the *V"iushki* quadrille on it—then he took his violin and with the same complete lack of difficulty played exactly the same thing.[24]

Scriabin's audio-spatial perceptions were flexible and precise: he could associate performed musical intervals with different spatial conditions—so the piano keyboard and the violin neck were equally comfortable for him, which speaks of the ease with which various audio-spatial equivalents can suggest themselves. This ease is, of course, a very good investment into virtuoso giftedness. Perhaps it was due to this giftedness that Scriabin spent very little time at piano exercises and yet maintained his marvelous pianist's form.

The jazz clarinetist and saxophonist Sidney Bechet mastered all variations of the clarinet, and all by himself. Each clarinet has its own arrangement of keys, and these keys are connected differently to the sounds they invoke. Ordinary musicians usually master two clarinets over the whole of a lifetime, in A and in B; these are the classical clarinets used in symphonic literature. Clarinetists need years to learn the saxophone, although the arrangement of these instruments and their technique of play have much in common.

Sidney Bechet took to the various different clarinets instantly, as if by magic. Somehow in the course of a single night, when he had to help out a friend, Bechet mastered an instrument he had never played before, the C saxophone. In the end he played all the saxophones in existence, his favorite being the little-used soprano sax. He also played the cornet, a variation of the trumpet. Louis Armstrong, a fellow New Orleans musician, recalled that Bechet's presence in a street parade made the whole orchestra sound powerful and penetrating (Chilton 1987). This characteristic sound stayed with Bechet his whole life and bedeviled studio sound engineers the world over.

Like many jazzmen, Bechet was self-taught. 'I myself learned to play by patterning my work after "*Big Eye*" Louis Nelson [he recalled]. In fact, Nelson gave me my first formal

---

[24] Prianishnikova, M. P. and Tompakova, O. M. (eds.) (1985) *Letopis' zhizni i tvorchestva Skriabina/ Scriabin's Life Story*. Moscow: Sovetsky kompozitor, p. 13.

instruction on the clarinet. After I had learned the rudiments from him I had to learn the rest for myself. That's what every young person has to do'.[25] Bechet's contemporaries were in awe of his talent and versatility: as one recalled, 'He'd take an E flat clarinet and play in the orchestra. He didn't know what key he was playing in, but you couldn't lose him. That's the truth. Never saw anything like it . . . And the notes that didn't work, he didn't mind that at all. That man was great'.[26]

Aural-spatial orientation and the plotting of the spatial equivalents of sound structures came to Bechet so easily that he learned new instruments with the same ease that a polyglot learns new languages. All the instruments were for him variants of an already-understood musical-spatial code. He never learned notes throughout his life, playing everything solely by ear. He grasped the musical sketch design as a complete whole and carried it over as such into the 'field of the instrument'. His sense of aural-spatial proportional relations never let him down; he was, in short, the rarest of natural virtuosi. Many self-taught musicians who lack the composer's talent and artistic giftedness of Sidney Bechet are nevertheless gifted with a sense of aural-spatial equivalence; this sense is a 'byproduct' of the architectonic ear. Some of these craftsmen can by themselves learn practically any instrument, and without (as in Bechet's case) ever learning to read notes. In Russian villages there are many such clever accordion, *balalaika* and *zhaleika* players who are in fact masters of all the folk instruments.

Aural-spatial associations are necessary to the virtuoso 'in order to hit the right notes'. But in order for the movements to be optimally comfortable and fast, he also needs aural-motor co-ordination. The fingers must respond to the order from the aural sectors of the brain extraordinarily quickly and precisely. The speed of this response depends on the clarity of the expressive ear and the sense of rhythm: if the sound from the very outset is penetrated by movement in the consciousness of the musician, if the sound 'lives', breathes and is 'verbally charged'—that is, it runs, leaps, hops, and skips—then it is easy for the artist to register this movement and physically express it. The leading role of the ear in the origin of aural-motor connections insures that these connections are easily formed; the music holds within it the optimal movements which express it—they are decoded in the music's expressive profile and rhythmic pattern. If the movement experience of the music, its rhythmic image in the consciousness of the performer, is sufficiently vivid and contrastive, then the hands will obey the order unconditionally. However the tasks which are assigned are never so unambiguous that they may not be changed or disregarded. The virtuoso often has to alter his playing strategy in favor of a better, more convenient one which he discovers as a result of his practice; and this process should flow lightly and quickly, for when the aural center issues another order, the hands fulfill it just as humbly and precisely as they did the first.

Natural virtuosity has musical-rhythmic origins. But there is another kind of virtuosity—or rather pseudo-virtuosity. This is produced by long hours of practice, given over in the

---

[25] Chilton, J. (1987) *Sidney Bechet. The Wizard of Jazz.* London: Macmillan, p. 12.
[26] Chilton, J. (1987) p. 14–15.

main to endless repetition of technically difficult passages. In this case the 'control center' of the performance is not in the aural centers of the brain: the hands instead work mechanically. It is very hard for such unfortunate 'virtuosos' to alter their physical movements, once learned, as these movements do not appear as reactions to orders from the ear and do not depend on such orders. Thus the torturous relearning may lead nowhere: once the mastered continuity of movement has been learned, the less-gifted artist cannot change it for a new, more successful one; hands functioning on 'automatic pilot' are very conservative. The same thing happens in sports: if in the course of his training an athlete has to change his strategy of motion, he can easily do so relying on his visual imagination: he can 'see' in his mind's eye how he should organize his movements, and his body will conform to this new image. But if the movement assignments are fulfilled mechanically it is extremely difficult to alter them and the athlete (or musician) in question becomes very inflexible in his 'virtuoso' development.

The musicality of movements, with their primordial orientation toward aural images, has allowed many extremely talented artists to correct shortcomings in their performance technique instantly. When the path from musical sound to movement equivalent is very short and direct, audio-motor flexibility saves artists from many hours of exhausting exercise at their instruments. The young Konstantin Igumnov both shocked and disappointed his teacher Sergei Zverev at their first session, of which the latter remarked:

> 'If he is going to play like this, nothing will come of lessons; technique will not develop. He must be put in order. If one can listen to him now, it is only thanks to his ability; but if this ability were not there, this hand placement and manner of play would yield something quite impossible.' They began working by playing on a simple table—so that the fingers, once risen, remained free. This was done twice a day for a half hour at a time. Then they moved on to a pair of Karl Cherny's etudes in slow movements, scales, and then to Beethoven and Weber. Everything went quickly, taking 3 months, from the beginning of October 1887, to Yuletide.[27] In that year the 15-year-old Igumnov entered the senior class ranks of the Moscow Conservatory.

The case of the quick readjustment of the young Igumnov demonstrates only that hand placement, like the entire virtuoso process, is 'ear-dependent'. As the great pianist Walther Gieseking noted: 'a trained and faultlessly controlled ear almost automatically relays to the nerves and muscles impulses which make the fingers play correctly'.[28] The same opinion was voiced by the famous pianist and professor at the Paris Conservatory Antoine Marmontel, under whose guidance Bizet and Debussy learned to play the piano: 'Fingers are like little horses which return to the stable by themselves'.[29] Beethoven, while awkward and uncouth in daily life, was an outstanding virtuoso: his body obeyed only orders from the 'aural center', no other orders having any sway over him at all (Ehrenwald 1984). Musical impressionability, sensitivity of the expressive ear, and the sense of rhythm,

---

[27] Cit. from Teplov, B. M. (1998) *Psihologiya i psikhofiziologiya individual'nyh razlichij/Psychology and Psychophisiology of Individual Differences.* Moscow-Voronezh: Modek, p. 121.

[28] Gieseking, W. (1975) Tak ya stal pianistom/So I've become a pianist. *Ispolnitel'skoe iskusstvo zarubezhnyh stran/Performing Art Abroad*, 7, p. 202.

[29] Long, M. (1978) *Za royalem s Debussy/At the Piano with Debussy.* Moscow: Sovetsky kompozitor, p. 13.

allow the performer to perceive scales as musical phrases climbing upward and hurtling down. Sometimes gifted artists cannot play mindless exercises at all but have brilliant success at virtuoso music.

In the majority of performance professions the artist's purely physical, athletic qualities have little or no significance. Glenn Gould's limitations in movement did not affect his playing, nor was the cellist Jacqueline Dupré hindered in hers during years of struggle against multiple sclerosis. The outstanding violinist Oleg Kagan played until his final days, although he was suffering from leukemia. Physical weakness and musical weakness correspond hardly at all, which illustrates once more the near-total extent to which virtuosity depends on the ear and musical-artistic sense of the musician rather than on his physical strength and adroitness. Among virtuoso musicians there are singularly unathletic people, fat people, and also people whose movements are elegant and optimally effective only as musical movements. Perhaps only conductors are an exception to this rule. As Ernest Ansermet observed:

> A condition of our profession is complete freedom of command over gestures—complete independence of movement of the hands and the inborn gift of expression through them. I had a friend who possessed everything necessary to be a conductor, but could not raise his hand without raising his upper torso at the same time—as a result of which the orchestra members could never tell which of these two gestures to follow. This shortcoming in the mastery of motor skills immediately jeopardized his career. In comparison, Italians who, as everyone knows, talk with their hands, are born conductors, at least as far as gestures are concerned.[30]

There are, however, no more great conductors in Italy than in other countries: physical predisposition to performance facilitates the achievement of virtuoso mastery only in the context of highly advanced musicality.

Virtuoso giftedness, including that of conductors, is the result of the motor-rhythmic saturation of musical perception. It is the moving physical transformation of musicality, thus there are practically no cases of great musical talents being deprived by nature of virtuoso abilities. Citing 'poor hands' is almost always unconvincing; these allegedly 'poor hands' are in fact connected to 'poor ears' and 'poor heads'. Such an opinion has been proffered by many outstanding music teachers who do not want to undertake the development of a virtuoso from a less-than-musically-gifted pupil. The connection of quickness and the musical qualities of young musicians was for them obvious, and thus they demanded that virtuosity was present in them from the very beginning as testimony to their musical talent. And not talent in its entirety, moreover, but only in its motor-rhythmic aspect—without which, however, the further development of the musician will proceed with significant difficulties. One of the students of the outstanding pianist Arthur Schnabel recalled:

> He simply would not tolerate ordinary technical shortcomings among his charges. A student who had played trills poorly, for example, was told that ' . . . thousands of people in the world can play trills wonderfully—and you're preparing to become a pianist without being able to do this'.[31]

---

30 Ansermet, E. (1976) *Besedy o muzyke/Talks on Music.* Leningrad: Muzyka, p. 100.

31 Schnabel, A. (1967) Moya zhizn' i muzyka/My life and music. *Ispolnitel'skoe iskusstvo zarubezhnykh stran/Performing Art Abroad*, 3, p. 84.

Paganini was just as categorical: 'A violinist who cannot on occasion produce, and clearly too, a hundred notes a second should renounce all hope of music—he will never benefit by the revolution my legacy will effect in the world of music'.[32] Paganini himself was a perfect example of the purest and most stunning virtuosity, which had absolutely nothing in common with endless practice on the instrument in question. His virtuosity often got by solely on the resources of his internal ear (Shulyachuk 1912); according to eyewitnesses, on a number of concert tours the maestro never picked up the violin except to perform. Paganini's aural-spatial and aural-motor connections were so strong in his imagination that they had no need of constant reinforcement.

Music generates its own motor-movement 'portrait' in the perception of the listener. If someone is possessed of virtuoso giftedness, then the timbre of sound, the character of its touch and its articulation in and of themselves engender in the musician precisely those movements necessary to produce precisely that sound. If a teacher demonstrates only the sound result without explaining how exactly it can be achieved, the gifted pupil has the ability to 'learn by ear'. The teachers of the young Yehudi Menuhin, Enker, and Persinger, did not assist the future virtuoso much at all, leaving everything to his incomparable talent. As Menuhin recalled in later years:

> To teach vibrato Anker would shout 'Vibrato! Vibrato!' With never a clue given as to how to do it. Indeed I would have obeyed him if I could. . . I had already left Anker's tutelage and was perhaps six or seven years old when, lo and behold, one bright day my muscles had solved the puzzle. By such strokes of illumination, the solution proving as mysterious as the problem and leaving one almost as blind as before, most violinists learned their craft.[33]

> No more than Sigmund Anker did Persinger reveal to me the mysteries of the violin. He demonstrated and I imitated, winning achievement by ear without detour through the conscious mind. What he gave me as a musician was insight into music, and as a teacher a degree of devoted attention which I only later discovered not all teachers were capable of.[34]

Many virtuosos grasped the secrets of sound production on their own instruments from the 'hands' of the music itself. Ross Russell, the biographer of Charlie Parker, notes:

> The exposure to the music was itself invaluable. Charlie's inner ear soaked up the sound and mood of Kansas city jazz. If he didn't know how a note was to be produced, he knew how it should sound. Everything was filed away for future reference, to be sorted out later. Charlie's lonely, questing spirit was being saturated to the core of its being with the Negro idiom of the blues, upon which saxophone playing in Kansas City was actually based.[35]

The ability to 'attune to the sound' and attain its muscular equivalent is particularly important in the vocalist's art. Nothing testifies more directly to the vocalist's talent than his inclination toward the imitation of sound, even toward parody. This speaks to the sharpness of his audio-motor connections, wherein aural sensation and aural command

[32] Courcy, G. de (1957) *Paganini, the Genoese*, vol.1. Norman: University of Oklahoma Press, p. 115.
[33] Menuhin, Y. (1979) *Unfinished Journey*. London: MacDonald and Jane's, p. 28.
[34] Menuhin, Y. (1979) *Unfinished Journey*. London: MacDonald and Jane's, p. 33.
[35] Russell, R. (1972) *Bird lives!* New York: Charterhouse, p. 63.

beget an exact response from the glottal muscles and the vocal chords. The legendary tenor Mario Lanza was a fine parodist. One of his friends recalled:

> He was a sincere enthusiast of all things vocal. We used to have passionate discussions until all hours of the night about the relative merits of the masters. He had an uncanny knack for recognizing voices and imitating them. If he could only have crawled out of his own skin and listened to his own voice he might have lived his whole life differently.[36]

Lanza learned to sing by listening for days on end to recordings of Enrico Caruso (who died on the day Mario was born). The virtuoso's instinct suggested to the young Mario the correct vocal movements which engendered the subtle sensation of timbre and articulation. The unity of emotive, motor, and spatial sense of a sound in the context of the expressive ear psychologically eased the interactions between and among these components: the perceived sound, with its timbre-dynamic characteristics, flowed into the movement of the muscles and vocal chords, giving birth to exactly that sound. Such is the musical perception of the virtuoso singer who can learn the vocalist's art.

In order to play as a virtuoso does—wherein the hands or voice can follow the ear without interference—complete naturalness in the position of the entire body and all its muscles is necessary. An instructor cannot 'attach' a student's muscles to his ears, nor can he endow his charge's musical imagination with the ability to make motor-rhythmic associations; but he *can* help the student assume the position of hands and body which will hinder his ear and fantasy the least. Pablo Casals was forced to be his own teacher, the one who put the entire performing apparatus into proper order; instructors at the beginning of the twentieth century, when Casals began his music studies, were still using methodology under which everything mechanical and reminiscent of an automaton was considered 'best'. As the great cellist later recalled:

> It was entirely obvious to me that if they teach you to play with the bow hand cramped by tension and with your elbows tightly pinned to your sides, then the result is both unnatural and extremely uncomfortable. But this was exactly the way cello playing was taught at that time. In fact, that was not the worst of it: as we were learning pieces we were supposed to hold a book under the right arm, in the armpit! I decided that all this was stupid.[37]

The result of the young Casal's umbrage was a new, free-style manner of play which he continued ever after.

Other musicians also strove for the same kind of freedom. Arthur Schnabel noted that in his playing style,

> The hands were always relaxed, the movements rounded, variable and free. During a performance the entire body was to be as free as the music itself. Music is a chain of continuous changes. If during the process of performance the position of the body remains unchanged, with the hands

---

[36] Callinicos, C. (1960) *The Mario Lanza Story*. New York: Robinson, p. 121.

[37] Kazal's, P. (1977) Radosti i pechali. Razmyshleniya Pablo Kazal'sa, povedannie Albertu Kanu/ Joys and sorrows. Reflections by Pablo Casals as told to Albert E. Kahn. *Ispolnitel'skoe iskusstvo zarubezhnyh stran/Performing Art Abroad*, 8, p. 243.

becoming immobile, then play will become extremely difficult. That is why such playing technique demands enormous preparation—ten hours a day.[38]

The necessity of marathon practice sessions arises from the incorrect positioning of the body and hands: if one acquires naturalness and freedom of movement, exhausting sessions sitting over the instrument will be unnecessary—just as they proved unnecessary to many outstanding musicians. As one student of Josef Hoffman and Ferrucco Buzoni recalled, the two masters could not bear 'practice':

> Is there really no more efficient use of time, no more useful undertaking than 'practice'? [Hoffman] pronounced the word 'practice' with the same light irony that Buzoni did when speaking of the necessity of 'repeatedly playing [pieces] on the piano'. Each regretted the loss of this time at work—time which could not reward them either mentally or morally.[39]

Chopin was required by his circumstances, as were many of the great composers, to give lessons; he had many pupils, and strove to render their technique natural to the maximum extent possible. Toward this end he violated many of the stereotypes of musical pedagogy. For example, he ignored the unwritten rule that the pianist's drills should begin with C-major scales, with the hands on the white keys. Comfort of the hands required that the long fingers be on the black keys—so Chopin began with E major and B major scales, in which the natural contours of the hand helped in the play. One of his former students recalled that 'More than everyone else, [Chopin] feared the dulling of his students' senses. When he somehow gathered from me that I practiced up to six hours a day, he became very angry and forbade me to study for more than three'.[40] As a great musician, Chopin knew that virtuosity did not proceed from the number of hours spent with the instrument, but rather from the correct positioning of hands and body and, primarily, from the quality of aural-motor co-ordination, wherein the ear and the imagination lead the movement of the musician's fingers and hands.

The technology of the psychology experiments used in studying virtuoso mastery and virtuoso giftedness is, of necessity, very complex. For the best understanding of musical virtuosity it would be necessary to study it as a part of musical creativity. However, the greater part of the musical-psychological experiments conducted to date relates to the cognitive psychology of music, which studies the perception of pitch and time in music, and the basic pitch-rhythm elements. Under this scheme of things the study of real music making is moved to the back burner, so to speak. The focus on musical-creative activity has not yet become the dominant approach that is becoming a cause of dissatisfaction for some researchers (Aiello 1994; Kirnarskaya and Winner 1999; Wolpert 2000); scholarly

---

[38] Schnabel, A. (1967) Moya zhizn' i muzyka/My life and music. *Ispolnitel'skoe iskusstvo zarubezhnykh stran/Performing Art Abroad*, 3, p. 145.

[39] Barinova, M. (1961) *Vospominaniya o I.Gofmane i F.Buzoni/Memoirs on J. Hoffman and F. Buzoni*. Moscow: Muzyka, p. 31

[40] Cit. from Milshtein, Y. (1967) *Sovety Shopena pianistam/Chopin's Advice to Pianists*. Moscow: Muzyka, p. 105.

research and science are only now embarking on the study of musical performance and musical composition. Nevertheless, there exists a body of research data which appeared in the context of comparisons of musicians and non-musicians Koelsch *et al.* 2000; LaBarba *et al.* 1992; Micheyl *et al.* 1997; Schweiger and Maltzman 1985). For example, the center for controlling the fingers of a violinist's left hand, as a group of psychologists led by Thomas Elbert discovered (Elbert *et al.* 1995), is extended in the brain in comparison to the analogous brain center which governs the movements of the left hand of non-musicians.

The development of musicians' hands is more left/right even than that of non-musicians. The former fulfill motor-test functions equally well with either hand, while in right handed non-musicians the superiority of the right hand is quite significant. As Rosamund Shuter-Dyson and Clive Gabriel report (1981), these data were gathered by psychologists M. Wyke and Asso in the 1970s. In all similar experiments there has been no indication as to whether this difference between musicians and non-musicians is inherited or acquired: whether these particular skills appeared as a result of musical activity or the inverse—meaning that people with a natural predisposition toward musical activity are inclined to pursue it—remains an open question. In any case, even the limited data now available on the psycho-physiology of virtuoso giftedness speak of its neuropsychological roots, demonstrating that playing an instrument is not simply a skill or an ability of external origin. This skill and this ability are psychologically so significant that they are even capable of changing the parameters of the human brain.

The virtuosity of the performing artist, like any other riddle of talent, will never be entirely puzzled out. The giftedness of the virtuoso is a part of musical talent, one of its manifestations and not a separate psycho-physiological attribute. Virtuosity is the consequence of a particular quality of one's hearing of music, a particular involvement with it and a particular keenness of aural-spatial and aural-motor associations. The experience of the great musicians tells us one thing: that quick and precise play is the result of vividness and clarity of musical ideas, the result of the psycho-motor experience of music. The best way to the musical Olympus is through development of the expressive ear and the sense of rhythm, and the development of aural-spatial associations. Long periods spent banging away at 'practice' lead not to the heights of musical virtuosity but to physical and psychological exhaustion. The old saw about repetition being the mother of learning is too simple, naive and ineffective for a musician whose play should produce a festival-like impression of the evenness, sparkle and beauty of the sound. This kind of play was called, in Chopin's day, *a perle*—play which shone like a pearl.

The artistic giftedness of the performer

Music, dance, and the dramatic arts were inseparable in antiquity, composing a syncretic whole in which sound, movement, and bodily grace complemented and inspired one another. Ancient rituals filled all that went on with an aura of magic: the mystical sensation of becoming one with higher forces was created in music, dramatic action, and dance.

The common center of attention on the ancient 'stage' were priests and shamans endowed with the gift of deciphering the mysteries of the world; together with them were the performers, who by song and gesture attempted to relay the message of the people to the deity above. This role was extremely serious and significant; singers, dancers, and conjurers of spirits were considered exceptional people, blessed with a particular gift of insight and communication with the gods. The phylogenesis, or historical origin, of artistic activity is connected with religious rituals of the pagan era, which is why even to the present day society beholds the image of the artist with such seriousness, such profundity and even with a trace of fetishism. The genetic complement of the human race, having adopted and refined over the course of thousands of years a particular attitude toward the artist, continues to pass it along by dint of our natural biological conservatism. Just as the relationship was in the past, so it is now: those who are on stage give those in the audience a feeling of proximity to a higher spiritual source; and irrespective of whether or not they recognize this, the public submits to the power of the artist just as did their distant ancestors at the dawn of civilization. Carrying the sacred torch is an honored assignment, and the person who is distinguished by artistic talent more easily becomes the idol of the crowd than does the one endowed with power. Spiritual power is acknowledged as the most significant, and by tradition of human society this power belongs to the artistic class. Leaders and rulers are often beloved of the people only to the extent that their artistic talent is strong and convincing—however skillfully they can make themselves correspond to the image which the collective unconscious associates with itself.

The arts of the stage were threatened with extinction many times during the course of the twentieth century. According to the prognoses of the skeptics, movies and television would surely bury the art of the theater; and live music making would be crushed under the weight of recordings, television, and radio. But the genetic memory of the race retains a need for direct contact between artist and public. No manner of screen can replace the magical union which forms between stage and audience; the arts of the stage are just as eternal as humanity's eternal memory, which retains phylogenetic traces of the origin of the theater, music, and dance. Just like the ancient shaman and conjurer, the Artist going out on stage must win a clear victory over his audience—and over himself. The stage is like a boxing ring, a symbol of the spiritual space where one saw, in the most ancient times, the confluence of all worldly powers—of the gods and men who challenge them, and the fellow clansmen hearkening to this struggle and becoming witnesses to the mysterious affinity between man and the Universe.

The stage arts are a model of life, with all its attendant risk and danger. Paralleling our daily reality, in the stage arts there are no 'second takes' or 'rough drafts'. In contrast to literature, film, and the fine arts, in which the artist creates carefully and gradually, the stage arts are spontaneous and improvisational: like a soldier on the battlefield, like a mountain climber conquering the heights, and simply like a man making his way through the one life he is given to lead, the Artist is given no right to make a mistake. He works like a tightrope walker without a net; his art does not admit corrections or inaccuracies.

The Artist is required to create his masterpieces in the here and now: it is from this that the audience experiences a feeling of having been selected—they are present at a unique event which will never be repeated anywhere in exactly the same way as they are seeing it here today.

The Artist, feeling a burden of responsibility before his art, his talent, and the public, enters into the same state of holy trepidation experienced by the chosen of the gods in antiquity. The risk of retreating and allowing a mistake in the ritual of spiritual unification being performed was then and is now very great: the muse of inspiration must visit the artist right now, practically on command. While in the arts of poetry, painting, or composing symphonies there is an accepted (and sometimes considerable) 'lag time' between the artistic demand and its fulfillment—that is, between the image of the future work and its actual appearance—in the art of the stage there is no such thing: the artistic idea and its embodiment exist simultaneously, and the work leading up this embodiment takes place in the past, in the process of practice and repetition. This fusion of time is, from the point of view of the psychology of the creative process, unnatural; it increases the psychological tension attendant to the artistic activity, and with it its emotional incandescence.

By force of will the Artist unconsciously carries the past into the present: everything he has worked out ahead of time, all his most fortunate discoveries and the best variations of music and body movement must come together in the real-time act of performance. The complete acquisition of the creative idea, insight into it, and recognition of what it means must descend on the Artist before a great swath of the public—and whether or not this serendipitous tripartite visitation actually takes place depends on two conditions: the degree of preparation of the Artist and his artistic motivation. The only person who can convey to an audience the idea within a musical message is one who thirsts to do this, someone whose spiritual nature is attuned to giving of, from and through oneself before the public. This, indeed, is artistic talent, which in the psychological sense is the same for actors, dancers, and musicians.

The musician recreates on stage a performable composition. Will he be able to recreate the best variant of performance, the one which he at this point mentally pictures as supreme and final? Here there is the same risk that the composer faces, when his imagination occasionally offers up for his approval bad imitations of bad originals. So it is that the Artist can settle upon less than the best of his creative discoveries. If he has prepared insufficiently—if his judgment of a work has not been finally formed, leaving an inadequate number of performance alternatives from which his esthetic sense can make its choice—then failure may be waiting for him when he reaches the stage: he may well perform in a mode at once pale, banal, and unexpressive. If the Performer is secure in his interpretation, if this interpretation is prepared and thought through multiple times, then a different, in fact opposite danger may await him: the performance threatens to lose its immediacy and improvisational freshness, it can seem unconvincing. Thus the risks of over-preparation and a resulting sterility can lie in wait for the Artist in the same way that shortcomings of mastery—insufficient physical and mental preparation of a composition—can imperil him, and thus the presentation itself.

The fear of performing below his capabilities, a fear no one knows better than he himself, makes the Artist nervous. This nervousness is conveyed in all languages by a particular word, a word which does not convey ordinary fear. Neither the fear of death on the field of battle, the fear of injury on the athletic field, nor the fear of failure on an examination is denoted with this special word or phrase—*Lampenfieber* in German, *trac* in French, and *stage fright* in English. The French *trac* is the most psychologically oriented; it conveys continuous alarm summoned forth by circumstances beyond human control—something with an overtone of another gallicism, the term *force majeure*. The German *Lampenfieber*, for its part, relays something of the fear of public-ness—literally a fear of being exposed to the light, of attracting attention. The English *stage fright* and its Russian synonym *estradnoe volnenie* do not analyze the condition in question, but simply proclaim its difference from various *other* fears and disturbances. 'As for me, only the word "torture" can convey what I feel before a concert', confessed the virtuoso cellist Grigory Piatigorsky.

> I know that on the stage, awaiting me, is an ordinary chair which will turn into an electric chair in which I will seat myself, despite my mortal terror, and will then appear collected and quite ready for my public execution. Nervousness can be called forth by fear of forgetting the notes, the novelty of the composition (if it is premiering), worry over acoustics in a new venue, and also doubts over the instrument itself, as it may for some reason turn out to be in less than perfect repair and ideally tuned. The weather can be too dry or too raw and, in the end, the worst of all—the realization that you are insufficiently prepared and are torturing yourself with remorse.[41]

All the fears which artists experience can be dissipated by a normal person in a few minutes. It takes little to demonstrate to the Artist that today's weather is no better or worse than it always is; that he knows the composition at hand extremely well; that his instrument is in perfect working order; that the public is, as always, favorably inclined toward him; and that his preparation for the concert has been marvelous. To the disinterested observer it is immediately obvious how completely irrational and superstitious stage fright is, how inexplicable it is by any objective criteria. The universal nature of this fright—which is experienced by the most refined of classical musicians and the most rough-edged of rock performers—speaks to its lack of connection to the nervous system and to a rather deeper entrenchment in the performer. As the Rolling Stones remarked:

> Y'know like just before we're going onstage, right, and everyone's a bit nervous, but we're all too busy tuning up and having a good drink and generally . . . uh, fortifying ourselves. But those guys like Bowie and Lou Reed—you shouldn't see 'em, they're petrified. Like everyone is standing around shaking and being totally paranoid. There's no sense of . . . jollity. It's like watching slow torture. You've never seen anything like it.[42]

[41] Piatigorsky, G. (1970) Violonchelist. *Ispolnitel'skoe iskusstvo zarubezhnyh stran/Performing Art Abroad*, 5, p. 149.

[42] *Rolling Stones in their own Words* (1977) London: Omnibus Press, p. 46.

Stage fright is familiar to all musicians—to novices and stars, to young and mature, to highly gifted and moderately equipped; about 20 percent of performers blame it for distorting their lives and careers (Fehm and Hille 2005; Kenny and Osborne 2006). The irrational origin of stage fright is confirmed by the fact that it can be treated only by hypnosis, probing the depths of the unconscious. Harry Stanton (1994) conducted an experiment in which he divided the students of a conservatory, all of whom had undergone testing for stage fright beforehand, into two groups. The first group underwent weekly 3-hour hypnotherapeutic relaxation sessions, with breathing exercises and visual imagery. The second group was treated by standard psychotherapy sessions in which doctors addressed the subconscious fears of the subjects, attempting to convince the students by rational means of the complete pointlessness and futility of stage fright. After 6 months both groups were again tested for stage fright.

Significant improvement was registered only in the first group, which confirmed the utter inability of standard psychotherapeutic methods in comparison to hypnosis. Unfortunately, Stanton reported nothing about the most important question—to what extent, if any, the relief of the tortures of stage fright was reflected in the quality of the students' subsequent performances; and thus, whether the sessions were, in fact, necessary at all.

Dutch psychologists Johannes van Kemenade, Maarten van Son, and Nicolette van Heesch (Kemenade *et al.* 1995) compiled some interesting data on stage fright which shed light on its origins. They studied 155 professional orchestra musicians from the best ensembles in Holland. Some of the musicians spoke of stage fright so intensely that it adversely affected both their professional and personal lives. Those especially susceptible began to worry weeks or even months before a major performance. At first glance these claims appear to be rather exaggerated: after all, an orchestra musician, unlike a conductor, is generally not the subject of universal attention at a concert; the individual orchestra musician sits in the shadows—yet nevertheless, it transpires, he can experience very significant stage fright. This suggests that the German *Lampenfieber* is misleading: stage fright may well *not* be connected with the fear of exposure as such.

It is not the mere fact of public exposure that concerns the Artist, but rather the necessity of publicly fulfilling an extremely important mission that makes him torture himself with baseless and irrational fears. The fear that plagues the Artist is a reflection of the ancient trepidation before the heavenly source of his art, a source with which he communicates as one side of a dialogue. The higher powers, which he must summon to commune with other mortals, may turn their backs on him and refuse to evince their good graces. The Artist's fear is similar to the fear of the pagan priest before the gods, the fear of early civilized man before the Scythian who guarded the secrets of the world and did not wish to share them. The connection of activities on the stage with early pagan rituals is manifest in the 'holy terror' which the Artist experiences just before he goes out onto the stage: he, a mortal, will be communicating with a god, on equal footing—and the public will judge whether he is worthy of the assigned mission. This fear has a phylogenetic origin and is not connected with the relative religiousness of the Artist, who may be a confirmed atheist and yet subconsciously feel himself Prometheus carrying the sacred fire to the world of mortals.

Stage fright is a phenomenon known only to people of mature mind, those who have long since departed the innocence of childhood. Someone who knows of the existence of higher powers and senses their presence in his life can only quake before them. There have been, of course, certain fortunate souls who, not understanding their mystical role and not recognizing the idea behind it, do not know the meaning of stage fright. For a period, at least. The transition from not knowing to knowing—and then knowing only too well—is demonstrated in the example of pianist Glenn Gould, one of the best-known victims of stage fright in an extreme form. Gould confessed that

> I didn't become very serious until I was perhaps ten or eleven, when I really began to work with the idea of a career. It was something to sit and think about when I was bored with the school teacher, as I always was; and it was also a wonderful escape from my fellow students, whom I was always getting wrong with.[. . .] It was all part of a game, really. In those days one was blissfully unaware of the responsibility. I just wish I could feel that way again. Now you accomplish the same thing by sedatives.[43]

In the end, Gould decided to free himself from the now-or-never burden of the attempt to attain perfection, which ever haunts the musical performer, and work only in a studio as a recording artist. It is altogether possible that his sense of artistic responsibility, given his predisposition toward religion, was more strongly felt than in other artists, and he simply could not tolerate the state of continuous stage fright which resulted.

Arthur Schnabel likewise knew nothing of stage fright in his youth. Despite an early maturity of mind and senses, which often marks the wunderkind, Schnabel maintained a psychological infantilism (another common trait) almost to the age of 20.

> At that time I was shamelessly lazy and prepared my concert programs, so to speak, at the last moment. I would even spend most of the day of the concert playing billiards—then I would dash home, quickly change clothes, down several cups of strong black coffee, make it to the concert hall just a bit after the audience, and 'dive' into the music. This was unforgivable laxness. And I now recall it with a sense of fear and trembling.[44]

The young pianist had no sense of artistic responsibility, one of the catalysts of stage fright; thus fright retreated and did not torture him. Subsequently he was visited by both ills: responsibility and fear of failure go hand in hand; if the responsibility is before higher powers, then the fear reaches almost celestial heights.

The recognition of his mission as an intermediary elevates the Artist in his own eyes: he overflows with pride, and he does not want to hear about anything else or involve himself in anything other than his calling. As guitarist Eric Clapton expressed:

> I'm not interested in guitar technique but in people and what you can do to them via music. I'm very conceited and I think I have a power—and my guitar is the medium for expressing that power.

[43] Payzant, G. (1984) *Glenn Gould. Music and Mind*. Toronto: Fayard, p. 11.
[44] Schnabel, A. (1967) Moya zhizn' i muzyka/My life and music. *Ispolnitel'skoe iskusstvo zarubezhnykh stran/Performing Art Abroad*, 3, p. 87.

I don't need people to tell me how good I am; I've worked it out by myself. It's nothing to do with the person behind that guitar who is trying to find an outlet.[45]

Clapton—whose feats on the guitar inspired a 'Clapton is God' graffiti campaign early in his career—was himself in no doubt about who (or what) was behind his performance, emphasizing that his self-expression as an artist had a higher goal, one which very much resembled a goal formulated by Alexandre Pushkin well over a century before in the poem *Prorok* (The Prophet): 'Arise, O Prophet, hark and see, fill with my will, cross earth and sea, and with my Word—light ye the hearts of men'. The understanding of his exalted mission makes the artist seek, indeed strive towards, meetings with the public. He dreams of such meetings and cannot conceive of himself *not* communicating with the audience whom he has been called to enlighten. 'How many imaginary concerts I have given', recalled the pianist Marguerite Long. I remember playing for hours on end before a nonexistent audience. The illusion was so complete that I felt an absolutely soaring happiness'.[46]

The strength of the stage fright, which the Artist experiences as a sign of his responsibility before the mission entrusted to him, should turn into the energy requisite for a higher level of concentration when performing the task itself. Knowledgeable musicians of the day maintained that the great conductor Arturo Toscanini was always so focused that he would not have flinched if the ceiling had caved in on top of him—he would have gone right on directing. As Gerald Moore, an outstanding pianist and accompanist for many great vocalists, has maintained:

Every professional knows that the most important thing, after you have come onto the stage but before the first note is sung or played, is to gather yourself into a state of maximum concentration. Any and all thoughts which are not related to the performance of the work at hand must be banished from the mind. The musician must pass along a message—that is his immediate task. Often the difference between a great artist and an ordinary performer lies only in the fact that the latter requires much more time to reach the peak of his form—he does not know how to concentrate himself quickly. This ability to concentrate oneself is the alpha and omega of the performer's art.[47]

The performance-sermon, which the Artist awaits from within himself, demands the utmost concentration of all his spiritual energies.

The Artist performs a sacred role on the stage, and his function as an intermediary gives him a certain psychological similarity with the higher religious figure—Christ, Buddha, Mohammed, all of whom are held to have brought people a higher knowledge; to have experienced a sacred awe before the importance of their great mission; and to fulfill this mission were prepared to sacrifice themselves for the sake of others. Stage fright is a sign of the Artist's sense of having been selected and of his willingness to make the greatest sacrifice. As Pushkin wrote, discovering the psychological reality of the creative process, 'At length Apollo demanded of the poet a sacred sacrifice'. The genre of artistic creation is, in

[45] Pidgeon, J. (1985) *Eric Clapton*. London: Vermilion, p. 36.

[46] Long, M. (1981) Za royalem s Gabrielem Fore/At the piano with Gabriel Foret. *Ispolnitel'skoe iskusstvo zarubezhnyh stran/Performing Art Abroad*, 9, p. 19.

[47] Moore, G. (1987) *Pevets i akkompaniator/Singer and Accompanist*. Moscow: Raduga, p. 41.

the psychological sense, entirely immaterial: a café singer or a music hall artist feels himself just as called to his task as does an outstanding conductor or a classical actor playing Hamlet. The psychological condition of the Artist is embedded in him from humanity's earliest days, and does not waver according to current fads and genre interests.

The Artist loves his audience with the same devoted love of which the discoverers of great truths and the founders of world religions proved themselves capable. This need for love is present in him to a much greater degree than it is in ordinary mortals. The young Mozart never tired of asking his parents and sister 'Do you love me?' This was not the normal coquettishness of a child but rather a foretaste of the fate of an artist. Charlie Parker's mother recalled of her son: 'He was the most affectionate child you ever saw. He'd call in from the next room 'Mama, are you there? Mama, I love you!'[48] Even as an adult, Elvis Presley was distinguished by his unusual sensitivity, which extended to collecting teddy bears, symbols of love, and attachment to home. The artist's love for the audience, to which he devotes all his strength and life itself, requires an answering love. The fear of not receiving this love in return, of being rejected by the audience, torments the Artist, increasing his stage fright. If he did not love his public, the Artist could not go onstage as to Golgotha—an act of self-torture, a sacred public ritual by the Artist which could not take place without this great love.

The sole remedy for and salvation from stage fright, which accompanies every entrance onto the stage, is that which allows the Artist to master himself after the first few moments on stage: the reciprocal love he feels from the audience. As the *Rolling Stones*' Mick Jagger recalled of the group's period of wildest popularity:

> There was a period of six months in England [when] we couldn't play ballrooms any more because we never got through more than three or four songs every night, man. Chaos. Police and too many people in the places fainting. We'd walk into some of those places and it was like they had the Battle of the Crimea going on, people gasping, things hanging out, chicks choking, nurses running around with ambulances . . . Scream power was the thing everything was judged by as far as gigs were concerned . . . You know that weird sound that thousands of chicks make when they're really letting it go. They couldn't hear the music. We couldn't hear ourselves play as a band on stage and we forgot all about it.[49]

Only from the standpoint of someone whose audience experience is limited to attending academic concerts does this represent something wild, something beyond the bounds of the civilized. Far from it: this act of liberation of both artists and public, with the attendant union of the two on some higher plane, recalls the state of ecstasy reached by the pagan priests at their moment of contact with the celestial powers. The highest reward for these priests was the special spiritual state reached by the public, in which the human mind cedes control and the spontaneous energy of Nature bursts forth. To return to people the sensation of universality—this is one of the Artist's goals; and when the public begins to feel that this goal has been reached, when the audience thanks the Artist for making it possible for people to cross beyond the boundaries and restrictions of daily life—the Artist can feel that

[48] Russell, R. (1972) *Bird Lives!* New York: Charterhouse, p. 109.
[49] *Rolling Stones in their own Words* (1977) London: Omnibus Press, p. 23.

his mission has been accomplished. The love of the audience is the signal that the Artist's energies have hit their mark, arousing in people powers of whose existence they themselves had not even suspected.

In an interview with the Russian newspaper *Obshchaia Gazeta* the pianist Polina Osetinskaya described that state of spiritual unity with the audience as the reward one receives for enduring stage fright:

> Every time before I come out on stage I walk around in the wings so mournfully that people who see me then are literally frightened. I hold my head in my hands and shout 'Why aren't I a home-maker?' It's true, once I am out on stage I understand that it's probably better if I don't join the ranks of the homemakers, that I'm just fine here on stage. Life on stage is the truest, the most sincere and the most authentic state of existence of all those which one experiences in life. It's there, in the first place, that you exchange a huge wave of energy with people in the concert hall. And also with the composer, with God, with the piano and with yourself. And when all these energies come together in one place—that is, in you—it is a completely magical sensation. Beyond that, of course, this is also in a certain sense a question of power: you are *making* these people in the hall listen to you. In my life I have never seen people who, having completely felt this state of mastery of minds, were able to resist it. The sense of the stage grasps people like a narcotic—maybe even more powerfully than that. It is not a question of glory, but of a particular power which has been granted you and which you can put to use for good.[50]

In rock music the psychological experience of mutual love between the Artist and the public is exactly the same. The Artist is fed by the energy flowing from the audience and transforms it into energy for his art, then returns this energy to the public in his performance. As Robert Plant, lead singer for the group Led Zeppelin, put it, there is a 'frightening power' involved, something that renders artist and audience utterly unlike their quotidian selves:

> Without the audience throwing back vibrations I just couldn't do it. I couldn't extend myself. When we're on stage and you're looking out into those thousands of faces it just seems to pour out of me. By allowing your mind to be free and open, you get a new dimension going and the audience comes back at us. I suspect that you could put a lot of the group's success down to that.[51]

The Artist senses on the stage the complete realization of his creative powers, his total claim on his audience and their need for him. In the sensing of this strength, power and maximal self-realization the Artist can 'drown' his stage fright, turning it into creative energy and giving it a new quality. The fear of not being understood is fatal for the Artist. For the Artist whom the public does not accept and does not love does not receive confirmation of his mission, which is a mission dedicated to these people. Until this confirmation is received, the Artist is doomed to remain an unrequited lover, tortured by the fear of never receiving love in return. 'You cannot perform in fear', as Marguerite Long has written, 'you have to play despite it. In truth, this kind of fear resembles the pangs of love, and people quickly forget about it'.[52]

50 D.Kirnarskaya 'Poliushka-Polya', *Obschaya gazeta*, 9 August 2001, p. 16.
51 *Led Zeppelin in their own Words* (1981) London: Omnibus Press, p. 77.
52 Long, M. (1981) Za royalem s Gabrielem Fore/At the piano with Gabriel Foret. *Ispolnitel'skoe iskusstvo zarubezhnyh stran/Performing Art Abroad*, 9, p. 37.

Loving his public as he does, the Artist wants to know it intimately, to become one with it and understand its innermost strivings. When the Artist senses himself a part of the audience, he feels more assured on stage. Elvis Presley was proud of the fact that at heart he remained just another guy, just like the ones in his audience (Presley 1977); he liked to compare himself to a truck driver (which he had once been) or a bus driver. And that *persona* was in fact his notional hero, the one with whom spiritual unity and identification was critical for Elvis to be able to perform. Jazzman Sidney Bechet left his properly bourgeois family home at the age of 16 in order to lose himself amid the throngs of New Orleans jazz afficianados (Chilton 1987). He played at every venue he possibly could, including restaurants and bars whose reputations were so dubious that their owners preferred to serve liquor in paper cups, thereby limiting the damage when the fighting would break out. The very names of these cultural establishments speak volumes: *The Rat Hole, Cemetery Courtyard, The Hole in the Wall.* The young saxophonist played at weekend stevedore picnics, in funeral processions, and on advertising bandwagons which plugged dance halls, boxing matches and the virtues of local dentists. Bechet later acknowledged that he did not regret a single day of this 'school', as it served him in an indispensable way: it allowed him to *really* get to know his audience.

Fritz Kreisler sought the attention of his audience at those places such an audience preferred—the expensive cafés and restaurants of Vienna, the places where Kreisler himself was a regular (Yampolsky 1975). The compositional and artistic aspirations of the virtuoso violinist were closest to popular music in a sentimental-bourgeois vein, his audience was middle class and gravitated toward the unchallenging comfort of sweet trills and flows. In his desire to be closer to his audience, Kreisler almost ruined his career: like many performing artists, he was seduced by the atmosphere of wealth and ease which he himself created and passed along in his works; had it not been for his American wife, the great violinist might have died in the clutches of demon rum. Like his performer colleagues, Kreisler greatly valued moments of real communication with his audience. As he wrote: 'When you have the blood of a virtuoso in your veins, the pleasure of coming out on stage makes all the suffering worthwhile. [It is so great that] one would perform for free, in fact. What am I saying? One ought really to pay for such a privilege'.[53]

Continuous stage fright is the psychological fuel of artistic activity as well as, at the same time, the cross the Artist must bear. Under the burden of constant tension, he sometimes shows a tendency toward 'antisocial antidepressants'. In the rock music milieu one finds extreme means of relief from the Artist's anxiety—drunken debauches, orgies and narcotics; in the more refined venue of theatrical performers, alcohol is the accepted means. Among classical musicians one finds much less of either of these two approaches, but there is nevertheless a reaction to the permanent stage fright that these performers also suffer—an unending stress, to which one must accustom oneself as the constant companion of creativity. Mark Schaller (1997) has demonstrated that artistic success and

---

[53] Cit. from Yampolsky, I. (1975) *Fritz Kreisler.* Moscow: Muzyka, p. 36.

fame only strengthen a need for self-destruction in the Artist. The higher he rises on the stairway to glory, the more dangerous it becomes to fall down. The fear of losing the love of the audience turns into a recurring nightmare which the Artist tries to overcome with the help of drugs and alcohol. Kurt Cobain, famous as the leader of the group *Nirvana*, could not cope with the burden of fame, entailing as it did for him a fear of rejection and oblivion; the terror of imagined loss was so strong that he killed himself. Suicide is the most extreme expression of intolerable stage fright which can grow into a chronic fear of losing the love of the audience once and for all. Such cases are extraordinarily rare; they speak of a disruption of the psychological balance between creative tension and the euphoria of mutual love that the Artist feels in the response from the audience, its attraction to him and empathy with him. Yet the exception proves the rule: without contact with the public, without constant assurance of its love for him, the Artist cannot go on—and yet he cannot give up stage performance, the pursuit to which he has dedicated his talent. Thus the life of the Artist courses between the burden of stage fright and the unbearable thought, if he loses the ability to perform, of never experiencing it again.

The talent of the Artist and that of the creator are connected in many ways. When Boris Pasternak observed that 'The goal of creativity is the giving of oneself', he had all creativity in mind—poetic, musical, scientific, and so on. The desire to deliver the message which people should receive from the artist inspires him, forces him to overcome all barriers which prevent him from being heard. In a psychological sense the Composer, the creator of the musical message, is quite close to the Artist-performer, who takes over the message, makes it his own and is ready to pass it along to others. The talent of the Composer and the Performer has the same phylogenetic roots: both of them were in earliest antiquity participants in and inspirers of collective musical improvisation, and each sees his goal as communicating with the audience with the help of music. Thus the vast majority of Composers possess performing talent, and if Fate ordains that they cannot occupy themselves with composing alone, then they can, like Rakhmaninov, become outstanding virtuoso artists.

Yet in order to understand the essence of artistic giftedness, the exception is more important than the rule. For example: the gifted composer Anatoly Lyadov could make music before friends with stunning mastery, amazing everyone with the lightness and elegance of his performing style. Yet Lyadov could not, and did not want to, play before the public. In particular he could not and did not want to be a conductor, which for him, as a composer for orchestra, would be particularly desirable. One of Lyadov's contemporaries recalled:

> In the performance of music before the public, a conductor, like any artist, must be strong enough to be able to defeat the inertia of that thousand-headed hydra in the hall, to rivet the attention of the mysterious crowd to the music being performed. But Lyadov simply did not have the elements in his character to achieve that kind of effect, if only because he had no interest at all in the opinion of the audience: in concert he never felt the breath of the crowd behind his back, sensing no psychic connection with it at all.[54]

54 Lyadov, A. (1916) *Zhizn, portret, tvorchestvo/Life, Portrait, Creative Work*. Petrograd, p. 25.

Lyadov was exceptionally gifted musically, but not so artistically. Artistic talent presupposes, beyond the sensing of one's mission as the emissary of art itself, a further love for the audience and a desire for direct communication with it. This second component of artistic giftedness was lacking in Lyadov, and it excluded him from a career as a virtuoso pianist or conductor.

Non-artistic people often do not experience stage fright because they do not strive to win the love of the public and are not afraid of being rejected by it. But much more often one encounters cases in which unartistic people are unbelievably agitated by the thought of an upcoming concert, the specter of failure torturing them almost as much, if not more, than it does the highly gifted virtuosos. Such people are not saved by the love of music, which turns away fear from the gifted musician and helps him concentrate on the musical tasks at hand; and they are not saved by the signs of success, the 'vibrations' within the concert hall which support and inspire an artist. The ungifted artist can think only of himself, of how terrible he looks and how inevitable it is that he is going to ruin everything.

There is a famous incident involving the pianist Osip Gabrilovich (Mark Twain's son-in-law): it seemed to Gabrilovich that throughout a certain concert he was giving the great Buzoni was listening in the back row. Out of fear that he would not please the famous maestro, the young pianist made a hash of the entire concert; and when it turned out that no Buzoni had been lurking in the back row after all, Gabrilovich had no one to blame but himself. His boundless pride and vanity had played him false. This pride sometimes masks itself as stage fright, but in reality it is deeply opposed to it. If stage fright arises from a heightened sense of responsibility and love of the audience, then pride proceeds from rather less exalted sources, sources absolutely alien to art and creativity. He who claims he wants to be an artist, but in reality is only tortured by a thirst for success and is afraid of not realizing his own ambitions—this would-be artist will hardly inhabit Parnasse; the temple of the muses rejects such pseudo-priests, not admitting them to the ranks of the true servers.

Edgar Coons, Louise Montello, and John Perez (Coons *et al.* 1995) conducted a study of a group of young pianists, measuring each individual's level of salivary immunoglobin a week before an examination. When the level of this hormone in the body is low, it is a sign of depression; when high, of raised spirits. The hormone is in fact produced as a reaction to stress, which is why it is often called exactly that, the 'stress hormone'. For every organism the level of salivary immunoglobin in a state of calm is different, and a rise or lowering is measured against this natural norm. In addition to hormonal measurements, all the participants were also tested to mark general levels of self-assurance and sense of being in demand. Two hours after the exam, all the subjects were tested for stress hormone. In those subjects who were by nature sure of themselves and sensed they were appreciated, the stress hormone rose, and they experienced a rise in spirit and a sense of exhilaration. Conversely, in those who had shown in previous testing a lack of self-assuredness and feelings of unwantedness, the level of stress hormone declined; they felt depressed and exhausted.

Edgar Coon and his colleagues' results can be cast as testimony to the varied psychological content of examination stress: that which is subjectively experienced by all the subjects as stage fright in reality has a different origin and a different psychological sense. Self-assured and appreciated student musicians experience genuine stage fright: their confidence and sense of being in demand speak to their recognition of their artistic giftedness; their experience from previous performances allows them to look at their prospects with optimism, and they are nervous in the same way that genuine artists are, with a nervousness that elates and inspires. Students who are weak and unsure of themselves know their limited possibilities from previous performances and do not expect anything good of themselves; their agitation is not the stage fright of the Artist who wants to fulfill the mission he has been assigned and win the love of the audience. The fretting of the weak student is, in psychological terms, simply the fear of failure. This is the fear a student who does not know the laws of Newton feels before a physics exam, or a student who does not know the Pythagorean theorem before a math test; this fear has nothing to do with stage fright, although they show similar symptoms of anxiety and discomfort. Different results from measurements of the stress hormone demonstrate the different physiology and psychology of nervous agitation, its different meaning for students with different levels of musical giftedness.

A group of psychologists from Slovenia led by Dennis Drayna (Drayna *et al.* 2001) did a related study using 104 student musicians from the Lubliana Academy of Music to examine the relationship between the level of stage fright experienced and the internal and external criteria of success in the public performances the young musicians gave. The stage fright which the subjects themselves spoke of served as the independent variable. Other parameters were examined for dependence/independence from stage fright and the extent of their connection to it. The researchers polled students who evaluated their performances highly and remained satisfied with them: the correlation between stage fright and positive internal evaluation was high—just as in the previous experiment, where stage fright inspired the confident and successful students; and those who positively evaluated their performances were always very agitated beforehand. Artistic success and stage fright always accompany one another, and in this study not a single exception to this rule was noted.

However, when the researchers tried to establish whether stage fright leads to objectively measurable results—musical prizes, competition awards, and the like—they could find no direct correlation. The statistical base they used contained data on all the students who experienced strong agitation before a public performance. Some of them were experiencing pure pre-exam nervousness, but since the psychologists were using the students' own testimony, it came out that almost everyone suffered from nervousness but only a few received rewards. In other words, no correlation at all existed between nervous agitation and objectively identified musical success.

The psychologists' conclusions confirmed that by itself, nervousness does not herald success and does not lead to it. What is important is not the subjective experience of distress, but its genuine psychological meaning, which becomes clear only when the performer is on the stage. The general consensus among practicing musicians is that the degree of stage fright a performer experiences is a reliable index of his artistic giftedness: it is, thus, a natural indicator of musical talent. A decade ago the Polish psychologist Maria Maturzewska described the situation as follows:

> One can posit a hypothesis that there exists a certain optimal level of stage fright, one which provides for the greatest activation of intellectual and energy resources in a person. This optimal level is different for different people. Everything that raises it, lowers the person's effective ability to act. But if the level of stage fright is too low, this speaks to a low level of demand and a lowered need for self-realization. The level of stage fright is different for students who are gifted and those who are less brilliant. Talented students experience stage fright which mobilizes them and strengthens their self-projection; on middling students, by contrast, stage fright has a completely opposite effect.[55]

The reason for the differences Manturzewska points to is the different psychological content of the anxiety and distress which people experience: the gifted musician experiences real stage fright, while the musician lacking talent suffers from pre-exam stress and the pangs of egotism, through which he fears one more revelation of his own artistic poverty.

Stage fright is a sort of sanitation engineer of the concert stage. It will not allow onto the stage people who are not suitably adapted and not gifted. Here stage fright plays its 'clearing the air' role: it stops the person who seeks glory but lacks the internal resources to secure it. Yet the greatest danger for art lies not in the person who gets too nervous and, tortured by an ungratified ego is forced to leave the stage; worst of all are the so-called 'conceited ambitious'. These people do not undergo real stage fright because they are not real artists; nor do they suffer the torments of pride, since they do not doubt for a moment their immeasurable worth—a self-confidence which derives from a total deafness to things esthetic and an inability to render any kind of real self-evaluation. Unless rotten tomatoes fly onstage from the audience, these pseudo-artists will remain completely satisfied with their performance and will even take an icy silence from the hall as a sign of success. Possessed of boundless energy and self-assurance, these untalented ambitious performers are capable of insinuating themselves further along in the field than one would expect. In the end, sometimes, they can only be stopped by letting the public have the last word on them: the people's wisdom can sort things out well enough and free art from the services of false servants of the muses.

For centuries the public has successfully fulfilled this role as 'sanitary engineer' of the stage arts. In earliest antiquity the public was a full-fledged participant in the mass rituals within whose confines were formed the arts of theater, music, and choreography. The public was the final goal of artistic presentation, its addressee and judge. The participation of the public in the birth of a work of art give the former special status: it was never a casual observer of artistic life; the public was rather a partner with the Artist in the process of creation, and thus the Artist's strivings were aimed at it—and he was rewarded for this. A given person may be incompetent and artistically undeveloped, but upon becoming a member of the magic

[55] Manturzewska, M. (1994) Les facteurs psychologiques dans le développement musical et l'évolution des musiciens professionnels. In *Psychologie de la musique*, (ed. A. Zenatti). Presses Universitaires de France, p. 274.

society of the concert hall this person is transformed. All present in the auditorium during a concert or play exchange unseen impulses, they intuitively attune themselves to each others' wavelengths and perceive the invisible 'messages' of the leaders of the hall—people no one chooses, but whose role is silently acknowledged by everyone. He who can evaluate what is going on before the audience in effect judges and infects his partners in the artistic process with his attitude. The public assembled in a theater or concert hall is a special psychological entity, a collective personality inspired by the recognition of its own role as co-creator and addressee of the art at hand. And this public, as a rule, does not make mistakes.

Sometimes the public is incapable of understanding the latest word in art. Yet it is impossible to blame the public alone in the initial failure of *Carmen* or *La Traviata*. Subsequent generations cannot feel the atmosphere of the premiere evening, the degree of appropriateness of the means and methods used by the artists, the degree of preparation of the artists to perform the new work, and so on. After several performances these failures turned into triumphs. So was it not the fault of the artists and theater management that the public could not be won over?

It is impossible to overestimate the role of the public, which for centuries has controlled the life of the stage. The public can neither be fooled nor bought off; it can only be attracted and taken prisoner. Over the last hundred years, the public has accepted certain laws of politesse—and thus voluntarily deprived itself of the right to judge art. At this point, audiences will not go below a sort of wan applause to express displeasure. But in all likelihood the further development of culture will return to the public its original role. Without the public, which punishes and pardons, the stage cannot exist. The history of art over the last century tells us that an external 'stage pass' in the form of the opinion of the audience is just as necessary as the internal 'pass', whose role in the theater, music and choreography is played by stage fright, the invariable companion of artistic giftedness.

Courage every day: the creative gift and the 'Great Career'

Viewed from outside, artists seem to be creatures of heightened sensitivity. They must possess a particular refinement: where others grasp only the general content and direction of a movement of thought, the Artist sees an entire Universe of sensation and ideas. He perceives art more subtly and in more detail than do others; he is extraordinarily responsive and impressionable. He is capable, like Glinka, of becoming so enthralled with a piece of music that he forgets to live, as it were: his pulse stops. As Pushkin put it, without embarrassment, 'I weep at the very thought'. This sensitivity and vulnerability is a sign of the gift of intrapersonal intelligence, as psychologist Howard Gardner has called it. This means that the Artist, the Composer, the Actor, and various other servants of the muses are natural psychologists. Love of the audience unavoidably combines in the soul of the Artist with the love of man, with the understanding of his weaknesses and with sympathy for his problems. Without a deep humanism and a philosophical empathy with mankind no manner of artistic intelligence is possible.

In the psychological sense every Artist resembles a sensitive membrane which vibrates at the slightest touch. Yet the reality of his onstage presence puts on him different, completely opposing demands. On the stage he must be all but a god: everything must work for him, he must be a model of mastery and inspiration. But at any given moment during the hubbub of daily life the Artist may find himself completely disinclined toward this. Here he differs from the Artist-creator, who may choose his own time and place to meet his Muse. For the performing artist the concert schedule is law, prosaic, and beyond appeal. A concert cannot be postponed, not a day later nor an hour later; such an extreme measure can be invoked only as the greatest of exceptions. Only stars of such magnitude that they have no fear of ruining their careers may (occasionally) allow themselves such things.

On the day when the Artist is supposed to stand before the public in the full glory of his talent, he may have a toothache, the electricity may have gone out in his apartment, he may have learned that the festival which he has dreamed of playing at has not invited him, and so on. For that matter, during the concert itself a string may break on him, an inexperienced conductor may, out of stage fright, lead at such a furious tempo that a singer or pianist is simply unable to keep up—but it is too late to change anything. The Artist may also forget the music: though this rarely happens, the possibility hangs over the head of all performing artists like the sword of Damocles every time they go out onto the stage. Recalling these and similar misfortunes the pianist Gerald Moore remarked that 'Every performer, when he is playing, must feel himself a commander on the field of battle. All manner of unexpected things may happen, but he must always find the means to stop the hemorrhaging and set things right'.[56]

The gifted pianist Margarita Long, a rather delicate woman, was nevertheless a great aficionado of bullfighting. A public concert was for her the same test of will and courage as was a struggle against a bull in the *corrida*. Once she was obliged to play a Chopin concert on a piano with a broken pedal, which multiplied all the difficulties of the virtuoso composition many times over. 'In order to master the public', she wrote, 'one must first master oneself. In essence this is a question of self-restraint. One must know how to remain calm and retain clearness of mind. I repeat again: "Do not despair"—that has been my foundation in life'.[57]

Any concert artist would subscribe to this maxim. The life of the touring stage performer teaches the Artist to take incidents of unexpected unpleasantness as the norm, and to take them on with all the weapons one can muster. Once on the day he was to give a concert in Holland the cellist Grigory Piatigorsky went skating, fell on the ice and broke his thumb. He had no time to get to a doctor and it was impossible to explain what had happened to the public. As the cellist later recalled:

> During the concert the thumb on my right hand was so red and swollen I could hardly hold the bow. I squeezed the thumb into my fist and that way played through to the end of the first part of the Dvorak concert. We began the Adagio. The pain became unbearable, and before the end of this beautiful section, tears began rolling down my cheeks. After such a touching performance many at

56 Moore, G. (1987) *Pevets i accompaniator/Singer and Accompanist*. Moscow: Raduga, p. 169.
57 Long, M. (1981) Za royalem s Gabrielem Fore/At the piano with Gabriel Foret. *Ispolnitel'skoe iskusstvo zarubezhnyh stran/Performing Art Abroad*, 9, p. 29.

the concert were weeping along with me. It was a triumph, and echoes of that evening returned to me for a long time after the doctor had removed the cast from my thumb.[58]

Readiness to meet the unexpected and an ability to find a way out of any unfortunate situation—these are qualities connected with the particularities of artistic talent. On the one hand, the musician is wholly given over to the piece he is performing, he creates as though improvising. At the same time, however, the Artist possesses the rare gift of being able to look at himself from the outside at any juncture: during a moment of impassioned involvement his mind stays cool and clear, continuing to control each movement and gesture. A newspaper correspondent once asked Elvis Presley: 'When you shake and quake when you sing, is that a sort of involuntary response to the hysteria of your audience?' To which Elvis answered 'Involuntary? I'm aware of everything I do at all times—but it's just the way I feel'.[59]

In the course of the creative process one and the same person invents and composes, thinking up new combinations of elements all the time; meanwhile, a second 'I' evaluates the proffered 'production' in accordance with the original concept. Similarly, during a performance one part of the Artist's consciousness is directly engaged in creative work, while another part of it controls this process and corrects, if need be, what is developing on the stage. Action and observation, creation and control take place simultaneously—a facility of 'twin vision' which very few people can claim. The Artist is adapted to this because he is also a creator, composer, and founder of that which he must now perform, and the creative process is naturally built on the simultaneous ability to create and the ability to control. These two abilities presuppose a particular composure and mobility of mind without which the creative act cannot proceed.

Following the Composer, or being the Composer himself, as happens in rock music, the Performer becomes 'two-headed', taking on a twin vision which predisposes him to sang-froid and self-control of a special kind. These are additional aspects of the creative giftedness of the Artist, its reverse side—thus it is hard to find a talented musician who cannot control himself completely during a concert. The creative cast of mind draws with it a particular cast of personality, as though forging and training it, perforce changing a subtle and sensitive person into a strong and resourceful one—one capable of taking on any unexpected development from a position of readiness.

The creative career of the musician, both the Composer and the Performer, is rife with vicissitudes. The musician needs an enormous self-assurance in his calling, stoicism in adversity and a creative optimism which again and again inspires him to achieve success and recognition. The psychological roots of this kind of optimism lie in the nature of creativity: the Composer and the Performer often have to reject ideas that come to mind because they do not pass the control of their esthetic sense. Arthur Honegger defined talent as 'the courage to begin everything over again'. In creativity it is always necessary to

---

[58] Piatigorsky, G. (1970) Violonchelist/ Cellist. *Ispolnitel'skoe iskusstvo zarubezhnyh stran/Performing Art Abroad*, 5, p. 153.

[59] *Elvis in his own Words* (1977) London-New York: Omnibus Press, p. 108.

continue the search for the best solution; this necessity is a natural component of the creative process without which it cannot exist. The Composer and the Performer accustom themselves to continuous searching; the nature of creativity will not allow them to rest on their laurels, satisfied with known entities; and in developing their careers, they subconsciously bring their creative habits into the real orbit of their life patterns: to search, to reject unsuccessful solutions in favor of successful ones as one continues on ahead.

The difficulties which the Artist meets along his path are often connected with creative competition. The Artist must always be at the peak of his form, replenishing his creative palette. If one of his colleagues turns out to be more resourceful, showing more initiative in the search for new artistic ideas, the talented Artist will take the colleague's success as a stimulus and a lesson. That is exactly how the king of the pre-war French cabaret singers, Maurice Chevalier, took the success of the young singer Charles Bouquot:

> I no longer was the public's favorite; where I had been invited to perform for three seasons, two were now more than enough. The blow was a heavy one—but a very useful one as well. I understood how sensitive the barometer of success was. The rise of Bouquot had been so unexpected! I had to analyze it. That Bouquot was moving ahead while I was slipping backward was unarguable. But why? Well because during the past year, playing in the *Folies Bergére*, I had not given concerts, I had not toured, had not sought out new songs, and had not varied my devices. And Bouquot? Well now, after his tremendous success am I supposed to give up? We shall see about that![60]

Chevalier understood that he had simply lost his pacing temporarily, and now he had to do what he always did—seek new solutions and new directions. For the talented there is nothing more natural: they are always, because of their psychological predisposition, prepared for creative competition—and thus for the kind of lifetime success story which Russians call *bol'shaia kar'era*, the Great Career.

Pushkin's principle that you are 'your own supreme judge' is always in force for the gifted Composer-Artist. He often encounters a lack of understanding on the part of the public, and must fight against it, must convince the audience that he is right. This self-assurance and conviction of one's rightness are also consequences of creative giftedness. In the creative process the Composer-Artist must reject external influences: only in doing so, in overcoming such influences, can he find his own voice and artistic self. His talent leads the Artist down a road of its own, a road on which he rejects imitation and variant copying as he creates his own manner of writing and his own style of performance. He must affirm himself in a struggle with the inertia of his own thinking. He is ready to go against everyone; in a sense he does that in his creative work, and if the necessity of entering the battle for success and recognition arises, the talented artist will fight to the end. Many gifted musicians have had to challenge the lethargy and inertia of the public, and only rarely have any of them retreated. Creativity taught them other norms of behavior which they carried over into their lives.

---

60 Sheval'e, M. (1977) *Moi put' i moi pesni /My Way and My Songs*. Moscow: Iskusstvo, p. 60.

The great Handel reached the height of his achievement in his later years, when he began to compose his oratorios. Only a select few among the music lovers of the period, people who truly valued high art, understood Handel's strivings and supported him. Fortunately, among this small number was a man of power and influence: George II of England, who was a genuine lover of music and an admirer of Handel's work. The king ordered the performance of the oratorios in spite of the resistance and tut-tutting of his court, whose members preferred Italian opera. In splendid isolation the king sat beneath the arches of the Cathedral and listened to the works of the great Handel. His court made jokes about it. It was claimed that once Lord Chesterfield arrived at the Covent Garden opera theater and asked another worthy in attendance 'Why are you not listening to the oratorio? Is it not being played today?' 'Yes it is', replied the courtier, 'and I suppose it has already started by now. In order not to disturb the king in his seclusion, however, I left before it started'.[61]

In spite of such attacks, of which he was perfectly well aware, Handel continued to go his own way and achieved recognition. The public came to value his innovation, perceived the greatness of his ideas, and eventually turned him into a living classic for all Englishmen to enjoy. Forty years had not passed since his death before virtually the entire country was gathering together for great Handel festivals, which became the early models for the music festivals of today.

The Composer and the Artist are forced to live without rest. Their imaginations are constantly engaged in invention; they can create only when they have many variants from which to make creative choices. Lacking that, inspiration simply will not visit them—the creative idea, not finding the appropriate combinations of musical elements and different performance variations, cannot find the single best and may die unfulfilled. Therefore the mind of the Composer-Performer resembles a factory which works round the clock to produce new sound combinations and shades of sound. The musician must demonstrate enormous patience, begin all over again, wait, and keep working—until Fortune smiles on him. Patience and stubbornness are part of the Composer-Performer's gift. Without them he could not produce anything.

The same qualities are necessary for the artistic Great Career: recognition comes to him who knows no fatigue and is ready to cultivate success like a patient gardener tends a capricious plant. The world of art does not tolerate the frail and the proud; it rejects them, opening the way to those who can put failure aside and continue their toil as though nothing had happened. This kind of stoicism is particularly necessary in conditions of having to write or play a great deal in order, as some artists say, not to 'run out of ammunition' and thus give the patron reason to turn to other performers. The artist must make his peace with the fact that in the conditions of a sweatshop system, and that is exactly what the show business and pop music businesses are, he cannot simply create one masterpiece after another. The artist must accept this, grumbling and cursing his fate, battling

[61] Kushenov-Dmitrevsky, D. F. (1831) *Liricheskiy museum/Lyrical Museum*. St.Petersburg: Kushenov-Dmitrevsky, p. 28.

fatigue and despair, and once again get down to work. This is just what Verdi did: after the successes of *Nabucco* and *The Lombardians* he had a series of failures. He was not yet a mature master of the operatic genre; his style was still developing and he had to accept modest successes and even some fiascoes (*The Two Foscaris, Alzira*). In a letter to a friend written in 1845 he wrote:

> Thanks for the news of *Alzira* but more for remembering your poor friend, condemned continually to scribble notes. God save the ears of every good Christian from having to listen to them! Accursed notes! How am I, physically and spiritually? Physically I am well, but my mind is black, always black and will be so until I have finished with this career that I abhor. And afterwards? It's useless to delude oneself. It will always be black. Happiness does not exist for me.[62]

Having poured out his soul to his close friend, Verdi set out on a new stage of his career: within a few years he produced a trio of masterpieces which made him great—*Rigoletto, La Traviata*, and *Il Trovatore*. These were the rewards for his patience and signaled victory over the despair which is at some point the lot of every Artist.

Creative labor demands certain specific psychological skills which are formed in the depths of the creative process: an elevated level of self-criticism and a readiness to look failure right in the eye without flinching; the 'courage to begin everything over again', as Honegger put it; a readiness to search continuously; a certain bravery, a sureness of one's own rightness; and endless patience. It is traditionally posited that these martial qualities are not part of the frail and artistic natures of those who create—yet this assumption has no basis in reality. Creative personalities are ideally suited for the struggle for recognition and success: it is not accidental that the majority of the great talents in the end reach glory by their own means, pulling themselves to the heights of the career ladder. Rather it is due to the nature of their character, which was formed in the womb of creativity itself.

One may note certain exceptions to this in the characteristic style of the notional heroes of certain gifted creators: Schubert's shy and wandering youthful poet and Wolf's ever-despairing and doubtful hero, for example, incline their creators to a way of life incompatible with the Great Career. Yet such exceptions serve merely to prove the rule: the majority of the talented can and do reach glory and recognition. If this were not so, and the creative gift turned people into hermits, the world would be barren of geniuses and gifted people generally. Fortunately for all of us, the talented do not let their chances go by: they are inspired toward success by the characteristics of the fighter and the strategist, which is what they are.

Stress as the companion of creativity

The expression 'creative torture' is often applied to performers and artists. Their entire lives are one long search—a search which has no guarantee of ending in success. The artist begins his path with no assurance that he will reach his goal; he begins a new composition unsure whether his concept is a true one or whether he will make a mistake, as

---

62 Walker, F. (1982) *The Man Verdi*. The University of Chicago Press.

Glinka did, for example, with his mistaken conception of the Cossack Symphony. How many uncompleted sketches, plans, and ideas are tossed along the wayside by the Artist! Some of them are unusable because society and the audience are simply not ready for them; others turn out to be untimely because the Artist himself has not yet reached complete maturity. Still others prove architectonically unsound—the plan conceived for them could not become a stimulus to action.

Every creative step involves the examination of variants and the choice of the best among them: there is a continuous creative metronome beating 'idea-reject-idea-reject' —and this can become extremely wearing. The unending beat creates psychological stress; the risk of creative failure haunts the Artist at every stage; the continual uncertainty of success and the overcoming of this feeling demands great expenditures of energy and extraordinary will power. To an outside observer it may seem that creative people are by nature dark and gloomy: they are under constant pressure, and social *politesse* rarely appears as one of their defining attributes. A nephew of the composer Nikolai Metner, having observed his uncle as the latter was composing away, recalled:

> With my own eyes I saw how that dear family member, the wonderful and childlike Uncle Kolya, who used to make the funniest and cutest faces for me—I saw how this man turned into, to use Pushkin's words, someone wild and stern, full of 'shouting and rebellion', and so forbidding in his severe concentration that he had become completely alien. I could not figure out how these two faces could belong to one and the same person.[63]

The Artist creates in order to express himself and his time. Yet what he is striving toward does not lend itself to being touched, measured, or seen. He wants to achieve beauty and perfection—but no one can ever really define exactly what these are. He wants to reach understanding and recognition—but these too are ephemeral, and could evaporate at any moment. The Artist is constantly bumping up against the fact that his daily process reality and his goals do not correspond to those of the majority of people, who seek peace, order, and well-being. Why, for what does the Artist turn his back on everything that others want and strive toward the chimeras of inspiration, creativity, and the creation of masterpieces? The unspoken conflict between the Artist and those close to him is exacerbated by stress, under whose influence the Artist passes his entire life. As soon as riches appear on the Artist's horizon, he sees in them the means for alleviating the undefined nature of his existence. As Verdi wrote in one of his letters: 'I will be a millionaire, a millionaire! At least it's something definite, unlike those mythological phantoms—"fame," "honor," "celebrity"'.[64]

It is generally recognized that creativity is the main engine of progress and the sole justification for man's earthly existence. Yet for all that, society hardly thirsts for progress and innovation; in the psychological sense it is, rather, 'routine-ocentric'. Henry Ford, no

---

[63] Metner, N. (1981) *Stat'i, materialy, vospominaniya/Articles, Materials, Memoirs*. Moscow: Sovetsky kompozitor, p. 67.
[64] Walker, F. (1982) *The Man Verdi*. The University of Chicago Press.

stranger to success at evaluating the desires of common people, claimed that the ordinary man feared nothing so much as the necessity of thinking something over and making changes. At three levels of organization, society, group, and individual, humans locate a certain 'harmonic point', a balance of strengths, interests, and possibilities which allows them to avoid violating the normal course of events and maintain the status quo. But the Creator, Inventor, Artist, and Performing Artist are all obsessed with change, they thirst for it. Offering up the fruits of their creative labors, they invade the ordered world of Things As They Are and stir everything up. If in scientific discoveries society can see a certain prospective utility for itself, however distant, in artistic discoveries it sees nothing of the kind: artistic discoveries are not our daily bread, so to speak. The Artist often feels himself an uninvited guest in society's home, forced to wait in the entrance hall for a time before finally being invited into the living room. Mozart found himself literally in this situation when he was looking for work in Paris in 1778: when he would finally get an audience in some home, the pomaded aristocrats would go on chatting away, drawing, sewing, telling stories—his music was no more necessary to them than the warbling of a canary in a cage. Mozart at length won his right to be creative, but with enormous difficulty and regrettable consequences, as 10 years of this 'freedom' cost him his life. And though his name was known all over Europe, although he was the idol of all music lovers of his time, he continued to live in need: then as now, a name and reputation do not of themselves necessarily correlate with rewards and material well-being.

Some Artists of the past were able to support themselves by their creative labor; the majority of these fortunate souls worked in the entertainment genres or served as adornments to the powers that be. Those who did neither of these were condemned to a bitter struggle for the mere chance to do what they were called to do. This struggle multiplies stress many fold, stress which carries within it both the creative process itself and conflict with society. The impossibility of reconciling creativity with the attainment of life's necessities can kill the Artist; the list of geniuses and great talents who died from this failure (or died young) would make a volume of its own. Schubert, Mussorgsky, and Hugo Wolf would be at the head of the list of musicians who fell in this struggle.

The Artist's organism defends itself against stress with the help of laziness. For certain periods the Artist does not want to do anything at all—he wants to forget about everything and drop out of the game altogether. He tries to forget about the sources of his eternal unease and psychological pressure: he no longer wants or needs either his own creative work or the struggle that goes with it. The great guitarist Eric Clapton said,

> I think all musicians are lazy, I think that's one of the best parts about us. . . .. I've got to force myself into a position where I think if I don't go out and play, I'll go broke. Because playing isn't everything. You've got your home life, you build up a little kind of empire—your house and a woman and people that depend on you. You can't just lie back, you've got to pretend that you're actually on the verge of bankruptcy, so that you can go out and graft. Otherwise you just sit back and get fat and do nothing at all.[65]

---

65 Cit. from John Pidgeon (1985) *Eric Clapton*. London: Vermilion, p. 108.

Beyond this defensive laziness, the Artist's organism continually demonstrates various caprices and 'breaks down'. The reason and proximate cause of these breakdowns is the stress which constantly accompanies the Artist's life: creative searching, stage fright, quarrels with intimates, and strangers who do not understand his struggle. With these constant tensions the organism refuses to work and comes up instead with ailments and illnesses. Though constantly required to be in excellent physical shape, the Artist in reality can never be certain that he has reached it. 'In my entire life', confessed the Bolshoi Theater soloist Sergei Migai, 'I have sung in good health four times'.[66] The ballerina Ekaterina Maksimova has said that for a ballerina something is always ailing: your hands, a foot, your back, or everything at once. A permanent state of ill health, the result of unending nervous stress, becomes for the Artist the natural setting of his life.

Creative stress and the conditions of the Artist's life which when it intensifies summon forth not only the desire to rest and do something else, but to go even further—to shed the heavy burden of responsibility before one's talent, before the public and before one's still uncreated works. The Artist wants to get lost in the crowd, become one of the many who seek only well-being, comfort, and the pleasures of hearth and home. The burden of talent at times becomes so unbearable that the Artist dreams of not playing, not composing, not performing, and not leading the life of a roving minstrel. Once three geniuses, the violinists Leopold Auer, and Henrik Wieniawsky and the pianist Nikolai Rubinstein, found themselves in Baden-Baden (Ginzburg 1966). The musicians decided to try their fortunes in a casino. Perhaps with beginner's luck, the trio soon found themselves way ahead. Rubinstein, the leader of the three-man 'enterprise', was elated: now they could give up concerts altogether, he was thinking; they would be rich and happy, they would enjoy their peace and quiet. All their concerts were cancelled. But then Dame Fortune turned her back on the musicians: Rubinstein, the financial director and principal player in the group, lost his shirt. Thus ended one attempt to leave the natural self behind; the Artist, tormented by continual stress, will try all manner of things for relief.

The creative process and his position in society expose the Artist to continuous nerve-wracking problems. These are not only a necessary accompaniment of creative life, but also its breeding ground as well, a peculiar prerequisite for the appearance of the Artist and the Performing Artist in the world of mortals. Psychologists have noted that gifted people in their childhood years much more often encounter nervous stress than do their non-gifted peers. As Ellen Winner has observed:

> Levels of early parental loss in creators are over three times as high as levels in the population at large, which have been reported to be somewhere between 6 percent and 8 percent. The only other groups with such high levels of parental loss are delinquents and depressive or suicidal psychiatric patients.[67]

[66] Nesterenko, E. (1985) *Razmyshleniya o professii/Thoughts on Profession*. Moscow: Iskusstvo, p. 18.
[67] Winner, E. (1996) *The Gifted Children*. New York: Basic Books, p. 299.

The childhood years of geniuses are often marred by stresses unconnected with orphan status or abandonment. The parents of such people are often highly affected and emotionally unsound. Beethoven's father suffered from alcoholism and was extremely unstable. Paganini's father beat him and was abnormally strict. Tender and caring relatives in the families of geniuses tend to be the exception rather than the rule, and thus the geniuses who later emerge into fame do not consider their childhood an oasis of pleasant memories. Paganini entered into his diary a sobering citation from the musings of the great Italian poet Leopardi:

> The most beautiful and fortunate age of man is tormented to such a degree with a thousand anxieties, fears and labors of education and instruction that a grown-up man, even in the midst of all the unhappiness caused by disillusionment and tedium of life and the deadening of imagination would yet not accept to return to childhood if he had again to suffer what he suffered then.[68]

No doubt many of the greats would subscribe to the poet's sentiment.

Suicide statistics confirm the tendency of the Artist and the Performing Artist to seek an escape from stress of the most radical kind. Steven Sack has made a special study of this problem, concluding:

> The standard federal occupational code definition of artist encompasses authors, musicians, composers, actors, directors, painters, sculptors, craft artists, artist printmakers, and dancers. Suicide data analysis was limited to ages 21–64. Logistic regression techniques indicated that being an artist elevated suicide risk by 112 percent relative to non-artists.[69]

One could comment on these results as an example of the chicken-or-egg dilemma: creators are twice as inclined toward suicide as ordinary people. But is that tendency a reaction to their life, so full of stress beyond measure—or does the tendency to become a creator simply appear more often in people who are unstable and endowed with certain elements of psychosis? For the time being both propositions must be considered valid as science offers no answer to the question.

One thing is clear: creativity and stress are connected both psychologically and socially. While a normal person avoids negative emotions and difficult experiences, nature itself seems to draw the creative person towards these. Deliberating on this subject, psychologists sometimes frighten themselves with their own propositions: some of them have put forth the idea that childhood stress facilitates the birth of talent (Feldman 1980, 1988; Ilyin 2004; Segalin 1925; Winner 1996), a pampered and spoiled child has a much smaller chance of becoming a creator in either the arts or the sciences than the child who was hounded and constantly suffered emotional problems. These problems and grim thoughts seem to inspire creative energy and provoke the growth of the imagination.

There are entirely natural neuropsychological bases for such conclusion. It is well known that the three I's—inspiration, intuition, and imagination—are located in the right hemisphere of the brain. This is where creative thought, creative impulse, and

[68] Cit. from Courcy, G. de (1957) *Paganini, the Genoese*, vol. 1. Norman: University of Oklahoma Press, p. 25.
[69] Stack, S. (1997) Suicide among artists. *Journal of Social Psychology*, 137, p. 129.

creative motivation are all born. The right hemisphere generalizes, synthesizes, and perceives the world in extraordinarily integrated terms; it does not have the power to reason and divide things into parts—yet it gives birth to images. All of this would have no particular bearing on psychosis, stress, and negative emotions if not for one thing: the experiencing of stress and sadness, dissatisfaction, and annoyance, and various other unpleasant emotions is also to a great extent localized in the right hemisphere (Medushevsky 1993; Bekhtereva *et al.* 1977; Scherbatykh 2006).

The right hemisphere is older, predating in the order of creation the clear and logical left side. Primitive man, lost in the wilds of nature, had much more reason to be grim than to rejoice: he was governed by stress all the time, the oldest and most unpleasant of feelings, as he was constantly dealing with loss and catastrophe. His emotional base was largely one of sadness. When man became a more reasoning being, his thoughts became a source of positive emotions: his ability to calculate, predict the course of events and react accordingly is connected with thought. Reason and the left hemisphere took upon themselves the pleasant responsibility of making man joyful. People who suffer from damage to the left hemisphere are usually very gloomy; people with a damaged right hemisphere are idiotically happy.

Stress calls forth strong negative emotions which unavoidably stimulate the creative right hemisphere. Addressing his negative experiences, man arouses in himself the sleeping powers of imagination and fantasy. Much of the things in which the right hemisphere feels itself strong are activated as a result of some activity in a negative emotional context. A saddened and anxiety-ridden person unconsciously 'shakes up' his right hemisphere, arousing it. And once it is in an aroused, active state, it begins to produce creative energy, to give birth to motivation toward creative work, and to stimulate the images of fantasy. Without addressing the right hemisphere it is hardly possible to set the creative process in motion—and the active means of doing that is to summon stress by creating an outburst of negative emotion.

Stimulation of the right hemisphere with the help of negative experiences is one of the most effective ways of creating the psychological conditions for creativity. The reverse is also true: creatively gifted people, which means people with a highly developed right hemisphere, are automatically drawn, when the activity of that hemisphere rises, toward negative emotions. They are more likely to be sad than happy; they are easily offended and easily embittered. However, since they are Artists, they do not subconsciously fear and avoid these states of mind as most other people do; indeed, they even seek them out, summon them, knowing that such conditions are, in fact, very conducive to creativity. It was altogether appropriate for Grigory Piatigorsky to note, after creating a masterpiece of performance despite the terrible pain of a broken thumb: 'It is a strange profession. One can be in wonderful form, physically and in spirit—and yet do almost nothing to one's own satisfaction. At the same time, one can be unwell and in unfavorable conditions give the very best one has to give'.[70]

---

[70] Piatigorsky, G. (1970) Violonchelist/Cellist. *Ispolnitel'skoe iskusstvo zarubezhnykh stran/Performing Art Abroad*, 5, p. 153.

The romantic poet asks 'What is a poet's life without suffering/what is the sea without storms?' While there is no doubt a certain logic in all this 'productivity from the negative', one should not make the mistake of assuming that an attraction toward suffering or, even more so, the artificial arousal of the right hemisphere with the aid of stressful conditions can make anyone a creative personality. The role of such arousal is that of an accompanist; the structure of talent is too multifaceted, with too many components, skills, and qualities going into creative activity, for the general activation of the right hemisphere to have a decisive role. A talented individual may produce perfectly well without immersing himself in a condition of woe and suffering; stress is by no means a necessary precondition for creativity, but rather one of a number of catalysts which may serve, all other conditions being equal, as a 'launching mechanism'.

An ungifted person who is seized by negative emotions will not become talented, just as a child who lives in conditions of continual stress will not become talented simply for that reason. There are many times more people who experience the pressure of circumstances and emotional discomfort than there are talented people, and there is no demonstrated cause-and-effect relationship or directly proportional relationship between stress and talent. Yet it must be noted that in the life of a gifted child, suffering brings with it an early emotional maturity which itself acts a stimulant of creative growth. The gifted child and adolescent encounter the resistance of people and circumstances mainly when they have certain defined intentions which they are trying to realize. So it is that many musical talents 'bring on their own problems' when, against their parents' wishes they decide to become musicians—and their early childhood, pre-teen, and adolescent years were passed in a condition of constant stress. This was the case for Schumann, Berlioz, Mussorgsky, Tchaikovsky, Sidney Bechet, Duke Ellington and several others. The lives of wunderkinds—Mozart, Beethoven, Paganini, and their like—were no less difficult under the relentless exploitation of egotistical fathers.

The creativity of the Artist is connected with continuous stage fright, which never lets him rest on his laurels. But stage fright alone is not enough to provide the impulse for creative performance: a person whose 'suffering organ' does not keep in practice risks falling into emotional apathy and finding himself in a state of good-naturedness that is fatal for an Artist. As Konstantin Igumnov put it:

> In some performers the inner life proceeds so smoothly that in the end absolutely nothing bothers them. At that point there arises the danger that in their musical performance there will be no content. Unfortunately, this kind of personal placidity, leveling all human experience, can be found all too frequently among performers.[71]

The history of culture and art testifies that in the most fortunate countries, where life is free of tragedy, there are lesser great talents. And in contrast to them, countries whose histories are shot through with contradictions and catastrophes are rich in talented individuals. By the same token, the times of great historical watersheds, eras of tragedy which

---

[71] Teplov, B. M. (1998) *Psihologiya i psikhofiziologiya individual'nyh razlichij/Psychology and Psychophisiology of Individual Differences.* Moscow-Voronezh: Modek, p. 147.

create great tensions in society, give rise to many talents. This takes place thanks to the significant spiritual content which tragic eras bear within themselves, psychologically stimulating people's creative energy. Asked by the present author why Russia has been so rich in musically talented souls, Yehudi Menuhin replied simply and to the point: 'Because they have suffered so much'.

Summing up our discussion of the gifted Performer, we shall note certain fundamental skills and qualities he must possess:

1 The talent of the Performer is phyilogenetically connected with the talent of the Composer: they have a common origin and hark back to sources of musical art in the form of collective improvisation. Despite the external dissimilarities in activity, the essence of the giftedness of the Performer consists in his ability to become a co-author with the Composer, recreating a work as he performs it on stage.

2 The virtuoso giftedness of the Performer is an extension of his expressive ear and sense of rhythm. It derives from the liveliness and sharpness of the aural-spatial and aural-motor connections. The problems of virtuosos are problems of synthesis and ease of transition from the aural modality into others: the factor of quantitative accumulation of motor skills is not the most effective means of developing virtuosos.

3 The artistic giftedness of the Performer unites him with all who perform on stage: the musical performer is as artistically gifted as the dramatic actor or dancer. The talent of the Artist relies on the ancient sensation of oneself as a priest and an envoy, called to pass along an important message. The artistic nature involves a feeling of responsibility before one's mission and a feeling of love for the audience, for whom this mission is being performed. Stage fright is an indication of artistic talent, as it derives from it directly.

4 The talent of the Artist is connected with a certain strength of spirit, courage and patience. In the creative process are discovered the same qualities of personality which allow someone to scale the heights of a career. Thus the great talents who were not able to make themselves known were the exception. A great talent draws a person to a Great Career.

Part 4

The structure of musical talent

The structure of musical giftedness is a reflection of the path of development which music has followed over the entire course of human history. Musical talent was arranged and formed together with musical activity, and deep within its very core. The first part to emerge was the expressive ear for music, reflecting the affective and communicative qualities of music. Next came the sense of rhythm, which brought forth musical movement, thus creating musical time. The expressive ear and the sense of rhythm served as the basis for the further development of the music of earliest man: relying on the sense of timbre and quality of sound articulation as well as the ideation of musical movement (its accentual nature and structural orientation), the analytical ear, the next stage in the development of musical talent, could then be born. This stage signaled the mastery of musical language with the help of the awareness of stable aural pitch patterns, motifs, and melodic phrases as well as modal regularities. This process had its origins in speech and took place simultaneously with the formation of verbal language, using the phonological, lexical, and syntactic mechanisms of articulated thought.

The complex of musical abilities relied on a motivational nucleus (the expressive ear) which makes up the center of human musicality, the basis of our ability to decode the content of a musical message and react to it. The operational apparatus of musical abilities which allows for the compilation of aural *gestalts* and pitch-rhythmic structures consisted of the sense of rhythm and the analytical ear. The apex of the operational mechanisms of musical abilities became the internal ear, whose appearance signaled the ability to imagine organized sequences of pitch-rhythmic structures, or musical expressions. The musical memory retained these expressions and facilitated their reproduction. With the help of the complex of musical abilities—the expressive ear, the analytical ear, and the sense of rhythm—humans could master different musical patterns and acquire musical language: they could understand, remember, and reproduce musical expressions.

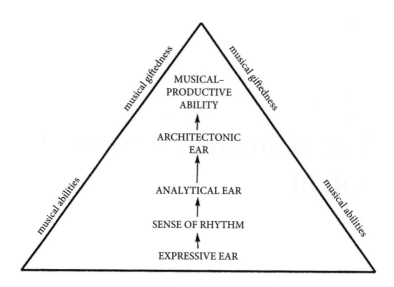

The architectonic ear represented the next stage in the development of musical talent belonging already to its creative part—musical giftedness. This is the step at which active mastery of musical language begins, signaling the transition from ability to giftedness, from absorption, mastery, and the ability to reproduce the already-mastered to productive musical activity. The architectonic ear presumes an understanding of the stylistic and genre-specific patterns of musical speech, the mastery of the skills necessary for the construction of a musical text. From the general-linguistic rules of the formation of musical structures, from the level of musical phonology, lexicon and syntax which are the province of the analytical ear, the architectonic ear leads a musical thought to the recognition of stylistic and individual particularities of texts and groups of texts. The sign of the completed formation of the architectonic ear is the esthetic sense, with its understanding of the integrity of a text, of its beauty and its internal proportionality. The architectonic ear allows man to approach the first phase of musical creation, the variant copying of stylistic-genre models on the basis of learned musical-stylistic algorithms, which are the regular patterns of the connections of musical elements and blocks.

The ability to produce music is the second constituent element of musical giftedness, the second component of the compositional ability of man. This ability makes up the combining nucleus of musical giftedness which invents and produces a multitude of new musical elements and structures. The musical-productive ability is the generative center of the composing process on the basis of which the architectonic ear constructs a new musical whole, completing the selection of useful and essential combinations and rejecting the unnecessary and unsuccessful. The giftedness of the composer presupposes the coordinated work of the musical-productive ability of the left hemisphere of the brain and the architectonic ear, with mostly right hemisphere (quasi-spatial) orientation. The complex of musical talent absorbing both basic musical abilities helping to better acquire musical skills plus musical creativity (giftedness) represents the highest stage of the development of musicality. It is not one more step in the development of abilities, but a qualitative leap forward on the level of musical thought. Musical talent as a particular complex of psychological properties and qualities is not formed by the training of basic musical abilities: its appearance is separated from them by many stages in the development of the human brain leading to musical creativity. These stages cannot be attained and surpassed in the course of a single human lifetime if talent itself is not present in a person as an innate gift.

The model of the structure of musical talent may serve as a starting point for the study of other forms of talents, each of which has analogs to the functions performed by the psychological components of musical talent. The analog of the expressive ear for music is the basis of any talent. This can be found in the depths of the past, when one or another form of human activity was born. The idea of this activity, its role in the survival of the human species was clearer then than they are now, and the essence of the function itself was more apparent. The analog of the expressive ear is the motivating element of any form of giftedness, the ideational core on which the second structural component of abilities is developed, the one that is functionally analogous to the sense of rhythm. The disassembly and assembly of space-time processes and their grouping is attendant to all forms of activity: the operator of the *gestalt*, fragmentation and summarizing processes which make up the basic content of activity, is found under the analog of 'sense of rhythm'.

The analog of the analytical ear in the context of a model of different forms of giftedness is the 'sense of language', the linguistic ability which manages the grammar and syntax of a given form of activity. Any ability uses a certain linguistic system, and life inside this system, its internal hierarchy, is organized with the help of the analog of the analytical ear, the 'systems operator' of the given form of giftedness. After it comes the analog of the achitectonic ear, which manages 'stylistic formation' in the context of the given activity. It controls the algorithms with the help of which copies of objects created during the activity can be made. The analog of the architectonic ear is a component of any talent: as distinct from abilities, which manage the initial organization of material and the organization of the 'manner of execution' of the activity, the architectonic ear answers for the activity's integrity on the level of the created 'texts'. The analog of musical-productive ability is the supplier of ready-made 'building blocks' for the given form of activity. It can create the elements from which objects are built and it can vary them, creating new 'blocks' and putting together finished structures. The quality of these structures will be assessed by the esthetic sense, relying on the resources of the 'architectonic ear'.

At the extreme poles of the model of talent are its motivational nucleus, the analog of the expressive ear, and the 'instigator' which brings about the activity, the analog of musical-productive ability. Between these are three structural 'operators' leading the process of activity from motivation to realization: the *gestalt*, or space-time operator, the systems (linguistic) operator and the operator of the integrity of the text. Additions to the content of this model are possible in the context of a particular activity, and musical activity and musical talent provide examples of how a talent's structure is made and what segments it consists of.

The phylogenetic model of musical talent presupposes the following basic tenets:

1 The lower strata of the model are of earlier origin that the higher, which were formed and grew from those below over the course of hundreds of thousands of years. The psychological properties and qualities belonging to the lower strata of abilities and talent had been formed very long ago and are more firmly embedded in the human genetic memory; more people possess them than possess the higher and later properties and qualities.

2 The higher one goes on the phylogenetic model; fewer people possess each of the components in comparison with those possessing the lower-placed components. For the full function of a talent the complete possession of its structural elements is essential. Those people who are possessed of the highest lying talent components must be recruited from those who possess the lower, otherwise talent will lose its structural integrity, and its quality and level will invariably suffer.

3 The phylogenetic model of musical talent is a model of an ideal talent, representing a theoretical construct. In practice, for the functioning of the whole of the structure of musical talent it is sufficient that each of the attendant components be greater than zero, that is be present at a minimally acceptable level. Only outstanding composers and performers possess all the components of the model at a high level of development. The rest of the professional and amateur musicians do not need this kind of 'component completeness'; their abilities and giftedness are defined by the specifics of their particular activities. The talent of a music teacher will differ from that of a music critic or a music editor, and the success of these people at their activities will not depend to a decisive degree on the completeness and quality of their musical talent.

4 The training of a musical talent should take phylogenetic structure into account. The order of appearance of the components in phylogenesis should lie at the base of the methodological principles used in musical pedagogy. The lower lying components should be dealt with before those higher on the structure. Observing this principle will facilitate the acquisition of musical skills and make musical education more effective altogether.

Part 5

The education of a musician

Musical talent and heredity

Does the apple fall far from the tree?

Is it possible to raise a musical talent? Are musical abilities the product of culture and upbringing or is man simply born with them? It is not really possible to offer authoritative answers to questions like these, but in any case it's possible to suppose that musical abilities have a more direct relationship with biology and genetics than the abilities of a lawyer or a bookkeeper. Music appeared much earlier than many other human occupations; familiarization with and mastery of various musical forms happened and happens spontaneously, involuntarily, in a process that might be called musicalization—a process that requires no special educational institutions.

Some psychologists and part of the general public assume that the first years of life determine the subsequent development of talent and its very existence (Dowling 1988; Miller 1989; Starcheus 2003; Szabo 1999; Welch 2000). In early childhood it is possible to stimulate a person's natural giftedness; if it is a question of musical talent, then the child must be surrounded by a stimulating musical environment: she should hear a great deal of music, listen to how her parents, friends, and acquaintances make music, and, insofar as she can, join in with them. Her musical ear and sense of rhythm should nurture musical impressions even as they become more and more acute. The conditions of the musical development of a child in her early years determine the child's musical future—or so goes the widespread popular wisdom. But is this true?

To what extent does the musical environment provided by music-loving parents facilitate the establishment of musical talent? And is the widely held opinion that 'The apple doesn't fall far from the tree' true in things musical? Do musical children grow up in musical families? A group of psychologists led by Joel Wapnick (Wapnick *et al.* 2000) resolved to find the answer to a question that lies at the base of musical pedagogy: what is most important in the formation of a musician—natural giftedness, the support of parents, or a good instructor? Wapnick's group interviewed 260 gifted student-musicians whose success was clear to everyone. These young talents were invited to special summer camp for gifted youths. The researchers' interviews involved not only the students themselves, but their parents and music teachers as well. All three groups were expected to offer their opinions on the question of who or what influenced the identification and development of the young musician to the greatest degree. The gifted youths themselves did not deny the pleasure of ascribing their success to their own talent and toil; parents and instructors did not play, the students felt, decisive roles. The parents, on the other hand, were quite convinced that without their support their children would never have achieved what they had—the victories in competitions, the medals, and all the rest. The parents, for their part, never mentioned any particular gifts the children might have had. The teachers agreed with their pupils, giving full marks to the giftedness and hard work of the latter— while not forgetting to mention their own long and selfless labor with their charges. All the participants in the study equated the good result with their own efforts, considering the input of the other 'sides' to the common cause of much less value. Beyond illustrating the natural human weakness of taking success as the fruit of one's own labor (and failure as the result of unfavorable circumstances), this experiment yet again revealed the multiplicity of 'centers of influence' on the creative success of a young musician. The result of another very similar experiment was not the less telling (Evans *et al.* 2000): parents, teachers, and outstanding music students, each of those groups, thought this particular group was the true author of the success story happening: 'Differences among these attribution patterns are surprising, but are consistent with research that suggests that individuals often make causal attributions that are self-serving giving a good deal of credit to their own characteristics or influence'.[1]

The composers of numerous questionnaires and polls have often attempted to identify the principal factor, among the many involved, in this success. Psychologists have tried to predict the degree of musicality of a child based on a known level of musicality of the parents. The proverbial dilemma of the chicken or the egg inevitably arose in this kind of inquiry, however: the parents of unmusical children were, as a rule, unmusical themselves, and thus it was unclear whether their children's indifference to music derived from a lack of opportunities to hear it at home or from the unmusicality of their parents being passed along genetically. The same was noted in musical families: the children of parents who liked to sing and play musical instruments were themselves musical. As Rosamund Shuter-Dyson and Clive Gabriel noted from their study of English schoolchildren:

> It could be argued that the parents who had had music lessons and kept up their playing were those who had talent and that their children had inherited their gifts. But equally it could be held that the parents' playing had contributed to raising the children's musical level and that parents who have themselves had music lessons are more likely to encourage their children to learn.[2]

John Shelton (1965) likewise conducted a statistical study of English schoolchildren, dividing them into two groups: musical and non-musical. According to Shelton's results, 91.6 percent of non-musical children come from non-musical families. This statistic can be read in two ways: the children are unmusical because of the unmusical environment in which they grew up; or perhaps they are lacking in musical abilities because their parents were similarly lacking, and their 'tin ear' was simply passed along as a legacy. The situation with musical children is not so clear cut. Some 16.6 percent of musical children come from musical families; 61.1 percent of musical children come from moderately musical families; and the remaining 22.2 percent come from clearly unmusical families. This last

[1] Evans, R. J., Bickel, R., and Pendarvis, E. D. (2000) Musical talent: Innate or acquired? Perceptions of students, parents, and teachers. *Gifted Child Quarterly*, 44, p. 80.
[2] Shuter-Dyson, R and Gabriel, C. (1981) *The Psychology of Musical Ability*. London: Methuen, p. 202.

number, contrary to the superficial view, speaks to the inheritance-based origins of giftedness: a child from an extremely unmusical family can become musical herself thanks only to natural inclinations which lead her to music, as her environment and immediate surroundings cannot alone stimulate musical development.

Musical environment according to all these data is not a 'number one' condition for the establishment of musical talent; musical children most often do not need a stimulating musical environment, and grow up in moderately musical or entirely unmusical families. These results fly in the face of commonly accepted prejudices, as they prove that the scientific and general view, that is, science and common sense, do not always go hand in hand. Common sense would incline one toward the opinion that the apple, after all, does not fall far from the tree, so musical children should have musical parents—which is not the case. The same common sense suggests that it is unlikely that musical children can be born into unmusical families—which is also incorrect a good 22.2 percent of the time. But the reverse 'theorem'—that an extremely unmusical person comes from an extremely unmusical family—in fact tends to be true almost about 90 percent of the time.

Shelton's research results indirectly confirm the experiments of Henry Moog (1976), an expert in the musical psychology of children. Moog studied the musical reactions and musical behavior of 3 year olds who grew up in families whose levels of musical development were incomparably diverse. In his classic work *The Musical Experience of the Pre-School Child* Moog observed:

> The home environment had no substantial influence on the subjects: our testing tasks were performed no differently by children who had no musical impressions to draw on and children who were most advanced in this category. In terms of activity and quality, the musical reactions among children who listened to music from morning to night and children whose musical exposure was extremely limited were, for practical purposes, the same.[3]

Similar experiments require us to re-examine the role of the family circle in the formation of a child's musicality—and perhaps, despite the accepted wisdom, dismiss it as a deciding factor. L. A. Sosniak (1985) worked with highly gifted young pianists beginning their careers as soloists, and with the pianists' parents as well. All the young musicians came from moderately musical families in which the attitude toward music was one of benign indifference. The parents began to take an active interest in music only after their child began a systematic study of it; before that their interest had not exceeded the bounds of the usual listener's curiosity. Yet they did not have the slightest desire to broaden their child's musical studies; if it had not been for the music teacher, the youthful gift would have remained altogether without support. Sosniak's data agree entirely with those of Shuter-Dyson and Shelton: 61 percent of musical children come from moderately musical families and 22 percent from unmusical families. In other words, 83 percent of the children who love music and show a great interest in it do so on their own initiative—at their hearts' request, you might say, and in spite of their parents' wishes.

---

[3] Moog, H. (1976) *The Musical Experience of the Pre-school Child*. Trans. C. Clarke. London: Schott.

Some parents do not understand the attraction of children to music, which they consider a trivial fancy. Sometimes parents are prepared to broaden their children's interest in music, but when talk turns to a musical career, parents do not see the choice as a particularly promising one. At this point the child takes on the role of the Persecuted Artist while the parents take the side of Society, which seeks a 'practical application' for everything. Despite widespread opinion to the contrary, the majority of young musicians in fact go against the will of their parents when they choose their career; and parents do not simply *not force* them to commit themselves to music, but quite actively *hinder* exactly that, which the research of Sosniak and Wapnik illustrates convincingly.

John Sloboda and Michael Howe (1991) conducted a research project in a special school for musically gifted children. One group of students, designated Group A, was composed of the highly gifted—children who could boast of victories in musical competitions and solo performances on stage. The second group, Group B, consisted of the moderately gifted—pupils whose musical successes were altogether satisfying for all concerned but who demonstrated nothing out of the ordinary in achieving them. Differences between the two groups in terms of behavior and personal qualities emerged, paralleling those between the highly gifted and the moderately gifted in any field. Group A children devoted less time to their principal instrument than did those in Group B, distributing their time more evenly, as the authors note, among different instruments; and the great achievements of the A students required less effort on their part than did the moderate accomplishments of their B comrades. As Liszt put it, 'a genius immediately reads the whole word while others are examining syllables'. This principle clearly holds for the talented when they are compared to their less-talented peers.

Group A students were interested in a great many things and had the time to explore them. They took up playing several instruments at once; read a great deal; went to performances and exhibitions; and spent time with their friends. Group B pupils were more narrowly focused and committed: they played only their principal instruments, expending all their energies there; had fewer outside interests; and led a more restricted lifestyle. These results agree with the opinions and data often mentioned in the journals *Gifted Child Quarterly, Roeper Review and High Ability Studies*. Long-term observations over the gifted and talented prompt the extraordinary breadth and openness of talented people: their interest extends to questions and subjects which concern neither themselves directly nor even the business they have committed themselves to. The talented are characterized by a lively interest in life and culture; they demonstrate a multi-channeled style of thought and perception which allows them to process the most varied information, accumulating and releasing it later into the orbit of their own creative work.

The less gifted, on the other hand, are forced to give their all to their chosen profession, and must pay a considerable price for what is, in effect, an incorrect choice: their professional accomplishments, despite the significant expenditure of energy, do not greatly reward either the principals themselves or those around them. This is especially true for moderately gifted children and teenagers pushed by their parents and dreaming of the world stars' fame. Their efforts do not enrich the field in which they work. In the end, the less-gifted strugglers may lose everything—friends, free time, the chance for a happy and rewarding life—and all of it sacrificed to an *idee fixe*, a myth, a fetish which can bring them neither creative satisfaction nor a great career. Such are 'anti-success' stories hiding under the roofs of many Russian special music schools where some students are wrongly focused on the great soloists' future.

The results of Sloboda-Howe experiment correspond with the results obtained earlier (Kirnarskaya 1989b; Tarasova 1988): the pupils in 'Group A' come from moderately musical families; those of 'Group B' come from more musical backgrounds—families in which the parents are professional musicians. But the extremely musical environment, the active involvement of the parents in the musical life of the child, the rich musical impressions from earliest childhood—all this did not have a deciding influence on the formation of the talent of the 'Group B' students. Despite the impressive array of possibilities and advantages for fostering talent, the 'B' children could not bring them to bear and remained on a middling level. Their peers from 'Group A', without these advantages, created them—by themselves and for themselves—with their interest in and love for music. The absence of active 'musical stimuli' in their childhood did not prevent them from demonstrating significant musical giftedness in their years of study in school. Judith Monsaas and George Engelhard (1990), looking at the competitive spirit and the desire to achieve of talented young people in athletics and music, also noted that home environment didn't play a decisive role here yielding to the teenagers' own drive and motivation.

Under such circumstances one might suppose that gifted pupils owed their success to their teachers, who proved to be more qualified and demanding than their colleagues. However, in schools for musically gifted children in both England and Russia the teaching is done by professors of extraordinarily high qualifications; these are performing artists and experienced masters whose reputations are beyond question. These professors may have students from Group A and Group B in the same classes—which testifies to the fact that the influence of a pedagogue is not decisive, or all the students of certain teachers would emerge as A-Group pupils, and the students of certain others as B-Group types.

Studies on the origins of musical children show that the conditions and environment of musical education do not have a decisive influence on the appearance of musical giftedness. Neither can teachers pretend to an exclusive role in the establishment of musical talent. Thus the question naturally arises: if it is not the environment, not the conditions of early development, and not the efforts of qualified instructors, then what *does* influence the appearance of musical talent? Is it not natural to assume that a person is simply born with greater musical potential than many others and that outstanding talent is a gift of nature itself later developed and polished by hard work? (Ilyin 2004; Krutetsky 1998; 2006; Rubinstein 1973; Winner 1996; 2000). Of course, here we are looking at a talent of someone who is bound to rouse millions' admiration, but not at the one who is playing in a local band or helping a little child to count 'a-one, and-two'. . . Those latter careers are accessible for all of us who are ready to pursue them, and the shy servants of Her Majesty Music, we are flinging our doors broadly to meet with delight and passion her true and unique priests—Homo Musicus by fate and fortune.

The origin of musical abilities

Natural and biological origins of musical abilities are commonly claimed by citing the prehistoric evidence of man's musicality. If this musicality had been formed as part of the life process instead of simply being granted at the outset, then neither animals nor infants would demonstrate any evidence of musical abilities. But the opposite is the case: birds make music, as do dolphins and certain species of apes—the brains of chimpanzees and makaks have special sections responsible for musical functions. Infant humans, for their part, demonstrate a rather high level of musicality, distinguishing melodies and even remembering certain ones which they heard before birth.

Music making is a pastime common to all races, nationalities, and cultures. Life at its earliest stages, the primitive levels of civilization, is unavoidably connected with music—as is life at the other end of the civilization spectrum, the most developed stages: the paragons of the Information Age make and consume music just as hungrily as did their earliest ancestors. The demand for music and the ability to create it never disappear under any circumstances; one hears music during war and peace, everywhere where people are, even though cultures and value systems can differ in the extreme. These cultural contrasts do not affect music; music may change in form but it always remains with people—which speaks of the deep genetic entrenchment of music making, the remarkable strength of its natural roots.

Music formed the human brain over the course of millions of years. Certain musical functions were assigned to certain sections of the brain. It's mainly the right hemisphere that answers for processes of musical synthesis and unity while the left hemisphere for processes of musical analysis and the disassembly of music into its constituent elements. The left hemisphere is more connected with musical movement and rhythm, while the right with aural-spatial associations. In the human brain a special section was formed, the auditory cortex, which processes musical information, relying on sound signals of different pitches. In the left hemisphere there is a special section called the *planum temporale* which is enlarged in people who have perfect pitch; and young violinists (if they began studying music before age 7) have in their brains a special 'embassy' for the fingers of the left hand—the connection between the brain and the fingers is more defined and more durable than in others. Data from neuropsychology, physical anthropology, and ethnography, as well as evidence from early childhood development studies suggest that music is a natural phenomenon, with a pre-cultural nature—and that no sort of artificial stimulus is necessary for an individual to begin demonstrating his status as *Homo musicus*. As Isabelle Peretz puts it:

> Many of the arguments presented here are directed against strong claims about an exclusively cultural perspective on music. My intention is to show that such claims are neurobiologically questionable . . . Music is an autonomous function, innately constrained and made up of multiple modules that overlap minimally with other functions (such as language).[4]

---

[4] Peretz, I. (2006) The nature of music from a biological perspective. *Cognition*, 100, p. 25

There is considerable periodical literature on the ability of infants to distinguish pitch, identify subtle differences in the structure of melodies and on the ability of a listener up to the age of 6 months to remember melodies heard before birth. The theme of infant musical capability which exceeds expectations has been the subject of dissertation research: the works of Brian Satt (1984) and Ronald Polverini-Rey (1993) at the California School of Professional Psychology have established that infants in the first months of life demonstrate a certain conservatism in musical taste, falling asleep more readily to lullabies which their mothers sang to them before their birth; D. Shaw (1991) from the same School has reported that mother and infant understand one another better if the mother took music lessons before giving birth. These and other studies, including broad research by Sandra Trehub and her colleagues, have led the scholarly community to the conclusion that man is born already endowed with a defined musical potential.

Marie Balaban and her colleagues (Balaban *et al.* 1998) resolved to determine the earliest stage at which neuropsychological musical specialization appears in an infant. It is known that adults perceive musical contour with the right hemisphere of the brain, spatially— but if the same motif is repeated in another pitch, the operation of comparison will be carried out by the left hemisphere. Scientists tested 8-month-old infants at both functions, judging their reaction with the help of a turn of the head in the direction of a lighted toy. It turned out that the infants had already formed a 'music specialization' of the brain hemispheres which worked exactly like that of adults. The authors concluded that the basic musical functions of the brain are inborn and given to humans at the outset of life already in working order.

Further, a group of psychologists led by Michael Lynch (1990) discovered that infants of different ethnic origins distinguish false notes in both their native tonalities and in those of other cultures: Caucasian (white) children are able to tell when something is out of tune in the Javanese tonal system *pelog*, while Indonesian children detected tuning errors in the European tonal system of major and minor keys. Adults tested for the same ability performed much worse: cultural conservatism limited their auditory resources, making the musical concepts of 'ours' and 'others' nowhere near as equivalent as they were to the children. Researchers joyfully made the conclusion that nature prepares humans to perceive all musical cultures without prejudice—only subsequent upbringing constricts our musical horizons.

Specialists never tire of marveling at the auditory potential of infant listeners. D. B. Chamberlain (1988) has chronicled the ability of infants to identify the same melody played at completely different tempos as well as rhythmic changes which disrupt melodies. Chamberlain holds that the strategies of musical perception and the processing of musical information used by adult listeners are already present in infancy. This phenomenon has been termed *perceptive competence*, and has been the subject of a special study by Sandra Trehub and her colleagues who made the following conclusion:

> On the basis of the developmental data presented, infants, young children, and adults appear to perceive novel melodies in fundamentally similar ways. Surprisingly, dramatic differences in

processing capacity and cumulative exposure between infancy and adulthood are not matched by qualitative leaps in musical processing but rather by subtle quantitative changes.[5]

Adult listeners, in reality, simply realize and refine over the course of a lifetime the auditory resources given to them at birth.

An experiment directed by Jenny Saffran and her colleagues (2000) confirmed the significance of man's inborn auditory resources. The subjects of the experiment were 7-week-old children, and the task they were asked to perform was simple: to listen to a 10-minute segment of a Mozart clavier sonata once a day over 2 weeks. Then, after a 2-week break from their listening, all the subjects (and their mothers) were brought to a laboratory where the children were played the same segment again, along with a control segment—a new selection from a different Mozart sonata. Despite the long break, the children recognized the familiar melody; beyond that, they could distinguish the beginning of the familiar segment from its middle, showing a preference for the beginning. The psychologists conducting the experiment were stunned by the ability of the children's memory to differentiate, and by its very capacity—which will by no means be retained by all subjects in the future: experiments with children emerging from infancy discourage rather than evoke optimism as far as human auditory capacities are concerned.

The ability of kindergarten-age children to distinguish changes appearing in variations on a given theme does not differ from the ability of second or fourth grade children to do the same. Vincent Kantorski and Gregory DeNardo (1996) became convinced of this, playing for audiences of children Mozart's Variations on the theme 'Ah, vous dirai-je, Maman'. The school-aged children outdid the kindergartners only in one instance—when, five seconds into the beginning of the fourth variation, they could identify a major–minor contrast between this variation and the basic theme. The distinction of 'major–minor' is not a natural ability, but an acquisition which one makes fairly late in the development of musical perception, as one enters European musical culture; hence, a few years of musical experience make a big difference in one's grasp of it. But overall the researchers were in fact rather surprised that at such a sensitive age musical experience had no significant influence on the auditory capabilities of their subjects: 'There were no significant differences among grades (age groups) in the proportion of students registering a perception of change in the first, third, and fifth seconds of any of the variations'.[6] The percentage of 'sharp-eared' subjects among groups of ascending ages does not increase, concluded Kantorski and DeNardo, which speaks to the natural origins of perceptive competence.

Many researchers have noted significant differences among children in their ability to sing, repeat musical figures, and remember them. Kira Tarasova, a Russian specialist in child musicality, has addressed this (1988); Sandra Trehub and her colleagues (Trehub *et al.* 1984), for their part, have demonstrated that 5-month-old infants perceive the difference

[5] Trehub, S., Schellenberg, E. G., and Hill, D. S. (1997) The origins of music perception and cognition: a developmental perspective. In *Perception and Cognition of Music* (eds J. Sloboda, I. Deliege, *et al.*). Hove, UK: Psychology Press/Erlbaum, p. 103.

[6] Kantorski, V. J. and DeNardo, G. F. (1996) An assessment of children's discrimination of change when listening to a theme and variations form. *Psychomusicology*, 15, p. 69.

between melodies with the same contour but with different sound order. These young listeners deserve our applause, as not all adults are capable of making such fine distinctions. But psychologists have not failed to note that these brilliant results were in fact shown by only half the subjects of the experiment. It is entirely possible that in 10 years time, from the half denoted as 'sharp-eared' infants will emerge children who can sing on key and remember familiar melodies—whereas those who cannot will be traced back to the other half, the group who did not stand out for their aural abilities at the age of 5 months. The more modest musical accomplishments of some infants in comparison with others can in no way be explained by differences in experience and upbringing, which underlines once again the inborn character of human musicality.

Peter Noy (1968) has noted that highly musical children demonstrate heightened interest in sounds while still in infancy. In this respect they resemble the great composers and performers—who are indeed most likely drawn from their ranks. Noy points out that sound is the principal communicative canal between mother and child, and children with a heightened sensitivity to the nuances of communication have a tendency to become particularly musical. Their ear for intonation, evincing a curiosity about sounds and sound communication, already harbors a potential for development into advanced musical ability, and perhaps into real talent. The musicality of these children emerges so early, in Noy's view, precisely because it is an innate quality, present from birth.

The most convincing evidence of the inborn nature of musical ability is drawn from experiments with identical twins, whose auditory capabilities are identical. Billie Thompson and Susan Andrews (2000) asked 136 pairs of identical twins and 148 pairs of fraternal twins between the ages of 18 and 74 to determine whether there were false notes in familiar tunes played for their benefit. Both members of each pair of twins grew up in the same family, so the influence of environment was the same in each case. The identical twins, in the end, showed much greater similarity in their answers. Researchers concluded that the influence of heredity on the level of auditory development was close to 80 percent, with the subjects demonstrating 'no effect of shared environment'. This conclusion was reached using special statistical techniques from the field of genetic modeling. The other research group experimenting with pitch processing of identical vs. fraternal twins came to the same conclusions: the influence of shared genes is more important that shared environments, with a heritability of 70–80 percent (Drayna et al. 2001).

Research on perfect pitch has confirmed beyond doubt the innate character of this phenomenon. As recounted above, a paper before the American Society for Human Genetics presented an analysis of 600 people with absolute pitch. Twenty-five percent of their brothers and sisters also possessed the same gift—whereas among musicians without perfect pitch only 1 percent of the siblings were so endowed. Genes played the decisive role in the development of perfect pitch, concluded the assembled scholars. The case for genetic inheritance of non-perfect pitch also has scientific evidence behind it, though not as weighty. Experiments of this kind always allow a certain margin for error, since the experimenters can only study those children and parents who agree to take part in the study. Experiments with relatives demonstrate that the closer the relationship of the subjects, the more likely (and the closer) will be the similarities in the level of auditory characteristics. Unrelated subjects show no correlation, while twins have a very close connection. This tendency confirms the theory of an inherited mechanism for the transfer of musical abilities—that is, their innate and genetic origins.

Family as the carrier of musical talent

In the well-known Nature vs. Nurture debate, if we speak of outstanding examples of great talent and great achievement, the scales are clearly tipping in the direction of Nature. A number of previously mentioned studies have confirmed that the environment and the conditions under which talent is developed in early childhood have no direct bearing on whether or not it flourishes subsequently: favorable formative circumstances do not make the children of professional musicians or from musical families more gifted than they are anyway. Beyond this, musical talent has an inborn origin; this is indicated by the results of various experiments with infants, twins, and people with perfect pitch. Thus a certain contradiction arises. On the one hand, musical talent is innate in origin and is not formed in the very early years of life—those most sensitive to external influences. On the other hand, this talent is not inherited: musical children often appear in the families of merely middlingly musical or even marginally musical parents. At the same time absolute unmusicality, if you will, is almost one hundred per cent inherited: extremely unmusical children come from extremely unmusical families.

Yet all these seemingly contradictory assertions are in fact congruent with the inherited nature of musicality. The fact of the inheritance of total *un*musicality appears very significant in this regard: the absence of an inherited characteristic is passed along 100 percent of the time, and if the parents are healthy and have no hereditary ailments then one may predict with assurance that their children will be healthy and will not have inherited ailments. So it is with musicality: its absence is assiduously passed along by heredity and directly from the parents. The mechanism for direct inheritance of existing characteristics, including hereditary illnesses, occurs genetically with a much lower probability. If one parent suffers from a hereditary illness, the illness will be passed along to the next generation at an instance of only 50 percent. So it is with talent: if one parent is gifted, this giftedness will occur in the children half the time. But if the other parent lacks giftedness altogether or is only very modestly endowed, then the possibility of giftedness occurring as a 'present' for the couple's children decreases dramatically. Isn't it why traditional upper echelons of society evince such resistance to *mesalliances* in marriage: to maintain a line of 'blue blood' and various abilities acquired over centuries, doesn't it behoove one to marry someone similar in genetic makeup to oneself? A lowering of the intellectual and cultural level by the second parent could decrease the probability of the children of an 'unequal' marriage inheriting high ability levels either.

Presumably, musicality is inherited—but it is often inherited from relatives other than parents. Who then is its carrier? To pursue this question L. Gedda and colleagues (Gedda *et al.* 1961) conducted an experiment using the members of the Choir of the Sistine Chapel in Rome. This group is composed of boys from 11 to 15 years of age, all blessed with an excellent ear and a fine memory for music. Gedda assembled as many of the boys' relatives as he could—brothers, sisters, uncles, aunts, cousins, and so on—and tested their acoustic abilities. As a control he used an analogous group of boys the same age but chosen acoustically at random, without pre-selection for a musical ear. Relatives of the control group members also participated. There was no doubt that boys from the Sistine Chapel would get higher marks in musical tests than their random peers. But what about their relatives? Neither group of relatives consisted of professional musicians. However, the 'Sistine' relatives overwhelmingly surpassed the relatives of the non-Sistine boys in aural characteristics. It bears noting here that analogous experiments done directly with the parents of musical children have always shown a much lower correlation, leading researchers to conclude that the carrier of musicality was not merely the immediate family of a musical child, but in fact his extended family—his entire family tree.

Henry Wing (1963) has also done considerable work in the search for the carrier of inherited musicality. Wing collected data on the number of musical instruments in the homes of musical children. There turned out to be a direct correlation between the number and the children's musicality: if in a given home both a piano and a guitar were found, there was a higher probability of a musical child living there than if there were either one instrument or the other. When the psychologist determined the origin of the instruments, it turned out that they were in the main left there by music-making relatives, some of whom had died and some of whom had moved elsewhere. And even if the parents did not themselves play them, the instruments remained in the homes as fond legacies. The larger the number of instruments, in some families there were three or four different ones, the more likely it was that there were significant musical abilities in the family tree, representing an extended family with a high 'musical aggregate'. This kind of musicality turned up with significant probability among the children of such families— independent of the musicality (or lack of it) of the parents. This pattern is all the more significant for the fact that Wing chose as the independent variable not simply the aural characteristics of the children, but also their architectonic ear, esthetic sense and musical taste, all of which he measured in his tests.

In order to assess the connection of a given individual's musical giftedness with that of his extended family, one may provisionally divide the musically talented into several groups according to the degree of their manifestation and the strength of their musical gifts. The first group is made up of professional musicians. Information on them has already been proffered here, in the accounts of research using the Sistine choir group, the school for gifted children and the beginning concert pianists. These experiments point to a certain 'spreading out' of musical giftedness as it courses through a family's history, notable particularly among musical children who become professional musicians. These children inherited their musicality from their relatives, most likely from those whom Wing described: amateur musicians, the family's music lovers.

Observing the patterns of appearance and disappearance of giftedness in family trees, geneticists have noted that the extended family appears to have as a sort of 'hidden agenda'—

the production of genius. For genius occurs as the realization of the foreordained 'destiny' of a family, its role in the greater human scheme of things. Giftedness builds up over time in a family, broadening and deepening its roots until the tree in question presents the world with a full-fledged genius. This idea was expressed by the Russian geneticist Nikolai Dubinin, and has been confirmed by examples from the biographies of leading lights of the music world (Dubinin and Glembotsky 1967).

A family's path toward the production of genius is connected with an ever more significant concentration of giftedness. The greater this concentration becomes (and the more self-evident the giftedness), the closer the family is to the birth of a genius. If one takes the world's great composers, of which there have been no more than a few dozen, one sees that the concentration and depth of the family's musicality becomes all-consuming in the genetic pool. The composers' biographies indicate not merely immediate families which are musical or notable musicality in the extended families, but an extraordinary distribution of musical talent among various members of the tree, encompassing not only the immediate family of the genius but the families of his relatives as well. (We should note here that data on the extended families of the great *performers* of music is unfortunately sparse. Unlike the biographies of the great composers, the performers' biographies have been researched only fitfully, with the musicality of their extended families often neglected. In any event, the data we do have indicate a clear pattern: outstanding musical performers do not appear *ex nihilo*, but are born in families into which musicality has long since implanted itself).

The great conductor Arturo Toscanini was born into the family of a tailor in the city of Parma. The family was a music-making one: the house was regularly filled with song, and the father, his craft notwithstanding, was a devoted music and theater lover who spent much of his time at the local opera house. Young Arturo was sent off by his father without a second thought to the Royal Music School, where he began to study the cello. Material considerations also played a role: the tailor's family lived in poverty, whereas the best students at the music school received scholarship support from the age of nine onward. The young Toscanini excelled; by the age of 13 he began earning extra income working with Parma's orchestras (Toscanini 1974).

Another outstanding conductor, Herbert von Karajan, was the son of a successful Vienna physician. Von Karajan's uncle (his father's brother) was a well-known engineer and a great music lover. In the von Karajan family music was heard continuously; as his older brother Wolfgang took piano lessons, young Herbert hid behind a partition and learned all the pieces by heart (Osborne 1991). Though his practical parents were not enthusiastic about giving their second son over to music as well (as they assumed naming one son after Mozart was sufficient), Herbert at length overcame their resistance, demanding and receiving music lessons of his own. After the father gave in, it soon became clear that he had been right to do so: once Herbert was allowed to pursue his own instincts, the rest, as the saying has it, was history.

The violinist Fritz Kreisler came from an extraordinarily musical family. The father, as in the von Karajan family, was a well-known physician. The family house was often host to quartet groups, in which Kreisler senior was an active participant. The young Fritz began playing the violin after a fashion at the age of 3: a cigar box served as the body of the fiddle, and shoelaces made a makeshift bow. Soon the young improviser was playing along with the visiting quartets, and by the age of 7 he was enrolled in the Vienna Conservatory—from which he graduated at the age of 10 with a gold medal. Recalling his childhood years later, Kreisler remarked that 'It may be that I became a professional musician for the very reason that my father unconsciously wanted to fulfill in me his own unrealized dreams of being a violinist'.[7]

The same was true for David Oistrakh: his father was a great lover of music, but did not become a professional musician. As Oistrakh recalled

> No matter how hard I search my memory, I cannot recall myself as a child without a violin. I was three and a half years old when my father brought home a toy violin, which I 'played', so to speak, fondly imagining myself a street musician—a melancholy profession, and one widespread in Odessa at that time. I got so carried away with this make believe street fiddling that when at age five I finally got my first real violin and started taking music lessons, the pursuit of music simply took me over altogether.[8]

Gifted fathers with unrealized musical talent comprise a sort of 'mini-pattern' among the biographies of outstanding performers and selected composers. Paul McCartney's father played in an amateur jazz orchestra and gave up his longtime interest in the trumpet only when forced to do so by dental problems (*Paul McCartney in his own Words* 1983). Recalling this unrequited love, the elder McCartney gave young Paul a new trumpet as a birthday present. But the latter had no interest in learning to play it, dreaming instead of success as a singer—which simply could not be combined with horn playing. Paul traded in the trumpet for a guitar and triumphantly brought it home, after which the senior McCartney made peace with his son's musical independence and encouraged him to expand his musical horizons further. The outstanding Russian composer Aleksandra Pakhmutova was likewise encouraged by her father, a power station construction worker and great music lover who taught himself to play Chopin waltzes, Beethoven sonatas and classical symphonies with great facility on the piano. Indeed, Nikolai Pakhmutov provides a good illustration of what the concept of a 'highly gifted' person can really encompass: not only was he a wonderful pianist, but an accomplished water color artist, photographer, and radio technician as well.

Rather less is known about the musical abilities of the mothers of the world's outstanding musicians. That said, there are nevertheless certain cases that may be taken as representative (or at least illustrative), among which is that of the family of the great twentieth-century tenor Mario Lanza. Lanza's father, Antonio Cocozza, was clearly the head of the household in what was a very musical family; employed as a minor clerk, he had had a passion for playing the French horn in his youth. Returning from the battlefields of World War I, Antonio walked into a bakery in Philadelphia and saw behind the counter the proprietor's charming daughter, Maria Lanza—who turned out to be a devoted music

[7] Yampolsky, I. (1975) *F. Kreisler*. Moscow: Muzyka, p. 37.
[8] Oistrakh, D. (1978) *Moi put'. Vospominania, statii, interviu, pisma. /My way. Memoirs, Articles, Interviews, Letters*. Moscow: Muzyka, p. 131.

lover and particular devotee of singing (Callinicos 1960). The singing career Maria dreamed of was not to be her lot—but rather that of the son she bore Antonio. After the couple were wed, their household was constantly filled with music; Antonio, an invalid from the war, was an opera fanatic and passed along this devotion to his son Mario—who took his beloved mother's last name as he made his career, and later maintained that he learned to sing by imitating the family's phonograph records of the great Caruso.

Niccolo Paganini's life developed from a similar scenario: the violinist's father was a stevedore by trade but a fanatic music lover. At the first opportunity he abandoned his laborer's life to become a singing teacher and mandolin salesman (Courcy de 1957). He mercilessly drove Niccolo and his other sons to realize the dream he could not fulfill himself—that of becoming a real professional musician—and clearly had good reason to do so. In any case, the frequency with which one encounters this kind of passionate devotion to amateur music making among the parents of outstanding musicians makes one think that these musicians are recruited from the ranks of those 16.6 percent of musical children (as psychologists have reported) whose parents in *their* time showed signs of an advanced musicality.

All the same, methodologies for the inheritance of musical talent are by no means limited to the multi-generational strengthening of giftedness and its movement into and throughout extended families. There are also contrary examples of a fairly radical nature. George Gershwin, for instance, grew up in the family of a small-time entrepreneur who barely managed to keep himself financially afloat operating a series of small businesses (Jablonski 1987). The senior Gershwin had little business acumen; the bars, baths and other enterprises he put his heart into developing all went bust—which in turn led to merciless nagging by his wife. Mrs Gershwin was not a musical soul, but rather a very practical type who loved to have herself photographed wearing fine furs. She did not encourage her son's musical interests, although she did pay for his music lessons—which was something she viewed as socially appropriate for the family and conducive to aspirations toward middle-class status. The Gershwins' relatives, immigrants from Russia, stayed home for the most part. All told, it is quite difficult to determine who in the (sizeable) extended family of the Gershwins' evinced particular musical abilities and successfully passed them along to George.

Equally mysterious is the origin of the musical talent of the great pianist Arthur Rubinstein, who was in heaven as a youth when left alone with the piano in the living room of his family's prosperous home. As he later recalled:

> Half in fun half in earnest, I learned to know the keys by their names, and with my back to the piano I would call the notes of any chord, even the most dissonant one. From then on it became mere child's play to master the intricacies of the keyboard, and I was soon able to play with one hand, later with both, any tune that caught my ear... All this, of course, could not fail to impress my family—none of whom, I must now admit, including grandparents, uncles, and aunts, had the slightest musical gift... By the time I was three and a half years old my fixation was so obvious that my family decided to do something about this talent of mine.[9]

---

[9] Rubinstein, A. (1973) *My Young Years*. London: Jonathan Cape, p. 5.

Similar cases may also be found among the great composers. It has proven impossible to discover any signs of musical giftedness in the extended family of Gluck. This phenomenon has led Rosamund Shuter-Dyson and Clive Gabriel (1981) to posit an 'untraceable hereditary factor' which led to the appearance of the great musician. Biographies like those of Gluck and Arthur Rubinstein are, in any case, the exceptions that prove the rule. Genetic patterns act as tendencies and probabilities—not with the absoluteness of laws. If we were examining fruit flies instead of outstanding musicians, the exceptional reproductive rate of the former would allow us to isolate such an 'untraceable factor' or at least make some reasonable suppositions about it; but when the subject is people who are in the main deceased, whose family genealogy no one pursued with any particular interest during the principals' lifetime, then it becomes unsurprising that the tracks of musical giftedness throughout the Gluck or Rubinstein families remains lost in the depths of history.

The study of the genealogies of the great composers indicates that their forbears possess more serious potential for producing musical greatness in future generations than do the ancestors of outstanding performers. If the parents of the latter tend to be great lovers of music, and some of them even music makers of a sort, the forbears of the great composers usually go considerably further: their interest exceeds the merely significant, as they themselves play expertly and have the ability to improvise—rendering themselves composers of a sort in their own right. Some relatives of the great composers have been professional musicians, and in a number of cases the fathers of future geniuses. The biography of Francois Couperin, the reigning genius of French music at the turn of the seventeenth–eighteenth centuries, is extremely revealing in this respect.

Couperin's great grandfather Maturin was a country jurist; grandfather Charles chose a career in trade, but was an active music maker, playing the organ (Tessier 1926). Charles' three sons all became professional musicians: the oldest son, Louis, was heard playing the organ by the well-known music master of the time Jacques de Chambonnier, who whisked him off to the capital where he was made royal organist of the court. Along with Louis to Paris went the youngest son Charles, to whom was born in 1668 a son—this was Francois, soon to become the leading musician of his day. The middle brother, Francois' uncle (for whom he was named), gave lessons on the harpsichord; this was a man of a happy disposition and the artistic temperament of a true Frenchman. As contemporaries recalled of this uncle: 'He was a short gray-haired man who loved good wine. He was glad to continue a music lesson when a carafe of wine and some bread were placed in front of him on the harpsichord cover—and he would continue the lesson for as long as the carafe kept being refilled'.[10] Couperin's biography recounts the steady widening of the 'musical field' around him: his father was not merely a music lover, but in time a professional musician himself. His two paternal uncles were also professional musicians, and one of them, Louis, became an outstanding composer. The concentration of musical giftedness among the relatives of the great composer Francois Couperin was very great indeed, far exceeding the analogous concentration one finds in the family trees of great performers.

[10] Tessier, A. (1926) *Couperin*. Paris: Henri Laurens, p. 29.

The family of the nineteenth-century Russian composer Anatoly Lyadov was also very musical—and in various different spheres. Lyadov's father Konstantin was a conductor at the imperial theaters; Konstantin's brothers included one cellist with the imperial ballet, one pianist, one conductor, and one chorister with the imperial opera, while his two sisters, Anna and Elena, were a fine pianist and a chorister of the Italian opera respectively. The conductor-brother's daughter, Vera Lyadova (Lyadov's cousin) became a famous operetta singer. This singular concentration of musical giftedness in one family can be considered exceptional. It is entirely possible, on the other hand, that if Mozart's father Leopold had had as many siblings as Konstantin Lyadov, all the senior Mozarts would have become professional musicians. But history does not recognize the hypothetical mood, so the potential of a different Mozart family tree will remain unexplored. Yet the family history of the Lyadovs is in any case very revealing, as it speaks to the extraordinary strength and breadth of inherited musical giftedness in the genetic stock of the great composers. Nothing similar appears in the backgrounds of the great performers, where in the majority of cases one finds merely a single music-loving parent.

The family of the composer Sergei Rakhmaninov fits this pattern. Sergei's paternal uncle Arkady was a dilettante composer who wrote some 150 musical works in several genres. Sergei's father Vasily was an expert amateur pianist who also had considerable improvisational skill (Rakhmaninov 1964). Sergei's first cousin, the son of the composer's paternal aunt Julia, was the outstanding pianist Alexandre Ziloti. Sergei's sister Elena was accepted at 17 into the Bolshoi Theater troupe (but died soon thereafter). In the family tree of the Rakhmaninovs one finds not only the 'gene of advanced musicality' but a 'composer's talent gene' as well. We may assume that the higher level of musical giftedness came about through the inheritance from a higher level of giftedness in the preceding generation of ancestors, rather than a medium level of giftedness which is not connected with the gift for composition. The giftedness of the older generation of the clan also emerged in the younger generation: Rakhmaninov's father Vasily and uncle Arkady passed along their talent not only to composer Sergei, but also to his cousin Alexandre and his sister Elena.

The extended family of composer Jacques Offenbach was likewise very musical. Offenbach's father was a professional musician who gave flute, guitar, violin, and voice lessons—a musical diversity which itself speaks of significant talent. In Offenbach's native Cologne the family trio of young Jacques, brother Julius and sister Isabelle made quite a name for itself (Decaux 1958). In the family of the composer Georges Bizet the mother's side was extraordinarily musical: Bizet's two maternal uncles were great singers, Camille as first tenor at Rheims and Francois as an outstanding vocal instructor, while the composer's mother, Amie Delsart, became an outstanding pianist. Bizet's father Adolphe was by trade a barber—but being a music fanatic he also tried his hand as a singing teacher, although he had no genuine talent, it seems, and brought little to the calling beyond his passionate love for music (Khohlovkina 1954).

Dmitry Shostakovich's mother was a professional pianist and a graduate of the St. Petersburg Conservatory, while his father was a fine singer. Alexsandre Skriabin's mother had a promising future as a concert pianist but died young. Musical-maker Andrew Lloyd Webber could claim both parents as musicians; the composer Edison Denisov's father could improvise and play by ear and his mother simply adored music. In some instances, if the family in question was of noble stock and financially well off, it is difficult to establish with any real sense of accuracy just how musical the clan actually was—or might have become: the majority of the Russian noble class, for example, did not work for a living; their musicality, whatever it was, could thus be defined only on an amateur scale. As Modest Tchaikovsky, his brother's biographer, recalled: 'According to stories my mother and father told, my paternal uncle, Pavel Petrovich, was possessed of enormous musical abilities—he could play entire overtures and other pieces by ear, wonderfully and fluently, without reading a note'.[11] This kind of musicality can be termed exceptional, going far beyond the bounds of the devotion to music typical of the standard educated music lover.

Outstanding performers, as a rule, do not come from such all-encompassingly musical families—and the 'composer's gene' is not visible in their family trees. Such a situation might be explained by the fact that in a family where there are few children, the breadth of giftedness within the clan may not have 'room' to appear, merely remaining in the wings as a potential or latent presence. In support of this reasoning one can cite examples of musical families with many children, such as the family of the outstanding violinist Jacques Thibauld. Thibauld's father was the first violinist of an opera orchestra. Two of Jacques' brothers, both marvelous pianists, went on to head conservatories in Buenos Aires and Bordeaux. A third brother, an outstanding violinist, died at an early age, while a fourth brother was an excellent cellist and became head of the conservatory in Oran. All told, only two of the seven Thibauld brothers showed no musical gifts whatsoever (Thibaud 1953).

Some psychologists, in insisting on the hereditary origins of musical talent, reach rather further than conventional analysis might warrant. J. Mjoen (1926) could not believe that a certain pianist of world-class stature could come from a family with two entirely unmusical parents. Mjoen went to extraordinary lengths in researching the woman's family tree, and in the end successfully proved that the pianist was in fact the illegitimate daughter of a well-known musician. There was no truly scientific basis for his suspicions: the hereditary transfer of 'high musicality', as we have seen, is a regular pattern rather than an absolute law. One can add another just-named pattern to the number of hereditary tendencies for musical giftedness: the greater the gift of the musician, the wider and deeper the musicality of the relatives who came before him.

The average professional musician finds in his family tree a certain 'musical point' which appears sporadically among the generations and is never of too high a range. Outstanding performers are 'narrowing' the circle of musicality to the members of their families—their fathers are often musically gifted but could not become professional

----

[11] Tchaikovsky, M. I. (1903) *Zhizn' P.I.Tchaikovskogo/Life of Pyotr Iliych Tchaikovsky*. Moscow: Izdatelstvo Jurgensona, p. 41.

musicians for one reason or another and see the fulfillment of their musical dreams in the successful careers of their sons. The extended families of the great composers seem to go through 'rehearsals' before giving birth to a genius; among the forbears of the latter are signs not only of musical giftedness, but of fully realized composer's talent.

The musicality of the family lineage of an outstanding musician is, as a rule, very broad; it includes not only the musician himself, his parents, and other relatives of the preceding generation, but his siblings as well. The case of the Bach brothers is well known: three sons of the great Johann Sebastian Bach—Philip-Emmanuel, Johann Christian, and Wilhelm Friedeman Bach—were all outstanding composers. Felix Mendelsohn's sister Fanny was an outstanding pianist, as was Mozart's sister Nannerl. Haydn's brother Michael was also an outstanding musician and a fine composer. Larger families insure not only the survival of the family line, but the survival of talent embedded in that line. Wolfgang Amadeus Mozart was the seventh child in his family, although only him and his sister Nannerl survived into adulthood: it is sobering to think of what the world would have lost if Anna and Leopold Mozart had decided to limit the number of their children.

Analysis of biographical details provides material for well-grounded hypotheses and speculations if not to say 'evidence' of the innate character and inheritability of musical talent (and is it really possible to gain real evidence when potential 'subjects'—those few boasting world fame and glory as musicians, are unaccessible for experimental work?). There may be some comfort in the fact that each human being figures somewhere in an invisible 'line of genius': with the birth and upbringing of children, every parent brings closer the point of appearance of the genius genetically programmed as the acme of this particular lineage, its yet unrevealed goal. The development of talent, granted by nature, and the search for pairs capable of genetically strengthening that talent, comes about at the behest of fate itself—for only destiny knows in advance of a coming burst of genius, the appearance of a talent whose very parents have no idea they are matched to create even as they search determinedly for one another.

Teacher and pupil

Can a musical ear be developed?

Every new skill one acquires, every step one takes forward in some area of knowledge, is naturally associated with the expenditure of effort. Teachers and their pupils try to measure the extent of this effort objectively in order to assess three things: what the result of their labor was; whether this result was in fact worth the effort; and what can and should be done in the field, meaning what direction should be chosen to make further progress, if such is deemed possible. Common sense tells us that directed study of any sort is never a hindrance; indeed, it and perhaps only it can bring the student closer to the intended goal. But is it always possible to reach that goal? Are not the efforts of young musicians sometimes like those of a traveler approaching the horizon—a point which is defined as constantly receding as one advances toward it, remaining always the same distance away? Or perhaps there is some sort of musical magic wand, the waving of which can transform one from a musical dwarf to a giant by the sudden multiplication of a person's musical resources?

Such questions are not easily answered by conducting psychology experiments: the learning conditions of each beginning musician are too individualized to generalize about; the abilities, the strengths, and weaknesses, of each music pupil are likewise too differentiated for summary judgments; and finally, both the methods of each instructor and the pedagogical talent said instructor brings to the process can only be x factors in any attempted formula for musical development.

Beyond this, research experiments on the effectiveness of music lessons cannot (or should not) be single-shot affairs; they must be, rather, longitudinal, as the psychologists put it—extended, systematic, and involving many years of observation. But this type of analysis is done considerably less often than one-time testing, as it demands, obviously, considerably greater expenditures of time and means. In sum, the music world can probably best estimate where best to put the greatest part of its instructional resources by contrasting its own working observations with whatever scientific data are available, thus making only provisional judgments on the psychological potential of various of the methodologies now being used in musical pedagogy.

Many students in beginning-level musical schools would like to improve their aural capabilities, their 'ear for music'. Researchers studying the development of aural perception are looking at the influence of methodology on the development of the ear under conditions as close as possible to those of natural music making. The results of these experiments show how various methodologies influence children's aural capabilities.

Music instructor Joanne Rutkowski (1996) has studied this influence on the most natural of all methods—singing. Rutkowski wanted to find the extent of dependence that existed between the study of singing and the native ability of the analytic ear—one's sense of musical pitch. She was ready to assume that systematic instruction in singing would refine and sharpen the sense of pitch among those tested. Before the experiment 14 kindergarten children were tested for pitch. After this initial testing the children played musical games and sang songs over the course of a year. In addition to the usual music classes in school, the children took voice lessons several times a week with individual instructors. The control group of children from the same kindergarten had no individualized instruction and no special small-group voice lessons, but in all other respects enjoyed the same music instruction—the same regiment of songs and games—that the experimental subjects did. At the end of a year it turned out that the specially trained children exceeded those of the control group only in vocal skills. In no other area did the subject children's sense of pitch change at all, suggesting that systematic study of voice does not influence or improve one's sense of pitch.

Music teacher Beverly Martin (1991) conducted a study of the effects of gesture, syllable, and letter association in the development of the musical ear. Students in the first grade sang and memorized short motifs over the course of 17 weeks at the beginning of each music class (for 9 minutes, thrice a week). Three groups took part in the experiment: one went about the assigned task in the standard way; the second incorporated hand and arm gestures into the learning process; and a third accompanied their singing with cards which denoted the different sounds. Over the course of 17 weeks all three groups supplemented their singing with visual impressions of the same motifs written as letters on the blackboard. After all three groups had undergone various hearing tests it emerged that none of the methodologies offered any particular advantage: the association of the musical motifs with gestures, letters, and notes served the same fruitless end, as none of the students' aural capabilities were improved.

In the context of the broadening and methodological diversification of practices in the development of the musical ear in many countries, these experiments appear fairly naive. They involve non-professional methodologies of developing aural skills, and take place in kindergartens and the early elementary school years. The addition of a half-hour a week of musical training, no matter how systematic, cannot be expected to produce significant results. In the opinion of many teachers the process of development of the musical ear is long and demands great effort; achieving real success with a 'judicious minimal investment' simply will not work. Joanne Rutkowski's methods are more natural and calculated to work over a long period, but the content of the singing lessons and the methodology used by the instructor may also not have been the most effective—hence the lower-than-expected results.

Further, despite the fact that any given experiment in this area can be rendered suspect on methodological grounds, their relative distance in time also lends conviction to their conclusions: the experiments described above stand in a line of similar efforts, not one of whose results contradict any of the others', although they were carried out under different conditions, using different children and different teachers—the experiments cited above, conducted in the United States in the mid-1990s, and those in England in the 1970s yielded the same results. R. Piper and D. Shoemaker (1973) report that 90 twenty-minute lessons thrice a week in a specially created musical program did nothing to improve the aural capabilities of pre-school age children. Another well-known researcher in the area of musical abilities, Edwin Gordon (1979), worked with a group of students over a period of 2 years in an attempt to increase their musical-ear capacities; the subjects demonstrated no significant improvement over that prolonged period. There was an improvement in test scores of all students involved, Gordon reports, but the improvement fell within the range of the test's built-in margin of error, rendering them ephemeral from the outset. It is especially indicative, in the end, that none of the students tested after 2 years of special instruction could demonstrate a gain in ability relative to anyone else in the group—or a loss, for that matter. In other words, no students profited more or less than their peers from the training, which speaks directly of the remarkable stability of the aural abilities that humans are endowed with.

Indeed, all the results gained by all the researchers in this area reinforce traditional skepticism at the idea that the analytical ear can be seriously influenced one way or another. Experiments of this kind simply provide another indication of the 'conservatism' of the ear, which cannot be improved by mere practice. The researchers remind the musical community that in the course of music making, musical games, singing, and reinforcement with gestures and visual associations, the aural capabilities do not expand. And if the achievement of any effect at all depends on extremely intensive study, beyond that undertaken for existing studies, will temporary expenditures be sufficient? Are such measures critical to success? And if achieving success depends using a super-professional instructor who is an expert in the particular methodologies for influencing aural capabilities, then how important will it be to 'drag along' into this process someone with merely adequate aural data? And will such a person's general musicality and musical responsiveness grow along with the intensive aural training she receives?

Professional means of training the musical ear are also not always effective. This was amply demonstrated by the work of Gerard Fogarty, Louise Buttsworth, and Philip Gearing (1996). They took a group of 87 student musicians aged 17–50 years and examined the extent to which their ability to correctly intone a melody could be influenced by the study of *solfeggio*—special vocal exercises (called 'aural training' in Britain) aimed at the development of the ear and the acquisition of music-reading ability. To increase the breadth and accuracy of the results, musicians of different specialties and instruments were chosen. All the subjects were given intonation tests three times over the course of an academic year. As the researchers concluded, a repeated measures analysis of variance failed to find evidence of either overall improvement in student performance across the three test administrations, or any significant differences on the intonation tests between musicians of different instrumental families. Results indicate that intonation tests tap an ability that is not significantly modified by training, is more or less the same across different instrument families, and is related to success in music training programs. This concerns the internal ear and the sense of tonality, which is what pitch discrimination depends on. The experimenters did not discover significant improvement in this ability during the period in which the subjects practiced *solfeggio*.

Particularly conservative is the musical memory, which is a reflection and continuation of the human internal ear. Polish researcher Jan Horbulewicz (1963) examined the musical memory of some 473 children entering music school (at the elementary-school level). After retesting his subjects several years later, Horbulewicz concluded that music studies were not a decisive factor in the development of musical memory, and that the pace at which memory grows is not influenced by music studies either. He further noted, with particular emphasis, the same condition that Edwin Gordon had called attention to: after 10 years of study in the same program, significant individual differences remain in the students' abilities: the best remain the best and the worst remain the worst. As Rosamund Shuter-Dyson and Clive Gabriel commented apropos of measuring musical memory among more- and less-experienced musicians (in experiments conducted by a group led by S. E. Gaede): 'Of great interest to the music educator is that musical experience had no effect on the results, which were as true for the experienced musicians (as defined in the experiment) as for the inexperienced. This result suggests that those aspects of musical ability used in the experiment are not trainable to any great extent'.[1]

Unlike the traditional testing and experimental probing of knowledge, skill, and functionality that all music teachers and their pupils recognize, psychological testing measures instead abilities, that is the psychological instruments with whose help people acquire knowledge, skills, and functional accomplishment. While knowledge and functional accomplishment obviously grow and become more complex in the course of activity in a given field, abilities remain unchanged—such is the possible supposition from psychological research. The eminent Russian psychologist Sergei Rubinstein (1973) held that abilities are defined by the quality of the processes of analysis and synthesis and the generalization of relationships: abilities, Rubinstein maintained, are the operational apparatus of human consciousness, helping us to receive information systematically, analyze it, and create the algorithms necessary for action. Abilities as a psychological operating system, as a sort of psychological tool chest of the conscious mind, are not the same as skills, which are acquired with abilities' help. Abilities simply explain the speed and quality with which we master skills, and thus explain the differences in these areas among individual people. Abilities determine the action strategy of a person and the methods of absorbing and refining information which he brings to bear.

It is entirely possible to master increasingly complex functions while employing strategy which is not altogether adequate. Every *solfeggio* instructor knows that certain students, possessed of a good sense of tonality, can write out rather difficult musical dictations, quickly jotting them down note for note without error. In the course of doing this, however, no overall picture of the musical fragment in question is being formed in the

---

[1] Shuter-Dyson, R. and Gabriel, C. (1981) *The Psychology of Musical Ability*. London: Methuen, p. 264.

students' consciousness: they don't remember the piece in terms of structure or the relationships of its musical elements. However the result is obvious: with a good sense of tone but a bad ear for harmonics or a bad musical memory, one can still successfully take difficult musical dictation.

Does this successful dictation of more complex musical fragments give proof of further development of the musical ear and memory? No, it does not: the strategy for dealing with the material remains the same; thus a new level of quality in the processes of analysis and synthesis will not be reached, meaning a new level of the processing of musical information will not be attained.

The practice of determining chord progression—when the student replaces the harmonic ear with the melodic—is analogous: the student in the main hears the bass voice, and by means of selection from among a limited number of possibilities she correctly names the chords. She does not demonstrate any sort of harmonic ear in this process: the appearance of mastering a complex function is in place, but there has been no development in ability. An increase in the students' fund of knowledge and an increased complexity in the functions they have mastered in no way speaks of the development of their aural characteristics—this is what the results of psychological testing may convincingly show. As Evgeny Ilyin, the researcher of abilities and talent, puts it:

> It is not surprising that taken broadly any change in the activity's effectiveness and quality is taken as an indicator of the abilities' development, and the fact that a student gains knowledge and skills creates an illusion of such development easily happening. Thus the selection problem is also dismissed: why bother if the abilities are easily developed (due to the individual working style acquisition, due to the changing of the attitude to work or due to skills and knowledge increase)? Just consider that skills and knowledge acquisition or working out the learning style—all depends on the extent and level of the abilities present—only this shows how 'ability development' concept is in fact wrong.[2]

At some point the methods of processing information which a particular ability has at its disposal will cease to be effective. To take the case of writing musical dictation, for example: performing this function at a faster pace or with a fragment of more complex harmonic composition will lead to a situation in which the 'note after note' strategy of perception will not help: for the fulfillment of a more complex task a different strategy will be necessary, qualitatively different processes of analysis and synthesis than the ones available to the given ability. That is the point at which an individual's 'ceiling' is reached: the person cannot execute more difficult tasks no matter how much effort she puts into the process because her abilities cannot provide a strategy for performing the action necessary to do the job. There may be a will, but there simply cannot be a way.

Music educators and teachers in some cases speak of having noted a threshold beyond which further training does not yield improvement. Changing the practice methodology can in such cases provide a certain gain, but as a rule this is temporary, unstable and to a certain extent ephemeral. This is why even the most resolute and assiduous music

---

[2] Ilyin, E. (2004) *Psikhologia individualnikh razlichii/The Psychology of Individual Differences*. St.-Petersburg: Piter, p. 226–7.

students do not become Mozarts—systematic practice yields incremental rises in knowledge and functionality, but it cannot spur a qualitative growth in the abilities with which a given person is naturally endowed in the first place. An old acquisition strategy can maintain its effectiveness for a long period, but not forever; a breakthrough will emerge, and the medicine prescribed for such a breakthrough can only be a realistic evaluation of the abilities of one's pupils.

The absence of ability superiority between more- and less-experienced and more- and less-educated people is clear from the example of the comparison of musicians and non-musicians. It is broadly stated that musicians exceed non-musicians only when they are provided with musical contexts in which to work and familiar conditions too. Boris Teplov, citing his colleagues' experiments, wrote:

> Musically educated people are superior to non-musicians in terms of sensitivity to pitch mainly in the confines of the minor and first octaves—that is, in the zone primarily used in music. In lower and higher registers the difference in sensitivity to pitch among these two groups is insignificant.[3]

The musician's ear feels particularly unsure of itself when psychologists ask it to perform exercises involving atonal music. Here the functions acquired during musical training and associated normally with the music of the preceding eras is of no help, and the musicians make mistakes exactly like those made by people with no musical background at all (Starcheus 2003). This applies to professional musicians with average aural characteristics (who make up the majority). Musicians with exceptional aural capabilities cope with the tasks given them in atonal musical contexts just as successfully as they do with standard tonal ones. The differences noted by psychologists in the performance of subjects with different musical-system backgrounds simply demonstrate that the superiority of the professionals is sometimes connected not with the superiority of their abilities, but rather with their considerable compilation of knowledge, skill, and functional accomplishment. The smallest deviation from familiar tasks in the testing procedures immediately reveals this heretofore hidden truth.

Clifford and Kate Madsen (2002) conducted the research where musicians, non-musicians, and children were supposed to recognize a familiar tune among others, not highly contrasting to the target one. Musicians supposed that their superiority will turn undoubtful and children will be simply unable to accomplish such task. How wrong they were. Children's results were totally compatible with that of the musicians', and the only undoubtful thing here was the difference in skills and experience between all participants in spite of which 'the weakest' (children) easily came along with 'the strongest' (musicians) in this musical memory 'contest' (Madsen and Madsen 2002).

In the course of a person's life, the discovery, manifestation, and realization of her abilities and gifts goes on apace—but the same cannot be said of their qualitative growth and development: the musical abilities of the majority of adults are entirely comparable with those of children. Researchers investigating musical perception have confirmed this,

---

[3] Teplov, B. M. (1985) Psihologiya muzykal'nyh sposobnostei/The psychology of musical abilities. In *Izbrannie trudy, t. I/Selected Works*, vol.I, (ed. M. G. Yaroshevsky). Moscow: Pedagogika, p. 143.

noting that the qualities of fragmentariness, non-exactitude, timbre-textured orientation, and diffusion—are all characteristics which adults share with children. It is enough to recall the experiment conducted by Lyle Davidson (1994) in which he asked adult subjects to create a means of notation for recording the song 'Happy Birthday'. The adults' aural development and musical thinking proved no more advanced than those of 8-year-old children.

The musical tastes of a society confirm the limitations of its aural resources. Societies clearly tend to prefer simple music to complex: the widespread popularity of rock and roll and pop music in comparison to classical can be explained to a certain extent in bio-psychological terms. Rock and pop music are close to the oldest of musical roots, for in them lives the spirit of improvisation and collective joy which gave life to the musical art form in earliest antiquity. These forms of music are closely connected in their original essence with nature: for the appreciation of the great mass of compositions in the popular musical genres one does not need a refined analytical ear or a great musical memory. Rock and pop fanatics may, of course, possess such qualities, along with other advanced musical abilities; it is just that in these particular genres they have no need to use them.

Following from the phylogenetic model of giftedness and the attendant concept of the origin of talent, the aural capabilities of the majority of people cannot be otherwise. The natural processes which dictate the genetic development of the human race are simply too conservative; biological evolution takes place too slowly. Abilities and giftedness are in greater measure a natural and psychological rather than a socio-cultural phenomenon. Many thousands of years went by before the sense of rhythm, and then the analytical ear, arose from the depths of our expressive hearing. This was a process which included many stages in the development of the human brain, the development of human consciousness and of the power of speech. An exceptional ear and musical memory, which only a few of us possess, are natural gifts culled over the course of an enormously long period of human development. Each new stage in the growth of abilities signals the next step in the path of development of the human species, and no individual human is given to cover the whole way in a brief period of study. It is hardly surprising that the apex of aural evolution is reached by only a select few. *Homo Sapiens* and *Homo Musicus* as a biological species do not develop that fast, and the majority of the representatives of humankind may well be at the same stage of aural development at which our distant ancestors arrived. Only those capabilities of our psyche and musicality which arose before the others—the expressive ear and the sense of rhythm, in this case—are comparatively widespread among the species as a whole. The abilities acquired later are distributed considerably less widely, and no matter how hard we strive, there is no such thing as leaping across a chasm in two jumps: no one's efforts can compensate for the unfathomably long time it took nature to create the higher properties of the musical mind on her own.

The phylogenetic approach simply confirms certain assumptions coming from psychological experiments and practical experience: that abilities are not so much developed, but simply manifest themselves and are brought to their full fruition in the reality of putting them to use. The only things which actually grow are the knowledge, skills, and functional applications which abilities help foster—the technological 'equipment' a person can bring to bear and the volume of information at his command. The most effective method of development of abilities can probably be the repetition of the phylogenetic path of evolution, the repetition of the steps of the development of the ear and musical thinking which mankind has taken. The student would move from an awareness of the expressiveness of sound, from the penetration into the character and ideational under-pinnings of musical communication, to the secrets of musical movement, the mastery of the language of the body through rhythm, and on to the organization of musical time.

A radical improvement of the musical ear, a genuine enrichment of its capabilities, would be connected with a sort of 'phylogenetic theatricalization' of the instruction process whereby the student would relive, as it were, the enormous evolutionary stage of the devel-opment of tonality [lad], the formation of musical morphology, lexicon, and syntax—it would be as though the student created music and its language right alongside primitive man. Other methods, based on the mechanical repetition of known musical elements, are only marginally effective, as practice has shown. They treat the symptoms rather than the illness, trying through the increase of functional improvement via the mastery of algorithms to qualitatively affect abilities. Only a specific labor—that very labor which reproduces the labor the human species exerted throughout the difficult period of the establishment of the musical ear—can help a music student rise to the next evolutionary level in the development of musicianship. That will possibly be the most natural and effective avenue.

There exists one more possibility of retaining natural musical potential that children display at the very earliest stages of the establishment of the musical ear. Some children show a fairly high level of aural development which planes off later in life. We can sup-pose relying on the research data that a high level of musicality and the good ear that accompanies it begin with a heightened attention on the child's part to sound as a whole, to its expressive possibilities. A musically gifted child wants to communicate by means of sound, the method which seems to her the most natural and desirable. According to the observations of parents, musically gifted children begin to sing before they begin to speak—repeating the phylogenetic path of the development of hearing and speech. The natural path of development of a good ear is connected with the child recognizing the expressive capabilities of sound—they are something she understands; and wishing to use these capabilities, her aural potential remains on a high level. At the base of the retention of these resources lies motivation, a particular motivation connected with the expressive ear; this is a musical necessity for the youngster, one which she has already managed to sense.

The key to the musical development of the child and of the student lies precisely here, in the growth of her musical motivation—her love for music and understanding of its possibilities. This path is the most natural and the most phylogenetically justified. So moved humanity—first defining the goal of the movement, its imagined result, and then finding the capability of reaching the goal, making the desired end a reality. That is exactly how abilities develop. Their base and cornerstone is motivation. In supporting musical motivation, making it a more and more conscious endeavor, one can awaken the aural reserves in a person—in fact, they themselves unfold, following the lead of the person's conscious intent. One can only agree with Boris Asafiev, who held that music 'is a world of ideation which values both that which sounds and that which sound gathers around it—the rays of thought whose very reason for being music is'.[4] Focusing these rays, turning them into sound—this is the surest way to develop musical abilities, the best catalyst of these abilities' natural growth.

Ustanovka: mindset for success

Every beginning musician wants Dame Fortune to smile on him, and everyone knows the signs of her favor: a natural musical gift is, of course, essential—for without that no other circumstances, no matter how favorable, will avail one anything. Starting early in life, at age 5 or 6, is also a kind of blessing: the mind is open, the pupil's receptivity is still at a point where it exceeds all imaginable boundaries. It would likewise be a considerable plus if the young musician's parents understood and supported him—and did so without shaking a stick at him or turning the house into a 'musical boot camp'. It is also extraordinarily desirable to engage an outstanding music teacher, as early as possible and for the long haul, who could become a second father or second mother to the pupil. It would likewise be good for the student to demonstrate her accomplishments in public, though such performing would be limited and would not have as its goal the creation of a concert *wunderkind*. All these wishes apply equally to those who will want to become professional musicians and those who will remain amateurs. In practice, however, these ideal conditions are apportioned by Fate to almost no one; reality invariably turns out to be a good deal less charitable, and the would-be musician has to find within himself the resourcefulness to gain his own foothold in music, and then continue on the long path without falling by the wayside. In the language of psychology, that initial foothold has been called the *set*; it carries connotations of both *mindset* and *attitude* as well. In Russian, in any case, it is termed *ustanovka [oo-stahn-off-kah]*—which we will use here—and might best be described as the point at which one is totally attuned to and entirely ready for successful engagement in a specific activity.

The *ustanovka* theory was first propounded by the Georgian psychologist Dmitry N. Uznadze (1886–1950). This theory directs a person's attention to the internal components of success and to an individual's particular relationship to an activity (as external circumstances are not always under our control). Change yourself and you change both who you are and your relationship to the matter at hand—and you raise the probability of success in your undertaking; such is the unspoken message of *ustanovka* theory. As Uznadze notes:

> '*Ustanovka*, as has been observed more than once, is not an experience of a private nature or some sort of defined motor activity on the part of the subject. It is, rather, a specific modification of the subject as such and as a whole; thus it makes no sense to present it as an intellectual process or any

---

[4] Asafiev, B. (1926) *De Musica*. St. Petersburg, p. 33.

other psychological process. It expresses the complete readiness on the part of the subject to take on a defined activity. Thus one cannot say that *ustanovka* in all instances signifies the understanding of a single body of knowledge. Undoubtedly *ustanovka* and the activity in which it is brought to realization are connected, and it is understood that in every individual case we are talking about an *ustanovka* which leads to this or that particular activity'.[5]

In our case, of course, the concern is a musical-creative activity connected with a musical-creative *ustanovka*. A person forms within herself a certain and definite view of everything connected with music and musical creation; she is ready to interpret her musical activity and the circumstances surrounding it in a particular context. Her relationship to her work as a musician, to the entirety of its active inputs and human connections, determines creative development and future success. *Ustanovka*, like all things in the psychological sphere, is often intuitive and involuntary, it cannot be formed artificially: in it find reflection both the nature of the musician's gift, its strengths, and weaknesses, and the human characteristics that make up the musician's individuality, including her cultural and social bearings and the particularities of her family upbringing. The musical-creative *ustanovka* is, in short, the whole of the person whose soul is attuned to the musical wavelength; this soul guides the musician in her path toward success and itself makes up one of the subject's principal components.

The student musician mastering the basics of play on his instrument and a musical genius are not comparable entities in terms of the dimensions of their respective gifts; yet at the same time there is much that is common between them. Each has a certain defined musical-creative *ustanovka*—a kind of unarticulated psychological force, which assists them in their work. Psychological issues concerning a common undertaking can bring together otherwise incompatible people, and this commonality allows every student, without reference to her future career or musical goals, to become familiar with the experience of outstanding musicians and take from that experience something useful for herself—to learn just what the musical-creative *ustanovka* of major musical talents was and to attempt to attune herself to that very mode. *Ustanovka*, as distinct from one's level of giftedness, is something which one can consciously act upon: to feel and understand the context of one's activity in the same way, at least to some extent, as this was (and is) done by the outstanding musicians—such in itself is a step closer to success, it points to a process of formulating success through one's own action and one's own thoughts.

All the outstanding musicians are unbelievably possessed by music. This enormous love and devotion to art make up part of their talent and, of particular importance here, stand at the very source of that talent. The desire to speak the language of music and to communicate with people with the help of musical forms, are things sensed by the Composer and Performer like an unconquerable attraction to one's art. 'Love should be the point of departure', writes the outstanding pianist Arthur Schnabel, 'the love

---

5 Uznadze, D. (1997) *Teoria ustanovki/The Theory of Set*. Moscow-Voronezh: Modek, p. 441.

of music. This is one of my most firm convictions: love always imparts a certain knowledge, whereas knowledge very rarely gives rise to something akin to love'.[6]

The pianist's entire way of life was subordinated to this love and flowed from it: the lessons he gave consisted in large part of listening to music and 'pursuing' it as one pursues an intended bride.

The critical moment of the young Schnabel's day was successfully getting in line early enough at the Vienna Opera's box office; it opened at 3:00 p.m. and one had to stand in line until the beginning of the performance itself at 7:00 p.m. Schabel often spent these hours in diverting chatter with Arnold Schoenberg, who took a place in line next to him. In addition to loving music as such, the future pianist loved to talk about it with knowledgeable people; happily, he had the opportunity to walk about the outlying areas of Vienna with Johannes Brahms. Despite the fact that the latter talked little enough about music (concerning himself more with the question of whether or not it was time to feed his infant child again), the young Schnabel could never sacrifice these walks together for any other pursuit—as a result of which his study time was severely limited: after Brahms, after the opera, and after a 2-hour wait for a lesson from maestro Leshetitsky (who scheduled the lesson for 10:00 but began it at noon), the future star of the concert circuit had only 3 hours a day for independent study. This was enough for him, because these hours were grounded on a solid base of listening to music and thinking about it, which in turn derived from an attraction to the art of music which can only be described as mad.

Leo Tolstoy is said to have described the diversity of humans' love for one another with the epigram 'There are as many kinds of love as there are hearts to do the loving'. This is also true of other kinds of love, however—the love of music, for one, can manifest itself in highly individualized ways; and the way of life of a given musician defines itself, in the end, by which particular music the artist chooses to make the principal object of his passion and what kind of behavior that music demands of him. The great violinist Pablo Sarasate committed himself to virtuoso genres. He was an artist of the musical revue, in the best sense of that term; those who heard him reported that they could not have imagined such purity, clarity, equanimity, and fluidity from the violin, along with such peerless bowmanship, had they not witnessed the unique talent of Saraste for themselves (Ginzburg 1966). Virtually everyone who heard him described Saraste as a genius—to which he himself replied 'Genius! I practice fourteen hours a day for 37 years, and now they call me a genius!' If Saraste had loved another kind of music he could have limited himself to a less demanding practice regimen, but his ideal—stunning violin virtuosity—demanded precisely this kind of labor. Virtuoso music resembles to a certain extent an ideally functioning machine—and the performer who commits himself to this machine becomes just such a machine himself. Saraste's work *ustanovka* was 'machine-ness', and his genius lay in the fact that he could work at his metier precisely as much as was

[6] Schnabel, A. (1967) Moya zhizn i muzyka/My Life and Music. *Ispolnitel'skoe iskusstvo zarubezhnykh stran/Performing Art Abroad*, 3, p. 140.

demanded by his love for the technique of violin play. For a performer of another cast such uniquely accomplished, all-encompassing virtuoso play would not be a critical necessity. Yet it was exactly to this perfection of technique that Saraste committed all his artistic energies; and he did not complain that these energies had to be so great: those truly in love never complain of sacrifices made in the name of the very love which so consumes them.

Konstantin Igumnov and Alexandre Scriabin were in their youth fashionable pianists of the 'salon' variety. They were attracted to music that was at once vibrant and sparkling and yet intimate and refined as well. They each showed an extraordinary respect for Chopin—for his soft, singing and penetrating intonation. This internal aristocratism and freedom could appear only as a consequence and reflection of a corresponding way of life which the young pianists chose for themselves. And this way of life created for them just that creative *ustanovka* which was optimal for them. Igumnov recalled:

> In general I studied music rather irregularly. At first all manner of school problems interfered with my music lessons, and then later I sometimes led a kind of 'disorganized lifestyle', especially when I found myself in the circles of patrons of the arts. There I made my way into society, and wore a top hat. There were oceans of invitations, the day would pass before I noticed it was gone, and I went to bed quite late.[7]

Scriabin distinguished himself with even more social activity and became a favorite of Moscow salons. According to Igumnov, he followed Chopin's instructions to his pupils to practice 3 hours daily—which from the standpoint of a virtuoso performer of the musical revue level is unforgivably little. But neither Scriabin nor Igumnov was a revue virtuoso—just as Chopin himself had not been. A musician of the social salon category needs a certain spontaneity of play, an unrehearsed and anti-mechanical quality even bordering on carelessness. The musical-creative *ustanovka* of an artist gives rise to a defined practice regime; and this *ustanovka* itself, in turn, depends on the genre and type of music which the musician commits himself to performing.

The initial requirement in the formation of a musical-creative *ustanovka* is the attunement of the musician to a particular artistic image. The love for music of a particular kind is the artist's choice—his visiting card, so to speak. It is as if the young musician is rehearsing a role which he will be playing in the future; the imagined hero of the neophyte, being his role model, directs the latter's style through these 'rehearsals', thus forming his musical-creative *ustanovka*. Musicologist Vyacheslav Medushevsky (1993) calls this hero 'the intonational character of the style'. These are views, moods and habits of a certain historical prototype that are forming the composer's 'voice' and underlie all what he has to say. The requirements of the notional hero are met as a first order of business: if he is extremely disciplined and operates like clockwork, if he is oriented towards the calculable and visible parameters of activity, such as purity and agility, technical brilliance and the absence of any roughness whatsoever, then the apprentice artist will form an appropriate

---

[7] Teplov, B. M. (1998) *Psihologiya i psikhofiziologiya individual'nyh razlichij/Psychology and Psychophisiology of Individual Differences.* Moscow-Voronezh: Modek, p. 131.

creative *ustanovka* and guard himself against any intrusions from outside interests or influences. If the intonational hero is, on the contrary, of the wide-open, capricious, and unpredictable type, then the rising artist will be likewise—in which case his musical-creative *ustanovka* will lead him to a socially active lifestyle into which his work will fit easily; emotionally, socially, and psychologically his creative work will be part of this lifestyle, dovetailing with it precisely.

In the Renaissance era the figure of the Composer (and of a creator in general) was somewhat different from what later centuries would come to understand by it. Working in the arts signified, first of all, status of a master, an expert in the accepted compositional devices of the day and their most winning applications. The mind of the composer in the fifteenth and sixteenth centuries was similar to the mind of a builder, an architect, and an engineer who elaborates his project with the greatest attention and exactitude. Success depended on the degree of refinement of the composer's mathematized mind, on the cleverness with which he was able to arrange voices and motifs, fitting together a proportionate and harmonic musical structure. The composer Palestrina was, by his lifestyle and attitude toward his work, a man of his times: pragmatic and businesslike. Strict discipline and self-regulation were part of his *ustanovka* in both life and art, fitting together and complementing each other.

Palestrina's life and art were part of the same *modus*—that of a person who created reality. As Henry Coates points out in his study of Palestrina:

> It is difficult to imagine the creator of the Missa Papae Marcelli engaged in producing wine and selling it by the barrel; building and buying house property and letting it out; or to think of him as devoting one part of his day to the somewhat dingy business of a furrier's shop and the other part to writing music of such rare beauty as the Missa Assumpta. Yet he did these things.[8]

Palestrina's musical-creative *ustanovka* included an attitude toward himself as creator and activator; that *ustanovka*, being as all-encompassing as any *ustanovka*, defined both Palestrina's way of life and the type of organization of his music practice sessions, being dispersed as they were among obligations of various kinds.

Observing the lifestyle and creative working regimen of the outstanding musicians, the student can absorb the salient principals of both: love of music, interest in it and a striving, above all things, to satisfy exactly this interest rather than to fulfill various and sundry demands of discipline; there also develops a musical-creative *ustanovka* from this very same love, from the musical preferences of the student which guide one to a particular lifestyle and practice regimen. An appropriately chosen lifestyle and practice regimen themselves lead a musician to success: his musical-creative *ustanovka* will work for him. Therefore the musician, like anyone else, needs to 'find himself'—to form a natural system of demands on himself and evaluations of the accomplished, on the basis of a model he understands; relying on these he can move ahead, rising to new creative heights. It will no doubt seem that there is no universality in this arrangement; what is good and useful for one artist may be useless and harmful to another. The internal *ustanovka*, the model

[8] Coates, H. (1948) *Palestrina*. London: J. M. Dents and Sons, p. 15.

and the idea of the chosen musical activity in the chosen genre will lead the musician after them, as he seeks to express in his creative work both himself and the times in which he lives.

If we examine the musical-creative *ustanovka* of the outstanding musicians in all its complexity—as both an aggregate of the individual musician's unarticulated demands on himself and a subconscious formulation of his musical goals, we find one very important characteristic: an extraordinary confidence in the individual's own powers. Outstanding musicians believe that 'the impossible is possible'—and make it so. As Yehudi Menuhin wrote:

> It was a conviction that supreme effort of concentration or prayer could release one from natural laws. Similarly I believed myself capable of performing miracles in music. That only the passage of time accumulates skill and insight was a fact my faith easily ignored: if I really applied myself to learning a work today I should know it by tomorrow, I was sure, and no doubt this confidence that all things were possible brought many things within reach.[9]

An indistinct conception of what will later emerge as music exists in the minds of both the Composer and the Performer, compelling them forward toward the hour of their as yet ill-imagined triumph. This hour has not yet come, there are no visible signs of its approach, but the internal conceptualization of future creative accomplishments already inspires the artist and eases the burdens of his daily life. Thus the young Haydn, turned out of his home into the streets of Vienna, was nevertheless certain, before he had composed anything or distinguished himself in any way, that his calling was to compose music (Geiringer 1982). He did not know how to compose, had never studied composition, he played the harpsichord and the violin tolerably but without distinction—he was, in short, just like hundreds of other boys who found themselves, as their voices began to change, no longer useful to church choirs. But Haydn firmly believed in his destiny; and it found him, of course. It was this belief which helped him through the years of poverty and obscurity, and helped him rise above the routine of life in the Esterhazy estate and resist the pull of his minor responsibilities there. At age 17 this unemployed chorister somehow knew that he would become a great composer; and that is what he did.

This extraordinary belief in oneself, a concomitant of genius everywhere, raises those who possess it to both unbelievable diligence and to an equally unbelievable laziness. Bach was an extremely industrious sort: the routine he committed himself to, prayer and praise, hailing the Lord and mourning the sinfulness of the world, demanded contemplation and an unhurried approach, as such themes needed to be worked through carefully and in detail. So Bach's creative task excluded frivolity and carelessness. He knew that his works were not in vain, he was sure that the word he said would be listened to: his belief in his creative powers gave rise to enormous energy and a formidable will to work. A conviction in the necessity of his work and in its lasting value allowed the creator to tolerate the inhuman pressure which he put upon himself. The '*ustanovka* of genius' which is characteristic of the creator, helps him cope with his own weakness and fatigue.

---

[9] Menuhin, Y. (1979) *Unfinished journey*. London: MacDonald and Jane's, p. 31.

The exact opposite of the great Bach was Gioachino Rossini, a roue and sybarite who was a great admirer of life's varied and various pleasures. Whatever had to be done would be put off by Rossini as long as possible—but in the end everything did get done, on time, and brilliantly in the bargain. As a beginning composer he was once given 6 weeks to produce an opera. For a month Rossini enjoyed life, using the advance he received for the opera. Then over the course of 2 weeks he wrote a duet and an aria every day, succeeding in getting the opera done on time, albeit including a number of mistakes with corrections in penciled ink (for which he was also criticized).

Rossini's music carried the stamp of immediacy and the breadth of the composer's fantasy: if he had labored hours on end to put his compositions into final form, Rossini could not, perhaps, have achieved the effect that he did. In any case, his belief in himself helped him avoid panic when the 'moment of truth' arrived, and he worked to deadlines as calmly and assuredly, as though he had no particular responsibilities to be concerned about. Rossini's 'ustanovka for genius' was the assurance of a composer working in the genre of pop music—which, to a significant extent, was the category to which the opera of his day belonged. Rossini's aural resources and his knowledge of contemporary opera style were great indeed, and he could at a moment's notice mobilize his entire 'musical storehouse' for use in his work. While he lazed away, he replenished this storehouse, listening to music on the street, in taverns, at carnivals, and in the theater. He had no need to 'grind gravel' to produce uniquely beautiful variant copies in contemporary opera style, and his lightheartedness was firmly based on the solid foundation of self-recognition: Rossini was sure of the efficacy of his compositional method, and proved the correctness of this judgment every time with the results of his creative activity.

In the music community the view that the first instructor plays a decisive role continues to hold sway. If a young talent is not fortunate from the very beginning with his instructor, and if this ill luck continues for some years, then many are ready to cross him off the list of potential musical stars. Fatalism of this kind is unwarranted: the biographies of the outstanding musicians recount an *ustanovka* of independent development among them, with the role of the instructor, even the first one, nowhere near as important as is held in some quarters. The young Niccolo Paganini began studying the mandolin before the age of 6; his first teacher was his father, a former stevedore. The future violinist caught sight of his first violin only at age 7, and his first instruction from a professional music teacher came 2 years later. This was an orchestra violinist who did not put excessive effort into his endeavors in musical pedagogy. Over the course of the next 3 years Paganini changed teachers twice; of the second of these, the famous professor Giacomo Costa, Paganini recalled years after becoming a violin legend: 'I think back with pleasure on the painstaking interest of good old Costa, to whom, however, I was no great delight since his principles often seemed unnatural to me and I showed no inclination to adopt his bowing'.[10]

The great talents are obstinate types, with their own particular and peculiar views of art—and they are quite ready to alter 'in their own image' the well-known and accepted

[10] Courcy de, G. (1957) *Paganini, the Genoese*, vol.1. Norman: University of Oklahoma Press, p. 33.

norms of play on their instruments. The stars of the future are extremely critical, take nothing on faith, and thus are inclined to change teachers with some frequency—or to dispense with them altogether. Gifted musicians have no qualms about being left one-on-one with music—their musical *ustanovka*, after all, presupposes independent communication with the musical muse—and in contrast to the middling music students they are quite ready to be satisfied with minimal prompting and guidance. They are capable of grasping the essence of a musical moment instantly, without outside help, and then moving on to the next moment in the same spirit of independent discovery.

The education of the gifted musician is often an unsystematic business, with constant changes of instructors, instruction methodologies, and disciplines under study. The average musician, in contrast, studies under a standard model and submits to a system which has been worked out over centuries. The highly talented musician seeks opportunities which correspond exactly to his needs, as the education of a talent is as individual as the talent himself. This is particularly true of composers, who organize for themselves not so much elementary-level musical education as a kind of acquaintance process with music. Their biographies can serve as refutations of all the everyday 'accepted wisdom' associated with the early training of professional musicians.

The first teacher of many musical geniuses strayed far from the expected: instead of laying down the fundamentals of mastery, as traditional musical pedagogy prescribes, these teachers spoiled their charges and paid little attention to their clearly unusual musical abilities. Such was the case with Louisa Volgeborn, whose claim to footnote status in history rests on having given the 6-year-old Alexandre Dargomyshky his first music lessons (Pekelis 1966). She was gentle and lenient with the child, hardly looking after his musical development at all. So it was as well with the young George Gershwin's first teacher, one Mr Goldfarb, the conductor of a military orchestra whose lessons with Gershwin culminated in Rossini's *William Tell Overture* (Jablonski 1987). Gershwin's subsequent teacher, the brilliant instructor Charles Hambitzer, was so outraged by what Goldfarb had done with his pupil that he threatened half in jest to shoot the man—without, as the story has it, placing an apple on his head beforehand.

The time from 8 years to 14 years are considered decisive in the fate of a developing musician: if he does not succeed in becoming a professional during this period, then the probability of creative success becomes almost entirely ephemeral. This formulation applies to all students—except the greatest talents. Dargomyzhsky's story is evidence of this. At the age of 8 the future composer met a certain Adrian Danilevsky, who tore up all the boy's opuses and turned him away from composition altogether (as he himself was a failed composer and suffered from an artistic inferiority complex). Putting Danilevsky behind him, Dargomyzhsky turned to studying the violin under the guidance of an orchestra violinist. Eventually, by the age of 15, Dargomyzhsky resolved to learn the basics of the composer's trade, moving hopefully (if in vain) to the tutelage of a competent but unspectacular composer named Schoberlechner. Of the latter Dargomyzhsky later wrote:

> None of his compositions leave the public or the experts entirely satisfied. The first consider him too dark, while the second think him a mediocrity. *Gospodin* Schoberlechner makes sacrifices at

two altars, yet his wishes are fulfilled at neither of them; he chases two rabbits at once and, it may well be, catches neither.[11]

After 2 years of study with Shoberlechner, Dargomyzhsky left him for a vocal and music theory instructor named Zeibich who was an actor and singer in a German troupe in St Petersburg.

The *ustanovka* for creative independence, which distinguishes outstanding musicians from all others, made Alexandre Dargomyzhsky strive constantly toward the ideal—and not having found it, uncompromisingly strive on further. All the future opera composer's searching was connected with an unarticulated desire on his part to write for the theater; for this he needed to be able to play the piano and violin reasonably well so that he could understand at least the rudiments of orchestra play. He also needed to have a certain sense of composition in general, and of vocal composition in particular. All these needs were in fact fulfilled by Dargomyzhsky's unexceptional teachers, each adding his own part. But the principal accomplishment of the composer's youth did not owe to his music lessons with mediocre teachers, but to other sources: his impressions from the theater and the wealth of stories, fables, and *bon mots* which issued forth during the family gatherings at the famed Dargomyzhsky household. These evenings created an appreciation for satire, humor, and theatrical declamation in the youth. Alexandre was a great admirer of French opera, which was famous for its interest in the world of drama and letters; theatrical music and the musical theater formed the ear and the talent of the future master.

While some outstanding musicians, such as Dargomyzhsky, had mediocre instructors, others spent their early years simply communing with music, having for a brief time studied under real pedagogical experts who instantly put the young talents on the right track. So it happened with Liszt and Igumnov. And there are examples of others who found in their early teachers not only invaluable instruction but real friendship as well: thus Schnabel found Leshetitsky, Oistrakh found Stoliarsky, and Rakhmaninov found Zverev. Yet no matter how their fates' were entwined, all the gifted musicians were in the end guided by an *ustanovka* for creative independence. One could say about each of them what Rosen Cheer, a professor of composition at Harvard, said of his pupil Leonard Bernstein: 'There wasn't much to teach him. He knew most of it by instinct'.[12]

The gift of learning from music itself distinguishes the truly talented, as the testimony of Fritz Kreisler confirms: 'I am convinced of this: the fact that I heard Joachim and Rubinstein was the most important event of my life, having an incalculably greater meaning for me than all my years of study in the conservatory'.[13]

The musical-creative *ustanovka* of outstanding musicians is distinct in its particulars; the path of formation of a great talent and an ordinary professional are in many ways incomparable. Yet the experience of a genius may serve as a kind of vector, a point of reference which can be of help in establishing the appropriate psychological orientation

[11] Cit. from M. Pekelis (1966) *A. S. Dargomyzhsky*. Moscow: Muzyka, p. 124.
[12] Peyser, J. (1987) *Bernstein*. New York: Beech Tree Books, p. 53.
[13] Yampolsky, I. (1975) *Fritz Kreisler*. Moscow: Muzyka, p. 15.

for the student musician, who should establish his own musical-creative *ustanovka* with one eye on what the masters have done. In this way the student musician can rise above himself and bring his creative potential to its maximum development. Like all the great musicians, the student at any level of giftedness will love music and become genuinely devoted to it. He will search for his musical self and his musical interests, leading a life-style which corresponds to the artistic image he has chosen. He will believe in his own future and sense his future success before it happens, and teach himself, seeking different educational opportunities and methods based on his own needs and the demands of his creative muse.

The music teacher

The music teacher is a very important figure in the musician's biography. And the further a musician is from genius, the more significant and all-encompassing is the role of the instructor. How many people enjoy music and make music all their lives thanks to the pedagogical talent of their music teacher; and how many people are deprived of that pleasure simply because a music teacher was insufficiently sensitive, insufficiently quali-fied, or simply insufficiently interested in doing the job well. Many outstanding talents have tried on the role of the music teacher, and much that is useful can be learned from the experience of outstanding instructors—as from outstanding pupils as well. Music teachers can use the experience of the former as models for their own methods, while music students can use the same experience to create standards for the ideal teacher with whom they would eventually like to study. The alpha and omega of music teaching are love for the student and an understanding of the difficulties he/she is going through. The instructor is like a military commander leading his troop(s) ahead to a victory which is still a long way distant; it is his calling to bring this victory closer psychologically, never to let discouragement gain a foothold, and to encourage belief in the final victorious outcome.

It would be wonderful to make every musical exercise interesting and comprehensible, of course, but this is not always feasible; the teacher has to inspire the pupil to labor on through the otherwise tedious and burdensome parts of the learning program. In this the teacher is practically a psychotherapist, as processes such as learning correct hand posi-tions on the keys or the fretboard, finding the optimal movements for fingers and hands, and adjusting the student to the methods of play best suited to a particular instrument—all these demand a level of patience and care not found in all adults (not to mention children). Sharing his experience with his teaching colleagues, the great pianist and piano teacher Alfred Cortot wrote:

> One should never forget that music drills, with their complicated rules, and the difficulty of initial contacts with the instrument, which give no musical enjoyment at all, can make the undertaking seem utterly useless to beginners unless you take care to remind them of the results which will come in the future, and inspire them with good humor, interesting examples or comparisons young minds can comprehend.[14]

---

14 Cortot, A. (1965) *O fortepiannom iskusstve/On the Art of Piano Playing*. Moscow: Muzyka, p. 83.

But no matter how hard the teacher tries to keep things interesting, the young pupil always wants to play outside or play with the cat; sometimes even the minimum investment demanded by the teacher can seem too much. Here again the instructor needs the unusual talent of the psychologist: he needs to determine whether the child is showing laziness or reluctance because the tasks assigned to him are too great and his abilities simply do not approach the level necessary to accomplish them; or is it just another case of a childish desire for unlimited freedom, which becomes greater as the years go by. The desire for personal freedom tends to be more pronounced among boys than girls—for whom the phrase 'because you have to', if voiced by parents or teachers, can be sufficiently convincing. A boy, on the other hand, reacts badly to any form of force or coercion.

As experiments measuring the expressive ear have demonstrated, there are exactly as many musically inclined boys as there are musically inclined girls (Kirnarskaya and Winner 1999). But getting a boy to study music is many times harder, owing both to the force of social custom—music is not among the traditionally male enthusiasms—and to certain objective difficulties in the instruction process. A boy who studies something with difficulty and without interest will sooner abandon the onerous subject than will a girl. Leaving aside the great talents who adored music and looking instead at the future music lovers and amateur musicians, one notes that these latter souls sometimes require coercion. The only limitations on the teacher and the pupil's parents in such cases should be those of tact and wisdom. Ilya Musin, an outstanding instructor who taught many conductors, tried to study the violin at first, then switched to the piano. Recalling those years Musin wrote:

> The first steps in my 'pianistic activity' did not seem to me to yield much more enjoyment than those I had taken on the violin. In the beginning touching the keyboard with my fingers appeared just as pointless. I became confused and upset when it turned out that you had to play different notes with each hand. The fact that I did not give up this enterprise as I had the violin can be put down to my father. Every day, when he came home from work, he sat me down at the instrument and made me practice for exactly one hour. What torture that hour was! But my father was implacable. And now I bow low before him and thank him for making me overcome my early resistance.[15]

At that critical moment, when the student encounters his first difficulties, the instructor must mobilize all his mastery, all his imagination, his ability to invent associations between music and the outside world, to make connections between music and the child's life (his favorite fairy tales, stories, songs, and movies, for example) so that the subject is not dry, does not become a series of tedious and repetitive exercises in which one has to adroitly shuffle one's fingers for reasons a child does not really understand. There is always the opportunity to take things more slowly, so as not to hurry the beginner— making sure along the way that the tasks are neither too difficult nor too boring. On the teacher's approach during the first years of study Alfred Cortot has written: 'Stimulate, do

[15] Musin, I. (1995) *Uroki zhizni. Vospominania dirizhera/Lessons of Life. Conductor's Memoirs.* St.Petersburg: Prosvetitelskoe izdatelskoe ob'edinenie Dean–Adia-M, p. 7.

not discourage. Never let the student play bad music. To the extent possible inspire love for music rather than simply for the piano'.[16]

Severity is the most sensitive instrument in the pedagogical arsenal. Not knowing how to find the key to a student's heart, not knowing how to interest her using musical exercises which match her abilities, many teachers turn into the equivalent of a musical Cerberus—and students, in turn, coming to recognize this as something of a sign of the teaching profession, begin to accept 'maestros' of this kind as the norm. Roland Persson did a questionnaire-based study of the attitude of organ students to their teachers. While Persson emphasized that the teachers in question did not have special pedagogical training (which limited their potential for success, in his view), the general image of the instructor which emerged from his study was not, in any case, a very attractive one:

> Tentative findings suggest that, inherent in a context of Western art and music are strong expectations about how a master performance teacher should behave; this causes students to reconstrue harsh and insensitive treatment as something positive and necessary. The maestro role appears to be product-oriented rather than person-oriented, suggesting that students lacking in self-assurance and independence may fare badly under such tutelage.[17]

The authoritarian method of teaching is a sign of pedagogical weakness, the inability to get through to the student with more 'democratic' methods—and, more important, a sign of an inability to instill in the student a love for music which would render the instructor's wishes and the student's the same, and stimulate the student to strive for perfection. As Yehudi Menuhin recalled:

> Music was something very alive to me, an essential means of expression, and I suspect that unending, hours of work on dull material might well have blunted rather than polished my interpretation... I have since seen how very rigid teaching of music, such as has been systematized in Russia, can steam-roller individual expressiveness into anonymous brilliance, so that only the most irrepressible survive the course with personality and musicality intact.[18]

There is a good deal more than a grain of truth in Menuhin's reproaches. Leaving aside the individual foibles of all instructors, their personal styles of communication, and idiosyncratic methodologies, the fact remains that in the case of the specialized music schools of musically-rich Russia, the system of instruction which has settled in is exactly the one which the great violinist warned about. Success at any price, virtuosity before all—including the student as a person; the main thing is to create not an individual performer but a sort of musical machine which could be, as one 'well-wisher' suggested, plugged into an electrical outlet—and music would issue forth. There are indeed results from this institutional arrangement: completed compositions show an extremely high level of difficulty and have an entirely professional appearance—but this is achieved at a price of strict regimentation and hours upon hours of exhausting practice sessions. Here the instructor's role is less that of helping and supporting the student and more of

---

[16] Cortot, A. (1965) *O fortepiannom iskusstve/On the Art of Piano Playing.* Moscow: Muzyka, p. 87.

[17] Persson, R. S. (1996) Studying with a musical maestro: a case study of commonsense teaching in artistic training. *Creativity Research Journal*, 9, p. 46.

[18] Menuhin, Y. (1979) *Unfinished Journey.* London: MacDonald and Jane's, p. 67.

directing sufficient psychological pressure to make him fulfill the demanding regimen. The student's parents are the initial allies in putting this ambitious policy into practice; they believe that their child will be the one to carry forward the banner of Oistrakh and Stern, and not somebody who ends up listlessly turning the pages for the orchestra's ninth chair and yawning as he looks up enviously at the latest maestro occupying the podium.

This micro-world has its own criteria for success and its own rewards: trips to competitions, concert performances, prestigious prizes, and scholarships. There are also certain ephemeral goals: a brilliant international career, ecstatic reviews, enormous honoraria, and success and glory. Only very few reach these heights—and they are most often those who have no need of the 'athletic-competition' style of instruction and practice, but rather musicians who could have reached the highest levels by themselves, with only their devotion to music and their talent to thank. As Anna Kantor, the famous teacher of Evgeny Kissin, the music star, answered in a personal conversation when asked to reveal her secret as his instructor: 'Just do nothing and don't be on his way'.

Those who do not reach the heights, the 'pseudo-soloists' who remain behind, are said to be victims (as one so often hears now) of false advertising on the part of the teachers. They convinced the children and their parents that success was not a matter of one's level of giftedness, but rather of zeal and force of will; these people believed that enormous patience could work miracles and move mountains. Yet after many years the majority of those who passed through this pedagogical 'school' came to believe that their self-denial led to an incredible one-sidedness in their development: the child who mastered Liszt's *Etudes* had no time for Pushkin's *Onegin* and no idea why Archimedes cried 'Eureka!' The *ustanovka* for a professional musical career common to schools for gifted children has ruined more than one life: the person not suited for such a career and lacking genuine talent is forced to stretch himself almost to the breaking point simply to achieve the norms designated as criteria for success in such schools. The children are not offered an alternative: from their ranks are supposed to issue forth a corps of uniformly strong and well-prepared musical 'pros' capable of making their way through the 'strainer' of conservatory entrance exams. If someone drops out of one of these special schools, it is considered almost a tragedy; this mathematically undereducated and not too literate young 'soldier' now faces only the prospect of teaching in a musical school for ordinary children— the lot of the middling musician, which cannot not but seem fairly dim to him now.

The pedagogical methods accepted in the specialized music schools are also adopted for use by the teachers in the regular music schools. The professional prestige of these teachers depends on the number of prizes and awards won by their charges, on such obvious and easily calculated indicators as victories in competitions and admissions into professional musical institutions. The music teacher is prepared to be proud of exactly this kind of success. In reality, however, there is only one real criterion of his mastery: the percentage of students who remain in his class in relation to the number who entered it. That is all, that is, to enthrall people with music, to support and develop a young person's interest in it, to convince him to give music more attention than sports, foreign languages, drawing, and other enthusiasms.

Some of these passions are far from mutually exclusive, but the master of musical pedagogy can work things out so that music can always occupy an honored position among the voluntary pastimes of a child (and then a teenager). To give society one more active listener and music lover—such is the single and solitary task the music teacher should set before himself. In previous eras all teachers of musical instruments and vocals, including the great and famous, taught the art of music in a family, where the only goal was the all-around cultural development of the child—without music the upbringing of an educated member of society, a member of the intelligentsia or an aristocrat, was considered incomplete. One-sided development—when a student tries to play ever more complicated pieces from the 'adult' repertoire—threatens to stifle the learner's musicality: someone who spends all his free time with an instrument is necessarily limited in his cultural outlook, reading little and knowing less, and will ultimately turn into only a middling musician. For a musician does not actually play with his fingers, but with his head, his heart, the whole of his personality, and the entire breadth of his understanding of life and art. A musician literally cannot exist if he commits all his time to music alone; he needs to live, spend time with people, go to the theater, and so on. And he also needs, finally, a critical dose of 'down time'—time spent in doing nothing in particular, relaxing, 'goofing off'. It is simply not possible to become a gifted composer or performer by sitting in a musical cage.

Art does not demand sacrifices—this is the actual truth, and all the posturing one hears about the necessity of forgoing many of life's pleasures for art's sake is nothing more than hypocrisy. In fact, art does not tolerate any limitations of human liberty; grasping this, gifted music teachers never force their charges to practice too much. The Petersburg music instructor Alexandre Villoin—the teacher of Anton and Nikolai Rubinstein, both pianists of genius—had this advice to offer on limiting the spade work of one's charges:

> It is enough for the youngest pupils to practice for an hour a day, at first. Those somewhat older may generally practice music for no more than an hour and a half or two hours [a day]; those who have reached full development of their physical skills should not exceed three hours of practice, with ten-minute breaks each hour. This is the regimen I used with the two Rubinsteins, and I continue to use it successfully to this day.[19]

Outstanding teachers have always given preference to 'music over technique'; while each is impossible without the other, of course, each nevertheless lends a certain accent to the student's attention when doing expressive exercises. Behind the mere notes the teacher sees a thought, a body, an image; and he strives to help the student feel this image and pass it along in the music. The pedagogical wisdom here consists in understanding the nature of musical virtuosity, which much more easily and naturally arises from the depths of the music, from its idea and essence and cannot be achieved by any manner (or number) of mechanical exercises. To help a student understand a work of music is to help him play it. The first teacher who really inspired the young Menuhin was the outstanding violinist and composer George Enescu. Recalling his lessons with Enescu, Menuhin noted:

> What I received from him—by compelling example, not by word—was the note transformed into vital message, the phrase given shape and meaning, the structure of music made vivid. I was ready

19 Cit. from Barenboim, L. (1957) *Anton Rubinstein*. Moscow: Muzyka, p. 29.

to receive it. Music was hardly dead for me; it was a fierce passion, but I had never known it to have such clear and vital form before.[20]

In the music community it has long been known that a brilliant musician and a brilliant music teacher are not necessarily one and the same person. There are people who are gifted musicians as well as gifted instructors; there are also people who are talented music teachers, especially in vocals, but have never performed on stage and were never stars of the popular concert circuit—yet nevertheless possess the secret of teaching people to become stars, proving by their example that the talent of a composer and a performing artist is one thing, while the talent of a music instructor is another altogether. The pedagogue and the artist have different psychological mindsets; they are drawn by and towards different goals and the object of their influence is likewise different: the individual person, the future musician is not like the audience of a concert hall; by the same token, the influence of someone's play on the public and the influence of someone's understanding of the musical art on a specific individual are also not identical. One-on-one communication assumes a certain exchange of energy, the creation of a kind of common spiritual space, if you will, which the instructor creates for himself, for the music and for his musical charge.

All who have had occasion to make the acquaintance of outstanding musician-pedagogues remark on the aura, the charged space, the whirlwind which envelops everyone who comes under these people's influence. 'Leshetitsky had no method', recalled Arthur Schnabel of his great teacher. 'His instruction was something far greater than a method. It was a kind of current, which strove to liberate the artistic energy hidden in the student. The student was given a task, not a formula.[21] Or as Leonard Bernstein recalled of his teacher, the great conductor Sergey Koussevitsky, whom he knew as an adult: 'He taught his pupils by simply inspiring them. He taught everything through feeling, through instinct and emotion. Even the purely mechanical matter of beating time, of conducting four beats in a bar became an emotional experience instead of a mathematical one'.[22]

For gifted students a gifted teacher is a blessing, a knowing and experienced friend with whom they can share their creative problems and from whom they can get answers to questions which would take far longer to resolve by themselves. For those who simply love music and want to devote themselves to it, a gifted teacher is a conductor and task master who explains the hidden and reveals the mysterious. There is only one category of student for whom 'too good a teacher' may be dangerous: this is the 'somewhat gifted' student whom a talented instructor can raise above the level expected for one of moderate endowment by inspiring and supporting him, by using his special energy and commitment to music, so that in effect this modest creative potential is multiplied well beyond its natural bounds. With this teacher, and only with him, sensing his approving presence, students can work miracles—because it is he who arouses in them a genuine interest in music and the desire to become musicians. But once the modestly gifted student finds

[20] Menuhin, Y. (1979) *Unfinished Journey*. London: MacDonald and Jane's, p. 71.
[21] Schnabel, A. (1967) Moya zhizn' i muzyka/My life and music. *Ispolnitel'skoe iskusstvo zarubezhnykh stran/Performing Art Abroad*, 3, p. 133.
[22] Bernstein, L. (1982) *Findings*. New York: Simon and Schuster, p. 186.

himself alone, left to his own devices with his own moderate resources, the miracle evaporates into thin air. In the history of pedagogy and performance there are examples of students who demonstrate brilliant results under a certain teacher, but upon moving on to another suddenly find themselves as lost as an infant deprived of a mother's breast.

The magic of human communication, the magic of the psychological alloy of man-to-music-to-man, are unlikely ever to be entirely understood. The talent of the music teacher is Sphinx-like in its intricate combination of musical and pedagogical sources, both of which are critically important. The interpenetration and interaction of the understanding of music, along with a human infectiousness which passes this understanding to others—these are the elements which make up this rare gift. Every student who plans a musical career for himself must for a time take leave of his favorite teacher for his own good, or he risks making a mistake by exaggerating by several factors his own creative possibilities. A student who shows brilliant results and has an excellent teacher needs to test himself: perhaps what is coming out is not music as such, but a 'man-and-music' combination, created by the talent of the teacher and leading the student into the misapprehension that he himself is the musician. A person with real musical talent stands independent: he and his teacher never resemble conjoined twins who cannot risk separation for fear of losing their lives. On the contrary, all the great musicians strove to strike out on the road to independence as soon as possible; if a young musician lacks such a drive, there is reason to be concerned about him. On the other hand, all those students who are not counting on professional musical careers can thank their lucky stars that their talented music teacher opened new horizons for them. Without the happy chance of meeting such a teacher, their whole lives would have been different—less joyful and less inspired.

Every teacher faces the difficult prospect of accurately assessing the abilities of his pupil. The teacher knows better than anyone how hard it is to earn one's daily bread through music; how great the commitment to one's art must be to do so; and how great a talent must be if one is to become a professional musician. On this aspect of pedagogical responsibility the outstanding trumpeter and music teacher Timofei Dokshitzer has written:

> You cannot make an artist from a person who does not have a natural gift. You cannot teach something that is granted from on high, at birth. A person who lacks creative initiative is supported by the instructor's tutelage like a man on stilts: take away the stilts, stop whispering to him and nudging him and he'll inevitably fall from the musical heights. The teacher should try everything to wean a student away. If nothing works, one must say, honestly and straightforwardly, 'Give it up, don't waste your time, this isn't your calling. Take up something else while you are still young.' It isn't always easy to do this, but a teacher who is preparing someone for life has a responsibility for this person's future—so he is obliged to do it. And he should do it in good time, so that 5–8 years of labor don't go to waste.[23]

Radical pronouncements from the music teacher are only necessary when the student insists on a professional career; in all other cases music lessons can only bring good into people's lives, and they should be continued as long as they remain interesting to the

---

23 Dokshitzer, T. (1995) *Iz zapisnikh knizhek trubacha/From the Trumpeter's Notes*. Moscow: Kompozitor, p. 61.

student and capable of engrossing him. According to the data available, it is never too late begin studying a musical instrument; indeed, there is no greater misapprehension in the field than that a 'late start' is fatal to a person's musical development. A musical gift can make itself known at any stage of life; there have been cases of concert performers who began their musical training as adolescents and even later. Composers, for their part, are traditionally numbered among music's 'late bloomers'; among the best known of these are Edison Denisov, who began his study of music at 16, and the great Aram Khachaturian, who began his path in music at the record-setting late age of 19.

American champions of the slogan 'Music is for everyone forever' often bring up a case specially organized to demonstrate the wisdom of these words. Dr. Roy Ernst was the dean of the faculty of music education at the prestigious Eastman School of Music in Rochester, New York. He assembled a jazz orchestra composed of performers aged 60 to 85—not one of whom had played a musical instrument before joining the group. The orchestra proved to be such a success that it started to tour. Success stories of adults starting to study music at their mature age are not always known; the more valuable is each experience reported and analyzed (Iritani 2002).

The early appearance of musical talent is more often the exception than the rule: the majority of gifted musicians made themselves known as such only at age 12 and later, when a person begins to emerge from childhood, form a distinct personality and recognize his own uniqueness. Music, like all art forms, is an expression of a person's inner being, his spiritual powers; as everyone knows, self-awareness and spiritual maturity do not arrive in childhood—the process of discovering a musical talent simply confirms this well-known truth. Gifted music teachers recognize this pattern; they instill in the student a love and understanding of music, ease his entry into the world of music and support him. For the time being they do not expect miracles, as they know that miracles, if such are indeed part of nature's plan for an individual, will not occur until student crosses the physical and psychological frontier of puberty, leaving childhood behind forever. That is the point at which he will take on and exhibit new qualities—creative independence and a distinctive voice—which had existed only embryonically and passed unnoticed before. The only people who develop differently are those in the category of musical *wunderkind*. Theirs is a separate story—indeed, a separate fate—and one without which any account of musical education would be incomplete.

The phenomenon of the musical *wunderkind*

The fate of the *wunderkind*

A *wunderkind* is a tiny virtuoso whom one cannot behold without a feeling of astonishment. He may still be small enough to walk upright under a table, yet he plays the violin (or the piano or some other instrument) with assurance. While their peers are playing with dolls or soccer balls the wunderkinds are already touring as concert artists. They give performances, receive ovations, are written up in the media, and bring their parents significant honoraria for their concerts. Their teachers are proud of them; they are indeed wonder-children, with bright futures looming before them. Many people, upon hearing wunder-kinds play, assert that the arresting artistic sense and technical mastery of their play puts these child musicians ahead of many adults. Others are more skeptical, maintaining that all the praise should be divided at least by two—half should go to the undeniable mastery of the wonder-child, and the other half to the little rose-colored jumper and short pants; if he weren't so small, goes the theory, there would be nothing remarkable about the performance. In any event, the general piety which society demonstrates before these wonder-children is well expressed in a remark attributed to conductor Zubin Mehta: after a performance by 7-year-old violinist Sarah Chang, Mehta is said to have exclaimed 'She must have learned that in a previous life!'

The parents, of course, are the first to notice wonder-children. If music is being played somewhere in the house and someone is playing an instrument, the child will appear—and attach himself to the player, try to take the lead; the parents will note with amazement how easily the child copes with a task assigned by a music teacher to an older brother or sister. Such was the way the talent of a number of wunderkinds first came to the attention of their parents: Arthur Schnabel immediately played works which his sisters were studying—although no one had taught him how to play a single note; Herbert von Karajan learned the entire repertoire of his older brother with no outside help; and a chubby little Fritz Kreisler accompanied the members of the family quartet on his tiny violin. The wunder-kind wants to and can make music, and immediately confirms this with his play: he does not need to be helped, nor does he need to be prompted to try his hand at music. If there is music playing, the wunderkind takes this as a directive for action and begins to play immediately by ear. His remarkable ear for music, his astonishing exactitude and the breadth of his musical memory surprise everyone around him—and if there is a musician among the group, the status of the wunderkind will immediately be recognized.

In the psychology community it has been assumed for some time that the ideal environment for the wunderkind is that of a family which offers support and help, yet at the same time is also very demanding and has high expectations. This portrait of an ideal wunderkind family is basically correct—but it cannot take into account motives such as parental ardor and maniacal over-involvement in the development of the young talent. Often the father of a gifted youth wants to satisfy his own ambitions, and sometimes his unrealized dreams of glory and a great career, through a talented son: 'Let *him* make it, at least', thinks the father of his promising offspring. So it was with the classic wunderkind-father Leopold Mozart: a gifted violinist, composer and teacher, he nonetheless did not succeed in making a great career for himself, as his dreams and ambitions exceeded the creative potential he was endowed with. Having seen the young treasure, Wolfgang, in his arms, Leopold began to identify psychologically with him, to the point of depriving the boy of the right to live his own life and simply be who he was. Father Leopold treated Wolfgang almost as a possession which he could use at his own discretion. He got used to thinking and acting this way while Wolfgang was small, and as a consequence never wanted to give up this proprietary approach.

The concerns of parents over the development of a child's talent are not infrequently tinged with self-interest. Indeed, Leopold Mozart is the rule rather than the exception. The childhoods of wunderkinds who go on to become geniuses are by no means always idyllic and filled with parental tenderness. The parents of wonder-children practically compete with one another in strictness and exacting demands toward their gifted offspring. Paganini's father beat and starved him, while forcing him to spend whole days playing the violin. Beethoven's father, a violinist of middling skill, dreamed of creating from his son a second Mozart and raised the child with canings and reproaches. Friedrich Wiek cruelly exploited his gifted daughter, the piano wunderkind Clara; he was ready to die before seeing her become Schumann's wife, and only a court freed the girl from her father's clutches (and his designs of living off her earnings). Leopold Mozart likewise entertained notions of riding on Wolfgang's coattails; the impossibility of bringing this plan to fruition brought him to deprive his genius son of any inheritance. Yet despite their external circumstances, the wunderkinds survived and continued to create—which speaks directly to the natural origins of their talent and to the innate character of their abilities, which did not fade out due to parental overprotection or too early concert experience.

Yet not all wunderkinds fall victim to parental ambition. Adam Liszt loved his son, genuinely delighted in his talent and, in order to show him to the world, arranged concerts for him. When it became necessary, Adam took the boy to Carl Czerny, who practically saved him from 'artistic overdose'. The parents of Arthur Schnabel, Arthur Rubinstein, and many others did not try to pry advantage from the early-appearing gifts of their children; they found them good teachers and gave them the freedom to develop.

The wunderkind becomes known as such thanks to his concert performances. At the age of 7 or 8 he begins to appear on stage and lives the life of an adult artist. Yehudi Menuhin made his debut at Carnegie Hall at the age of 7, and from that time forward combined his music studies and 'work'. Anton Rubinstein began to perform at the same tender age and, as he expressed it himself, from the age of 11 served 'as my own teacher'. Certain wunderkinds have not been involved in regular concert performing—but certainly could have, if they had chosen to. So it was with the young Modest Mussorgsky. His talent had been noted by the age of 5; at 7 he could play complex pieces by Liszt. The well-known Petersburg music teacher Anton Gerke was brought in to teach the gifted boy, and at age 9 Mussorgsky gave a public concert of John Field; at age 12 he made a tremendous success at a charity concert at the home of the stats-dama Riumina. Gerke, who was normally strict and unsentimental with his pupils, was so moved by Mussorgsky's progress and performances that he presented the boy with a Beethoven sonata As-dur. Had it not been for the outlook on work of the gentry class from which he came, Mussorgsky could certainly have begun to give concerts—but his mother simply would not hear of it. Other children performed on stage, making their names for the future and providing for the welfare of their families. Up to the age of puberty and transition into adulthood this was not difficult for them: their childlike artistic grace and the innocent absence of stage fright are considerable advantages. 'At that age I took the stage everywhere and every time without the slightest hesitation', recalled Anton Rubinstein. 'I simply looked at concerts as a game, as something fun—that is, I treated them as a child, because I was a child'.[1]

The relations between the wunderkind and his teacher are unlike those of the latter with other future artists. The 'educability' of the wunderkind is so phenomenal, his ability to grasp everything quickly so exceeds all imaginable bounds, that the instructor has only to hint at the correct artistic device—to show or simply tell how one does this or that—and the wunderkind is off, racing ahead with giant steps and without asking for further explanation. This is why so many wunderkinds, 'spoiled' from several years of independent study, can so easily extract themselves from the crisis wrought of the irregularity of their education and set themselves on the right path. As Carl Czerny recalled upon first seeing the 11-year-old Liszt at the piano:

> The child looked weak and pale, and when he played he rocked back and forth on the chair like a drunk; I thought he was just about ready to fall off. His play, as well, was utterly irregular, unclear and off-putting. He did not have the faintest idea of what fingering was and completely randomly he threw his fingers around the keyboard. But despite all that I was amazed by the talent the child had been granted by nature … When at his father's request I gave him three themes for improvisation, I became even more convinced of his remarkable abilities: without any knowledge of harmony as such, he inserted into his improvisation an idea of genius. He quickly learned every song and was so accustomed to playing spontaneously that soon he could play the most difficult songs at sight, as if he had been studying them for a long time.[2]

The example of the young Liszt is very illustrative: mistakes which would have been fatal to an ordinary musician were simply an organic part of the beginning stage of his artistic biography. He performed, he sensed the audience—and that was more important than

[1] Rubinstein, A. (1889) Avtobiographicheskie zapiski/Autobiographical Notes. St-Petersburg, p. 11.
[2] Cit. from Milshtein, Y. (1999) *Ferenz Liszt*. Moscow: Kompozitor, p. 36.

correct fingering and appropriate placement of the hands. With the adaptability characteristic of the wunderkind he easily relearned what he had taught himself 'incorrectly' and went on from there. The same easy correctives came to the wunderkind Konstantin Igumnov when he fell into the hands of Sergei Zverev. After 6 months the former was flourishing as a conservatory student without a single technical flaw in his repertoire.

This kind of super-adaptability allows wunderkinds to get along practically without teachers. Liszt spent a year and a half with Czerny; Rubinstein studied 4 years with Alexandr Villoin before becoming a European celebrity at the age of 11. Paganini studied irregularly with various teachers—some of whose qualifications, especially at the early stages of the violinist's education, were rather dubious. The 13-year-old Paganini was at length sent to Parma at the behest of the patron of the arts Di Negro in order to study under the leading violinist of the city, maestro Alessandro Rolla. But Rolla sent the boy away, since he felt there was nothing he could teach him—the young virtuoso already knew and could do everything. What takes an ordinary musician years to master is handled by the wunderkind in months. The speed with which he processes and assimilates information—musical information for a musical wunderkind, or, say, mathematical information for his mathematical counterpart—literally approaches the unbelievable.

The brilliant beginning of the wunderkind's career leads one to expect an equally brilliant continuation. Certainly all parents of beginning virtuosos expect this. But the statistics assembled by scholars point elsewhere—to, for example, only a 10 percent success rate among former wunderkinds in their future creative development (Slonimsky 1947). The outstanding contemporary cellist and former wunderkind Yo Yo Ma is even less optimistic, putting the figure at 2 percent (personal conversation with Ellen Winner). Perhaps he was exaggerating in a flight of frustrated empathy, having seen too many others' shattered careers while on his own path to becoming a mature virtuoso. In any case, only a very small number of the children who raise great expectations are fated to fulfill them. All statistics are, in some sense, relative; but the sign on the gates of Hell which reads 'Abandon hope all ye that enter here' to a significant extent applies to the wunderkinds who have decided to scale the musical Olympus: the probability of success for anyone who sets foot on the path of an artistic career at the same age as Mozart is very slim indeed.

The little violinist, whose violin is barely larger than he is, and the little pianist, whose feet do not reach the pedals—these images are at once captivating and touching. So it is that wunderkinds, with society's particular curiosity about and attention to children and childhood, have remained in fashion for some three centuries now. But for the wonder-children themselves this 'fashion' bodes no good; the majority of them, rather, fall victim to it. As Ellen Winner has noted:

> Out of more than seventy musical prodigies who blossomed in San Francisco in the 1920s and 1930s, only six (including Yehudi Menuhin and Leon Fleischer) went on to become well-known soloists. We do not know what happened to the others, but probably some became orchestra members or music teachers, while others left music altogether. The myth that prodigies have brilliant futures is strengthened by the fact that many eminent and creative people throughout history showed exceptional abilities as children. We forget that this does not imply the reverse—that exceptional

children become adult creators. Most gifts never fully develop. Many gifted children burn out. A major difficulty in probing the connection between childhood giftedness and adult creativity is that we so rarely have any record of the many gifted children who have stopped developing their abilities.[3]

The cessation in development which Winner refers to raises emotional difficulties and issues of self-esteem for the former wunderkind. Not having lived up to the expectations of teachers and parents, having 'quit the race', he feels empty and useless. His fate is not infrequently a tragic one. Knowing this, Debussy wrote in one of the reviews: 'Petite Bleu' reported to us recently on the existence of a miraculous child whom he calls, a bit prematurely, the new Mozart. I hope that this Pierre Chagnon turns out to be one who shows us the way—but I would wish for the child himself rather less popularity'.[4] Alas, Debussy was right. Today the name of this 'new Mozart' remains virtually unknown to the world.

The bright beginnings and inglorious endings of the short careers of the majority of wunderkinds leave psychologists with a rather difficult task—finding an answer for why the wonder-children burn out. Is the problem a lack of pedagogical intervention—or the opposite, too much interference by the teacher? Are ambitious parents at fault, through hyper-exploitation which exhausts the child and deprives him of all stimulus for further growth? Or perhaps in the very nature of the wunderkind there are certain defects which determine his early creative demise. In the end one can only turn to the established facts, to the observations of the wunderkinds' teachers and parents. One can also recall the biographical details of people who succeeded in becoming outstanding creative talents, and compare them with the life stories of those who did not reach the heights of an artistic career. The elements which distinguish genuine wonder-children—the ones who 'really made it', as Americans say—from the 'pseudo-wunderkinds', who remained 'geniuses in short pants', can surely point researchers in the right direction.

The non-creative giftedness of the wunderkind

The simplest explanations for the failure of the wunderkind may be dismissed fairly easily. One cannot prove that over-ambitious parents are at fault: the fathers of Mozart and Paganini set all the records for tyrannical parental exploitation—yet their wonder-children brought glory to the family name and never gave a hint of burning out. Their talent was so great that the desires of their fathers coincided with their own, and no manner of cruelty or bullying could dissuade them from pursuing their music. A lack of parental pressure likewise fails as an explanation for wunderkind burnout: in the comfortably bourgeois milieu of the Schnabel and Rubinstein families, where the prospect of a musical career for a son and heir was viewed somewhat askance and by no means encouraged, the two outstanding pianists nevertheless grew up quite nicely—and their lack of concert experience at an early age did nothing to hinder their ascent to creative heights later on. No matter what the family's attitude, too hot, too cold, or somewhere in

[3] Winner, E. (1996) *Gifted Children*. New York: Basic Books, p. 279.
[4] Debussy, K. (1964) Stat'i, retsenzii, besedy/Articles, Reviews, Interviews. Moscow: Muzyka, p. 113.

between, the wunderkind remains what he is; the family's sole influence, it seems, is on the psychological comfort of the child and the subsequent pleasantness or bitterness of his childhood memories. The wunderkind's creative result, however, depends very little on family circumstances.

The quality of pedagogical interaction with the young genius also does not appear to be a decisive factor in his fate. The teacher may be very good, as Theodor Leshetitsky was with Schnabel, or he may be quite the opposite; the adult Arthur Rubinstein would not even speak of his teachers, as he felt that they had left him with extraordinarily little. The wunderkind may from his earliest years employ the advice of a great master—or he may just as soon be self-taught; neither one nor the other guarantees initial success or insures against subsequent failure. No matter who does the teaching and no matter how he does it, the teacher cannot produce a winning lottery ticket for the pupil's success or doom his career, either. A lack of brilliant teachers did not keep Menuhin from becoming an international virtuoso. Two of his instructors in childhood (Messrs. Enker and Persinger) were in fact typical violin teachers and did not earn the title of maestro. At the same time there are wonderful pedagogue-musicians who can remember several wunderkinds who 'quit the race'. Van Cliburn, who studied under the marvelous instructor Rosina Lhevinne, did not become an international virtuoso: his first triumph was his last, and his wonderful professional training with Lhevinne could not protect him.

It's possible to suppose that the reasons for wunderkind burnout are internal, related in some way to the particular nature of these people's thought processes—one quality of which may be to turn at a certain point from free flow into a kind of braking action. 'Wunderkind-ism' is a childhood of hypertrophic levels of perception, extraordinary educability and an innate sense of how systems work. All children easily grasp the structural principles of set systems, as we see first of all in their acquisition of their native language (or of several languages spoken in a household). The rules of a language, the combination of its various elements, are something children understand as a spatial field whose laws have unity and coherence. One does not need to explain these laws to children, as they deduce them for themselves. Children learn the use of a computer by playing around with it. In one region of India scientists set up a computer with an internet connection; within a month, without any instruction whatsoever, all the illiterate children of the neighborhood were computer literate and were busily surfing the worldwide web to amuse themselves (Ramzaev 2001). In exactly the same way children can amaze their elders as they play with Rubik's Cube: arranging all the colored surfaces in the right sequence is nothing to them—child's play, as the telling phrase has it—yet their parents can take hours to figure out the same process.

Possibly, it is this kind of innate understanding of systems which helps children become wunderkinds. A trait which is normally simply a childhood peculiarity is developed in wonder-children to an extraordinary degree. Every wunderkind chooses for himself a particular element-base—for one it may be musical structures, for another, visual elements, for a third, patterns of thread which he arranges on his fingers. The wunderkind effortlessly creates in his subconscious a set of rules for putting together the figures, notes, words, phrases, and various other structural units he needs for his system to work. Ellen Winner recounts the case of a wunderkind named Stephen who had an amazing ability to create and decipher systems of abstract symbolic figures in all manner of contexts. Like that of all wunderkinds, Stephen's talent expressed itself in areas in which no life experience was necessary. As Winner relates:

> He began to read without instruction at age three, while studying lists of songs on cassette tapes. He also began to write at three and by four was able to read cursive. He drew complex maps, charts, and diagrams, but he had no interest in drawing observationally or in color. He mastered highly technical computer-programming books at age eight, and he began to write programs in a variety of computer languages. He was fascinated with foreign languages and different alphabets. One of his amusements for years was to invent new alphabets. When he played chess, he seemed more interested in recording his moves in chess notation than in actually moving the pieces, much as he seemed to prefer playing with music notation to playing music.[5]

The passion of the wunderkind for quasi-linguistic manipulations is spread over a relatively narrow range. Some wunderkinds like to create systems of visual representation, adding visual elements one to another and committing to memory their typical formations; musical wunderkinds are capable of remembering typical conjunctions of musical structures and constructing variations on them (which is why they are capable of improvisations in styles familiar to them). The workhorse of the wunderkind is his ability to reproduce, which in the end is the root structure beneath all his phenomenal abilities. The childhood ability to copy, along with the ability to uncover systemic algorithms, reaches extraordinary degrees in the wunderkind. Memory for the 'combinability' of differentiated elements, which is what all ability with languages is based on, forms the basis of the wunderkind's abilities. If for the ordinary child the understanding and replication of a musical construction represents a difficult problem, for the wunderkind the construction appears in his consciousness seemingly by itself, as though inherently obvious. What goes with what and how it does it is self-evident to the wunderkind. No manner of manipulation, rearrangement, or transformation within a structure he knows can present any kind of problem for him.

Exceptional ability in systematic thinking and a phenomenal memory are the first signs of 'wunderkindism' which are noticed by those in the child's immediate environment. The example of a Hungarian boy named Erwin Neregazi is widely known among psychologists and pedagogues, as he was the subject of a psychological monograph (Revecz 1925). Erwin's father was a singer at the Budapest opera. Before reaching the age of 1 year, the boy was singing along with his father; in his second year he could competently reproduce his father's repertoire; and a year later he could play on the piano everything that he could sing. The child then demonstrated an ability to play Beethoven sonatas through four times—in the process committing them to memory for subsequent play by heart. Yet after these brilliant early successes, Erwin's debut in the United States led to nothing in particular. He turned out to be a typical 'pseudo-wunderkind'

---

[5] Winner, E. (1996) *Gifted Children*. New York: Basic Books, p. 91.

who failed to live up to the hopes and expectations of those around him. His subsequent fate came to interest no one, and the tragic anti-climax of Erwin Neregazi, like that of so many others in this category, is not the subject of further discussion in the literature on the subject.

If the wunderkind's memory were a pure memory, like that of a tape recorder, there would be no question of improvisation in familiar styles or composition of musical medleys and pot-pourri. Ervin and other wunderkinds do these things marvelously, relying on the elements of constructions they know and making new constructions from them by using the same principles. Knowing this, Schumann declined to comment one way or another on the altogether musically grammatical compositions of the young Anton Rubinstein: 'The first work of a gifted youth', wrote Schumann, 'is the work of a piano virtuoso who has already received all kinds of vociferous praise. The question of whether or not he is also possessed of an outstanding creative gift cannot be resolved *pro* or *con* on the basis of a first composition'.[6] The young Rubinstein had turned out a rendition of the contemporary romantic style; Schumann could not determine on the basis of anything copied whether the boy had a composer's imagination—which is what distinguishes the wunderkind from the beginning composer.

Child performers have an extraordinary ability to copy others. The Russian pianist Marya Barinova, a student of Joseph Hoffman and the author of a memoir about him, retained this simulative ability past childhood into her early youth. She recalled:

> Not long before I finished my studies when Hoffman was supposed to go to America, in the summer of 1905, I was learning Chopin's *Polonaise in D-Flat Minor*. When I came to my lesson, Hoffman played it for me. Wishing to hear his criticism of my performance of the polonaise, I asked his permission to repeat it myself. When he had heard me play, Hoffman announced that he was not going to play anything else for me because I copied his execution exactly.[7]

This is typically what wunderkinds do. They copy their teachers' playing, or copy the playing they hear on recordings. Given their amazing aural capabilities, there is nothing strange in this: they recall the tiniest nuances in someone else's playing and reproduce them. The natural children's abilities of mimicry, simulation, and imitation reach extraordinary heights in wunderkinds. One can assume that Van Cliburn came under the powerful influence of his teacher Rozina Lhevinne, whose animatedly Russian style of play he adopted with great success. Certain adults, by virtue of the infantilism which remains with most wunderkinds, retain their extraordinary abilities into their early youth—which only serves to delay for a time the inevitable collapse of their careers.

Those who have studied the wunderkind phenomenon have noted an Achilles heel. The wonder-children are never composers, not even to the smallest degree. The execution of variant copies in familiar styles has little in common with composition. The wunderkind

---

[6] Rubinstein, A. (1889) *Avtobiographicheskie zapiski/Autobiographical Notes*. St.Petersburg, p. 36.

[7] Barinova, M. (1961) Vospominaniya o I.Gofmane i F.Buzoni/Memoirs on J. Hoffman and F. Buzoni. Moscow: Muzyka, p. 39.

can improvise in a certain (known) manner, but he cannot create a manner of his own. Speaking of the maturing of the compositional ear for music, Boris Asafiev wrote:

> Usually between the ages of four and six, musicians who will display strong creative gifts in the future begin to demonstrate a particular activization of the ear in the as yet unconscious culling from all the sound around them those particular 'ingredients' which will prove useful for the musical memory—which is no longer a passive fund, as soon something original will issue forth from this archival reserve. Here we must be careful to clearly distinguish all manner of wunderkindism from those very rare cases of people who really have the abilities of compositional selectivity and the reworking of aural impressions.[8]

The composer is to a large extent the antipode of the wunderkind and his pattern of thought: the former masters and copies something *other*, while the latter produces something of his *own*. These two abilities are psychologically very far apart—which is why the majority of composers were not wunderkinds. Although beginning composers tend to variant copying, simulation as a general strategy is entirely foreign to them: copying is their instrument but not their purpose. The young Shostakovich was not a wunderkind. He had the ability to improvise in a manner which resembled any style, even the most diverse kinds of music which he would hear. This ability was also possessed by the entirely mediocre musician Bruni, with whom Shostakovich studied. The boy did not impress with any particular technical brilliance at the piano, and thus the well-known virtuoso Alexsandre Ziloti was led to remark, upon hearing him: 'The youth will not make a musical career for himself, as he does not have the abilities. But, of course, if he really wants to study music, well ... let him study'.[9] The young Shostakovich cried all night over this. Yet another 'expert', less musically qualified than Ziloti, it would seem, saw in the youth something else altogether. 'At some friends' place I met a very young man, almost a boy', recalled the writer Isaac Babel, 'and immediately, from the first glance, I sensed in him an unusual personality—something remarkable and endowed with a particular and exalted gift'.[10]

Babel had spied that spiritual source from which springs all creativity, including the musical; from this source grew Shostakovich the composer, who had no reason to be a wunderkind. Composing is the highest stage of musical talent. Outstanding performers, even if they were wunderkinds, are endowed with the gift of composition at least to a certain extent. In their play as teenagers one already senses a significant creative independence—one hears a particular musical content which is not a reproduction of the play of other performers. Failed wunderkinds lack this independence; they have phenomenal musical abilities but no musical talent, no creative potential—and that which was touching in a child cannot be, in an older youth, the cause of admiration. When people speak of the collapse or failure of a wunderkind, they unconsciously have in mind the loss of certain qualities which the subjects possessed before. Yet no such losses have taken place.

---

[8] Asafiev, B. V. (1952) Sluh Glinki/Glinka's ear. In *Izbrannie trudy/Selected Works*, vol.1. Moscow: Izdatelstvo Akademii nauk, p. 231.

[9] Meyer, K. (1998) *Shostakovich*. St.-Petersburg: Kompozitor, p. 22.

[10] Meyer, K. (1998) *Shostakovich*. St.-Petersburg: Kompozitor, p. 23.

As they grow older the wunderkinds in fact lose only a certain artistic spontaneity and the ideal on-stage self-possession which many child performers have. There is nothing else they can lose.

That which is stunning to see in a child's performance inspires hardly any reaction at all when it appears in the play of a youth. The fact that someone can play ultra-complex compositions from an adult repertoire means little after the age of 14. And the fact that someone plays the most difficult virtuoso etudes, sonatas, and other works from the musical 'stratosphere' will elicit merely the remark 'Everybody plays all those' if the subject is a teenager rather than a child. The wunderkind can easily exhaust the interest of society, and if there is no sense from him of a creative individuality, if his performing does not engage people, then the career of the child may be considered unrealized.

The infectiousness of the performing artist, his ability to 'take over the hall', is connected less with the quality of his abilities—the analytical ear, the sense of rhythm, and even the architectonic ear—as with the quality of his creative giftedness. And this giftedness, in turn, is unimaginable without the active, creative motivation which is one of its constituents. Like the young Shostakovich, the outstanding Performer senses in himself a significant spiritual content which he wants to pass along. The wunderkind takes only the surface of a composition, its external structures, and does not penetrate further into the internal workings. The wunderkind's ability to recreate and copy does not produce creative motivation and will not grow into it. In his understanding of music the wunderkind does not extend to the strata of thought invested in a composition, and has no desire to give that thought expression.

If there is no creative motivation, then there is no creative conception—without which, in turn, no creative result can ensue. The motivational inadequacy of wunderkinds was confirmed during an experiment conducted in the United States in 1998 in which the present author and others were measuring the expressive ear for music (Kirnarskaya 2006). The subject group included 15 wunderkinds, all winners of various international children's competitions. Those of them who had a poor expressive ear, which also means a weak motivation for musical communication, ceased to amaze anyone with their playing in a few years, and did not become professional musicians. The other gifted children, with a good expressive ear, showed the opposite: they later flourished, and the quality of their playing became better. Their musical nature gave them the chance to show themselves creatively, to demonstrate who they were—while the pseudo-wunderkinds did not strive for such self-expression and probably did not grasp what the term meant.

If the structure of the abilities of a wunderkind lacks a motivational block, the career of the child in question is relegated to a gradual withering away. This fate speaks of the fact that even phenomenal abilities do not grow into talent, and no efforts by teachers, parents, or the wunderkind himself can succeed in transforming one into the other.

An ordinary miracle

In the music community the word wunderkind has come to be used rather loosely. In schools for gifted children, regular outbursts of wunderkind-ism are something both desired and expected—and thus at the slightest indication of ability exceeding the norm, teachers and parents munificently bestow the title of wunderkind upon a child. In reality, the 'outburst' in question may amount to nothing more than being able to play, at 7–9 years of age, an adult repertoire and several difficult etudes. In the psychological and social sense such boys and girls are not wonder-children at all, of course; there is nothing at all miraculous in their performance. Adding oil to the fire beneath this imitation-wunderkind boomlet, in any case, was the music teacher and pianist Karl Martinsen (2003), who coined a term for the collective description of a particular array of brilliant musical abilities—a marvelous ear, a prodigious musical memory, and the statistical signs of a virtuoso—dubbing them the 'wunderkind complex'. The truth is, however, that one may possess all these wonderful abilities and still not be a wunderkind: the levels at which very capable children and wunderkinds perform are, in fact, not at all comparable.

The wunderkind, irrespective of his ultimate fate and the extent of his gifts, demonstrates capacities which are, put simply, phenomenal and amazing. While merely able children study away at 'adult' works over the course of several weeks or months, practicing stubbornly all the while, the wunderkind masters the same material in the course of a couple of days—and occasionally a couple of hours. The speed with which the wunderkinds process information can be compared with nothing else. Further, the wonder-children further assemble enormous repertoires, similar to those of adult artists. Everything they have ever learned, anywhere at any time, remains in their active memories, without the aid of practice or repetition. What the able child does quickly, the wonder-child does instantaneously; what the former learns easily but not without effort, the wunderkind masters as an amusement, in merely playing around. The final product which the able child produces is encouraging; what issues from the wunderkind is stunning. In the course of a decade or two, a major metropolis will see many hundreds of capable children, but only a few dozen wunderkinds.

The unique abilities of the wonder-children are really only comparable with the analogous abilities of the so-called *idiot savants*. These people distinguish themselves in the same areas as the wunderkinds: mathematics, painting and drawing, and music. Musical savants strike one with their exceptional aural capacity: they 'shine through' a composition and then copy it without so much as an erasure. They can create pot-pourri from familiar works, and even improvise in styles which they know (Lamont 1998; Miller 1999; Treffert 1989). Unlike wunderkinds, however, the savants suffer from a pronounced deficit of mental capability: they have no command of logic, do not communicate in speech, have no ongoing relations with the outside world, and are incapable of abstract thought. Their IQ levels are extremely low. Savants suffer from autism, an ailment in which people enclose themselves in a narrow range of their own activities and do not venture out. The autistic, as is the case with many psychologically disturbed people, do not suspect that they are suffering from an ailment and take life for what it is. The classic popular representation of the autistic person is that rendered by Dustin Hoffman in the film *Rain Man*, in which the character Raymond, emotionally stunted and socially estranged, lives in a world of self-imposed stereotypes: he always eats the same number of fish sticks, always sleeps by the window, and regularly retreats, when he perceives a threat, into the repetition of movie dialogue memorized in childhood.

Robyn Young and Tom Nettelbeck (1995) conducted a study of a 12-year-old autistic boy, whom they designated TR in their account. The boy had an unusual ability to concentrate, a remarkable memory, and could absorb information with amazing speed. As with all savants, TR spoke very badly and could not pursue logical thought on even the simplest level. His musical abilities, on the other hand, were extraordinary: like other musical savants he had perfect pitch and could reproduce large fragments of music after a single hearing. As the researchers noted: 'TR's ability to recall and perform structured music in diatonic and whole-tone systems was dependent on his familiarity with musical structure. TR demonstrated competence in improvisation and composition, albeit restricted by adherence to structural representations of familiar musical rules'.[11]

The musical abilities of savants are connected psychologically with other rare abilities which they possess. In observing savants' habits and predilections, scientists are drawing ever closer to understanding the cognitive strategy such people use, and the behavior of savants may shed light on their methods of processing information—including musical information. Ellen Winner, the author of a substantial monograph on gifted children (1996), has done significant work on artist-savants. These people possess a surprising ability to recreate reality on paper: when other children draw little sheep and symbolic figures, savant-children scrupulously record in their drawings all the details of objects they have seen. While they normally draw from memory, the detail and degree of verisimilitude do not suffer for this. As Winner notes:

> These descriptions suggest a kind of memory in which conceptualization and understanding do not intervene, a kind of tape-recorder memory that requires no effort and admits no thought. It could be argued that this kind of non-comprehending memory would lead to excessively realistic rendering. Savants may, in fact, draw complex objects with precision because, when looking at the object, they see it merely as a cluster of lines and shapes, not as a three-dimensional object.[12]

Winner proposes that savants use an 'element to element' strategy, when the object appears from the 'hemming' of the scrap-fragments, each of which is perceived entirely formally. The same formalism is distinguishable in the savants' perfect pitch. Oliver Sacks, an expert on perfect pitch and its neuro-psychological coordinates, has written: 'The precocious appearance of absolute pitch, its relative isolation from conceptual, verbal, and even general musical powers and its remarkable incidence in individuals with Williams syndrome and autism suggests that it may be a savant talent'.[13]

The left-hemisphere of the brain is enlarged in all people with perfect pitch, including savants; this is the section of the brain which controls speech patterns. Yet despite the hypertrophic *planum temporale*, savants, like other autism victims, suffer from speech

[11] Young, R. L. and Nettelbeck, T. (1995) The abilities of a musical savant and his family. *Journal of Autism and Developmental Disorders*, 25, p. 231.

[12] Winner, E. (1996) *Gifted Children*. New York: Basic Books, p. 127.

[13] Sacks, O. (1995) Musical ability. *Science*, 268, p. 621.

defects, usually including non-mastery of verbal language. An experiment performed at the University of Glasgow's Institute for Biomedical Research may shed light on this apparent contradiction: the highly developed left hemisphere and the *planum temporale* must not meet with the speech deficit which hinders all savants. A group of scientists led by Pamela Heaton (Heaton *et al.* 1999) studied an autistic child called S., who showed remarkable musical abilities, for 4 years. Unlike many savants, S. did not suffer from mental defects and could reason logically; his social skills were well below the norm, however. His communication problems were so great that the whole of his behavior was considered by doctors 100 percent autistic: the child lacked any connection with the outside world. He had perfect pitch, and like all savants he remembered and played familiar music by ear. The group concluded:

> This S. demonstrated absolute pitch ability and outstanding analytical capacities within the musical domain. His musical information processing style might be accounted for by a tendency to focus on local rather than global aspects of musical stimuli, and in addition illustrates a case study of exceptional ability in the absence of musical talent.[14]

The group studying S. noted an extremely important aspect of the abilities of savants: the seemingly unique activity of savants is in fact completely lacking in conscious thought. The operational abilities of savants, which manipulate musical elements and remember musical structures, have nothing at all in common with talent as a function of and capacity to communicate a certain specified artistic content. Their reproduction of music and any other material takes place on a purely formal mechanical level; it is the mere stringing together of detached elements. These elements come together into some sort of whole only in the perception of the audience; for the savant himself the whole exists only as a sum, as the aggregate of certain 'bricks' which have been arranged in a certain way: he sees the bricks but not the building. The savant does not understand the category of thought; his activity is not directed toward anything or conditioned by anything. This is why he neither talks to nor deals with others: he has nothing to tell them and no expectations of them.

Subject S. could speak, which by itself demonstrates that the absence of speaking abilities is not a principal characteristic of autism (though it is widespread among autists). This common absence of the power of speech is most likely a result not of an operational deficiency, so to speak, but rather of an ideational one. Possibly, an autistic person does not communicate less because of physical restraints than because he does not want to—and here the extraordinarily developed *planum temporale*, the home of both perfect pitch and the speech functions, can alter nothing. The autistic savant has no motivation to interact with others; he feels no necessity to do so. 'Light' autism, as described by the Pamela Heaton and her colleagues, underlines the essence of all aspects of autism: extreme deficits of emotion and ideation, damage to the centers of communication and interaction—but none to the operational components of speech ability. The speech

---

[14] Heaton, P., Pring, L., and Hermelin, B. (1999) A pseudo-savant: a case of exceptional musical splinter skills. *Neurocase*, 5, p. 503.

apparatus may not function because its starter mechanism, the need for contact, does not engage.

Among wunderkinds, or rather among the vast majority of them, those who do not become outstanding artists, the same deficit may be evident. In adolescence, when the childhood ability to copy weakens, these former wonder-children no longer 'light up' the auditorium because they have no impulse for interaction with the audience; their play is without substance, even though it may be at the virtuoso level and performed 'smoothly'. And at the same time, their manipulative abilities, the ease of operation with the musical elements which they demonstrate, is very similar to the analogous activity of savants. Ellen Winner has noted the psychological similarity between wunderkinds and savants: 'Despite the differences that do certainly exist between savants and prodigies in art and music, savant gifts in these domains are close enough to those of prodigies to provide strong evidence against the IQ myth even for music'.[15]

Psychological parallels between prodigies and savants really exist, including analogous appearances of abilities, similar attention to particular at the expense of general, gathering details instead of grasping the whole, and, finally, insufficiencies in emotional and communicative qualities. Subject S., with whom the Pamela Heaton's group worked, closely approaches the wunderkinds while remaining a savant. On the psychological level he is almost normal, with the exception of the 'communication failure' he demonstrates. The problems of the wunderkinds who could not complete a test to measure the expressive ear for music are neither as obvious nor as acute as the problems of S., but they are on the same plane, that of communication.

In March 1996 at a conference of musical psychologists in Cambridge, England, a blind 14-year-old savant, referred to as P., performed on the piano. His play elicited amazement, based on the fact that P. was entirely lacking in mental abilities. His performance was extraordinarily colorless, vacant, and unexpressive, which reflected the total absence in P. of an expressive ear for music. It is no surprise that savants, unlike wunderkinds, do not give concerts—no one could stand to listen to the play of a savant for long. Wunderkinds do not normally evince this kind of emotional-communicative deficit in their performance, as they sufficiently faithfully reproduce the play of other artists and their instructors. But in their behavior and in their appearance overall some of them not infrequently recall the behavior and appearance of autistic children.

Wunderkinds tend to be extraordinarily withdrawn in their practice sessions and show a lack of interest in communicating with their peers and family members. This self-immersion is normally written off as the typical withdrawal demonstrated by geniuses; yet this may be misapprehension, as real geniuses—and here Mozart provides a textbook example—are not withdrawn at all. They like people and are open to them. The submersion into a world of their own which wunderkinds pursue, and the isolation reached by some of them, may in fact be signs of a very mild form of autism. The wonder-children may be healthy, but these hints of autism are nevertheless indications of a neuropsychological

---

15 Winner, E. (1996) *Gifted Children*. New York: Basic Books, p. 115.

predisposition towards autism, which appears in the characteristic profile of their abilities: absolutely perfect pitch, a hypertrophic memory, and a single-element-based view of structures combined with an atrophied level of contact with the world. There are cases in which 'burned out' wunderkinds are recorded as demonstrating clear signs of autism and significant episodes of psychological distress, up to and including suicide attempts (Winner 1996). In any event, further research needs to be done to confirm or refute the assumption that the closeness in behavior parallels between the two groups—wunderkinds and autists— reflects a closeness in the psychological origins of their phenomenal abilities.

The extraordinarily rare cases of 'true' wunderkinds—those who manage to remain at or even exceed their performance levels of childhood—are entirely unlike the 'false' wonder-children one sees most often. The eminent St Petersburg music teacher Marina Wolf, an instructor with many wonderful pianists to her credit, maintains that the wunderkind is 'an early manifestation of an intense spiritual life'. Those things which in the 'pseudo-wunderkind's' musical life occupy the last places—the artistic mission, the image, a striving to communicate through music—are for the genuine wunderkind matters of primary importance.

Wonder-children, with Mozart in the lead again, show a heightened need for love. This exceptional need for interaction and sympathy arises early in their lives and continues throughout them. But that is not all: wunderkinds amaze all who know them with their remarkable maturity of spirit, unusual wisdom, and the subtlety of their minds. Recounting for his son the story of the boy's early childhood, Mozart's father recalled:

> When a child you've been more serious than boyish, and while you were sitting at the clavier all absorbed with music, there wasn't a stir. Your face expression was so solemn, that looking at the early blossom of your talent and your always serious and thoughtful little face, many shrewd people from different countries expressed their doubts whether you were destined for long life.[16]

Those wunderkinds who are fated to leave a mark in the historical record possess two psychological characteristics which are, to some extent, mutually exclusive. They are at once blessed with a hypertrophic receptivity in childhood and with an unusual ability to master musical systems and the rules that govern them; and they are no worse than the 'false' wunderkinds and idiot savants at remembering and performing music. At the same time they have an inclination toward composition—the sign of true musical talent. In their childhood compositions, as in those of the young Prokofiev, one already sees their creative 'I' at work: the piano pieces Prokofiev wrote as a 10-year-old bear the stamp of the abruptness and theatricality which were to be hallmarks of his work thereafter. In this awkward and unprofessional work one already hears the characteristic 'Prokofiev note'.

Wonder-children resemble adults in their independence of manner. As a 3-year-old Sidney Bechet would stubbornly stand on the street listening to any little passing band; his parents were incapable of making him come home (Chilton 1987). He showed the same stubbornness when his parents would not give him a clarinet to play: he stole his older brother's instrument and played it until the instrument was finally officially given

---

[16] Chicherin, G. (1970) *Mozart*. Leningrad: Muzyka, p. 117.

to him as a Christmas present. Bechet loved to watch as adults played music; he would forever find ways to run off and listen to the music at the circus or hang around real clarinetists, with whom spending time was for Bechet the highest form of blessing. Young Bechet studied the clarinet on his own, and by the age of 8 had become a complete virtuoso on the instrument. He had all the characteristics of an adult artist: a maniacal attachment to music, a tremendous need for musical interaction, and a rare (even among adults) firmness of character and understanding of his goals.

In his childhood Arthur Schnabel always sought the company of his elders. From infancy until the age of 30 he preferred to make friends among people old enough to be his father (Schnabel 1967). His closest friend was Johannes Brahms—who was in fact old enough to be his grandfather. The adults recognized the entirely unchildlike intellectual and spiritual level of young Arthur: at soirees staged by and for his elders, when children of his age were being put to bed, Schnabel was left to remain with the adults and treated as an equal in their conversations. The other children were jealous of these exceptional privileges, and Schnabel received his first slap in the face from one of the boys staying over at his house: all the children had been trundled off to bed after dessert, while young Arthur continued to play the social lion as though that were the normal thing to do.

The performance of a talented wunderkind is indeed unique; no one who has heard such a presentation will forget it. The performance bears the purity and openness of childhood, a complete giving up of oneself to the music—and yet at the same time the listener senses the wisdom and consciousness of an adult performance. The wunderkind lives in two worlds at once, that of childhood and adulthood, and he harvests honey from both flowers, as it were: remaining a child, artless and at times naive, he also reminds one of a prophet of old with his depth of understanding of the ways of the world and his gift of insight. Such indeed was the violin wunderkind Jacques Thibauld. Perhaps the untimely death of his mother, when the boy was only two, brought about his early maturity. He began to study the violin only at age 9, after the death of his brother Hippolite, an extraordinarily gifted violinist (Thibaud 1953). By age 11, Jacques was already giving concerts. Having heard the boy play, the virtuoso Eugene Ysaye told Thibaud's father, 'You know that I am a man who tells the truth: your son plays better than I do'.

Science does not yet know the reasons for such early maturity in wunderkinds. It really is a miracle of nature, quite real and inexplicable: what you have is an adult in the form of a child. Neuropsychological studies may shed light on the methods of information processing which wunderkinds employ, but explaining their phenomenal spiritual growth, which turns them from children into adults overnight, remains beyond the realm of the scientific. The most convincing 'explanation' remains that offered by Zubin Mehta for the impossibly mature performance of the 7-year-old Sarah Chang: she must have acquired the necessary skill and experience in a previous lifetime.

Predicting the dawn or sunset of the wunderkind's gift is extraordinarily difficult: science is still in the data-compilation stage, at the level only of offering hypotheses. One of these theories is that noted above concerning psychological similarities between failed wunderkinds and savants, notably the proximity of activity parameters for both groups.

Part of this idea is the extraordinary role which is played in the development of the gifted young musician's motivational core of talent: suffering from a 'communicative deficiency', with a weak intonational ear and unarticualted musical-creative requirement, many winderkinds cease to demonstrate that they are gifted musicians.

Musical pedagogues Larry Scripp and Lyle Davidson conducted a statistical experiment, the result of which could be interpreted in favor of the innate character of both the success and failure of wunderkinds in their later careers: 'Neither early detection of giftedness nor intensive early training in an artistic domain assures smooth passage through later levels of development'.[17]

The authors noted the secondary role of external influences on the development of the wunderkind's abilities; but they refrained from offering an opinion of their own as to the reasons for the onset and disappearance of these abilities. Ellen Winner, in advancing her theory, avoids leaping to conclusions—but she does note a hallmark difference between 'genuine' and 'false' wunderkinds: 'The ability of [the former] adolescents to attain a state of flow while working in their area of gift was far more predictive of commitment than was academic ability, family support, or other personality factors'.[18]

She emphasizes the leading role of motivation—or *drive*, as the British and Americans refer to it—in any creative activity, including that of the wunderkind. A comparison of the triumph of certain wonder-children and the collapse of others points to the same thing: among the former there is a spiritual, cultural, and emotional fullness of talent—as well as the potential for love and reflection, which moves talent, and can raise it to the heights of glory and a brilliant career. Society rejects everything else, assuring us all of the wisdom of Polish writer Stanislas Lem, who said: 'Man needs only man'. Abilities which do not serve the ends of mutual understanding and bringing people closer together are ultimately of no value, and no manner of musical slight of hand on the part of the 'false' wunderkinds, no matter how deftly rendered, can obviate this truth.

[17] Scripp, L. and Davidson, L. (1994) Giftedness and professional training: the impact of music reading skills on musical development of conservatory students. In *Beyond Terman: Contemporary Longitudinal Studies of Giftedness and Talent. Creativity Research Series* (ed. R. F. Subotnik, K. D. Arnold *et al.*). Norwood, NJ: Ablex Publishing Corporation, p. 209.

[18] Winner, E. (1996) *Gifted Children*. New York: Basic Books, p. 29.

Part 6

Homo musicus

The human race has become accustomed to referring to itself grandly and in Latin—
Homo sapiens, Reasoning Man. With this title we separate ourselves from unthinking
Nature and mark ourselves as her master. But Reasoning Man in fact began to reason
fairly late in the evolutionary game, and thus science, the proof and prover of the
complete development of his reasoning powers, was likewise a late arrival.

Art and music are older than science, and indeed older than thought itself: in art man
expresses his relationship to nature and life, with the ideational process dissolving into
sensation and blending into it entirely. Art as the creative self-expression of man and the
method of his interaction with the world arose earlier than abstract thought and science.
This means that the human brain was originally formed in the venues of art—songs,
dances, and rituals. It was formed when man covered the walls of his cave with magical
drawings, it was formed when he made rhymes and sang songs—and only then, after the
passing of many millennia, did this brain chart the course of the planets, open the secrets
of matter, and discover the laws of natural evolution.

So *Homo musicus*—Musical Man, who creates, performs, and listens to music—is older
than *Homo sapiens*. Man made music of a sort even when he did not know how to
measure things or count them properly, and the very concept of numbers was still but
a glimmer in his brain. He made music when he could not find the reason for natural
phenomena, the rain, hail, and drought around him. He made music before he had
learned to work the land and before he could build a boat to cross the sea. Music was
already, in the most distant antiquity, the concentration on feeling and thought in our
primitive ancestor. Music helped man relate to those near him, and played a part in the
appearance of the Word (since it preceded this event). Before the formulation of mathematics as a science there was present in the rhythm of music the essence of proportions,
symmetry, and the relationship of things in time; geometry did not exist, yet in the songs
man sang there was already a concept of higher and lower, of different 'points in space'
which indicated different ranges of sound. Earliest man thought with the help of music
even before he came upon abstract thought and learned to use concepts. Man's mental
abilities were assembled over thousands of years in the framework provided by the art of
Music, a framework left distinct as evolution moved on.

Civilization has recognized the leading role of music in the development of the human brain. The ancient Greeks spoke of the harmony of the celestial sphere, assuming that music resounded in the cosmos and expressed its laws: if one did not know and understand music, one could not comprehend nature. The earliest Chinese considered music the formula of peace, likening the relationship of sounds to the relationship of any and all sizes, shapes, and objects. In Europe in the Middle Ages music was set alongside geometry and astronomy as one of the sciences. Man has never divorced music from thought, considering it both a part of thought and to a certain extent its source. Thinking as such and the procedures of thought—comparison, apposition, analysis, and synthesis, the division of things and their assembly into a whole—exist organically in music. Indeed, it is entirely possible that these functions proceeded from music to the realm of abstract thought, creating a psychological bridge between the world of art and that of science, between emotional-sensory thought and that which we now call abstract-logical.

Music and Thought are inseparable: the second derived from the first, forming itself in the musical depths throughout the entirety of the phylogenetic process; thus a man wishing to order his thoughts naturally, wishing to return to the psychological sources of thought, and to give thought over completely to nature—such a man must inevitably turn to music. He must become *Homo musicus* in order to return in future to *Homo sapiens*—such was the process of the evolution of the human brain, and there is nothing more sensible in the development of one's mental powers than to turn to their musical source. To think in music and to gain a foot-hold for abstract reasoning in music is easier than doing without it. Learning to think in sounds and then taking one's acquired ability into other spheres—this is a psychologically organic process, as it relies on the natural course of evolution. Thus the human race was formed, and in precisely this way is formed the thinking pattern of every individual human who recognizes himself as the product of evolution and a bearer of its traditions.

Music and the schools

Over the many centuries of its development European culture maintained a 'musical accent' which played an active role in the educational process. In the European universities of the Middle Ages and the Enlightenment music was studied alongside the other more 'useful' sciences. All this changed in the eighteenth century when the sacred began to retreat before the temporal, the spiritual before the practical, and man began to think more about 'contemptible utility' than about the development of his own being. Efforts were put into knowledge, skills, and technique, while the development of abilities as such and the expansion of mental powers was considered a matter of secondary importance.

In the industrial and post-industrial eras society witnessed the unprecedented growth of science, a development once regarded as the fruit of the educational process set right, in the appropriate 'pragmatic' mode. In doing this, however, society forgot the most important thing: the human brain evolves slowly; the talents we observe today and observed yesterday are the fruit of genetic development which took place over many centuries. This simply means that the flourishing of scientific thought and mental giftedness can be ascribed to the educational process of preceding centuries, in whose depths was formed modern man's natural thought process. To a much greater degree man's mental resources flow from the genetically 'accumulated baggage' of thought than from the direct process of education through which any given man may pass.

In the second half of the twentieth century society encountered, alongside the stunning successes of science and industry, a certain 'mechanization' of thought, a formalization of a kind. Modern society saw the ascent of the 'executive' approach toward man over the creative. A person was seen as a subject acting on instructions and capable of fulfilling a limited range of operations—but fulfilling this limited range very well indeed, since he is 'tasked' with precisely that. Relating to oneself as to a function became the predominant approach among youth, a significant portion of which lost its taste for creativity and creative self-expression, preferring to master instructions rather than waste oneself on creative tension, and in the end expanding one's free time to the maximum. In the long run such a philosophy can lead humanity to the degeneration and loss of its creative potential: a man who does not see himself as an independent spiritual entity ceases to produce ideas and ceases to be the engine of growth of his society and culture. The 'consumer society' is dangerous for this exaggeratedly mechanical approach to humanity, which threatens to cut human creative potential short.

At the onset of the third millennium the pedagogical communities within many societies have recognized the limitations and dangers of mechanical functionalism in our understanding of man and his social role. In recent years the pedagogical fraternity in the developed countries has been attempting to re-examine the philosophical bases of education, turning its attention to the traditions under which education had been unthinkable outside of art and broadly included art both as a subject and as a method of instruction. Art fed human giftedness at the dawn of history and continued to feed it later, when the study of science and the study of art, as an inseparable tandem, established the core and content of education. Now, when the excessive pragmatism of education threatens the very future of Talent, the future of the creative powers of humanity, the most farsighted among the teaching community are relying on art, and within art particularly on Music, to expand the mental powers of their students and help them overcome difficulties in the educational process.

The University of Chicago stands in the avant-garde of this pedagogical movement. A group of professors at Chicago's School of Education made a study of the academic progress of some 25 000 elementary school pupils from 1992 to 1998. These children studied in an expanded curriculum which included broad use of music and the arts. Such programs have been included among the required courses in the curricula of many American experimental schools, whose principals understand the leading role of art in the development of a student's intellect and in the mastery of necessary life skills (Catterall *et al.* 1999). The program was designated the Chicago Arts Partnership in Education (CAPE).

The researchers paid special attention to the success of children from families of lower socio-economic status; students from non-CAPE schools served as the experiment's control. The results of the study indicated that children in the experimental group did much better across the entire spectrum of school subjects, and did much better on the special tests designed for the experiment than did the students in the control group. The arts-intensive students outperformed their control-group peers in both mathematics and reading skills. Significantly, the differences were especially evident among students at the sixth grade level—that is, among students on the brink of their teenage years, when thought patterns begin to take on adult characteristics. Children from disadvantaged socio-economic backgrounds in particular distinguished themselves by their high rates of growth in academic achievement and test-taking ability; for them the art studies proved to be even more advantageous than for their more-advantaged peers.

The exceptional effectiveness of music as a stimulator of success in elementary school and in academic endeavors generally has been confirmed by the studies of Polish musicians done by Maria Manturzewska (1978). Certain representatives of society (without close ties to the realm of music) suggested that perhaps the great time commitments demanded by the preparation for a professional music career left musicians lacking in basic knowledge and generally be less intellectually developed than members of other professions. Nothing of the sort, it turned out, was true: a careful study of the biographies of Poland's leading musicians and testing of the nation's younger generation of musicians confirmed a commendable facility with language among both groups, as well as a highly developed capacity for logical thought. Two of the benchmarks of successful elementary education—command of one's native language and essential mathematical skills—were in fact more evident among the musicians than among other professionals in the society at large.

Given the possibility to study music, children become more creative, more inventive, and on the whole more smart. These effects mostly occur in the elementary school years, prompting that in the 'critical period' of a child's development a broad road towards music is something to be provided by our educational system (Crncec et al. 2006; Hodges 2005; Schellenberg 2006; 2005; 2003; Schellenberg et al. 2007; Schlaug et al. 2005). And those who benefit most from exposure to music, are possibly the disadvantaged: a group of them, suffering from Williams syndrome, could enhance their understanding of mathematics under the influence of special music enrichment program. Authors of this research regret that a well-known craving for music these children demonstrate usually remains ignored in their curricula (Reis et al. 2003).

The experience of the outstanding Japanese music teacher Shinitsu Suzuki is likewise revealing. Suzuki advocates beginning the study of the violin at a very early age and encourages parental involvement in the educational process: mothers play an active role in their children's music lessons, helping oversee them and standing in for the music teacher when the child is at home. Suzuki's idea, no doubt, was to create a 'nursery' for the musically talented. In practice, however, the Suzuki plan fostered the general mental development of the students far more than it did their musical proclivities. Jean-Pierre Mialaret reports about Maria Serafine's work with a group of 34 eleven year olds who had completed the Suzuki program. Their memories were better developed than those of their peers, they better understood the nature of hierarchical relationships, recognized the division of spatial and other structures onto planes better, and could manipulate various hierarchical structures their peers could not (Mialaret 1997). Similarly, Gael Orsmond and Leon Miller (1999) found in a study of a group of 58 children aged 3–6 years—half of whom were Suzuki students and half lacking any musical preparation whatsoever—that after 4 months of classes the Suzuki group had far surpassed the others in the development of visual-motor skills.

A number of studies carried out in different countries show the beneficial effects of music on the intellectual growth of children. The effectiveness of music's influence on humans, especially during the childhood period of heightened receptivity, is explained by the intimate connection between musical arts and the brain, developed over the entire course of human evolution. Musical and non-musical functions were housed in the same compartments of the brain, so that it was impossible to touch and activate the musical functions without touching the others as well. Thus music stimulates brain activity across the board because musical functions are spread out widely in the brain, taking in all its compartments. Musical pursuits optimize the brain's work, which cannot but help in the most variegated of mental labors. Musical functions are to be found in the right and left hemispheres and practically in all parts of the brain including the oldest, cerebellum, and the most intellectually advanced, the frontal lobes (Levitin 2006); listening to, composing, and performing music require a constant exchange of information between different parts of the brain and active interaction in perception and creativity. Other forms of mental activity hardly call forth such coordination and parallelism, which speaks to the harmonizing influence of music on brain activity and the strengthening of interaction among brain structures under the influence of music and music making.

Music reorganizes the functions of the brain—such was the conclusion of T. N. Malyarenko (1996). Over the course of 6 months Malyarenko's experiment had 4-year-old children listen to classical music for an hour a day; the control group spent the same daily hour involved in typical kindergarten pursuits involving no music at all. Subsequent testing of the children using electroencephelographic examinations revealed that in the 'musical' children the alpha-rhythm of various parts of the brain stem had become more coordinated and, the researcher noted, more 'connected and coherent'. It's possible to interpret these results as speaking to a greater 'cooperation' among the sections of the brain, or to say that the benefits derive from more relaxed, tension-free work of the brain mechanisms. It was emphasized that these changes, whatever their actual source, took place without any active engagement of the children in the musical process—what happened simply happened because music was playing in the immediate environment. This speaks of the enormous power of music's influence, and to the genuinely intimate connection between the art of music and the human brain.

Assymetria between the hemispheres of the brain is less pronounced among musicians; during brain activity the hemispheres easily succeed one another and pass along various functions to each other. This pattern was revealed in an experiment conducted by Lutz Jaencke and his colleagues (Jaencke et al.1995). The subjects in the experiment consisted of two groups—one of right-handed musicians, the other of left-handed non-musicians. The musicians, it turned out, had a less pronounced predominance of right hand over left.

Since the left brain hemisphere governs the right hand, and the right hemisphere the left, the scientists interpreted this result as proof of less-developed brain specialization—a demonstration of greater equality of the hemispheres among musicians in comparison with non-musicians. Gottfried Schlaug and his colleagues (Schlaug *et al.* 1995a) also demonstrated that in musicians the size of the *corpus callosum*—the section of the brain which answers for communication between hemispheres and also for sensory-motor connections—was also greater. Musicians generally boast a much more active connection of sight, sound, and movement than non-musicians; a musician will react sooner and more effectively to a visual or aural signal than a non-musician. This pattern is particularly evident among those who, while not becoming professionals, began to study music before the age of 7 (Elbert *et al.* 1995).

Teaching methodology at the elementary school level focuses to a great extent on the development of analytical skills: the pupil is required to disassemble material put before him into constituent parts (a rule, a law, an observed relationship, a fragment of text); to work on/over each part separately; and finally to form a complete picture of the overall process under examination. Analytical skills are also indispensable in the study of languages, where one must master the structure of words and sentences, and in the study of mathematics, where one must know what various formulas consist of and how to balance others. Music aids considerably in the formation of analytical thought patterns since it is by nature hierarchical: even minor motifs and musical phrases can be understood as the products of smaller sub-motifs and intervals. In pursuing music people learn to think hierarchically: the rules for forming hierarchical structures are imprinted in the intellect—smaller units coalesce into greater ones, and these in turn become parts of an even greater musical whole. The important role of the analytical left hemisphere in mature musical perception is a broadly accepted assumption: activization of the left hemisphere during music studies furthers the mastery of analytical skills, first and foremost in the study of the exact sciences.

Vanessa Sluming and John Manning (2000) at the University of Liverpool made a study of the style of self-directed school work among secondary school students. The concept of style included: different motivations for performing the work (internal and external); ability or inability to work in isolation; capacity or incapacity to concentrate in a noisy environment; and the self-perception of the subjects as students who rely on self-discipline or students who require external guidance. The study showed that students who studied music were more independent, requiring neither external stimuli or assistance. And that is exactly the working style of the musician: she practices alone, she has no one to turn to for support, and she must spend several hours a day with her instrument, interacting with no one and experiencing no external pressure. Musicians and former musicians are more free spirited and focused pupils, and these traits are so widely known that scientific data only serve to confirm the stereotypical characteristics of musical children.

Judith Burton and her colleagues (Burton *et al.* 2000) initiated a project involving the active introduction of art into school curricula. At the core of the project was a single principle: systematic musical studies for all the children. The project studied 2046 pupils from 12 American middle schools. In analyzing the results of their project the researchers concentrated on personality development among the children and growth of their intellectual capacities—and, consequently, on the rise of their grades in school. The project designers noted that the children began to think creatively: they proposed multiple solutions for every problem, their solutions were more original, and they did not scrimp on time or effort in their search for the best variant. The art program participants were better able to articulate their thoughts, could better summarize diverse information and interacted better with their teachers and peers. The teachers in the art-program schools noted that the children became more self-assured, no longer doubting their own abilities in reading, math, and general academic subjects. The project's authors came to the conclusion that 'It appears that a narrowly conceived curriculum, in which the arts are either not offered or are offered in limited and sporadic amounts, exerts a negative effect on the development of critical cognitive competencies and personal dispositions'.[1]

All the available research agrees in one principal finding: music stimulates the work of the brain. Strategically located, as it was, alongside the very sources of human intelligence, music cannot but help in the brain's work, since thought patterns were formed for practical purposes over the course of evolution. Abstract reasoning and scientific methods of examining the world grew from the heart of concrete and sensory thought and from artistic thought. Of all the forms of art, music is the most abstract and structured; studying music it is easier to develop patterns of thought which will prove necessary for the pursuit of any work of the mind. Music improves the results of students in all subjects across the board, promoting better self-discipline among those who practice it. Parents who understand the role of music in the development of children will have more occasions to be proud of their offspring than parents who see music studies as merely extra-curricular or frivolous. Music is the best of teachers, a teacher who can change ways of thinking instead of presenting pre-digested facts. Music, indeed, teaches one to think: the brain educated by music can get everything it needs. The musical student simply does not have problems at school—such is the wisdom confirmed through decades of observation by educators and psychologists.

Music and the talents of Caesar

As a military leader the great Julius Caesar earned his glory in no small measure because of his ability to do several things at once. Caesar's imitators have been many as the temptation to 'embrace the unembraceable', to take on more than can reasonably be done, is always among man's greatest: we want to watch the football game—as we glance through a textbook, study for tomorrow's exam and talk with a friend on the telephone. For some people a striving to retain and strengthen such multi-channeled receptivity and 'splintering-up' of one's attention is neither a sign of caprice nor an effect of absent-mindedness, but rather a necessity of life. There are many professions in which one must react to simultaneous signals from many inputs, where an instant compilation of

---

[1] Burton, J., Horowitz, R., and Abeles, H. (2000) Learning in and through the arts: the question of transfer. *Studies in Art Education*, 41, p. 256.

information from a variety of sources is necessary—and leads to an instant decision based on them. The reception of a signal, its analysis, and the formulation of a response to it take place, in many instances, simultaneously; as they push a button in answer to a preceding signal, dispatchers and complex machine operators are often required at the same time to take in a subsequent signal, which itself demands a very quick response. Put briefly, the ability to do several things at once is indispensable in many professions and in our daily endeavors, from automobile drivers and simultaneous interpreters to airline pilots and air traffic controllers.

In order to think in 'multiple channels', analyze different sources of information, make appropriate decisions and implement them, the asset of first and foremost value is the ability not to be nervous. The *Journal of Sports Medicine* (Szmedra and Bacharach 1998) reported a study of the effect of music on runners in which 25 young athletes did their training—with music and without it. After the training sessions, blood samples were taken from the athletes to measure the level of lactates in their systems; lactates are produced by the body as a result of stressful muscle exertion. It turned out that the runners who trained while music was being played had lower levels of lactates in their blood—meaning that music has the ability to lower and lessen muscle stress.

Timo Krings (2000) obtained analogous results in a different experiment: he asked a group of non-musicians and a group of pianists to perform identical sets of finger exercises. Both groups performed the exercises well, yet subsequent measurements of blood flow in the brain among both groups showed that the non-musicians were more tense than the pianists in completing the tasks: put otherwise, the achievement of equal success at the exercises came at a physiologically 'higher price' for the non-musicians. The researcher interpreted the results as a confirmation of a greater effectiveness of brain function among the pianists: control of complex motions came easier to them, demanding lesser expenditures of energy. The successes of Caesar under such circumstances are literally waiting around the corner for whoever seeks them: expending less in every area of endeavor, the musical person leaves himself a reserve of energy which can be used for other tasks. And if we bear in mind that the musician experiences the benevolent, stress-reducing influence of music on his muscles over the course of an entire lifetime, then it is all the more possible for him to pursue several procedures at once: he is stable, his muscles are accustomed to feeling relaxed and at ease, his body is prepared to take on different challenges.

Beyond calm and the ability to expend energy reserves economically the Caesar model demands attentiveness and concentration, as it requires a tenacity of perception which allows one to retain the residue of fleeting perceptions for later analysis. Neuropsychologists have noted that musicians retain the traces of an explicit aural incident for some 7.84 seconds, while non-musicians retain it for only 1.42 seconds (Starcheus 2003). It is not only that musicians keep sound impressions in their memories longer; their sense of hearing creates a tendency to retain the residue of all sensory inputs. Musicians in many instances turn out to be more attentive and have better memories than others because the habit of musicians to 'listen up' and react sensitively to external impulses has long since become second nature to them.

The acid test for qualifying as a multi-tasking Caesar is, of course, sight reading. Nothing compares with this function in terms of quantity of simultaneously performed actions: the performer must look at the notes, glancing a bit ahead in order to gauge what he will have to do in the immediate future. At the same time his hands must play that which his eyes fixed upon some time in the past and decoded as the instruction to be carried out. Thus the sight reading musician works in two regimes at once, combining the past and the future. He has to recognize in time the structures he is playing because he has to fill in those elements which his eye may not have caught or inadvertently dropped with his own 'imaginings' and constructs. A backward–forward movement of the eye is the sight reader's constant occupation, and this process, as researchers attest, takes place some five or six times per second during performance of the most complex physical actions which a musician simultaneously controls and coordinates.

A group of psychologists under the leadership of Frances Truitt (Truitt *et al.* 1997) set an experiment involving eight sight-reading pianists. The researchers wanted to measure what effect greater and lesser qualification would have on the sight reading process. The criteria for the subjects' fulfillment of the tasks were two: the time gap between seeing the notes and the movement of the hands, and the time the subject spent looking ahead at the notes upcoming before actually playing. The more qualified and experienced pianists looked ahead further, took in more extensive fragments of the piece and retained them longer in their memory. And for all this they needed shorter glances at the musical text than did the less-qualified pianists. The researchers concluded that the qualified pianists knew how to use their time with maximum effectiveness and concentration: they received the most information in the shortest period and could successfully combine a regime of direct action with one of planning for the future.

Sight reading is one of the indexes of musical ability, and great musical talents invariably demonstrate phenomenal mastery in this realm. To run one's eye over the large vertical field of a musical score and then immediately look at the next vertical field—without losing the idea and attendant connection of the musical structures at hand—is something that by no means all gifted musicians can do. For this one truly needs the talents of Caesar. Some geniuses display their ability to read scores almost coquettishly, as Glinka once recalled, having seen Liszt perform in Paris: 'He played Chopin's mazurkas, nocturnes and etudes, indeed all the bright and fashionable music, very nicely—but with a shade of over-mannered nuances. Then he played at sight several pieces from [my own] *Ruslan*, using a handwritten score which no one else had ever seen—and to our general amazement he didn't miss a note'.[2] The volume of information processed by Liszt (particularly if one recalls Glinka's penmanship) is beyond comparison. To say that he passed this particular test amounts to an understatement which is itself beyond comparison.

The musician who sight reads very quickly, almost unconsciously, segments the score and divides it into fragments, in the process indicating 'points' of his progress. Two researchers (Drake and Palmer 2000) set an experiment with a group of 60 pianists, both

---

[2] Glinka, M. (1954) *O muzyke i muzykantah/On Music and Musicians*. Moscow: Gosmuzgiz, p. 75.

children and adults. The secret of good sight reading ability, they concluded, lay exactly there:

> Increased anticipatory behavior and a greater range of planning is to appear with skill and practice. A strong positive relationship between the mastery of temporal constraints and planning abilities within performance suggests that these two cognitive indicators are closely related and may arise from segmentation processes during performance. Examination of sequence timing may explicate planning abilities that underlie many complex skills.[3]

Tim Griffiths (2000) at Newcastle Medical School has demonstrated the ability of musicians to plan their actions correctly. Griffiths concentrated on a relatively simple task: 18 musicians and 18 non-musicians were asked to keep time by tapping a baton along with fragments of classical music. The musicians kept time more accurately, were distracted less often, and, most important, could act on different levels of musical structure: they could keep time at larger intervals, accompanying only whole phrases or half-phrases, or at smaller ones, on each measure or beat. The non-musicians could not easily fathom this kind of hierarchical arrangement. Griffiths concluded that musicians are able to organize events mentally at greater time intervals and can more fully perceive the hierarchy of such events.

The Caesar-like tendencies of musicians are extraordinarily useful in many kinds of activities. Everything we do represents, to a certain extent, a conscious organization of discrete events, actions, and processes. The English word deadline, with its clear reference to the consequences of failure, gives an indication of the importance the marketplace puts on exactitude and timeliness in contemporary business. When sight reading music on his instrument, the musician constantly finds himself in deadline conditions measured in parts of seconds; in these conditions he has to look at the notes, mentally process new information, look back at what has just passed and plan the future. Does success at this multiple tasking not render him 'like unto Caesar'?

Music and social communication

Music and speech have gone hand in hand since the earliest times. They share a common function: social communication. Music and speech bring about intellectual and emotional exchange between humans, employing the venue of sound toward the end of mutual understanding. With the help of music and speech a man learns of the moods of other humans, how they regard one event or another or the whole of life as such—and how these views may differ from his own. A proper understanding of 'we and they' is one of the most fundamental social skills which we attain in the communicative process; and music contributes significantly to the acquisition and refinement of this skill.

Music is varied and multifaceted: there is simply no such thing as a social group, a nationality or a historical period that has not created a music of its own which distinguishes it from other groups, nationalities, and eras. The musician, the person who plays

---

[3] Drake, C. and Palmer, C. (2000) Skill acquisition in music performance: relations between planning and temporal control. *Cognition*, 74, p. 1.

or enjoys music, perforce becomes accustomed to a variety of feelings, points of view, behavior patterns, and the means of their expression in sound; he knows that some 'musics' are monotonal and deliberately paced, others are prolix and fitful, still others are simple and disingenuous even as others are extraordinarily elegant and deeply imagined. The musician lives among worlds of sound filled to overflowing with different senses and sensations, and takes these riches as the norm—which in turn renders for him the very concept of 'we and they' less dramatic and fraught with conflict than it is for other people. He takes the 'they' in question, the 'other', not through the filter of his brain but rather directly and with his senses, allowing him at times to do something wholly remarkable: he begins to include 'them' with 'us' because their 'otherness' does not repel—it attracts, engages him, and wins him over. Studying the musical tastes and preferences of various social groups Bethany Bryson has concluded that people with knowledge of music are drawn toward pluralism. As he noted in the *American Psychological Review*: 'Political tolerance is associated with musical tolerance. Broad familiarity with music genres is significantly related to education, and cultural tolerance constitutes multicultural capital as it is unevenly distributed in the population and evidences class-based exclusion'.[4]

People who enjoy a high degree of musical culture accept 'otherness' more easily and are less inclined to repulse and negate it. These people are, in politics and social life generally, more likely to hold views described as liberal. This same conclusion was reached by a group of four American psychologists led by Donald Fucci (1996). The Fucci study examined rock and roll fans, aficionados of early jazz, and classical music lovers. The last of these, with the great variety and complexity of classical music, were tolerant towards both jazz and rock, whereas the rock and jazz groups were more strict and selective, preferring in the main only their own music. The authors concluded that a broad musical perspective facilitates social communication and mutual understanding between and among different social layers. Put otherwise, musical education, if broad and universally included in school curricula, could serve as one of the cornerstones of a stable social environment since it leads to a psychological transformation in people: they turn those who had been 'they' into new members of 'we'.

Psychologists confirm that the basis of social adaptation resides in two skills: the ability to find alternative solutions and the ability to see the consequences of one's actions. People who have mastered these skills have the 'right stuff' required of leaders and administrators. The study of music, in fact, greatly facilitates the development of these very skills. Lilja Ulfarsdottir and Philip Erwin (1999) conducted a study of social adaptability among children studying music and non-musical children; the former proved considerably more socially flexible than the latter. The music-oriented group was not content with a single solution to a problem, searching for others if the first proved inadequate. Thanks to the livelier imaginations among the musical group, moreover, the children in it were more easily able to picture various outcomes of a problem's resolution; with that knowledge, the

---

[4] Bryson, B. (1996) 'Anything but heavy metal': symbolic exclusion and musical dislikes. *American Psychological Review*, 61, p. 884.

musical children restrained themselves from radical approaches and answers much more easily than did their non-musical peers.

Martin Gardiner's study (2000) of felons and petty criminals in Rhode Island provides particularly convincing evidence on this point. Studying the police data on thousands of offenders in the highest frequency period for crime (up to age 30), Gardiner correlated arrest records with youth participation in musical activities. The conclusion was starkly revealing: between these two conditions there was a clearly defined inverse relationship. The more and more often a young person took part in musical activities, the less likely he or she was to have a run-in with the judicial system. People who could sight read music were wholly absent from the police blotter; indeed, the most interesting result of the Gardiner study was the discovery of a 'rising curve of musicality': a typical musical education merely lowered the likelihood of antisocial behavior, while one which included independent composition and performance all but eliminated it. And at the top of the scale, the complete mastery of complex musical skills, it turned out, excluded criminal activity altogether. This would seem to be food for thought for educators and administrators around the world.

One of the habits which musical education inculcates—that of listening to someone else and understanding him—makes musicians less rigid and more tolerant individuals. Yet at the same time the musicians' qualities of independence do not suffer in the least, as the Australian scholars Louise Buttsworth and Glen Smith concluded (1995). Buttsworth and Smith gave personality tests to some 255 professional musicians and discovered in their subjects an unusual combination of psychological attributes. On the one hand, the musicians demonstrated more sensitivity and intuitiveness than is found in the general population, while on the other, the musicians were more emotionally stable than non-musicians. This rare matching of sensitivity and intuition with internal calm would make musicians practically ideal secret agents—James Bond take note—though for present purposes we will simply mark the extraordinary social adaptability that derives therefrom. In short, musicians see and feel a great deal, yet they are difficult to upset and less given to bouts of insecurity than their fellow citizens—a fortuitous combination indeed.

Music and the word

The unity of music and speech is recognized by scholars everywhere. It is practically clear that the two are drawn from common roots and have a common origin (Nazaikinsky 1967; Masataka 2007; Mithen 2006; Richman 1993; Patel 2003; 1998; Saito and Maekawa 1993; Tervaniemi *et al.* 2006; Zatorre *et al.* 2002). Both a written text and a musical score are understood as a conscious communication of thought conveyed in a particular format. Both music and speech consist of sound-phonemes joined into 'word-signs' which in turn form finished phrases and expressions. The structure of both, moreover, depends on a linear arrangement of consecutive elements organized in accordance with certain rules. Musical scholars long took the expressions 'musical language' and 'musical speech' metaphorically, although the closeness of music and speech, the similarity of their hierarchical structures and methods of functioning, more than hinted at a closeness whose nature was real and actual rather than analogous. As early as the late 1960s the musicologist Eugene Nazaikinsky wrote:

> An examination of the connections of music and speech shows also that it is not the details and not music's imitation of certain speech locutions which unite our perceptions of the two, but rather patterns which they share in common. And it is here, in fact, that we should search for the inter-connections of music and speech, as it is here that these ties are much more significant and varied than it was possible to suppose.[5]

Recent neuropsychological research has left no doubt that music and speech are psychological relatives, if you will. They are controlled either by the same or by neighbouring sections of the brain; if an injury or illness victim loses the use of the sections which govern speech, there is a 50 percent likelihood that he will also lose the analogous musical functions: aphasia (loss of speech) and amusia (loss of the ability to perceive and create music) very often resemble each other (Benton 1977; Jacome 1984; Patel 2005; Peretz *et al.* 1997; Piccirilli *et al.* 2000). Very often if a patient cannot read words, he cannot read musical notes either; if he does not recall familiar melodies, then he cannot remember familiar verses either—both of which leave neuropsychologists to note with regularity the similarity between the musical and speech impediments among one and the same patients. The other half of the aphasia cases, in which the speech failure is not accompanied by amusia (and the reverse, where amusia occurs without aphasia) is explained by the relative autonomy of the musical and speech functions, each of which has its own locality in the brain. Deep connections between speech and music in the human brain were recently once more confirmed: 'Not only language has syntax and semantics—music has them, too, and both linguistic and musical syntax (as well as semantics) are processed with partly identical, and largely overlapping neuronal mechanisms'.[6]

The coincidence or lack of it between failures of speech and musical functions depend on the area of the brain responsible for the disorder. This question was treated in the July 1992 issue of *Science*, in which a special study by a group of four psychologists was published. These psychologists, led by Justine Sergent, worked with professional pianists, studying the sections of the brain which helped them first to read notes, and then bring their perception of the written score to life as music on the keyboard. It turned out that the sections of the brain which took part in the musical process were located immediately alongside those sections which governed analogous verbal operations. If a sick or injured person is 'lucky', and the damaged part of the brain is localized, then one of the functions, either speech or music, will be retained; if he is 'unlucky' and the damage turns out to be wider, then it will affect both the musical and speech sections responsible for analogous operations and the patient will suffer from both aphasia and amusia. Injury and illness statistics indicate that the 'lucky' and 'unlucky' are divided equally: half the patients lose

5 Nazaikinsky, E. (1967) Rechevoi opyt i muzikalnoe vospriatie/Speech experience and music perception. *Esteticheskie ocherki/Essays on aesthetics*, 2, p. 282.
6 Koelsch, S. and Fritz, T. (2007) Neuronale Korrelate der Musikverarbeitung. *Verhaltenstherapie und Verhaltensmedizin*, 28, p. 23.

both functions and half retain one of them, the reason for which is elaborated in the study.

It is now clear that music and speech are neuropsychological 'neighbors'. In all probability the musical sections of the brain, which arose earlier, were forced to make room for and concede some of their brain 'territory' to the verbal sections of the later-developing speech function. In this process the familial relationship of the 'neighbors' and the exchange of information between them was retained for many thousands of years, creating in the brain a unified speech-music space. The origins of this space were laid by singing; music 'took in' speech and 'raised' it in its bosom. The first speech as such was in fact still a kind of speechified music, in which the affective and communicative functions were melded into one. To a considerable extent the transition from *Homo musicus* to *Homo sapiens* took place within the framework of this speech-music; the separation of the latter from the former was signaled by the appearance of independent speech produced by a purely verbal language. Singing—the most fundamental testimony to the speech-music connection and its embodiment—remains to this day a tool for aiding the development of speech.

Psychologists regularly point out the benevolent effect of singing on child development, and particularly the development of speech. Rosamund Shuter-Dyson and Clive Gabriel (1981), summarizing the considerable research on the effect of intensive singing study on the development of children's speech, noted in particular the success of those children involved in singing practice. They began to speak earlier, and their speech was more complex; they immediately began to compose sentences of three words, while other children reached this stage only several months later. Magda Kalmar (1982) has reported analogous experience from an experiment with 3 year olds studying singing under the Kodaly system. Over the course of 3 years the success of the test group in verbal development proved incomparably greater than that of the control group without Kodaly training.

A study by Canadian neuropsychologists Willy Steinke, Lola Cuddy, and Lorna Jakobson (2001) summarized the available data on this issue. The study dealt with amateur musicians who suffered from amusia but retained the speech function unimpaired. A patient could not recognize a familiar instrumental melody—the overture to the *Barber of Seville*, for example, or Mozart's *Fortieth Symphony*; but if he heard a familiar song, the same patient could immediately remember the name of the song and the words. The words of the song, retained in the patient's memory, helped him remember the melody, the lyric 'drawing' the music along with it. The music and the words of a song are sufficiently autonomous so that the words could survive in the patient's memory while the music had been erased; but at the same time the melody and the word phrases were connected enough so that one could bring back the other, rescuing it from oblivion. If the words survived, then the music does as well. A song is a construct of remarkable durability, occupying a 'double bed' in the human brain: its textual and musical components are both connected and yet at the same time relatively independent.

The Canadian experiment showed that the retention of the word could bring music back to life. The reverse process—of greater interest to musicians—had in fact already been demonstrated by the work of Daniel Jacome (1984). A patient suffering from the worst form of aphasia undertook a program of self-treatment; no medicines or treatments had helped him, his powers of speech were completely destroyed—but he began instinctively to whistle familiar tunes. This was not a professional musician, merely someone who enjoyed music. Over the course of 2 years of self-directed whistling therapy, the patient's power of speech returned to him—which physicians regarded as some sort of miracle. Music had given birth to speech and once more confirmed its role as the initiator of speech, its direct stimulator. Music has demonstrated this function in other conditions as well, when reading-deficient children have caught up with their peers with the help of musical exercises. A group of researchers led by Irwing Hurwitz (1975) worked with a group of child dyslexics who had problems mastering speech and reading. With music lessons, the dyslexic group brought their reading skills to the level of the control group and approached the level of children with no speech defects whatsoever. Here, as with the patients suffering from aphasia, music 'cured' the children, bringing their speech development into the normal range.

A memory for words serves as a reliable indicator of verbal ability. The millions who study foreign languages dream of developing their word memory. Probably, one way of developing this facility is the systematic study of music. In 1998 three psychologists performed the experiment in which the subjects, female college students, were asked to memorize a battery of words. One group of students consisted of girls who had studied music to the age of 12; the other group had no such experience. The 'musical' group far exceeded the non-musicians in word retention, although the music studies of the group members had taken place some 10 years earlier (Chan *et al.* 1998). These results were once more confirmed in an identical research, this time with children, who after a year of intensive music studies showed a dramatic verbal memory improvement (Ho *et al.* 2003).

It is not accidental that many poets and prose writers have been musically gifted individuals. The writer and dramatist Pierre Beaumarchais, one of the most interesting performers of the eighteenth century, was often invited to the royal court to play the harp; Leo Tolstoy was knowledgeable about music and loved it, with musicians regularly visiting his home. Stendhal and Roman Rolland had both knowledge and talent that might have been envied by their professional musician-contemporaries; the works on music and biographies of outstanding composers written by these two remain unsurpassed to this day. Thomas Mann was one of the most musically educated people of the first half of the twentieth century. His novel *Doktor Faustus*, written under the influence of his friendship with Arnold Schoenberg and Theodor Adorno, tells more about music and the psychology of its creators than dozens of scholarly studies. The writer E. T. A. Hoffman, one of the greatest romantics, was a marvelous composer, producing the opera *Undine* (*The Mermaid*). Jean-Jacques Rousseau himself, the great philosopher and writer, can also be found at the origins of the French comic opera: a dilettante composer, Rousseau wrote the opera *The Country Wizard* which became the 'hit' of the mid-eighteenth century. It is likely that the intimate connection of music and the word at the intonation level explains the closeness of the musical and verbal talents: composers try to write verses, creating romances for their own texts, even as poets and prose writers produce and listen to music.

By the third millennium the connection of music and speech at the level of the human brain is no longer arguable. This connection explains the oft-noted 'help' which music offers in the study of language, in the mastery of reading skills and in the alleviation of speech deficiencies. *Homo musicus*, as orator and listener, enjoys significant advantages over others because he has mastered the semantic key to speech—the intelligent intoning which he senses and understands in more detail than does his non-musical peer. Thus the musician and the musical child read better, begin to speak sooner, and do so more effectively. In the beginning was the Sound, from which the Word developed—such was the course of evolution, through which man acquired the power of speech and continues to exercise his verbal abilities to this day.

Music and mathematics

Music is mathematical and mathematics is musical. In both the idea of numbers and their relationship is of paramount importance. There is no area of music in which numbers do not serve as the final methodology for describing what happens: in each measure there are a set number of beats which are characterized by set dependencies and proportional relationships; rhythm divides the time into units and establishes numerical ties between them; the musical form is based on the idea of similarity and difference, identity and contrast—which goes back to the principles of multiplication and symmetry, and which form quasi-geometrical musical concepts. In addition music is process-oriented, while mathematics essays to describe processes of the most diverse kinds in abstract categories—the category of transformation, on which the whole of music's formal structure rests, is extremely mathematical. In both mathematics and music beauty and harmony bring with them creative thought; it is not accidental that mathematicians say 'The only true solution is the one that is beautiful'. It is not a chance that mathematical concepts reveal themselves via music and music in its turn is better understood in connection with mathematics. This was brilliantly demonstrated by Jeanne Bamberger and Andrea Disessa, who worked with groups of children and in the end concluded that

> Students' inquiry into the bases for their perceptions of musical coherence provides a path into the mathematics of ratio, proportion, fractions, and common multiples. In a similar manner, we conjecture that other topics in mathematics—patterns of change, transformations and invariants—might also expose, illuminate and account for more general organizing structures in music.[7]

Spatial intuition and the category of movement play an immense role in mathematical creativity. In studying musical communication Roger Kendall and Edward Carterette have noted that 'Mathematicians say that they operate not in symbols but rather in

---

[7] Bamberger, J. and Disessa, A. (2003) Music as embodied mathematics: A study of mutually informing affinity. *International Journal of Computers for Mathematical Learning*, 8, p. 123.

undefined metasymbolic mental forms and motor sensations'.[8] Do these 'mental forms and motor sensations' not resemble the 'deep structures' of musical creations, the simultaneous multi-modal forms from which the composer's fantasy takes wing? Composers frequently admit that their method differs only a little from the mathematical. The outstanding conductor Ernest Ansermet has noted this, pointing out that 'Between music and mathematics there is an undoubted parallelism. Each of them represents action in imagination, which frees us from the incidental nature of practical life'.[9]

Ansermet underscored the abstract character of musical and mathematical material, which lacks real or direct analogues elsewhere, as well as the generalizing nature common to the bases of both. Many leading musicians have shone as mathematical talents, including the aforementioned Ansermet, who is at once a professional mathematician and the leading conductor of Stravinsky. Leonid Sabaneev, a graduate of the mathematics department of Moscow University, was a marvelous pianist and composer (as well as a friend of Scriabin). The composer Edison Denisov taught mathematics at Tomsk University. The outstanding cellist K. Y. Davydov, moreover, took a degree in physics and mathematics and, as his contemporaries recall, showed 'stunning abilities in pure and applied mathematics: in his apartment he long kept a model of the railroad bridge which he had invented and which, according to specialists in that field, was worthy of serious attention'.[10]

In a large study involving 25 000 American elementary school pupils studying in special arts-enhanced curricula, it was particularly noted that the children studying music showed a markedly higher propensity to excel on mathematics tests than did their non-musical peers (Catterall *et al.* 1999). For children from 'underprivileged families' the progress in mathematical testing was especially noteworthy: of the underprivileged eighth graders in the music-inclusive curriculum, 21 percent had high mathematics scores, compared to only 11 percent of the non-music students—a full 10 percent difference. By the tenth grade the gulf had widened: here some 33 percent of the underprivileged who took music showed high math scores, while among their socio-economic peers the figure was only 16 percent—meaning the differential had added an additional 7 percent in only two years. Research by J. M. Cheek and L. R. Smith (1999) reached similar results: eighth grade students who were learning to play musical instruments proved much better at mathematics than students without such study. The particular standouts in the group were the pianists, whose math scores actually won a competition.

The coincidence of musical and mathematical giftedness became a subject of interest to psychologists. At first there arose a supposition about the coincidence of aural resources between musicians and mathematicians: the musical ear is to a significant degree analytical, which might be one of the reasons for the musicality of mathematicians and the mathematical abilities of musicians. But the experiments of three psychologists led by William R. Steinke (1997) disproved this hypothesis. They tested a hundred individuals with

8 Kendall, R. and Carterette, E. (1990) The communication of musical expression. *Music Perception*, 8, p. 129.
9 Ansermet, E. (1976) *Besedy o /Talks on Music*. Leningrad: Muzyka, p. 52.
10 Ginzburg, L. (1950) *K. Y. Davydov*. Moscow: Muzgiz, p. 6.

a good musical ear; but these people demonstrated no superiority over a like number of others who lacked such an ear in abstract thought and mathematical abilities. The musical ear was not in and of itself a component of mathematical thought and did not correlate with it.

The essence of the psychological connections between musical and mathematical abilities became clearer when scientists turned their attention to the exaggeratedly abstract nature of musicians' perceptions. Russian psychologist Elena Artemieva studied various groups of students assigned the task of describing the visible world with the help of a variety of categories. She noted that 'The group of students from the music school stood out in particular. With them, unlike the others, the quantity of geometrical and objective indicators exceeded the quantity of direct-sensory and evaluative-emotional indicators'.[11]

Accustomed to noting the proportional-symmetrical quasi-spatial relationships within the musical form, and accustomed to processing in their consciousness a variety of hierarchically subordinated structures lacking obvious objective analogues, musicians carry over their skills of spatial-geometric perception into the real world.

Artemieva's conclusions corresponded with the opinion of Sherman VanderArk and Daniel Ely (1993) who had studied groups of music students and biology students as they listened to music. After the listening sessions the level of cortisol in the students' blood was measured; a rise in the level would indicate that the listeners were occupied with abstract thoughts, while a decline would show a more sensory concreteness and emotion-alism of perception. The music students' cortisol rose and the biologists' sank, leading to the conclusion that musicians are extraordinarily abstract in their method of perceiving things.

An international group of eight psychologists under the leadership of Herve Platel (1997) organized a large-scale experiment to determine the zones of responsibility of sections of the brain for this or that musical function. The subjects were six Frenchmen, young men without musical background, who were assigned to listen to music and musical fragments—short melodies, rhythmic passages, and series of sounds. The men's musical perception proved to be, on the neuropsychological level, very analytical: the processing of musical information was done by those sections of the brain which traditionally bore responsibility for operations demanding logic. These findings could seem rather unusual to those who subconsciously placed music into the emotional frame.

Similar results were obtained by two German specialists in the neuropsychology of music, Marianne Hassler and Niels Birbaumer (1986), when they compared male musi-cians and non-musicians in their late-teenage and early adult years. The musician-subjects' spatial operations, traditionally pertaining to the right hemisphere, were,

---

[11] Artemieva, E. U. (2007) *Psikhologia sub'ektivnoi semantiki/The Psychology of Subjective Semantics.* Moscow: LKI, p. 62.

compared to those of the non-musicians, somewhat mixed in with the left hemisphere—owing, most likely, to the musicians' particularly analytical 'bent'. The non-musicians (and female musicians, as well) carried out their spatial procedures in the right hemisphere. These differences may be interpreted as confirmation of the particular nature of spatial representations in male musicians: without losing touch with the orderly right hemisphere, the male musicians' spatial representations took on a certain analytical character because of their partial involvement with the left hemisphere. Is this not a particular sign of musical talent? The overwhelming majority of outstanding composers are in fact male, while the majority of professional musicians are female. Perhaps the preponderance of compositional talent among men is connected with the specifics of their spatial thinking. In a study carried out in 1992 involving 117 adult musicians and 120 musicians in their teens, Marianne Hassler noted the general superiority of musicians over non-musicians in quality of spatial thought, as the musicians performed significantly better than their non-musical peers on spatial tasks. These conclusions were made on the basis of 8 years of observation of all the subjects.

The data of modern neuropsychology confirm the heightened analytical nature of perception and the high quality of spatial operation of the 'musical brain'. This offers some explanation for the frequent coincidence of musical and mathematical giftedness in the same people. When Maria Manturzewska conducted a study comparing the mathematical abilities of the strongest and weakest music students, she found that those of the former exceeded those of the latter by several magnitudes; the most gifted musicians were also the most gifted mathematicians (1978). Another practical (if anecdotal) demonstration of the proximity of musical and mathematical inclinations can be found in the doctoral dissertation of Paul Vernon (1931) at Cambridge University, which reports that in the 1927–1928 academic year some 60 percent of the physics and mathematics professors at Oxford University were also members of the university music society—while a mere 15 percent of the professors in all other disciplines belonged. The gifted mathematicians needed music much more than did all the others combined.

Observations drawn from experience have led science to make a serious supposition that musical and mathematical operations are related both psychologically and in content. In occupying himself with music, man develops and trains his mathematical abilities—the significance of which, in our pragmatic age, can hardly be disputed.

***

Music soothes us emotionally. Music enriches us mentally. Music aids the growth of our fundamental human abilities, those of logical thought and the mastery of speech and writing. Music is, from the standpoint of the psychological mechanisms which govern it, extraordinarily close to the most basic intellectual skills of man, which in great part came together thanks to music—and did so in the 'nursery' of music making. Music furthers the development of the social qualities valued by man, rendering him more tolerant and more able to perceive one of Them as one of Us. An enormous number of remarkable and merely successful people who did not become musicians nevertheless love music and make music as they can; among them are kings and presidents, politicians and business people, famous artists and actors. Many important companies and firms, including computer giants and leading banks, prefer to hire employees with some musical education or background. And they are right to do so, as music expands and strengthens all the spiritual and intellectual possibilities of man. Music is so multifaceted and involved with all the human qualities that there cannot be a musician who could not excel in any sphere of activity—for the title *musician* itself signifies a superlative, everywhere and in all things: the most disciplined, the quickest, the most accurate, the most thoughtful. A broad implementation of musical studies—in kindergartens, schools, and colleges, at all possible levels—would allow everyone in our society to discover and develop the abilities each possesses, to the greatest extent possible and to the common benefit of all.

References

Abert, H. (2007) *W. A. Mozart*. Yale University Press.

Abrams, R. M., Griffiths, K., Huang, X. *et al.* (1998) Fetal music perception: the role of sound transmission. *Music Perception*, 15, 307–17.

Adachi, M. and Trehub, S. E. (1998) Children's expression of emotion in song. *Psychology of Music*, 26, 133–53.

Aggleton, J. P, Kentridge, R. W., and Good, J. M. (1994) Handedness and musical ability: a study of professional orchestral players, composers, and choir members. *Psychology of Music*, 22, 148–56.

Aiello, R. (1994) Can listening to music be experimentally studied? In *Musical Perceptions* (ed. R. Aiello and J. Sloboda), pp. 273–82. New York: Oxford University Press.

Alajouanine, T. (1948) Aphasia and artistic realization. *Brain*, 71, 229–41.

Alcock, K., Wade, D., Anslow P., and Passingham, R. (2000) Pitch and timing abilities in adult left-hemisphere-dysphasic and right-hemisphere-damaged subjects. *Brain and Language*, 75, 47–65.

Aldridge, D. (1995) Music therapy and the treatment of Alzheimer's disease. *Clinical Gerontologist*, 16, 41–57.

Alexeev, E. (1986) *Rannefol'klornoe intonirovanie/Early Folklore Intoning*. Moscow: Sovetsky kompozitor.

Ansermet, E. (1976) *Besedy o muzyke/Talks on Music*. Leningrad: Muzyka.

Appleton, J. H. (1993) Epilogue: implications for contemporary music practice. In *Psychology and Music: The Understanding of Melody and Rhythm* (ed. T. J. Tighe and W. J. Dowling), pp. 215–19. Hillsdale, New Jersey: Lawrence Erlbaum.

Aranovsky, M. G. (1974) O psihologicheskih predposylkakh predmetno-prostranstvennyh sluhovyh predstavleniy/ On psychological prerequisites of object-spatial aural imaging. In *Problemy muzykal'nogo myshleniya/Problems of Musical Thought* (ed. M. G.Aranovsky), pp. 252–71. Moscow: Muzyka.

Aranovsky, M. G. (1991) *Sintaksicheskaia structura melodii/Syntactic Structure of Melody*. Moscow: Kompozitor.

Aranovsky, M. G. (1998) *Muzykal'nyi tekst. Struktura i svoistva/MusicText. Structure and Properties.* Moscow: Kompozitor.

Artemieva, E. U. (2007) *Psikhologia sub'ektivnoi semantiki/The Psychology of Subjective Semantics.* Moscow: LKI.

Asafiev, B. V. (1923) *De Musica*. Petersburg.

Asafiev, B. V. (1952) Sluh Glinki/Glinka's ear. In *Izbrannie trudy/Selected Works*, vol.1, pp. 289–331. Moscow: Izdatelstvo Akademii nauk.

Asafiev, B. V. (1971) *Muzikalnaia forma kak protsess/Musical From as a Process.* Leningrad: Muzyka.

Avratiner, V. (1971) *Vnutrenniy slukh pianistov/ Internal Ear of Pianists.* Neopublikovannaia rukopis/ Unpublished manuscript.

Bailey, J. (1983) Music structure and human movement. *Perceptual and Motor Skills*, 7, 237–58.

Bain, B. (1978) The cognitive flexibility claim in the bilingual and music education research traditions. *Journal of Research in Music Education*, 26, 76–81.

Balaban, M. T., Anderson, L. M., and Wisniewski, A. B. (1998) Lateral asymmetries in infant melody perception. *Developmental Psychology*, 34, 39–48.

Balonov, L. and Deglin, V. (1974) *Slukh i rech dominantnogo i nedominantnogo polusharii/Hearing and Speech of Dominant and Non-Dominant Hemispheres.* Leningrad: Nauka.

Baldwin, B. and Stecher, L. (1925) *The Psychology of the Preschool Child.* New York: Appleton.

Bamberger, J. and Disessa, A. (2003) Music as embodied mathematics: a study of mutually informing affinity. *International Journal of Computers for Mathematical Learning,* 8, 123–60.

Banton, L. J. (1995) The role of visual and auditory feedback during the sight reading of music. *Psychology of Music,* 23, 3–16.

Barbarotto, R., Capitani, E., and Laiacona, M. (2001) Living musical instruments and inanimate body parts? *Neuropsychologia,* 39, 406–14.

Barenboim, L. (1957) *Anton Rubinstein.* Leningrad: Muzgiz.

Barinova, M. (1961) *Vospominaniya o I.Gofmane i F.Buzoni/Memoirs on J. Hoffman and F. Buzoni.* Moscow: Muzyka.

Barwick, J., Valentine, E., West, R., and Wilding, J. (1989) Relations between reading and musical abilities. *British Journal of Educational Psychology,* 59, 253–57.

Baum, S., Owen, S. V., and Oreck, B. A. (2004) Talent beyond words: identification of potential talent in dance and music in elementary students. In *Artistically and Musically Talented Students. Essential Reading in Gifted Education* (ed. E. Zimmerman), pp. 57–72. Thousand Oaks, CA: Corwin Press.

Becker, H. and Becker, G. (1989) *Giacomo Meyerbeer: a Life in Letters.* London: Helm.

Bekhtereva N., Bunzen, P., and Gogolitsin, Y. (1977) *Mozgovie kodi psikhicheskoi deyatelnosti/The Brain Codes of Psychological Activity.* Leningrad: Nauka.

Belenkaya, L. (1992) Ob uslovnyh refleksah na vremya u muzykantov/On conditioned reflexes for time among musicians. In *Muzykal'naya psihologiya/Psychology of Music* (ed. M. Starcheus), pp. 94–7. Moscow Conservatory.

Bell, J. C. (1987) Music and the elderly. *Educational Gerontology,* 13, 147–55.

Benbow, C. P. and Lubinski, D. (1993) Psychological profiles of the mathematically talented: some sex differences and evidence supporting their biological basis. In *Ciba Foundation Symposium 178: The Origins and Development of High Ability* (ed. G. R. Bock and K. Ackrill). Chichester, NJ: Wiley.

Benton, A. L. (1977) The amusias. In *Music and the Brain* (ed. M. Critchley and R. A. Henson), pp. 378–97. London: Heinemann.

Berlioz, G. (1962) *Memuary/Memoirs.* Moscow: Muzyka.

Bernstein, L. (1982) *Findings.* New York: Simon and Schuster.

Berry, C. (1990) On the origins of exceptional intellectual and cultural achievement. In *Encouraging the Development of Exceptional Abilities and Talents* (ed. M. Howe), British Psychological Society.

Besson, M. and Faieta, F. (1995) An event-related potential (ERP) study of musical expectancy: comparison of musicians with nonmusicians. *Journal of Experimental Psychology: Human Perception and Performance,* 21, 1278–96.

Besson, M., Faieta, F., Peretz, I., and Bonnel, A.-M. *et al.* (1998) Singing in the brain: independence of lyrics and tunes. *Psychological Science,* 9, 494–98.

Biasutti, M. (1990) Music ability and altered states of consciousness: an experimental study. *International Journal of Psychosomatics,* 37, 82–5.

Bigand, E., Filipic, S., and Lalitte, P. (2005) The time course of emotional responses to music. In *The Neurosciences and Music II: From Perception to Performance* (ed. G. Avanzini, L. Lopez, S. Koelsch, and M. Manjno), pp. 429–37. New York: New York Academy of Sciences.

Bispham, J. C. (2006) Rhythm in music: what is it? Who has it? And Why? *Music Perception,* 24, 135–42.

Blacking, J. (1973) *How Musical is Man?* London: Faber and Faber.

Boltz, M., Schulkind, M., and Kantra, S. (1991) Effects of background music on the remembering of filmed events. *Memory and Cognition,* 19, 593–606.

Boltz, M. G. (1998) Singing in the brain: independence of lyrics and tunes. *Perception and Psychophysics*, 60, 1357–73.

Bouchard, T. J., Lykken, D. T., McGue, M., Segal, N. L., and Tellegen, A. (1990) Sources of human psychological differences: the Minnesota study of twins reared apart. *Science*, 250, 223–8.

Boucher, R. and Bryden, M. P. (1997) Laterality effects in the processing of melody and timbre. *Neuropsychologia*, 35, 1467–73.

Bouhuys, A. L., Bloem, G. M., and Groothuis, T. G. (1995) Induction of depressed and elated mood by music influences the perception of facial expressions in healthy subjects. *Journal of Affective Disorders*, 33, 215–26.

Boulez, P. (1995) Le temps musical. In *Homo Musicus: Readings in Psychology of Music* (ed. M. Starcheus). Moscow Conservatory, pp. 66–75.

Boult, A. (1975) Mysli o dirizhirovanii/Thoughts on conducting. *Ispolnitel'skoe iskusstvo zarubezhnyh stran/Performing Art Abroad*, 7, 136–90.

Boyle, D. J. (1970) The effect of prescribed rhythmical movements on the ability to read music at sight. *Journal of Research in Music Education*, 18, 307–18.

Brackbill, Y., Adams, G., Crowell, D. H., and Gray, M. L. (1966) Arousal level in neonates and older infants under continuous auditory stimulation. *Journal of Experimental Child Psychology*, 4, 178–88.

Brancucci, A. and Martini, P. S. (1999) Can children with autistic spectrum disorders perceive affect in music? An experimental investigation. *Neuropsychologia*, 37, 1445–51.

Brittin, R. and Sheldon, D. (1995) Comparing continuous versus static measurements in music. *Journal of Research in Music Education*, 43, 36–46.

Brophy, J. and Good, T. (1973) *Individual Differences: Toward an Understanding of Classroom Life.* Holt: Rinehart and Winston.

Brown, S., Martinez, M. J., and Parsons, L. M. (2006) Music and language side by side in the brain: a PET study of the generation of melodies and sentences. *European Journal of Neuroscience*, 23, 2791–803.

Brown, W. A., Sachs, H., Cammuso, K., and Folstein, S. E. (2002) Early music training and absolute pitch. *Music Perception*, 19, 595–97.

Brownley, K. A., McMurray, R. G., and Hackney, A. C. (1995) Effects of music on physiological and affective responses to graded treadmill exercise in trained and untrained runners. *International Journal of Psychophysiology*, 19, 193–201.

Bruner, J. C. (1990) Music, mood, and marketing. *Journal of Marketing*, 94–104.

Bryantseva, V. N. (1985) *Frantsuzskaya komicheskaya opera XVIII veka: puti stanovlenia i razvitia janra/ The French Comic Opera of the XVIIIth Century: The Trends of Formation and Development of the Genre.* Moscow: Muzyka.

Bryson, B. (1996) 'Anything but heavy metal': symbolic exclusion and musical dislikes. *American Sociological Review*, 61, 884–99.

Burns, M. T. (1988) Music as a tool for enhancing creativity. *Journal of Creative Behavior*, 22, 62–9.

Burroughs, G. E. and Morris, J. N. (1962) Factors involved in learning a simple musical theme. *British Journal of Educational Psychology*, 32, 18–28.

Burton, J., Horowitz, R., and Abeles, H. (2000) Learning in and through the arts: the question of transfer. *Studies in Art Education*, 41, 228–57.

Buttsworth, L. M. and Smith, G. A. (1995) Personality of Australian performing musicians by gender and by instrument. *Personality and Individual Differences*, 18, 595–603.

Callinicos, C. (1960) *The Mario Lanza Story.* New York: Robinson.

Cappelletti, M., Waley-Cohen, H., Butterworth, B., and Kopelman, M. (2000) A selective loss of the ability to read and write music. *Neurocase*, 6, 332–41.

Cassidy, J. W. and Ditty, K. M. (2001) Gender differences among newborns on a transient otoacoustic emissions test for hearing. *Journal of Music Therapy*, 38, 28–35.

Cattell, R. (1982) *The Inheritance of Personality and Ability. Research Methods and Findings.* New York-London: Academic Press.

Catterall, J. S. (1998) Involvement in the arts and success in secondary school. In *Americans for the Arts Monographs*, 1, No. 9, November.

Catterall, J. S., Chapleu, R., and Iwanaga, J. (1999) *Champions of Change: The Impact of Art on Learning.* UCLA Graduate School of Education and Information Studies.

Ceci, S. J. and Liker, J. (1986) A day at the races: a study of IQ, expertise, and cognitive complexity. *Journal of Experimental Psychology: General*, 115, 255–66.

Ceci, S. J. (1990) *On Intelligence … More or Less: A Bio-Ecological Treatise on Intellectual Development.* New Jersey: Prentice Hall.

Chabris, C. F., Steele, K. M., Bella, S. D., Peretz, I., and Dunlop, T. *et al.* (1999) Prelude or requiem for the 'Mozart effect'? *Nature*, 400, 826–28.

Chamberlain, D. B. (1988) The mind of the newborn: increasing evidence of competence. In *Prenatal and Perinatal Psychology and Medicine* (ed. P. Fedor-Freybergh and M. L. Vogel), pp. 5–22. Park Ridge, NJ: Parthenon Publishing.

Chan, A. S., Ho, Y. -C., and Cheung, M. C. (1998) Music training improves verbal memory. *Nature*, 396, 128.

Chandler, S., Christie, P., Newson, E., and Prevezer, W. (2002) Developing a diagnostic and intervention package for 2- to 3- year-olds with autism: outcomes of the frameworks for communication approach. *Autism*, 6, 47–69.

Chang, H. W. and Trehub, S. E. (1977) Auditory processing of relational information by young infants. *Journal of Experimental Child Psychology*, 4, 324–31.

Cheek, J. M. and Smith, L. R. (1999) Music training and mathematics achievement. *Adolescence*, 34, 759–61.

Chicherin, G. (1970) *Mozart*. Leningrad: Muzyka.

Chilton, J. (1987) *Sidney Bechet, the Wizard of Jazz*. London: Macmillan.

Chin, C. S. (2003) The development of absolute pitch: a theory concerning the roles of music training at an early developmental age and individual cognitive style. *Psychology of Music*, 31, 155–71.

Chipman, A. (2000) Janacek and Sibelius: the antithetical fates of creativity in late adulthood. *Psychoanalytic Review*, 87, 429–54.

Christianson, H. (1938) *Bodily Rhythmic Movements of Young Children in Relation to Rhythm in Music.* New York: Teachers College Contribution, No. 736.

Clynes, M. (1986) Music beyond the score. *Communication and Cognition*, 19, 169–94.

Coates, H. (1948) *Palestrina*. London: J. M. Dents and Sons.

Coon, H. and Carey, G. (1989) Genetic and environmental determinants of musical ability in twins. *Behavior Genetics*, 19, 183–93.

Coons, E. E., Montello, L., and Perez, J. (1995) Confidence and denial factors affect musicians' postperformance immune responses. *International Journal of Arts Medicine*, 4, 4–14.

Cortot, A. (1965) *O fortepiannom iskusstve/On the Art of Piano Playing*. Moscow: Muzyka.

Cossentino, J. and Shaffer, D. (1999) The math studio: harnessing the power of the arts to teach across disciplines. *Journal of Aesthetic Education*, 33, 99–109.

Courcy de, G. (1957) *Paganini, the Genoese*. Norman: University of Oklahoma Press.

Crncec, R., Wilson, S. J., and Prior, M. (2006) The cognitive and academic benefits of music to children: facts and fiction. *Educational Psychology*, 26, 579–94.

Crummer, G. C., Walton, J. P., Wayman, J. W., Hantz, E. C. *et al.* (1994) Neural processing of musical timbre by musicians, nonmusicians, and musicians possessing absolute pitch. *Journal of the Acoustical Society of America*, 95, 2720–7.

Csikszentmihalyi, M. and Csikszentmihalyi, I. S. (1993) Family influences on the development of giftedness. In *Ciba Foundation Symposium 178: the Origins and Development of High Ability*, (ed. G. R. Bock and K. Ackrill). Wiley.

Csikszentmihalyi, M., Rathunde, K., and Whalen, S. (1993) *Talented Teenagers: The Roots of Success and Failure.* New York: Cambridge University Press.

Cunningham, J. and Sterling, R. (1988) Developmental change in the understanding of affective meaning in music. *Motivation and Emotion*, 12, 399–413.

Cutietta, R. A. and Haggerty, K. J. (1987) A comparative study of color association with music at various age levels. *Journal of Research in Music Education*, 35, 78–91.

Cutietta, R. A. and Booth, G. D. (1996) The influence of metre, mode, interval type, and contour in repeated melodic free-recall. *Psychology of Music*, 24, 222–36.

Cytowic, R. E. (1976) Aphasia in Maurice Ravel. *Bulletin of the Los Angeles Neurological Society*, 41, 109–14.

Dark, V. J. and Benbow, C. P. (1990) Enhanced problem translation and short-term memory: components of mathematical talent. *Journal of Educational Psychology*, 82, 420–29.

Dark, V. J. and Benbow, C. P. (1991) The differential enhancement of working memory with mathematical versus verbal precocity. *Journal of Educational Psychology*, 83, 48–60.

Darrow, A. (1987) An investigative study: the effect of hearing impairment on musical aptitude. *Journal of Music Therapy*, 24, 88–96.

Davidson, J. W. (1993) Visual perception of performance manner in the movements of solo musicians. *Psychology of Music*, 21, 103–13.

Davidson, L. (1994) Songsinging by young and old: a developmental approach to music. In *Musical Perceptions*, (ed. R. Aiello and J. Sloboda), pp. 99–130. New York: Oxford University Press.

Davidson, J. W., Howe, M. J., Moore, D. G., and Sloboda, J. A. (1996) The role of parental influences in the development of musical performance. *British Journal of Developmental Psychology*, 39, 21–35.

Davies, J. (1978) *The Psychology of Music.* London: Hutchinson.

Davies, J. (1994) Seeds of a false consciousness. *The Psychologist*, 7, 355–6.

Debussy, K. (1964) *Stat'i, retsenzii, besedy/Articles, reviews, Interviews.* Moscow: Muzyka.

Decaux, A. (1958) *Offenbach, roi de second empire.* Paris: P. Amiot.

Deliége, I., Melen, M., Stammers, D., and Cross, I. (1996) Musical schemata in real-time listening to a piece of music. *Music Perception*, 14, 117–60.

Delis, D., Fleer, J., and Kerr, N. H. (1978) Memory for music. *Perception and Psychophysics*, 23, 215–18.

Delogu, F., Lampis, G., and Belardinelli, M. (2006) Music-to-language transfer effect: may melodic ability improve learning of tonal languages by native nontonal speakers? *Cognitive Processing*, 7, 203–7.

Demorest, S. M. and Serlin, R. C. (1997) The integration of pitch and rhythm in musical judgment: testing age-related trends in novice listeners. *Journal of Research in Music Education*, 45, 67–79.

Deutsch, D. (1972) Mapping of interactions in the pitch memory store. *Science*, 175, 1020–2.

Deutsch, D. (1978) Delayed pitch comparisons and the principle of proximity. *Perception and Psychophysics*, 23, 227–30.

Deutsch, D. (ed.) (1999) *The Psychology of Music.* San Diego: Academic Press.

DeWitt, L. A. and Samuel, A. G. (1990) The role of knowledge-based expectations in music perception: evidence from musical restoration. *Journal of Experimental Psychology: General.* 119, 123–44.

Dibben, N. (1999) The perception of structural stability in atonal music: the influence of salience, stability, horizontal motion, pitch commonality, and dissonance. *Music Perception*, 16, 265–94.

DiCarlo, N. S. (1994) Internal voice sensitivities in opera singers. *Folia Phoniatrica et Logopaedica*, 46, 79–85.

Di Giammarino, M., Hanlon, H., Kassing, G., and Libman, K. (1992) Arts and aging: an annotated bibliography of selected resource materials in art, dance, drama and music. *Activities, Adaptation and Aging*, 17, 39–51.

Dogantan-Dack, M. (2006) The body behind music: precedents and prospects. *Psychology of Music*, 34, 449–64.

Doig, D. (1941) Creative music I: music composed for a given text. *Journal of Educational Research*, 33, 263–75.

Doig, D. (1942) Creative music II: music composed on a given subject. *Journal of Educational Research*, 35, 345–55.

Doig, D. (1942) Creative music III: Music composed to illustrate given musical problems. *Journal of Educational Research*, 36, 241–53.

Dokshitzer, T. (1995) *Iz zapisnikh knizhek trubacha/From the Trumpeter's Notes*. Moscow: Kompozitor.

Don, A., Schellenberg, G., and Rourke, B. (1999) Music and language skills of children with Williams syndrome. *Child Neuropsychology*, 5, 154–70.

Dowling, W. J. and Fujitani, S. (1971) Contour, interval and pitch recognition in memory for melodies. *Journal of Acoustic Society of America*, 49, 524–31.

Dowling, W. J. (1988) Tonal structure and children's early learning of music. In *Generative Processes in Music* (ed. J. Sloboda), pp. 113–28. Oxford: Clarendon Press.

Dowling, W. J. (1993) Procedural and declarative knowledge in music cognition and education. In *Psychology and Music: The Understanding of Melody and Rhythm* (ed. T. J. Tighe and W. J. Dowling), pp. 5–18. Hillsdale, N.J.: Lawrence Erlbaum Associates.

Drake, C. and Palmer, C. (2000) Skill acquisition in music performance: relations between planning and temporal control. *Cognition*, 74, 1–32.

Drake, C., Penel, A., and Bigand, E. (2000) Tapping in time with mechanically and expressively performed music. *Music Perception*, 18, 1–24.

Drake, C. and Bertrand, D. (2003) The quest for universals in temporal processing in music. In *The Cognitive Neuroscience of Music* (ed. I. Peretz and R. Zatorre), pp. 21–31. New York: Oxford University Press.

Drayna, D., Manichaikul, A., de Lange, M., Snieder, H., and Spector, T. (2001) Genetic correlates of musical pitch recognition in humans. *Science*, 291, 1969–72.

Dubinin, N. P. and Glembotsky, Y. L. (1967) *Genetika populiatsii i selektsia/Genetics of Population and Selection*. Moscow: Nauka.

Duke, R. A. (1989) Musicians' perception of beat in monotonic stimuli. *Journal of Research in Music Education*, 37, 61–71.

Duke, R. A., Geringer, J. M., and Madsen, C. K. (1991) Performance of perceived beat in relation to age and music training. *Journal of Research in Music Education*, 39, 35–45.

Durkin, K. and Townsend, J. (1997) Research note: influence of linguistic factors on young school children's responses to musical pitch tests: a preliminary test. *Psychology of Music*, 25, 186–91.

Eerola, T., Jarvinen, T., Louhivuori, J., and Toiviainen, P. (2001) Statistical features and perceived similarity of folk melodies. *Music Perception*, 18, 275–96.

Efrusi, E. (ed.) (1939) *Muzykal'noe vospitanie nachinauschih pianistov v rukah pedagoga-pianista/Music Education of Piano Beginners in Piano Teacher's Hands*. Moscow: Pedagogika.

Ehrenwald, J. (1984) *Anatomy of Genius*. New York: Human Sciences Press.

Eitan, Z. and Granot, R. Y. (2006) How music moves: musical parameters and listeners' images of motion. *Music Perception*, 23, 221–47.

Elbert, T., Pantev, C., Wienbruch, C., and Rockstroh, B., *et al.* (1995) Increased cortical representation of the fingers of the left hand in string players. *Science*, 270, 305–7.

Ellington, D. (1973) *Music is my Mistress.* New York: Da Capo Press.

Ellis, M. C. (1996) Field dependence-independence and the discrimination of musical parts. *Perceptual and Motor Skills*, 82, 947–53.

Elvis in his own Words (1977) London-New York: Omnibus Press.

Ericsson, K. A. and Polson, P. G. (1988) An experimental analysis of a memory skill for dinner-orders. *Journal of Experimental Psychology: Learning, Memory and Cognition*, 14, 305–16.

Ericsson, K. A. (1999) Creative expertise as superior reproducible performance: innovative and flexible aspects of expert performance. *Psychological Inquiry*, 10, 329–33.

Ericsson, K. A., Krampe, R. T., and Heizmann, S. (1993a) Can we create gifted people? In *Ciba Foundation Symposium 178: the Origins and Development of High Ability* (ed. G. R. Bock and K. Ackrill). Chichester, NJ: Wiley.

Ericsson, K. A., Krampe, R. T., and Tesch-Romer, C. (1993b) The role of deliberate practice in the acquisition of expert performance. *Psychological Review*, 100, 363–406.

Ericsson, K. A. and Charness, N. (1995a) Expert performance: its structure and acquisition. *American Psychologist*, 49, 725–47.

Ericsson, K. A. and Charness, N. (1995b) Abilities: evidence for talent or characteristics acquired through engagement in relevant activities. *American Psychologist*, 50, 803–4.

Ericsson, K. A., Charness, N., Feltovich, P., and Hoffman, R. R. (eds) (2006) *Cambridge Handbook of Expertise and Expert Performance.* Cambridge, UK: Cambridge University Press.

Evans, R. J., Bickel, R., and Pendarvis, E. D. (2000) Musical talent: Innate or acquired? perceptions of students, parents, and teachers. *Gifted Child Quarterly*, 44, 80–90.

Eyesenck, H. J. (1950) Know your own IQ; criterion analysis: an application of hypothetico-deductive method to factor analysis. *Psychological Review*, 57, 38–53.

Eysenck, H. J. (1990) Biological dimensions of personality. In *Handbook of Personality: Theory and Research* (ed. L.A. Pervin), pp. 244–76. New York: Guilford.

Eysenck, H. J. and Barrett, P. T. (1993) Brain research related to giftedness. In *International Handbook of Research and Development of Giftedness and Talent* (ed. K. A. Heller, F. J. Munks, and A. H. Passow). New York: Pergamon.

Eysenck, H. J. (1995) *Genius: the Natural History of Creativity.* New York: Cambridge University Press.

Fehm, L. and Hille, C. (2005) Behnenangst bei Musikstudierenden/Performance anxiety in music students. *Verhaltenstherapie und Verhaltensmedizin*, 26, 199–212.

Feierabend, J. M., Saunders, T. C., Holahan, J. M., and Getnick, P. E. (1998) Song recognition among preschool-age children: an investigation of words and music. *Journal of Research in Music Education*, 46, 351–59.

Feld, S. (1984) Sound structure as a social structure. *Ethnomusicology*, 28, 383–409.

Feldman, D. H. (1980) *Beyond Universals in Cognitive Development.* Norwood, NJ: Ablex.

Feldman, D. H. (1988) Creativity: dreams, insights, and transformations. In *The Nature of Creativity*, (ed. R. J. Sternberg), pp. 271–97. Cambridge University Press.

Finney, S. A. (1997) Auditory feedback and musical keyboard performance. *Music Perception*, 15, 153–74.

Fitch, W. T. (2006) The biology and evolution of music: a comparative perspective. *Cognition*, 100, 173–215.

Fogarty, G., Buttsworth, L., and Gearing, P. (1996) Assessing intonation skills in a tertiary music training programme. *Psychology of Music*, 24, 157–70.

Fowler, W. (1981) Case studies of cognitive precocity: the role of exogenous and endogenous stimulation in early mental development. *Journal of Applied Developmental Psychology*, 2, 319–67.

Fraisse, P., Pichot P., and Claironui, G. (1949) Les aptitudes rythmiques. Etude comparée des oligophrénes et des enfants normaux. *Journal de psychologie normale et pathologique,* 309–30.

Frances, R. (1958) *La perception de la musique.* Paris: Vrin.

Franek, M., Mates, J., Radil, T., Beck, K. *et al.* (1994) Sensorimotor synchronization: motor responses to pseudoregular auditory patterns. *Perception and Psychophysics,* 55, 204–17.

Fredrickson, W. E. and Johnson, C. M. (1996) The effect of performer use of rubato on listener perception of tension in Mozart. *Psychomusicology,* 15, 76–86.

Fredrickson, W. E. (1999) Elementary, middle and high school student perceptions of tension in music. *Journal of Research in Music Education,* 47, 44–52.

Freeman, J. (1990) The intellectually gifted adolescent. In *Encouraging the development Of Exceptional Skills and Talents* (ed. M. J. Howe), pp. 89–108. British Psychological Society.

Fucci, D., Petrosino, L., Banks, M., and Zaums, K. (1996) The effect of preference for three different types of music on magnitude estimation-scaling behavior in young adults. *Perceptual and Motor Skills,* 83, 339–47.

Fujihara, T. and Tagashira, N. (1984) A multidimensional scaling of classical music perception. *Japanese Journal of Psychology,* 55, 75–9.

Furnham, A. and Allass, K. (1999) The influence of musical distraction of varying complexity on the cognitive performance of extroverts and introverts. *European Journal of Personality,* 13, 27–38.

Furtwaengler, W. (1953) *Entretiens sur la musique.* Paris: Albin-Michel.

Gaede, S. E., Parsons, O. A., and Bertera, J. H. (1978) Hemispheric differences in music perception: aptitude vs. experience. *Neuropsychologia,* 16, 369–73.

Gagné, F. (1993) Constructs and models pertaining to exceptional human abilities. In *International Handbook of Research and Development of Giftedness and Talent* (ed. K. A. Heller, F. J. Munks, and A. H. Passow), pp. 63–85. New York: Pergamon.

Gagné, F. (2004a) An imperative, but, alas, improbable consensus! *Roeper Review,* 27, 12–14.

Gagné, F. (2004b) Transforming gifts into talents: the DMGT as a developmental theory. *High Ability Studies,* 15, 119–41.

Gagné, F. (1985) Giftedness and talent: reexamining a reexamination of the definitions. *Gifted Child Quarterly,* 29, 103–12.

Gammond, P. (1975) *Scott Joplin and the ragtine era.* London: Abacus.

Gannon, P. J., Holloway, R. L., Broadfield, D. C., and Braun, A. R. (1998) Asymmetry of chimpanzee planum temporale: humanlike pattern of Wernicke's brain language area homolog. *Science,* 279, 220–22.

Ganschow, L., Lloyd-Jones, J., and Miles, T. R. (1994) Dyslexia and musical notation. *Annals of Dyslexia,* 44, 185–202.

Garcia, E. (2000) Gustav Mahler's choice: a note on adolescence, genius, and psychosomatics. *Psychoanalytic Study of the Child,* 55, 87–110.

Gardiner, J. M., Kaminska, Z., Dixon, M., and Java, R. I. (1996) Repetition of previously novel melodies sometimes increases both remember and know responses in recognition memory. *Psychonomic Bulletin and Review,* 3, 366–71.

Gardiner, M., Fox, A., Knowles, F., and Jeffrey, D. (1996) Learning improved by arts training. *Nature,* 381, 284.

Gardiner, M. (2000) Music linked to reduced criminality. MuSICA Research Notes, VII–I. Available at: http://www.musica.uci.edu

Gardner, H. (1971) Children's sensitivity to musical styles. Harvard Project Zero, Technical Report, No. 4.

Gardner, H. (1983) *Frames of Mind*. London: Heinemann.

Gardner, H. (1993) *Multiple Intelligences: The Theory in Practice*. New York: Basic Books.

Gardner, H. (1995) Why would anyone become an expert? *American Psychologist*, 50, 802–3.

Gardner, H. (1997) *Extraordinary Minds*. New York: Basic Books.

Gates, A., Bradshaw, J. L., and Nettleton, N. C. (1974) Effect of different delayed auditory feedback intervals on a music performance task. *Perception and Psychophysics*, 15, 21–5.

Gazzaniga, M. S. (1985) *The Social Brain: Discovering The Networks of the Mind*. New York: Basic Books.

Gedda, L. *et al.* (1961) L'eredita delle attitudini musicali. *Processions of 2-nd International Congress of Human Genetics*, Rome.

Gieseking, W. (1975) Tak ya stal pianistom/So I've become a pianist. *Ispolnitel'skoe iskusstvo zarubezhnyh stran/Performing Art Abroad*, 7, 191–284.

Geiringer, K. (1982) *Joseph Haydn*. Berkelee: University of California Press.

Geringer, J. M., Cassidy, J. W., and Byo, J. L. (1996) Effects of music with video on responses of nonmusic majors: an exploratory study. *Journal of Research in Music Education*, 44, 240–51.

Ginzburg, L. S. (1950) *K.Y.Davydov*. Moscow: Muzgiz.

Ginzburg, L. S. (1966) *Vidauschiesia skripachi/Outstanding Violinists*. Leningrad: Sovetsky kompozitor.

Giomo, C. J. (1993) An experimental study of children's sensitivity to mood in music. *Psychology of Music*, 21, 141–62.

Glinka M. (1954) *O muzyke i muzykantah/On Music and Musicians*. Moscow: Gosmuzgiz.

Goolsby, T. W. (1994a) Eye movement in music reading: effects of reading ability, notational complexity, and encounters. *Music Perception*, 12, 77–96.

Goolsby, T. W. (1994b). Profiles of processing: eye movements during sightreading. *Music Perception*, 12, 97–123.

Gordon, E. (1978) *Pattern Sequence and Learning In Music*. Chicago: G.I.A Publications.

Gordon, E. (1979) Developmental music aptitude as measured by the primary measures of music audiation. *Psychology of Music*, 7, 42–9.

Gosselin, N., Peretz, I., Johnsen, E., and Adolphs, R. (2007) Amygdala damage impairs emotion recognition from music. *Neuropsychologia*, 45, 236–44.

Gotell, E., Brown, S., and Ekman, S.-L. (2002) Caregiver singing and background music in dementia care. *Western Journal of Nursing Research*, 24, 195–216.

Gotell, E., Brown, S., and Ekman, S.-L. (2003) Influence of caregiver singing and background music on posture, movement, and sensory awareness in dementia care. *International Psychogeriatrics*, 15(4), 411–30.

Gregersen, P. K., Kowlasky, E., Kohn, N., and Marvin E. W. (1999) Absolute pitch: prevalence, ethnic variation, and estimation of the genetic component. *American Journal of Human Genetics*, 65, 911–13.

Gregersen, P. K., Kowlasky, E., Kohn, N., and Marvin E. W. (2000) Early childhood music education and predisposition to absolute pitch. *American Journal of Medical Genetics*, 98, 280–82.

Griffiths, T. D. (2000) Musical hallucinosis in acquired deafness. Phenomenology and brain substrate. *Brain*, 123, 2065–76.

Griffiths, T. D., Rees, A., Witton, C., Cross, P. M., Shakir, R. A., and Green, G. G. (1997) Spatial and temporal auditory processing deficits following right hemisphere infarction: a psychophysical study. *Brain*, 120, 785–94.

Gromko, J. E. (1993) Perceptual differences between expert and novice music listeners: a multidimensional scaling analysis. *Psychology of Music*, 21, 34–47.

Gromko, J. and Poorman, A. (1998) Why has musical aptitude assessment fallen flat? And what can we do about it? *Journal of Research in Music Education*, 46, 173–81.

Gross, M. U. (1993a) Nurturing the talents of exceptionally gifted individuals. In *International Handbook of Research and Development of Giftedness and Talent* (ed. K. A. Heller, F. J. Munks, and A. H. Passow). New York: Pergamon.

Gruhn, W. (2006) The appearance of intelligence in music: connections and distinctions between the concepts of musical and general intelligence: a review. In *Intelligence: New research* (ed. L. V. Wesley), pp. 115–32. Hauppauge, New York: Nova Science Publishers.

Gudmundsdottir, H. R. (1999) Children's auditory discrimination of simultaneous melodies. *Journal of Research in Music Education*, 47, 101–10.

Gundlach, R. H.(1935) Factors determining the characterization of musical phrases. *American Journal of Psychology*, 47, 624–43.

Gyarmathy, E. and Herskovits, M. (1999) Cue utilization in communication of emotion in music performance: Relating performance to perception. *Pszichologia: Az MTA Pszichologiai Intezetenek folyoirata*, 19, 437–58.

Habe, K. (2000) Vpliv izvajalske anksioznosti na uspesnost glasbenega nastopanja /The interrelationship between performance anxiety and efficiency of solo music performance. *Horizons of Psychology*, 9, 103–20.

Hagen, E. H. and Bryant, G. A. (2003) Music and dance as a coalition signaling system. *Human Nature*, 14, 21–51.

Hallam, S. (1998) The predictors of achievement and dropout in instrumental tuition. *Psychology of Music*, 26, 116–32.

Halpern, A., Bartlett, J., and Jay, W. (1998) Perception of mode, rhythm and contour in unfamiliar melodies: effects of age and experience. *Music Perception*, 15, 335–55.

Halpern, J. (1992) Effects of historical and analytical teaching approaches on music appreciation. *Journal of Research in Music Education*, 40, 39–46.

Hantz, E. C., Kreilick, K. G., Braveman, A.L., and Swartz, K. P. (1995) Effects of musical training and absolute pitch on a pitch memory task: an event-related potential study. *Psychomusicology*, 14, 53–76.

Hantz, E. C., Kreilick, K. G., Kananen, W., and Swartz, K. P. (1997) Neural responses to melodic and harmonic closure: an event-related-potential study. *Music Perception*, 15, 69–98.

Hargreaves, D. (1986) *The Developmental Psychology of Music*. Cambridge: Cambridge University Press.

Hargreaves, D. (1999) Children's conception and practice of musical improvisation. *Psychology of Music*, 27, 205–7.

Haroutounian, J. (2000) Perspectives of musical talent: a study of identification criteria and procedures. *High Ability Studies*, 11, 137– 60.

Haroutounian, J. (2002) *Kindling the Spark. Recognizing and Developing Musical Talent*. Oxford University Press.

Hassler, M., Birbaumer, N., and Feil, A. (1985) Musical talent and visual-spatial abilities: a longitudinal study. *Psychology of Music*, 113, 99–113.

Hassler, M. and Birbaumer, N. (1986) Witelson's Dichaptic Stimulation Test and children with different levels of musical talent. *Neuropsychologia*, 24, 435–40.

Hassler, M., Birbaumer, N., and Feil, A. (1987) Musical talent and visual-spatial ability: onset of puberty. *Psychology of Music*, 15, 141–51.

Hassler, M. and Nieschlag, E. (1991) Salivary testosterone and creative musical behavior in adolescent males and females. *Developmental Neuropsychology*, 7, 503–21.

Hassler, M. (1991) Maturation rate and spatial, verbal, and musical abilities: a seven-year longitudinal study. *International Journal of Neuroscience*, 58, 183–98.

Hassler, M. (1992) Creative musical behavior and sex hormones: musical talent and spatial ability in the two sexes. *Psychoneuroendocrinology*, 17, 55–70.

Heath, S. B., Soep, E., and Roach, A. (1998) Living the arts through language and learning: a report on community-based youth organizations. In *Americans for the Arts Monographs*, 2, 1–20.

Heaton, P., Hermelin, B., and Pring, L. (1998) Autism and pitch processing: a precursor for savant musical ability. *Music Perception*, 15, 291–305.

Heaton, P., Pring, L., and Hermelin, B. (1999) A pseudo-savant: a case of exceptional musical splinter skills. *Neurocase*, 5, 503–9.

Heller, K. A. (1993) Scientific ability. In *Ciba Foundation Symposium 178: the Origins and Development of High Ability*, (ed. G. R. Bock and K. Ackrill). Chichester, NJ: Wiley.

Hendrikson, A. E. and Hendrikson, D. E. (1980) The biological basis for individual differences in intelligence. *Personality and Individual Differences*, 1, 3–33.

Hepper, P. G. (1991) The musical foetus? An examination of fetal learning before and after birth. *Irish Journal of Psychology*, 12, 95–107.

Hevner, K. (1936) Experimental studies of the elements of expression in music. *American Journal of Psychology*, 48, 246–68.

Hevner, K. (1937) The affective value of pitch and tempo in music. *American Journal of Psychology*, 49, 621–30.

Hitz, R. (1987) Creative problem solving through music activities. *Young Children*, 42, 12–17.

Ho, Y.-C., Cheung, M.-C., and Chan, A. S. (2003) Music training improves verbal but not visual memory: cross-sectional and longitudinal explorations in children. *Neuropsychology*, 17, 439–50.

Hodges, D. A. (2005) Why study music? *International Journal of Music Education*, 23, 111–15.

Hoffman, I. (1934) *Fortepiannaya igra/Piano Playing*. Moscow: Pedagogika.

Hollingworth, L. S. (1942) *Children above IQ 180: Origin and Development*. Yonkers, NY: World Books.

Honegger, A. (1963) *Ya - kompozitor!/I am a Composer!* Leningrad: Muzyka.

Honegger, A. (1979) *O muzikalnom iskusstve/On the Art of Music*. Leningrad: Sovetsky kompozitor.

Holopova, V. (2000) *Muzyka kak vid iskusstva/Music as the Art Form*. St-Petersburg: Lan'.

Horbulewicz, J. (1963) *The Development of Musical Memory*. Doctoral Dissertation. Danzig: Higher School of Education.

Horikoshi, T., Asari, Y., Watanabe, A., Nagaseki, Y. *et al.* (1997) Music alexia in a patient with mild pure alexia: disturbed visual perception of nonverbal meaningful figures. *Cortex*, 33, 187–94.

Horn, J. L. (1986) Intellectual ability concepts. In *Advances in the Psychology of Human Intelligence*, vol. 3 (ed. R. J. Sternberg). Hillsdale, NJ: Erlbaum.

Hoskins, C. (1988) Use of music to increase verbal response and improve expressive language abilities of preschool language delayed children. *Journal of Music Therapy*, 25, 73–84.

Howard, D. M., Rosen, S., and Broad, V. (1992) Major/minor triad identification and discrimination by musically trained and untrained listeners. *Music Perception*, 10, 205–20.

Howe, M., Davidson, J., and Sloboda, J. (1999) Innate talents: reality or myth? In *The Nature-Nurture Debate: The Essential Readings. Essential Readings in Developmental Psychology* (ed. S. Ceci and W. Williams), pp. 257–89. Malden, MA: Blackwell Publishing.

Howe, M. J. A. (1982) Biographical information and the development of outstanding individuals. *American Psychologist*, 37, 1071–81.

Howe, M. J. A. (1990) *The Origins of Exceptional Abilities*. Oxford: Blackwell.

Howe, M. J. A. (1995) What can we learn from the lives of geniuses? In *Actualizing Talent: A Lifelong Challenge* (ed. J. Freeman, P. Span, and H. Wagner). London: Cassell.

Howe, M. J. A., Davidson, J. W., Moore, D. G., and Sloboda, J. A. (1995) Are there early childhood signs of musical ability? *Psychology of Music*, 23, 162–76.

Howe, M. J. A. (1996) The childhoods and early lives of geniuses: combining psychological and biographical evidence. In *The Road to Excellence: The Acquisition of Expert Performance in the Arts and Sciences* (ed. K. A. Ericsson). Hillsdale, NJ: Erlbaum.

Huf, P. A., Parker, S. P., Corbo, M. P., and Stevens, K. M. (1996) Effect of music training on monaural perception of pitch and rhythm. *Perceptual and Motor Skills*, 82, 843–51.

Hulse, S. H. and Page, S. C. (1988) Toward a comparative psychology of music perception. *Music Perception*, 5, 427–52.

Hurwitz, I., Wolff, P. H., Bortnick, B. D., and Kokas, K. (1975) Nonmusical effects of the Kodaly music curriculum in primary grade children. *Journal of Learning Disabilities*, 8, 45–51.

Ilari, B. and Polka, L. (2006) Music cognition in early infancy: infants' preferences and longterm memory for Ravel. *International Journal of Music Education*, 24, 7–20.

Ilyin, E. (2004) *Psikhologia individualnikh razlichii/The Psychology of Individual Differences*. St.-Petersburg: Piter.

Iritani, T. (2002) Learning to play music in later adulthood: a personal perspective focusing on the piano. *Psychomusicology*, 18, 132–41.

Ivanchenko, G. V. (2001) *Pskhologia vospriatia muzyki: problemi, podkhodi, perspektivi/The Psychology of Music Perception: Problems, Approaches, Prospects*. Moscow: Smysl.

Ivanov, V. V. (1983) Khudozhestvennoe tvorchestvo, funktsionalnaia asymmetria i obraznie sposobnosti cheloveka/Artistic creativity, functional assymetry and imagery abilities of man. *Trudi po znakovim systemam/Semiotic Systems' Research*, 635, 3–14.

Iwanaga, M. (1994) Synchronous changes of psychophysiological responses and tone pressure: effect of musical training. *International Journal of Psychophysiology*, 18, 71–4.

Izumi, A. (2000) Japanese monkeys perceive sensory consonance of chords. *Journal of the Acoustical Society of America*, 108, 3073–78.

Jablonski, E. (1987) *Gershwin*. New York: Doubleday.

Jackendoff, R. and Lerdahl, F. (2006) The capacity for music: what is it, and what's special about it? *Cognition*, 100, 33–72.

Jacome, D. E. (1984) Aphasia with elation, hypermusia, musicophilia and compulsive whistling. *Journal of Neurology, Neurosurgery and Psychiatry*, 47, 308–10.

Jaencke, L., Schlaug, G., and Steinmetz, H. (1997) Hand skill asymmetry in professional musicians. *Brain and Cognition*, 34, 424–32.

Jaques-Dalcroze, E. (1965) *Le rythme, la musique et l'education*. Lausanne: Foetisch.

Jentschke, S., Koelsch, S., and Friederici, A. D. (2005) Investigating the relationship of music and language in children: influences of musical training and language impairment. In *The Neurosciences and Music II: From Perception to Performance* (ed. G. Avanzini, L. Lopez, S. Koelsch, and M. Majno), pp. 231–42. New York: New York Academy of Sciences.

Johnson, S. M. (1998) Listening to the music: emotion as a natural part of systems theory. *Journal of Systemic Therapies*, 17, 1–17.

Jones, M. R. and Pfordresher, P. Q. (1997) Tracking musical patterns using joint accent structure. *Canadian Journal of Experimental Psychology*, 51, 271–91.

Jones, M. R. and Yee, W. (1997) Sensitivity to time change: the role of context and skill. *Journal of Experimental Psychology: Human Perception and Performance*, 23, 693–709.

Jung, C. G. (1981) *The Archetypes and The Collective Unconscious* (1981 2nd edn Collected Works vol. 9, Part 1), Princeton, NJ: Bollingen.

Juniu, S., Tedrick, T., and Boyd, R. (1996) Leisure or work? Amateur and professional musicians' perception of rehearsal and performance. *Journal of Leisure Research*, 28, 44–56.

Juslin, P. N. (1997) Emotional communication in music performance: a functionalist perspective and some data. *Music Perception*, 14, 383–418.

Juslin, P. N. (2000) Cue utilization in communication of emotion in music performance: relating performance to perception. *Journal of Experimental Psychology*, 26, 1797–813.

Kalmar, M. (1982) The effects of music education based on Kodaly's directives in nursery school children: from a psychologist's point of view. *Psychology of Music, Spec. Issue*, 63–8.

Kanellopoulos, P. A. (1999) Bodily intention in children's improvisation and composition. *Psychology of Music*, 27, 175–91.

Kantorski, V. J. and DeNardo, G. F. (1996) An assessment of children's discrimination of change when listening to a theme and variations form. *Psychomusicology*, 15, 69–77.

Karno, M. and Konecni, V. (1992) The effect of structural interventions in the first movement of Mozart's symphony in G minor of aesthetic preference. *Music Perception*, 10, 63–72.

Kaspersen, M. and Gotestam, K. G. (2002) A survey of music performance anxiety among Norwegian music students. *European Journal of Psychiatry*, 16, 69–80.

Kastner, M. P. and Crowder, R. G. (1990) Perception of the major/minor distinction: IV. Emotional connotations in young children. *Music Perception*, 8, 189–201.

Kawamura, M., Midorikawa K., and Kezuka M. (2000) Cerebral localization of the center for reading and writing music. *NeuroReport*, 11, 3299–303.

Kazal's, P. (1977) Radosti i pechali. Razmyshleniya Pablo Kazal'sa, povedannie Albertu Kanu/ Joys and sorrows. Reflections by Pablo Casals as told to Albert E. Kahn. *Ispolnitel'skoe iskusstvo zarubezhnyh stran/Performing Art Abroad*, 8, 231–78.

Keating, D. P. and Bobbitt, B. L. (1978) Individual and developmental differences in cognitive-processing components of mental ability. *Child Development*, 51, 39–44.

Kendall, R. and Carterette, E. (1990) The communication of musical expression. *Music Perception*, 8, 129–64.

Kemenade, J., Son, M., and Heesch, N. (1995) Performance anxiety among professional musicians in symphonic orchestras: a self-report study. *Psychological Reports*, 77, 555–62.

Kenny, D. T. (2005) A systematic review of treatments for music performance anxiety. *Anxiety, Stress and Coping: An International Journal*, 18, 183–208.

Kenny, D. T. and Osborne, M. S. (2006) Music performance anxiety: new insights from young musicians. *Advances in Cognitive Psychology*, 2, 103–12.

Kessen, W., Levine, J., and Wendrich, K. A. (1979) The imitation of pitch in infants. *Infant Behavior and Development*, 2, 93–100.

Khohlovkina, M. (1954) *Georges Bizet*. Moscow: Muzgiz.

Kilgour, A. R., Jakobson, L. S., and Cuddy, L. L. (2000) Music training and rate of presentation as mediators of text and song recall. *Memory and Cognition*, 28, 700–10.

Killian, J. N. (1991) The relationship between sightsinging accuracy and error detection in junior high school singers. *Journal of Research in Music Education*, 39, 216–24.

King, C. D. (1972) *The Conservation of Melodic Pitch Patterns by Elementary School Children as Determined by Ancient Chinese Music*. Unpublished doctoral dissertation, Ohio State University.

Kirnarskaya, D. (1988) Sovremennie predstavleniya o muzykal'nyh sposobnostyah/Contemporary views on musical abilities. *Voprosy psihologii*, 2, 137–47.

Kirnarskaya, D. (1989a) Muzykal'no-yazykovaya sposobnost' kak komponent muzykal'noi odarennosti/Music-language ability as the component of musical giftedness. *Voprosy psihologii*, 2, 47–56.

Kirnarkskaya, D. (1989b) Razdum'a u konservatorskogo poroga/Thoughts on the conservatory's threshold. *Sovetskaya muzyka*, 5, 47–59.

Kirnarskaya, D. (1992) Opyt testirovaniya muzykal'noi odarennosti na vstupitel'nyh ekzamenah/Musical giftedness' testing at the conservatory entering examinations. *Voprosy psihologii*, 1–2, 158–63.

Kirnarskaya, D. (1995) Music-language ability as a component of musical talent. In *The First East-West Conference in General Psychology*, pp. 298–303. Banska Bystrica: Matej Bel University.

Kirnarskaya, D. (1997) *Muzykal'noe vospriyatie/Music Perception*. Moscow: Kimos-Ard.

Kirnarskaya, D. (1999) Psihologicheskiy portret kompozitora, napisannyi im samim/Psychological portrait of a composer written by himself. In *Problemi psikhologii tvorchestva/ Psychology of Creativity Research* (ed. E. Vyazkova), 183–205.

Kirnarskaya, D. and Winner, E. (1999) Musical ability in a new key: exploring the expressive ear for music. *Psychomusicology*, 16, 2–16.

Kirnarskaya, D. (2006) *Teoreticheskie osnovi i metodi otsenki muzikalnoi odarennosti/Theoretical Foundations and Methods of Testing of Musical Giftedness*. St. Petersburg: St. Petersburg University.

Kliegl, R., Smith, J., and Baltes, P. B. (1989) Testing the limits and the study of adult age differences in cognitive plasticity of a mnemonic skill. *Developmental Psychology*, 25, 247–56.

Koelsch, S. (2005) Neural substrates of processing syntax and semantics in music. *Current Opinion in Neurobiology*, 15, 207–12.

Koelsch, S., Gunter, T., Friederici, A. D., and Schroeger, E. (2000) Brain indices of music processing: 'nonmusicians' are musical. *Journal of Cognitive Neuroscience*, 12, 520–41.

Koelsch, S., Schroger, E., and Gunter, T. C. (2002) Music matters: preattentive musicality of the human brain. *Psychophysiology*, 39, 38–48.

Koelsch, S. and Fritz, T. (2007) Neuronale Korrelate der Musikverarbeitung/Neural correlates of music processing. *Verhaltenstherapie und Verhaltensmedizin*, 28, 23–38.

Kondrashin, K. (1976) *Mir dirizhera/ Conductor's World*. Leningrad: Muzyka.

Konen, V. (1971) *Claudio Monteverdi*. Moscow: Sovetsky kompozitor.

Konishi, M. (1994) Pattern generation in birdsong. *Current Opinion in Neurobiology*, 4, 827–31.

Konovalov, V. F. and Otmakhova, N. A. (1984) EEG manifestations of functional asymmetry of the human cerebral cortex during perception of words and music. *Human Physiology*, 9, 250–55.

Korredor, H. (1960) *Besedy s Pablo Kazal'som/Conversations with Pablo Casals*. Leningrad: Gosmuzizdat.

Krampe, R. T. and Ericsson, K. A. (1996) Maintaining excellence: cognitive-motor performance in pianists differing in age and skill level. *Journal of Experimental Psychology: General*, 125, 331–59.

Kratus, J. (1989) A time analysis of the compositional processes used by children ages 7 to 11. *Journal of Research in Music Education*, 37, 5–20.

Kratus, J. (1994) Relationships among children's music audiation and their compositional processes and products. *Journal of Research in Music Education*, 42, 115–30.

Krings, T. (2000) Pianists have more efficient brains. *Neuroscience Letters*, 278, 189–98.

Krumhansl, C. L. (2002) Music: a link between cognition and emotion. *Current Directions in Psychological Science*, 11, 45–50.

Krumhansl, C. (1997) An exploratory study of musical emotions and psychophysiology. *Canadian Journal of Experimental Psychology*, 51, 336–52.

Krutetsky, V. (1998) *Psikhollogia matematicheskikh sposobnostei shkolnikov/The Psychology of Schoolchildren's Mathematical Abilities*. Moscow: Institut prkticheskoi pskhologii.

Kuhn, T. L. and Booth, G. D. (1988) The effect of melodic activity, tempo change, and audible beat on tempo perception of elementary school students. *Journal of Research in Music Education*, 36, 140–55.

Kushenov-Dmitrevsky, D. F. (1831) *Liricheskiy museum/Lyrical Museum*. St. Petersburg: Kushenov-Dmitrevsky.

LaBarba, R. C., and Kingsberg, S. A., and Martin, P.K (1992) Cerebral lateralization of unfamiliar music perception in nonmusicians: *Psychomusicology*, 11, 119–24.

LaBarba, R. C. and Kingsberg, S. A. (1990) Cerebral lateralization of unfamiliar music perception in nonmusicians: a dual task approach. *Cortex*, 26, 567–74.

LaFuente, M. J., Grifol, R., and Segarra, J. *et al.* (1997) Effects of the Firstart method of prenatal stimulation on psychomotor development: the first six months. *Pre- and Peri-Natal Psychology Journal*, 11, 151–62.

Lamar, H. B., Jr. (1989) *An Examination of Congruency of Musical Aptitude Scores and Mathematics and Reading Achievement Scores of Elementary Children.* Unpublished doctoral dissertation, University of Southern Mississippi.

Lamb, S. J. and Gregory, A. H. (1993) The relationship between music and reading in beginning readers. *Educational Psychology*, 13, 19–27.

Lamont, A. (1998) Music, education, and the development of pitch perception: the role of context, age, and musical experience. *Psychology of Music*, 26, 7–25.

Lamont, A. and Dibben, N. (2001) Motivic structure and the perception of similarity. *Music Perception*, 18, 245–74.

Leader, L.R., Baillie, P., and Martin, B. *et al.* (1982) The assessment and significance of habituation to a repeated stimulus by the human fetus. *Early Human Development*, 7, 211–19.

Lecanuet, J. P., Graniere-Deferre, C., Jacquet, A.-Y., and DeCasper, A. J. (2000) Fetal discrimination of low-pitched musical notes. *Developmental Psychobiology*, 36, 29–39.

Led Zeppelin in their own Words (1981) London: Omnibus Press.

Lehmann, A. C. (1995) The acquisition of expertise in music: efficiency of deliberate practice as a moderating variable in accounting for sub-expert performance. In *Perception and Cognition of Music* (ed. I. Deliége and J. A. Sloboda). Hillsdale, NJ: Erlbaum.

Lehmann, A., Sloboda, J., and Woody, R. (2007) *Psychology for Musicians: Understanding and Acquiring Skills.* UK: Oxford University Press.

Lemeshev, C. (1987) *Iz biograficheskih zapisok. Stat'i, besedy, pis'ma, vospominaniya/From Biographical Notes. Articles, Talks, Letters, Memoirs.* Moscow: Sovetsky kompozitor.

Levi-Strauss, K. (1983) *Strukturnaya antropologiya/Structural anthropology.* Moscow: Nauka.

Levitin, D. J. and Bellugi, U. (1998) Musical abilities in individuals with Williams syndrome. *Music Perception*, 15, 357–89.

Levitin, D. J. (1999) Absolute pitch: self-reference and human memory. *International Journal of Computing Anticipatory Systems*, 4, 255–66.

Levitin, D. J. and Rogers, S. E. (2005) Absolute pitch: perception, coding, and controversies. *Trends in Cognitive Sciences*, 9, 26–33.

Levitin, D. J. and Menon, V. (2005) The neural locus of temporal structure and expectancies in music: evidence from functional neuroimaging at 3 Tesla. *Music Perception*, 22, 563–75.

Levitin, D. J. (2006) *This is Your Brain on Music.* New York: Plume.

Lim, S. and Lippman, L. G. (1991) Mental practice and memorization of piano music. *Journal of General Psychology*, 118, 21–30.

Lizst, F. (1959) *Izbrannie stat'i/Selected Articles.* Moscow: Muzyka.

London, J. (2001–2002) Some theories of emotion in music and their implications for research in music psychology. *Musicae Scientiae*, Spec Issue, 23–36.

Long, M. (1978) *Za royalem s Debussy/At the Piano with Debussy.* Moscow: Sovetsky kompozitor.

Long, M. (1981) Za royalem s Gabrielem Fore/At the piano with Gabriel Foret. *Ispolnitel'skoe iskusstvo zarubezhnyh stran/Performing Art Abroad*, 9, 15–38.

Long, N. H. (1972) Music discrimination tests – their construction, assumptions and uses. *Australian Journal of Music Education*, 11, 21–5.

Lowery, H. (1929) Musical memory. *British Journal of Psychology*, 19, 397–404.

Lundin, R. W. (1958) What next in the psychology of musical measurement? *Psychological Record*, 8, 1–6.

Lundin, R. W. (1963) Can perfect pitch be learned? *Music Educational Journal*, 49, 49–51.

Lyadov, A. (1916) *Zhizn', portret, tvorchestvo/Life, Portrait, Creative Work.* Petrograd. Izdanie popechitelnogo soveta dlya pooschrenia russkikh kompozitorov i muzikantov/Publishing of board of trustees for the encouragement of Russian composers and musicians.

Lynch, M. P., Short, L. B., and Chua, R. (1995) Contributions of experience to the development of musical processing in infancy. *Developmental Psychobiology*, 28, 377–98.

Lynch, M. P., Eilers, R. E., Oller, D. K., and Urbano, R. C. (1990) Innateness, experience, and music perception. *Psychological Science*, 1, 272–76.

Madsen, C. K. (1997) Emotional response to music as measured by the two dimensional CRDI. *Journal of Music Therapy*, 34, 187–99.

Madsen, C. K. and Madsen, K. (2002) Perception and cognition of music: musically trained and untrained adults compared to sixth-grade and eighth-grade children. *Journal of Research in Music Education*, 50, 111–30.

Madsen, C., Geringer, J., and Wagner, M. (2007) Context specificity in music perception of musicians. *Psychology of Music*, 35, 441–51.

Mahler, G. (1964) *Pis'ma, dokumenty/Letters, Documents*. Moscow: Muzyka

Maikapar, C. (1938) *Gody ucheniya/Years of Studies*. Moscow-Leningrad.

Mainwaring, J. (1933) Kinaesthetic factors in the recall of musical experience. *British Journal of Psychology*, 23, 284–307.

Malyarenko, T. N. (1996) Music alters children's brainwaves. *Human Physiology*, 22, 76–81.

Mantle, J. (1989) *Fanfare: The Unauthorised Biography of A. L. Webber*. London: M. Joseph.

Manturzewska, M. (1994) Les facteurs psychologiques dans le développement musical et l'évolution des musiciens professionnels. In *Psychologie de la musique*, (ed. A. Zenatti), pp. 259–90. Presses Universitaires de France.

Manturzewska, M. (1978) Psychology in the music school. *Psychology of Music*, 6, 36–47.

Marshall, C. (1982) Towards a comparative aesthetics of music. In *Cross-cultural Perspectives on Music* (ed. R. Falck and T. Rice). Toronto: University of Toronto Press.

Manturzewska, M. (1979) Results of psychological research on the process of music practising and its effective shaping. *Bulletin of Council of Research for Music Education*, 59, 59–61.

Manturzewska, M. (1990) A biographical study of the life-span development of professional musicians. *Psychology of Music*, 18, 112–39.

Martin, B. A. (1991) Effects of hand signs, syllables, and letters on first graders' acquisition of tonal skills. *Journal of Research in Music Education*, 39, 161–70.

Martin, P. J. (1976) *Appreciation of Music in Relation to Personality Factors*. Unpublished doctoral dissertation, University of Glasgow.

Martinsen, K. (2003) *Metodika individualnogo prepodavania igri na fortepiano/Methods of Individual Piano Teaching*. Moscow: Vlados.

Masataka, N. (1999) Preference for infant-directed singing in 2-day-old hearing infants of deaf parents. *Developmental Psychology*, 35, 1001–05.

Masataka, N. (2007) Music, evolution, and language. *Developmental Science*, 10, 35–9.

McAdams, S., Winsberg, S., Donnadieu, S., and De Soete, Geert *et al.* (1995) Perceptual scaling of synthesized musical timbres: common dimensions, specificities, and latent subject classes. *Psychological Research*, 58, 177–92.

McAdams, S. (1996) Audition: cognitive psychology of music. In *The Mind-brain Continuum: Sensory Processes* (ed. R. R. Llinas, P. S. Churchland *et al.*), pp. 251–79. Cambridge, MA: MIT Press.

McDermott, J. and Hauser, M. (2005) The origins of music: innateness, uniqueness, and evolution. *Music Perception*, 23, 29–59.

McDougall, R. (1902) The relation of auditory rhythm to nervous discharge. *Psychological Review*, 9.

McLeish, J. (1968) *Musical Cognition*. London: Novello.

McNamara, P., Flannery, K. A., Obler, L. K., and Schachter, S. C. (1994) Special talents in Geschwind's and Galaburda's theory of cerebral lateralization: an examination in a female population. *International Journal of Neuroscience*, 78, 167–76.

Medushevsky, V. (1993) *Intonatsionnaya forma muzyki/The Intonation Form of Music.* Moscow: Sovetsky kompozitor.

Menuhin, Y. (1979) *Unfinished Journey.* London: MacDonald and Jane's.

Merkur, B. (2000) Synchronous chorusing and human origins. In *The Origins of Music* (ed. N. L. Wallin, B. Merkur, and S. Brown). Cambridge, MA: MIT Press.

Metner, N. (1981) *Stat'i, materialy, vospominaniya/Articles, Materials, Memoirs.* Moscow: Sovetsky kompozitor.

Meumann, E. (1894) Untersuchungen zur psychologie und aesthetik des rythmus. Philos. Studien, 10.

Meyer, K. (1998) *Shostakovich.* St.-Petersburg: Kompozitor.

Meyer, L. B. (1956) *Emotion and Meaning in Music.* Chicago: University of Chicago Press.

Mialaret, J. -P. (1997) *Explorations Musicales Instrumentales chez le Jeune Enfant.* Paris: PUF

Micheyl, C., Carbonnel, O., and Collet, L. (1995) Medial olivocochlear system and loudness adapation: differences between musicians and non-musicians. *Brain and Cognition*, 29, 127–36.

Micheyl, C., Khalfa, S., Perrot, X., and Collet, L. (1997) Difference in cochlear efferent activity between musicians and non-musicians. *Neuroreport*, 8, 1047–50.

Midorikawa, A. and Kawamura, M. (2000) A case of musical agraphia. *Neuroreport*, 11, 3053–7.

Mikhailov, A. (1993) V. A. Motsart i K. F. Morits, ili o videnii slukhom/W. A. Mozart and K. F. Moritz, or on visualization via ears. In *Problemy tvorchestva Motsarta/Problems of Mozart's Creative Work* (ed. E. Tchigareva), pp. 60–71. Moscow Conservatory.

Milhaud, D. (1995) *My Happy Life.* London: Marion Boyars.

Miller, L. B. (1989). Children's musical behaviors in the natural environment. In *Music and Child Development* (ed. J. C. Peery *et al.*), pp. 206–24. New York: Springer-Verlag.

Miller, L. (1999) The savant syndrome: intellectual impairment and exceptional skill. *Psychological Bulletin*, 125, 31–46.

Milliman, R. E. (1982) Using background music to affect the behavior of supermarket shoppers. *Journal of Marketing*, 46, 86–91.

Milshtein, Y. (1967) *Sovety Shopena pianistam/Chopin's Advice to Pianists.* Moscow: Muzyka.

Milshtein, Y. (1999) *Ferenz Liszt.* Moscow: Kompozitor.

Miluk-Kolasa, B., Obminski, S., Stupnicki, R., and Golec, L. (1994) Effects of music treatment on salivary cortisol in patients exposed to presurgical stress. *Expeimental and Clinical Endocrinology*, 102, 118–20.

Mitani, J. C. and Marler, P. (1989) A phonological analysis of male gibbon singing behavior. *Behaviour*, 109, 20–45.

Mithen, S. (2006) *The Singing Neanderthals: The Origins of Music, Language, Mind, and Body.* Cambridge, MA: Harvard University Press.

Miyazaki, K. (1995) Perception of relative pitch with different references: some absolute pitch listeners can't tell musical interval names. *Perception and Psychophysics*, 57, 962–70.

Miyazaki, K. and Ogawa, Y. (2006) Learning absolute pitch by children: a cross-sectional study. *Music Perception*, 24, 63–78.

Mjoen, J. (1926) Genius as a biological problem. *Eugenic Review*, 17, 242–57.

Mockel, M., Rocker, L., Stark, T., Vollert, J., Danne, O., Eichstadt, H., Muller, R., and Hochrein, H. (1994) Immediate physiological responses of healthy volunteers to different types of music: cardiovascular, hormonal, and mental changes. *European Journal of Applied Physiology*, 68, 451–59.

Moen, I. (1991) Functional lateralisation of pitch accents and intonation in Norwegian: Monrad-Krohn's study of an aphasic patient with altered 'melody of speech'. *Brain and Language*, 41, 538–54.

Monaghan, P., Metcalfe, N., and Ruxton, G. (1998) Does practice shape the brain? *Nature*, 394, 434.

Monsaas, J. and Engelhard, G. (1990) Home environment and the competitiveness of highly accomplished individuals in four talent fields. *Developmental Psychology*, 26, 264–68.

Moog, H. (1979) On the perception of rhythmic forms by physically handicapped children and those of low intelligence in comparison with non-handicapped children. *Bulletin of Council of Research in Music Education*, 59, 73–8.

Moog, H. (1976) *The Musical Experience of the Pre-school Child*. London: Schott.

Moore, G. (1987) *Pevets i akkompaniator. Vospominaniya. Razmyshleniya o muzyke/Singer and Accompanist. Memoires. Thoughts on Music*. Moscow: Raduga.

Moorhead, G. E. and Pond, D. (1941) *Music of Young Children I. Chant*. Santa Barbara, CA: Pillsbury Foundation for Advancement of Music Education.

Mueller, J. and Hevner, K. (1956) Studies in music appreciation. *Journal of Research in Music Education*, 4, 3–25.

Munte, T. F., Kohlmetz, C., Nager, W., and Altenmuller, E. (2001) Superior auditory spatial tuning in professional conductors. *Nature*, 409, 580.

Musin, I. (1995) *Uroki zhizni.Vospominania dirizhera/Lessons of life. Conductor's Memoirs*. St.Petersburg: Prosvetitelskoe izdatelskoe ob'edinenie Dean–Adia-M.

Nakada, T. (1998) Brain area for reading musical scores. *NeuroReport*, 2, 343–9.

Nazaikinsky, E. (1967) Rechevoi opyt i muzikalnoe vospriatie/Speech experience and music perception. *Esteticheskie ocherki/Essays on Aesthetics*, 2, 245–83.

Nesterenko, E. (1985) *Razmyshleniya o professii/Thoughts on Profession*. Moscow: Iskusstvo.

Nestiev, I. (1973) *Zhizn' Sergeya Prokof'eva/Life of Sergey Prokofiev*. Moscow: Sovetsky kompozitor.

Neuhaus, G. (1999) *Ob iskusstve fortepiannoi igry/On the Art of Piano Playing*. Moscow: Klassika-XXI.

Newton, G. de (1959) *Selection of Junior Musicians for Royal Marines School of Music: An Evaluation of H. D. Wing's Test*. Senior Psychologist's Department, Admiralty, London.

Nichols, B. L. and Honig, A. S. (1995) The influence of an inservice music education program on young children's responses to music. *Early Child Development*, 113, 19–29.

Nikolaev, A. (1964) *Arkhitektor Carlo Rossi/Architect Carlo Rossi*. Leningrad: Iskusstvo.

Nilsonne, A. and Sundberg, J. (1985) Differences in ability of musicians and nonmusicians to judge emotional state from the fundamental frequency of voice samples. *Music Perception*, 2, 507–16.

Noy, P. (1968) The development of musical ability. *Psychoanalytic Study of the Child*, 23, 332–47.

O'Connor, N. and Hermelin, B. (1987) Visual and graphic abilities of the idiot savant artist. *Psychological Medicine*, 17, 79–90.

Oistrakh, D. (1978) *Moi put'. Vospominania, statii, interviu, pisma/My Way. Memoirs, Articles, Interviews, Letters*. Moscow: Muzyka.

Okaichi, Y. and Okaichi, H. (2001) Music discrimination by rats. *Japanese Journal of Animal Psychology*, 51, 29–34.

Olsho, L.W. (1984) Infant frequency discrimination. *Infant Behavior and Development*, 7, 27–35.

O'Neill, C. T., Trainor, L. J., and Trehub, S. E. (2001) Infants' responsiveness to fathers' singing. *Music Perception*, 18, 409–25.

Orlov, H. (1992) *Drevo muzyki/The Tree of Music*. Washington-St.-Petersburg: Kompozitor.

Orsmond, G. I. and Miller, L. K. (1999) Cognitive, musical, and environmental correlates of early music instruction. *Psychology of Music*, 27, 18–37.

Osborne, R. (1991) *Conversations with Karajan*. Oxford: Oxford University Press.

Osgood, N. J. (1993) Creative activity and the arts: possibilities and programs. In *Activity and Aging: Staying Involved in Later Life* (ed. J. R. Kelly), pp. 174–86. Newbury Park, CA: Sage Publications.

Ostwald, P. (1966) Music and human emotions. *Journal of Music Therapy*, 3, 93–4.

Ostwald, P. (1973) Musical behavior in early childhood. *Developmental Medicine and Child Neurology*, 15, 367–75.

Otte, A., De Bondt, P., Van der Wiele, C., Audenaert, K., and Dierckx, R. A. (2003) The exceptional brain of Maurice Ravel. *Medical Science Monitor*, 9, 133–8.

Oyama, T., Yamada, H., and Iwasawa, H. (1998) Synesthetic tendencies as the basis of sensory symbolism: a review of a series of experiments by means of semantic differential. *Psychologia*, 41, 203–15.

Palmer, C. (1996) On the assignment of structure in music performance. *Music Perception*, 14, 23–56.

Palmer, C. and Drake, C. (1997) Monitoring and planning capacities in the acquisition of music performance skills. *Canadian Journal of Experimental Psychology*, 51, 369–84.

Panksepp, J. (1995) The emotional sources of 'chills' induced by music. *Music Perception*, 13, 171–207.

Patel, V. L. and Groen, G. J. (1991) The general and specific nature of medical expertise: a critical look. In *Toward a General Theory of Expertise: Prospects and Limits* (ed. K. A. Ericsson and J. Smith), pp. 93–125. New York: Cambridge University Press.

Patel, A. and Peretz, I. (1997) *Is music autonomous from language? A neuropsychological appraisal.* In *Perception and Cognition of Music* (ed. J. A. Sloboda and I. Deliége), pp. 191–215. Hove: Psychology Press.

Patel, A. D. (1998) Syntactic processing in language and music: different cognitive operations, similar neural resources? *Music Perception*, 16, 27–42.

Patel, A. D., Peretz, I., Tramo, M., and Labreque, R. (1998) Processing prosodic and musical patterns: a neuropsychological investigation. *Brain and Language*, 61, 123–44.

Patel, A. D. (2003) Language, music, syntax, and the brain. *Nature Neuroscience*, 6, 674–81.

Patel, A. D. and Daniele, J. R. (2003) An empirical comparison of rhythm in language and music. *Cognition*, 87, B35–B45.

Patel, A. D. (2005) The relationship of music to the melody of speech and to syntactic processing disorders in aphasia. In *The neurosciences and Music II: From Perception to Performance* (ed. G. Avanzini, L. Lopez, S. Koelsch, and M. Manjno), pp. 59–70. New York: New York Academy of Sciences.

Paul McCartney in his own words (1983) New York: The Putnam Publishing Group.

Payzant, G. (1984) *Glenn Gould. Music and Mind.* Toronto: Key Porter Books.

Pekelis, M. (1966) *A. S. Dargomyzhsky.* Moscow: Muzyka.

Peretz, I. and Morais, J. (1993) Specificity for music. In *Handbook of Neuropsychology*, 8, (ed. F. Boller and J. Grafman), pp. 373–90. Amsterdam: Elsevier Science Publishers.

Peretz, I. (1996) Can we lose memory for music? A case of music agnosia in a nonmusician. *Journal of Cognitive Neuroscience*, 8, 481–96.

Peretz, I., Belleville, S., and Fontaine, S. (1997) Dissociations entre musique et langage apres atteinte cerebrale: un nouveau cas d'amusie sans aphasie/ Dissociations between music and language after cerebral damage: a new case of music deficits without aphasia. *Canadian Journal of Experimental Psychology*, 51, 354–67.

Peretz, I., Gagnon, L., and Bouchard B. (1998) Music and emotion: perceptual determinants, immediacy, and isolation after brain damage. *Cognition*, 68, 111–41.

Peretz, I. and Gagnon, L. (1999) Dissociation between recognition and emotional judgment for melodies. *Neurocase*, 5, 21–30.

Peretz, I. and Gagnon, L. (1999) Dissociation between recognition and emotional judgements for melodies. *Neurocase*, 5, 21–30.

Peretz, I. and Zatorre, R. (eds) (2003) *The Cognitive Neuroscience of Music.* New York: Oxford University Press.

Peretz, I. (2005) The nature of music. *International Journal of Music Education*, 23, 103–5.

Peretz, I. and Sloboda, J. (2005) Music and the emotional brain. Introduction. In *The Neurosciences and Music II: From Perception to Performance* (ed. G. Avanzini, L. Lopez, S. Koelsch, and M. Manjno), pp. 409–11. New York: New York Academy of Sciences.

Peretz, I. (2006) The nature of music from a biological perspective. *Cognition*, 100, 1–32.

Perlman, M. and Krumhansl, C. L. (1996) An experimental study of internal interval standards in Javanese and Western musicians. *Music Perception*, 14, 95–116.

Persson, R. S. and Robson, C. (1995) The limits of experimentation: on researching music and musical settings. *Psychology of Music*, 23, 39–47.

Persson, R. S. (1996) Studying with a musical maestro: a case study of commonsense teaching in artistic training. *Creativity Research Journal*, 9, 33–46.

Petsche, H. (1996) Approaches to verbal, visual and musical creativity by EEG coherence analysis. *International Journal of Psychophysiology*, 24, 145–59.

Petzold, R. G. (1966) *Auditory perception of musical sounds by children in the first six grades*. Cooperative Research Project No. 1051, University of Wisconsin.

Peynircioglu, Z. F., Tekcan, A. I., Wagner, J. L., Baxter, T. L., and Shaffer, S. D. (1998) Name or hum that tune: feeling of knowing for music. *Memory and Cognition*, 26, 1131–7.

Peyser, J. (1976) *Boulez. Composer, Conductor, Enigma*. London: Cassell.

Peyser, J. (1987) *Bernstein*. New York: Beech Tree Books.

Pfordresher, P. Q. and Palmer, C. (2006) Effects of hearing the past, present or future during music performance. *Perception and Psychophysics*, 68, 362–76.

Piccirilli, M., Sciarma, T., and Luzzi, S. (2000) Modularity of music: evidence from a case of pure amusia. *Journal of Neurology, Neurosurgery and Psychiatry*, 69, 541–45.

Pick, A. D., Gross, D., Heinrichs, M., and Love, M. *et al.* (1994) Development of perception of the unity of musical events. *Cognitive Development*, 9, 355–75.

Pidgeon, J. (1985) *Eric Clapton*. London: Vermilion.

Pineau, M. and Bigand, E. (1997) Effet des structures globales sur l'amorcage harmonique en musique/ The influence of global structures on the beginnings of harmony in music. *Annee Psychologique*, 97, 385–408.

Piper, R. M. and Shoemaker, D. M. (1973) Formative evaluation of a kindergarten music program based on behavioral objectives. *Journal of Research in Music Education*, 12, 145–52.

Piro, J. M. (1993) Laterality effects for music perception among differentially talented adolescents. *Perceptual and Motor Skills*, 76, 499–514.

Pitt, M. A. (1994) Perception of pitch and timbre by musically trained and untrained listeners. *Journal of Experimental Psychology: Human Perception and Performance*, 20, 976–86.

Platel, H., Price, C., Baron, J. C., Wise, R., Lambert, J., Frackowiak, R., Lechevalier, B., and Eustache, F. (1997) The structural components of music perception: a functional anatomical study. *Brain*, 120, 229–43.

Plomin, R. (1988) The nature and nurture of cognitive abilities. In: *Advances in the Psychology of Human Intelligence* (ed. R. Sternberg), 4, pp.1–33. Hillsdale, NJ: Lawrence Erlbaum Associates.

Plomin, R. and Thompson, L. A. (1993) Genetics and high cognitive ability. In *Ciba Foundation Symposium 178: The Origins and Development of High Ability* (ed. G. R. Bock and K. Ackrill), pp. 67–79. Chichester, England: Wiley.

Polverini-Rey, R. A. (1993) *Intraterine Musical Learning: The Soothing Effect on Newborns of a Lullaby Learned Prenatally*. Unpublished doctoral dissertation. California School of Professional Psychology.

Ponomarev, Y. (ed.) (1983) *Issledovanie problem psihologii tvorchestva/ The Psychology of Creativity Research*. Moscow: Nauka.

Presley, E. (1977) *Elvis in his own Words*. London-New York: Omnibus Press.

Prianishnikova, M.P. and Tompakova, O.M. (eds) (1985) *Letopis' zhizni i tvorchestva Skryabina/ Scriabin's Life Story*. Moscow: Sovetsky kompozitor.

Prokofiev, S. (2003) *Dnevniki/Diaries*. Moscow: Klassika-XXI.

Protopopov, V. (ed.) (1947) *Pamyati Sergeya Ivanovicha Taneeva/In the Memory of Sergey Ivanovich Taneev*. Moscow-Leningrad: Muzgiz.

Poincaret, H. (1910) *Matematicheskoe tvorchestvo/Creativity in Mathematics*. Yuriev.

Piatigorsky, G. (1970) Violonchelist/Cellist. *Ispolnitel'skoe iskusstvo zarubezhnyh stran/Performing Art Abroad*, 5, 127–215.

Radvansky, G. A., Fleming, K. J., and Simmons, J. A. (1995) Timbre reliance in nonmusicians' and musicians' memory for melodies. *Music Perception*, 13, 127–40.

Rakhmaninov, S. (1964) *Literaturnoe nasledie. Pis'ma, vospominaniya, interv'yu/Literary Works. Letters, Memoirs, Interviews*, vol. 1. Moscow: Muzyka.

Rameau, J.-F. (1934) Traktat o garmonii/Treatise on harmony. In *Materialy i dokumenty po istorii muzyki/Materials and Documents on History of Music*, vol. 2. Moscow: Academia.

Ramzaev, M. (2001) *Internet dlia nachinauschikh/Internet for beginners*. Moscow: Aquarium.

Rawlings, D. and Ciancarelli, V. (1997) Music preference and the five-factor model of the NEO Personality Inventory. *Psychology of Music*, 25, 120–32.

Renzulli, J. S. (1978) What makes giftedness? Reexamining a definition. *Phi Delta Kappan*, 60(3), 180–4, 261.

Repp, B. H. (1995) Expressive timing in Schumann's 'Traumerei': an analysis of performances by graduate student pianists. *Journal of the Acoustical Society of America*, 98, 2413–27.

Repp, B. H. (1996) The art of inaccuracy: why pianists' errors are difficult to hear. *Music Perception*, 14, 161–84.

Repp, B. H. (1997) The aesthetic quality of a quantitatively average music performance: two preliminary experiments. *Music Perception*, 14, 419–44.

Repp, B. H. (1998a) Obligatory 'expectations' of expressive timing induced by perception of musical structure. *Psychological Research*, 61, 33–43.

Repp, B. H. (1998b) Variations on a theme by Chopin: relations between perception and production of timing in music. *Journal of Experimental Psychology: Human Perception and Performance*, 24, 791–811.

Repp, B. H. (1998c) The detectability of local deviations from a typical expressive timing pattern. *Music Perception*, 15, 265–89.

Revecz, G. (1925) *The Psychology of a Musical Prodigy*. New York: Harcourt, Brace and Company.

Richman, B. (1993) On the evolution of speech: singing as the middle term. *Current Anthropology*, 34, 721–22.

Rideout, B. E. and Taylor, J. (1997) Enhanced spatial performance following 10 minutes exposure to music: a replication. *Perceptual and Motor Skills*, 85, 112–14.

Ries, N. L. (1987) An analysis of the characteristics of infant-child singing expressions: replication report. *Canadian Journal of Research in Music Education*, 29, 5–20.

Rimsky-Korsakov, N. A. (1911) *Muzykal'nie stat'i i zametki/Papers and Notes on Music*. St.-Petersburg: Jurgenson.

Rimsky-Korsakov, N. A. (1982) *Letopis' moei muzykal'noi zhizni/The Story of My Life in Music*. Moscow: Muzyka.

Rizzo, M. and Eslinger, P. J. (1989) Colored hearing synesthesia: an investigation of neural factors. *Neurology*, 39, 781–4.

Robazza, C., Macaluso, C., and D'Urso, V. (1994) Emotional reactions to music by gender, age, and expertise. *Perceptual and Motor Skills*, 79, 939–44.

Rock, A. M., Trainor, L. J., and Addison, T. L. (1999) Distinctive messages in infant-directed lullabies and play songs. *Developmental Psychology*, 35, 527–34.

Rolling Stones in their own Words (1985) London: Omnibus Press.

Rosner, B. S. and Meyer, L. B. (1986) The perceptual roles of melodic process, contour, and form. *Music Perception*, 4, 1–39.

Rosner, B. S. (1999) A cross-cultural investigation of the perception of emotion in music: psychophysical and cultural cues. *Music Perception*, 17, 101–14.

Ross, D. A., Gore, J. C., and Marks, L. E. (2005) Absolute pitch: music and beyond. *Epilepsy and Behavior*, 7, 578–601.

Rossolimo, G. I. (1893) *K phisiologii muzikalnogo talanta/Towards the Physiology of Musical Talent.* Moscow.

Rubinstein, A. (1889) *Avtobiographicheskie zapiski/Autobiographical Notes.* St.-Petersburg.

Rubinstein, S. L. (1960) Problemi sposobnostei i voprosi psikhologicheskoi teorii/The problems of abilities and the questions of psychological theory. *Voprosi psikhologii/Questions of Psychology*, 3, 3–15.

Rubinstein, A. (1973) *My Young Years.* London: Jonathan Cape.

Ruggieri, V. and Katsnelson, A. (1996) An analysis of a performance by the violinist D. Oistrakh: the hypothetical role of postural tonic-static and entourage movements. *Perceptual and Motor Skills*, 82, 291–300.

Russell, R. (1973) *Bird Lives!* New York: Charterhouse.

Russo, F., Windell, D., and Cuddy, L. (2003) Learning the 'Special Note': evidence for a critical period for absolute pitch acquisition. *Music Perception*, 21, 199–27.

Rutkowski, J. (1996) The effectiveness of individual/small-group singing activities on kindergartners' use of singing voice and developmental music aptitude. *Journal of Research in Music Education*, 44, 353–68.

Rytsarev, S. (1987) *Christof Villibal'd Glyuk/ Christoph Willibald Gluck.* Moscow: Muzyka.

Sabaneev, L. (1925) *Vospominaniya o Skriabine/ Memoirs of Skryabin.* Moscow: Izdatelstvo Sabashnikovykh.

Sacks, O. (1995) Musical ability. *Science*, 268, 621.

Saffran, J. and Griepentrog, G. (2001) Absolute pitch in infant auditory learning: evidence for developmental reorganization. *Developmental Psychology*, 37, 74–85.

Saffran, J. R., Loman, M. M., and Robertson, R. W. (2000) Infant memory for musical experiences. *Cognition*, 77, 15–23.

Saito, N. and Maekawa, M. (1993) Birdsong: the interface with human language. *Brain and Development*, 15, 31–9.

Salk, L. (1960) The effects of the normal heartbeat sound on the behaviour of the newborn infant: implications for mental health. *World Mental Health*, 12, 168–75.

Salk, L. (1961) The importance of the heartbeat rhythm to human nature: theoretical, clinical, and experimental observations. In *Proceedings of the Third World Congress of Psychiatry*, pp. 740–46. Toronto: University of Toronto.

Salk, L. (1962) Mother's heartbeat as imprinting stimulus. *Transactions of the New York Academy of Sciences*, 24, 753–63.

Salomonsson, B. (1989) Music and affects: psychoanalytic viewpoints. *Scandinavian Psychoanalytic Review*, 12, 126–44.

Satt, B. J. (1984) *An Investigation into the Acoustical Induction of Intrauterine Learning.* Unpublished doctoral dissertation, California School of Professional Psychology.

Sawyer, R. K. (1998) Effect of music on spatial performance: a test of generality. *Creativity Research Journal*, 11, 11–19.

Schaller, M. (1997) The psychological consequences of fame: three tests of the selfconsciousness hypothesis. *Journal of Personality*, 65, 291–309.

Schapov, A. P. (1934) *Etyudy o fortepiannoi pedagogike/Etudes on Piano Teaching.* Moscow: Muzgiz.

Scheerer, M., Rothmann, E., and Goldstein, K. (1945) A case of 'idiot savant': an experimental study of personality organization. *Psychological Monographs*, 58, 1–63.

Schellenberg, E. G. (1996) Expectancy in melody: tests of the implication-realization model. *Cognition*, 58, 75–125.

Schellenberg, E. G. and Trehub, S. E. (1996) Natural musical intervals: evidence from infant listeners. *Psychological Science*, 7, 272–77.

Schellenberg, E. G. (2003) Does exposure to music have beneficial side effects? In *The Cognitive Neuroscience of Music* (ed. I. Peretz and R. Zatorre), pp. 430–48. New York: Oxford University Press.

Schellenberg, E. G. (2005) Music and cognitive abilities. *Current Directions in Psychological Science*, 14, 317–20.

Schellenberg, E. G. (2006) Long-term positive associations between music lessons and IQ. *Journal of Educational Psychology*, 98, 457–68.

Schellenberg, E. G., Nakata, T., Hunter, P. G., and Tamoto, S. (2007) Exposure to music and cognitive performance: tests of children and adults. *Psychology of Music*, 35, 5–19.

Schellenberg, G. E. and Trehub, S. E. (2008) Is there an Asian advantage for pitch memory? *Music Perception*, 25, 241–52.

Scherbatykh, Y. V. (2006) *Psikhologia stressa/The Psychology of Stress.* Moscow: Eksmo.

Schlaug, G., Jaencke, L., Huang, Y., and Staiger, J. F. *et al.* (1995a) Increased corpus callosum size in musicians. *Neuropsychologia*, 33, 1047–55.

Schlaug, G., Jaencke, L., Huang, Y., and Steinmetz, H. (1995b) In vivo evidence of structural brain asymmetry in musicians. *Science*, 267, 699–701.

Schlaug, G., Norton, A., Overy, K., and Winner, E. (2005) Effects of music training on the child's brain and cognitive development. In *The neurosciences and music II: From perception to performance*, (ed. G. Avanzini, L. Lopez, S. Koelsch, and M. Manjno), pp. 219–30. New York: New York Academy of Sciences.

Schmuckler, M. A. (1997) Expectancy effects in memory for melodies. *Canadian Journal of Experimental Psychology*, 51, 292–305.

Schnabel, A. (1967) Moya zhizn' i muzyka/My Life and Music. *Ispolnitel'skoe iskusstvo zarubezhnykh stran/Performing Art Abroad*, 3, 63–192.

Schneider, W. (1993) Acquiring expertise: determinants of exceptional performance. In *International Handbook of Research and Development of Giftedness and Talent* (ed. K. A. Heller, F. J. Munks, and A. H. Passow). New York: Pergamon.

Schoenberg, A. (1949) *Style and Idea.* New York: Philosophical Library.

Schoegler, B. (1998) Music as a tool in communications research. *Nordic Journal of Music Therapy*, 7, 40–9.

Schon, D., Semenza, C., and Denes, G. (2001) Naming of musical notes: a selective deficit in one musical clef. *Cortex*, 37, 407–21.

Schon, D. and Besson, M. (2005) Visually induced auditory expectancy in music reading: a behavioral and electrophysiological study. *Journal of Cognitive Neuroscience*, 17, 694–705.

Schweiger, A. and Maltzman, I. (1985) Behavioural and electrodermal measures of lateralization for music perception in musicians and nonmusicians. *Biological Psychology*, 20, 129–45.

Scripp, L. and Davidson, L. (1994) Giftedness and professional training: the impact of music reading skills on musical development of conservatory students. In *Beyond Terman: Contemporary Longitudinal Studies Of Giftedness And Talent. Creativity Research Series* (ed. R. F. Subotnik, K. D. Arnold *et al.*), pp. 186–211. Norwood, NJ: Ablex Publishing Corporation.

Seashore, C. E. (1919) *The Psychology of Musical Talent.* New York: Silver Burdett.

Seashore, C. E. (1938) *The Psychology of Music.* New York: McGraw-Hill.

Segalin, G. (ed.) (1925) *Klinicheskiy arkhiv genialnosti i odarennosti/Clinical Archive Of Genius and Giftedness.* Sverdlovsk: Uralskiy institut psikhiatrii.

Seifert, M. and Hadida, A. L. (2006) Facilitating talent selection decisions in the music. *Management Decision*, 44, 790–808.

Sekowski, A. (1988) Personality predictors of music achievement. *Polish Psychological Bulletin*, 19, 131–7.

Senyshyn, Y. (1999) Name that tune: identifying popular recordings from brief excerpts. *Canadian Journal of Education*, 24, 30–41.

Sergeant, D. C. (1969) Experimental investigation of absolute pitch. *Journal of Research in Music Education*, 17, 135–43.

Sergeant, D. C. and Roche, S. (1973) Perceptual shifts in the auditory information processing of young children. *Psychology of Music*, 1, 39–48.

Sergeant, D. C. and Vhatcher, G. (1974) Intelligence, social status, and musical abilities. *Psychology of Music*, 2, 32–57.

Sergent, J., Zuck, E., Terriah, S., and MacDonald, B. (1992) Distributed neural network underlying musical sight-reading and keyboard performance. *Science*, 257, 106–9.

Seroff, V. (1943) *Dmitri Shostakovich: The Life and Background of a Soviet Composer.* New York: Alfred A. Knopf.

Shaw, D. (1991) *Intrauterine Musical Learning: A Study of Its Effects on Mother-Infant Bonding.* Unpublished doctoral dissertation, California School of Professional Psychology.

Shelton, J. S. (1965) *The Influence of Home Musical Environment Upon Musical Response of First-Grade Children.* Unpublished doctoral dissertation, George Peabody College for Teachers.

Shepard, R. N. and Levitin, D. J. (2002) Cognitive psychology and music. In *Foundations of Cognitive Psychology: Core Readings* (ed. D. J. Levitin), pp. 503–14. Cambridge, MA: MIT Press.

Sheval'e, M. (1977) *Moi put' i moi pesni/My Life and My Songs.* Moscow: Iskusstvo.

Shilling, W. A. (2002) Mathematics, music, and movement: exploring concepts and connections. *Early Childhood Education Journal*, 29, 179–84.

Shlifstein, S. I. (1975) *Musorgsky. Khudozhnik. Vremya. Sudba/Mussorgsky. The Artist, The Time, The Destiny.* Moscow: Muzyka.

Shulgin D. I. (1998) *Priznanie Edisona Denisova/Edison Denisov's Confession.* Moscow: Kompozitor.

Shulyachuk, I. (1912) *Paganini.* Moscow: Izdatelstvo Sytina.

Shuter-Dyson, R. and Gabriel, C. (1981) *The Psychology of Musical Ability.* London-New York: Methuen.

Shuter-Dyson, R. (1994) Le probléme des interactions entre hérédité et milieu dans formation des aptitudes musicales. In *La psychologie de la musique*, (ed. A. Zenatti), pp. 211–49. Presses Universitaire de France.

Siegel, J. A. (1976) Judgment of intonation by musicians: further evidence for categorial perception. *Research Bulletin No. 375*, University of Western Ontario.

Siegel, J. A. and Siegel, W. (1977) Absolute identification of notes and intervals by musicians. *Perception and Psychophysics*, 21, 143–52.

Siegel, J. A. and Siegel, W. (1976) Categorical perception of tonal intervals: musicians can't tell sharp from flat. *Perception and Psychophysics*, 21, 399–407.

Siegler, R. S. and Kotovsky, K. (1986) Two levels of giftedness: shall ever the twain meet? In *Conceptions of Giftedness*, (ed. R. J. Sternberg and J. E. Davidson). Cambridge University Press.

Simonton, D. (2000) Creative development as acquired expertise: theoretical issues and an empirical test. *Developmental Review*, 20, 283–318.

Simonton, D. K. (1999) Talent and its development: an emergenic and epigenetic model. *Psychological Review*, 106, 435–57.

Sloboda, J. A. (1984) Experimental studies of musical reading: a review. *Music Perception*, 2, 222–36.

Sloboda, J. A. (1985) *The Musical Mind: The Cognitive Psychology of Music.* London: Oxford University Press.

Sloboda, J. A., Hermelin, B., and O'Connor, N. (1985) An exceptional musical memory. *Music Perception*, 3, 155–70.

Sloboda, J. A. (1991) Music structure and emotional response: some empirical findings. *Psychology of Music*, 19, 110–20.

Sloboda, J. A. and Howe, M. J. A. (1991) Biographical precursors of musical excellence: an interview study. *Psychology of Music*, 19, 3–21.

Sloboda, J. A. and Howe, M. J. A. (1992) Transitions in the early musical careers of able young musicians: choosing instruments and teachers. *Journal of Research in Music Education*, 40, 283–94.

Sloboda, J. A., Davidson, J. W., and Howe, M. J. A. (1994a) Is everyone musical? *The Psychologist*, 7, 349–54.

Sloboda, J. A., Davidson, J. W., and Howe, M. J. A. (1994b) Musicians: experts not geniuses. *The Psychologist*, 7, 363–4.

Sloboda, J. A. (1996) The acquisition of musical performance expertise: deconstructing the `talent' account of individual differences in musical expressivity. In *The Road to Excellence: The Acquisition of Expert Performance in the Arts and Sciences* (ed. K. A. Ericsson). Erlbaum.

Sloboda, J. A., Davidson, J. W., Howe, M. J. A., and Moore, D. G. (1996) The role of practice in the development of performing musicians. *British Journal of Psychology*, 87, 287–309.

Sloboda, J. A. and Deliége, I. (eds.) (1996) *Musical Beginnings: Origins and Development of Musical Competence.* London: Oxford University Press.

Sloboda, J. A. (2005) *Exploring the Musical Mind: Cognition, Emotion, Ability, Function.* UK: Oxford University Press.

Sloboda, J. A., Wise, K. J., and Peretz, I. (2005) Quantifying tone deafness in the general population. *Annals of the New York Academy of Sciences*, 1060, 255–61.

Slonimsky, N. (1947) *The Road to Music.* New York: Dodd Mead and Company.

Sluming, V. A. and Manning, J. T. (2000) Second to fourth digit ratio in elite musicians: evidence of musical ability as an honest signal of male fitness. *Evolution and Human Behavior*, 21, 1–9.

Smith, J. D. (1997) The place of musical novices in music science. *Music Perception*, 14, 227–62.

Smith, J. D., Nelson, D. G., Grohskopf, L. A., and Appleton, T. (1997) What child is this? What interval was that? Familiar tunes and music perception in novice listeners. *Cognition*, 52, 23–54.

Smith, L. D. and Williams, R. N. (1999) Children's artistic responses to musical intervals. *American Journal of Psychology*, 112, 383–410.

Snyder, R. F. (2000) The relationship between learning styles/multiple intelligences and academic achievement of high school students. *High School Journal*, 83, 11–21.

Sogin, D. A. (1997) An exploratory study on contingent verbal feedback for accuracy of intonation in musical performance. *Perceptual and Motor Skills*, 84, 217–18.

Sosniak, L. A. (1985) Learning to be a concert pianist. In *Developing Talent in Young People* (ed. B. S. Bloom). Ballantine.

Sosniak, L. A. (1990) The tortoise, the hare, and the development of talent. In *Encouraging the Development of Exceptional Abilities and Talents* (ed. M. J. A. Howe). British Psychological Society.

Spearman, C. (1904) 'General Intelligence', objectively determined and measured. *American Journal of Psychology*, 15, 201–93.

Spiegler, D. M. (1967) *Factors Involved in the Development of Prenatal Rhythmic Sensitivity*. Unpublished doctoral dissertation, West Virginia University.

Stack, S. (1997) Suicide among artists. *Journal of Social Psychology*, 137, 129–30.

Stadler, E. S. (1990) Vocal pitch matching ability in children between four and nine years of age. *European Journal for High Ability*, 1, 33–41.

Stankov, L. and Spilsbury, G. (1978) The measurement of auditory abilities of blind, partially sighted, and sighted children. *Applied Psychological Measurement*, 2, 491–503.

Stankov, L. and Horn, J. L. (1980) Human abilities revealed through auditory tests. *Journal of Educational Psychology*, 72, 19–42.

Stanton, H. E. (1994) Reduction of performance anxiety in music students. *Australian Psychologist*, 29, 124–7.

Starcheus, M. (2003) *Slukh muzikanta/The Musician's Ear*. Moscow: Moscow conservatory.

Starr, A., Amelie, R. N., and Martin, W. H. *et al.* (1977) Development of auditory function in newborn infants revealed by auditory brainstem potentials. *Pediatrics*, 30, 831–9.

Steinke, W. R., Cuddy, L. L., and Holden, R. R. (1997) Dissociation of musical tonality and pitch memory from nonmusical cognitive abilities. *Canadian Journal of Experimental Psychology*, 51, 316–35.

Steinke, W. R., Cuddy, L. L., and Jakobson, L. S. (2001) Dissociations among functional subsystems governing melody recognition after right-hemisphere damage. *Cognitive Neuropsychology*, 18, 411–37.

Steinmetz, H. (1996) Structure, function and cerebral asymmetry: in vivo morphometry of the planum temporale. *Neuroscience and Biobehavioral Reviews*, 20, 587–91.

Sternberg, R. J. (1993) Procedures for identifying intellectual potential in the gifted: a perspective on alternative 'metaphors of mind'. In *International Handbook of Research and Development of Giftedness and Talent* (ed. K. A. Heller, F. J. Munks, and A. H. Passow). New York: Pergamon.

Stevens, C. and Latimer, C. (1997) Music recognition: an illustrative application of a connectionist model. *Psychology of Music*, 25, 161–85.

Stokowski, L. (1943) *Music for All of Us*. New York: Simon and Schuster.

Storfer, M. D. (1990) *Intelligence and Giftedness: the Contributions of Heredity and Early Environment*. San-Francisco: Jossey-Bass.

Stough, C., Kerkin, B., Bates, T., and Mangan, G. (1994) Music and spatial IQ. *Personality and Individual Differences*, 17, 695.

Stratton, V. N. and Zalanowski, A. H. (1989) The effects of music and paintings on mood. *Journal of Music Therapy*, 26, 30–41.

Strauss, R. (1975) Razmyshleniya i vospominaniya/Thoughts and memoirs. *Ispolnitel'skoe iskusstvo zarubezhnykh stran/Performing Art Abroad*, 7, 24–98.

Stravinsky, I. (1971) *Dialogi/Dialogues*. Leningrad: Muzyka.

Struve, B. (1952) *Puti nachal'nogo razvitiya yunykh skripachei i violonchelistov/The Ways of Early Development for Junior Violinists and Cellists*. Moscow: Muzgiz.

Stwolinski, G., Faulconer, J., and Schwarzkopf, A. B. (1988) A comparison of two approaches to learning to detect harmonic alterations. *Journal of Research in Music Education*, 36, 83–94.

Super, C. (1976) Environmental effects on motor development: the case of 'African infant precocity'. *Developmental Medicine and Child Neurology*, 18, 561–7.

Szabo, M. (1999) Early music experience and musical development. *General Music Today*, 12, 17–19.

Szmedra, L. and Bacharach, D. W. (1998) Effect of music on perceived exertion, plasma lactate, norepinephrine and cardiovascular hemodynamics during treadmill running. *International Journal of Sports Medicine*, 19, 32–7.

Takeuchi, A. H. and Hulse, S. H. (1993) Absolute pitch. *Psychological Bulletin*, 113, 345–61.

Taniguchi, T. (1991) Mood congruent effects by music on word recognition. *Shinrigaku Kenkyu*, 62, 88–95.

Tarasova, K. (1988) *Ontogenes muzikal'nikh sposobnostei/The Onthogenesis of Musical Abilities*. Moscow: Pedagogika.

Taylor, E. M. (1941) A study of the prognosis of musical talent. *Journal of Experimental Education*, 10, 1–28.

Tchaikovsky, M. I. (1903) *Zhizn' P.I.Tchaikovskogo/Life of Pyotr Iliych Tchaikovsky*. Moscow: Izdatelstvo Jurgensona.

Teplov, B. M. (1947) *Psikhologia muzikal'nikh sposobnostei/The Psychology of Musical Abilities*. Moscow: Pedagogika.

Teplov, B. M. (1985) Psihologiya muzykal'nyh sposobnostei/The psychology of musical abilities. In *Izbrannie trudy, t. I/Selected Works*, vol. I, (ed. M. G. Yaroshevsky), pp. 42–222. Moscow: Pedagogika.

Teplov, B. M. (1998) *Psihologiya i psikhofiziologiya individual'nyh razlichij/Psychology and Psychophisiology of Individual Differences*. Moscow-Voronezh: Modek

Terman, L. M. (1916) *The Measurement of Intelligence: An Explanation of and Complete Guide for the Use of the Stanford Revision and Extention of the Binet-Simon Intelligence Scale*. Boston: Houghton Mifflin.

Terman, L. M. and Oden, M. H. (1947) *The Gifted Child Grows up: Twenty-five years' Follow-up of a Superior Group*. Stanford, CA: Stanford University Press.

Terman, L. M. and Merrill, M. A. (1973) *Stanford Binet Intelligence Scale: Manual for the Third Revision Form L. M.* Boston: Houghton Mifflin.

Tervaniemi, M., Szameitat, A. J., Kruck, S., Schroger, E., Alter, K., De Baene, W., and Friederici, A. D. (2006) From air oscillations to music and speech: functional magnetic resonance imaging evidence for fine-tuned neural networks in audition. *Journal of Neuroscience*, 26, 8647–52.

Terwogt, M. M. and Van Grinsven, F. (1988) Recognition of emotions in music by children and adults. *Perceptual and Motor Skills*, 67, 697–8.

Tessier, A. (1926) *Couperin*. Paris: Henri Laurens.

Thackray, R. (1969) *An Investigation into Rhythmic Abilities*. London: Novello.

Thackray, R. (1972) *Rhythmic Abilities in Children*. London: Novello.

Thaut, M. H., Rathbun, J. A., and Miller, R. A. (1997) Music versus metronome time-keeper in a rhythmic motor task. *International Journal of Arts Medicine*, 5, 4–12.

Theiler, A. M. and Lippman, L. G. (1995) Effects of mental practice and modeling on guitar and vocal performance. *Journal of General Psychology*, 122, 329–43.

Thibaud, J. (1953) *Un violon parle: souvenirs de Jaques Thibaud*. Paris: del Duca.

Thompson, B. M. and Andrews, S. R. (2000) Genetic correlates of musical pitch recognition in humans. *Intergrative Physiological and Behavioral Science*, 35, 174–88.

Thompson, W. F., Schellenberg, E. G., and Husain, G. (2001) Arousal, mood, and the Mozart effect. *Psychological Science*, 12, 248–51.

Thompson, L. A. and Plomin, R. (1993) Genetic influence on cognitive ability. In *International Handbook of Research and Development of Giftedness and Talent* (ed. K. A. Heller, F. J. Monks, and A. H. Passow). New York: Pergamon.

Thorpe, L. A. and Trehub, S. E. (1989) Duration illusion and auditory grouping in infancy. *Developmental Psychology*, 25, 122–7.

Tillmann, B., Bigand, E., and Madurell, F. (1998) Local versus global processing of harmonic cadences in the solution of musical puzzles. *Psychological Research*, 61, 157–74.

Torff, B. and Winner, E. (1994) Don't throw out the baby with the bath water. *The Psychologist*, 7, 361–2.

Toscanini, A. (1974) *Vospominania. Biograficheskie materialy/Memoirs. Biographical Materials.* Leningrad: Muzyka.

Trainor, L. J. and Heinmiller, B. M. (1998) The development of evaluative response to music: infants prefer to listen to consonance over dissonance. *Infant Behavior and Development*, 21, 77–88.

Trainor, L. J. (2006) Innateness, learning, and the difficulty of determining whether music is an evolutionary adaptation. *Music Perception*, 24, 105–10.

Treffert, D. A. (1989) *Extraordinary People.* London: Bantam Press.

Trehub, S.E., Bull, D., and Thorpe, L. A. (1984) Infants' perception of melodies: the role of melodic contour. *Child Development*, 55, 821–30.

Trehub, S. E., Cohen, A. J., Thorpe, L. A., and Morrongiello, B. A. (1986) Development of the perception of musical relations: semitone and diatonic structure. *Journal of Experimental Psychology: Human Perception and Performance*, 12, 295–301.

Trehub, S. E. and Thorpe, L. A. (1989) Infants' perception of rhythm: categorization of auditory sequences by temporal structure. *Canadian Journal of Psychology*, 43, 217–29.

Trehub, S. E., Schellenberg, E. G., and Hill, D. S. (1997) The origins of music perception and cognition: a developmental perspective. In *Perception and Cognition of Music* (ed. I. Deliége and J. Sloboda), pp. 103–28. Mahwah, NJ: Erlbaum.

Trehub, S. E. and Nakata, T. (2001–02) Emotion and music in infancy. *Musicae Scientiae*, Spec. Issue, 37–61.

Trehub, S. E. and Hannon, E. E. (2006) Infant music perception: domain-general or domain-specific mechanisms? *Cognition*, 100, 73–99.

Trevarthen, C. (2002) Consonance and dissonance of musical chords: neural correlates in auditory cortex of monkeys and humans. *Enfance*, 54, 86–99.

Truitt, F. E., Clifton, C. Jr., Pollatsek, A., and Rayner, K. (1997) The perceptual span and eye-hand span in sight reading music. *Visual Cognition*, 4, 143–61.

Ulfarsdottir, L. and Erwin, P. (1999) The influence of music on social cognitive skills. *The Arts in Psychotherapy*, 26, 81–4.

Upitis, R. (1992) *Can I Play You My Song? The Compositions and Invented Notations of Children.* Portsmouth, NH: Heinemann.

Upitis, R. (1995) Fostering children's compositions: activities for the classroom. *General Music Today*, Spring, 16–19.

Uznadze, D. N. (1997) *Teoria ustanovki/The Theory of Set.* Moscow-Voronezh: Modek

VanderArk, S. D. and Ely, D. (1993) Cortisol, biochemical, and galvanic skin responses to music stimuli of different preference values by college students in biology and music. *Perceptual and Motor Skills*, 77, 227–34.

VanderArk, S. D. and Ely, D. (1992) Biochemical and galvanic skin responses to music stimuli by college students in biology and music. *Perceptual and Motor Skills*, 74, 1079–90.

Veldhuis, H. A. (1984) Spontaneous songs of preschool children. *Arts in Psychotherapy*, 11, 15–24.

Vernon, P. E. (1931) *The Psychology of Music With Special Reference to its Appreciation, Perception, and Composition.* Unpublished doctoral dissertation. Cambridge University.

Volkenshtein, V. (1931) *Dramaturgiya/The Drama.* Moscow-Leningrad: Academia.

Vollmer-Haase, J., Finke, K., Hartje, W., and Bulla-Hellwig, M. (1998) Hemispheric dominance in the processing of J. S. Bach fugues: a transcranial Doppler sonography (TCD) study with musicians. *Neuropsychologia*, 36, 857–67.

Vygotsky, L. (1993) *Mishlenie i rech/Thought and Speech.* Moscow: Prosveschenie.

Wallin, N. L., Merker, B., and Brown, S. (eds.) (2000) *The Origins of Music.* Cambridge, MA: The MIT Press.

Walker, F. (1982) *The Man Verdi.* The University of Chicago Press.

Walter, B. (1969) *Tema s variatsiami: avtobiografia/Theme with Variations: Autobiography*. Moscow: Muzyka.

Wapnick, J., Mazza, J. K., and Darrow, A. A. (2000) Musical talent: innate or acquired? Perceptions of students, parents, and teachers. *Journal of Research in Music Education*, 48, 323–36.

Ward, W. D. and Burns, E. M. (1978) Singing without auditory feedback. *Journal of Research in Singing*, 1, 24–44.

Warren, J. (2003) Maurice Ravel's amusia. *Journal of the Royal Society of Medicine*, 96, 284–7.

Waterman, M. (1996) Emotional responses to music: implicit and explicit effects in listeners and performers. *Psychology of Music*, 24, 53–67.

Waters, A. J., Townsend, E., and Underwood, G. (1998) Expertise in musical sight reading: a study of pianists. *British Journal of Psychology*, 89, 123–49.

Waters A. J. and Underwood, G. (1999) Processing pitch and temporal structures in music reading: independent or interactive processing mechanisms? *The European Journal of Cognitive Psychology*, 11, 531–53.

Watson, K. B. (1942) The nature and measurement of musical meanings. *Psychological Monographs*, 54.

Webern, A. (1975) *Lektsii o muzyke.Pis'ma/Lectures on Music. Letters*. Moscow: Muzyka.

Weinberger, N. M. (1995a) Dynamic regulation of receptive fields and maps in the adult sensory cortex. *Annual Review of Neuroscience*, 18, 129–58.

Weinberger, N. M. (1995b) The musician's brain. *MuSICA Research Notes*, VII–I. Available at: http://www.musica.uci.edu

Welch, G. F. (2000) The ontogenesis of musical behaviour: a sociological perspective. *Research Studies in Music Education*, 14, 1–13.

Welch, G. F. (1994) The assessment of singing. *Psychology of Music*, 22, 3–19.

Werner, L. A. and Marean, G. C. (1996) Human Auditory Development. Boulder, CO: Westview Press.

White, B. W. (1954) Visual and auditory closure. *Journal of Experimental Psychology*, 48, 234–40.

Wieser, H. G. and Walter, R. (1997) Untroubled musical judgement of a performing organist during early epileptic seizure of the right temporal lobe. *Neuropsychologia*, 35, 45–51.

Wiggins, J. H. (1994) Children's strategies for solving compositional problems with peers. *Journal of Research in Music Education*, 42, 232–52.

Williamon, A. and Valentine, E. (2000) Quantity and quality of musical practice as predictors of performance quality. *British Journal of Psychology*, 91, 353–76.

Wilson, B. A., Baddeley, A. D., and Kapur, N. (1995) Dense amnesia in a professional musician following herpes simplex virus encephalitis. *Journal of Clinical and Experimental Neuropsychology*, 17, 668–81.

Wilson, D. (1994) Letter to *Early Music List*.

Wing, H. D. (1963) Is musical aptitude innate? *Review of Psychology of Music*, 1, 1–7.

Wing, H. D. (1968) *Tests of Musical Ability and Appreciation*. Cambridge University Press.

Winner, E. (1996) *Gifted Children*. New York: Basic Books.

Winner, E. and Martino, G. (1993) Giftedness in the visual arts and music. In *International Handbook of Research and Development of Giftedness and Talent* (ed. K. A. Heller, F. J. Munks, and A. H. Passow). New York: Pergamon.

Winner, E. (2000) The origins and ends of giftedness. *American Psychologist*, 55, 159–69.

Wolpert, R. S. (2000) Attention to key in a nondirected music listening task: musicians vs. nonmusicians. *Music Perception*, 18, 225–30.

Worthy, M. D. (2000) Effects of tone-quality conditions on perception and performance of pitch among selected wind instrumentalists. *Journal of Research in Music Education*, 48, 222–36.

Yampolsky, I. (1975) *F. Kreisler*. Moscow: Muzyka.

Yarbrough, C., Karrick, B., and Morrison, S. J. (1995) Effect of knowledge of directional mistunings on the tuning accuracy of beginning and intermediate wind players. *Journal of Research in Music Education*, 43, 232–41.

Yeung, A., McInerey, D., and Russel-Bowie, D. (2001) The effect of music on anxiety. *Australian Journal of Psychology*, 53, 125–33.

Young, R. L. and Nettelbeck, T. (1995) The abilities of a musical savant and his family. *Journal of Autism and Developmental Disorders*, 25, 231–48.

Zatorre, R. J., Belin, P., and Penhune, V. B. (2002) Structure and function of auditory cortex: music and speech. *Trends in Cognitive Sciences*, 6, 37–46.

Zenatti, A. (1980) *Tests Musicaux pour Jeunes Enfants*. Issy-les-Moulineaux: Editions Scientifiques et Psychologiques.

Zentner, M. R. and Kagan J. (1998) Infants' perception of consonance and dissonance in music. *Infant Behavior and Development*, 21, 483–92.

Ziv, N. and Goshen, M. (2006) The effect of 'sad' and 'happy' background music on the interpretation of a story in 5 to 6-year-old children. *British Journal of Music Education*, 23, 303–14.

Index